KT-146-469

ALASTAIR SAWDAY'S

Special
places to stay

FRENCH BED & BREAKFAST

Edited by Ann Cooke-Yarborough and Emma Carey

Typesetting, Conversion & Repro:	Avonset, Bath
Design:	Caroline King & Springboard Design, Bristol
Mapping:	Springboard Design, Bristol
Maps:	Bartholomew Mapping Services, a division of HarperCollins Publishers, Glasgow
Printing:	Stige, Italy
UK Distribution:	Portfolio, Greenford, Middlesex
US Distribution:	The Globe Pequot Press, Guilford, Connecticut

Published in November 2001

Alastair Sawday Publishing Co. Ltd
The Home Farm Stables, Barrow Gurney, Bristol BS48 3RW
Tel: +44 (0)1275 464891 Fax: +44 (0)1275 464887
E-mail: info@specialplacestostay.com Web: www. specialplacestostay.com

The Globe Pequot Press
P. O. Box 480, Guilford, Connecticut 06437, USA
Tel: +1 203 458 4500 Fax: +1 203 458 4601
E-mail: info@globe-pequot.com Web: www.globe-pequot.com

Seventh edition

ISBN 1-901970-22-1 in the UK

ISBN 0-7627-1247-3 in the US

Printed in Italy

The publishers have made every effort to ensure the accuracy of the information in this book at the time of going to press. However, they cannot accept any responsibility for any loss, injury or inconvenience resulting from the use of information contained therein.

ALASTAIR SAWDAY'S

Special

places to stay

FRENCH BED & BREAKFAST

This being human is a guest house...
... Be grateful to whoever comes
because each has been sent
as a guard from beyond.
Rumi 1207-1273

The
Globe
Pequot
press

Guilford
Connecticut, USA

Alastair Sawday Publishing
Bristol, UK

Contents

Contents

Contents

Contents

Acknowledgements

Not everyone thrown into the deep end will learn to swim. But Emma Carey, tossed - benignly of course - into assistant editorship of this hugely popular book has flourished. It must be admitted that she was taught to swim by Ann Cooke-Yarborough, who has produced so many editions, so brilliantly, from her base in Paris. Annie Shillito, the previous editor, has also been on permanent stand-by. However, Emma's delightful manner with everybody has won praise from many a French B&B owner and she has poured herself into another triumphant edition of a marvellous book. I congratulate her.

Many devoted inspectors have added their support marshalled by Ann Cooke-Yarborough who has also done a great deal of the inspecting and the lion's share of the writing. So this book continues to owe much to her zeal and deep skills.

Such a magnum opus would never see the printing press without in-depth support back at base: Julia Richardson, Annie Shillito, Rachel Brook, Laura Kinch, Sheila Clifton and Jenny Purdy. Let me not forget Russell Wilkinson whose web site adds so much to the work of all of our books and whose bottomless patience has rescued many of us from computer-driven madness. Finally, the atmosphere in our office has made the production of the book so much more fun than it might have been; for that I can thank everybody, but especially Nicola Crosse and Sarah Bolton, the sort of people with whom we all want to work.

Alastair Sawday

Series Editor:................ Alastair Sawday
Editors:.........................Ann Cooke-Yarborough, Emma Carey
Managing Editor:......... Annie Shillito
Production Manager:.... Julia Richardson
Administration:............. Rachel Brook, Marie Hodges, Laura Kinch
Accounts:...................... Jenny Purdy
Inspections:.................. Douglas Arestegui, Richard & Linda Armspach, Chantal Le Bot, Colin & Alyson Browne, Jill Coyle, Meredith Dickinson, Sue Edrich, John Edwards, Robin Fleet, Georgina Gabriel, Susan Gill, Michèle Goëmon, Anna Halama, Diana Harris, Susan Luraschi, Jo-Bell Moore, Joanna Morris, Caroline Portway, Lynne Wooster, Elizabeth Yates
Additional writing:....... Brendan Flanagan, Elizabeth Yates
Illustrations:................. Aymeric Chastenet
Additional photos:........ D Paillard (no. 222), R Thomas (no. 709)

Special thanks, too, to those people not mentioned here who visited - often at short notice - just one or two houses for us.

A word from Alastair Sawday

This book is still a source of deep satisfaction to me, even after eight years. It was our first baby, produced in a mad rush of enthusiasm, as babies often are. No market research, no experience and few skills. But we somehow hit the right button and have sold nearly 100,000 copies. That means that about half a million people (I guess) have probably used it - which means that a great deal of good regional food has been eaten, multitudes of local shops have had mini-boosts to their businesses and thousands of bed-nights have been spent in the homes of good, hard-working people rather than in the hotels of corporations and faceless companies. I am told that friendships have blossomed (if only the book had been out before the Hundred Years' War).

Much as I cherish all our other guides, all built on the French model, this one still has that very special idiosyncratic theme that is peculiar to France. Its houses and their ways are as gloriously varied as its wines and cheeses. With this book you can plunge safely into many social adventures. You will meet farmers and wine-growers, artists and entrepreneurs, aristocrats and bohemian businessmen; people from other countries too who've settled here, seduced by a French way of life. They will all throw open their doors, greet you with warmth, and either sweep you into their lives or leave you to meditate upon your own good fortune. Some of their houses are breathtakingly lovely. All stand ready to receive you.

After years of using this book myself I am struck by one particular phenomenon: it enables you to do pretty well whatever you want in France. It is the 'ultimate' reference book, because it contains over 760 people, or groups of people, who will be glad to help you. Thus, if you want a horse-riding holiday, someone here will be able to arrange it for you. They'll then put you in touch with others and before you know it your whole holiday is 'sorted'. Cyclists, walkers, ski-ers, artists, sailors - whoever you are, this book will provide you with the network of friends and support of which until now you could only dream.

Alastair Sawday

Introduction

What to expect from a French B&B • Choosing the right place • Directions and maps • Bedrooms and bathrooms • Dinner • Prices • Telephoning • Booking • Paying • When to arrive • Children and pets • Feedback

What's special about staying in French B&Bs?

That it can be tremendously exciting. You will meet some wonderful people running the *chambres d'hôtes* (French for 'bed and breakfast') in this guide, people from all walks of life - aristocrats and artisans, painters and *paysans*, teachers, writers, retired globetrotters. So many opportunities for enriching exchange are there for the taking. Some readers have formed enduring friendships with owners or other guests. And although most of our owners are simply down-to-earth, friendly individuals living in reliably French houses, they are all passionate about their area, have a touch of originality and they don't believe that the *porte-monnaie* is the only thing that counts.

How we choose our Special Places

We search for the best of everything and write a book without fixed boundaries. If we discover a place where the art of hospitality is practised with flair, good humour and commitment, we want to include it. We evaluate each place on its own merits, not by comparison. We visit every house - atmosphere, welcome and value for money are key considerations. We like people who do their own thing, though eccentricity is no excuse for poor standards. Good views are more important than deluxe toiletries, good walks more important than jacuzzis.

What to expect

Expect to feel a privileged guest and to have a fascinating glimpse into a French way of life. But if you are new to B&B, remember these are not hotels - in a B&B you are a paying guest in someone's home so please don't expect hotel-like surroundings or services.

Don't imagine that your towels will be changed daily, that your childrens' toys will be gathered or that your late request for a vegetarian meal will produce anything more exciting than an omelette. Let your hosts know of any special needs well ahead and take your own tea-bags if you're particular.

Breakfast is usually 'Continental' with fruit juice, home-made jams and the freshest bread. Occasionally fruit, eggs, cheese or meats will be offered, or you can ask; there may be a supplement to pay.

Although owners love guests to stay more than one night, they usually expect you to be out during the day - they have their own lives to lead so they can't be on hand all the time. If they are happy for you to be around, check which parts of the house or garden you may use during the day.

Introduction

Choosing the right place for you

Read carefully, sleep happily

Do remember to interpret what you see and read in this book. If you opt for a working farm, expect cockerels to crow or tractors to set off at dawn. If you choose a "rambling château with old-fashioned bathrooms" there could be some draughty corridors and idiosyncratic plumbing.

Check on anything that is really important to you before confirming your booking, e.g. whether the swimming pool will be ready to use at Easter, whether the bicycles available have been promised to other guests.

A problem well defined is half-way solved

If you find anything we say misleading (things do change in the lifetime of a guide), or you think we miss the point - if for example you were led to expect a very child-friendly house and were surprised by elegant white carpets and delicate ornaments at toddler height - please let us know.

And do discuss any problem with your hosts at the time - they are the only ones who can do something about it immediately. They would be mortified to discover, too late, that you were, for example, cold in bed when extra blankets could easily have been provided.

Non-French owners

Our aim is essentially to guide readers to meetings with French families in their homes so non-French owners have a smaller chance of being chosen. But many of you have written to say how good it can be to relax in your native tongue from time to time, so we include a reasonable number of 'foreigners'. The choice is yours.

How to use this book

Finding the houses

The entry number, in colour at the bottom left of each entry, is the number to use when looking for places on the map pages (NB Paris flags are not positioned geographically).

Our maps

The General Map of France is divided into the same regions as the Contents and marked with the page numbers of the detailed maps. The detailed maps are not designed to be used as road maps; they show roughly where the B&Bs are and should be used with a large-scale road atlas or map such as Michelin or Collins.

Introduction

Directions

Except for two-way motorway exits, our directions take you to each house from one side only. We name the French roads with the letters they carry on French maps and road signs:

A = *Autoroute*. Toll motorways with junctions that usually have the same name/number on both sides.
N = *Route Nationale*. The old trunk roads that are still pretty fast, don't charge tolls, but often go through towns.
D = *Route Départementale*. Smaller country roads with less traffic.

Our directions are as succinct as possible. For example:
From A7 exit Valence Sud A49 for Grenoble; exit 33; right D538a for Beaumont 2.5km; right at sign for 800m; house on right.
Interpretation: Take A7 motorway going north or south; leave at junction named 'Valence Sud' and get onto motorway A49 going towards Grenoble; leave this road at junction no. 33 and turn right onto road no. D538a (the 'a' means there are liable to be roads numbered 538c, 538e... in the vicinity) towards Beaumont for 2.5km until you meet a meaningful sign (often *Chambres d'Hôtes*, or the name of the house); turn right at this sign; the house is 800 metres down this road on the right.

Bedrooms

In this book 'double' means one double bed, 'twin' means two single beds, 'double/twin' means two single beds that can be made up into a large double. A 'triple' or 'family' room may have any mix of beds (sometimes sofabeds) for 3, 4 or more people. A 'suite' may be one large room with a sitting area or, like an 'apartment', it will have two or more interconnecting rooms and one or more bathrooms. An apartment is more likely to be self-contained and may have a small kitchen. A 'studio' is a bedroom with a bathroom and a small sitting and kitchen area. A 'duplex' is on two floors; the upper floor is often an open mezzanine. Extra beds and cots for children, at an extra cost, can often be provided; ask when booking.

Bathrooms

There's a wonderful variety of washing arrangements in French homes - we've done our best to make the layouts clear: bathrooms directly off the bedroom = 'with'; not directly off the bedroom but not shared = 'private'; shared with others = 'sharing'. Most, but not all baths have shower attachments. A 'continental' bath is a half or three-quarter-size tub with a shower attachment. Bathrooms are generally good but if you are wary of quirky arrangements go for the modernised places (which are probably more expensive).

Introduction

Dinner - Table d'Hôtes

Don't miss the opportunity to eat honest - even gourmet - food in an authentic family atmosphere. However, dinner absolutely must be booked beforehand. It won't be an option every day but do please turn up if you have booked it - it's distressing to prepare a meal that no-one comes to enjoy. Very few places do lunch but occasionally picnics can be provided; this is not always mentioned in the entry so ask the owners.

New, stringent laws copied from the hotel sector about kitchen equipment, hygiene and taxation are making it harder for house owners who would like to offer their guests dinner occasionally to do so without its becoming a bureaucratic and financial assault course. Because of these hassles, some owners don't mention meals but may provide an occasional dinner if asked.

Dinner, including wine?

The number and type of courses you will be offered for dinner varies and we have not attempted to go into details, although price may be an indicator. When wine is included this can mean a range of things, from a standard quarter-litre carafe per person to a barrel of table wine; from a very decent bottle of local produce to, in some rare cases, an excellent estate wine. Whatever it is, it is usually good value but please do not abuse your hosts' *vin à volonté* (unlimited wine with meals).

If there is no *table d'hôtes,* we give an idea of other places but beware, rural restaurants stop taking orders at 9pm and close at least a day a week.

Closed

When given in months, this means for the whole of both months named, so 'Closed: November-March' means closed from 1 November to 31 March.

Prices

The Euro becomes legal tender in the Euro Zone on 1 January 2002; the French Franc is to be phased out by 17 February 2002. Our prices are listed exclusively in Euros. We have rounded them off to the nearest 50 cents so you may find some prices differ by a few cents from those printed. There is a Euro/Franc/£/$ conversion table at the back of the book.

The price or price range is for two people sharing a room and it includes breakfast. Prices are presumed to be for 2002 but are not guaranteed, so please check. A price range may mean there are rooms at different prices or that the difference is seasonal. There will often be a reduction for single occupancy of a double room, even if it's just the cost of a breakfast. An extra person can often be accommodated for a small extra sum.

Introduction

Reductions

Most French B&Bs offer reductions for longer stays; some have attractive half-board terms or special prices for children. Do ask when you book.

Symbols

Symbols and their explanations are listed on the last page of the book. Use them as a guide rather than an unequivocal statement of fact and double-check anything that is important to you.

Gîte space for … people (shown in italics at the end of the description) allows you to assess what the total population staying on the property may be. Some places are *Gîtes d'Etape* i.e. they welcome walkers, cyclists or riders who are often catered for; others are *Gîtes de Séjour* or *Gîtes Ruraux* - self-contained, holiday houses. We have not inspected these *gîtes* and are not necessarily recommending them.

Types of houses

For a definition of *château, bastide, mas* see 'French words & expressions' at the back of the guide (where most French words used in the descriptions are explained).

Practical Matters

Telephoning/Faxing

All telephone numbers in France have ten digits, e.g. (0)5 05 25 35 45.

You should know that:

- the initial zero (bracketed above) is for use when telephoning from **inside** France only, i.e. dial 05 15 25 35 45 from any private or public telephone;

- when dialling from **outside** France use the international access code, then the country code for France - 33 - followed by the last 9 digits of the number you want, e.g. 00 33 5 15 25 35 45;

- numbers beginning (0)6 are mobile phone numbers;

- to telephone from France
  - to Great Britain: 00 44 then the number without the initial zero,
  - to the USA, 00 1 then the number.

Télécartes phone cards are widely available in France and there are plenty of telephone boxes, even in the countryside (they often take only cards).

Introduction

Booking

It is essential to book well ahead for July and August, and wise for other months. You may receive a *Contrat de Location* (Tenancy Contract) as confirmation. It must be filled in and returned, probably with a deposit, and commits both sides to the arrangement.

Remember not to telephone any later than 9pm or 9.30pm at the latest and that Ireland and the UK are one hour behind the rest of Europe. Some country folk have been quite upset by enquiries coming through when they were fast asleep.

Deposits

Some owners ask for a deposit - many readers have found it virtually impossible or ridiculously expensive to do this by direct transfer, so here are two suggestions:

- Send the appropriate amount of Euro banknotes with your confirmation by 'International Recorded' mail or send an ordinary cheque, which the owner will destroy when you arrive (so no-one pays the charges); when you leave, they will ask you for cash for your whole stay.

Paying

Most B&B owners do not take credit cards but where they do they will have our credit card symbol. Virtually all ATMs in France take Visa and MasterCard. Euro travellers' cheques should be accepted, other currency cheques are unpopular because of commission charges.

Taxe de séjour

This is a small tax that local councils are allowed to levy on all visitors paying for accommodation. Some councils do, some don't. So you may find your bill increased by a Euro or two per person per day.

Tipping

B&B owners do not expect to be tipped - they would be taken aback. If you encounter extraordinary kindness you may feel a 'thank you' letter, Christmas card or small gift would be appropriate.

Arriving

Most owners expect you to arrive between 5 and 7pm. If you come earlier, rooms may not be ready or your hosts may still be at work. So, if you are going to be late (or early, unavoidably), please telephone and say so.

Introduction

No-shows

Most owners hope you will treat them as friends, with sensitivity and punctuality. It's obviously upsetting for them to prepare rooms, even meals, and to wait up late for 'guests' who give no further sign of life. So if you find you are not going to take up a booking, telephone right away.

By the way, there is a tacit agreement among some B&B owners that no-show + no-call by 8pm, even 6pm in some cases, can be taken as a refusal of the booking and they will re-let the room if another guest turns up. This may be mentioned in italics at the end of the description of the place and some people may charge cancellation charges.

Children

Our symbol 🧸 shows where children are welcome with no age restrictions. Elsewhere, they may be welcome with restrictions as indicated in italics at the end of the description. e.g. *Babies only,* because of an unfenced pool.

Pets

Our 🐾 symbol tells you which houses generally welcome them but you must check whether this means the size and type of your pet and whether it will be in the house/in your room/in an outhouse. Your hosts will expect animals to be well-behaved and that you will be responsible for them at all times.

Subscriptions

Owners pay to appear in this guide; their fee goes towards the high production costs of an all-colour book. We really do only include places and owners that we find special. It is not possible for anyone to buy their way in.

Disclaimer

We make no claims to pure objectivity in judging our *Special Places to Stay*. They are here because we like them. Our opinions and tastes are ours alone and this book is a statement of them; we hope you will share them. We have done our utmost to get our facts right but apologise for any mistakes that may have crept in. Sometimes, too, prices shift, usually upwards, and 'things' change. We should be grateful to be told of any errors and changes.

The Environment

We try to reduce our impact on the environment where possible by:

- planting trees to compensate for our carbon emissions (as calculated by Edinburgh University): we are officially a Carbon Neutral® publishing

Introduction

company. The emissions directly related with the paper production, printing and distribution of this book have been made Carbon Neutral® through the planting of indigenous woodlands with Future Forests.

- re-using paper, recycling stationery, tins, bottles, etc.

- encouraging staff use of bicycles (they're loaned free) and car sharing.

- celebrating the use of organic, home- and locally-produced food.

- publishing books that support, in however small a way, the rural economy and small-scale businesses.

- encouraging our owners to follow recommendations made by the Energy Efficiency Centre to make their homes more environmentally friendly.

www.specialplacestostay.com

Our web site has online entries for many of the places featured here and in our other books, with up-to-date information and direct links to their own email addresses and web sites. You'll find more about the site at the back of this book.

Feedback

Finally, a huge Thank You to those of you who take the time and trouble to write to us about your *chambres d'hôtes* experiences - good and bad - or to recommend new places. This is what we do with them:

- Poor reports are followed up with the owners in question: we need to hear both sides of the story. Really bad reports lead to incognito visits after which we may exclude a house.

- The relevant owners are informed when we receive substantially positive reports.

- Recommendations are followed up with inspection visits where appropriate. If we include one of yours, you receive a free copy of the edition in which that house first appears.

We love your letters and value your comments, which make a real contribution to this book, be they on our report form, by letter or by email to frenchbandb@sawdays.co.uk. Or you can now visit our website and write to us from there.

Bon Voyage - Happy Travelling!

Ann Cooke-Yarborough

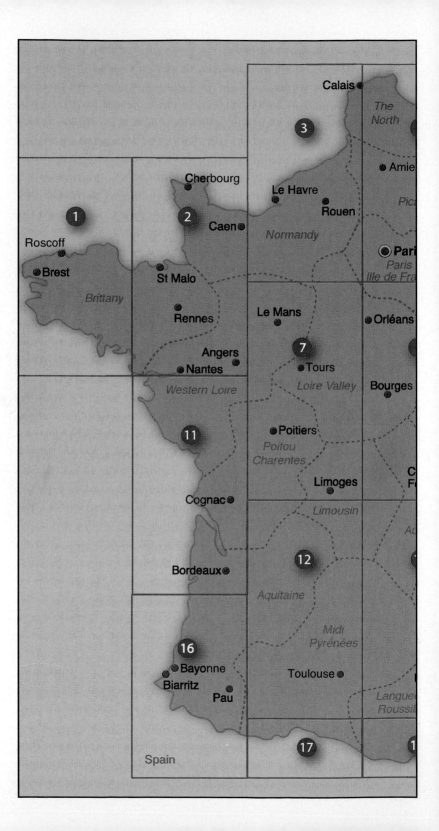

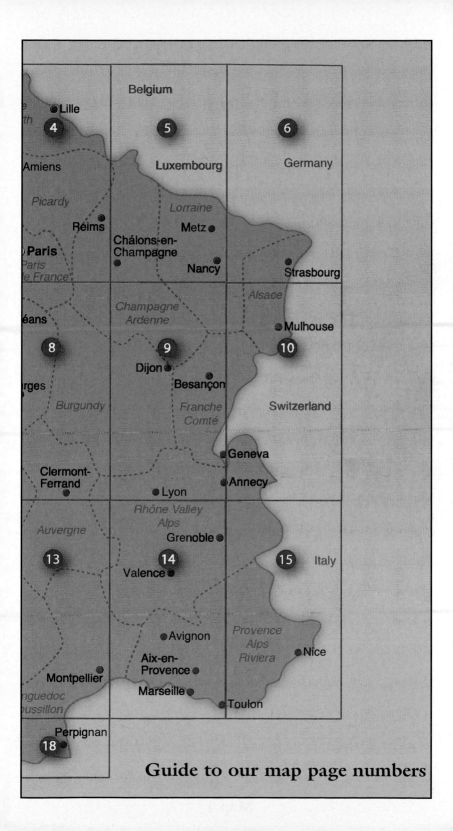

Guide to our map page numbers

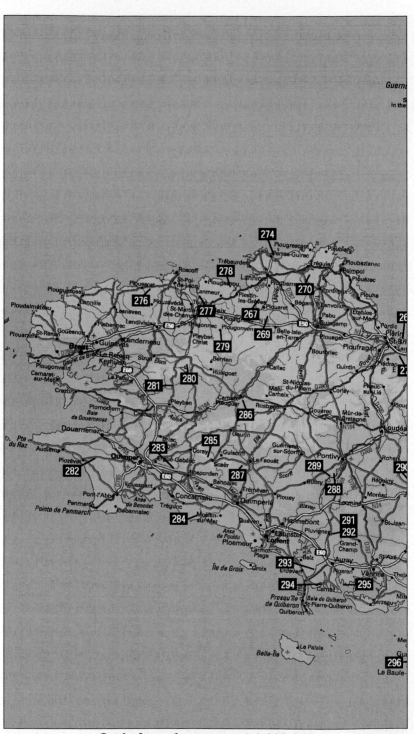

Scale for colour maps 1:1 600 000
(1cm:16km or 1 inch:25.25 miles)

Map 1

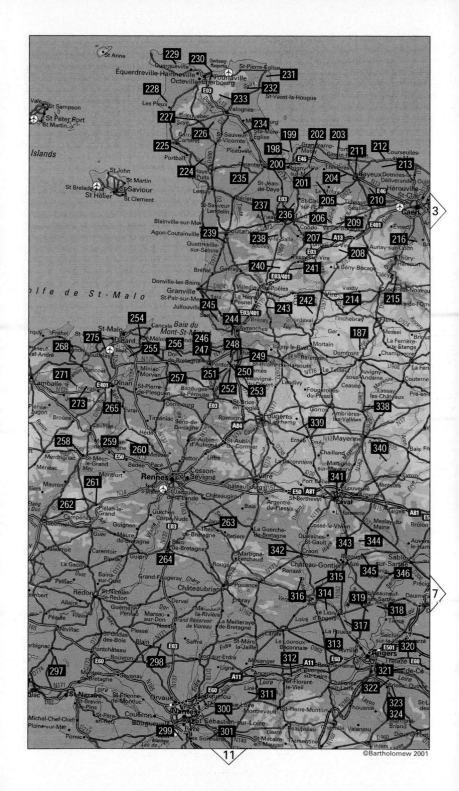

©Bartholomew 2001

Map 2

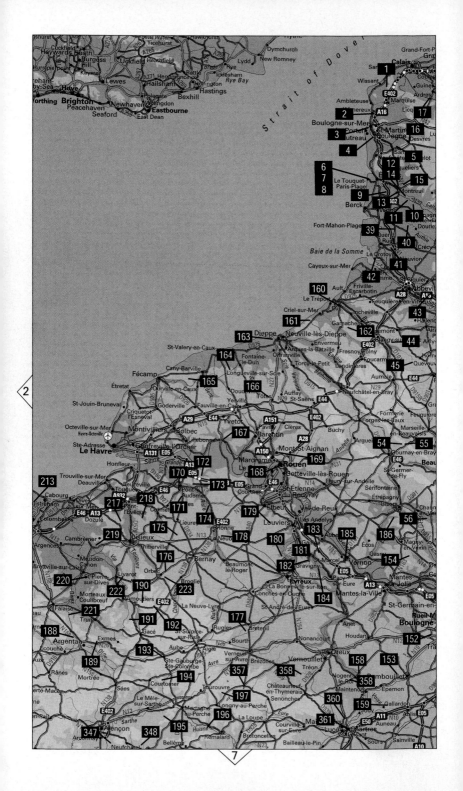

Map 3

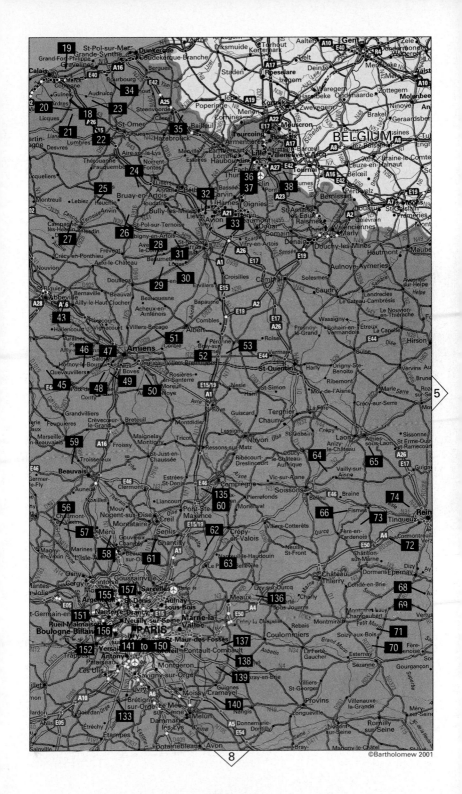

Map 4

©Bartholomew 2001

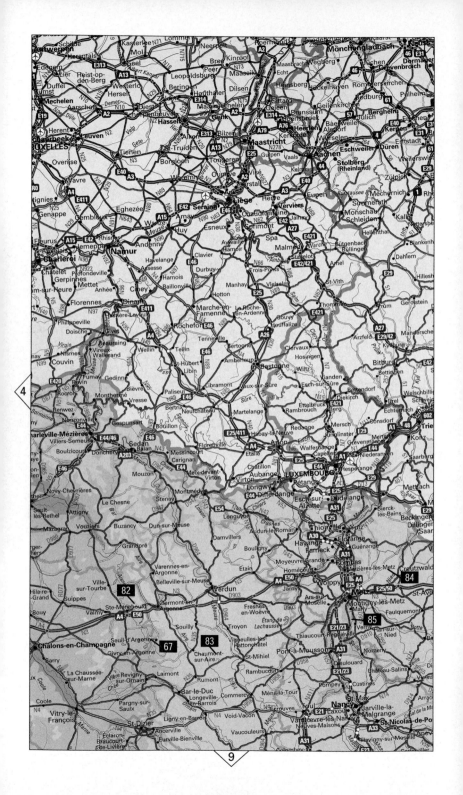

Map 5

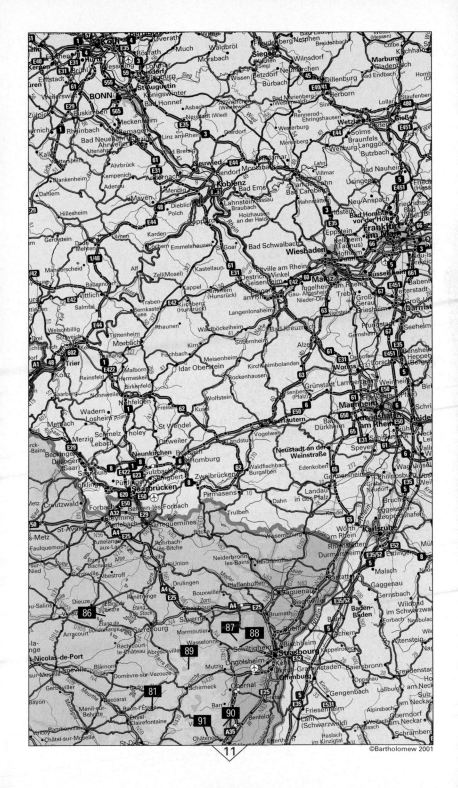

©Bartholomew 2001

Map 6

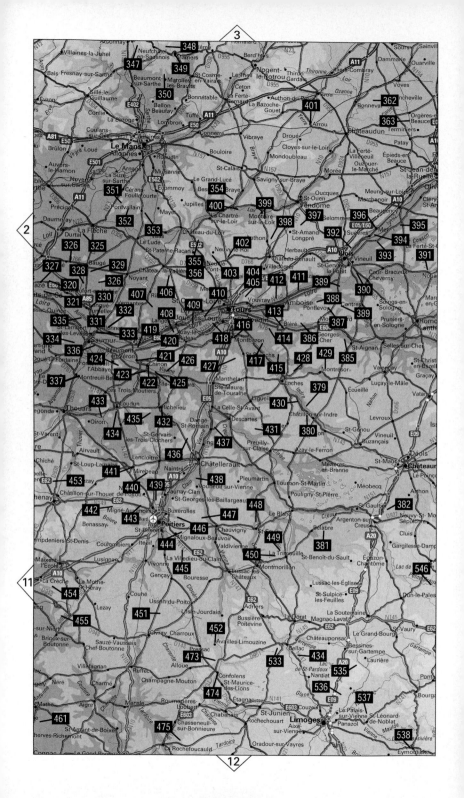

Map 7

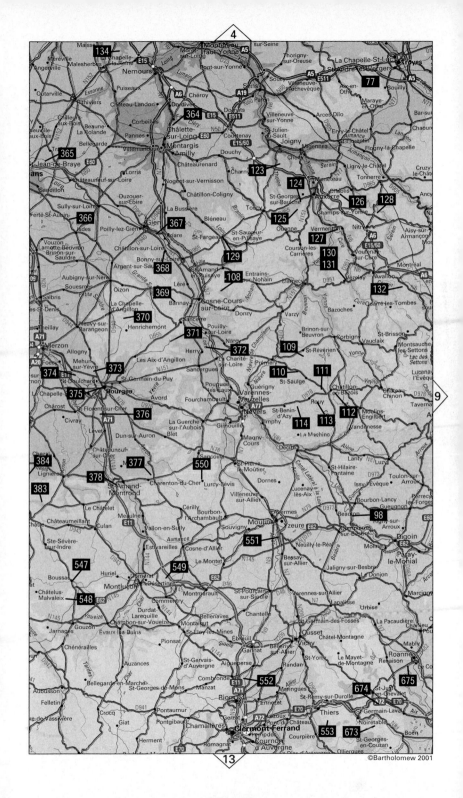

Map 8

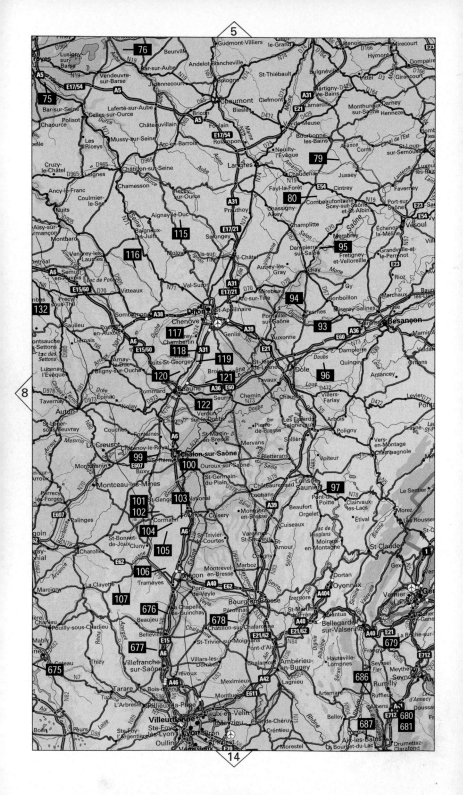

Map 9

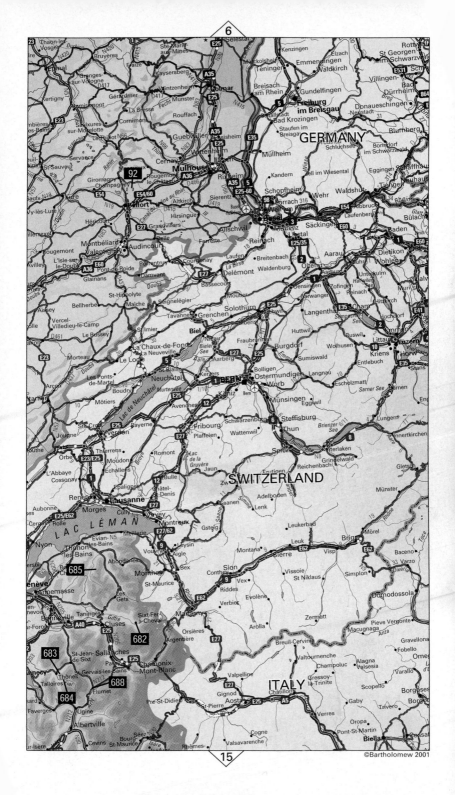

©Bartholomew 2001

Map 10

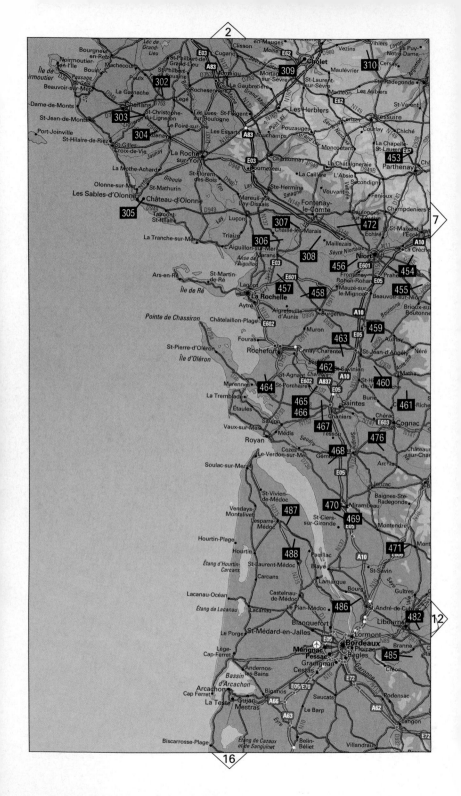

Map 11

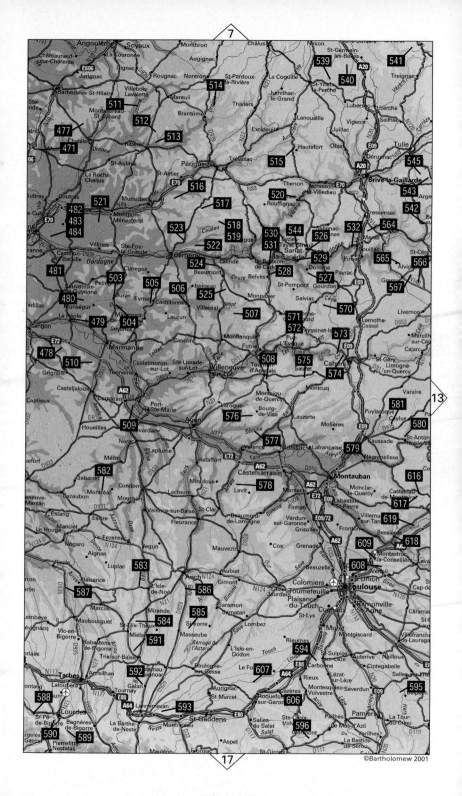

Map 12

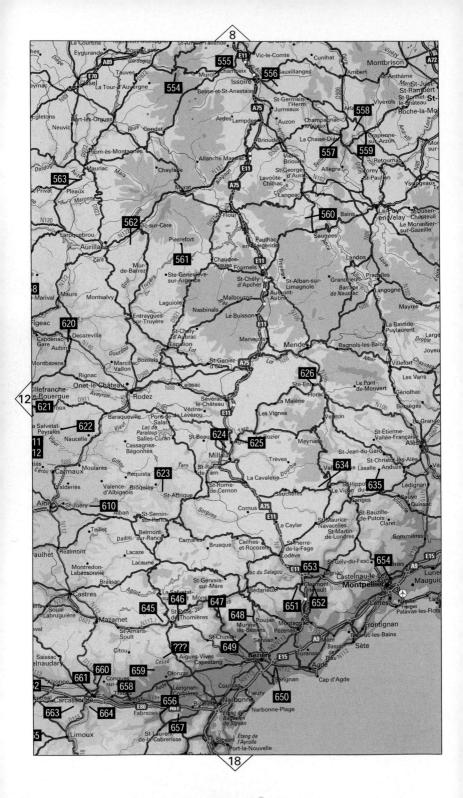

Map 13

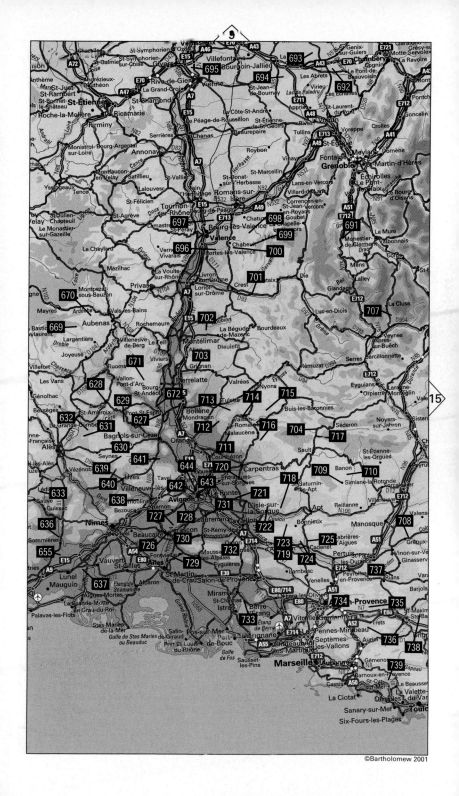

Map 14

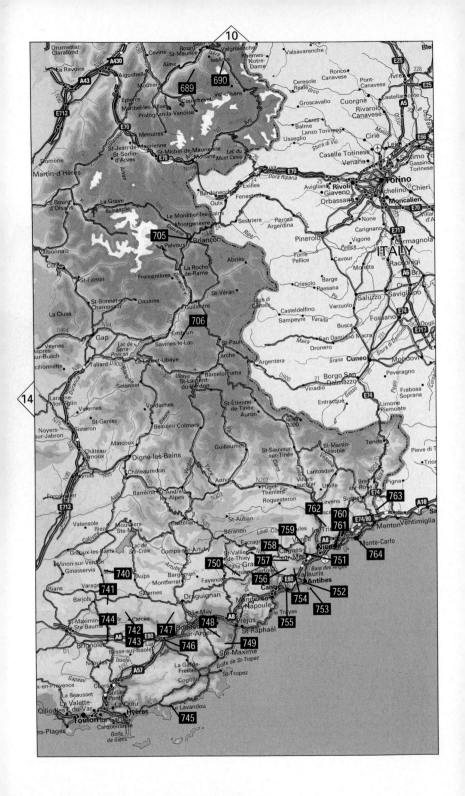

Map 15

©Bartholomew 2001

Map 16

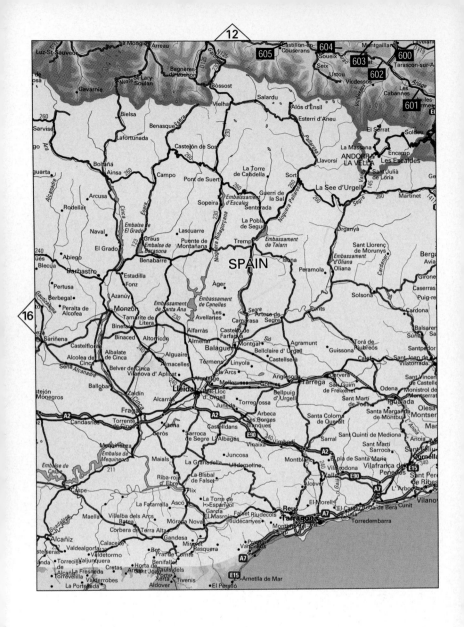

Map 17

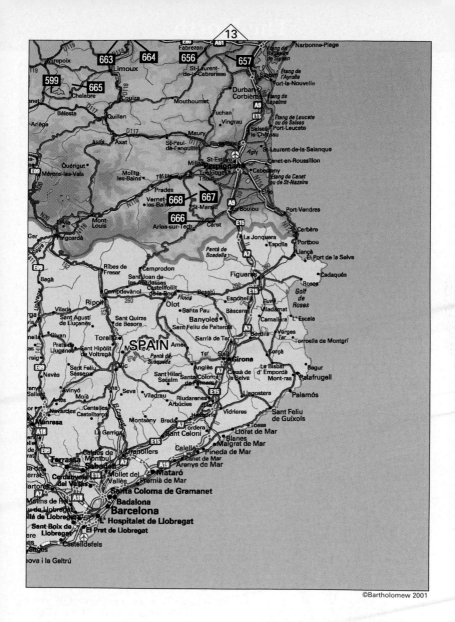

Map 18

Your dark, lively hostess will flash her quick smile and lead you into her house of surprises. The little low frontage opens onto a most unexpected open-plan, double-height living space where modern and family pieces - a superb heavy table made from a pair of convent doors, a baby grand piano, an immensely high carved *fiancée's armoire* (the French girl's bottom drawer) - sit comfortably together and a picture window brings the garden indoors for breakfast. Upstairs, a gallery leads to the pretty, attic bedrooms where rafters frame dormer windows and crochet bedcovers create that old French country atmosphere.

Rooms: 1 double, 1 triple, 1 suite for 4; all with shower or bath & wc.

Price: €43 for two.

Meals: Dinner €15, including wine & coffee.

Closed: Christmas & New Year.

Calais-Boulogne autoroute A16, exit 9 for Hervelinghin on D244. In village, house on right before church.

Catherine & Jean-Marc Petitprez
La Leulène
708 rue Principale
62179 Hervelinghen
Pas-de-Calais
Tel: (0)3 21 82 47 30
E-mail: laleulene@aol.com

The North

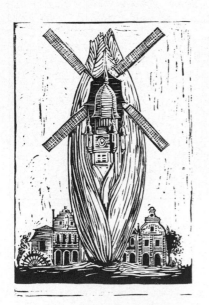

On the flat, fertile plains of Flanders, among the swathes of wheat and maize, grow windmills, belfries and the arcaded streets of lovely old Arras.

Entry No: 1   Map: 3

Perfect for a first or last night to your French holiday or a good place from which to explore the 'Opal Coast', made fashionable by the British in the thirties. *Monsieur Hulot's Holiday* mirrors the atmosphere of the little seaside town and this ravishingly exuberant house on the front. Mary's décor is soberly luxurious, in keeping with the period: white linen, wooden floors, carefully-chosen fabrics and furniture. She speaks excellent English and has acquired some good English habits - she may offer you a cup of tea in the beautiful room looking out to sea. Her huge and delicious breakfast takes place here too.

Rooms: 2 doubles, 2 twins, all with bath or shower & wc.

Price: €60-€75 for two.

Meals: Wide choice of restaurants locally.

Closed: Never.

From A16 exit 3 to Wimereux. In town, go to sea front. House about halfway along promenade, 100m left of Hôtel Atlantic (with your back to the sea).

Mary Avot
La Goelette
13 Digue de Mer
62930 Wimereux, Pas-de-Calais
Tel: (0)3 21 32 62 44
Fax: (0)3 21 33 77 54
E-mail: lagoelette@nordnet.fr
Web: www.lagoelette.com

Entry No: 2   Map: **3**

Distinguished is the word: well-groomed rooms and a very elegant hostess whose B&B philosophy is founded on trust and respect. An effervescent animal-lover, she says her guests have "opened the world to her". Huge, heavy family furniture, a great high-arched floral hall, dining space and French upholstered upright chairs for 12 in the common areas. The 'Big Bedroom' is fabulous, its bathroom almost more so; the top-floor suite is more Modern Rustic. All fascinating, capturing the flavour of one particular (and lovable) kind of France. Just 100 yards from the lovely old walled town of Boulogne.

Rooms: 1 double with bath & wc; 1 triple with shower & wc on different floor; 1 suite for 4 with shower, sharing wc.

Price: €45.50 for two.

Meals: Wide choice of restaurants within ramparts, walking distance.

Closed: January.

Follow signs for 'Vieille Ville'. Rue Flahaut is off Boulevard Mariette which runs below the ramparts on the northern side of the city past the Porte des Dunes.

Simone & Édouard Delabie
26 rue Flahaut
62200 Boulogne sur Mer
Pas-de-Calais
Tel: (0)3 21 31 88 74

Entry No: 3   Map: **3**

The golden stone of the old farmhouse is easy on the eye as you arrive, flowers flourish in the front, the big garden and orchard go down to the river behind, but there are only a few horses in the stables now; the main stud farm is further away. Madame is lively and fun when relaxed although your hosts have a busy life and may be a little preoccupied. The bedrooms, in a self-contained outbuilding which looks out onto the courtyard and wooded hills, have simple, modern décor - the new double has a canopied bed - and the living room is also straightforward. A good family stopover. *Gîte space for 9 people.*

Rooms: 2 doubles, 1 twin, all with shower & wc; 1 double with bath & wc.

Price: €42-€49 for two; reduction 2 nights or more.

Meals: Auberge in village.

Closed: Christmas & New Year.

From Boulogne D940 to St Léonard; at 2nd lights, left on small road to Echingen (no sign); in village centre, left in tiny street imm'ly after sharp bend; left first gateway.

Jacqueline & Jean-Pierre Boussemaere
Rue de l'Eglise
62360 Echinghen
Pas-de-Calais
Tel: (0)3 21 91 14 34
Fax: (0)3 21 91 06 41
E-mail: jp-boussemaere@wanadoo.fr

Entry No: 4   Map: **3**

Behind its flat face, the house unfolds round the courtyard, over the porch, into an unexpectedly lovely garden. It is a generous *Notaire's* house (the shield signals his office) with original mouldings, tiles and fireplaces. Big, prettily traditional French rooms have antiques, good rugs on wooden floors, modern bathrooms and there's a gloriously original attic *salon* for guests with all the furniture gathered in the centre. Breakfast includes *clafoutis* if you're lucky. The village is genuinely unspoilt, your hosts have a similar well-bred, olde-worlde air to them and modernity intrudes very little in the form of traffic noise at night.

Rooms: 1 double, 2 twins, all with bath or shower & wc.

Price: €40 for two.

Meals: Good restaurant 5km.

Closed: Never.

From Boulogne N1 S towards St Léonard & Montreuil for approx. 15km. In Samer, take road that goes down to right of church; house on left, near top of hill.

Joëlle Maucotel
127 rue du Breuil
62830 Samer
Pas-de-Calais
Tel: (0)3 21 87 64 19
        (0)6 77 83 04 74
Fax: (0)3 21 87 64 19

Entry No: 5   Map: **3**

These two are fabulously alive and attentive, cultivated and communicative. Georges is an Orson-Wellesian figure, well able to talk at the same time as gentle but determined Marie... a sort of irresistible double act. The well-proportioned house is an architectural flourish, the contents a pleasing mix of antique and modern. Guest rooms, with their own entrances, have pretty bedding, one or two antiques and good bathrooms. The only possible drawback is the Holiday Inn opposite but it's a quiet family hotel, the sea is just 10 minutes away through the trees and there's stacks to do locally. Perfect for children, lots of talk and fun. And Georges paints extremely well.

Rooms: 1 double, 1 twin, both with bath & wc.

Price: €60 for two.

Meals: Wide choice of restaurants within walking distance.

Closed: 15 November-15 March.

From A16 Le Touquet exit; through Etaples; follow signs for Le Touquet centre. After 4th lights, take 2nd right towards Holiday Inn. 2nd house on right opposite telephone box.

Georges & Marie Versmée
Birdy Land
Avenue du Maréchal Foch
62520 Le Touquet
Pas-de-Calais
Tel: (0)3 21 05 31 46/
       (0)3 27 46 39 41
Fax: (0)3 21 05 95 07

Entry No: 6   Map: **3**

The tufted dunes whisper in the westerly sea breeze or the easterly road hum: walk out and join others on the path to the beach. Guests have the whole top floor here: dark, dynamic Elena brings breakfast to the flame-covered table in the bright living room or the dune-view veranda. Her décor is pretty with modernistic touches (viz. the bendy wire clock), sofas round a log stove for chilly evenings and snug, individual bedrooms (minimal storage space). Plus sand-yachting and fashionable resort life at your feet. *Entire apartment also available to rent.*

Rooms: 2 doubles, 1 triple, 1 twin, plus 2 bathrooms which can be shared, or private for a supplement.

Price: €45-€51 for two.

Meals: Restaurants in Le Touquet.

Closed: Never.

At entrance of Le Touquet head for 'Base Nautique Sud'. Then towards Rue de Paris; head straight towards dunes. Villa on top of hill.

Elena Desprez
La Crête des Dunes, Avenue Blériot
62520 Le Touquet
Pas-de-Calais
Tel: (0)3 21 05 04 98
Fax: (0)3 21 05 04 98
E-mail: contact@bnbletouquet.com
Web: www.bnbletouquet.com

Entry No: 7   Map: **3**

On a former English polo pitch sits this neat house in a fabulous garden: curly iron chairs, overflowing pots, quiet glades and tame wild rabbits - the perfect place to retire with a favourite book. Inside, the entire length of a gnarled trunk stretches across the ceiling, English florals and comfy sofas jostle with ethnic rugs and terracotta tiles, bedrooms are warm peaches and cream, ivory and tidy baby-blue stripes with old pine, cream carpets, lacy cotton cushions. Lucie is an attentive hostess who looks after her guests with easy-going elegance, though Nixon the Golden Labrador will steal any show.

Rooms: 1 family suite with wc & separate bathroom; 2 doubles with separate bathrooms; 1 double with bath & wc.

Price: €46-€50 for two.

Meals: Restaurants Le Touquet 1.5km.

Closed: January.

From A16 exit Le Touquet/Étaples for Le Touquet; across bridge, over big r'about (McDonalds) then left at 2nd traffic light; drive 150m down on left.

Lucie & Serge Bournoville
Le Polo
Allée des Pâquerettes
62520 Le Touquet
Pas-de-Calais
Tel: (0)3 21 05 18 14
Fax: (0)3 21 05 36 98
E-mail: bournovilles@minitel.net

Entry No: 8   Map: **3**

Madame Horel is a true Breton: she makes forty crêpes every morning to complete her already copious and delicious breakfast served in the plant-filled conservatory, built onto one end of the Horels' modern house and overlooking the garden. This garden is Madame's ruling passion - she says she is incapable of letting someone sleep in a room without fresh flowers: you could even choose the season of your visit according to your floral preferences. Her bedrooms are full of thoughtful touches - sweets by your bed, hairdryers - to add to the pretty, feminine décor.

Rooms: 2 triples, 1 double, all with shower & wc.

Price: €45 for two.

Meals: 3 restaurants in St Josse.

Closed: Never.

From A16 exit 25 for Rang du Fliers; right at 1st roundabout onto D140 towards Merlimont; at 2nd roundabout take D143 for Le Touquet; at 3rd r'bout right on D144E to St Josse & follow signs.

Marie-Thérèse & Maurice Horel
Les Buissonnets
67-70 chemin des Corps Saints
62170 St Josse
Pas-de-Calais
Tel: (0)3 21 84 12 12
Fax: (0)3 21 84 12 12

Entry No: 9   Map: **3**

Le Saule has been recommended by many in terms such as "the best cowshed I've ever stayed in". Others claimed they'd had their "best breakfast in France" here. And we know that the Trunnets' smiles are genuine, their delight in your company unfeigned, their converted outbuilding handsome and perfectly finished (down to mosquito nets on windows), if a touch characterless, and beds excellent (one equally smart guest room is in the main house). Monsieur is only too happy to show you the flax production process (it's fascinating), while Madame will be baking yet another superb cake for tomorrow's breakfast.

Rooms: 1 double, 3 triples, all with shower & wc.

Price: €46 for two.

Meals: Choice of restaurants in Montreuil, 6km.

Closed: Never.

From A16 exit Montreuil. Just before town right at traffic lights & left towards Brimeux on D349. In Brimeux left at junction, pass church, house on right, signposted.

M & Mme Germain Trunnet
Ferme du Saule
20 rue de l'Église
62170 Brimeux
Pas-de-Calais
Tel: (0)3 21 06 01 28
Fax: (0)3 21 81 40 14

Entry No: 10　　　Map: 3

A calm unaffected welcome and not even a cockerel to disturb the peace. Madame is as kindly and down-to-earth as you would expect of someone who brought up nine children on the farm. The farmhouse, "built in 1724 by Lovergne", has a natural family feel. Rooms are simple: the twin in the main house has country fabrics and a wooden floor; the double off the little rose garden is darker, more intimate. Breakfast can include cheese and home-made jam or fresh baguettes and croissants; Madame is a fount of local knowledge and loves getting to know her guests properly, so do stay on.

Rooms: 1 double, 1 twin, both with shower & wc.

Price: €35-€41 for two.

Meals: Restaurants in Montreuil sur Mer 3km.

Closed: December-February.

From A16 exit 26 to Montreuil; D349 for Hesdin; through Beaumerie St Martin; first right at signpost.

Jeanne-Marie & Francis Locqueville
L'Overgne
62170 Beaumerie St Martin
Pas-de-Calais
Tel: (0)3 21 81 81 87

Entry No: 11　　　Map: 3

As the name implies, it was indeed the home farm of the nearby Carthusian monastery and Anne, who manages to run the B&B, bring up three delightful children and teach part-time, is a charming, thoughtful hostess. Her talent and taste are in the guest rooms - hard to believe they were once pigsties, now transformed into pretty bedrooms, not over-large but very comfortable. Breakfast, which may include crêpes, is served in the enchantingly decorated kitchen/diner. Part of the monastery is open to visitors - a pleasant after-breakfast discovery - or you can play a game of tennis on the home court (lessons available too).

Rooms: 1 double, 1 triple, both with shower & wc.

Price: €43 for two.

Meals: Choice of restaurants in Montreuil, 4km.

Closed: Never.

From A16 exit Montreuil sur Mer onto N1 direction Le Touquet/Boulogne. At lights right to Neuville then right on D113. Pass 2 other Chambres d'Hôtes - house on left next to abbey.

Anne Fourdinier
Ferme de la Chartreuse
62170 Neuville sous Montreuil
Pas-de-Calais
Tel: (0)3 21 81 07 31
Fax: (0)3 21 81 07 31

Behind the pretty face hides the wonder of an extraordinary free-standing wooden staircase, a local speciality in the 17th century. Two gracious rooms up here: high ceilings, parquet floors, space and no clutter - the primrose and moss twin over the street has elegant original cupboards; the custard and wine double over the back is cosily alcoved. Families will like the privacy of the snugger room across the yard: pretty blue head cushions and duvet-clothed bunks. Your hosts used to run a bistro and Madame is the jolliest, laughingest hostess we know.

Rooms: 1 twin with corner bath & wc; 1 double, 1 family room for 4, both with bath & wc.

Price: €46 for two.

Meals: Full choice of restaurants on doorstep.

Closed: Never.

In Montreuil, drive to top, Place Darnétal; house on right facing square.

M & Mme Louchez
77 rue Pierre Ledent
62170 Montreuil sur Mer
Pas-de-Calais
Tel: (0)3 21 81 54 68
E-mail: louchez.anne@wanadoo.fr

A modern bungalow with the heart of traditional French country life. When your hosts handed the family farm on to the next generation, they wanted to go on doing B&B in their new house. The road is at the front, big windows let in the green that wraps the land at the back and it has a real family feel: photos and mementoes everywhere, in the comfortable guest rooms too, with their good, pretty bathrooms. Madame, clearly a natural at grandmothering, might even mind your baby if you want to go off to sample the bright lights of Montreuil. Friendly and impeccable, it is excellent value and an ideal stopover.

Rooms: 1 double with bath & wc; 1 quadruple with shower & wc.

Price: € 38 for two.

Meals: Good choice of restaurants in Montreuil, 3km.

Closed: Never.

In the walled garden the ancient dovecote sings with life; the house feels almost Gothic on a dark night in its bare, white-stoned simplicity - perfectly restored for lovers of the soberly authentic. The vaulted oak and stone dining room is a great rarity; bedrooms and bathrooms are remarkable in artistry and personality: lit candles, old mirrors, appropriate pictures, bits of bronze and brass, rich tapestry and patchwork fabrics - unusual yet utterly inviting. Madame is flexible and helpful, breakfasts are full of light, space and home-made jams, her passions include rescuing animals and collecting 1900s dress-dummies. A fine balance of sobriety and fantasy.

Rooms: 2 doubles, 1 suite for 4, all with bath & wc.

Price: € 50 for two.

Meals: Wide choice of restaurants 5km.

Closed: Never.

From A16 exit Montreuil sur Mer N1 for Le Touquet/Boulogne; at lights right to Neuville; right D113 for 200m; house on right.

From Montreuil D901 to Neuville. There, on sharp bend, D113 past La Chartreuse to Marles/Canche; 2km to village centre. House on right at crossroads after tight bend - go slowly!

Hubert & Christiane Fourdinier
30 rue de la Chartreuse
62170 Neuville sous Montreuil
Pas-de-Calais
Tel: (0)3 21 81 95 05
Fax: (0)3 21 81 95 05

Mme Dominique Leroy
Manoir Francis
62170 Marles sur Canche
Pas-de-Calais
Tel: (0)3 21 81 38 80
Fax: (0)3 21 81 38 56

Entry No: 14   Map: **3**

Entry No: 15   Map: **3**

Jean-Loop will always be remembered as France's first astronaut but he is less known for running a B&B in his old spaceship. Over tea and a mouth-watering scone, talk space as a flight simulator whisks you off to the Milky Way - the effect is quite stunning. Experience zero gravity with a complimentary cocktail before dinner - this engaging space vet just winks when you ask what's in it - then choose from a Franco-Nasa fusion of pill-shaped meals - three courses with coffee and petit fours in one remarkable tablet. For those who revel in totally unnatural pleasures.

Rooms: 5 converted laundromat tumble-dryers.

Price: 1 eurostar. Owner charges a constellation fee.

Meals: Don't take the headache pills by accident.

Closed: Black Holeday Monday.

Go to the nearest comic shop and browse in the sci-fi section.

Capt. Jean-Loop P. Card
Astronef
L'Espace
La Frontière Finale
Pas-de-Calais
E-mail: flymetothemoon@once.pleaset
Web: www.spritedaway.com

Entry No: 16   Map: 3

The 'Cloths of Gold' has been an inn since 1640 and Christine's open, joyful welcome fits the tradition - she will receive you like old friends. She uses colour well too: the warm, bright little guest dayroom is a reflection of her dynamic personality; the bedrooms - blue, yellow, green and red - are equally fresh and bright, with good modern furniture and some pretty fabric effects. Three of them give onto the street but Ardres, a delightful little town, is extremely quiet at night while the green and gentle garden gives a country feel at the back.

Rooms: 1 twin, 2 doubles, 1 family, all with shower & wc.

Price: €45 for two; reduction 2 nights or more.

Meals: Restaurants within walking distance.

Closed: Never.

From Calais A16, exit 17; N43 to Ardres; right after church - house on corner on left.

Christine & François Borel
Les Draps d'Or
152 rue Lambert d'Ardres
62610 Ardres, Pas-de-Calais
Tel: (0)3 21 82 20 44
Fax: (0)3 21 82 20 44
E-mail: draps.dor@freesbee.fr
Web: www.drapsdor.fr.st

Entry No: 17   Map: 3

A warm, eager couple, she the artist, he the earthy do-er, and an unusual house of genuine character: a big converted stable block, a glass and brick screen, a 'little house' (two rooms prettily independent here) and the creeper-covered stable walls (horses welcome to share with the children's ponies) enclose the garden and old stone pond in an embrace of bricks, arches and columns - a deliciously sheltered, other-worldly feel. The house has space and interesting 1930s furniture; plants, pictures and objects abound; bedrooms, lightly decorated with Françoise's stencils and hand-painted furniture, are fresh and welcoming. It's a delight to be here.

Rooms: 2 twins, 1 suite, each with shower & wc; 1 triple with shower; wc on floor below.

Price: € 52 for two.

Meals: Dinner occasionally available € 18, including wine & coffee; restaurants 1km.

Closed: Never.

From Calais A16 exit 17 for St Omer, RN43. Pass Les Attaques, Pont d'Ardres, first r'bout at Bois en Ardres; before 2nd r'bout left Rue de Saint Quentin for 1km; green gate.

Françoise & Thierry Roger
Le Manoir de Bois en Ardres
1530 rue de St Quentin
62610 Ardres, Pas-de-Calais
Tel: (0)3 21 85 97 78
Fax: (0)3 21 36 48 07
E-mail: roger@aumanoir.com
Web: www.aumanoir.com

Entry No: 18   Map: 4

All is tranquil at Meldick. The long dining room windows look out onto the pond and the fields beyond - hard to imagine that two terrible wars were waged here, but one of Madame's fascinating treasures is a real collection of medals and badges from those days. She has huge energy, a beautiful 1930s house that is a delight to be in and simply loves doing B&B because she enjoys the contact so much. Rooms are colour-themed, good-sized, carefully decorated and finely furnished; the family room is enormous! You are definitely welcomed as friends into the Houzets' home.

Rooms: 2 double, 2 twin, 1 room for 4, all with bath or shower & wc.

Price: € 50 for two.

Meals: Good restaurant 5km.

Closed: Never.

From A16 exit 19 to Marck. There, right on D940 then immed. left to Le Fort Vert, through Marck. At Le Fort Vert, right onto D119. House 3km along on right

Jean & Danièle Houzet
Manoir du Meldick
2528 ave du Général de Gaulle
Le Fort Vert
62730 Marck, Pas-de-Calais
Tel: (0)3 21 85 74 34
Fax: (0)3 21 85 74 34
E-mail: jeandaniele.houzet@free.fr

Entry No: 19   Map: 4

An open, smiling, intelligent family who 'do' wine-tastings and will sell you wine and honey, they are delightful people. The big park is soft and appealing and lots of animals wander around; the closeness to ferry ports is seductive although the nearby main road and TGV line may disturb some people. Straightforward and simple are the key words here - no luxury and showers behind curtains. Breakfast is in the separate guest quarters (or the family kitchen for very early starts), where basic pine furniture and slatting grace the smallish rooms, and windows look onto lawn and trees. *Gîte space for 11 people.*

Rooms: 2 triples, both with shower, sharing wc; 1 quadruple with shower & wc.

Price: €34.50-€38 for two.

Meals: Restaurants nearby.

Closed: Never.

This organic dairy farm is run with passion by your hosts who receive you in their square old house at the end of the tree-lined drive and ply you with organic-based food. Lut, from Belgium, is a quiet, sensitive and unpretentiously warm mother of two boys - her genuine welcome will touch you. Your rather minimalist double-aspect room spreads comfort with its finely friezed walls and there's a tiny room off it with a refrigerator. It is reached from the (somewhat disappointing) sitting room, not used by the family when guests are here, but the romantic garden is great with its rose bowers and little formal hedges.

Rooms: 1 double with shower & wc.

Price: €43 for two.

Meals: Dinner €17, incl. wine & coffee.

Closed: Never.

From A26 exit 2 onto N43 for Calais. Wolphus on left 1km after junction, with woods beside road. Be careful turning in.

Jean-Jacques Behaghel
La Ferme de Wolphus
62890 Zouafques
Pas-de-Calais
Tel: (0)3 21 35 61 61
Fax: (0)3 21 35 61 61
E-mail: ferme.de.wolphus@wanadoo.fr

From A26 exit 2 towards Licques; through Tournehem & Bonningues lès Ardres; left after village to farm.

Lut & Jean-Michel Louf-Degrauwe
La Ferme de Beaupré
129 rue de Licques
62890 Bonningues lès Ardres
Pas-de-Calais
Tel: (0)3 21 35 14 44
Fax: (0)3 21 35 57 35
E-mail: degrauwelut@minitel.net

Bobble-edged curtains and squat, plush chairs fight for the retro stakes in the hall. Here, you will meet the nicest, simplest farming folk imaginable, worn and naturally gracious after a lifetime on the land. Madame laughs easily and cooks French country meals, eaten in true conviviality and praised to the skies by readers, with home-grown ingredients (even the *kir* is made with raspberry *maison*). Rooms are simply, carefully authentic with old wooden beds, marble-top chests, one superb carved wardrobe and bed, small showers, lots of light. A real French experience - catch it before it disappears into the hi-tech millennium!

Rooms: 1 double, 1 twin, both with shower & wc.

Price: € 33 for two.

Meals: Dinner € 15, including wine & coffee.

Closed: Never.

From A26 exit 2 on N43 towards St Omer. 3km after Nordausques, right to Nortleulinghen. In village, right to church and right into Rue de la Mairie.

M & Mme Noël Martin
8 rue de la Mairie
62890 Nortleulinghen
Pas-de-Calais
Tel: (0)3 21 35 64 60

Entry No: 22   Map: 4

A lovely old lady in a genuine old farmhouse! She talks lots, in French, and otherwise relies on radio and telly for company. Hers is a piecemeal family house with comfortable old furniture and masses of photographs (a tribe of grandchildren). Rooms are rustically attractive: well-decorated with good beds and windows onto the peace outside. Madame loves cooking her delicious country dishes for visitors and many readers have praised her natural hospitality. Ask to see the exquisite vaulted stables - built for cows and carthorses, fit for thoroughbreds and prizewinners.

Rooms: 2 doubles, 1 with cot & child's bed, all with shower & wc.

Price: € 32.50 for two.

Meals: Dinner € 14, including wine & coffee.

Closed: November-March.

From A26 exit 2 for Tournehem, over N43, follow to Muncq Nieurlet, on towards Ruminghem. House on left, about 1.5km after leaving Muncq Nieurlet, at signpost.

Mme Françoise Breton
La Motte Obin
62890 Muncq Nieurlet
Pas-de-Calais
Tel: (0)3 21 82 79 63

Entry No: 23   Map: 4

Gina's welcome is as genuine and unpretentious as her house, set in calm countryside with neither cockerels nor dogs to alarm your early morning. There are informal wine-tastings at dinner and in the outbuilding - where guests are welcome to use the cooking equipment - and *pétanque* tournaments in summer. Madame calls her guest rooms *La Verte, La Rose, La Bleue...* and there are two other cosy ones under the roof of this 200-year-old farmhouse (mind your head up there!). Your hostess cares deeply that everyone should be happy and creates a really homely atmosphere.

Rooms: 3 doubles, 2 triples, all with bath or shower & wc.

Price: €42-€46 for two.

Meals: Dinner €18.5, including wine & coffee.

Closed: Never.

The Battle of Agincourt (remember your *Henry V*?) was in 1415, right here; this house, tower and all, was built in 1750. You imagine hearing the clanking of swords? Open your eyes and you may indeed see medieval knights passing - that's just your hosts on their way to re-enact a battle: they love their local history and tales of ghosts and archers, soldiers and horses. The pretty guest rooms, called *Voyage, Romantique, Retro...*, are in an attached wattle-and-daub house with its own dayroom and log fire. Breakfast is in a room crammed with bric-a-brac in the tower. Huge fun.

Rooms: 3 doubles, 1 triple, all with shower & wc (1 behind curtain).

Price: €46 for two.

Meals: Restaurant 1km; choice 6-15km.

Closed: Never.

From Calais A26, exit 4 to Thérouanne then D341 to Auchy au Bois (12km). Right at Le Vert Dragon restaurant. 1st left; 2nd house on right after church.

From St Omer D928 for Abbeville. At Ruisseauville left for Blangy-Tramecourt; at next x-roads, left for Tramecourt; house 100m along.

Gina Bulot
Les Cohettes
28 rue de Pernes
62190 Auchy au Bois
Pas-de-Calais
Tel: (0)3 21 02 09 47
Fax: (0)3 21 02 81 68
E-mail: temps-libre-evasion@wanadoo.fr

Patrick & Marie-Josée Fenet
La Gacogne
62310 Azincourt
Pas-de-Calais
Tel: (0)3 21 04 45 61
Fax: (0)3 21 04 45 61

You can see it has character and history and... two dining rooms: one has a unique '1830s-Medieval' fireplace, the other is classical French with coffered ceiling, deeply carved door frames, a vast Louis XIII dresser. In an outbuilding, guest rooms are simpler and more modern, each with some old furniture and a neat shower room, one with its own kitchen and garden. Madame loves telling tales of the house and its contents, has a couple of goats in the quiet garden (but weekend racetrack in the valley), will do anything she can to be of service to guests. Both your hosts work constantly on their beloved house - good folk.

Rooms: 2 doubles, 3 twins (2 on ground floor), all with shower & wc.

Price: €38 for two.

Meals: Choice of restaurants within walking distance; self-catering possible.

Closed: Never.

From St Pol sur Ternoise, D343 NW for Fruges. Just after entering Gauchin Verloingt, right Rue de Troisvaux; right Rue des Montifaux. House on right.

Marie-Christine & Philippe Vion
Le Loubarré
550 rue des Montifaux
62130 Gauchin Verloingt
Pas-de-Calais
Tel: (0)3 21 03 05 05
Fax: (0)3 21 41 26 76
E-mail: mcvion.loubarre@wanadoo.fr

Entry No: 26   Map: 4

The Garrels left lively Lille for the country, exchanging staying in B&Bs for running their own. They love meeting guests, both young and old, and children from the village play in their yard. Bedrooms round the pretty courtyard have wonky timbers, cream tiled floors, pastel colours and modern bathrooms - a joint effort: Madame's ideas executed by Monsieur. The family room snugly holds all you'll need with, upstairs, toys, books, twin beds tucked beneath eaves - a dream den. Walk in the hills and woods behind - one of the delightful donkeys will happily accompany you.

Rooms: 1 double, 1 duplex for four, both with shower, wc & kitchenette; 1 double with shower & wc.

Price: €42 for two; €61 for four.

Meals: Restaurants 3-4km; self-catering possible; BBQ.

Closed: Never.

From Hesdin D928 towards St Omer; 1st left D913 through Huby St Leu to Guisy; signposted.

Martine & Marc-Willam Garrel
La Hotoire
2 place de la Mairie
62140 Guisy
Pas-de-Calais
Tel: (0)3 21 81 00 31
Fax: (0)3 21 81 00 31
E-mail: a.la.hotoire@wanadoo.fr

Entry No: 27   Map: 4

An exceptional mix of place and people. After 12 years, this dynamic family - all eight of them - have almost finished rebuilding their château and getting covered in paint, brightening their escutcheon while running a publishing house in Paris and leading a brilliant social life - phenomenal energy, fascinating people, natural hospitality that makes up for any residual damp or possible winter chill. Built in 1745, the château has striking grandeur: come play lord and lady in vastly beautiful chandeliered, ancestored *salons*, enjoy an aristocratically graceful bedroom with big windows and a good bathroom and walk the rolling green parkland as if it were your own.

Rooms: 4 doubles/twins, all with bath or shower & wc.

Price: €90 for two.

Meals: 2 restaurants within 4km.

Closed: Never.

From Arras towards St Pol le Touquet N39 5km; left on D75 to Avesnes le Comte; towards Doullens/Grand-Rullecourt 4km. Château in village square, signed.

Patrice & Chantal de Saulieu
Château de Grand-Rullecourt
62810 Grand Rullecourt
Pas-de-Calais
Tel: (0)3 21 58 06 37
Fax: (0)1 41 27 97 30
E-mail: Isaulieu@routiers.com
Web: www.saulieu.com/chateau/

Entry No: 28　　　　　Map: 4

The stately face has been lifted and it looks grander than ever, surrounded by its great park and orchards producing delicious apples by a method called 'Reasoned Agriculture'. Inside, it is a warm, embracing country house with a panelled breakfast room, a perfectly amazing, museum-worthy, multi-tiled gents cloakroom and, up the wide old stairs, delightful bedrooms, some very big, mostly done with fresh pine furniture and good strong colours on wooden floors with old fireplaces or mirrored armoires. Quiet and intelligent, Sylvie will make you feel deeply welcome in her redecorated rooms while serenely managing her young family. *Gîte space for 4 people.*

Rooms: 2 triples, 1 double, 2 suites for 4, all with bath or shower & wc.

Price: €46 for two.

Meals: Choice of restaurants 5-8km.

Closed: January.

From Doullens N25 towards Arras for 17km. In L'Arbret, first left to Saulty and follow signs.

Emmanuel & Sylvie Dalle
82 rue de la Gare
62158 Saulty
Pas-de-Calais
Tel: (0)3 21 48 24 76
Fax: (0)3 21 48 18 32

Entry No: 29　　　　　Map: 4

You may just come for lovely old Arras or the military cemeteries of the Vimy Ridge but the rural simplicity of this low house, hugging its little garden behind the church, could entice you to stay longer. The very personal rooms with their air of family history are a delightful mix of modern fabrics and interesting antiques: spriggy wallpaper among the timbers, an unusual old desk in the ground-floor room, a super multi-purpose piece on the red-carpeted landing - an armchair/desk/bookcase - said to have belonged to Jules Verne..., plus well-fitted bathrooms. Madame is shyly proud of her house and serves a generous, imaginative breakfast.

Rooms: 2 doubles, 1 twin, all with bath or shower & wc.

Price: € 30 for two.

Meals: Basic bar/restaurant 7km.

Closed: Never.

Madame is warmly relaxed and attentive, the pivot of her much-photographed family, and is passionate about interior design: beautifully-made curtains, gently-matched papers and fabrics, old-fashioned touches here (crochet, carving), modern details there in good comfortable bedrooms. Monsieur's domain, the sheltered garden going down to the little river, is splendid (swings for the children too) and the lime trees are a fitting backdrop to this imposing old manor built in soft grey stone. It originally belonged to the château next door and the drive is still flanked by a fine laurel hedge. A gentle, civilised place to stay.

Rooms: 1 family suite, 1 double, both with bath or shower & wc.

Price: € 44 for two.

Meals: Choice of restaurants 4-7km.

Closed: Never.

From Arras N25 towards Doullens. At Bac du Sud right on D66 to Gouy en Artois and Fosseux. House near church.

Geneviève Delacourt
3 rue de l'Église
62810 Fosseux
Pas-de-Calais
Tel: (0)3 21 48 40 13
Fax: (0)3 21 48 40 13

From Arras, N39 towards Le Touquet. After 6km under railway bridge, 1st left along D56 to Duisans. House first on left.

Annie & Patrick Senlis
Le Clos Grincourt
18 rue du Château
62161 Duisans
Pas-de-Calais
Tel: (0)3 21 48 68 33
Fax: (0)3 21 48 68 33

They are wonderful in their unexpected town farmyard! A retired couple of real farmers, he silently earthy, loving to stay at home and do his garden, she comfortably maternal, delighting in her freedom to discover the rest of the world at last and indulge her collectionitis. Their equally typical farmers' house is old-fashioned, pretty and utterly stuffed with bits of china, glass, copper and pewter while the genuine *chambres d'hôtes* (formerly their daughters' rooms: Delphine and Cloé) are family-furnished and draped with all sorts and conditions of crochet. A splendid place, street at the front, fields at the back, farmyard and creeper-covered old house in between - and such a friendly welcome.

Rooms: 1 double, 1 triple, with shower/bath & wc.

Price: € 30 for two.

Meals: Dinner € 11, inc. wine & coffee.

Closed: Never.

The Peugniez are lovely, gentle people whose children have grown and flown; they still farm (cereals only now, having given up beef) and enjoy good company. Their house, a typical example of careful northern French brick-building and as splendid as the 19th-century brewery across the road with its curious double swastika emblem, is simple and most welcoming with a warm family feel and no pretensions. The attic-floor guest rooms have screened-off showers, old timbers and floorboards and make a good-value stopover. And don't forget that fascinating old Arras is thoroughly worth a day trip.

Rooms: 3 doubles, 1 twin, 1 quadruple, all with shower, sharing 2 wcs.

Price: € 34 for two.

Meals: Restaurants in village.

Closed: Christmas & New Year.

A26 from Calais, exit Aix-Noulette for Liévin. Head for 'centre ville', then Givenchy. House is 300m past little park.

From A1 exit 16 on N50 to Arras for 2km; left to Fampoux. In village follow Chambres d'Hôtes signs. House on right

M & Mme François Dupont
Ferme du Moulin
58 rue du Quatre Septembre
62800 Liévin
Pas-de-Calais
Tel: (0)3 21 44 65 91

Dominique & Marie-Thérèse Peugniez
17 rue Paul Verlaine
62118 Fampoux
Pas-de-Calais
Tel: (0)3 21 55 00 90
Fax: (0)3 21 55 00 90

Entry No: 32   Map: 4

Entry No: 33   Map: 4

You will receive a marvellous welcome and be treated with immense care by the competent, smiling owners of this fine old house and its opulent garden. The marble-floored hall strikes you first, then the sober breakfast room, the multitudinous stuffed animals in the dining room and another stylish room with painted panelling. Bedrooms are big and most inviting and all is impeccably clean, orderly and utterly French. A very good, and genteel, stop for those going to and from the ferry, it is just 2-3 minutes' stroll from the town centre and excellent value.

Rooms: 2 doubles, both with shower & wc.

Price: €40 for two.

Meals: Good restaurant 100m.

Closed: Never.

Helped by the innate character of the solid old house (the original frieze in the hall is superb), Béatrice has applied her artist's talent and imagination to wonderful effect in the four guest rooms. One has Roman ruins on the walls and columns for bedside tables; another is all mahogany; all are light and harmonious with marble fireplaces, hand-painted furniture and big shower rooms. Roger is as friendly and helpful as his wife; their three teenagers are well-mannered; their dinners are based on real Flemish specialities and this very Flemish-minded area is probably the most interesting in northern France.

Rooms: 1 twin, 3 doubles, all with shower & wc.

Price: €60 for two.

Meals: Dinner €20, inc. wine & coffee.

Closed: Never.

From Calais A16 E exit 23b into Bourbourg. From Place de l'Hôtel de Ville the street (aka Rue de l'Hôtel de Ville) is left of the town hall as you face it.

From A25 exit 28 on N225/A25 for Lille; exit 13 on D948 for Poperinghe; imm'ly right to Goderwaersveld; D139 to Boeschepe; house next to windmill.

Marilou & Jacques Van de Walle
25 rue des Martyrs de la Résistance
59630 Bourbourg
Nord
Tel: (0)3 28 22 21 41
E-mail: jacques.van-de-walle@wanadoo.fr

Roger & Béatrice Maerten
340 rue de la Gare
59299 Boeschere
Nord
Tel: (0)3 28 49 45 73
Fax: (0)3 28 49 45 73
E-mail: info@boeschepe.com
Web: www.boeschepe.com

Entry No: 34   Map: 4

Entry No: 35   Map: 4

Lille is a richly interesting city where plain façades often hide unsuspected beauties. Jeannine Hulin's townhouse reflects her personality: artistic - kitchen and *salon* show masterly use of colour - and warm, she loves having guests. You breakfast at a tiled table in the bright kitchen or in the flower-filled conservatory above the garden. Original floor tiles, stripped pine doors and masses of plants add atmosphere. The big bedroom is lovely with matching sleigh bed, wardrobe and desk, antique white linen and mirrors, and your delightful bathroom has a claw-footed bath. *Happy to collect from train station.*

Rooms: 1 double with private bath, 1 twin with shower, both sharing wc on floor below.

Price: €40-€41.50 for two.

Meals: Choice of restaurants in town.

Closed: Never, please book ahead.

Chantal is a charming hostess, her welcome more than compensates for an unremarkable modern house on a city street. And there's a lovely surprise: the picture window in the uncluttered living room gives onto a garden full of flowers where you can relax after exploring the treasures of Lille. The bedrooms are small, cosily-carpeted, pleasing and there's a little kitchen for guests. Chantal, bright, energetic and typically French, used to teach English (speaks it perfectly) then adapted her house especially to receive guests. Yves has good English too, and will dine with you - they both enjoy having an open house.

Rooms: 2 doubles, both with shower & wc; 1 twin with bath & wc.

Price: €35-€45 for two.

Meals: Dinner €15, inc. wine & coffee.

Closed: Never.

From A1 exit 20 onto D917 towards Fâches Ronchin - Lille for 4km. At traffic lights (Boulangerie Paul on corner) left; 1st right is Rue des Hannetons.

From Calais/Dunkerque A25 for Lille, exit 4; 1.5km; right at lights to Wattignies. 3 km straight; left for C.R.E.P.S/village centre. Pass church on left. House on right.

Jeannine Hulin
28 rue des Hannetons
59000 Lille
Nord
Tel: (0)3 20 53 46 12
Fax: (0)3 20 53 46 12
E-mail: jeanninehulin@diapason
Web: www.caramail.com

Yves & Chantal Le Bot
59 rue Faidherbe
59139 Wattignies
Nord
Tel: (0)3 20 60 24 51

Entry No: 36   Map: **4**

Entry No: 37   Map: **4**

This classic French farmyard is reached through a 17th-century archway facing the old stables where you will find your bedroom. In a fairly standard conversion job, rooms have been carefully colour-co-ordinated in simple cottagey style and the showers are welcomingly wide: a whole family could have fun in there. Your hosts particularly like having children - they have three of their own. Breakfast, which includes their own milk and yogurt, wholemeal bread and waffles in winter, is a feast you can have at any time from 6am to noon. An ideal family base and really good value.

Rooms: 2 doubles, 1 twin, 1 triple, all with shower & wc.

Price: €37 for two.

Meals: Dinner €12, including wine & coffee.

Closed: Never.

From A27 (Lille-Doornik) exit 'Cité Scientifique' for Cysoing. In Sainghin, leave church on right, continue 600m, right on Rue du Cimetière, across junction into Rue Pasteur; farm 800m on right.

Dominique Pollet
Ferme de la Noyelle
832 rue Pasteur
59262 Sainghin en Mélantois
Nord
Tel: (0)3 20 41 29 82
Fax: (0)3 20 79 06 99

Entry No: 38   Map: **4**

Explanation of Symbols

Farm or vineyard.

Children welcome.

Pets welcome.

Vegetarian food by arrangement.

Organic or home-grown produce used.

Certified disabled facilities available.

Accessible to guests of limited mobility.

No smoking anywhere.

Smoking restricted.

Owners have pets.

Credit cards accepted.

Some degree of English spoken.

Bikes for hire or on loan.

Good hiking from village.

Swimming pool.

Behind the low façade are many riches: all is just so, rather like a dolls' house, down to the requisite ornaments - Madame's perfect plaything. The impression is of character and antiques with some modern bits. The big living room has pink walls, beams, marble floor and fireplace and there is an almost overwhelmingly pretty breakfast room: *objets trouvés*, plants and a Thai howdah sofa. The two first-floor rooms, one reached by an outside staircase, can communicate if you want a suite. Smart and mostly pink, they have lovely linen, good bathrooms, beams and views over church and garden. And Monsieur has lots of interesting things to tell.

Rooms: 2 double/triples, both with shower & wc.

Price: €57 for two.

Meals: Choice of restaurants 5km.

Closed: Never.

From Paris A16, exit 24 (25 from Calais); N1 for Montreuil/Boulogne for 25km. In Vron left to Villers sur Authie; right on Rue de l'Église (opp. café). At end of road, left up unpaved lane; house on left.

Pierre & Sabine Singer de Wazières
La Bergerie
80120 Villers sur Authie
Somme
Tel: (0)3 22 29 21 74
Fax: (0)3 22 29 39 58

Picardy

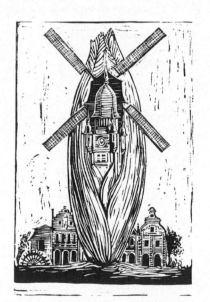

Rolling, river-run, loam-rich Picardy where Gothic fervour travels on wild wings from gargoyles' throats over corn and beet fields, twice fed by the Europe's young blood, past chip-makers' chimneys, out to the misty bird sanctuary and the long low sea.

Entry No: 39   **Map:** 3

Picardy

Through the gate and into a vast other world of green and watery peace beside the Authie. The superlative modern house marches round an astonishing courtyard of 'giant bonsais' and sculpted creatures. Living is done in a huge fan-beamed room with marble floor, rich rugs, super antiques and doors to the veranda for breakfast. Sleeping is done upstairs in the guest wing: original and succulent rooms, great use of colour, wood and exotica, fine bathrooms. One fishing lake, one bird-breeding lake, two rowing boats, paddocks and woods. Your hosts' delight is infectious: they are lively, interesting and fun - so is Shogun their PR dog. *Pets by arrangement.*

Rooms: 3 doubles, 1 suite, all with shower & wc.

Price: €74 for two.

Meals: Restaurants 300m-5km.

Closed: Never.

Your hosts have restored their fine brick house with respectful imagination: a lesson in that deceptively simple sobriety that turns every patch of colour, every rare object into a rich reward. Basics are white, ivory, sand; floors are pine with ethnic rugs by big new beds; blue, ginger or red details shine out and great-grandfather's Flemish oil paintings are perfect finishing touches. One big white bathroom is empty bar a flame-clothed table and a little round window that looks onto ponds and the setting sun. Drink in the white-panelled, open-hearthed, brown-leather sitting room, revel in the pale, uncluttered dining room - and Claudine's good food. A glamorous, welcoming couple. *Gîte space for 6 people.*

Rooms: 3 doubles, 1 suite, all with shower or bath & wc.

Price: €73.50 for two.

Meals: Dinner €21.

Closed: Never

From A16 exit 24 N1 to Vron; right D175 to Argoules; left D192 for Nempont; in Valloires Abbey car park: Chemin des Moines; gate 150m on left.

From A16 exit 24 towards Boulogne through Bernay en Ponthieu then first left; through Arvy, 1km beyond turn left to Le Thurel after great barn.

Michèle Harfaux
La Vallée Saint Pierre
Chemin des Moines, Valloires
80120 Argoules, Somme
Tel: 03 22 29 86 41
Fax: 03 22 29 86 48
E-mail: michele@vallee-st-pierre.com
Web: www.vallee-st-pierre.com

Claudine & Patrick van Bree-Leclef
Le Thurel
Relais de Campagne
80120 Rue, Somme
Tel: (0)3 22 25 04 44
Fax: (0)3 22 25 79 69
E-mail: lethurel.relais@libertysurf.fr
Web: www.lethurel.com

It's enchanting: from its knoll, the house looks down the lush garden, across the front and out to the shimmering bay. Madame is a delight too, happy to impart her deep knowledge of this area to visitors; her cooking is locally inspired, light and refined like herself, and to dine in her antique-furnished room beneath the modern tapestry would be a privilege. Up the steep stairs, the big room, full of ocean light, is pale and attractive with lots of pine and a perfect little shower room. The pretty, smaller room across the landing has blue-quilted nesting beds. *Mme happy to babysit. Gîte space for 4 people.*

Rooms: 1 double, 1 twin/double sharing shower & wc.

Price: €53 for two.

Meals: Dinner €19, wine €7; restaurants in village.

Closed: January.

From A16 exit Rue for Le Crotoy 10km; at r'bout follow to 'La Plage' to end; left Rue Jean Vadicocq; No 19 on right after playground.

Micheline Knecht
19 rue Jean Vadicocq
80550 Le Crotoy
Somme
Tel: (0)3 22 27 80 15
Fax: (0)3 22 27 80 15

Entry No: 42   **Map:** 3

Joanna is amazing: founder of a tribe of 33, she is no ordinary granny. Her little old house, an 18th-century townsman's weekend house in a pretty village, displays a highly original flair for interior décor - daring colour combinations, strong wallpapers, highly modern bathrooms, antiques and modern pieces, crochet, plush and wickerwork - and her artistic gift with clay. It all works brilliantly and she has a great sense of fun. Her ancient garden stretches away from formal box to wild grass and the hills. Breakfast on organic jams in the conservatory among the artworks. One delicious bedroom is reached through the kitchen.

Rooms: 1 double, 1 suite for 3, 1 suite for 5, all with shower or bath & wc.

Price: €43-€49 for two.

Meals: Barbecue available; choice of restaurants in Abbeville.

Closed: Christmas.

From Boulogne A16, Abbeville/St Riquier exit. At first roundabout, to Vauchelles lès Quesnoy. House on main square opposite church.

Mme Joanna Crépelle
Place de l'Eglise
80132 Vauchelles lès Quesnoy
Somme
Tel: (0)3 22 24 18 17
Fax: (0)3 22 24 18 17
E-mail: joanna_crepelle@yahoo.fr

Entry No: 43   **Map:** 3

A genuine northern château, but above all a family house. Madame, mother of four lovely-mannered children and lover of things outdoor - dogs, horses, gardening - reigns with energy and a refreshingly natural attitude: what matter if a little mud walks into the hall? In pleasing contrast is the formal dining room with its fabulous patterned parquet floor, vast table, family silver and chandeliers, and excellent food. Up the brilliant ginger-clothed staircase, the comfortable rooms may seem slightly worn: they are gradually being rejuvenated. Come for lively hospitality not smart château bedrooms. *Gîte space for 20 people.*

Rooms: 1 double, 1 suite for 4, both with bath or shower & wc; 2 doubles sharing bathroom.

Price: €53.50-€61 for two.

Meals: Dinner €17, inc. wine & coffee.

Closed: Never.

From Abbeville, N28 for Rouen. At St Maxent, D29 to Oisemont; D25 for Sénarpont. Signposted on edge of Foucaucourt.

Mme Élisabeth de Rocquigny
Château de Foucaucourt
Foucaucourt Hors Nesle
80140 Oisemont, Somme
Tel: (0)3 22 25 12 58
Fax: (0)3 22 25 15 58
E-mail: chateaudefoucaucourt@wanadoo.fr
Web: www.chateaudefoucaucourt.com

Entry No: 44   Map: 3

These calm, hospitable people were first in the Somme to open their house, a very fine building with an extraordinary staircase, for B&B. Monsieur, who is Dutch, grows several thousand tulips in serried ranks. He also makes honey, cider and calvados (ask to see the vaulted cellars) and keeps that supremely French animal a *trotteur* mare. Madame, a solid citizen of local stock, was Mayor of the village for 24 years. Bedrooms, smaller on the second floor, are comfortable and uncluttered, views are peaceful, the panelled dining room a proper setting for a good breakfast. A great place to stay. *Gîte space for 13 people.*

Rooms: 1 double with shower & wc; 3 triples, all with shower & basin, sharing wc.

Price: €37-€40 for two.

Meals: Barbecue & guest kitchen available; good restaurants 12km.

Closed: Never.

From Abbeville N28 towards Rouen for 28km; left at Bouttencourt D1015 to Sénarpont; D211 towards Amiens for 4.5km; left into Le Mazis; follow Chambres d'Hôtes signs.

Dorette & Aart Onder de Linden
3 rue d'Inval
80430 Le Mazis
Somme
Tel: (0)3 22 25 90 88
Fax: (0)3 22 25 76 04

Entry No: 45   Map: 3

The Guérins, gentle, cultured refugees from city madness, have restored their ancient farmhouse on its sloping site to timbered glory and shrubby delight. She "learned gardens" in England, he loves working with wood - the windows in the gable ends illustrate their respectful creativity. Rooms in the main house, not huge but uncluttered, are pretty, fresh and... timbered, with floral quilts and compact bathrooms; one, in bright green and sand colours, wraps itself round a vast chimney breast. The barn houses two slightly larger rooms and a cooking/eating area. Peace, good food, a warm family atmosphere and an Evrard grand piano in the hall. *Gîte space for 12 people.*

Rooms: 3 triples, 1 double, 1 twin, all with bath or shower & wc.

Price: €40 for two.

Meals: Dinner €13, including wine & coffee.

Closed: Never.

From A16 exit 18 to Quévauvillers; right on D38 through Bussy lès Poix. Last house in village, on left.

Francis & Françoise Guérin
1 rue de l'Église
80290 Bussy lès Poix
Somme
Tel: (0)3 22 90 06 73
E-mail: guerin.francis@free.fr

Entry No: 46   Map: 4

The ground-floor room, straight off the lovely garden, is white all over with pools of colour in the bed hangings, soft kilim rugs, dark polished antiques, old oils, gilt-framed prints; white doors open to a gorgeous bathroom (antique basin and taps) and a tiny sitting alcove. The upstairs room, soberly cosy, is softly clothed in grey-blue with a perfect little shower room. There's a little flask of port in each room. Madame is a painter and the peaceful picture of her garden, with bantams all about, deepens her friendly yet unintrusive welcome. Breakfast, served in a delightful room in the main house, is a most happy affair. *Gîte space for 2-4 people.*

Rooms: 1 double with bath or shower & wc.

Price: €40-€58 for two.

Meals: Restaurant 5km; choice 8km.

Closed: November-March.

From Amiens, N29 towards Poix; left on D162 to Creuse; signposted.

Mme Monique Lemaître
26 rue Principale
80480 Creuse
Somme
Tel: (0)3 22 38 91 50
Fax: (0)3 22 38 91 50

Entry No: 47   Map: 4

The Richoux love horses, the place's roots go back 1000 years to the age of myths, so they call it La Licorne (the unicorn). Relaxed and likeable people, they know all about local history and good hiking. You sleep in the former chapel, also a *gîte d'étape* (no B&B bookings when groups are here); there's a kitchen, a curious free-standing fireplace and a massive dining table which converts for snooker. Breakfast is brought to you here. You can light a fire, play snooker, use the kitchen, lounge in the garden. Under the rafters, one of the smallish bedrooms has the loo in the room. Nearby are water sports, fishing and Amiens' Gothic Cathedral. *Gîte space for 12 people.*

Rooms: 1 double, 1 triple, both with bath & wc.

Price: € 35 for two.

Meals: Self-catering available; restaurants 4km.

Closed: Never.

Madame's welcome is typically, warmly northern. Once a social worker, she is at ease with all sorts and has the most infectious laugh. Monsieur, a big-hearted, genuine, chatty countryman, is good company too, though they don't dine with guests. Bedrooms, each with separate entrance, have been recently redecorated and are furnished with panache, personality and all necessary modernities including good kitchenettes and bathrooms. Ask for the big room in the *grenier* (loft) - it's splendid. The lush green garden at the back has wrought-iron furniture, a lily pond and hens scratching in a large pen.

Rooms: 3 triples, all with shower, wc & kitchenette.

Price: € 37-€ 42 for two.

Meals: Dinner € 13, including coffee; many good restaurants in Amiens.

Closed: November-April, except by arrangement.

From Amiens N1 towards Beauvais for about 15km. Between St Sauflieu and Essertaux, right on D153 to Lœuilly; signposted.

From Amiens N1 south to Hébécourt. Opposite church follow Chambre d'Hôtes signs to Plachy Buyon.

Claudine & Bernard Richoux
Route de Conty
80160 Lœuilly
Somme
Tel: (0)3 22 38 15 19
Fax: (0)3 22 38 15 19
E-mail: richoux.bernard@wanadoo.fr

Mme Jacqueline Pillon
L'Herbe de Grâce
Hameau de Buyon
80160 Plachy Buyon
Somme
Tel: (0)3 22 42 12 22
Fax: (0)3 22 42 04 42

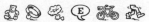

Entry No: 48 Map: 4

Entry No: 49 Map: 4

This house has a lovely face but the main road is very close. Guest bedrooms and sitting room, in a well-converted barn that gives onto the courtyard, are fairly blandly furnished with a mix of old and new, pleasing pine-slatted ceilings, fresh flowers in summer and good double-glazing against winter chill and road noise. If you arrive at a sensible time you may be offered a glass of home-made cider in the owners' living room at their unusual coffee table: a giant slice of fallen elm. Breakfast by the vast fireplace here is a feast and there's a very rare holly tree in the garden by the stables. Pony-and-trap rides in summer.

Rooms: 1 double, 1 twin, 1 triple, 1 suite, all with bath or shower & wc.

Price: €50 for two.

Meals: Dinner from €15, including wine & coffee.

Closed: Never.

From A16 Dury exit onto N1 S towards Breteuil and Paris. Arriving in Dury, left at traffic lights. House is first on right.

Alain & Maryse Saguez
2 rue Grimaux
80480 Dury
Somme
Tel: (0)3 22 95 29 52
Fax: (0)3 22 95 29 52
E-mail: alain.saguez@libertysurf.fr
Web: http://perso.libertysurf.fr/saguez/dury.html

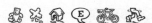

Entry No: 50 Map: 4

The emphasis here is on country family hospitality and Madame, smiling, uncomplicated and several times a grandmother, gives guests a big welcome. It's a paradise for children, the rambling garden has stone love-seats and two ponds, swings and a playhouse, while the old manor house has some fine architectural detailing and the feel of an adventure story. Your quarters are nicely independent beyond the hall, your living room leads down to the bedroom, there's plenty of space, a prettily draped bed and big square French pillows. Most of European history is at your doorstep, from Gothic Amiens to the battlefields of the First World War. *Gîte space for 7-8 people.*

Rooms: 1 suite for 2-4 with bath & wc.

Price: €50 for two, €65 for family of 4.

Meals: Auberge 6km.

Closed: December-March.

From Amiens D929 towards Albert. At Pont Noyelles, left onto D115 towards Contay; signposted in Bavelincourt.

M & Mme Noël Valengin
Les Aulnaies
15 Grande Rue
80260 Bavelincourt
Somme
Tel: (0)3 22 40 51 51

Entry No: 51 Map: 4

A watery paradise enfolds the village: the River Somme, acres of ponds, a canal flowing behind the old farmhouse. Guests can join the villagers fishing, boating or lazing on the edge. You can also fish in Madame's private pond. The decent-sized guest breakfast and sitting room has this view, as do the small, brightly-clothed and functional bedrooms. Here, Madame will help you prepare your day. In the evening, she serves excellent regional specialities in her big, gable-timbered, flower-filled dining room and there's a patch of green for sitting out by the farmyard. *Gîte space for 5 people.*

Rooms: 2 doubles, 1 twin, all with shower & wc.

Price: €43 for two.

Meals: Dinner €17, including wine & coffee.

Closed: Never.

From A1, Péronne exit onto D237 *westwards and immed. right on D146 towards Feuillères. Before village, D471 to Frise. First farm after bridge.*

Annick Randjia-Lépine
La Ferme de l'Écluse
80340 Frise
Somme
Tel: (0)3 22 84 59 70
Fax: (0)3 22 83 17 56

Entry No: 52   Map: 4

A dazzling house where within echoes without. The hill-shaped roof becomes a timbered vault way above swathes of natural-stone floor; the blocks of outdoor colour - holly, sky, poppy, cloud - reveal their functions inside (red for food, green for guestrooms...); the Picardy sky pours in and fills the vast minimally-furnished living space and your hostess shows shy pleasure at your amazement... then serves you superb food and intelligent conversation. Bedrooms are pure too: white walls, patches of colour, stone floors, excellent beds and bathrooms, 1930s antiques and touches of fun. Gourmet weekends can be arranged. Exceptional.

Rooms: 2 twins, with shower & wc; 1 family with bath & wc; 1 suite: 2 bedrooms, 1 bathroom & 1 shower room.

Price: €46 for two.

Meals: Dinner €18.50, including wine & coffee.

Closed: Never.

From A1 exit 13 onto N29 towards St Quentin. In Villers-Carbonnel, right at traffic lights onto N1/ for 5km to Fresnes-Mazancourt. House next to church.

Martine Warlop
1 rue Génermont
80320 Fresnes Mazancourt
Somme
Tel: (0)3 22 85 49 49
Fax: (0)3 22 85 49 59

Entry No: 53   Map: 4

Picardy

In a tiny brick hamlet, this listed courtyard farmhouse, owned by an interesting and sophisticated artist/journalist couple, has a sculpture garden and a thrillingly personal interior. Pascal has sculpted all the dark, metallically beautiful furniture, from superb beds to amusing loo-roll holders, giving the plain-coloured bedrooms an air of playful austerity. The old stable timbers show through, floors are coolly tiled, shower rooms are warmly ochre; the high white room is stunning. Meals are taken in the attractive living room where old and new (an old cider-press table bears Pascal's standard lamp) are a foil to Brigitte's fine cooking.

Rooms: 1 double, 1 triple, 1 quadruple all with shower & wc.

Price: €41 for two.

Meals: Dinner €14, including wine & coffee.

Closed: January.

From Gournay en Bray D930 for 8km; left towards Bellefontaine. Number 13 near the end of the hamlet.

Brigitte & Pascal Bruandet
13 hameau de Bellefontaine
60650 Hannaches
Oise
Tel: (0)3 44 82 46 63
E-mail: bellefontaine@free.fr
Web: bellefontaine.free.fr

Entry No: 54   Map: **3**

The warm, enthusiastic Verhoevens live in an old farmhouse in an idyllic village of handsome houses surrounded by rolling farmland and green woods. Cows graze in the field and apples grow in the small orchard. Furniture and décor are in various colours, textures and styles, all carefully chosen and placed. Guest rooms in the modern extension have good repro pieces too, and new mattresses. Monsieur is proud to have been a proper 'natural' farmer and Madame is every inch the chatty, friendly, elderly farmer's wife. She is also a charming hostess who loves tending her orchard and kitchen garden... and her guests.

Rooms: 2 doubles, both with shower, bath & wc.

Price: €40 for two.

Meals: 3 restaurants within 2km.

Closed: Never.

From Beauvais towards Le Tréport to Troissereux; D133 to Songeons; D143 towards Gournay en Bray. 1st village on leaving forest is Buicourt; house near church.

Eddy & Jacqueline Verhoeven
3 rue de la Mare
60380 Buicourt
Oise
Tel: (0)3 44 82 31 15

Entry No: 55   Map: **3**

In 1927 Auguste Perret, king of concrete, added a piece of design history to a pretty 18th-century house. His immense living room is squares in squares: panels, bookshelves, floor tiles, the huge table. Above is the green and puce (so's the bathroom) Perret-panelled bedroom with a flourish of columns, super 1930s furniture, terrace and vast view. Other rooms have lovely ethnic fabrics, much light, sophisticated bathrooms. Madame, who is Scottish, loves her house and enjoys sharing its delights. Monsieur is mad about horses; their pasture is part of the sweeping view from the quiet garden. And the train can carry you straight from the village to Paris... and back again.

Rooms: 1 double, 2 triples, all with bath or shower & wc.

Price: €50 for two.

Meals: Dinner €25, including wine & coffee.

Closed: Never.

From Calais A16 exit 13 (Méru) for Chaumont en Vexin. In Loconville, left to Liancourt St Pierre; right to post office & follow left into Rue du Donjon (no through road); high gate on left.

Fiona & Luc Gallot
La Pointe
10 rue du Donjon
60240 Liancourt Saint Pierre
Oise
Tel: (0)3 44 49 32 08
Fax: (0)3 44 49 32 08
E-mail: lucgallot@aol.com

Entry No: 56   Map: 3

Close the garden door and feel yourself secluded in this walled garden with grape-laden vine bower and a green corner for guests. Up an outside stair and into your room: the old hayloft, brilliantly converted with originality and red cushions on butter-yellow bedcover on a platform by the little window. The timbers glow their 300 years, there's space, shapeliness and a super little shower room; fridge and dining table too. The separate single is snug and pretty. Dine with your active, informative hosts by the old farm fireplace - he quietly acts as cook while she keeps you jolly company. A private place of peace, and so close to Paris.

Rooms: 1 double, 1 single, both with shower & wc.

Price: €46 for two.

Meals: Dinner €19, including wine & coffee.

Closed: Never.

From A16 exit 13 for Gisors & Chaumont en Vexin about 20km; after Fleury left to Fay les Etangs; 2nd left; house on left.

Philippe & Chantal Vermeire
Le Clos
3 rue du Chêne Noir
60240 Fay les Étangs
Oise
Tel: (0)3 44 49 92 38
Fax: (0)3 44 49 92 38
E-mail: philippe.vermeire@wanadoo.fr

Entry No: 57   Map: 4

The soft grandeur of 16th-century brick, the classic contrast of little four-part formal garden and great landscaped park fading into wooded hillside (with railway) behind, exquisite French manners and Irish warmth: Fosseuse mixes things perfectly. The grandest room, up the fine, terrifically worn stone staircase, has a vast, nobly canopied bed and a brand new bathroom. The sweetest is the double hidden over the library/breakfast room: open the panelling to find the secret stair. All have big windows over the park. Your deeply cultured hosts labour on to save their family home and genuinely enjoy sharing it with visitors.

Rooms: 1 suite, 1 double, all with bath & wc; 1 triple with shower & wc.

Price: €66-€70 for two; suite €100 for four.

Meals: Good choice of restaurants 2-10 km.

Closed: Never.

In the rose-climbed former bakery, where bread was once baked for humans - and potatoes for pigs - guests are now made very welcome in rooms with space, simple furniture, an Indian cotton throw at each bedhead, magnificent 17th-century roof timbers and sober carpets. There are two pretty breakfast rooms where the vast bread oven, beams and character have been preserved. Your active, quiet hosts have taste and humour and have turned their small farmhouse rooms into a lovely open-plan space with timber framing where you may dine with them in all simplicity and soak up the warm, natural atmosphere. *Gîte space for 13 people.*

Rooms: 1 quadruple, 1 triple, 2 doubles, all with shower & wc.

Price: €38 for two.

Meals: Dinner €12.50, including wine & coffee.

Closed: Never.

From A16 exit 13 for Esches (D923); in Fosseuse, château gate on right at traffic light.

From Beauvais N31 towards Rouen. Leaving Beauvais pick up signs to Savignies. Farm in village, 50m from church.

Shirley & Jean-Louis Marro
Le Château de Fosseuse
60540 Fosseuse, Oise
Tel: (0)3 44 08 47 66
Fax: (0)3 44 08 47 66
E-mail: chateau.fosseuse@wanadoo.fr
Web: www.france-random.com/chateau-de-fosseuse

Annick & Jean-Claude Leturque
La Ferme du Colombier
60650 Savignies
Oise
Tel: (0)3 44 82 18 49
Fax: (0)3 44 82 53 70
E-mail: ferme.colombier@wanadoo.fr

Picardy

Macquelines is ideal for families. The Hamelins, intelligent, smiling farmers, have thoughtfully installed swings, slides and a tennis court in their garden; the farm, surrounded by woods and fields, has an elegant cobbled farmyard at its heart. Cleverly-renovated cottages provide delightful, clean, modern rooms with pretty fabrics and good bedding; the 'best' room has a fine pale-wood Louis XVI cane bed. In a converted vaulted barn are two huge rooms: the games room has table football, ping-pong and a piano; the stone-walled sitting/breakfast room has a big log fire, comfortable chairs, an old dresser and painted jugs.

Rooms: 1 double, 1 twin, 1 family suite (twin & bunks), all with bath or shower & wc.

Price: €50 for two.

Meals: Choice of restauarants in Crépy, 9km.

Closed: January.

From A1 Senlis exit onto N324 to Crépy en Valois; D332 towards Lévignen and Betz. 3km after Lévignen right to Macquelines. Right at T-junc; farm immed. on right.

Philippe & Marthe Hamelin
Ferme de Macquelines
60620 Betz
Oise
Tel: (0)3 44 87 20 21
Fax: (0)3 44 87 20 21

Entry No: 60　　　　Map: 4

Le Rouge, Le Noir... et Le Blanc! Down from the rather dingy station road, the modern house, astonishing in its shiny black and red interior, turns through vast windows towards the peace of the Japanese-style garden. There your little studio-nest awaits you: a hideaway under the trees, all white paint, pine slats and restful natural fabrics with just a bright red door (and relatively little traffic noise). Come back to breakfast on a red stool at the black bar with your charming and interesting cosmopolitan hosts - Croatian architect and Anglo-French airport executive - or have it on your own front patio with the birds. Great for Chantilly and Paris.

Rooms: 1 twin/double with shower, wc & kitchen (studio).

Price: €63 for two.

Meals: Self-catering available.

Closed: Never.

From A1 exit Survilliers to N17 to Chantilly; left at château; at roundabout left again; under railway bridge & Rue Victor Hugo next right.

Sylviane Lokmer
30c rue Victor Hugo
60500 Chantilly
Oise
Tel: (0)3 44 57 63 91
Fax: (0)3 44 57 63 91
E-mail: miro.lokmer@wanadoo.fr
Web: www.vrbo.com/vrbo/2531.htm

Entry No: 61　　　　Map: 4

An enchantment for garden lovers who want real old château style but not plush bathrooms. Madame is still repairing her 200-year-old family home and garden, her great love: down past the old *lavoir* to the bottom, meet all the trees and shrubs, the stream, the pond, the island - a work of art. The house is elegantly well-worn, you breakfast in a darkly handsome room, sit in a totally French oak-panelled *salon*, sleep in 210-cm antique sleigh beds (tiny child's room off). The second bedroom is simpler, with Continental bath, and the washing arrangements not American standard. But Madame's passion for house and garden will convince you. *Children over 10 welcome.*

Rooms: Suite: 1 twin with en suite bathroom & wc, 1 twin with basin & wc, sharing bathroom.

Price: €92 for two.

Meals: Good auberge 3km; Senlis 8km.

Closed: 15 October-15 May.

From Senlis D330 for Borest/Nanteuil for 8km; right at cemetery; 1st right; across Place du Tissard towards big farm; left Rue de la Ferme; gates at bottom: No 1.

Hélène Merlotti
Château de Saint Vincent
1 rue Élisabeth Roussel
60300 Borest
Oise
Tel: (0)3 44 54 21 52
Fax: (0)3 44 54 21 52

Fear not! Behind the high brick walls and imposing archway is a secret garden with a goldfish pond, lots of interesting mementoes and a laughing, fun-loving lady - a retired chemist who loves her dogs, travelling and contact with visitors. Your beamed, fireplaced, mellow rooms, furnished like drawing rooms with old pieces and soft fabrics (and kettle etc), are in the original house; she lives in the brilliantly-converted barn, and all is harmony and warmth among the family antiques. Drink in the atmosphere and her talk of France, the French and the rest of the world. Rest in peace, rouse to the dawn chorus, then enjoy breakfast in the sunshine.

Rooms: 1 twin with shower & basin, 1 double with bath & basin, sharing wc.

Price: €50 for two.

Meals: Restaurants 4-6km.

Closed: Never, please book ahead.

From A1 exit 10 for Compiègne, 4km. By caravan yard right at small turning for Jaux. 1st right to Varanval, over hill. House on right opposite château gates.

Françoise Gaxotte
La Gaxottière
60880 Jaux Varanval
Oise
Tel: (0)3 44 83 22 41
Fax: (0)3 44 83 22 41

If you've always wanted to sleep in a tower, try this: the vast double bedroom and child's room across the landing have been imaginatively and most attractively housed in the octagonal tower, which is one of the charms of this delicious *troubadour*-style château. Jacques' family have been here for five generations and are likely to remain, judging by the tribe of exquisitely-behaved children he and Marie-Catherine have produced. In summer, breakfast and dinner (by arrangement) are served in the enchanting orangery. The old family home is indeed much loved and well used by these delightful people.

Rooms: 1 suite (double & single) with shower & wc.

Price: €45 for two.

Meals: Dinner €18, including (good) wine & coffee.

Closed: Never.

Genuine French generosity and real contact are here in the big old house, welcoming and warmly tatty with mix 'n' not-match wallpapers, posters on long corridors, funny old prints in bedrooms. The energetic owners are great fun and love their dinner parties in the dining room with its old family furniture, where guests of all nations communicate as the wine flows. They wouldn't dream of changing a thing for the sake of modern sanitising fashions - may they prosper! The rooms are simple and good; one has a ship's shower room, another a Louis XVI bed, all look onto green pastures.

Rooms: 1 suite for 4, 2 doubles, 1 twin, all with bath or shower & wc; 1 double, 1 twin with basins, sharing bathroom.

Price: €33.50-€45.50 for two.

Meals: Dinner €15.50, including wine.

Closed: 16 October-14 March, except by arrangement.

From A26 exit 13 for Laon. Round Laon bypass towards Soissons onto N2 for about 15km; left on D423 to Nanteuil la Fosse. Through Nanteuil, follow signs for La Quincy; château on right outside village.

From A26-E17, Laon/Chambry exit 13 on N2; 2nd left to Athies s/Laon; D516 to Bruyères & M.; left D967 for Fismes; Chérêt signed on leaving Bruyères.

Jacques & Marie-Catherine Cornu-Langy
La Quincy
02880 Nanteuil la Fosse
Aisne
Tel: (0)3 23 54 67 76
Fax: (0)3 23 54 72 63

Mme Monique Simonnot
Le Clos
02860 Chérêt
Aisne
Tel: (0)3 23 24 80 64

Entry No: 64　　　　　　Map: **4**

Entry No: 65　　　　　　Map: **4**

Ressons is a big, active farm out in the wilds, with an unspoilt house among rolling hills and champagne vineyards. Your hosts are hard-working, dynamic and good, even exciting, company; they also hunt. Madame, an architect, works from home, brings up three children *and* nurtures her guests. The deeply-carved Henri III furniture is an admirable family heirloom; rooms are colour-co-ordinated, beds are beautiful, views are stunning, dinners cooked with home-grown produce are excellent; bring rod and permit and you can fish in the pond. Arms are open for you in this civilised household.
Gîte space for 12 people.

Rooms: 1 double, 1 twin, both with bath, sharing wc; 2 doubles & 1 twin, sharing bath & 2 wcs.

Price: €39-€46 for two.

Meals: Dinner €16, wine €11-€15.

Closed: Christmas.

From Fismes D967 for Fère en Tardenois & Château Thierry 4km. DON'T go to Mont St Martin. Cont. 800m beyond turning; white house on left.

Valérie & Jean-Paul Ferry
Ferme de Ressons
02220 Mont St Martin
Aisne
Tel: (0)3 23 74 71 00
Fax: (0)3 23 74 28 88

SOME FALSE FRIENDS

Biologique & Organic
Produce called 'organic' in English is known as *de culture biologique* in French, *bio* for short. If you talk about *organique*, people may think you are having trouble with your organs.

Biscuit & Gâteau
Biscuit literally means 'twice cooked' and originally meant dehydrated army rations or the base for some sticky puddings. Sweet biscuits are usually called *gâteaux secs* or *petits gâteaux* ; savoury biscuits are *gâteaux d'apéritif*. At breakfast, *gâteau maison* will probably be a simple sponge-cake with jam or a French-style fruit cake, also called *cake* (pronounced cack).
Tourte: French for a pie with pastry on top, it only applies to savoury dishes.
Tarte: An open tart or flan.
Flan: Baked custard.
Tartine: Breakfast food. Usually, half a baguette sliced lengthwise and buttered; can be toasted before buttering, when it becomes a *tartine grillée*.
Une Pie: Magpie.
Un pis: (same pronunciation as *pie*) is an udder of any milking animal.
Scotch: Either adhesive tape or whisky - context is all.
Mousse: Mousse, as in chocolate; or foam, lather, froth, as on sea, soap, beer; or foam rubber; or moss.
Marmelade: Well-stewed fruit. 'Marmalade' is *confiture d'oranges amères* (jam made with bitter oranges).
Pomme de pin: Fircone. 'Pineapple' is *ananas*. *Pamplemousse* is 'grapefruit'.
Grappe Bunch, cluster. *Grappe de raisins* - bunch of grapes.
Raisin: Generic term for the fruit of the vine: the grape. One 'grape' is *un grain de raisin*. Steinbeck's book translates as *Les Raisins de la Colère*.
Raisins de Corinthe: currants (you can hear the etymology); *raisins de Smyrne* - sultanas; *raisins secs* - raisins!
Prune: Fresh plum; *pruneau* - prune.
Verger: Orchard. Many a greengrocers' shop is called *Aux Fruits du Verger*.
Trouble: Cloudy, murky - you can send that bottle of wine back.
Troublé: Troubled, disturbed.

Your hosts recently converted the stables and handed the farm over to their son but cows still graze and grandchildren come and go easily. Two rooms have their own ground-floor entrance; the third is upstairs in the owners' 'wing'; all three are done in brave contemporary colours that set off the mix of old and new furniture perfectly; bright and pleasing with lovely linen, good mattresses, clean-cut bathrooms. Madame is fun and an excellent cook (lots of organic and farm-grown ingredients), Monsieur is a whizz on local history; both are proud of their country heritage, wonderful with children and deeply committed to 'real B&B'. Great value.

Rooms: 1 double, 1 suite for 4, 1 quadruple, all with shower & wc.

Price: € 36 for two.

Meals: Dinner € 13, including wine & coffee.

Closed: Never.

From A4, exit Ste Menehould on D982 (382 on some maps) to Givry en Argonne. There, left on D54 to Les Charmontois (9km).

M & Mme Bernard Patizel
5 rue St Bernard
51330 Les Charmontois
Marne
Tel: (0)3 26 60 39 53
Fax: (0)3 26 60 39 53
E-mail: nicole.patizel@wanadoo.fr
Web: www.chez.com/patizel

Champagne-Ardenne

The angel of Reims smiles eternally upon the Kings of France anointed in his cathedral and upon the incomprehending soldier slain in the battlefields.
And the ephemeral bubbles burst on.

Entry No: 67   Map: **5**

Behind its sober façade, here is a beautiful and generously hospitable marriage of old and new, French and English. Didier, house-restorer supreme, makes champagne. Imogen, warm, relaxed and informed, has done designing, book-binding, teaching... and now runs two small children and this fine *Champenoise* house. They have decorated the guest rooms to great effect: two have space, light and luxurious sitting room/bathrooms; the smaller has a richly-canopied bed, a green and pink oriental atmosphere and a superb claw-footed bath. Work continues on the ground floor, Imogen is an excellent cook, champagne is served at dinner. You'll want to stay for ever. *Gîte space for 4 people.*

Rooms: 2 doubles, 1 twin, with bathrooms.

Price: €41 for two.

Meals: Dinner €21.50, including wine.

Closed: 2 weeks in September.

The quiet is so deep that the grandfather clock inside and the doves cooing in the trees outside can seem deafening. A timeless feel wafts through the new house from that clock, the pretty, traditionally-decorated bedrooms (sleigh beds and Louis Philippe furniture), the piano and a lovely old sideboard. Huguette and her husband, who runs the dairy farm, are generous hosts offering traditional unpretentious farmhouse hospitality. You can opt for champagne from their son-in-law's nearby vineyard, with a meal to match the quality of the wine and the welcome. *Gîte space for 14 people.*

Rooms: 2 doubles, 1 triple, all with bath or shower & wc.

Price: €42 for two.

Meals: Dinner €18, with wine; €24 with champagne.

Closed: Never.

From Calais A26 to Reims; N51 to Epernay; follow for Châlons en Champagne then to Avize; head for Lycée Viticole, house opp. Lycée.

From Châlons en Champagne D933 to Bergères (29km); right D9 through Vertus; left, follow signs to La Madeleine 3km.

Imogen & Didier Pierson Whitaker
Le Vieux Cèdre
14 route d'Oger
51190 Avize
Marne
Tel: (0)3 26 57 77 04
Fax: (0)3 26 57 97 97
E-mail: champagnepiersonwhitaker@worldnet.fr

Huguette Charageat
La Madeleine
51130 Vertus
Marne
Tel: (0)3 26 52 11 29
Fax: (0)3 26 59 22 09

Champagne-Ardenne

A wonderful woman who really understands hospitality and good food will welcome you to this impressive 17th-century farm with its two courtyards: it is all simple and real. In the converted stables: a living room with original mangers, log fire and kitchenette, then steep stairs up to two simply-decorated, warmly-carpeted, roof-lit rooms. In the main house: the third room, bigger and cosier with old furniture and a view of the pond. You breakfast next to the kitchen but dine at the big old table in the family *salon* on home-produced vegetables, eggs, poultry and fruit. Fabulous walks to be had in the great Forêt du Gault nearby.

Rooms: 1 twin, 1 double, 1 triple, all with shower or bath & wc.

Price: € 34 for two.

Meals: Dinner € 16, including wine & coffee.

Closed: Never.

The place bristles with cows, chickens, ducks, guinea fowl, turkeys, donkey, sheep, goats... children love this working farm with its friendly animals, and love the higgledy-piggledy buildings too; school groups come for visits. The house bristles with beams, the rooms are full of swags, flowers and antique bits, the piano swarms with candles and photographs and one bathroom is behind a curtain. Our readers have loved the house, the family and the food. Little English is spoken but the welcome is so exceptional, the generosity so genuine, that communication is easy. Superb outings in the area for all.

Rooms: 1 suite with shower & wc; 3 doubles, all with bath & wc (1 curtained off).

Price: € 43-€ 52 for two.

Meals: Dinner € 22 with wine, € 25 with champagne; restaurants 10km.

Closed: Never.

From Calais A26 to St Quentin; D1 to Montmirail; D373 for Sézanne, 7km. On leaving Le Gault left at silo; signposted.

From Epernay D51 for Sézanne; at Baye, just before church, right D343; at Bannay right; farm before small bridge.

Famille Boutour
Ferme de Désiré
51210 Le Gault Soigny
Marne
Tel: (0)3 26 81 60 09
Fax: (0)3 26 81 67 95
E-mail: domaine_de_desire@yahoo.fr

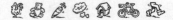

Muguette & Jean-Pierre Curfs
Ferme de Bannay
51270 Bannay
Marne
Tel: (0)3 26 52 80 49
Fax: (0)3 26 59 47 78

Entry No: 70   Map: 4

Entry No: 71   Map: 4

With their three children, they are a delightful young family, welcoming, available and friendly. The guest rooms and the terrace of their old family farmhouse, rebuilt in the 1920s after war destruction, look out onto the quiet courtyard: you can't hear the road, only the sound of the two running springs, so sleep till 11 if you like - that's the latest Nathalie serves freshly-squeezed fruit juice and masses of croissants (on the terrace in summer). The vast and very attractive bedroom suites are comfortably furnished and have everything you need. And there's a pretty pony in the field next door.

Rooms: 4 suites for 3/4, all with shower & wc.

Price: €46 for two.

Meals: Restaurant in village.

Closed: January-February.

From Reims D980 SW to Ville en Tardenois 20km; house in town centre opposite Crédit Agricole bank.

Nathalie & Éric Lelarge
Ferme du Grand Clos
51170 Ville en Tardenois
Marne
Tel: (0)3 26 61 83 78
Fax: (0)3 26 50 01 32

Entry No: 72   Map: **4**

Independent champagne growers, the Aristons delight in showing guests round vineyards and cellars (tastings included). Indeed, Madame, a wonderful person, started doing B&B for champagne buyers who did not want to leave after tasting! Through the flower-filled courtyard and up a private staircase, the bright, airy attic bedroom has beams, dormers, matching handmade curtains and covers, wicker furniture. Breakfast is served in the lovely old family house with fine jams made by Madame. Guests have use of a fridge and freezer - great for picnic provisions. *Latest bookings taken at 7pm. Gîte space for 6 people.*

Rooms: 2 doubles, both with bath & wc; 1 double with shower & wc.

Price: €41.50-€44.50 for two.

Meals: Choice of restaurants in Fismes, 11km.

Closed: Third week in August.

From Reims exit 22 (A4) for N31 Fismes to Jonchery sur Vesle. Left to Savigny sur Ardres (D386). Right through Serzy et Prin, Crugny; left on D23 to Brouillet. House on right, signed.

Remi & Marie Ariston
Champagne Ariston Fils
4 & 8 Grande Rue
51170 Brouillet, Marne
Tel: (0)3 26 97 43 46
Fax: (0)3 26 97 49 34
E-mail: champagne.ariston.fils@wanadoo.fr
Web: www.champagne-aristonfils.com

Entry No: 73   Map: **4**

The Harlauts are great company, love entertaining and are keen to provide good value so, although they produce their own marque of champagne and bottles are for sale, it is for the first-class food and the atmosphere that guests return. Dinner *en famille* is either in the dining room or on the terrace overlooking the garden. There are steep narrow stairs up to the warm, wood-floored, uncluttered guest rooms, two of which share a loo - a minor concern as everything is spotless and they make a good family suite. Great views over the plains of Reims, and do try the champagne cakes.

Rooms: 1 suite for 2/4, 1 room for 2/4, 1 double, all with shower & wc.

Price: €41.50-€44.50 for two.

Meals: Dinner €20, including aperitif/champagne, wine & coffee.

Closed: January & Easter.

Madame, French-speaking from Quebec, is a friendly, busy, chatty young mother of teenagers with a farming husband and parents-in-law 'through the wall'. She has the key to the fascinating church, a must. In this lovely setting, her own house, built in 1087 with two ancient towers, is the old priory, and has a superb pool. The rooms too are splendid: one is enormous with a huge stone fireplace, two queen beds, wattle walls in great timbers, more beams above, a simple bathroom. Others are most attractively modern. The excellent breakfast is also a great social occasion. "Better than any five-star hotel on all counts", said one reader.

Rooms: 2 quadruples, 2 triples, 1 family for 5, all with bath or shower & wc.

Price: €35-€45 for two.

Meals: Restaurant 10 mins walk.

Closed: Never.

From A26 exit 15 Reims La Neuvillette N44 towards Laon 2km; left to St Thierry; house in village.

From Troyes N71 SE for 22km. In Fouchères left D81 for Poligny; house just behind church.

Évelyne & Remi Harlaut
5 rue du Paradis
51220 Saint Thierry
Marne
Tel: (0)3 26 03 13 75
Fax: (0)3 26 03 03 65
E-mail: contact@champagne-harlaut.fr
Web: www.champagne-harlaut.fr

Sylvie Berthelin
Le Prieuré
Place de l'Église
10260 Fouchères
Aube
Tel: (0)3 25 40 98 09
Fax: (0)3 25 40 98 09

Entry No: 74   Map: 4

Entry No: 75   Map: 9

Champagne-Ardenne

Take a fascinating trip back in time. This was the family château's summer house for two centuries and has been their main house for one: Madame will show you the family books, lovely old furniture and mementoes and tell you the stories (e.g. Louis XIV's envoy to Peter the Great was an ancestor) in incredibly fast French. She has a wealth of information, a deep love of books (does her own bookbinding), a garden full of roses, each introduced by name, and a couple of horses in the paddock (there are racehorses elsewhere). She is hyperactive and loves to talk - it's great fun and deeply interesting

Rooms: 1 triple with shower & wc.

Price: €40 for two.

Meals: Dinner €16, including wine & coffee, children under 12 free.

Closed: Never.

The secluded old mill buildings house two owner families, a fish-tasting restaurant, several guest rooms and 50 tons of live fish - it's a fish farm! 500 fishers may gather, on Sundays, to catch trout in the spring water that feeds the ponds. Breakfast and *table d'hôtes* are shared with your enthusiastic hosts - they created this place from nothing 40 years ago - in the big beamy restaurant; groups come for speciality lunches. Bedrooms under the eaves are compact, small-windowed, simply furnished, prettily decorated in rustic or granny style, the larger annexe rooms are more modern. Great fun for children. Good English spoken.

Rooms: 4 doubles, 1 suite, all with bath & wc.

Price: €55 for two.

Meals: Dinner €17, including wine & coffee.

Closed: Never.

A26 to junction 22 (Troyes); N19 to Bar sur Aube; D384 to Ville sur Terre. Follow for Fuligny. House on long main street.

From Paris A5 exit 19 on N60 to Estissac; right Rue Pierre Brossolette; mill at end of lane (1km).

Nicole Georges-Fougerolle
Les Épeires
17 rue des Écuyers
10200 Fuligny
Aube
Tel: (0)3 25 92 77 11
Fax: (0)3 25 92 77 11

Édouard-Jean & Chantal Mesley
Domaine du Moulin d'Eguebaude
10190 Estissac
Aube
Tel: (0)3 25 40 42 18
Fax: (0)3 25 40 40 92

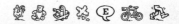

Entry No: 76   Map: **9**

Entry No: 77   Map: **8**

This large and splendid farmhouse is irresistible: for walkers, bird-watchers, fishermen there's a river and a fine park full of wildlife (come for the cranes in spring or autumn); for architecture buffs, the local half-timbered churches are one of the '100 most beautiful attractions in France'. Afternoon tea is served in the elegant panelled *salon*; dinner, possibly home-raised boar or carp, is eaten either communally or separately but not with your hosts, delightful as they are: they live in another wing and prefer to concentrate on their good *cuisine maison*. Bedrooms are comfortable and attractive. *Children over seven welcome.*

Rooms: 2 doubles, 2 twins, 1 suite, all with bath or shower & wc.

Price: €44–€53 for two.

Meals: Dinner €23, including wine & coffee.

Closed: Never.

In a typical sleepy French village, this is a place for getting out and about in several modes: there is riding (and space for 15 guest horses), pony-trapping, walking, mountain-biking, archery, orienteering and a bit of gentle ping-pong. It's a friendly place, simple and easy, with breakfast of home-made jams, fresh brioche and lots of coffee available until midday. Beyond the separate guest entrance, the pretty basic rooms are right for the price, warmly carpeted (after the corridor upstairs with its 'artexed' walls and 'lino' floor), thinly walled, with good storage space. *Gîte space for 19 people.*

Rooms: 3 doubles, 1 twin, sharing shower & wc.

Price: €30 for two.

Meals: Restaurant 5km.

Closed: Never.

From Troyes D960 to Brienne; D400 for St Dizier; at Louze D182 to Longeville; D174 for Boulancourt; house on left at 1st crossroads.

From Langres, N19 towards Vesoul. Left on D460 towards Bourbonne; right on D34; 3rd left to Velles. Through village to grass triangle; house on left.

Philippe & Christine Viel-Cazal
Domaine de Boulancourt
Boulancourt
Longeville sur la Laines
52220 Montier en Der
Haute-Marne
Tel: (0)3 25 04 60 18
Fax: (0)3 25 04 60 18

Alain & Christine Rousselot
Les Randonnées du Pré Cheny
52500 Velles
Haute-Marne
Tel: (0)3 25 88 85 93
Fax: (0)3 25 88 85 93
E-mail: randoprecheny@wanadoo.fr

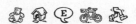

While restoring the house, the Poopes were enchanted to 'meet' the former owners, in the shape of faded old photographs in the attic. These inspired the décor of each splendid room - and one has an antique bread trough too. Evelyne and Michel adore doing B&B and do all they can to make you feel at home. Breakfast is deeply local: yogurt from the farm, honey from the village and Evelyne's home-made jam, while dinner may include such delicacies as Langres cheese tart with artichokes or flamed turkey; Michel is chief pastry-cook. He also paints very nicely while Evelyne does floral pictures.

Rooms: 1 double, 1 twin, both with shower, sharing wc; 1 triple, 1 suite, both with shower & wc.

Price: €34-€46 for two.

Meals: Dinner €12, including wine & coffee.

Closed: Christmas.

From A31 exit 7 to north Langres then N19 towards Vesoul for 30km. Right at Chambres d'Hôtes sign to Pressigny; house just after pond on left.

Evelyne & Michel Poope
Maison Perrette
24 rue Augustin Massin
52500 Pressigny
Haute-Marne
Tel: (0)3 25 88 80 50
Fax: (0)3 25 88 80 49
E-mail: POOPEMichel@net-up.com

Entry No: 80　　　　Map: **9**

OTHER FALSE FRIENDS
Accomodation: Adaptation or focussing of the two eyes.
Actuellement: A real pitfall, it means now, currently, at this time and not 'As a matter of fact'.
Les actualités: The news.
Éventuellement: Another pitfall, it means should the case arise, if necessary, possibly and not 'At last, In the end'.
Agenda: Diary.
Ordre du Jour: Agenda.
Compte-rendu/Procès verbal: Minutes (of a meeting, a court case).
Cheminée: Fireplace, flue or chimney stack (flue is also *le conduit de cheminée*). *Un feu dans la cheminée*? a delight on a cold night; *un feu de cheminée*? call the *Pompiers* (fire brigade).
Chaise percée: Commode.
Commode: Chest of drawers.
Christmas: Christmas card. Christmas used to be a religious and family event; the French would send their normal visiting card with handwritten New Year wishes any time between mid-December and the end of January. The custom of sending cards caught on some decades ago and the object was, naturally, given a smart if truncated English name.
Crime: Has a stronger, bloodier meaning in colloquial French: murder or assassination. Other unlawful acts are called *délits*.
Correspondance: Connections between flights, trains, metro lines.
Courrier: Post, mail, correspondence.
Dérangement: Disturbance (of person, routine), breakdown (of telephone).
En suite: can cause terrible confusion in France. In France, it does not mean 'room with its own bathroom'. It means a series of two or more connecting rooms. One booking for 'two en-suites', made with B&B hosts who speak good English, became a disaster when the owners reserved their one and only 'suite' for these English guests. On arrival, the two couples were distressed at having to fit into rooms where the double led to the twin which led to the shared bathroom. It's safer to ask for *Une chambre pour deux avec salle de bains* and omit the word 'suite' altogether.
Sensible: Sensitive (person, subject) or appreciable (difference, quantity).
Sensé(e): Sensible.

Lorraine

Vast views across lakes, woods and hills surround 'Grandma's Fields'. The house is like a chalet, all warm, glowing wood. Here, it's bed and breakfast *plus* afternoon tea and cake... and apparently Madame's chocolate-and-cherry is to die for. This is a quiet, bookish house (no telly), the perfect spot for a holiday of walking, swimming with the trout in the pond near the house, or reading. In autumn and spring you can go mushrooming and cook your catch in Madame's cosy kitchen. Breakfast, which can be French, German or English, to taste, is in here too. Supremely peaceful house, place and person.

Rooms: 2 doubles, sharing bathroom.

Price: €53.50 for two.

Meals: Use of kitchen & barbecue; restaurants in Senones 2km.

Closed: Never.

From Strasbourg A352 W then N420 to St Blaise la Roche (45km); right on D424 14km towards Senones to La Petite Raon; right after church for Moussey; 3rd left (after café) then left, left and left to house.

Storks still build their messy nests on the chimney stacks of breweries and biscuit factories where women once wore the giant bow as their traditional headdress.

Judith Lott
Les Champs Grandmère
Thiamont
88210 La Petite Raon
Vosges
Tel: (0)3 29 57 68 08
Fax: (0)3 29 57 68 83
E-mail: judelott@infonie.fr

A triumph! Monsieur's seemingly endless restoration of these venerable buildings - one house 400, the other 300 years old - is finished, and very nicely too: fine woodwork, stylish furniture, an intriguing gas chandelier (*gasolier*?) in the dining room, elegant terraces and a super garden with a children's play area. Madame is charmingly lively, her attractive rooms have goodnight chocolates, kettle kits, smallish shower rooms and lots of religion on view (bedside Bibles are French Catholic, not American Gideon). Hers is a genuine welcome, breakfast is a highlight and traffic noise seems minimal.

Rooms: 2 doubles, 1 twin, 1 triple, all with shower & wc.

Price: €39-€54 for two.

Meals: Restaurants 200m; self-catering in suite.

Closed: Never.

The lively, dynamic owners are justifiably proud of their deeply-adapted stables, built two centuries ago in local stone - out with the horses, in with the big, plush guest rooms: the suite even has its own telly and telephone, they are all done with taste and quality. Dinner is superb, a chance to sample some of the region's best dishes, course after course, wine after wine; Madame will join you for dessert and a chat. In the forest: an 'artists' path' to explore; in the garden: a golf practice area. An excellent stopover in a pretty, peaceful village between the ferries and Germany.

Rooms: 2 triples, both with shower & wc; 1 suite with bath, shower & wc.

Price: €64-€84 for two.

Meals: Dinner €25, including wine & coffee.

Closed: Never.

From A4 exit Ste Menehould; N3 for Verdun-Chalons; signposted in La Vignette, hamlet before Les Islettes; 1st building on left.

From Reims A4 exit 'Voie Sacrée' N35 for Bar le Duc; at Chaumont sur Aire D902 left to Longchamps sur Aire; D121 left to Thillombois; house next to château.

M & Mme Léopold Christiaens
Villa des Roses
La Vignette
Les Islettes
55120 Clermont en Argonne
Meuse
Tel: (0)3 26 60 81 91
Fax: (0)3 26 60 23 09

Lise Tanchon
Le Clos du Pausa
Rue du Château
55260 Thillombois
Meuse
Tel: (0)3 29 75 07 85
Fax: (0)3 29 75 00 72

Entry No: 82   Map: **5**

Entry No: 83   Map: **5**

A most interesting, unpretentious couple, they are passionate about the environment and keen to chat over dinner. He, a retired French architect, has won a prize for this brilliant conversion, she's Polish and paints (work in progress on the easel), patchworks (her work adorns your bed) and dances. It is good news, too, for vegetarians who like a change: Alina is a 'veggie' and will rustle up a hot *borsch* or a dish of *pierogi* (vegetable ravioli) though her talent stretches to delicious meaty things too. An excellent and friendly house with lovely rooms.

Rooms: 2 triples with shower & wc.

Price: €42 for two.

Meals: Dinner €16 (meat or fish) or €13 (vegetarian), including wine & coffee.

Closed: Never.

These ancient stones are heavy with history: the tower was part of the 13th-century defensive ring around Metz. It is now a typical farmhouse with 110 acres of cereal fields. Brigitte relishes her role as hostess, does it with great talent and makes friends easily. She also keeps goats, rabbits, a donkey and a dog. All the bedrooms are in another building, filled with her own remarkably good paintings and beautiful hand-painted furniture. There is a handsome breakfast room with great beams. A wonderful family and a friendly peaceful village (until work on the new Metz bypass starts).

Rooms: 1 triple, 1 double, both with bath & wc; 1 twin with shower & wc.

Price: €46 for two.

Meals: Restaurants 4km.

Closed: November-March.

From Metz D3 NE towards Bouzonville for about 21km, then right on D53a to Burtoncourt. House on left in main street.

From A31 exit 29 for Féy; right at junction; do not enter Féy, cont. for Cuvry; farm on edge of village past Mairie; signs.

Alina & Gérard Cahen
51 rue Lorraine
57220 Burtoncourt
Moselle
Tel: (0)3 87 35 72 65
Fax: (0)3 87 35 72 65

Brigitte & Jean-François Morhain
Ferme de Haute-Rive
57420 Cuvry
Moselle
Tel: (0)3 87 52 50 08
Fax: (0)3 87 52 60 20

Entry No: 84 Map: **5**

Entry No: 85 Map: **5**

A genuine family château where rooms, not big (apart from the twin) or super-luxurious, have the patina of long history in their antiques (carved armoires, *Voltaire* armchairs, pretty writing desks) and the softness of bygone days in bedhead draperies, pastel fabrics and plush. The real style is in the utterly French many-chaired *salon* and the dining room - reached through halls and hunting trophies - with its huge square table and man-sized ceramic stove. Here you may share splendid meals with your lively, intelligent hosts - Monsieur a mine of local history, Madame skilfully attentive to all. And always fresh flowers.
Gîte space for 2 people.

Rooms: 3 doubles, 3 twins, all with bath & wc.

Price: € 68.50-€ 84 for two.

Meals: Dinner € 31-€ 38.50, including coffee; wine € 7.50.

Closed: 1 October-1 May.

From Nancy N74 for Sarreguemines/ Château Salins. At Burthecourt crossroads D38 to Dieuze; D999 south 5km; left on D199F; right D199G to château.

Livier & Marie Barthélémy
Château d'Alteville
Tarquimpol
57260 Dieuze
Moselle
Tel: (0)3 87 86 92 40
Fax: (0)3 87 86 02 05
E-mail: chateau.alteville@caramail.com

Entry No: 86   Map: 6

Your gentle-mannered hosts live in another house but are present, attentive and welcoming. Their pride and joy is Monsieur's woodwork: he has built these rooms in the old stables using different timbers, fitting shower rooms ingeniously into the space available, making stairs, delicately painting the eaves. There is a quiet courtyard with a garden; breakfast, with fresh juice, home-made jam and cakes, is in a room by the road. Rooms sparkle and English-speaking offspring are home after 8pm - ring then if you need to (but not too late). *Gîte space for 11 people.*

Rooms: 2 duplex, 3 doubles, all with shower (1 behind curtain) & wc.

Price: € 39-€ 48 for two.

Meals: Restaurants Pfettisheim 2-3 km; self-catering in duplexes.

Closed: Never.

From A4 exit 48. N63. Vendenheim/ Strasbourg. D64 for Lampertheim. At Pfulgriesheim, right on D31 to Pfettisheim. In village follow main road; signs.

Marie-Célestine Gass
La Maison du Charron
15 rue Principale
67370 Pfettisheim
Bas-Rhin
Tel: (0)3 88 69 60 35
Fax: (0)3 88 69 85 45

Entry No: 87   Map: 6

Alsace

A real old Alsatian farmhouse in the wine-growing area where you can be in a bustling village street one minute and your own peaceful little world the next. It's on a fairly busy main road but bedrooms, in the separate guest wing, are at the back; they are simple, small, yet comfortable. Your friendly hosts retired from milk and wine production to enjoy having more time for guests. Marie still teaches German; Paul serves breakfast in the garden or in the dining room with its brown tiles and blue walls. A great place to know at the start of the Route des Vins: so close to gorgeous, expensive Strasbourg, it is great value. *Gîte space for 6 people.*

Rooms: 3 doubles, all with shower & wc.

Price: €31-€35 for two.

Meals: Traditional restaurant 200m.

Closed: Never.

Just the place for the wine connoisseur! Deep in the heart of the Alsace wine country, spending a night in this charming place will give you a deeper insight into the finer points of wine reproduction. Built in the traditional Alsatian style, the timber-framed house is well-resinated. Madame, a delightful character, fully imbibed with all the local lore, is often away at her Drying Workshop - remember to water the geraniums in her absence. And don't miss the regular *Enlevage de cales*, the Barrel-Rolling Festival, which provides great fun for the locals and is a revolutionary experience for the occupants.

Rooms: 1 double with revolving doors.

Price: €5 for two, including VAT.

Meals: Restaurant Jet de Pierre is within a stone's throw.

Closed: Never, except in periods of heavy flooding.

From Saverne A4, exit 45 onto N404/N4 towards Strasbourg for 16km. Farm is in middle of the village of Marlenheim on left, before post office.

Paul & Marie-Claire Goetz
86 rue du Général de Gaulle
67520 Marlenheim
Bas-Rhin
Tel: (0)3 88 87 52 94

goetz.paul@wanadoo.fr

Follow the Route des Vins until you can go no further. Then ask a policeman.

Mme Tonneau
Rue des Embouteilleurs
67200 Buveurville
Bas-Rhin
E-mail: diogenes@wanadoo.fr

Entry No: 88   Map: 6

Entry No: 89   Map: 6

In gorgeous old Dambach, here at the centre of a working vineyard is a typical, geranium-dripping Alsatian house, built by the first Ruhlmann wine-grower in 1688. Wine buffs enjoy visiting the wine cellar and non-drinkers can taste the sweet water springing from the Vosges hills. The charming rooms, in the guest wing under the sloping roof, have new carpets and old family furniture (and there are two more banal overflow rooms); breakfast is served in the huge relic-filled guest dayroom: a wine press, a grape basket, a superb ceramic stove. Your friendly hostess speaks excellent English.

Rooms: 2 doubles, both with shower, sharing wc.

Price: € 36 for two.

Meals: 6 restaurants within walking distance.

Closed: December-March.

Young Madame Engel, who really loves receiving guests, will greet you with the warmest welcome and the finest Alsace cooking. The peaceful chalet, with breathtaking views of the mountains and forests, is just the place to enjoy both. All you need to do is breathe deeply, forget everything - and relax. The rooms are simply comfortable with signs of Monsieur's upholstering skills, geraniums cascading from every window, the views pouring in and a guest entrance. Breakfast tables are laden with goodies - try the home-made organic fruit jams and *kougelopf* (Alsace cake to the uninitiated).

Rooms: 2 doubles, 1 twin, all with shower & wc.

Price: € 56 for two.

Meals: Choice of restaurants nearby.

Closed: January.

Dambach is about 8km north of Sélestat on D35. House in village centre, about equidistant between the two town gates on main road.

From Colmar A35 & N83 Sélestat (exit 11); N59 & D424 to Villé; D697 to Dieffenbach au Val. Careful: ask for exact address as two other Engels do B&B!

Jean-Charles & Laurence Ruhlmann
34 rue Maréchal Foch
67650 Dambach la Ville
Bas-Rhin
Tel: (0)3 88 92 41 86
Fax: (0)3 88 92 61 81
E-mail: ruhlmann.schutz@wanadoo.fr

Doris Engel-Geiger
Maison Fleurie
19 route de Neuve Église
Dieffenbach au Val, 67220 Villé, Bas-Rhin
Tel: (0)3 88 85 60 48
Fax: (0)3 88 85 60 48
E-mail: infos@lamaisonfleurie.com
Web: www.lamaisonfleurie.com

The house is a gallery for Madame's hand-painted stencils (she'll teach you if you like). She and her artistic daughter often paint quietly on the landing. The top-floor pine-clad sitting room is a delight, like being in a boat; bedrooms are big and cosy, the suite in a separate building. Dinner with your hosts and possibly their grown children plus a few friends is a model of conviviality... and Madame should charge extra for her conversation! "Lucky is the traveller who stops here," said one reader. The garden leads out to forest, deer, red squirrels; nearby are golf, skiing and the *Ballons des Vosges* Regional Park.

Rooms: 1 double, 1 suite for 4, both with shower & wc.

Price: €46.50 for two; suite €69.50 for four.

Meals: Dinner €16.50-€20, including wine & coffee.

Closed: Never.

In a tiny village stands a mansion where fine materials and craftsmanship breathe elegance and loving care. Superbly personal taste and gentle light, glowing old floors and delicate mouldings make the generous spaces utterly seductive. Roland combs the auction rooms for lovely rugs, little bronzes, old mirrors and modern paintings; Fabienne hangs thick curtains, places pretty desks, solid oak or carved walnut armoires and soft sofas in vast pale-walled bedrooms. He gardens passionately, she cooks brilliantly - remarkable hosts, interior designers of much flair, they are fun and excellent company. With super-luxury bathrooms to boot, this is value indeed.

Rooms: 1 double/quadruple, 2 suites (2nd double in each is a sofabed), all with bath or shower & wc.

Price: €53.50-€61 for two.

Meals: Dinner €23, including wine & coffee.

Closed: Never.

From A36 exit 14 N83 for Mulhouse; in Les Errues left for Anjoutey and Étueffont; at r'bout right for Rougemont; left at first bend; house at end.

From Troyes A31 exit 6 Langres-Sud through Longeau, onto D67 through Gray towards Besançon. Cult on right 21km beyond Gray. Signposted in village.

Astride & Daniel Elbert
Le Montanjus
8 rue de la Chapelle
90170 Étueffont
Ter-de-Belfort
Tel: (0)3 84 54 68 63
E-mail: daniel.elbert@wanadoo.fr
Web: www.amiesenfranchecomte.com

Mme Fabienne Lego-Deiber
Les Egrignes
70150 Cult
Haute-Saône
Tel: (0)3 84 31 92 06
Fax: (0)3 84 31 92 06
E-mail: lesegrignes@wanadoo.fr

It defies description: the gaunt exterior, part of the town's 15th-century fortress, imposes - but wait. Guy, novelist, traveller and collector, bought the two-metre-thick walls and, with an architect's help, built a house within them - his pride and joy. The huge ground-floor rooms, open to the public, are gorgeous; the breakfast room is suspended from the ceiling of the *salon*; bedrooms, all differently, artistically marvellous, have luxy bathrooms and great views - like sleeping in a modern palace. It could be overwhelming but Guy and Lydie are such a super couple that it's unforgettably moving. *Children over five welcome.*

Rooms: 4 doubles, 1 twin, 1 triple, all with bath or shower & wc.

Price: € 68.50 for two; reduction for 2 nights or more.

Meals: Restaurants 2 minutes walk.

Closed: Mid-October-mid-March.

As part of its vast (100m²) suite, this château has one of the most extraordinary bathrooms this side of the Saône: panels hung with old engravings, a sunken bath and an Italian chandelier contribute to an atmosphere of elegant luxury even a five-star place would be hard put to match; bedroom and sitting room are just as amazing. All this and a family feel. Antiques, attention to detail, a charming hostess with an easy laugh, make this a very special place. Dinner, carefully chosen to suit guests' tastes (if you want snails, you'll have to ask), is exquisitely presented on Gien porcelain and served on the terrace in summer. Untouched 18th-century living. *Gîte space for 1 person.*

Rooms: 1 suite for 3, with bathroom.

Price: € 66 for two.

Meals: Dinner € 16, including wine & coffee; light supper € 8.

Closed: September-mid-May.

From A36 exit 2 onto D475 to Pesmes (20km). House at top of village on left.

From A36 exit 3 onto D67 towards Gray 35km. Entering Gray, right on D474; fork left on D13 to Beaujeu and Motey sur Saône. There left to Mercey; signposted in village.

M & Mme Guy Hoyet
La Maison Royale
70140 Pesmes
Haute-Saône
Tel: (0)3 84 31 23 23
Fax: (0)3 84 31 23 23

Bernadette Jantet
Le Château
70130 Mercey sur Saône
Haute-Saône
Tel: (0)3 84 67 07 84

Entry No: 94   Map: **9**

Entry No: 95   Map: **9**

The fabulously renovated neo-classical mansion and its stylish owners can be unhesitatingly recommended for an authentic taste of *la vie de château*. All rooms, with proper period furniture, engravings and family portraits, look out over the fine *Directoire*-style park. Guests have their own breakfast and sitting rooms and the Oppelts are most welcoming in English that is adequate but not fluent. Madame, as elegant as her house, unintrusively provides for all and Monsieur, whose pride and joy is that park, is pleased to be told that ten years of painstaking work have been worthwhile.

Rooms: 3 doubles, 1 suite, all with bath & wc.

Price: €75-€105 for two.

Meals: Auberge 4km.

Closed: Never.

Your organic-wine-grower hosts are the gentlest, most generous couple imaginable whose son runs wine-tasting sessions for them – and you. Their fairly average home, a converted wine merchant's house, distinguished by that wonderful welcome, offers rooms under the roof, a lovely view of orchards and meadows, a brook to sing you to sleep. There's also a fine dresser carved with the lion of Franche-Comté, their delightful art gallery (Madame does embroidery but shows other artists' paintings) and a tempting garden at the back where a play house awaits children. And anyone may play the piano here or golf just down the road.

Rooms: 1 twin, 1 suite for 4, both with shower & wc.

Price: €38 for two.

Meals: Dinner €11, including coffee. Wine €6-€11 per bottle.

Closed: Never.

In Lons le Saunier towards Chalon/Bourg en Bresse. After SNCF station left on D117 towards Macournay then D41 to Vernantois. Left before church & follow signs to Rose Art.

From Besançon, N73 to St Vit. Then left through town and right onto D203 to Salans; château in village.

Béatrice & Claus Oppelt
Château de Salans
39700 Salans
Jura
Tel: (0)3 84 71 16 55
Fax: (0)3 84 79 41 54

Monique & Michel Ryon
Rose Art
8 rue Lacuzon
39570 Vernantois
Jura
Tel: (0)3 84 47 17 28
Fax: (0)3 84 47 17 28

Entry No: 96   Map: 9

Entry No: 97   Map: 9

A beautiful spot, the Loire at the bottom of the garden, a fascinating host - Monsieur has retired to share his time between his house and his guests. His English nanny made him for ever at home with the English language and culture and he enjoys discussing his many interests over dinner: the region, its history and architecture, his print and corkscrew collections; he's also passionate about cooking (and wine, and art...) The 18th-century, entirely lived-in château has no end of family furniture and treasures, a boat for guests' use and the Pilgrim's Path (GR 13) passing close by. A chance to sample the pleasing lifestyle of the French provincial aristocracy.

Rooms: 2 doubles, 2 twins, 1 suite for 4, all with bath & wc.

Price: €53-€76 for two.

Meals: Dinner €23, including wine & coffee.

Closed: 31 December-1 April.

Burgundy

St Claude makes the prince of pipes,
Canon Kir mixes his inimitable vine-fruit nectar,
the fat snail creeps to marry parsley and garlic,
the best wines fetch fabulous sums in the courtyards of Beaune: *À table!*

From Digoin D979 towards Bourbon Lancy for 25km. In St Aubin, 1st left at sign Les Lambeys; house on right.

Etienne de Bussierre
Les Lambeys
71140 St Aubin sur Loire
Saône-et-Loire
Tel: (0)3 85 53 92 76

Entry No: 98   Map: 8

A fantastic ceramic stove as big as two men dominates the panelled breakfast room of this 17th-century royal hunting lodge. The whole place has an air of exaggeration: over-generous stairs, ingenious double windows, highly voluptuous decoration, all totally French with floral wallpapers and embroidered bedcovers in magnificent bedrooms, 1930s tiled bathrooms (one whirlpool) and stained glass panels. Marie knows everyone in wine-growing and will help you all she can over another cigarette. And Burgundy has so much to offer, as well as superb wines.

Rooms: 1 twin with bath & wc; 1 double & 1 twin sharing shower & wc; 1 triple & 1 twin sharing bath & wc.

Price: € 61-€ 76 for two; suite € 122 for four.

Meals: Dinner € 24, including wine & coffee.

Closed: Never.

From Chalon sur Saône N80 for Montceau les Mines 9km; exit 31 on D981 for Givry; follow Complexe Sportif signs; 2nd on right.

The guest rooms of this former abbey are in the 17th-century pigeon tower: those hollows are where the original occupants roosted. Ring at the wrought-iron gates for your young hosts, the easiest of people - it's all pleasingly eccentric and fun. There's a ground-floor sitting room with a twin room off it - ideal for children - and in the tower itself is that amazing bathroom with the main bedroom on a mezzanine floor above. Breakfast, a relaxed family affair, is a short walk through the park to the château kitchen; dinner may be in the graciously faded dining room.
Gîte space for 5 people.

Rooms: 1 quadruple with bath & wc.

Price: € 56.50 for two.

Meals: Dinner € 23, including wine & coffee.

Closed: Never.

From A6 exit Chalon south, N6 towards Varrennes le Grand; D6 towards Le Lac de Laives to La Ferté. Press intercom at large iron gates at crossroads marked La Ferté.

Marie & Daniel Lacroix-Mollaret
Manoir du Clos de Vauvry
3 rue des Faussillons
71640 Givry Poncey, Saône-et-Loire
Tel: (0)3 85 44 40 83
Fax: (0)3 85 44 53 54
E-mail: closdevauvry@multimania.com
Web: www.multimania.com/closdevauvry

Jacques & Virginie Thenard
Abbaye de la Ferté
71240 Saint Ambreuil
Saône-et-Loire
Tel: (0)3 85 44 17 96
Fax: (0)3 85 44 17 96
E-mail: thenardjacques@aol.com

Nobles is a place to die for with oceans of history behind it (a prehistoric *menhir* stands in the grounds) and charming owners bursting with more restoration ideas: they are passionate about it. Monsieur cultivates the vines and the wine: wine production started here in the 10th century. The bedrooms, in a renovated building near the main 13th-15th-century château, are fresh and unfussy in the stylish way so many are in France - the bigger one is a gem, with its superb beams, vast mezzanine and little veranda. Breakfast is in the château, a delightfully lived-in listed monument. Irresistible.

Rooms: 1 triple, 1 family, both with bath or shower & wc.

Price: €70 for two.

Meals: 5 restaurants within 5km.

Closed: November-March.

Children love it here: they can watch the goats being milked in the clean, enclosed farmyard, even help if they (and the nannies) like. There are horses too. Your hard-working hosts, with two children of their own and sensitive to the needs of families, have made a large family room at the top of the old stone farmhouse. Bathrobes are provided for grown-ups, so everyone feels cared for. All six rooms are sparkling and charmingly simple. People return, not only for the relaxing experience but also to stock up on the home-made cheeses, mouth-watering jams and local wines that the family make and sell.

Rooms: 2 doubles sharing shower & wc; 2 twins with shower & wc; 2 family suites with shower, wc & kitchen.

Price: €47-€52 for two.   *56*

Meals: Self-catering in two rooms; restaurant nearby.

Closed: Never.

From Tournus D14 for Cormatin. Passing Brancion on right cont. on main road for 1.5km. Towers opposite on bend.

From Tournus D14 towards Cluny. At Chapaize, D314 to Bissy sous Uxelles. House next to church.

Bertrand & Françoise de Cherisey
Château de Nobles
71700 La Chapelle sous Brancion
Saône-et-Loire
Tel: (0)3 85 51 00 55

Pascale & Dominique de La Bussière
La Ferme
71460 Bissy sous Uxelles
Saône-et-Loire
Tel: (0)3 85 50 15 03
Fax: (0)3 85 50 15 03
E-mail: dominique.de-la-bussiere@wanadoo.fr
Web: www.m-fjsolutions.com/BB/

Entry No: 101   Map: 9

Entry No: 102   Map: 9

What goes on behind the scenery? You can discover how the theatre really works here, where farmhouse B&B is combined with a thriving theatre and art gallery. In June and July the local group of actor-winegrowers, *La Mère Folle*, founded in 1981 by Jean-Paul, perform in their converted barn. Régine, a musician, helps with productions. Busy, artistic people, they create an atmosphere of relaxed energy, take their B&B very seriously and offer good rooms with comfortable beds, modern décor of pale wood, original beams and, generously, *Grand-père's* excellent Cubist paintings.

Rooms: 4 doubles, 1 twin, all with bath or shower & wc.

Price: €45 for two.

Meals: Bistro in village, 2km, otherwise 6km.

Closed: November-February.

From A6 exit Tournus; D56 for Lugny. 3km after Chardonnay right on D463 & follow signs to Chambres d'Hôtes/Théâtre Champvent.

Régine & Jean-Paul Rullière
Le Tinailler
Manoir de Champvent
71700 Chardonnay
Saône-et-Loire
Tel: (0)3 85 40 50 23
Fax: (0)3 85 40 50 18

Do explore the woods and gardens of this 13th-century château - they are beautiful and tours of the cellars and the *Route des Vins* can be arranged; Monsieur is a cellar master. The excellent guest rooms are in the *maisons vigneronnes*, the old vine workers' cottages, except one room, more 'period' with its small four-poster (and more expensive), which is in the château. Madame manages with charming efficiency, aperitifs in the cellar are part of the evening ritual and Monsieur may surprise you with an enormous bottle of cognac after a dinner of regional dishes made with home-grown vegetables. A most welcoming place. *Gîte space for 16.*

Rooms: 2 twins, 1 double/twin, 1 triple, all with bath & wc.

Price: €77-€99 for two.

Meals: Dinner €20-25, including wine & coffee.

Closed: January.

From A6 exit to Tournus; in centre right on D14. Château on left of D14 between Ozenay & Martailly, 9km from Tournus.

Marie-Laurence Fachon
Château de Messey
71700 Ozenay
Saône-et-Loire
Tel: (0)3 85 51 16 11
Fax: (0)3 85 32 57 30
E-mail: vin@demessey.com
Web: www.demessey.com

You can see the pretty 12th-century church from the house, which is only 17th-century... It has been renovated with superb attention to detail, including excellent bathrooms. Monsieur, elderly, charming and very chatty with lots of tales to tell, is totally French, right down to his cigarettes. He'll take good care of you, will have a welcoming log fire in winter, share his love of this famous wine-making region and provide a feast of local produce for breakfast (on the terrace when days are long and warm) - jams, honey, bread, cheeses and pâtés - which should set you up perfectly for a heady day's visit to the vineyards.

Rooms: 2 doubles, both with shower or bath & wc.

Price: €44 for two.

Meals: Excellent restaurant nearby.

Closed: Never.

From Tournus, D14 towards Cormatin for 12km; left on D163 towards Grévilly. After 200m right to Grévilly; across T-junction; house 100m on left: outside village, just below church.

Claude Depreay
Le Pré Ménot
71700 Grévilly
Saône-et-Loire
Tel: (0)3 85 33 29 92
Fax: (0)3 85 33 02 79

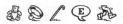

The lovely stones and cascading geraniums outside, the silk flowers, frilly lampshades and polished furniture inside have an old-world charm. The breakfast room is cosily stuffed with bric-à-brac, bedrooms are family-simple. Madame was a florist: she arranges her rooms as if they were bouquets, is always refreshing them and might put a paper heart on your pillow wishing you *bonne nuit*. She doesn't refuse children but may well be happier if you arrive with a little dog under your arm. She or her husband can do winery visits for non-Francophones. Ask for one of the larger rooms; the smallest feels cramped.

Rooms: 3 doubles, all with bath or shower & wc.

Price: €38-€46 for two.

Meals: Choice of restaurants 3-5km.

Closed: Sundays in winter.

From N79 exit La Roche Vineuse. Left to Charhay lès Macon (not La Roche Vineuse); left for Sommeré. Up hill following EH signs - house at top on left; bell on wall by gate.

Éliane Heinen
Le Tinailler d'Aléane
Sommeré
71960 La Roche Vineuse
Saône-et-Loire
Tel: (0)3 85 37 80 68
Fax: (0)3 85 37 80 68

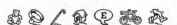

Burgundy

The authentically worn old manor house has immense personality. Madame, with her unorthodox sense of humour, is "quite a character" too. She wants visitors to see that it was built by a 19th-century *parvenu* (some delightfully OTT bits) and is now inhabited by artists (watercolours and weavings). Choose activity: cycling, walking, horse-riding; or gentility: contemplate mountain scenery, play the Érard baby grand, browse through the local guides and histories in the library. Super but smallish old-decorated rooms, fine modern bathrooms. Give Madame time to come to the door - she may be deep in the garden. *Gîte space for 10 people.*

Rooms: 1 double with bath, shower & wc; 1 suite for 5 with shower, wc & kitchen.

Price: €38-€40 for two.

Meals: Self-catering in suite; restaurant 5km.

Closed: Never.

Language no obstacle: the Duchets are natural hosts and easy communicators. Their engagingly cottagey old farmhouse is full of character and space beneath its sweeping roof - exposed beams and old tiles are part of Monsieur's fine renovation job. Madame is a charming, enthusiastic hostess, keen to provide her guests with authentic country hospitality. Rooms, traditionally decorated and comfortable, include a pleasant living room with books and games. Breakfast (home-made jams) and dinner are eaten with the family; Madame is Portuguese and will make national specialities if asked - a real treat.

Rooms: 2 doubles, both with shower & wc.

Price: €46 for two.

Meals: Dinner €20, including wine & coffee; children €9.

Closed: November-Easter.

From Mâcon, N79 for Cluny. At Berzé le Châtel, N79-D987 for Charolles to exit Clermain-Matour-Trambly; D987 to Trambly. Left past church; house on left.

From Cosne sur Loire, D114 to St Loup; left on D114; Chauffour is between St Loup and St Vérain; follow Musée de la Machine Agricole then Chambres d'Hôtes.

François & Florence Gauthier
Les Charrières
71520 Trambly
Saône-et-Loire
Tel: (0)3 85 50 43 17
Fax: (0)3 85 50 49 28
E-mail: gauthierflorence@minitel.net

Elvire & René Duchet
Chez Elvire
Chauffour
58200 St Loup
Nièvre
Tel: (0)3 86 26 20 22

Entry No: 107   Map: **9**

Entry No: 108   Map: **8**

The whole atmosphere of generous, well-organised hospitality and rural peace generated by your hosts and their surroundings is exceptional. Bedroom shutters open onto country views and a curved double staircase leads down to a kempt lawn where, rather endearingly, chickens may be roaming. Inside are open fires, antique beds (with antique monogrammed bedclothes), sympathetic period decorations and an atmosphere of secluded comfort. Madame Bürgi's cakes and jams are incomparable, all organic and home-made - if only breakfast could be more than once a day! Delicious dinners, too *Gîte space for 2 people.*

Rooms: 6 doubles/twins, all with bath or shower & wc.

Price: €60-€77 for two.

Meals: Dinner €33, including wine & coffee; restaurant in village.

Closed: Never.

Huge fun for families: horses and ponies for rides or tours of several days; country discovery courses for children and themed weekends such as camping, lambing, map-making/reading; sheep-rearing to observe. The new, energetic owners, who broke away from city jobs, have given the whole place a fresh look - bright paintwork and cheerful fabrics - but are keen to keep the overall farm atmosphere. Your children may romp with theirs, you can head for the national mountain biking centre (550km of marked track) or just 3km away you can immerse yourself in water sports. *Overnight farm stopover for 19.*

Rooms: 1 double & pullout beds for children, with shower & wc.

Price: €40 for two.

Meals: Dinner €14 including wine & coffee; 2 restaurants in St Saulge, 1 in Prémery.

Closed: Never.

From Nevers, D977 to Prémery. D977 bis for Corbigny; St Révérien is 15km on; signposted.

From Prémery, D38 for St Saulge; Gîte d'Étape sign at junction of D38 and D181 to St Martin.

Bernadette Bürgi & Florent de Beer
La Villa des Prés
58420 Saint Révérien
Nièvre
Tel: (0)3 86 29 04 57
Fax: (0)3 86 29 65 22
E-mail: contact@villa-des-pres.com
Web: www.villa-des-pres.com

Laurence & Philippe Kneuss
Basse Cour de St Martin
58330 Sainte Marie
Nièvre
Tel: (0)3 86 58 35 15
Fax: (0)3 86 58 22 83
E-mail: phkneuss@club-internet.fr
Web: www.bassecour-stmartin.com

Inside the house, immaculately restored by the owners, you find good antique furniture and elegant décor with plenty of interesting wallpaper and stupendous bathrooms. Outside, if you come at the right time of year, you'll be surrounded by fields of sunflowers for ever and beyond. Your modest, friendly hosts clearly enjoy sharing their 1690s house and its 115 hectares of parkland. They are happy to suggest activities - visiting local châteaux, lovely canalside walks, pony rides. Monsieur takes English lessons and is keen to flex his linguistic muscles with any willing volunteers - he has an impressive Burgundy accent!

Rooms: 4 doubles, all with bath or shower & wc.

Price: €43-€54 for two.

Meals: Self-catering possible; restaurant 5km.

Closed: Never.

From Château Chinon, D978 through Châtillon en Bazois for Nevers 4km (past Alluy); after service station, right on D112 for Bernière; house on left after 1.5km.

Colette & André Lejault
Bouteuille
58110 Alluy
Nièvre
Tel: (0)3 86 84 06 65
Fax: (0)3 86 84 03 41
E-mail: lejault.c@wanadoo.fr
Web: perso.wanadoo.fr/bouteuille

What a welcome! The Perreaus may meet you with a glass of something special; wonderful folk, full of *joie de vivre*, their house and farm are full of life, human and animal. They breed cattle and horses, and summer foals dance in the buttercup meadows - a lovely backdrop to the terrace and swimming pool. They also have a sideline in organic vegetables - Madame, who is a delight, loves her big *potager*, you will love its fruits. You stay in the big loft of the old farmhouse where bright, finely-furnished bedrooms share a large sitting room and a sweet little breakfast room. A tremendous place for enjoying the good things in life. *Gîte space for 10 people.*

Rooms: 2 twins, 2 doubles, sharing 2 showers & separate wcs; 1 double with shower & wc.

Price: €50 for two.

Meals: Dinner €15, including wine & coffee.

Closed: Never.

From Nevers D978 towards Château Chinon. 3km before Châtillon right on D10 towards Alluy. In St Gratien left on C3 to La Marquise; 800m on right.

Huguette & Noël Perreau
La Marquise
58340 Saint Gratien Savigny
Nièvre
Tel: (0)3 86 50 01 02
Fax: (0)3 86 50 07 14

The garden sweeps down to the lake, the sun sets over it, you can borrow the owners' small boat and row on it, or fish, or canoe, or windsurf, and there's a private beach that guests can use - a perfect place to go with children. Breakfast includes home-produced honey and *viennoiseries*. The big, bright rooms are French classic with gilt-framed mirrors, round tables in modern bathrooms and that particular type of wallpaper. They are a super couple, she level-headed, he loving to joke, who create a relaxedly family atmosphere. Madame is taking English lessons, but her genuine welcome already transcends the language barrier. *Gîte space for 10.*

Rooms: 2 triples, 1 double, all with bath or shower & wc.

Price: €43-€46 for two.

Meals: Self-catering possible; restaurants nearby.

Closed: Never.

Farmyard heaven in a priory. Marie-Georges, an energetic shepherdess and artist, loves to be surrounded by people and animals: there are sheep, horses, dogs, goats, ducks and chickens; she runs 'Nature Days', stencilling, wool-dyeing and other courses in the converted stables, for adults and children. The Ryans (he English, she French) came to this handsome old country priory to enjoy the countryside and they thrive on activity. Meals are happy family events in the old farm kitchen, with fresh eggs and home-grown vegetables. The large, cosy *chambre d'hôtes* has its own entrance off the courtyard. There's camping here too. *Gîte space for 4 people.*

Rooms: 1 suite for 4, with shower & wc.

Price: €40 for two.

Meals: Dinner €15, including wine & coffee.

Closed: Never.

From Nevers D978 to Rouy; D132 to Tintury, right on D112 to Fleury (signposted Fertrève); first right after village, up to lake, turn right; signposted.

From Decise N81 to Cercy la Tour; D26 towards St Benin d'Azy for 5km; right to Diennes Aubigny. Large house next to church, through farm gates.

Michel & Marie-France Guény
Fleury La Tour
58110 Tintury
Nièvre
Tel: (0)3 86 84 12 42
Fax: (0)3 86 84 12 42

Douglas & Marie-Georges Ryan
La Réserve
58340 Diennes Aubigny
Nièvre
Tel: (0)3 86 50 05 29
Fax: (0)3 86 50 05 29
E-mail: lareserve@free.fr
Web: www.saute-mouton.com

Entry No: 113   **Map:** 8

Entry No: 114   Ma

Tarperon is uniquely French and an ageless charm breathes from the ancient turrets, fine antiques, paintings and prints; Soisick is modern and good fun, with her sense of humour and her unstuffy formality - if you can't find her, walk in and make yourself at home, she's not far. The rooms are full of family furniture in an utterly uncontrived, fadedly elegant, lived-in décor; the bathrooms are family style with lots of unusual bits. Dinner, superbly cooked by Claudine and Soisick, is a treat. Also: lovely gardens, fly-fishing, painting courses - stay two or three days to enjoy it all properly.

Rooms: 3 doubles, 1 twin, 1 triple, all with bath or shower & wc.

Price: €60 for two.

Meals: Dinner €23, including wine & coffee.

Closed: 2 November-20 March.

The Gounands receive guests so warmly in their modern house with its fabulous valley views over historic Alesia (Julius Caesar fought the Gauls here in 52 BC). Having lived in Africa, they came to escape the rat race, build and decorate (slightly garishly) this house, become Mayor of the village (Monsieur has now retired but will describe it all over a *kir*) and offer spotless rooms, good mattresses, high-quality bathrooms to lovers of peace and wine, walking and medieval villages (lovely dawn chorus too). Choose Madame's good cooking or your own in the well-equipped, open-sided summer house that Monsieur designed for the garden.

Rooms: 1 double, 1 twin, both with curtained shower, sharing wc.

Price: €34 for two.

Meals: Dinner €12, including wine & coffee.

Closed: November-Easter, except by arrangement.

From Dijon N71 for Châtillon sur Seine, 62km; right D901 for Aignay. Tarperon signed on D901.

From Dijon N71 for Châtillon sur Seine; after Courceau D6 left and follow signs; house on D19A near junction with D6.

Soisick de Champsavin & Claudine Raillard
Manoir de Tarperon
21510 Aignay le Duc
Côte-d'Or
Tel: (0)3 80 93 83 74
Fax: (0)3 80 93 83 74
E-mail: manoir.de.tarperon@wanadoo.fr

Claude & Huguette Gounand
Villa le Clos
Route de la Villeneuve
21150 Darcey
Côte-d'Or
Tel: (0)3 80 96 23 20
Fax: (0)3 80 96 23 20
E-mail: claude.gounand@libertysurf.fr

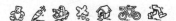

You cannot forget the lifeblood of Burgundy: wine buffs will love the twisting drive along the *Route des Vins* into the gravelled courtyard of this fine old wine-grower's house. Your courteous host knows a lot about wine and loves to practise his English, so sample an aperitif in his atmospheric stone-arched cellar, (if you're not a wine fan there are locally-pressed fruit juices too). The house has a classic stone staircase and generous windows, the comfortable and homely bedrooms are reached by outside steps, the breakfast room has flagstones and ochre-coloured walls. In summer, breakfast is in the well-kept, willow-draped garden.

Rooms: 1 double, 1 twin, 1 family, all with shower & wc.

Price: €50-€56 for two.

Meals: Excellent restaurant 300m.

Closed: Never.

The entrance to the fine gardens and house may seem narrow but don't get it wrong: you are very welcome and can always leave the car outside. The generous warmth of the ochre-tinted, green-shuttered façade extends indoors where a beautiful Alsatian ceramic stove stands proud beside huge plants in the sunny breakfast room and the double-aspect guest rooms are airy and florally friezed. Interesting prints on the walls too. Your hosts are chatty and friendly. Monsieur teaches economics, Madame gave up a high-powered marketing job to care for two small children and the visitors she so enjoys receiving.

Rooms: 1 triple, 1 twin, 2 doubles, 1 family suite, all with bath, shower & wc.

Price: €70-€85 for two.

Meals: Restaurant 1km.

Closed: Never.

From Lyon N on A6 exit Nuits St Georges, then N74 towards Dijon. After approx. 13km left to Marsannay la Côte.

From A31 exit Nuits St Georges; N74 for Dijon; at Vougeot r'bout head for Gilly centre; 1st right after station.

Jean-Charles & Brigitte Viennet
34 rue de Mazy
21160 Marsannay la Côte
Côte-d'Or
Tel: (0)3 80 59 83 63
Fax: (0)3 80 59 83 28
E-mail: viennet.jean-charles@wanadoo.fr
Web: perso.wanadoo.fr/gite.marsannay

André & Sandrine Lanaud
La Closerie de Gilly
16 avenue du Recteur Bouchard
Gilly lès Cîteaux
21640 Vougeot, Côte-d'Or
Tel: (0)3 80 62 87 74
Fax: (0)3 80 62 87 74
E-mail: as.lanaud@wanadoo.fr

Entry No: 117   Map: 9

Entry No: 118   Map:

Ancient rafters, white-swathed roof windows, little florals - the bedrooms, one with a ladder up to the children's mezzanine, are sweetly charming, just like the wide rose-bordered terrace where breakfast is served on fine days. The Dufouleur wine is pretty good too - they are one of the old wine-growing families and Madame willingly prepares light suppers of local cheeses, salad and choice of estate wines. There's history beneath the old stones: the house stands on the remains of the Duke of Burgundy's 13th-century castle (he was Hugues de Quincey) and the little church is floodlit at night. Perfectly quiet, ideal for wine-lovers.
Children over 3 welcome.

Rooms: 1 triple with bath & wc; 1 double with shower & wc; loft for children.

Price: € 58 for two.

Meals: Supper € 11.

Closed: Never.

In its attractive hilltop village, the endearingly higgledy-piggledy 18th-century house has space and a big welcome for all. Its cheerful, plain rooms all have independent entrances and Françoise's hand decoration of some of the furniture lends an artistic flourish: "neither marble nor satin, but wood and plaster, whiteness and colour" is how she defines her décor. Breakfast in the big, all-in-together kitchen features honey from Henri's hives. You may meet him in the evening and hear about life as a beekeeper: he is genuinely fascinating, Françoise clearly enjoys people, dinners are moments of sharing and mirth.

Rooms: 1 quadruple, 1 triple, 1 double, all with shower or bath & wc.

Price: € 35 for two.

Meals: Dinner € 14, including wine & coffee.

Closed: December-February.

From A31 exit Nuits St Georges for Gerland-Seurre 3km; right to Quincey; house opposite church.

From Nuits St Georges, N74 for Beaune. At Corgoloin, D115 to Magny lès V.; cont. for Pernand Vergelesses; house almost immed. on right leaving Magny.

Chantal Dufouleur
Place de l'Église
21700 Quincey
Côte-d'Or
Tel: (0)3 80 61 13 23
Fax: (0)3 80 61 13 23
E-mail: dufouleurchantal@wanadoo.fr
Web: perso.wanadoo.fr/gite.nuits-saint-georges/

Françoise Giorgi
Maison des Abeilles
Route de Pernand-Vergelesses
21700 Magny lès Villers
Côte-d'Or
Tel: (0)3 80 62 95 42

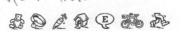

Entry No: 119   Map: 9

Entry No: 120   Map: 9

Burgundy

'Red Beeches' is a 200-year-old hunting lodge where the garden is full of flowers, the trees are centenarians and breakfast has the savour of yesteryear: yogurt, fresh bread and home-made jam - a past one wouldn't mind revisiting regularly. Your hosts extend the warmest of genuine welcomes to the weary traveller - lots of towels, superb bed linen, beautifully-judged colour schemes (Madame paints and knows about colour), fine furniture, a sprig of flowers, all combine to provide a soothing and reviving environment. The cottage is a deliciously independent blue hideaway with a working fireplace.

Rooms: 1 double, 1 twin, both with bath & wc.

Price: €77-€81 for two.

Meals: Wide choice of restaurants 10km.

Closed: Never.

Here you will find space, warmth, good taste, intelligent company and a pretty terrace for breakfast - and so many musical events in summer. Madame is open and at ease - her house reflects her natural elegance. All is harmony in her renovated and not over-furnished manor with its pale colours, old tiles and rugs, modern art and big, soft-textured bedrooms (one more intimate and carpeted). The soft Burgundian light pours in through the big windows in the main rooms and the little village is quietly authentic. A highly civilised house and family.

Rooms: 2 triples, 1 double, all with bath or shower & wc.

Price: €64 for two.

Meals: Good restaurants locally.

Closed: Mid-October-April.

From A31 exit 1 onto D35 E towards Seurre for about 3km; right to Quincey and on to Antilly (4km). House on right.

From A6 Beaune/Chagny exit onto D973 towards Dole & Seurre for 10km. In Corberon house signposted up on left.

Jean-François & Christiane Bugnet
Les Hêtres Rouges
Antilly
21700 Argilly, Côte-d'Or
Tel: (0)3 80 62 53 98
Fax: (0)3 80 62 54 85
E-mail: leshetresrouges2@wanadoo.fr
Web: www.leshetresrouges.com

Chantal & Alain Balmelle
L'Ormeraie
21250 Corberon
Côte-d'Or
Tel: (0)3 80 26 53 19
Fax: (0)3 80 26 54 01
E-mail: cab.abc@wanadoo.fr

Entry No: 121   Map: **9**

Entry No: 122   Map:

So very grand, so very French, this 19th-century manor set back from the lime-tree-shaded square. Persian carpets on parquet floors, antiques and good, firm beds grace the large, luminous rooms and bathrooms are well-fitted and finished. In winter a wood fire burns in the sitting room. Madame has taken great pains over her immaculate home, puts you at your ease in these rather formal surroundings and enjoys talking to guests. Should she have to be out when you arrive, she'll leave a note on the door. "B&B perfection," wrote one reader, "for style, beds, hostess!" *Well-behaved children welcome. Minimum stay 2 nights July-September.*

Rooms: 1 double/twin with shower & wc; 1 double, 1 twin sharing bath, shower & wc.

Price: €53-€68 for two.

Meals: Dinner €20, including wine & coffee; low season only.

Closed: Never.

From Paris A6 exit for Joigny; D89 for 10km to Senan; Place de la Liberté after church on right.

Mme Paule Defrance
4 place de la Liberté
89710 Senan
Yonne
Tel: (0)3 86 91 59 89

All you have to do is ring at the huge gates and enter and this superb château is your home for the night. You will indeed be welcomed as family by this charming young couple, their little girl, their pedigree Schnauzer dogs (Madame breeds them) and their parakeets - all delightful. Downstairs, the thick-walled, vaulted dining and sitting rooms support the rest of the house, an impressive and original alternative to deep foundations. An oak staircase leads up to the charming, period-furnished bedrooms with views over roofs and woods. Meals come with home-grown veg and good wine from the Septiers' cellar. *Gîte space for 5 people.*

Rooms: 2 doubles, both with shower & basin; 2 doubles; all sharing 2 bathrooms & wc in corridor.

Price: €60 for two.

Meals: Dinner €30, including wine & coffee.

Closed: Never.

From A6 exit Auxerre Nord towards Auxerre 0.5km; right D158 for Perrigny/St Georges/Villefargeau. At Relais de la Vallée restaurant, left twice, château at end of road, after riding school.

Jacky & Marianne Septier
1 allée du Château
89240 Villefargeau
Yonne
Tel: (0)3 86 41 37 38
Fax: (0)3 86 41 27 25
E-mail: marianne.septier@wanadoo.fr
Web: perso.wanadoo.fr/marianne.septier/

Burgundy

A fantastic collection of 16th-century fortified farm buildings complete with towered château, where the Brodards live. The good-size guest rooms in the converted barn are simply decorated with some interesting pieces of old furniture and sparklingly clean, tiled bathrooms. Your host - who is something of a jam expert - prepares breakfast in the *salon*/breakfast room with its tearoom-style round tables, open fire and courtyard view. Great countryside, only 10 minutes' walk from the pretty village with its gourmet restaurant, and a healthy cycle ride from Auxerre.

Rooms: 5 doubles/twins with shower & wc.

Price: €57.50 for two.

Meals: Restaurants in village or 3km.

Closed: Never.

Simplicity and attention to detail are Madame's keynotes and her harmonious, quirky house - 'Gothic' windows even in the attic, 'Victorian' panelling, superb old patterned floor tiles - thoroughly endorses the warm and friendly central theme. Up two floors, the simply-furnished bedrooms have sloping ceilings, ancient rafters and not one common wall. Breakfast by the old bread oven or outside before learning to 'grow' truffles, consulting Monsieur on the estate wine you'll take home (the cellar is below the house), or setting off for Auxerre. A child-friendly house belonging to the nicest possible people.

Rooms: 4 doubles, 1 suite for 4, all with bath or shower & wc.

Price: €45-€65 for two.

Meals: Restaurant 2km; Auxerre or Chablis 10km.

Closed: 15 December-15 January.

From A6 exit Auxerre Nord onto N6 towards Auxerre; right towards St Georges; straight across all r'bouts to traffic lights. In Chevannes first left; last house on leaving village.

From Auxerre, D965 towards Chablis; after passing under A6 motorway, 3km on, house on right. Do not go to Venoy.

Claude & Marie-Claude Brodard
Château de Ribourdin
89240 Chevannes
Yonne
Tel: (0)3 86 41 23 16
Fax: (0)3 86 41 23 16

François & Françoise Choné
Domaine de Montpierreux
89290 Venoy
Yonne
Tel: (0)3 86 40 20 91
Fax: (0)3 86 40 28 00

The handsome millhouse, completely surrounded by a rushing river and its own lake where Leigh has sunk a brilliant natural-looking swimming pool, is reached via a narrow, private bridge. Wander the beautiful grounds or settle yourself in the most inviting sitting room, complete with roaring log fire when it's cold. Leigh and Cinda are relaxed and easy hosts who delight in sharing their watery world. There's a canoe, and balloon flights can be arranged. The big, light bedrooms are freshly decorated with good bathrooms and the mill race is generally noisier than the road. *Gîte space for 6 people.*

Rooms: 3 doubles, 1 twin, 1 triple, 1 suite for 4, all with bath/shower & wc. Extra beds possible.

Price: €50-€68 for two.

Meals: Restaurants close by.

Closed: Never.

These young owners have brought vitality to their handsome old house with a clever conversion that lets in stacks of light - perfect for the exhibition of local artists' work: water colours, oils and sculptures. Corinne has decorated each bedroom as if it were her own, they are all comfortable and colourful with co-ordinated headboards and bedspreads and good bathrooms. She loves her flower and vegetable garden too, meals are definitely worth booking (she also runs courses for groups interested in traditional French cooking) and you may choose from Pascal's excellent cellar of Yonne wines.

Rooms: 2 doubles, 1 twin, 1 family for 4, all with shower or bath & wc.

Price: €51 for two.

Meals: Dinner €19, including wine & coffee.

Closed: Never.

From Auxerre N6 towards Avallon for 22km. Just before Vermenton village nameplate, sharp right, double back and cross bridge.

From A6 exit Nitry towards Tonnerre for 7km, right at crossroads signed Chambres d'Hotes; left to Môlay then Arton - house opposite 'lavoir' (wash hut).

Leigh Wootton & Cinda Tarasoff
Le Moulinot
89270 Vermenton
Yonne
Tel: (0)3 86 81 60 42
Fax: (0)3 86 81 62 25
E-mail: lemoulinot@aol.com

Corinne & Pascal Collin
Le Calounier
5 rue de la Fontaine-Arton
89310 Môlay, Yonne
Tel: (0)3 86 82 67 81
Fax: (0)3 86 82 67 81
E-mail: info@lecalounier.fr
Web: www.lecalounier.fr

A picture of a place. Different architectural periods are joined by three big staircases and several small ones (not for the stiff-limbed, although one bedroom is in the stable block), giving a real sense of history. Parts are 14th century; it was once fortified and most of the moat remains; Louis XIV's cousin declined to stay long "because of the ghost". Madame is direct and knowledgeable, her big, old-fashioned guest rooms are idiosyncratic rather than luxurious, the heated swimming pool is tucked away in the three-hectare park. A very special, unpretentious place. *Can be tricky to find: ring for help if lost.*

Rooms: 2 doubles, 1 twin, all with bath or shower & wc.

Price: €65-€76 for two.

Meals: Restaurants nearby.

Closed: Never.

Ancient and atmospheric, Cabalus was a pilgrims' hospice built in the shadow of the revered Basilica on its *Eternal Hill*. A gallery of quietly intriguing, tempting objects and a coffee shop occupy the 12th-century vaulted hall: guests have that huge fireplace to themselves for breakfast. Rooms are simple, authentic, with good beds. Eccentric, Swiss and slightly shuffling, M Cabalus is the perfect gentleman with a fine sense of humour, Madame a most welcoming artist. An exceptional and inimitable house.

Rooms: 2 double, both with shower & wc; 2 doubles, both with shower but sharing wcs.

Price: €58-€75 for two.

Meals: Dinner €20, including wine & coffee.

Closed: Never.

From Mezilles D965 towards St Fargeau for 3.5km; small road on right towards Dannery, up to white fencing; tree-lined drive to manor house.

Mme Couiteas
Dannery
89170 Saint Fargeau
Yonne
Tel: (0)3 86 74 09 01
Fax: (0)3 86 74 09 01

In Vézelay centre, follow main street up to 'Basilique'. Park car and walk down main street. Ring at second door on right.

M Cabalus
Cabalus
Rue Saint Pierre
89450 Vézelay, Yonne
Tel: (0)3 86 33 20 66
Fax: (0)3 86 33 38 03
E-mail: contact@cabalus.com
Web: www.cabalus.com

Burgundy

The great stones and timbers of this house on the stone-paved hill, climbed by pilgrims over 500 years, vibrate with age and spirituality. A stone spiral staircase leads to the bedrooms; the double has a terrace overlooking the sublime Basilica; both are full of simple character. Madame, easy, unintrusive and a passionate rider, serves breakfast in her dining room with its huge fireplace and readers have enjoyed the utter Frenchness of it all. There are maps and advice for hikers and cyclists and a pretty little self-catering flat for longer stays. *Gîte space for 4 people.*

Rooms: 1 double, 1 twin, sharing shower & wc.

Price: €45 for two.

Meals: Good restaurants in Vézelay.

Closed: Never.

From Avallon D957 to Vézelay; up towards Basilica (Rue St Étienne becomes Rue St Pierre); turreted house 100m from Basilica.

Monique & Bertrand Ginisty
La Tour Gaillon
Rue Saint Pierre
89450 Vézelay
Yonne
Tel: (0)3 86 33 25 74
E-mail: b.ginisty@wanadoo.fr

Entry No: 131   Map: 8

Was that Rapunzel? Climb the winding stone stair to the top of the turret, push the big oak door, choose your four-poster, wallow in the ingenious Gothicky bathroom then lie and admire the brilliant hangings and 'authentic' lights: no need to let down your hair. All is as 12th-century as Madame can make it. The medieval atmosphere, called strange, stagey, fascinating by some, is completed by objects from the château's history, some as old as the Crusades. Madame is passionate about the place, most approachable and a talented cook - medieval dinners are served in the candlelit baronial kitchen/dining room. A stylish and romantic retreat.

Rooms: 1 quadruple (2 four-posters) with bathroom.

Price: €85 for two.

Meals: Dinner €15-€55, including wine & coffee (state your budget).

Closed: Never.

From Avallon, N6 for Saulieu. As you enter Ste Magnance, first house on right.

Martine & Gérard Costaille
Château Jaquot
2 route d'Avallon
89420 Sainte Magnance
Yonne
Tel: (0)3 86 33 00 22

Entry No: 132   Map: 9

Several centuries, ending with Art Deco, shape this old hunting lodge that was determinedly 'modernised' in the 1920s: high-windowed, fully-panelled dining room with extraordinary dressers, unbelievably moustachioed grandfather, fabulous bathroom fittings. It is exuberantly sober and shapely with Versailles parquet and fine fireplaces as well. Tae, from Chile, uses her perfect sense of style and colour to include these respected elements in her décor alongside richly baroque Chinese chairs and lots of South American pieces and paintings. Quiet spot, vast natural garden, joyous hosts, perfect for Chartres, Paris, Versailles.

Rooms: 2 suites for 5, both with bath & wc.

Price: €69 for two; €99 for four.

Meals: Good restaurants within walking distance.

Closed: Never.

Paris – Ile de France

From A10 exit 10 to toll gate, right after toll; right again on D27 to St Cyr sous Dourdan; continue for Arpajon; first house on left.

Claude & Tae Dabasse
Le Logis d'Arnières
1 rue du Pont-Rué
91410 St Cyr sous Dourdan
Essonne
Tel: (0)1 64 59 14 89
Fax: (0)1 64 59 07 46

"Ye who sit at a pavement café in Paris will see the whole world go by" under the all-seeing eye of the long-aproned, world-weary waiter who loves his City of Light but will never let you know it.

Entry No: 133   Map: **4**

Madame's delightful serenity must be fed by the natural air of real farm life that wafts in from the great wheat fields. Tractors come and go in the farmyard, the old horse grazes in the meadow, the five young children play in the sandpit, the dog dances in its pen. The Desforges have done an excellent barn conversion. You climb the steep stairs to the lofty raftered dayroom where breakfast is served (tea-making equipment, an old dresser, a comfortable sofa), and the simply pretty, good-sized bedrooms. One is furnished with grandmother's richly-carved, if short-bedded, Breton bridal suite, one with grandfather's brass bed; wardrobes are old, mattresses new.

Rooms: 3 doubles, 2 twins, all with shower & wc.

Price: €40 for two.

Meals: Choice of restaurants in Milly, 3km; picnic possible.

Closed: Mid-December–beginning February.

From A6 exit Cély en Bière for Milly La Forêt. At Milly, 1st r'bout towards Etampes; next r'bout, towards Gironville, turn right. Farm 2km on right.

Sophie & Jean-Charles Desforges
Ferme de la Grange Rouge
91490 Milly la Forêt
Essonne
Tel: (0)1 64 98 94 21
Fax: (0)1 64 98 99 91

Entry No: 134   Map: 8

A brilliant mixture! A 13th-century farmhouse with 1990s deluxe bathrooms; 20 minutes from high-tech CDG airport with a national hiking path (GR1) leading to forests just behind the house; a fluting Pan lording it over the manicured profusion of a prize-winning garden. Nothing is left to chance by your well-travelled, gracious and caring hostess. Royal breakfasts on rose-patterned porcelain in the peach-panelled *salon*; thirsty bathrobes to wear until changing for dinner which arrives in your room under silver cloches; interesting conversation in several languages. A form of perfection.

Rooms: 2 doubles/twins, 1 suite, all with bath & wc.

Price: €142 for two.

Meals: Dinner €40, including wine & coffee.

Closed: 2 weeks in February.

From A1 exit 'Soissons' on A104 towards Marne la Vallée then N2 towards Soissons 12km. Exit Othis. Through Othis on D13; at traffic light left to Beaumarchais. In village right after 1st speed bump.

Françoise Montrozier
12 rue des Suisses
Beaumarchais
77280 Othis
Seine-et-Marne
Tel: (0)1 60 03 33 98
Fax: (0)1 60 03 56 71

Entry No: 135   Map: 4

A gorgeous setting: green swards flowing down to a barge-carrying river, a cosmopolitan hostess perfectly in tune with her animal and plant companions. She loves people too, is quietly, intelligently attentive and wants you to enjoy her old family house, once home to the local tax collector/inn keeper, though the Neo-Gothic goblin-guarded fireplace once belonged to Alexandre Dumas. Madame's lamp collection is fascinating and her rooms are unostentatiously friendly with well-loved old furniture - the big balcony suite is our favourite looking way out to the hills beyond the River Marne. Keen walkers can follow the Canal de l'Ourcq all the way to Paris.

Rooms: 1 suite for 3 with shower & wc; 1 suite for 5 with bath & wc.

Price: €44-€59 for two.

Meals: Two good restaurants nearby.

Closed: November-February.

From A4 exit 18 onto N3 towards Paris through St Jean then 1st right to Armentières; straight on at junction, past church. House is last but one on right.

Denise Woehrlé
44 rue du Chef de Ville
77440 Armentières en Brie
Seine-et-Marne
Tel: (0)1 64 35 51 22
Fax: (0)1 64 35 42 95
E-mail: dverlet@aol.com

Entry No: 136   Map: **4**

The big informal garden merges into the fields with green corners and space for everyone, so don't worry about the new houses ahead. There's space in the high-beamed dayroom too, and at the fabulous table made of great old oak beams. Upstairs, the five simple, white-walled, softly colour-themed rooms, each with two beds on a mezzanine, are ideal for families. An old mirror or table or desk adds character and new shower rooms are cleverly designed. Isabelle has made the two larger, temptingly independent lodges most attractive. She and Patrick, with all the time in the world for their guests, are wonderful hosts. And there's Disney, *bien sûr*! *Gîte space for 8 people.*

Rooms: 1 triple, 4 quadruples, all with shower & wc.

Price: €47-€63 for two.

Meals: Dinner €15; restaurants 4km.

Closed: Never.

On A4 take exit 13 for Villeneuve le Comte. In Villeneuve follow signs for Neufmoutiers en Brie; follow Chambres d'Hôtes signs.

Isabelle & Patrick Galpin
Bellevue
77610 Neufmoutiers en Brie
Seine-et-Marne
Tel: (0)1 64 07 11 05
Fax: (0)1 64 07 19 27
E-mail: ipgalpin@club-internet.fr
Web: www.club-internet.fr/perso/ipgalpin

Entry No: 137   Map: **4**

Miles from Normandy, a sort of architectural cuckoo: an 'Anglo-Norman' face veneered onto a concrete skull concealing an unspoilt 1920s interior. Fascinating (great arched windows, red and black crested tiles), elegant ('Versailles' parquet), comfortable and beautifully furnished. The guest suite is as untouched as the blue-green panelled *salon*: stone walls, patterned parquet, marble fireplace and a delicious round sitting corner in the tower. Big breakfasts appear at the long dining table, your retired hosts will tell the history of grandfather's hunting lodge in good English (they still organise shoots) and their welcome is warmly French.

Rooms: 1 suite with bathroom & wc.

Price: €120 for two.

Meals: Variety of restaurants nearby.

Closed: Never.

The high blue doors open onto a pair of long, low stone buildings round a narrow courtyard, the apse of the medieval church looking benignly over the wall and a charming garden at the back. The Laurents are friendly, straightforward, gentle people (the marble bathroom is not their doing!) with ever a new project on the boil; they are 'junk-shop' hunters but they like to keep it uncluttered. They have two children who adopt stray cats, keep miniature ponies and will do all they can to make your stay peaceful and fruitful, including organising walks and making vegetarian meals (by arrangement) in the heavily-beamed, 1930s-furnished guest dining room.

Rooms: 1 triple with bath & wc; 1 suite for 5/6 with shower & 2 wcs; 1 suite for 4 with kitchen, shower & 2 wcs.

Price: €48 for two; €18 per extra person.

Meals: Dinner €19, including wine & coffee.

Closed: Never.

From A4 exit 13 to Villeneuve le Comte; right on D96 towards Tournan; after Neufmoutiers, 1st left on small road for 1.5km; white gates on left.

From A4 exit 13 to Villeneuve le Comte; right on D96 through Neufmoutiers to Châtres. House in village centre to left of church.

Hubert & Francine Charpentier
Manoir de Beaumarchais
77610 Les Chapelles Bourbon
Seine-et-Marne
Tel: (0)1 64 07 11 08
Fax: (0)1 64 07 14 48
E-mail: hubert.charpentier@wanadoo.fr
Web: www.le-manoir-de-beaumarchais.com

Dominique & Pierre Laurent
Le Portail Bleu
2 route de Fontenay
77610 Châtres, Seine-et-Marne
Tel: (0)1 64 25 84 94
Fax: (0)1 64 25 84 94
E-mail: leportailbleu@voila.fr
Web: perso.wanadoo.fr/leportailbleu/

Entry No: 138   Map: 4

Entry No: 139   Map: 4

Cereals and beets grow in wide fields and show-jumpers add a definite touch of elegance to the landscape. A generous farmyard surrounded by beautiful warm stone buildings encloses utter quiet and a genuine welcome from hosts and Labradors alike, out here where Monsieur's family has come hunting for 200 years (his great-grandfather was a surgeon with Napoleon's army). Family furniture (the 1900s ensemble is most intriguing) in light-filled rooms, spotless mod cons and a vast sitting room for guests with piano and billiards table. Your hosts are excellent tour advisers who can direct you to little-known treasures.

Rooms: 1 triple with shower & wc; 1 apartment for 4 with mini-kitchen, shower & wc.

Price: €47 for two.

Meals: Auberge in village (3 Michelin stars).

Closed: Christmas week.

Between the Seine and the Rue de Rivoli, a quiet back street conceals this old Parisian building. Inside is a city home of charm and elegance whose owners managed to salvage some of the ancient timbers from the renovator's clean sweep and who live happily among signs of great architectural age. It is beautifully done, like a warm soft nest, antique-furnished, with lots of greenery and interesting artwork. Madame greatly enjoys her guests and is a source of good tips on Paris. Monsieur is a university professor. The compact guest quarters down the corridor are nicely private with good storage space, pretty quilts, lots of light. *Mimimum stay 2 nights.*

Rooms: 1 twin with small bath/shower & wc.

Price: €70 for two.

Meals: This is Paris.

Closed: Summer holidays.

From A5 exit 15 on N36 for Meaux, 200m; 2nd right to Crisenoy after TGV bridge, through village; 1.5km to farm.

Metro: Châtelet or Pont-Neuf. (Between the Louvre and Notre-Dame.) Parking: Conforama car park, via Rue du Pont Neuf then Rue Boucher. Lift to 3rd floor.

Philippe & Jeanne Mauban
Ferme de Vert Saint-Père
77390 Crisenoy
Seine-et-Marne
Tel: (0)1 64 38 83 51
Fax: (0)1 64 38 83 52
E-mail: mauban.vert@wanadoo.fr

Mme Mona Pierrot
Châtelet district
75001 Paris
Tel: (0)1 42 36 50 65

Entry No: 140   Map: **4**

Entry No: 141   Map: **4**

Anna was lucky. She was able to buy the flat next to hers and turn it into a self-contained apartment for her 20-year-old son. You will be lucky if you stay here as the ochre-walled living room - a big blue sofa with comfy chairs sitting on herringbone parquet - has a wonderful selection of paintings on the walls by a now-famous once-starving Cypriot artist whom she befriended. Lucky again as this is right in the hustle-bustle of the Latin Quarter. An aperitif is offered when you dine in her husband's excellent Italian restaurant, downstairs. *Also available on self-catering basis.*

Rooms: 1 suite with shower, wc & kitchenette.

Price: €69 for two.

Meals: Paris is on your doorstep.

Closed: Occasionally.

Madame likes to treat her guests 'properly' and serves breakfast in silver coffee pots on fine linen before long views of the roofs and domes of Paris. The compact living room also contains a couple of deep sofas, an upright piano and Madame's collection of curiosities - well worth investigating. Bedrooms are simpler and perfectly comfortable with yet more interesting pictures. This is a trendy quarter with the Mosque, the colourful Rue Mouffetard and the quieter Jardin des Plantes, home of the Natural History Museum. Madame is quiet, a little shy, and most helpful. She also has a self-contained one-room apartment to let near Place de la République. *Minimum stay 2 nights.*

Rooms: 1 triple with shower; 1 double sharing bathroom; both sharing wc.

Price: €60-€68 for two.

Meals: This is Paris!

Closed: Never.

Metro: Maubert Mutualité, St Michel. RER: St Michel. Parking: Place Maubert, Pantheon.

Metro: Austerlitz. Parking: Rue Censier. Lift to 8th floor.

Anna Sartori
28 rue des Écoles
75005 Paris
Tel: (0)1 43 25 85 57
Fax: (0)1 43 25 85 57
E-mail: stefsart@clubinternet.fr

Mme Lélia Cohen-Scali
75005 Paris
Tel: (0)1 43 36 51 62
Fax: (0)1 45 87 94 16
E-mail: lelia1@noos.fr

The view of Notre Dame at the end of the road, her Gothic buttresses flying in the setting sun, is breathtaking. In this air, you catch centuries of history by osmosis. A few yards along, a great 17th-century doorway opens onto more ancient stones under the utterly Parisian porch. Old stone stairs bring you to a high-ceilinged, family-loved, unpretentiously ancient duplex flat where guests have a breakfast space beside the spiral staircase and a mezzanined, fireplaced room with high windows onto an unexpected green city garden - a "bowl of air" as they say, a huge privilege in Paris. Madame is polyglot, active in the city and quietly welcoming - she enjoys having guests.

Rooms: 1 room for 2-4 with bath & wc.

Price: €76 for two.

Meals: Restaurants nearby.

Closed: Never.

Metro: Maubert-Mutualité. RER/Metro: St Michel-Notre Dame. Parking: 'Lagrange' underground car park.

Mme Brigitte Chatignoux
75005 Paris
Tel: (0)1 43 25 27 20
Fax: (0)1 43 25 27 20

Outside it is smart Left Bank, inside are intelligence, sobriety and genuine style. Madame will welcome you into her vast, serene apartment - neither modern gadgets nor over-restored antiques, just a few good pieces, much space and light-flooded parquet floors. Beyond the dining room, the smaller, cosy guest room gives onto the big, silent, arcaded courtyard. Your multilingual hosts have lived all over the world; Monsieur, a retired engineer, still spends his days studying or teaching. Madame is as stylish and genuine as her surroundings and enjoys, in equal parts, renovating her old mill near Chartres and the company of like-minded visitors - she is worth getting to know.

Rooms: 1 twin with bath & wc.

Price: €76 for two.

Meals: Choice of restaurants within 5 minutes walk; St Germain des Prés 10 minutes away.

Closed: Never.

Metro: Solférino, Assemblée Nationale or Invalides. Parking: Invalides. Lift to 2nd floor.

Mme Élisabeth Marchal
National Assembly/Invalides district
75007 Paris
Tel: (0)1 47 05 70 21
(0)2 37 23 38 19

Entry No: 144   Map: 4

Entry No: 145   Map: 4

Paris – Ile de France

Within walking distance of the Luxembourg Gardens, the Monbrisons' intimate little flat, cluttered with books, paintings and objects from all over the world, has just one quiet, sunny, snug guest room with a king-size double/twin bed and its own bathroom. American Cynthia, a lively art-lover, and quintessentially French, and Christian, knowledgeable about history, wine and cattle-breeding, offer great hospitality and will take guests on special evening tours to historical city landmarks - they are attentive and intelligent hosts. Twice a week, the street market brings the real food of France to your doorstep and the neighbourhood is always alive with shops, cafés and restaurants.

Rooms: 1 double/twin with bath/shower & wc.

Price: €75 for two.

Meals: Dinner occasionally, by arrangement. Varying prices.

Closed: August.

Metro: Edgar Quinet or Montparnasse. Airport buses from Orly and Charles de Gaulle to Montparnasse (5 minutes walk).

Christian & Cynthia de Monbrison
Montparnasse district
75014 Paris
Tel: (0)1 45 38 68 72
Fax: (0)1 45 38 68 72

Entry No: 146   Map: 4

In a fine big 1930s building, on the sixth floor, with a superb view from its balconies across the Seine to the new André Citröen park, is this well-proportioned flat with big rooms, old family pieces, mementoes from distant travels and a well-loved, lived-in patina. The unfussy guest room is big too, with that tremendous view, two narrow single beds, endearingly old-fashioned tiling in the shower, the loo just down the passage. With the window open, you hear the traffic, somewhat muffled by leaves in summer. Madame, who still travels after all these years, has plenty of time for her guests and lends a very attentive, gracious ear to their own travellers' tales.

Rooms: 1 twin with shower & basin, sharing wc.

Price: €53 for two.

Meals: Choice of restaurants within walking distance.

Closed: July-mid-September.

Metro: Mirabeau, Église d'Auteuil, Exelmans. Bus: 72, 22, Petite Ceinture. Lift to 6th floor.

Mme Bargeton
Auteuil district
75016 Paris
Tel: (0)1 42 88 87 66

Entry No: 147   Map: 4

In a proudly moulded and bracketed 1900s building, this is a typical little Paris flat. Montmartre is within walking distance but not so close that you feel harassed by charcoal-waving portraitists. The wooden fireplace, the floorboards, the plasterwork are original; the décor is as young and lively as Françoise and Hervé themselves: theatrical bits and pieces, ivy growing all over your balcony, a dry garden inside with grasses and nests, gnomes and dollies. They love their foreign guests and are happy to share their knowledge of Paris, French food and wine with you. You will like their youth, their spontaneity, their sense of fun.

Rooms: 1 double sharing shower & wc.

Price: €70 for two.

Meals: Plenty of good restaurants nearby.

Closed: Never.

Metro: Guy Moquet.

Françoise & Hervé
Montmartre district
75018 Paris
Tel: (0)1 44 85 06 05
Fax: (0)1 44 85 06 14
E-mail: fforet@noos.fr

Your very proper elderly hosts exchanged an isolated Provençal villa for this colourful quarter of Paris where you hear a multitude of languages. The ninth-floor flat (yes, there is a lift) is all white walls, modern parquet floors and fine old family furniture. There are views right across Paris over to the Eiffel Tower and the Great Arch of La Défense, or up the hill to the Parc de Belleville, a super, surprising hillside patch of green above the city. Breakfast on the balcony or by the amazing glass-fronted wardrobe while Madame serves fresh pastries and tells you all about everything, and Monsieur twinkles shyly. *Some Spanish spoken.*

Rooms: 1 double with shower & private wc.

Price: €61 for two.

Meals: Wide choice of restaurants on the doorstep.

Closed: Never.

Metro: Belleville. Bus: 26. Parking: Ask owners. Lift to 9th floor.

Danièle & Bernard de La Brosse
Belleville district
75019 Paris
Tel: (0)1 42 41 99 59
Fax: (0)1 42 41 99 59
E-mail: daniele.delabrosse@libertysurf.fr

Entry No: 148   Map: **4**

Entry No: 149   Map: **4**

In one of the less gentrified, more genuinely *vieux Paris* parts of Paris, your kindly artist hosts live between two tiny gardens and a tall house. The simple guest room, with good double bed and new divan, modern furniture and a pretty mirror, shares a building with Sabine's studio and the next generation's ground-floor flat. Colours and fabrics are quiet and gentle, the bathroom old-fashioned, the tea-maker very welcome. The cosy family living room, in the main house, welcomes you for breakfast (French with a healthfood bias), or have it outside under the birdsung tree. Jules makes the organic bread and big, beautiful, black Janto, his guide dog, loves people.

Rooms: 1 triple with bath & wc.

Price: €60 for two.

Meals: Choice of restaurants within walking distance.

Closed: July-August.

Metro: Jourdain or Place des Fêtes.
Parking: Place des Fêtes.

Sabine & Jules Aïm
75019 Paris
Tel: (0)1 42 08 23 71
Fax: (0)1 42 40 56 04

Entry No: 150   Map: **4**

Your hosts, sophisticated lovers of art and animals, have decorated their elegant little 1830s manor with old oils, dreamy murals (Madame is the artist's agent), some fine antiques and comfortable sofas: it's a big family house with a lived-in air and happy dogs. Two comfortable guest rooms, one large, one smaller, are here. In the rose-filled garden, the hunting lodge has become a magnificent self-contained studio with complete kitchen and the old orangery has two very pretty, snug little rooms with roses peering through the windows. Fifteen minutes from Paris or Versailles and only nightingales are heard. *Spanish spoken.*

Rooms: 4 doubles, all with shower & wc; 1 suite with shower, wc & kitchen.

Price: €76 for two.

Meals: Dinner €15, including wine & coffee.

Closed: Never.

From A13 exit 6 on D186 for St Germain en Laye; D102 right 3.5km; D321 left 3km to Chatou; bear left Ave Clemenceau, right V. Hugo; right Garennes.
RER: A, for St Germain en Laye.

Françoise Pasquier
Les Impressionnistes
6 rue des Garennes
78400 Chatou
Yvelines
Tel: (0)1 30 53 20 88
Fax: (0)1 30 53 20 88
E-mail: pasquierpdsc@aol.com

Entry No: 151   Map: **4**

Behind the modest façade is a generous and lovely interior where Madame's very interesting paintings - she's an art teacher and definitely an artist - stand in pleasing contrast to elegant antiques and soft plush furnishings. Picture windows let the garden in and the wooded hillside rises beyond. The larger guest room is superb in blue draperies, fur bedcover and big bathroom; the smaller one with skylight and its own bathroom across the landing is excellent value. Madame, active and communicative, sings as well as she paints and enjoys cooking refined dinners for attentive guests; she is very good company. A short drive from Paris.

Rooms: 2 doubles (1 large, 1 small), both with bath & wc.

Price: €43–€58 for two.

Meals: Dinner €15, including wine & coffee.

Closed: Never.

From Paris A13 onto A12 towards St Quentin en Yvelines; exit on N12 for Dreux. Exit to Plaisir CENTRE; 1st exit off r'bout towards Plaisir Les Gâtines, 1st left for 400m; right into Domaine des Gâtines; consult roadside plan.

Mme Hélène Castelnau
7 rue Gustave Courbet
Domaine des Gâtines
78370 Plaisir
Yvelines
Tel: (0)1 30 54 05 15
Fax: (0)1 30 54 05 15
E-mail: hcastelnau@club-internet.fr

Entry No: 152   Map: **3**

From Morocco, Indonesia and reddest America, this great traveller has amassed carvings great and small, artefacts ancient and modern, inlays and filigrees in brass, lacquer and wood, and filled his family mansion. A collector's paradise (housemaid's hell?). All is exuberance and love of life and beautiful things, bedrooms are a feast of almost baroque décor: the Coca Cola room is devastatingly... Coke (surely a unique collection), the Indonesian bed overwhelmingly rich. Your host is very good company and on weekdays his delightful assistant Taïeb will take excellent care of you. There is also a loo/library and a three-legged cat, exotic fowl, stone boars and remarkable men to be met.

Rooms: 5 doubles, all with shower & wc; 1 suite for 5 with bath & wc.

Price: €52–€61 for two.

Meals: Three restaurants in village.

Closed: Never.

From N10 north of Rambouillet D937; D936 for Poigny la Forêt, 5km; left on D107 to Poigny; left up road by church; house on right.

François Le Bret
Château de Poigny
2 rue de l'Église
78125 Poigny la Forêt
Yvelines
Tel: (0)1 34 84 73 42
Fax: (0)1 34 84 74 38
E-mail: lechateaudepoigny@wanadoo.fr

Entry No: 153   Map: **3**

Utterly original, intelligent fun, a marriage of abundant creativity and scholarship: Hazeville is amazing. Your host has turned his refined château-farm, dated 1400s to 1600s, into a living show of his talents: huge abstract paintings, dozens of hand-painted plates and tiles, a dazzling 'Egyptian' reception room, kitchen and loo (oh yes) in the barn; the stables now house hi-tech artisans. Beautifully-finished guest rooms in the pigeon tower are deeply luxurious; generous breakfasts come on china hand-painted by Monsieur to match the wall covering; he also knows all the secret treasures of the Vexin. *Well-behaved children over seven welcome. Hot air ballooning possible.*

Rooms: 1 double, 1 twin, both with bath, shower & wc.

Price: €110 for two.

Meals: Wide choice of restaurants within 5-10km.

Closed: Weekdays & school term time.

From Rouen, N14 towards Paris. 20km before Pontoise, at Magny en Vexin, right onto D983 to Arthies. Left onto D81, through Enfer; château on left.

Guy & Monique Deneck
Château d'Hazeville
95420 Wy dit Joli Village
Val-d'Oise
Tel: (0)1 34 67 06 17/
 (0)1 42 88 67 00
Fax: (0)1 34 67 17 82

Entry No: 154   Map: **3**

This super couple of hard-working Parisians, he a burly, bearded epicurean, she lithe and energetic, are excellent company and really enjoy having guests. The garden studio, smart blue with soft pink oriental touches, is snugly designed with kitchen, (low-ceilinged) double sleeping platform and twin beds below. Be as independent as you like (you may subtract breakfast and do your own). In the house, above the sober wooden dining room and the colourful, cosy, booklined *salon*, the delightful bedroom has an elegant caned bed and big balcony over the 1920s colonnaded porch and garden. *10 minutes by train from Paris.*

Rooms: 1 double with shower & shared wc, garden studio (for four) with shower & wc.

Price: €58-€79 for two.

Meals: Dinner possible, by arrangement.

Closed: August.

Directions on request. Train: from St Lazare to La Garenne Colombes.

Chris & Jean-Jacques Billon
22 rue des Arts
92700 Colombes
Hauts-de-Seine
Tel: (0)1 47 60 11 92
Fax: (0)1 47 82 35 63
E-mail: cbillon@spray.fr

Entry No: 155   Map: **4**

In a classy block of flats in a smart Paris suburb lives a mild woman with a powerful brush. Ruth is an artist. You may share her atmospheric personal space: her studio is part of the splendidly mix-decorated living room - worn antiques to sit on, fashionable red table for breakfast, abstracts, collages, books - and perhaps the privilege of following a work in progress. Looking onto the quiet back garden, your simply-furnished, smallish room has all the necessities: writing desk, kettle, storage, light and live art; also a snug little shower room. One bed tucks under the other, the curtain is leopard-skin voile, the painting leaps off the wall. This is different - and real.

Rooms: 1 twin/double with shower & wc.

Price: € 53 for two.

Meals: Restaurants nearby.

Closed: Never.

Metro: Pont de Levallois (10 mins' walk). Bus: 174, 163, 164, 93, 82.

If you want to be close to the centre of Paris but still relax in the garden under the gazebo, then this is surely the place for you. Cecilia is Anglo-French and loves having people to stay in her comfortable 1950s suburban house. She enjoys a chat over the breakfast table, helping you plan the day ahead. Green is clearly her favourite colour. Rooms open directly onto the garden and are light and airy with replica tapestry wall hangings, chintzy curtains with net drapes, onyx figurine bedside lamps, potted plants and, I need hardly say, green carpets. *They can be let as gîtes. Italian spoken.*

Rooms: 1 double, 1 triple, both with shower, wc & mini-kitchen.

Price: € 64 for two.

Meals: Self-catering possible; restaurants nearby.

Closed: Occasionally.

From Paris Bd Périphérique exit Porte d'Asnières through Levallois, across Seine. Ask for map. Train: from St Lazare, 'Banlieue' train to Bécon Les Bruyères (6 minutes).

Ruth Himmelfarb
53 boulevard Victor Hugo
92200 Neuilly sur Seine
Hauts-de-Seine
Tel: (0)1 46 37 37 28
Fax: (0)1 46 37 37 28

M & Mme Bobrie
10 rue Denfert Rochereau
92600 Asnières sur Seine
Hauts-de-Seine
Tel: (0)1 47 93 53 60
Fax: (0)1 47 93 53 60
E-mail: ceciliasguesthouse@hotmail.com

The welcome is straightforward, the house unpretentious with that friendly, lived-in air, so what matter if it's sometimes just the oilcloth on the table? The Maréchals are amiable, down-to-earth farmers who lead a sociable life and love having their grandchildren around. Low-beamed bedrooms are modest but comfortable with imitation parquet floors, pastel colours and pretty bedcovers. In summer, meals can be taken under canvas in the flower-filled courtyard. Readers have told of hilarious evenings in approximate French and English over honest, family meals, often made with home-grown, chemical-free vegetables. *Gîte space for 18 people.*

Rooms: 3 doubles, all with bath or shower & wc.

Price: €41 for two.

Meals: Dinner €14, including wine & coffee.

Closed: Never.

From Dreux N12 to Broué; D305 to La Musse (La Musse between Boutigny & Prouais); 'Chambres d'Hôtes' signs.

Serge & Jeanne-Marie Maréchal
La Ferme des Tourelles
11 rue des Tourelles
La Musse
28410 Boutigny Prouais, Eure-et-Loir
Tel: (0)2 37 65 18 74
Fax: (0)2 37 65 18 74
E-mail: la-ferme.des-tourelles@wanadoo.fr

Entry No: 158   **Map:** 3

It feels easy, fun and intelligent. Your hosts are delightful: Virginie beautifully French, Richard a gentle Europeanised American and their two toddler sons. Down a long wooded drive and set in a big leafy garden, the old family house has tall windows, fine proportions and the air of a properly lived-in château: elegance and deep comfortable armchairs by the marble fireplace under crystal chandeliers. The top floor has been converted into five good rooms with sound-proofing, big beds, masses of hot water, rich, bright colour schemes... and just the right amount of family memorabilia: oils, engravings, lamps, old dishes.

Rooms: 1 triple, 4 doubles, all with shower & wc.

Price: €55-€60 for two.

Meals: Dinner available locally.

Closed: November-February.

From A11 exit Ablis on N10 for Chartres. At Essars, right to St Symphorien, Bleury & Ecrosnes. There right & immed. left to Jonvilliers, 2.5km. White château gates straight ahead.

Virginie & Richard Thompson
Château de Jonvilliers
17 rue d'Épernon
28320 Jonvilliers, Eure-et-Loir
Tel: (0)2 37 31 41 26
Fax: (0)2 37 31 56 74
E-mail: information@chateaudejonvilliers.com
Web: www.chateaudejonvilliers.com

Entry No: 159   **Map:** 3

Normandy

Did Queen Victoria really 'stop' here once? We'll never know, but the 17th-century hunting lodge is ideal for parties while the owners' house (19th-century over 12th-century cellars) has one huge guest room. Monsieur manages the Port and the Chamber of Commerce, Madame the house and garden, masterfully - she has lived here since she was six. Both are proud of their region, keen to share their knowledge and advise on explorations: nature, hiking, historical visits, excellent suggestions for wet days, dry days... A delightful, welcoming couple with natural generosity, elegance and manners and an open-minded approach to all.

Rooms: 1 triple, 1 double, 1 apartment for 5, all with shower & wc.

Price: €45 for two.

Meals: Dinner in Eu 2km, Le Tréport 4km; self-catering in apartment.

Closed: Never.

Take D49 to Eu. Before Eu turn left towards Forest of Eu/Route de Beaumont. House 3km on right.

Fierce pagan Vikings sailed warlike up the Seine in their long battle-boats... and settled into the rolling pastures to milk cows for Camembert and breed Christians for the Abbeys.

Catherine & Jean-Marie Demarquet
Manoir de Beaumont
76260 Eu
Seine-Maritime
Tel: (0)2 35 50 91 91
Fax:
E-mail: cd@fnac.net
Web: www.chez.com/demarquet

A dear little village house with a tiny garden overlooking the village green and a big garden behind - it's one of those semi-rural houses, modest yet authentically themselves. There's a small bedroom with ancient and modern furniture, good linen and mattresses; and a big one with floorboards and rugs, plain walls and *toile de Jouy* soft furnishings. Its beams are painted light blue. Two rooms are in a little building by the main house. The other is in the attic, big and comfortable. It is spotlessly clean, neat and genuine - with a big welcome. *"Très cosy, disent les Anglais"*.

Rooms: 3 doubles, all with shower & wc.

Price: €40 for two.

Meals: Restaurant in village.

Closed: Never.

Lapping up to the edge of the farm, the Forest of Eu is 9,300 hectares of green space to explore in an area of natural and historical delights (Louis Philippe and Queen Victoria begat the Entente Cordiale in the Château of Eu). But come here for the uncanny silence at night, the birdsong at dawn and your hosts' radiant smiles at all times - a heart-warming household where old-fashioned wallpapers and French good manners prevail, it has an authentic family atmosphere, masses of human warmth, not an ounce of hotellishness. *Gîte space for 10 people.*

Rooms: 1 suite with bath & wc; 1 suite, 1 double, both with wc, sharing shower.

Price: €31-€43 for two; suite €61-€86 for four.

Meals: Choice of restaurants 4-12km.

Closed: Never.

From Le Tréport D925 for Dieppe 15km; in Biville sur Mer right Rue de l'Église, No 14 faces you in middle of fork in road.

From A28 exit Blangy sur Bresle for Le Tréport to Gamaches; left at lights D14 to Guerville; follow to Melleville. Just before village ends, right Route de la Marette.

Marie-José Klaes
Le Clos Mélise
14 rue de l'Église
76630 Biville sur Mer
Seine-Maritime
Tel: (0)2 35 83 14 71

Etienne & Nelly Garçonnet
La Marette
Route de la Marette
76260 Melleville
Seine-Maritime
Tel: (0)2 35 50 81 65
Fax: (0)2 35 50 81 65

Entry No: 161   Map: **3**

Entry No: 162   Map: **3**

Golfers love it here: the house is hard by the third green. Green comes inside too, thanks to the exotic palms where a parrot may lurk. The light, modern house is a refreshing change, definitely creature-comfortable and copes well with the transition between '80s daring and '90s pleasing. Each room has space - terrace or mezzanine - television and plush modern décor with softening accessories from eastern worlds; no two bedrooms have walls in common. Your hosts are naturally friendly, interesting people and Madame is happy to give you a relaxing yoga lesson. You will feel cocooned here.

Rooms: 2 twins, 1 double, all with bath or shower & wc.

Price: €54-€58 for two.

Meals: Restaurants 1.5 km.

Closed: Never.

Simply irresistible. This gloriously restored and revived listed 17th-century château is surrounded by formal gardens designed by a pupil of Lenôtre with beech maze and lime tree avenues and a rose garden containing 900 species and 2000 varieties. The Prince (Syrian father, French mother) knows each one of them and the special attention it requires. The Princess makes rose-petal jelly for breakfast in the elegant dining room and also loves to prepare authentic 18th-century dishes from old recipes she has unearthed. The panelled bedrooms are delightfully cosy with canopied beds, proper bed linen, fluffy duvets and sweet-smelling bathrooms.

Rooms: 2 doubles, 1 twin, 2 suites, all with bath & shower & wc.

Price: €78-€128 for two.

Meals: Dinner €42, including wine & coffee.

Closed: Never.

From Dieppe D75 (Route du Littoral) W along coast for Pourville; at golf course, 1st left, 3rd house on right (signposted).

From A13 exit 25 Pont de Bretonne/ Yvetot. Through Yvetot for St Valéry en Caux. 2km after Ste Colombe, right towards Houdetot. Château 2km on left.

Alain & Danièle Noël
24 chemin du Golf
76200 Dieppe
Seine-Maritime
Tel: (0)2 35 84 40 37
Fax: (0)2 35 84 32 51
E-mail: villa-florida@wanadoo.fr
Web: perso.wanadoo.fr/villa-florida

Princesse Anne-Marie Kayali
Château du Mesnil Geoffroy
76740 Ermenouville
Seine-Maritime
Tel: (0)2 35 57 12 77
Fax: (0)2 35 57 10 24
E-mail: chateaumesnil.geoffroy@wanadoo.fr
Web: www.siteparc.fr/chateaumesnil

Entry No: 163   Map: 3

Entry No: 164   Map: 3

Nature lovers benefit: first, a view from your bed of the immaculate garden where pigeons, ducks and cats scurry; second, a long shower, fluffy towels and bathrobes; then breakfast with four kinds of bread; fishing and hiking at your back door, tennis a few miles away. And the family suite has welcome wet-weather entertainments. After an afternoon jaunt, you can read Madame's books, relax among the lovely antiques or make yourself something in the kitchen. She is most amicable and gracefully succeeds in caring for her teenage children while giving time to guests. *Gîte space for 7 people.*

Rooms: 1 triple with bath & wc; 1 suite with bath, shower & wc.

Price: €80 for two.

Meals: Restaurants in Valmont, 1 km.

Closed: Never.

From Dieppe D925 W for Fécamp 60km; left D17 to Valmont centre; left D150 for Ourville 1.2km; right Chemin du Vivier; house 2nd entrance on right (no. 4).

Dominique Cachera & François Greverie
Le Clos du Vivier, 4-6 chemin du Vivier
76540 Valmont, Seine-Maritime
Tel: (0)2 35 29 90 95
Fax: (0)2 35 27 44 49
E-mail: dc@le-clos-du-vivier.com
Web: www.le-clos-du-vivier.com

Madame was born here, has a winning smile and loves to talk (in French). Her house, which stands in a classic, square, poplar-sheltered Seine-Maritime farmyard, is 300 years old; the worn old stones and bricks and the less worn flints bear witness to its age - so does the fine timberwork inside. Otherwise it has been fairly deeply modernised, but the long lace-clothed breakfast table before the log fire (in winter) is most welcoming. The pleasant rooms are good if unremarkable and the only sounds are the occasional lowing of the herd and the breeze blowing in the poplars. *Gîte space for 10 people.*

Rooms: 1 triple with bath & wc; 1 double with shower & wc; 2 doubles sharing shower & wc.

Price: €36 for two.

Meals: Auberge 1km.

Closed: Never.

From Dieppe N27 towards Rouen 29km; right N29 through Yerville & towards Yvetot 4.5km; left D20 to Motteville; right to Flamanville. Rue Verte is behind church. Farm 300m on left; signposted.

Yves & Béatrice Quevilly Baret
La Ferme de la Rue Verte
76970 Flamanville
Seine-Maritime
Tel: (0)2 35 96 81 27

Madame, a blithe soul who is "on holiday all year", will give you a terrific welcome - nothing is too much trouble. The colourful, flowerful garden, her great love, is a wonder in almost any season, a hillside oasis of tumbling vegetation in the town (the road can seem noisy but it's all right at night). Her guest rooms are cosy and tempting, reflecting the history of the old house and her collecting flair. There is a dayroom for guests but breakfast is in the pretty family dining room. A very French house, full of character, excellent value and a good base for exploring the churches and villages that fill this area. *Gîte space for 4 people.*

Rooms: 2 doubles, 1 triple, 1 quadruple, all with shower & wc.

Price: €43 for two.

Meals: Choice of restaurants in village, 500m.

Closed: Never.

In the historic centre of lovely old Rouen, on an ancient street 100m from the Cathedral, stands this 17th-century family home. Monsieur enjoys sharing, in English, German or Norman and with much wry humour, the history of Rouen and the comfort of his lovely quiet townhouse. It is a treasure-trove of curios, with huge beams, big windows and Norman antiques. Bathrooms are a bit old-fashioned, breakfast generous and your reception generally cheerful. *Car park a short walk from house. Gîte space for 8 people.*

Rooms: 2 doubles, 1 twin, both with bathrooms (can be a suite with kitchen); 1 single, sharing bathroom.

Price: €50 for two.

Meals: Vast choice of restaurants on the spot.

Closed: Never.

From Rouen D982 towards Le Havre; under Pont de Brotonne, into Caudebec, right into Rue de la République (D131) towards Yvetot; No.68 is 500m on right.

On Cathedral-side embankment: at Théâtre des Arts, take Rue Jeanne d'Arc; Rue aux Ours 2nd on right but NO parking. Leave car in Bourse or Pucelle car parks, near house, and walk.

Christiane Villamaux
Les Poules Vertes
68 rue de la République
76490 Caudebec en Caux, Seine-Maritime
Tel: (0)2 35 96 10 15
Fax: (0)2 35 96 75 25
E-mail: christiane.villamaux@libertysurf.fr
Web: villamaux.ifrance.com

Philippe & Annick Aunay-Stanguennec
45 rue aux Ours
76000 Rouen
Seine-Maritime
Tel: (0)2 35 70 99 68

Entry No: 167 Map: 3

Entry No: 168 Map:

The solid-fronted, black-doored face hides a light, stylish interior with soul-lifting views across old Rouen to the spires of the Cathedral. Dominique, a keen and cultured Egyptologist, has a flair for refined decoration - as her paintings, coverings and country furniture declare. Oriental rugs on parquet floor, French windows to balcony and garden, feminine, unfrilly bedrooms, a stupendous orange bathroom. Nothing standard, nothing too studied, a very personal home and a lovely spot for a leisurely feast at her flower-decked breakfast table and a talk with her (her English is excellent) about her latest digs in Egypt.

Rooms: 1 double with bath & wc; 2 doubles, all with bath, sharing wc.

Price: €44-€49 for two.

Meals: Dinner €18, including wine & coffee.

Closed: October-November.

In Rouen follow Gare SNCF signs; Rue Rochefoucault right of station; left Rue des Champs des Oiseaux; over 2 traffic lights into Rue Vigné; fork left Rue Hénault; black door on left.

Dominique Gogny
22 rue Hénault
76130 Mont Saint Aignan
Seine-Maritime
Tel: (0)2 35 70 26 95
Fax: (0)2 35 52 03 52
E-mail: chambreavecvue@online.fr
Web: chambreavecvue.online.fr

Entry No: 169   Map: 3

Some sort of perfection? It is all pretty, picture-perfect deepest Normandy, from the fine old timbered cider-press building, built during the French Revolution and beautifully restored, to Monsieur's ship-shape garden groaning with flowers and fruit trees (he's an ex-naval man), and the soft, lacy, cottagey rooms - Madame's labour of love where her cut and dried flowers peek from every corner. Old lace, antique country beds, wardrobes and dressers from family treasure stores, the scent of beeswax hanging in the air and a gentle civilised atmosphere. And local specialities with cider for dinner.*Children over 10 welcome.*

Rooms: 2 doubles, both with shower & wc.

Price: €44.50 for two.

Meals: Dinner €21.50, including cider & coffee; restaurants nearby.

Closed: Never.

From Le Havre A131 towards Paris; cross Pont de Tancarville; D810 right, through Pont Audemer, onto D87 through St Germain Village; right on CV19 to Tricqueville; signposted (abt 50 km total).

Gaston & Michelle Le Pleux
La Clé des Champs
27500 Tricqueville
Eure
Tel: (0)2 32 41 37 99
E-mail: redmoon45@aol.com

Entry No: 170   Map: 3

10 years ago, this was a low-lying cottage in need of love and affection. Jean-Marc, with boundless energy and oodles of ideas, transformed it into a floral, country gem to stay, meet, eat - and have fun in. The house is a mix of sober and frivolous - old and modern pieces, rustic revival and leather, contemporary art and *brocante*. The garden will become exuberant too, as it matures. The bedrooms stand out in their uncomplicated good taste and plain fabrics but it's Jean-Marc who makes the place: candlelit dinners and sporting events, strawberry soup and laughter, flowers in your room and birdsong. Amazing.

Rooms: 1 twin with shower & wc; 1 double, 1 triple, 2 family, all with bath & wc.

Price: €48 for two.

Meals: Dinner €19, including wine & coffee; picnic possible.

Closed: Never.

From Pont Audemer D810 for Bernay 12km; right through St Siméon; up hill for Selles; house on left at top.

Jean-Marc Drumel
Le Coquerel
27560 Saint Siméon
Eure
Tel: (0)2 32 56 56 08
Fax: (0)2 32 56 56 08
E-mail: MOREAU-DRUMEL@wanadoo.fr
Web: perso.wanadoo.fr/chambreshotes/

Entry No: 171   Map: **3**

A brightly-coloured tanker is liable to appear from behind the trees heading for the Channel, or the great annual armada to come sailing past - such is the magic of this site on the banks of the Seine just below Rouen. The Laurents' garden goes down to the water's edge and they lend binoculars for bird-watching, maps and books for trail-exploring - it is a Panda (WWF) house. The big house is for guests, the owners have the thatched cottage next door. There are beams and panelling, antiques and windows onto that stunning view, a kitchen/diner, a very comfortable sitting room and Madame has all the time in the world for you. *Gîte space for 14.*

Rooms: 2 suites for 3, 2 quadruples, all with bath or shower & wc.

Price: €45 for two.

Meals: Dinner €13, including coffee (wine €10-€15, cider €4); self-catering possible.

Closed: Never.

From Pont Audemer D139 NE for 10km to Bourneville & continue D139 to Aizier. In village, left at Mairie towards Vieux Port; house on right.

Yves & Marie-Thérèse Laurent
Les Sources Bleues
Le Bourg
27500 Aizier
Eure
Tel: (0)2 32 57 26 68
Fax: (0)2 32 57 42 25

Entry No: 172   Map:

This charming couple now offer special food-and-wine breaks and cookery courses - a natural development as they are knowledgeable and inspiring about the subject and have a strong following. Nicky is English and a *Cordon Bleu* cook, Régis is French with great taste in all departments. There's still nothing nicer than waking up in one of the attractive antique- or ethnic-furnished rooms of their superbly-renovated farmhouse (great bathrooms too) and the stylish new dining room is now finished. The grounds just get prettier, strutted by poultry and overseen by black-headed sheep. Come and make the most of it! *Minimum stay 2 nights.*

Rooms: 2 doubles, 1 twin, 1 triple, 1 quadruple, all with bath or shower & wc.

Price: Half-board €107 for two.

Meals: Breakfast & dinner included.

Closed: Never.

From A13, Le Havre exit, on D139 towards Pont Audemer. In Fourmetot, left towards Corneville. Farm 1km from turning on left.

Régis & Nicky Dussartre
L'Aufragère
La Croisée
27500 Fourmetot, Eure
Tel: (0)2 32 56 91 92
Fax: (0)2 32 57 75 34
E-mail: regis@laufragere.com
Web: www.laufragere.com

You find it good-looking? You'll find its atmosphere is just as pleasing: this is a genuinely old Normandy farmhouse (apple trees abound), its lovely external timber frame enclosing a heart-warming antique clutter spread with excellent taste over bricks and beams, original tile floors and carved furniture. The delicious bedrooms are subtly lit by dormer windows, furnished country-style, pastel-hued and comfortably bathroomed. Monsieur is a charming gentleman, full of smiles. Madame is most attentive. Both are proud of their warmly cosy house and its ravishing garden with long views of the peaceful valley.

Rooms: 2 doubles/twins, 1 suite for 4, all with bath or shower & wc.

Price: €42-€45 for two.

Meals: Dinner €18.50, including wine & coffee.

Closed: September-April.

From Paris A13 exit 26; left on D89 to 'Médine' r'bout. Take Evreux/Appeville-Annebault; left immed. after Les Marettes sign then follow Chambres d'Hôtes signs.

Françoise & Yves Closson Maze
Les Aubépines
Aux Chauffourniers
27290 Appeville dit Annebault
Eure
Tel: (0)2 32 56 14 25
Fax: (0)2 32 56 14 25
E-mail: clossonmaze@wanadoo.fr

Normandy

One of the most delicious houses we know in Normandy, it is the newfound delight of your ex-Parisian hosts. It stands in a lush mature garden, overgrown here, tamed there, where typical timber-frame characters peer from the bushes, roses seek the sky and a stupendous walnut tree triumphs behind. Inside, Marie-Hélène, bright-eyed and eager, has used Jouy cloth and elegant colours to dress the marble fireplaces and polished floors with sober intelligence. In the quietly orange dining room, by the prettiest floral-fantasy tiled stove alcove, you will enjoy good food with a courteous gentleman and his happy wife.

Rooms: 2 twins, 2 doubles, all with shower & wc.

Price: €54 for two.

Meals: Dinner €19, including wine & coffee.

Closed: Never.

Madame did all the wallpapering herself! Tall, sophisticated and immaculate, she is naturally relaxed and welcoming and finds it normal that everyone sit at the same big table in the ochre and scarlet breakfast room. There is a family-friendly common room with billiards, table tennis, picnic table, refrigerator. Bedrooms are big and beautifully decorated (*merci Madame!*); *La Jaune* has superb views. No finery, a touch of faded grandeur and all-pervasive warmth characterise this splendid house of friendship.

Rooms: 2 family, 1 double, 1 twin, all with bath or shower & wc.

Price: €46 for two.

Meals: Choice of restaurants in Orbec.

Closed: Never.

From Evreux 13 for Lisieux 50km; entering Duranville right D41 for St Aubin de S. 2.5km; drive on right.

From Lisieux N13 towards Evreux 18km to Thiberville; then D145 towards Orbec 10km. Château on right about 50m after sign 'Le Grand Bus'.

Marie-Hélène François
La Charterie
27230 Saint Aubin de Scellon
Eure
Tel: (0)2 32 45 46 52 or
    (0)6 20 39 08 63

Bruno & Laurence de Préaumont
Château du Grand Bus
Saint Germain la Campagne
27230 Thiberville
Eure
Tel: (0)2 32 44 71 14
Fax: (0)2 32 46 45 81
E-mail: bruno.laurence.depreaumont@libertysurf.fr

Contradictions? The ancient fortress is 40 years old, the rickety old rail-less bridge over the moat is made of 1960s sleepers; impeccably classic bedrooms have starched linen and lacy bedcovers; downstairs is a collector's clutter of pictures, porcelain and old shoes. Madame, extraordinary and bohemian, changes from scatty gardener to lady for a gracious candlelit dinner with antique silver and deeply informed conversation about the arts illuminated with flashes of outrageous humour. Just one loo between three bedrooms is surely a small price to pay for time with this entertaining and cultured person, alone on her tiny island.

Rooms: 2 doubles, 1 twin, all with bath or shower, sharing wc.

Price: €61 for two.

Meals: Dinner €20, including wine & coffee.

Closed: January-February.

From Breteuil D141 for Rugles; through forest; at Bémécourt, left 300m after traffic lights into Allée du Vieux Château.

Mme Maryvonne Lallemand-Legras
Le Vieux Château
27160 Bémécourt
Eure
Tel: (0)2 32 29 90 47

Entry No: 177   Map: 3

Embraced by pastoral meadow and spreading lake, cushioned by soft woods, Hermos is a house of quiet history and family atmosphere. Outside, a typical 16th-century marriage of brick and stone and a baronial double staircase; inside, panels, mouldings, parquet floors, flowers all over. Madame is a most welcoming hostess, full of spontaneous smiles, whose family has owned the house for 100 years. She also gardens, organises seminars (not when B&B guests are here) and cares for two children. The large panelled bedrooms have refreshing colours, good beds, old wardrobes and windows onto the gentle world outside. Elegant and peaceful. *Gîte space for 20 people.*

Rooms: 1 quadruple with bath & wc; 1 triple with shower & wc.

Price: €42-€58 for two.

Meals: Choice of restaurants 2-8km.

Closed: Never.

From A13 exit Maison Brulée N138 for Bourgthéroulde & Brionne. 8km after Bourgthéroulde D83 left to Le Gros Theil; entering village, sharp right D92 & follow signs for 2km.

Béatrice & Patrice Noël-Windsor
Manoir d'Hermos
27800 Saint Eloi de Fourques
Eure
Tel: (0)2 32 35 51 32
Fax: (0)2 32 35 51 32
E-mail: manoirhermos@lemel.fr

Entry No: 178   Map: 3

So very French: old and new furnishings, tailored and natural garden, cultural references (Saint-Exupéry, author of the immortal *Petit Prince* and a friend of Madame's father, stayed here). The sensuous garden is full of old favourites: lilac, peonies, honeysuckle, fruit trees. Built in the 1500s, set in the middle of the village, the house is very old, very quiet and has an atmosphere that inspires ease and rest. Madame used to be an antique dealer so breakfast is served on old silver. She sculpts and paints and also restores the statues in the 15th-century church opposite the house. *Gîte space for 12 people.*

Rooms: 2 doubles, 1 triple, 1 quadruple (in cottage), all with shower & wc.

Price: €41 for two.

Meals: Dinner €14, including coffee; wine €12-15.

Closed: Never.

Your hostess is a real French lady of classic style. Strong, intelligent and gracious, she still bubbles with enthusiasm and energy after all these years of B&B. The 80m² yellow-tinted living room of her very French house has giant old beams, a huge Turkey rug on antique tiles and some choice relics from her time in Africa; the staircase is beautifully sculpted and the garden goes down to the river. Relaxing, impeccable bedrooms are thoroughly carpeted and she is rightly proud of her breakfast table with its pewter, intricately folded napkins and home-made delights. A most comfortable place, halfway between the wonders of Giverny and Rouen. *Gîte space for 4 people.*

Rooms: 1 double/twin, 1 suite for 5, both with bath & wc.

Price: €40-€44 for two.

Meals: In village or 6km away.

Closed: Never.

From A13 exit 19 to Louviers; D313 towards Elbeuf for 11km; left on D60 to St Didier des Bois. House with white iron gate opposite church.

From Paris A13 for Rouen; exit Louviers N154 for Évreux; exit Heudreville D71 to village. House in cul-de-sac opp. church.

Annick Auzoux
1 place de l'Église
27370 Saint Didier des Bois
Eure
Tel: (0)2 32 50 60 93
Fax: (0)2 32 25 41 83

Mme Janine Bourgeois
La Ferme
4 rue de l'Ancienne Poste
27400 Heudreville sur Eure
Eure
Tel: (0)2 32 50 20 69
Fax: (0)2 32 50 20 69

Entry No: 179   Map: **3**

Entry No: 180   Map: **3**

An elegant, listed 18th-century château, Émalleville has it all: landscaped and formal gardens, vast woodlands for walking (and autumn shooting), a tennis court, an ancient fallen mulberry that has rebuilt itself, two suites full of canopied beds in the château, other fine rooms in the converted dovecote. Breakfast is served in the *salle de chasse*: try the mulberry or wild plum jam; Parma ham and eggs are also a possibility. The lady of the manor's exquisite taste has weaved its magic from floor to ceiling, from Jouy print to antique wardrobe and you will feel like prince and princess here, just 30 minutes' drive from Giverny.

Rooms: 2 doubles, 1 double/twin, 2 suites for 4/5, all with bath or shower & wc.

Price: €80–€140 for two.

Meals: Restaurant 8km.

Closed: Never.

From A13 exit 'Louviers' on A154 towards Évreux, exit Caër/Gravigny on D155 for Acquigny. Through Boulay Morin, 500m after village, left to Émalleville; château opposite church.

Lilian Thieblot
Château d'Émalleville
17 rue de l'Église
27930 Émalleville, Eure
Tel: (0)2 32 34 01 87
Fax: (0)2 32 34 30 27
E-mail: chateau_emallevil@yahoo.fr
Web: www.multimania.com/chateauemallevil

Entry No: 181   Map: **3**

This charming Franco-Spanish couple spent over 20 years in Latin America then came back to renovate their 18th-century manor house between the coast of Normandy and the châteaux of the Loire - it vibrates with echoes of faraway places. Bedrooms aren't huge but are solidly comfortable with good furniture, interesting prints and immaculate bathrooms. There's a fully 'telecommunicating' study too; fresh breads and home-made jams (always a choice - from rhubarb to cherry) for breakfast at the huge Andean cedar breakfast table; a quiet, pretty garden and good conversation in English, French, Italian, Spanish or Catalan.

Rooms: 1 suite for 2, 1 family for 4, 1 double, all with bath or shower & wc.

Price: €41–€49 for two.

Meals: Auberges 5km.

Closed: Never.

From A13 exit 17 for Gaillon; W for Évreux D316 through Autheuil, St Vigor & up hill; right to Reuilly; house on road, 200m past Mairie on right.

Jean-Pierre & Amaia Trevisani
Clair Matin
19 rue de l'Église
27930 Reuilly
Eure
Tel: (0)2 32 34 71 47
Fax: (0)2 32 34 97 64
E-mail: clair_matin@compuserve.com

Entry No: 182   Map: **3**

Madame cooks beautiful Norman dishes with home-grown ingredients served on good china; also, remarkable tomato and banana jam for breakfast - be brave, it's worth trying. She has been doing B&B for years, is well organised and still enjoys meeting new people when she's not too busy. Guest quarters, independent of the house, have pretty French-style rooms, good bedding and excellent tiled shower rooms while the caringly-restored, listed 15th-century farmhouse, the duck pond, the peacocks and the furniture - each item carefully chosen, some tenderly hand-painted - all give it character. And it's excellent value. *Games room.*

Rooms: 1 triple, 2 doubles, 2 twins, both with shower & wc.

Price: €41 for two; €53 for three.

Meals: Dinner €16, including cider.

Closed: Never.

Eliane and Michel invested five years, great care and much good taste in restoring this lovely 19th-century farmhouse in a particularly pretty village. You stay in a self-contained part of the house with your own dayroom and breakfast area where there's lots of space to spread your legs in front of the fire. Bedrooms are spotless with *toile de Jouy* fabrics, beamed ceilings and polished floorboards. Outside, sweeping lawns run down to a pretty stream that meanders beneath high wooded cliffs. Éliane is passionate about her garden and loves to chat about it, pointing out the rich and the rare.

Rooms: 1 double, 1 twin, both with bath & wc.

Price: €44 for two.

Meals: Choice of restaurants nearby.

Closed: Never.

From Rouen N15 for Paris for 40km. At Gaillon right D10 towards La Croix St Leufroy for about 7km; in La Boissaye follow signs for Chambres d'Hôtes.

A13 exit 16 towards Cocherel; after 10km to Chambray; left at monument; left after 100m to Fontaine sous Jouy. In centre right Rue de l'Ancienne Forge for 800m; Rue de l'Aulnaie on right.

Clotilde & Gérard Sénécal
Manoir de la Boissière
Hameau de la Boissière
27490 La Croix Saint Leufroy
Eure
Tel: (0)2 32 67 70 85
Fax: (0)2 32 67 03 18

Éliane & Michel Philippe
L'Aulnaie
29 rue de l'Aulnaie
27120 Fontaine sous Jouy, Eure
Tel: (0)2 32 36 89 05
Fax: (0)2 32 36 89 05
E-mail: emi.philippe@worldonline.fr
Web: perso.worldonline.fr/chambre-fontaine/

Gorgeous!... and without a whiff of pretension. The Brunets, as delightful as their house, have the lightness of touch to combine the fresh best of modern French taste with an eye for authenticity - in a brand new house. There is light flooding in through recycled château windows on both sides of this classical narrow *maison de campagne*, eye-catching stretches of pine-floored corridor, handsome rugs, a brave mix of old and modern furniture and massive comfort. Exquisite.

Rooms: 3 twins, 2 doubles, all with bath or shower & wc.

Price: €84-€105 for two; reduction 2 nights or more.

Meals: Restaurants in village or 5km.

Closed: December-March, except by arrangement.

From A13 exit 14 towards Giverny. Entering Giverny left Rue Claude Monet. After church/Hotel Baudy first left Rue Blanche Hoshedé Monet for 1.2km; left on white arrow, imm'ly right on track for 800m, left to house.

Didier & Marie Lorraine Brunet
La Réserve
27620 Giverny
Eure
Tel: (0)2 32 21 99 09
Fax: (0)2 32 21 99 09
E-mail: ml1reserve@aol.com
Web: www.giverny.org/hotels/brunet/

Entry No: 185   Map: 3

The clean, cool River Epte, which Monet diverted at nearby Giverny to create the ponds for his famous *Nymphéas*, runs at the bottom of the pretty garden and bestows the same quality of serenity here. The house is beautifully furnished with family antiques and Madame, a strong, intelligent and inherently elegant person, willingly shares her extensive knowledge of all things Norman, including food. Rooms are stylish and quiet; one has an Art Deco brass bed designed by *Grand-père*; the attic twin is up steep stairs and under sloping ceilings.

Rooms: 2 doubles, both with shower or bath & wc.

Price: €50-€55 for two.

Meals: Dinner €20, including wine & coffee.

Closed: 16 December-14 March.

From Dieppe, D915 to Gisors. Cross Gisors; D10 for Vernon. In Dangu, Rue du Gué is beside River Epte; house with green shutters.

Nicole de Saint Père
Les Ombelles
4 rue du Gué
27720 Dangu, Eure
Tel: (0)2 32 55 04 95
Fax: (0)2 32 55 59 87
E-mail: vextour@aol.com
Web: vextour.ifrance.com

Entry No: 186   Map: 3

Normandy

Built in 1870, La Maigraire stands in pretty grounds and has its own fishing. Jean and his cousin François bought it in 1998 and did a brilliant restoration, carefully preserving the right atmosphere. Jean studied at the Louvre and worked as an interior designer and antique dealer before falling for La Maigraire. Luckily he had kept a little cache of pieces which look perfectly at home here. These attentive hosts will make you feel very welcome, providing delicious home-made jam for breakfast and perhaps even playing the piano while you have tea in the *grand salon*.

Rooms: 1 double, 1 suite for 2/3, both with bath or shower & wc.

Price: €72-€95 for two.

Meals: Several good restaurants in the area.

Closed: Never.

Peace is the norm not the exception in this deeply rural spot and you are unhesitatingly received into a warm and lively family - it feels good. Two rooms are in a converted outbuilding and have an appropriately rustic air - the upstairs room is bigger and lighter, the ground-floor room has a little private garden; both have beams, old wardrobes and mini-kitchens. The suite, ideal for families, is in the main house. Breakfast is at the family table, there are fresh flowers everywhere and your hosts have a genuine sense of country hospitality. Children are welcome to visit their son's farm next door. *Gîte space for 6 people.*

Rooms: 2 doubles, both with shower, wc & mini-kitchen; 1 suite for 4 with bath & wc.

Price: €35 for two.

Meals: Restaurant 5 km; self-catering in 2 rooms.

Closed: Never.

From D962, between Flers and Domfront, D260 towards Forges de Varennes & Champsecret for 1.5km; left into La Maigraire hamlet.

Jean Fischer
Château de La Maigraire
61700 Saint Bômer les Forges
Orne
Tel: (0)2 33 38 09 52
Fax: (0)2 33 38 09 52

From Argentan N158 for Caen. After sign for Moulin sur Orne next left. House 800m on left; signed (3.5km from Argentan).

Janine & Rémy Laignel
Le Mesnil
61200 Occagnes
Orne
Tel: (0)2 33 67 11 12

Entry No: 187   Map: 2

Entry No: 188   Map:

There's home-made elderflower cordial if you arrive on a hot day or a wonderful smell of hot bread may greet you: this converted manor-farm with its pigeon tower and duck stream has an unfussy family atmosphere. Your hosts have sheep, dairy cows, 300 apple trees (*Normandie oblige!*), work hard and are thoroughly integrated, as are their daughters. The bedrooms in the old dairy are light, soberly furnished with touches of *fantaisie* and Diana's very decorative stencils. Breakfast is superb, dinner should be an occasion to linger over and remember, both under the pergola in fine weather.

Rooms: 1 triple, 1 double, 1 twin, all with bath or shower & wc.

Price: €46-€50 for two; reduction for 2 nights or more.

Meals: Dinner €20, including wine & coffee.

Closed: December-February.

Debbie and Daniel, artistic young landscape gardeners new to the world of B&B, are thoroughly enthusiastic about it all: welcoming their guests to their pretty, unfussy rooms, improving the bathrooms, devising and preparing vegetarian menus to flatter taste and eye, redesigning the mature garden with its great old trees to include areas for Scent, Colour and Feel, developing the organic vegetable patch (free-range hens too). They have decorated the place with creative good taste, provide varied, healthy breakfasts and dinners and will take great care of your comfort and well-being.

Rooms: 3 doubles, all with shower & wc.

Price: €66-€78 for two.

Meals: Dinner €25, including wine & coffee.

Closed: Never.

From Vimoutiers D916 for Argentan. Just outside Vimoutiers fork left D16 for Exmes; D26 for Survie & Exmes.

Diana & Christopher Wordsworth
Les Gains
Survie
61310 Exmes
Orne
Tel: (0)2 33 36 05 56
Fax: (0)2 33 35 03 65
E-mail: christopher.wordsworth@libertysurf.fr

D579 from Lisieux to Vimoutiers; D979 for Alençon for 5km; left D12 for L'Aigle. In Ticheville, house signed on left.

Debbie & Daniel Armitage
La Maison du Vert
Le Bourg
61120 Ticheville, Orne
Tel: (0)2 33 36 95 84
Fax: (0)2 33 36 95 84
E-mail: mail@maisonduvert.com
Web: www.maisonduvert.com

Entry No: 189   Map: **3**

Entry No: 190   Map: **3**

Guest rooms, called *Spring, Summer, Autumn* and... *Cashmere*, have cane or brass beds, plain country décor and fresh flowers. Your hosts, caring, generous, sensitive farmers, enjoy contact and share their quiet sense of humour with each other, their guests and their children. Madame spoils you at breakfast and dinner with local honey and Camembert, her own poultry and rabbit from the field across the stream. Her home-made jam repertoire includes dandelion-flower and apple and meals are normally taken with the family - most convivial despite limited English. The sitting room, playroom and kitchen facilities are a bonus.

Rooms: 2 doubles, 1 triple, 1 quadruple, all with shower & wc.

Price: € 37 for two.

Meals: Dinner € 14, including wine & coffee.

Closed: Never.

There is something quintessentially *chambre d'hôtes* about Les Roches, unaffected, authentic, low-ceilinged and still recognisable since the thick creeper was stripped to reveal the flint and brick face dated 1696. Madame's breakfast remains old-style basic French but simple rooms with their old furniture and floral linen are being redone: the triple has already taken on a warm ochre glow and the corridor a soft pale finish that brings new light. But most memorable are Madame's bubbling laughter, her endearingly low-key husband and the smell of grass and countryside in the morning.

Rooms: 1 double, 1 triple, both with bath or shower & wc.

Price: € 40 for two.

Meals: Choice of restaurants within 3km.

Closed: Never.

From Argentan, N26 for L'Aigle & Paris. Left at Silli en Gouffern. At Ste Eugénie, last farm on left.

From Rouen N138 for Alençon, through Bernay to Monnai; right D12 for 2km; signposted; entrance on left - long drive to house.

Pierre & Ghislaine Maurice
La Grande Ferme
Sainte Eugénie
61160 Aubry en Exmes
Orne
Tel: (0)2 33 36 82 36
Fax: (0)2 33 36 99 52
E-mail: GHIS.P.MAURICE@wanadoo.fr

Gérard & Émilienne Bourgault
Les Roches
61470 Le Sap
Orne
Tel: (0)2 33 39 47 39

Entry No: 191   Map: **3**

Entry No: 192   Map: **3**

Looks angular? It's like that inside too, the staircase a monumental piece elbowing its way up to the second floor where a panoramic window lets in the whole sky. Grandmother's toy camel stands here in its 1905 skin: the house was built by her parents in 1910 to an open, American-style plan and sliding glass partitions give generous ground-floor spaces. Guest rooms are good too, much-windowed, soft-coloured, marble-fireplaced, old-mirrored. Impeccable and full of personality, the house is the pride and joy of your alert, eager hostess who laughs easily and manages her home and guests expertly.

Rooms: 1 twin with bath & wc; 1 suite for 4 with shower & wc.

Price: €50.50 for two.

Meals: Dinner €22, including wine & coffee.

Closed: December-February.

Barbara calls it her "corner of paradise" and her delight is contagious. Utter peace among the cattle-dotted Norman pastures - one woman, her horses, dogs and cats in a low-lying farmhouse, beautifully rebuilt "from a pile of stones", where old and new mix easily and flowers rampage all around. The lovely sloping garden is all her own work too - she appears to have endless energy. The pastel guest rooms, two upstairs, one with garden access on the ground floor, are attractive and have brand new bathrooms. Come by horse, or walk. Beautiful country and a sociable, interesting, horse-loving woman to welcome you.

Rooms: 1 twin, 1 double, all with bath or shower & wc.

Price: €46 for two.

Meals: Restaurant in village, 1.5 km.

Closed: Never.

From Argentan N26 E for 37km. Entrance 4km after Planches on right by small crucifix; long lime-bordered drive.

From Courtomer, past Mairie right after last building for Tellières. Left at crossroads for Le Marnis. Second lane on right.

Antoine & Nathalie Le Brethon
La Bussière
61370 Ste Gauburge Ste Colombe
Orne
Tel: (0)2 33 34 05 23
Fax: (0)2 33 34 71 47

Barbara Goff
Le Marnis
Tellières le Plessis
61390 Courtomer
Orne
Tel: (0)2 33 27 47 55
E-mail: barbaragoff@minitel.net

Entry No: 193   Map: **3**

Entry No: 194   Map: **3**

Helen and Rex will really look after you in the old Percheron farmhouse they have rescued and restored in this bucolic region, renowned for its breed of heavy horses. Feel free to potter on their land or venture further afield and come back to a friendly cup of tea and a delicious supper in the farmhouse kitchen. Helen may be English but you would never guess it from her cooking - it's probably more French than her neighbours'. *Normandie oblige*: Rex's company sells all sorts of things for horses. Rooms are comfortable and fresh in cream and white.

Rooms: 1 double, 1 triple, both with bath & wc.

Price: €46 for two.

Meals: Dinner €23, including wine & coffee; restaurants within 10km.

Closed: December.

From Mortagne au Perche D931 towards Mamers for 8km; right on D650 for Coulimer at small crossroads. House 800m on left, last of small group of houses.

Rex & Helen Barr
La Simondrière
61360 Coulimer
Orne
Tel: (0)2 33 25 55 34
Fax: (0)2 33 25 49 01
E-mail: prima@wanadoo.fr

Entry No: 195   Map: **3**

Fascinating hosts, they are retired doctors indulging their passion for beautiful countryside (they have 40 acres of it) and its wildlife, their garden, orchard and animals, music (the music room is truly special), mellow old buildings made comfortable without any loss of character, good food and fine wine and, of course, people. At breakfast, probably out on the terrace, there'll be fresh eggs, home-made chemical-free fruit, jams and yogurt. Two bedrooms have a private staircase in the main house, one double is in a separate building with a big upstairs bedroom and fabulous view. Go and discover this place!

Rooms: 2 doubles, 1 twin, all with shower or bath & wc.

Price: €85-€100 for two.

Meals: Dinner available locally.

Closed: Never.

From Verneuil-Avre D941 to La Ferté Vidame; D4 then D11 to Longny; D111 to Monceaux; right for Chapelle-Montligeon for 500m; left for Maison Maugis on D291 2.5km; right - sign.

Édith & Jean-Louis Grandjean
Domaine de l'Émière
61110 Maison Maugis
Orne
Tel: (0)2 33 73 74 19
Fax: (0)2 33 73 69 80

Entry No: 196   Map: **3**

Delightful people and a fascinating house. An ancestor fled to Scotland in 1789 and returned an Adam fan bringing trompe l'œil marble and Wedgwood mouldings. The Longcamps are a civilised, friendly couple: she organises chamber music in their big, log-fired drawing room; he makes top-class Camembert and mows his acres on Sundays. The elegant bedrooms have antiques, books, ancestral portraits, much soft comfort and a loo in a tower. The dining room with wrap-around oak panelling inlaid with precious woods is a fine setting for breakfast. Come and belong briefly to this wonderful world. Good walks start 2km away.

Rooms: 1 twin, 2 doubles, all with bath & wc.

Price: €95-€110 for two.

Meals: 2 good restaurants within 5 km.

Closed: Open April-November and by arrangement December-March.

Breakfast by the massive fireplace may be candle or oil-lamp-lit on dark mornings in this ancient fortress of a farm. It also has a stupendous tithe barn and a little watchtower turned into a delightful gîte for two. Madame is proud of her family home, its flagstones worn smooth with age and its fine country antiques so suited to the sober, high-ceilinged rooms - one has a shower in a tower, another looks over the calving field. Her energy is boundless, she is ever redecorating, cooking (excellent Norman cuisine), improving her rooms, much supported by her farmer husband. *Gîte space for 6 people.*

Rooms: 2 triples, 1 double, all with shower & wc.

Price: €46 for two.

Meals: Dinner €18, including cider.

Closed: Never.

From Verneuil sur Avre, N12 SW 24km to Carrefour Ste Anne. Left D918 for Longny au Perche for 4.5km; left D289 for Moulicent. House 800m on right.

From Bayeux N13 30km west; exit on D514 to Osmanville and on towards Grandchamp for 5km; left towards Géfosse Fontenay; house 800m along on left before church.

Jacques & Pascale de Longcamp
Château de la Grande Noë
61290 Moulicent
Orne
Tel: (0)2 33 73 63 30
Fax: (0)2 33 83 62 92
E-mail: grandenoe@wanadoo.fr

Gérard & Isabelle Leharivel
Ferme-Manoir de la Rivière
14230 Géfosse Fontenay
Calvados
Tel: (0)2 31 22 64 45
Fax: (0)2 31 22 01 18
E-mail: manoirdelariviere@mageos.com
Web: www.chez.com/manoirdelariviere

Normandy

A round pigeon tower and a private chapel complete the picture of this charming fortified working farm, parts of which are 15th century. Rooms are big with high beamed ceilings and there's a fine walled garden. The whole place has been carefully restored and it all feels unpretentiously stylish with a friendly, relaxed atmosphere. The bedrooms have been decorated quite beautifully, each with its own theme, mostly traditional variations with antique furniture and flowery fabrics, one in navy blue and white with nautical pictures. The sea is just a short walk away.

Rooms: 1 double, 1 twin, 1 suite, 1 family, all with shower & wc.

Price: €50 for two.

Meals: Choice of restaurants Grandcamp Maisy.

Closed: November-March.

Previously renovated in the 16th and 18th centuries..., the glorified farm has 30 rooms, fabulous tiled and parquet floors, classic French décor. At its centre, the grand panelled dining room has sun pouring in from both sides and views across the moat, over the formal garden with its swings and myriad plants down to the orangery. Breakfast is at separate tables here. The whole house is littered with woodcarvings and furniture made by Monsieur's father and bedrooms are, of course, splendidly, classically French. And Madame is a gracious and outgoing hostess. *Pets by arrangement.*

Rooms: 5 doubles, all with bath & wc.

Price: €55-€62 for two.

Meals: Choice of restaurants 7-12 km.

Closed: December-March.

From Bayeux N13 30km west; exit D514 to Osmanville and on towards Grandcamp for 4km; left D199a towards Géfosse-Fontenay for 400m then follow yellow signs on right.

From Cherbourg N13 to Isigny; right D5 for Le Molay; left near Vouilly church; château on right 500m.

François & Agnès Lemarié
L'Hermerel
14230 Géfosse Fontenay
Calvados
Tel: (0)2 31 22 64 12
Fax: (0)2 31 22 64 12
E-mail: lemariehermerel@aol.com

Marie-José & James Hamel
Château de Vouilly
Vouilly
14230 Isigny sur Mer
Calvados
Tel: (0)2 31 22 08 59
Fax: (0)2 31 22 90 58

Entry No: 199   Map: **2**

Entry No: 200   Map: **2**

It's all utterly rural. Madame is a quiet, kindly woman who creates an easy family atmosphere. Her son bakes delicious bread in the 18th-century oven he has restored and may produce cakes and *pâtisseries* of all sorts for tea. Rooms are simple country style. *La Chambre Ancienne*, definitely the best, has a low ceiling, antique beds and planked floor; shower rooms are rather old-fashioned. You might be able to fish on Madame's trout-stuffed pond nearby and they'll organise a boat ride across the bird-full *Marais* for you. There is a small camping site on the farm.

Rooms: 2 twins, 1 triple, all with shower & wc.

Price: € 37 for two.

Meals: Ferme-auberge 3km.

Closed: Never.

Do anything to stay here; the solid beauty of the old fortified farmhouse and the serenity of the *Marais* lapping at the lawn make it near-perfect. Your amiable and generous hosts, happy to wait up for you if you arrive late, love transmitting their deep knowledge of local history and wildlife: theirs is a WWF *Gîte Panda* with nature guides and binoculars on loan. Stretch your eyes across a luminous landscape of marshes and fields, watch storks nesting, the heron fishing in the pond, then negotiate the stone spiral up to big, comfortably simple rooms and sleep in bliss.

Rooms: 1 double, 1 twin, 1 suite for 5, all with bath or shower & wc.

Price: € 43 for two.

Meals: Dinner available locally.

Closed: October-Easter.

From Bayeux, D5 W through Le Molay Littry towards Bernesq & Briqueville. Right about 0.75km before Bernesq; Le Ruppaley on this road, signposted.

Marcelle Marie
Le Ruppaley
14710 Bernesq
Calvados
Tel: (0)2 31 22 54 44

From Bayeux N13 to La Cambe, D113 south. After 1km, D124 to St Germain du Pert (1.5km).

Paulette & Hervé Marie
Ferme de la Rivière
14230 Saint Germain du Pert
Calvados
Tel: (0)2 31 22 72 92
Fax: (0)2 31 22 01 63

Entry No: 201 Map: **2**

Entry No: 202 Map: **2**

A charming couple, she natural, strong and brave, he softly spoken and communicative, with three courteous, smiling sons, they have been enjoying B&B for 20 years now as well as running a large dairy herd. Their 300-year-old farmhouse contains two of the guest rooms; the family room is in the more recent extension with the breakfast room that leads onto the pretty patio. There's also a largish grassy area for run-around children. Rooms are floral, shiny floorboarded and have excellent beds and shower rooms. This is a good, reliable place to stay with a delightful family.

Rooms: 1 double, 1 triple, 1 suite for 4, all with shower & wc.

Price: €38-€41 for two; suite €55-€67 for four.

Meals: Restaurants St Laurent sur Mer, 4km.

Closed: Never.

How old is old? This house is 11th century, renovated in 1801... The brass-railed staircase and the drawing room are gracious but not grand; the dining room, with its huge fireplace and modern bar, is relaxed in its yellow and green garb. Madame uses colour well, mixing bright with soft, just as she mixes antiques with artificial flowers. Your hosts are warm people, taking you naturally into their family circle. The comfortable bedrooms look onto wide fields, the smaller attic room is perfect and the 'Norman' dinners have been praised to the skies.

Rooms: 1 double, 2 quadruples, all with shower or bath & wc.

Price: €40 for two.

Meals: Dinner €19, including wine & coffee.

Closed: Never.

From Cherbourg N13 S 76km; exit Formigny towards St Laurent sur Mer; after church right 800m: entrance on left.

From Bayeux N13 for Cherbourg; through Tour en Bessin, left on D100 for Crouay 1km. House on right.

Odile & Jean-Claude Lenourichel
Le Mouchel
14710 Formigny
Calvados
Tel: (0)2 31 22 53 79
Fax: (0)2 31 21 56 55
E-mail: odile.lenourichel@libertysurf.fr

Catherine & Bertrand Girard
Le Relais de la Vignette
Route de Crouay, Tour en Bessin
14400 Bayeux,Calvados
Tel: (0)2 31 21 52 83/(0)6 80 45 69 95
Fax: (0)2 31 21 52 83
E-mail: relais.vignette@wanadoo.fr
Web: perso.wanadoo.fr/relais.vignette/

The Abbey is right there, floodlit at night, in an exquisitely peaceful setting. The Fauvels' house was the monks' farm in the 15th century and ancient dreams hover over the stone staircase and the old beams - you may sleep like angels. One suite has quantities of antiques and *objets*; the other, in the little old monks' bakery, is more intimate, less elaborate. Monsieur, a retired breeder of cattle and horses, is quietly contemplative; Madame, a lively grandmother, is bright and attentive - very pleasant hosts and a thoroughly good, place. *Gîte space for 11 people.*

Rooms: 1 twin, 2 suites for 3, all with shower or bath & wc.

Price: €40 for two.

Meals: Restaurants 10km.

Closed: Never.

Up the drive, across the cleanest ever farmyard to this totally French house, to be met by a charmingly hospitable owner - she delights in gardening and cooking, her husband runs the dairy farm. Beyond the dinky little hall, the *salon* - high-backed chairs, beams, antimacassars - is a good place for a quiet read. The big sunny bedrooms are cosily frilly with quantities of lace, country furniture and gentle morning views over the garden dropping down to the pond. Special extras are the pond for fishing, paths for walking, home-made yogurt and cider - and pillows for the asking. *Small dogs welcome.*

Rooms: 2 doubles, 1 suite, all with shower & wc.

Price: €40 for two.

Meals: Dinner €18, including wine & coffee.

Closed: Never.

From Bayeux, N13 W for 14km; D30 for Trévières; 2nd right, 1st right, right again D29 for St Lô for 1km; right D124 to Écrammeville; signs (farm near church).

From Caen A13 for Cherbourg, exit Carpiquet/Caumont l'Éventé; 500m before Caumont, left at Chambres d'Hôtes sign.

Louis & Annick Fauvel
Ferme de l'Abbaye
14710 Ecrammeville
Calvados
Tel: (0)2 31 22 52 32
Fax: (0)2 31 22 47 25

Alain & Françoise Petiton
La Suhardière
14240 Livry
Calvados
Tel: (0)2 31 77 51 02
Fax: (0)2 31 77 51 02

Entry No: 205   Map: **2**

Entry No: 206   Map: **2**

You could scarcely find easier, friendlier hosts than Joseph and Marie-Thé who have quantities of local lore and advice to communicate, will join you for a farm supper at the long table in the fresh-flowered, log-fired (winter) guests' dayroom and create a generally fun-loving, relaxed atmosphere. There are animals and milking for children, table football and volleyball for teenagers, *pétanque* for all. They are simple, genuine people, as are their rooms (one has an ancient dresser set into the stone wall) and their welcome. This is superb value and far enough from the road not to suffer from much traffic noise.

Rooms: 4 suites for 3/4, all with bath or shower & wc, 1 with kitchen.

Price: € 32 for two.

Meals: Dinner € 13, including wine & coffee.

Closed: Never.

A place to indulge the senses: gorgeously flowered surroundings, bucolic walks (itineraries provided) and the farm with many-feathered with geese for *foie gras* (Madame knows how and does it all herself) and spit-roasting in winter. You are warmly greeted by your youngish hosts, the atmosphere is easy and if the big bedrooms are unremarkable, they are clean, with their own entrance, kitchen and sitting room. But you will come above all for Madame's talented cooking and genuine hospitality. Children are welcome: there are cots, games and bikes for them. *Gîte space for 7 people.*

Rooms: 2 triples (1 on ground floor), both with shower & wc.

Price: € 33 for two.

Meals: Dinner € 13, including wine & coffee.

Closed: December-February.

From A84/E401 exit 42 onto N175 towards Cahagnes for 2km; right following Chambres d'Hôtes signs to farm.

Joseph & Marie-Thé Guilbert
Le Mesnil de Benneville
14240 Cahagnes
Calvados
Tel: (0)2 31 77 58 05
Fax: (0)2 31 77 37 84

From Caen A84 towards Avranches; exit to St Martin des Besaces on D53; left D165 towards Brémoy; house on right 4km from St Martin.

Jacqueline & Gilbert Lalleman
Carrefour des Fosses
14260 Brémoy
Calvados
Tel: (0)2 31 77 83 22
E-mail: jg_lalleman@yahoo.fr

Entry No: 207   Map: 2

Entry No: 208   Map: 2

A solid, elegant Norman mansion with walled garden and summer house outside, billiards and two dining rooms inside, as one would expect. Andrew receives you in relaxed style, dynamic Elizabeth is present at weekends. Your sleeping and sitting rooms are on the airy first floor: generous light, glowing parquet, French and English antiques against pale walls. Downstairs, the sandy, creamy-white dining room is unusually frescoed; the oak-panelled, many-windowed dining room is beamed and fireplaced; both have seriously big tables. Andrew continues his restoration in excellent taste and it is all most comfortable and welcoming. *Gîte space for 7 people.*

Rooms: 1 triple, 1 twin, 2 doubles, all with bath or shower & wc.

Price: € 60-€ 65 for two.

Meals: Dinner € 21, including wine & coffee.

Closed: Christmas & New Year.

From Caen ring road exit 13 for Falaise; 9km, right to Bretteville sur Laize; continue to Barbery. House behind field on right, with high, green gates.

Elizabeth & Andrew Bamford
Les Fontaines
Barbery
14220 Bretteville sur Laize, Calvados
Tel: (0)2 31 78 24 48
Fax: (0)2 31 78 24 49
E-mail: lesfontaines@free.fr
Web: lesfontaines.free.fr

Entry No: 209   Map: 2

Through the wood and across the stream to the simplest, friendliest house you could imagine. It is about a century old while the Ameys have that timeless quality of solid country dwellers and will wrap you in blue-eyed smiles. Their unpretentious welcome is full of comfort and warmth. Most furnishings are in simple country style, bar two superb Norman armoires: walls are pastel, curtains lace, bathroom pink, towels small. Breakfast comes with incomparably good farm milk and butter; dinners are reliably Norman; the wisteria blooms. Lovely people, excellent value. *Gîte space for 6 people.*

Rooms: 3 doubles, all with basin, sharing bathroom & separate wc.

Price: € 31 for two.

Meals: Dinner € 14, including wine & coffee.

Closed: Never.

From Caen A84 towards Mt St Michel, exit 46 'Noyers Bocage'. Right on D83 towards Cheux for 1.5km; left to Tessel; signposted.

Paul & Éliane Amey
La Londe
14250 Tessel
Calvados
Tel: (0)2 31 80 81 12
Fax: (0)2 31 80 81 57
E-mail: paul.amey@wanadoo.fr

Entry No: 210   Map: 2

Normandy

A lovely old house of golden 17th-century stone stands beyond the great arched gate, its courtyard housing several tribes of animal and a games room. Also a cider-apple orchard; a fascinating military historian who takes battlefield tours (don't be daunted: arrange yours with him) and loves sharing his passion for the dramas that took place here; his gentle lady who serves her own jams plus fresh breads and croissants for breakfast; stone stairs to big, comfortably casual guest rooms; and a genuine family-friendly welcome just 15 minutes' walk from the Cathedral. *Gîte space for 6 people.*

Rooms: 2 doubles, 2 triples, all with shower & wc.

Price: €40-€45 for two.

Meals: Choice of restaurants in Bayeux, 1km.

Closed: Never.

The style is 'contemporary rustic' and your young hosts have done a great renovation job on their intriguing 18th-century house, preserving old stonework and beams, installing modern showers and decent beds. Mylène has brought pretty Provençal fabrics from her native Drôme, Christian is Norman and trained as a chef; both are friendly, relaxed and keen that their guests get a good glimpse of French country life. There's a wide choice of local and home-made breads and jams at breakfast, a barbecue and refrigerator you can use, table tennis and a couple of bikes for further exploration.

Rooms: 1 double, 1 suite for 3, both with shower & wc.

Price: €47 for two.

Meals: Restaurants nearby.

Closed: Never, please book ahead.

On Bayeux bypass, at Campanile Hotel D572 towards St Lô; 2nd right and follow signs to arched gateway.

From Caen D7 for Douvres 8km; left D404 for 5.5km; D79 to Courseulles sur Mer; D514 to Ver sur Mer. At village entrance 1st left Ave Provence, 1st right, 1st left cul-de-sac. House at end on right.

Lt-Col & Mrs Chilcott
Manoir des Doyens
Saint Loup Hors
14400 Bayeux
Calvados
Tel: (0)2 31 22 39 09
Fax: (0)2 31 21 97 84
E-mail: chilcott@mail.cpod.fr

Christian Mériel & Mylène Gilles
Le Mas Normand
8 impasse de la Rivière
14114 Ver sur Mer
Calvados
Tel: (0)2 31 21 97 75
Fax: (0)2 3 1 21 97 75
E-mail: lemasnormand@wanadoo.fr

Entry No: 211   Map: 2

Entry No: 212   Map: 2

It's just plain lovely, this little group of stone buildings with pretty bridge and terraces by the rushing stream. There's the age-old converted mill (for the family); the 'hunting lodge' (for guests) where Madame's talented decoration marries things past - antiques, old prints, photographs - and designer-hued present and you have your own dining room and kitchen; the blue, yellow and green garden, the woods for nut-gathering, beaches nearby, the stream for entertainment on the spot. Your hosts are sweet and love having families. *Italian spoken. Gîte space for 6 people.*

Rooms: 1 double with shower & wc; 1 double, 1 twin sharing shower & wc.

Price: € 48 for two.

Meals: Restaurants 2-3km; self-catering possible.

Closed: Never.

With a few sheep in the background and Mireille the gentle old donkey in the paddock, this is a typical old farmhouse, even down to the corrugated iron roof. The guest wing is in the converted stables, where the kitchen/diner has its original stone flags, and the manger. The rooms are country-comfortable, if a little scuffed, functional and spotless; one has a balcony onto the farm and the apple orchard (and road at the bottom) where all sorts of games await your pleasure. Your elderly hostess is friendly and glad to have your company.

Rooms: 1 double, 1 triple, both with shower & wc.

Price: € 38 for two.

Meals: Restaurants in Vire 2km; self-catering possible.

Closed: Never.

From Ouistreham D35 through Douvres & Tailleville; over D404; right at r'about entering Reviers - 2nd Chambres d'Hôtes on left.

From Vire centre, D524 for Tinchebray & Flers; house on right after 2km; signposted.

Patricia & Jean-Michel Blanlot
La Malposte
15 rue des Moulins
14470 Reviers
Calvados
Tel: (0)2 31 37 51 29
Fax: (0)2 31 37 51 29

Mme Marcelle Marie
La Gage
14500 Roullours
Calvados
Tel: (0)2 31 68 17 40
Fax: (0)2 31 68 17 40

What the house lacks in years is made up tenfold by your hosts' timeless, down-to-earth Norman hospitality. They are close to all things natural, plough their big veg patch with the cob in harness, will drive you along secret byways in a pony and trap while telling local legends, take you on night-time discovery walks, share organic dinners made to old forgotten regional recipes, offer good rooms where you wake to stunning views over the hushed hills of *La Suisse Normande*. Nothing gushy or corny, these are independent, strong, comforting people who genuinely care for your well-being and that of the land.

Rooms: 2 doubles, 1 twin, 1 suite, all with shower & wc.

Price: €35 for two.

Meals: Dinner €13, including wine & coffee.

Closed: Never.

The square-set château stands handsome still though the densely wooded park was devastated by the 1999 storm. Taste the "world's best cider" (so says Monsieur), admire yourself in myriad gilded mirrors, luxuriate in a jacuzzi or bare your chest to a power shower, play the piano, watch pop-up telly, appreciate Monsieur's very dry sense of humour and Madame's superb cooking, and lie at last in an antique bed in one of the great, deep-tinted bedrooms. The period ceilings, tapestries and furniture make this a real château experience; the people make it very human.

Rooms: 2 doubles, 2 suites, all with bath or shower & wc.

Price: €90 for two.

Meals: Dinner €40, including wine, calvados & coffee.

Closed: Never.

From Caen D562 towards Flers for about 35km; at Le Fresne D1 towards Falaise for 4km; house on right, signposted.

Roland & Claudine Lebatard
Arclais
14690 Pont d'Ouilly
Calvados
Tel: (0)2 31 69 81 65
Fax: (0)2 31 69 81 65

From Caen N158 for Falaise; at La Jalousie, right D23; right D235 just before Bretteville sur Laize; signposted.

Anne-Marie & Alain Cantel
Château des Riffets
14680 Bretteville sur Laize
Calvados
Tel: (0)2 31 23 53 21
Fax: (0)2 31 23 75 14
E-mail: acantel@free.fr

Françoise and Michel have been doing B&B for years, in one house or another, and are ever ready to welcome guests to their typically Norman house where space is well organised and you won't feel crowded in. Françoise will produce an excellent dinner for you, likely to centre around *confit de canard* and apple or plum tart, depending on the time of year. The rooms are not large but they are comfortably cheerful and look out onto a very pretty garden. The loudest sound you might hear is the odd lawnmower. *Apartment for 4-5.*

Rooms: 1 double, 1 triple, with bath or shower & wc.

Price: €60-€68 for two.

Meals: Dinner €18.50 including aperitif & coffee, wine €12-€14.

Closed: Never.

Views from this anciently, beautifully Norman house, a festival of timbers and stones, are pastoral bliss. Ancient layout too: half cottage, half manor, it has two narrow staircases, two bathrooms for four bedrooms, one on another floor. But such super Anglo-Canadian hosts - much travelled and cultured - who cook and talk easily and interestingly, such a personal dining room where Julia has hand-painted the beams, laid out her willow pattern china and hung her friends' paintings. And special bedrooms: mixed baroque, contemporary and cottage with velvet and quilt, floorboards and rugs. A quite lovely house in a deeply rural spot a stone's throw from Honfleur.

Rooms: 4 twins with 2 separate bathrooms (2 baths, 2 wcs & 2 showers).

Price: €38-€46 for two.

Meals: Dinner €18-23, including cider & coffee.

Closed: Never.

From Pont l'Évêque D579 towards Lisieux. At Le Breuil en Auge r'about D264 to Le Torquesne. 1st right after church, Chemin des Toutains. House is 500m further on.

From Pont l'Évêque D579 for Lisieux; at Fierville les Parcs left to Blangy; right on hairpin for Norolles/Lisieux; 1st left for Les Batailles; house on right.

Françoise Valle
Le Clos St Hymer
14130 Le Torquesne
Calvados
Tel: (0)2 31 61 99 15
Fax: (0)2 31 61 99 36

Julia Mclean
Domaine des Leudets
Blangy le Château
14130 Pont l'Évêque
Calvados
Tel: (0)2 31 64 61 79

Entry No: 217   Map: 3

Entry No: 218   Map: 3

Despite its make-believe face among the smooth green curves of racehorse country, it is genuine early 1600s. Inside is an equally astounding dining room built by one Mr Swann and resplendently carved, panelled and painted. Two big rooms - *Jaune* and *Verte* - see the sun rise, but *Saumon* is even better with its heavenly sunset prospect; one has a splendid old-style bath and tiling, all are incredible value. Madame, a beautiful Swedish lady, made all the curtains and covers. She and her diplomat husband are well-travelled, polyglot, cultured and make their B&B doubly special.

Rooms: 2 doubles, 1 twin, all with bath or shower & wc.

Price: €45-€55 for two.

Meals: Restaurant 1km.

Closed: 15 November-1 March.

From Caen N13 E towards Lisieux for 25km. At Carrefour St Jean, D50 (virtually straight on) towards Cambremer. 5km from junction, house signposted on right.

Christine & Arnauld Gherrak
Manoir de Cantepie
Le Cadran
14340 Cambremer
Calvados
Tel: (0)2 31 62 87 27

Oh! the soft colour and architecture, the honeysuckle in the walled garden, the roses, the orchards, the shutters, the view across the valley, the antiqued, characterful living room, Madame's delightful welcome... French bliss. The first date is precisely 1462: it was probably part of the Abbey. The garden is yours and you can fish for coloured carp in the pond. Rooms are good, one on the ground floor with age-old terracotta tiles, paintings, antiques and a leather armchair, the others on the first floor - all with long green views. Madame is full of fun but she often has to be out after lunch, so prefers you to arrive in the late afternoon if possible. *Gîte space for 12 people.*

Rooms: 1 double with shower & wc; 2 triples, 1 family, all with bath or shower, sharing 3 separate wcs.

Price: €41 for two; under 3s free.

Meals: Good choice of restaurants nearby.

Closed: Never.

From Lisieux D511 towards St Pierre sur Dives. Just before St Pierre D40 left towards Livarot for 1.5km; right to Berville; signposted.

Annick Duhamel
Le Pressoir
Berville
14170 Saint Pierre sur Dives
Calvados
Tel: (0)2 31 20 51 26
Fax: (0)2 31 20 03 03

Falaise was Duke William's home until he left his native Normandy in 1066 to conquer other shores but this typical Falaise house, in a dear, quiet little Norman village, is quite young, only dating from the 1600s. Monsieur's family have owned the pretty house for 100 years: he was born here and married a local girl. They are a sweet couple, quietly and unobtrusively attentive, and you will feel well tended, just like the large garden, clearly much loved with its flowery bower holding a stone table. Indoors are some superb pieces of family furniture - country French at its best - as well as crinkly pink lights and little bits of *brocante*.

Rooms: 1 suite for 4, 1 double/triple, both with shower & wc.

Price: €35 for two.

Meals: Restaurants Falaise, 3km; barbecue & picnic possible.

Closed: Never.

From Falaise D63 for Trun, 2km; 2nd left towards Villy lez Falaise for 1km; in village farm 1st on left after stop sign.

Alice & Gilbert Thomas
Ferme la Croix
14700 Villy lez Falaise
Calvados
Tel: (0)2 31 90 19 98

From the restored guest building you see the majestic manor displaying its timbered splendours - and breakfast is by the truly monumental fireplace over there in the very handsome dining room. Your smiley, eager hosts have put hearts and talent into this restoration. Gérard's eye for detail and Sopheakna's Cambodian origins inform the décor: Eastern antiques and contemporary art in perfect harmony with the stones and woodwork of the ancient frame; exquisite bedrooms, original crooked beams, painted or plain, seagrass matting and oriental rugs on smooth old terracotta tiles, fabulous, unusual bathrooms. Not one mistake: worth every cent.

Rooms: 3 suites for 2, with shower & wc.

Price: €115-€164 for two.

Meals: Supper tray in room €18; good restaurant 1km.

Closed: 15 October-30 March.

From Lisieux D579 to Livarot; left D4 to N-D de Courson; cont. 3km towards Orbec; left at top of hill: 500m down lane.

Gérard & Sopheakna Goy
Manoir de Courson
Notre Dame de Courson
14140 Livarot, Calvados
Tel: (0)2 31 32 30 69
Fax: (0)2 31 32 30 69
E-mail: gggoy@aol.com
Web: manoirdecourson.com

A delicious surprise: behind its small town frontage the house stretches deep into the garden where Dorothea and Claude, a charming and elegant couple, nurture roses, wisteria and myriad colourful plants; there's even a stream with a little bridge. The utterly quiet guest bedrooms and sitting room are in the old stables; one lovely room is the old coachman's quarters, up an extraordinary spiral wooden staircase which climbs to huge windows overlooking the light and luscious garden. This polyglot house reflects its owners' polytravels as well as their passion for gardening and it's all quite delightful.

Rooms: 1 apartment for 2/4, 1 double, both with shower & wc.

Price: €46 for two.

Meals: Choice of restaurants in Orbec.

Closed: Never.

The simple, authentic charm of the Jays' welcome is utterly fitting among the quiet marshes of the Regional Park where their B&B is a *Gîte Panda*, providing full information on the wildlife here: there's an excellent 8km circular walk mapped from the house. In their well-converted farmhouse, you climb the handsome stone stairs to big, beamed or raftered, beautifully furnished and peaceful rooms (even 7am church bells are in keeping). The Clays put everyone quickly at their ease, share their television, serve great breakfasts (home-made jams, own eggs) - and children love the goats, ducks and rabbits. *Gîte space for 12 people.*

Rooms: 2 doubles, both with bath or shower & wc.

Price: €35 for two.

Meals: Restaurants 5-17km.

Closed: Never.

Orbec 19km S of Lisieux on D519. Turn into village; house on main street next to L'Orbecquoise restaurant.

From La Haye du Puits, D903 for Barneville Carteret. At Bolleville, right on D127 to St Nicolas de Pierrepont; left before church; house on right after cemetery.

Dorothea Vaillère
62 rue Grande
14290 Orbec
Calvados
Tel: (0)2 31 32 77 99
Fax: (0)2 31 32 77 99

Richard & Jay Clay
La Ferme de l'Église
50250 St Nicolas de Pierrepont, Manche
Tel: (0)2 33 45 53 40
Fax: (0)2 33 45 53 40
E-mail: theclays@wanadoo.fr
Web: perso.wanadoo.fr/normandie-cottages-bed-and-breakfast

One of our best-loved owners in a newly-restored *longère* on the edge of this pretty little town, Madame has the same honest, open personality as ever and Monsieur, now retired, has time to spread his modest farmer's joviality. One side of the house is theirs, the other yours with its entrance, dining room with a vast old fireplace and little kitchen. There are old tiles, beams and lime-washed walls everywhere, plus the family photograph collection. The two rooms up the steepish outside stairs are small but well insulated, the ground-floor room is larger and the welcome is remarkable.

Rooms: 1 twin, 1 double, 1 triple, all with shower & wc.

Price: €38 for two; €46 for three.

Meals: Choice of restaurants 500m; self-catering possible.

Closed: Never.

From St Sauveur le Vicomte D15 to Portbail; entering town, right just before church Rue R. Asselin; over old railway: La Roque de Gouey 250m on right.

Bernadette Vasselin
La Roque de Gouey
Rue Gilles Poërier
50580 Portbail
Manche
Tel: (0)2 33 04 80 27

Surrounded by attractive farmland and well placed for the delights of Valognes, this secluded village house is run by a sweetly and peacefully hospitable elderly couple. They are very informative on local history and sights and their house, with its open fireplace, is typically French country style. The rooms, not big but comfortable, have new bedding and wallpaper and fine old family furnishings; we definitely preferred the attic room where you feel secret and snug, even if the loo is down a flight of stairs. There is a kitchen especially for guests.

Rooms: 1 double with shower & wc; 1 double with shower, wc on floor below.

Price: €30 for two.

Meals: Self-catering possible.

Closed: Never.

From Cherbourg, N13 to Valognes; D902 towards Bricquebec for 2km; left on D87 to Yvetot Bocage. At church, towards Morville and first left.

Lucienne Dubost
Le Haut Billy
Route de Morville
50700 Yvetot Bocage, Valognes
Manche
Tel: (0)2 33 40 06 74

Normandy

A laughing, smiling, talkative couple, your hosts aim to give you "the best of France, the best of England": theirs is an old Norman house with pretty fabrics, antiques from both countries, a collection of English china inside, wild French hares, kestrels and owls outside (there's a spyhole for observation). The twin is smallish, the studio room under the eaves is big and full of light. Both have good bathrooms and oodles of fluffy towels. Linda varies the daily menu, down to napkin colours and china; Ted, an expert on the Second World War, will take you round the landing beaches. They are passionate about their house and region; their delight is catching.

Rooms: 2 doubles, both with bath & wc; 1 twin with shower & wc.

Price: €54-€60 for two.

Meals: Dinner €18, including wine & coffee; picnics by arrangement.

Closed: Never.

From Cherbourg S towards Caen then D900 to Bricquebec via Le Pont; cont. for Valognes, past Intermarché, left at T-junct., left after 'Sapeurs Pompiers' for Les Grosmonts; 400m on right.

Ted & Linda Malindine
La Lande
Les Grosmonts
50260 Bricquebec
Manche
Tel: (0)2 33 52 24 78
Fax: (0)2 33 52 24 78
E-mail: la.lande@wanadoo.fr

Entry No: 227   Map: 2

Within this splendid group of buildings, a spectacular historical ensemble where hefty medieval walls shelter an elegant 18th-century manor from the wild sea (you can hear it one mile away), hosts and furnishings are irreproachably French and civilisation is the keynote - books, fine china, panelling, gilt mirrors, plush chairs, engravings. Your suite has ancient floor tiles, brand new bedding, a loo in a tower. Stay a while, make your own breakfast (home-made jam and fresh eggs available) in exchange for using the very grand dining room, and get to know your literary *châtelaine*. *Gîte space for 6 people.*

Rooms: 1 suite for 2-4 with shower & wc.

Price: €77 for two.

Meals: Restaurants 2-15km.

Closed: Never.

From Cherbourg D904 towards Coutances. 3km after Les Pieux, right D62 towards Le Rozel, right D117 into village. House just beyond village; signs.

Josiane & Jean-Claude Grandchamp
Le Château
50340 Le Rozel
Manche
Tel: (0)2 33 52 95 08
Fax: (0)2 33 52 95 08

Entry No: 228   Map:

Normandy

Old-fashioned hospitality in a modern house. You are just a mile from the (often) glittering sea and Michel, who makes submarines, is happy to share his passion for sailing and might even take you coast-hopping. His shipbuilding skill is evident here: the attic space has been cleverly used to make two snug rooms with showers and kitchenettes for evening meals; the landing makes a pleasant sitting area. A brilliantly quiet position, simple décor, spotless rooms and an open, chatty hostess who will rise early for dawn ferry catchers make it ideal for beach holidays and channel crossing alike. *Gîte space for 5-6 people.*

Rooms: 2 doubles, both with shower & wc.

Price: €37 for two.

Meals: 2 restaurants within 2km; self-catering.

Closed: Never.

From Cherbourg D901 then D45 W 13km to Urville Nacqueville; 1st left by Hôtel Le Beau Rivage; up hill D22 for 2km; 2nd left; signposted.

Michel & Éliane Thomas
Eudal de Bas
50460 Urville Nacqueville
Manche
Tel: (0)2 33 03 58 16
Fax: (0)2 33 03 58 16

Entry No: 229　　　　Map: 2

This old stone manor stands proudly on the Normandy coastal hiking path looking across the town and out to sea. It is spotless, not over-modernised, and furnished in very French style with lots of velvet, floral linen and marble-topped chests. Retired from farming, the sociable Guérards enjoy welcoming both their own family and guests whom they happily point towards the cliff walks and other sights worth the detour. You are in quiet country, just 6km from the ferries (the separate room with its own outside entrance is ideal for early ferry-catchers). *Gîte space for 7 people.*

Rooms: 1 double, 1 twin, both with bath & wc; outside stairs to triple room with shower & wc.

Price: €40.50-€45 for two.

Meals: Restaurants 3km.

Closed: Never.

From Cherbourg D901 to Tourlaville & for St Pierre Église. Right at lights for Château des Ravalet/Hameau St Jean; up hill to 'Centre Aéré', follow Chambres d'Hôtes signs (3km from lights).

Mme Guérard
Manoir Saint Jean
50110 Tourlaville
Manche
Tel: (0)2 33 22 00 86

Entry No: 230　　　　Map: 2

For over 800 years, great swaying pines, a wild coast and the sea have guarded this site where the English burnt the first castle in 1346. Lush lawns, many-hued flowers and white geese soften Nature's wildness. The manor's stern stone façade hides a warm, gentle, elegant welcome in rooms with superb fireplaces, good beds, big windows to let in the light and truly personal decoration: pictures, books (breakfast is taken in the library) and antiques. Madame, charming and knowledgeable, will enthrall you with tales from Norman history and provide detailed maps for hikers. Bask in it all. *Gîte space for 6 people.*

Rooms: 1 suite for 3, 1 double, both with shower & wc.

Price: €50 for two.

Meals: Auberge within walking distance.

Closed: Never.

What can we say? It's near-perfect. Incredibly, your beautiful, energetic hostess is a grandmother! A farmer's wife! He now breeds racehorses, she indulges her passion for interior decoration - her impeccable rooms are a festival of colours, textures, antiques, embroidered linen. You cannot fail to enjoy staying in this wonderful old building - they love having guests; the great granite fireplace is always lit for the delicious breakfast which includes local specialities; there is a richly-carved 'throne' at the head of the long table. A stupendous place, very special people. *Gîte space for 5 people.*

Rooms: 2 doubles, all with shower & wc; 1 twin with bath & wc; (1 overflow room for children).

Price: €46-€58 for two.

Meals: Good choice of restaurants in Barfleur, 3km.

Closed: Never.

From Cherbourg, D901 to Barfleur. There, D1 for St Vaast. After end of Barfleur sign, 2nd right, 1st left.

Mme Claudette Gabroy
Le Manoir
50760 Montfarville
Manche
Tel: (0)2 33 23 14 21

From Barfleur for Quettehous; branch right D25 for Valcanville. 2nd right; follow signs.

Marie-France & Maurice Caillet
La Fèvrerie
50760 Sainte Geneviève
Manche
Tel: (0)2 33 54 33 53
Fax: (0)2 33 22 12 50

Entry No: 231   Map: **2**

Entry No: 232   Map: **2**

A very special place but not for the stuffy or the luxury-seeking. This wonderfully ramshackle, unspoiled, even dilapidated château houses a delightful couple, their family and all the guests who come to share the hugely relaxed, some would find over-casual, atmosphere. There is a big garden to explore and variegated rooms with old-fashioned bathing spaces. The cavernous Mussolini Room has the balcony with views across the heart-shaped lawn. The *Colonial Room* has pith-helmets and mementoes, while the *Hat Room*... The Berridges do energetic themed weekends and there's a great value dinner deal for guests at the local bar. *Gîte space for 15 people.*

Rooms: 2 doubles, 1 twin, all with bath & wc (1 screened off); 1 quadruple, 1 triple sharing a bathroom.

Price: €40-€46 for two.

Meals: Simple restaurant 2km.

Closed: January, February & August.

From Cherbourg N13 for Valognes 12km; right D119 for Ruffosses; cross motorway bridge; follow blue & white signs.

Mark & Fiona Berridge
Château Mont Épinguet
50700 Brix
Manche
Tel: (0)2 33 41 96 31
Fax: (0)2 33 41 98 77
E-mail: epinguet@aol.com
Web: www.chateaulemontepinguet.co.uk

Entry No: 233   Map: **2**

"They are a delight", said our inspector. Monsieur has a fine dry wit and loves to chat, about everything - but especially politics. She, too, is a chatty country lady; anyone with a smattering of French would enjoy them enormously. They are retired farmers, deeply, proudly anchored in their marshy region. The old manor set among mature hardwoods and conifers has huge character and a small private chapel; a vast collection of egg cups over the great granite fireplace and endearingly haphazard, spontaneous décor. There is even some Art Deco furniture. Wonderful value in a natural and unsophisticated manner.

Rooms: 1 triple with bath & wc; 1 triple, 1 double sharing shower & wc.

Price: €30-€34 for two.

Meals: Small good-value restaurants locally.

Closed: Never.

From Cherbourg N13 south; exit Ste Mère l'Église into Ste Mère l'Église; follow signs for Pont l'Abbé; house signposted on right after 3km.

Albert & Michèle Blanchet
La Fière
Route de Pont l'Abbé
50480 Sainte Mère l'Église
Manche
Tel: (0)2 33 41 32 66

Entry No: 234   Map: **2**

Inside the stately 16th-century manor, up a twisty stone staircase, along a creaky corridor, is one of the finest B&B suites we know: canopies, carved fireplaces, a boudoir, rugs, prints and antiques, a claw-footed bath, windows onto lush gardens with ancient trees. The vast panelled dining room fills with light, the tiled, be-rugged guest sitting room is grand yet welcoming, your hosts are lively, cultured and fun. Belgian Yves is a busy and dynamic young retired businessman and English Lynne offers wonderful aromatherapy sessions and has created splendours in the gardens and by the two lakes.

Rooms: 1 apartment (1 double, 1 twin & child's bed) with bath & wc.

Price: €96 for two.

Meals: Restaurants 6-15 km.

Closed: December-February.

From Carentan D903 for La Haye du Puits; at Baupte (5km) right D69 to Appeville & on for Houtteville; 2nd lane on right; house on left.

Yves Lejour & Lynne Wooster
Le Manoir d'Ozeville
Appeville
50500 Carentan
Manche
Tel: (0)2 33 71 55 98
Fax: (0)2 33 42 17 79
E-mail: ozeville@aol.com

Entry No: 235   Map: 2

The younger Franco-American Buissons have given a thorough internal facelift to this typical 18th-century Normandy farmhouse with its old stables and outbuildings flanking the dark-gravel courtyard. Rooms are pretty-papered in peach or green, beds have new mattresses, the rustic furniture is locally made with marble tops, the watercolours are done by an aunt. It is all simple, fresh and most welcoming. Jean works during the week but Nancy, perfectly bilingual, is very present and loving her new B&B activity. There's a flower garden outside and swings for the children.

Rooms: 2 doubles, both with bath & wc.

Price: €30 for two.

Meals: Restaurants in St Lô 5km.

Closed: Never.

From Cherbourg, N13 and N174 to St Lô. At St Georges-Montcocq, D191 to Villiers Fossard. In village, right on C7; house is 800m on right.

Jean & Nancy Buisson
Le Suppey
50680 Villiers Fossard
Manche
Tel: (0)2 33 57 30 23

Entry No: 236   Map: 2

The totally French farmhouse is colourful, neat and immaculate; one room is pink-flavoured, the other blue, with bits of crochet, a Norman wardrobe or a brass bed and a clean, compact shower room each; the gloriously ostentatious blue bathroom is also yours for the asking - giant tub and plants rampaging. But most special of all is the charming, elegant Madame Lepoittevin - she's full of smiles and laughter, has an abundant collection of dolls and she and her husband rejoice in *la convivialité* of B&B. You can picnic in the garden or cook your own on the barbecue.

Rooms: 1 double with shower & separate wc; 1 double with shower & wc.

Price: € 35 for two.

Meals: Choice of restaurants 4-10km.

Closed: End February-mid-March.

The Osmonds greet guests with big smiles, stories and much useful local information - they are such spontaneously welcoming, down-to-earth country folk that people come back year after year. Madame, a delightful, humorous woman, plays the organ in the village church. Bedrooms have old family furniture (admire *grand-mère's* elaborately crocheted bedcover), really good mattresses, simple washing arrangements. It is all spotless and guests have a good-sized dayroom with lots of plants and a kitchen in the old cider press.

Rooms: 1 double with shower & wc; 1 twin, 1 double, both with shower, sharing 2 wcs.

Price: € 34 for two.

Meals: Restaurant 1km; choice St Lô 4km; self-catering possible.

Closed: Never.

From St Lô D972 towards Coutances, through St Gilles; house signposted on left, 4km after St Gilles, on D972.

From St Lô D999 towards Villedieu for 3km; right D38 towards Canisy. House 1km along on right.

Jean & Micheline Lepoittevin
Saint Léger
50570 Quibou
Manche
Tel: (0)2 33 57 18 41
Fax: (0)2 33 57 18 41

Marie-Thérèse & Roger Osmond
La Rhétorerie
Route de Canisy
50750 St Ébremond de Bonfossé
Manche
Tel: (0)2 33 56 62 98

Entry No: 237 Map: 2

Entry No: 238 Map: 2

Normandy

The place is so French: rich carpeting on floors and walls, highly floral linen, masses of toiletries (one room is up a steep wooden staircase). Monsieur breeds horses and riding is possible for very experienced riders; the less horsey can enjoy visiting the stables which have produced some great show-jumpers. Madame cooks all the food, including her own bread and croissants, and meals are served in the brownly beamed kitchen/diner. She and her husband are attentive hosts, it is all snug and homey, the setting is charming, among hills, woods and fields - this would be a delightful place for a winter visit, too. *Gîte space for 6 people.*

Rooms: 1 double, 2 twins, all with shower & wc.

Price: €30.5 for two.

Meals: Dinner €15, including wine & coffee.

Closed: Never.

From the conservatory you can wrap your eyes round the abundantly flowered garden - it is Madame's pride and joy and she'll tell you all about gardening and medicinal plants - while you spy on the squirrels in the lime tree and indulge in a sinfully-laden breakfast table (dare try the *Kousmine*, a muesli-type concoction to keep you energised all day). Three rooms are in a converted outbuilding, two in the enchanting main house. Beds are brass or carved wood; there are lace and pink and granny-style touches in keeping with an old farmhouse, plus some fine antiques. *Gîte space for 2 people.*

Rooms: 1 twin, 3 doubles, 1 triple, all with shower & wc, 1 with kitchenette.

Price: €38-€43 for two.

Meals: Restaurant in village, 1.5km.

Closed: 1 week in January & Sept.

From Coutances D971 for Granville; fork quickly left D7 for Gavray 1.5km; left D27 to Nicorps; through village; first right; house on left, sign.

From Percy D58 towards Hambye then immed. left on D98 towards Sourdeval for 1.5km. House signed on right.

M & Mme Posloux
Les Hauts Champs
La Moinerie de Haut
50200 Nicorps
Manche
Tel: (0)2 33 45 30 56
Fax: (0)2 33 07 60 21

Daniel & Maryclaude Duchemin
Le Cottage de la Voisinière
Route de Sourdeval
50410 Percy, Manche
Tel: (0)2 33 61 18 47
Fax: (0)2 33 61 43 47
E-mail: cottage.voisiniere@wanadoo.fr
Web: perso.wanadoo.fr/cottagedelavoisiniere

Deep in the Norman lushness, this ancient farmhouse, originally a sentinel post to the Torigny château, sheltered pilgrims on their journey to Santiago de Compostela. Today's travellers can also rest their weary bones at L'Orgerie - it is superbly welcoming. The dogs greet you as you sip your *pommeau* aperitif and share intelligent conversation with delightful hosts, then dinner is taken in the towering dining room with its gallery and massive granite fireplace. The house is invitingly dark and cosy with age, the bedrooms are snug and few will mind the loo being down the corridor. Amazing value.

Rooms: 1 double, 1 twin (family suite), sharing shower & separate wc.

Price: € 30 for two.

Meals: Dinner € 12, including wine & coffee.

Closed: Never.

From Caen N175 SW towards Rennes & Villedieu. At Pont Farcy left on D52 towards Vire for 3km; house signed on right (DON'T turn to St Vigor).

Jacques & Jacqueline Goude
L'Orgerie
50420 Saint Vigor des Monts
Manche
Tel: (0)2 31 68 85 58

Entry No: 241   Map: **2**

Real, rural France is here with these solid, earthy, farming folk and Madame, who is a bit shy, has a lovely sunny smile. She keeps lots of poultry, still hopes to breed rare strains such as Rouen duck and always encourages guests to visit Sourdeval on Tuesdays to see the cattle market in full swing. Their rooms are unpretentiously simple with candlewick bedcovers, old floor tiles, wooden wardrobes and views across the valley. The family room has two beds on a mezzanine. Guests breakfast at one long table and are welcome to watch the milking. Real people, real value. *Gîte space for 2 people.*

Rooms: Main house: 1 triple, 1 double sharing shower & separate wc. Cottage: family room for 5, shower & wc.

Price: € 29 for two.

Meals: Choice of restaurants 5km.

Closed: Never.

From Sourdeval D977 for Vire 6km. Just before end of Manche sign right towards Le Val. House 2km along on right.

Jeanne & Raymond Desdoits
Le Val
Vengeons
50150 Sourdeval
Manche
Tel: (0)2 33 59 64 16
Fax: (0)2 33 69 36 99

Entry No: 242   Map: **2**

Normandy

The château's origins are mixed - some bits 17th-century, others 18th; Madame is thoroughly French and has lived in Paris, the deeply rural south-west and now Normandy with her four wonderfully-mannered children, her Dutch partner and their peaceful Labrador. She is strong, easy-going, independent and has a fine sense of humour, the children are a delight, the grounds are lush and those rolling views carry your eye for miles. Home-made cake with breakfast, refined regional cooking for dinner (vegetarian if asked for early) which may include home-grown strawberries and herbs.

Rooms: 3 doubles, all with bath or shower & wc.

Price: €45-€64.50 for two.

Meals: Dinner €15, including coffee; wine €9.

Closed: Christmas & New Year.

From Villedieu les Poêles N175 /D524 for Vire 1.5km; right D999 for Brécey. After Chérencé le H. left through St Martin B. to sawmill; follow signs to Loges sur Brécey. House 2km along, 2nd left after wood.

Nathalie de Drouas
Château des Boulais
Loges sur Brécey
50800 Saint Martin le Bouillant
Manche
Tel: (0)2 33 60 32 20
Fax: (0)2 33 60 45 20

Entry No: 243　　　Map: 2

Madame is smiling and eager to please, not too reserved, not gushing - the sweetest old lady. Hers is a typical, 19th-century village house. Pleasant, country-style bedrooms have floral wallpapers and mats on polished wood floors. There's an inviting, armchaired reading corner on the landing plus a big dayroom with a fireplace. Breakfast is served here at the long 10-seater table. There are (free) tennis courts, a swimming pool and restaurants close at hand and the proximity to Mont Saint Michel is a natural advantage. (When calling to book, better to have a French speaker to hand.)

Rooms: 1 double, 1 triple, sharing bath & wc; 1 twin with shower & wc.

Price: €31-€34 for two.

Meals: Gourmet auberge next door.

Closed: Never.

From Avranches N175 for Pontorson; 3km after Précey, right to Servon.

Mme Marie-Thérése Lesénéchal
Le Bourg
6 rue du Pont Morin
50170 Servon
Manche
Tel: (0)2 33 48 92 13

Entry No: 244　　　Map: 2

It is said there are as many horses as inhabitants in the area: your hosts train racehorses and are also bringing up five children in this deep country spot by the sea - Mont St Michel can be seen from the roof windows. They are energetic and sociable, have lots of time for guests and really enjoy doing B&B. Your rooms and bathrooms are refreshingly minimalist in their white paint and duvets with simple country or wicker furniture. In the morning, you go through a huge, immaculate kitchen to the simply-furnished yellow and blue dining room for a very generous breakfast.

Rooms: 1 twin, 1 double, both with bath & wc.

Price: € 55 for two.

Meals: Restaurants 3km.

Closed: Never.

Three big new rooms and a dayroom, all at the other end of the farmhouse from the two older rooms, all facing Mont St Michel! And that view is definitely worth the detour - you can walk to the Mount in two hours, or they have bikes for you. In the enclosed courtyard there are passion-fruit and figs. The Gédouins keep cows and pigs; Annick, who used to teach, makes delicious jams; Jean is Mayor - the council meets in his kitchen. Rooms are in pretty, country-floral style and one now has wheelchair access. All is rural peace in this tiny village by the marshes and there is a warm and kindly welcome from both generations of Gédouins.

Rooms: 1 double, 1 twin, both with bath & wc; 1 triple, 2 family, both with shower & wc.

Price: € 35-€ 43 for two.

Meals: Restaurants 500m-2km.

Closed: Never.

From A13/N176 exit Avranches for Granville; over bridge; left D911 for Jullouville; in Dragey right before petrol station 1km; right for Dragey l'Église; house 800m on right.

Florence & Olivier Brasme
Belleville
Route de Saint Marc
Dragey l'Église
50530 Sartilly, Manche
Tel: (0)2 33 48 93 96
Fax: (0)2 33 48 59 75
E-mail: belleville@9online.fr

From A84 exit 33 for St Malo/Pontorson on N175 for 9km; right to Servon; at church right for 500m - farm on left.

Annick, Jean & Valérie Gédouin
Le Petit Manoir
21 rue de la Pierre du Tertre
50170 Servon
Manche
Tel: (0)2 33 60 03 44
Fax: (0)2 33 60 17 79

Entry No: 245   Map: **2**

Entry No: 246   Map: **2**

These are simple farming folk, smiling and hospitable in their 'château': it has been renovated and modernised virtually beyond recognition - but the farm buildings are genuine. Set back from the (still audible) main road, the house 'lives' on the other side where you discover the original pediment and healing views of hills and woods. Bedrooms, freshly decorated in pink/dark green or blue/white, are simple with brass or wooden beds and mirrored armoires. Breakfast is taken at the long and convivial family dining table and Madame is eager to help you plan your day. The Botanical Gardens in Avranches are superb and Mont St Michel so close.

Rooms: 1 double, with shower & wc; 3 doubles, all with shower, sharing wc.

Price: € 30-€ 37 for two.

Meals: Restaurants 1.5km or Avranches 3km.

Closed: Never.

The extension to the lovely old stone farmhouse, with great windows to luscious views of garden and lake, is for guests on rainy days but the generous continental farmhouse breakfast is served by your bright, chatty hostess at a long table in the inviting, country-furnished living room where obscure farm antiquities parade. Good, fresh and simple bedrooms, three with that lovely view. Your hard-working hosts - dairy herd and show jumpers - are good company and, although there may be 60 cows in the cowshed, 6 horses in the paddock and a motorway over the hill, you could hear a kitten dance, the peace is so complete.

Rooms: 2 doubles, 1 triple, 1 family, all with shower & wc.

Price: € 36-€ 52 for two.

Meals: Ferme-auberge 3km.

Closed: Never.

From Avranches D973 towards Granville, across Pont Gilbert; 300m after shopping precinct, 1st drive on left.

From A84 or N175 exit 34 for Mt St Michel 800m; left D998 for Juilley 4.2km; D566 for Ferme du Gd Rouet; signs.

Eugène & Huguette Turgot
Le Château
Marcey les Grèves
50300 Avranches
Manche
Tel: (0)2 33 58 08 65

Christian & Isabelle Fardin
Le Grand Rouet
50220 Juilley
Manche
Tel: (0)2 33 60 65 25
Fax: (0)2 33 60 02 70
E-mail: c.fardin@wanadoo.fr

Normandy

Monsieur, a joyous fellow, formerly a senior fire officer, is proud of his restoration of the old farm (the B&B is his project, Madame works in town). He is an attentive, positive host, full of smiles and jokes. And has indeed done a good job. Old granite glints as you pass the softly-curtained entrance to the duplex where the whirlpool bath is reached via a staircase banistered with oak manger rails; the airy triple has antique beds and brightly-coloured curtains; the white breakfast room with its welcoming granite fireplace is simple and good and the fields around are open for all so no need to worry about the road at the front.

Rooms: 1 triple with bath & wc; 1 family, 1 suite, both with shower & wc.

Price: €55 for two.

Meals: Restaurants in St James, 6 km.

Closed: Never.

From A84 exit 33; right at r'bout & uphill for about 300m to next r'bout; left then left again D998 for St James; house on right after 5km.

Laurence & Jean-Malo Tizon
Les Blotteries
50220 Juilley
Manche
Tel: (0)2 33 60 84 95
Fax: (0)2 33 60 84 95
E-mail: bb@les-blotteries.com
Web: www.les-blotteries.com

Entry No: 249   Map: **2**

Masses of flowers sweeten the air but this is definitely a working farm with 800 pigs and a high-tech milking shed that attracts interest from far and wide; you can watch too. The young owners enjoy contact with visitors and Madame pays special attention to breakfast - her apple tart is delicious. Then you can walk directly out into the lovely countryside to see the little chapel or the local château. The guest rooms, one in the house, the other with its own entrance, are simple and good. This place is as real, unpretentious and comfortable as ever.
Gîte space for 14 people.

Rooms: 2 doubles, each with shower & wc.

Price: €30 for two.

Meals: Good choice of restaurants 5km.

Closed: Never.

From Pontorson, N175 to Aucey la Plaine; follow signs to Chambres d'Hôtes La Provostière for 3km. Farm between Pontorson & Vessey.

Maryvonne & René Feuvrier
La Provostière
50170 Aucey la Plaine
Manche
Tel: (0)2 33 60 33 67
Fax: (0)2 33 60 37 00

Entry No: 250   Map: **2**

What a treat to stay in this gently grand, gracious château where the Count's family have lived since it was built in 1763. He and the Countess have lived in Paris and Chicago - theirs is an elegant, unstuffy lifestyle in which you are welcome to join. Bedrooms are beautifully furnished and decorated with personal touches, family portraits and embroidered linen sheets. Breakfast, including home-made jams and tarts served on fine china, is taken in the lovely, round, panelled and mirrored dining room. Its French windows give onto the grounds which come complete with lake and private chapel. *Spanish spoken. Gîte space for 6 people.*

Rooms: 2 doubles, 2 suites, all with bath & shower & wc.

Price: €115-€145 for two; €135-€145 for three.

Meals: Restaurants 7-15km.

Closed: Never.

An authentic farm B&B in a glorious setting - ivy on the walls, beamed attic bedrooms with fresh flowers, woodland walks, lake and château across the way - and an authentic farming family. Jean-Paul and Brigitte are a friendly, interesting couple, travel a lot and talk well. He is a dairy farmer and arbitrator, she is on the council. Meals (they are delicious) are taken in the lovely dining room with its huge fireplace. A splendid staircase leads you up to the good, snug, cottagey yet unfussy guest rooms. Children love it too - there are games galore and it is a working farm.

Rooms: 2 doubles, 2 family, all with bath or shower & wc.

Price: €38 for two.

Meals: Dinner €14, including wine & coffee.

Closed: Never.

From Avranches for Mt St Michel exit 34; N175 exit D40 Mt St Michel/Antrain; left for Antrain; left D308 for St Senier de Beuvron: château entrance 800m.

From Cherbourg A84 exit 34 for Mt St Michel/St Malo 600m; exit for Mt St Michel/Rennes D43 for Rennes. At r'about D40 for Rennes, 5.5km; D308 left; signs.

Régis & Nicole de Roquefeuil-Cahuzac
Château de Boucéel
50240 Vergoncey, Manche
Tel: (0)2 33 48 34 61
Fax: (0)2 33 48 16 26
E-mail: chateaudebouceel@wanadoo.fr
Web: www.chateaudebouceel.com

Jean-Paul & Brigitte Gavard
La Ferme de l'Étang
Boucéel
Vergoncey
50240 St James, Manche
Tel: (0)2 33 48 34 68
Fax: (0)2 33 48 48 53
E-mail: j.p.gavard@club-internet.fr

Le Gautrais is clean and comfortable, in solid farmhouse style. The old stable block, entirely modernised for B&B in the 1970s, has stripped wooden floors and easy furnishings, cots in the attic rooms and a kitchenette, making it ideal for family stopovers. The Balcony Room is in a league of its own with exposed timbers, country antiques and even... a (glassed-in) balcony. Madame is very quiet, "makes a superb soufflé" and mouthwatering Norman cuisine. The poetically-named but perfectly ordinary Two Estuaries motorway now provides quick access 1km away. *Gîte space for 6 people.*

Rooms: 1 triple, 1 double, 1 twin, 1 quadruple, all with bath or shower & wc.

Price: € 36 for two.

Meals: Dinner € 13, including wine & coffee.

Closed: Never.

From A84 exit 32 at St James then D12, following signs for Super U store for 900m towards Antrain. House on right.

François & Catherine Tiffaine
La Gautrais
50240 Saint James
Manche
Tel: (0)2 33 48 31 86
Fax: (0)2 33 48 58 17

GREETINGS

Good Morning and Good Afternoon are both translated as *Bonjour* (Good Day). Good Evening is *Bonsoir* which can also serve instead of *Bonne nuit* (Goodnight) when retiring to bed. Upon meeting, *Salut!* has, as its nearest equivalent, the American 'Hi' and, though it's less colloquial, the English 'Hello'. It is also used as a less formal expression of farewell than *Au revoir.*

FORMS OF ADDRESS

The French are generally more formal than the 'Anglo-Saxons'. For the example, they move less easily onto first-name terms. This reluctance is not a sign of coldness, they are not being unfriendly, it's simply a different way of relating to others, an Old National Habit to be respected, we feel, like any other tribal ritual.

The same applies to the question of when or if to progress from the formal *vous* form to the more familiar *tu*. If in doubt, wait for the signal from them as to when you have achieved more intimate status. A more quirky example is how to say 'Hello Mrs Jones'. It is considered rather familiar to say *Bonjour Monsieur Dupont* or *Bonjour Madame Martin*, i.e. to use their name. They just say *Bonjour Monsieur* or *Bonjour Madame*, which are not nearly as formal in everyday use as our 'Sir' and 'Madam'. And it means you have to worry less about remembering people's names.

Brittany

It's a privilege to stay in this amazing, artistic house where the traditional and the esoteric, the antique and the contemporary rub happy shoulders - a deeply aesthetic atmosphere, yet utterly without pretension, as is your hostess. She is warm and talented and has gathered some wonderful wooden artefacts; her husband is a brain scientist and they keep a quietly civilised, cultured house which like-minded guests will revel in. The guest rooms, all different, are beautifully furnished, full of interest and space and have good bathrooms.

Rooms: 3 doubles, 1 triple, all with bath, shower & wc.

Price: €70-€75 for two.

Meals: Wide choice of good restaurants nearby.

Closed: Never.

The sea! The rocks! Fear not fisherfolk – if the lighthouse cannot save you from wrecking on the reefs, the carved calvaries will send up prayers for your souls ashore.

From St Malo D155/D76 for Rennes; right at 'Irrigation' building before La Gouesnière; house 2nd on right (black gates).

Mme Françoise Duriez
La Haute Barbotais
35350 Saint Méloir des Ondes
Ille-et-Vilaine
Tel: (0)2 99 89 15 42

Entry No: 254   **Map:** 2

House and owner are imbued with the calm of a balmy summer's morning, whatever the weather - timeless simplicity reigns inside, modernity bustles on the village street outside the front door. Isabelle's talent seems to touch the very air that fills her old family house. There is nothing superfluous: simple carved pine furniture, an antique wrought-iron cot, dhurries on scrubbed plank floors, palest yellow or mauve walls to reflect the ocean-borne light, harmonious striped or gingham curtains. Starfish and many-splendoured pebbles keep the house sea-connected. The unspoilt seaside village is worth the trip too.

Rooms: 2 doubles, 1 twin, all with bath & wc; 2 doubles, both with shower & wc (1 fully equipped for the disabled).

Price: €44.5 for two.

Meals: Choice of restaurants in village.

Closed: Never.

Old bones: the largest mammoth skeleton ever discovered in Europe was found at Mont Dol; old stones: Mont St Michel is so close. But it's Marie-Madeleine who makes this place special. She is all attention: in winter, up before breakfast to lay the fire; in summer, she gives her all to garden and orchard. Gentle, bright-eyed Jean says that, tied to the farm, he "travels through his guests". Of course the wear and tear of returning guests shows in some of the linen - so what? Rooms are good, the fireplace huge, your hosts know and love their region intimately and the sea is just 3km away. *Stays of two nights or more preferred.*

Rooms: 3 rooms for 2-4 people, all with shower or bath & wc.

Price: €40 for two.

Meals: Choice of restaurants in Dol de Bretagne 4km.

Closed: Never.

From St Malo, N137 towards Rennes. 6km after St Malo, right on D117 to St Suliac (3km from N137 exit to village entrance). Road leads to Grande Rue down to port; house at top on right.

From St Malo N137 for Rennes 15km; exit N176 for Mt St Michel 12km. At Dol de Bretagne D80 for St Broladre 3km; left D85 for Cherrueix; house sign on right before 3rd little bridge.

Isabelle Rouvrais
Les Mouettes
17 Grande Rue
35430 Saint Suliac
Ille-et-Vilaine
Tel: (0)2 99 58 30 41
Fax: (0)2 99 58 39 41

Jean & Marie-Madeleine Glémot
La Hamelinais
35120 Cherrueix
Ille-et-Vilaine
Tel: (0)2 99 48 95 26
Fax: (0)2 99 48 89 23
E-mail: à venir

Entry No: 255   Map: **2**

Entry No: 256   Map: **2**

The little lakeside house is a dream, in the old bakery, far enough from the main house to feel secluded, snugly romantic and utterly seductive. The new, split-level room in the big house is larger and just as pretty. The whole place is idyllic, bucolic - the beauty of the setting takes you by surprise. You can fish or observe all sorts of water-dwelling folk. If your need for intimacy is deep, then Catherine will deliver breakfast and dinner (course by course) to your hideaway. But nicer still to join them at table; they are young and delightful and we have received nothing but praise for them.

Rooms: 1 double/quadruple in split-level room with *salon*, shower & wc; 1 double/quadruple in cottage with *salon*, shower & wc.

Price: €43-€54 for two.

Meals: Dinner €16, including wine & coffee.

Closed: Never.

Constantin is the perfect French townhouse: elegant, refined, light yet solidly comfortable, inside and out. The owners, he a photographer, she a watercolourist, have applied all their talent and taste to renovating it. The guest duplex, above Madame's studio in a separate little house, is fresh and romantic with home-sewn furnishings in restful colours - admire the curtains cleverly made from antique linen sheets. You may dine with your gentle, artistic hosts in their delicious white dining/sitting room and even take a painting course.

Rooms: Duplex for 4 with shower & wc.

Price: €42 for two.

Meals: Dinner €17, including wine & coffee.

Closed: Never.

From St Malo N137 to St Pierre de Plesguen; by church D10 towards Lanhelin for 1.5km; follow signs on right to Le Pont Ricoul Chambres d'Hôtes.

From Rennes N12 W for 36km exit St Méen le Grand. In town centre, back to Mairie, take Ave Foch between Crédit Agricole & Pharmacie. No. 39 on left.

Catherine & François Grosset
Le Pont Ricoul
35720 Saint Pierre de Plesguen
Ille-et-Vilaine
Tel: (0)2 99 73 92 65
Fax: (0)2 99 73 94 17
E-mail: pontricoul@aol.com

Catherine & Luc Ruan
Le Clos Constantin
39 avenue Foch
35290 Saint Méen le Grand
Ille-et-Vilaine
Tel: (0)2 99 09 53 09
Fax: (0)2 99 09 53 09
E-mail: luc.ruan@wanadoo.fr

Entry No: 257   Map: **2**

Entry No: 258   Map: **2**

On the fine Place du Vieux Marché, this, the oldest house in beautiful Bécherel, 'City of Books', has elegance and long country views. A woman of talent and refined taste, Monique speaks perfect English, loves people and, if you ask, will guide you round Caradeuc Park and the architecture of Bécherel. Guest rooms, each with its own entrance and a super bathroom, are across the patio in the 17th-century weaver's house. *Juliette*, the romantic, in cool blue and warm ochre, has a huge stone fireplace; *Joséphine*, of the roses, is prettily pink with pine furniture and garden view; *Marie* has a fascinating antique needlework theme.

Rooms: 1 double, 1 twin, 1 double/triple, all with bath or shower & wc.

Price: €50-€65 for two.

Meals: Dinner €16, including wine & coffee; crêperie in village.

Closed: November-March.

From St Malo N137 S for Rennes 43km. At Tinténiac exit, right D20 to Bécherel. House on main square near church.

Monique Lecourtois-Canet
Le Logis de la Filanderie
3 rue de la Filanderie
35190 Bécherel, Ille-et-Vilaine
Tel: (0)2 99 66 73 17
Fax: (0)2 99 66 79 07
E-mail: filanderie@aol.com
Web: www.filanderie.com

The atmosphere, history and utter silence of Quengo will call you back, not its cosiness or squeaky cleanliness. Madame, a straightforward, friendly *Bretonne*, once managed the 9,000 egg-laying hens. The château has a private chapel, a monumental oak staircase, marble fireplaces, 1900s wallpaper and about 30 rooms - too many corners for housework to reach every day; underfoot is a mosaic floor by Italian craftsmen, overhead are hand-painted beams by a local 19th-century artist. The bathroom has a claw-footed bath, bedrooms are old-fashioned too; the vast park offers a wood, a lake and an island. Amazing.

Rooms: 1 double, 1 triple, both with basin & bidet, sharing bathroom & 3 separate wcs.

Price: €34 for two.

Meals: Choice of restaurants 4-6km.

Closed: Mid-October-March.

From N24 for St Brieuc exit at Bédée D72 to Irodouer; 1st right before church; château entrance 600m on left.

Mme de Lorgerie
Château du Quengo
35850 Irodouer
Ille-et-Vilaine
Tel: (0)2 99 39 81 47

A delicious little 'French' garden - low walls, box hedges, giant camellia, masses of flowers and a herb patch - comes with the lovely 18th-century townhouse on the church square. Inside, there are hand-decorated beams, antiques from 25 years of dealing and from Madame's family (her grandmother lived here), plus an ocean-themed loo. A sumptuous breakfast is supplied by your lovely, leisurely hostess who's all covered in smiles with a soft young voice. She has Breton, Creuzois, Basque and Flemish origins and spent her childhood 'commuting' between Morocco and Brittany. This makes for a powerfully interesting old lady!

Rooms: 1 double, 1 suite, all with bath & wc.

Price: €46 for two; €77 for suite for four.

Meals: Choice of restaurants in town.

Closed: Never.

Merlin lived here. Well, in Brocéliande forest... and everyone knows he was a Breton not a Cornish wizard. From one bedroom you can see the forest only 500m away, from another, which has a little 18th-century marble fireplace that still works, you look out over fields. Big, bright, interesting decoration throughout thanks to Madame's good taste and new ideas in handling her lovely big old manor house. And old it is, mainly 1760s with some 15th-century bits. She serves breakfast as late as you want with real squeezed orange juice and is a most unusual, interesting companion. *Gîte space for 6 people.*

Rooms: 2 doubles, 1 suite for 4, all with bath or shower & wc.

Price: €46 for two.

Meals: Choice of restaurants 1-5km.

Closed: Never.

From Rennes N24 W for 27km to Plélan le Grand. House on church square: granite façade & ivy hedge.

From Rennes N24 SW to Plélan le Grand; right at church D59 towards St Malon sur Mel; 1st left: Chemin des Châteaux for 1km. House on top of small hill, entrance behind on left.

Mme Hubert de Floris
La Treberdière
Place de l'Église
35380 Plélan le Grand
Ille-et-Vilaine
Tel: (0)2 99 06 83 05

Mme Christine Hermenier
Manoir de la Ruisselère
35380 Paimpont
Ille-et-Vilaine
Tel: (0)2 99 06 85 94

Entry No: 261   Map: 2

Entry No: 262   Map: 2

A place for an intimate dinner by the fire in your own room - and breakfast here next morning. Each room has its own mini-garden with potted shrubs and front door, each now with private service and relatively little contact. Madame's passion for *brocante* and embroidery brings much individuality to the bedrooms and in her mini-boutique you can sit and read on an antique chair then buy it as you leave. They are a caring but busy couple so the atmosphere is not particularly *familiale*. It is in a tiny hamlet and very peaceful.

Rooms: 1 large suite for 5, 1 triple, both with shower & wc. 'Studio' also available.

Price: €49-€57 for two; lovers' night €122.

Meals: Dinner €16, including wine & coffee.

Closed: Never.

From Rennes D163/D41 S to Janzé; right D92 for La Couyère about 6km; house on right in La Tremblais: yellow gate & sign. Park behind.

Claudine & Raymond Gomis
La Raimonderie
La Tremblais
35320 La Couyère
Ille-et-Vilaine
Tel: (0)2 99 43 14 39
Web: www.la-raimonderie.com

Entry No: 263   Map: **2**

Fear not, the farm mess is forgotten once you reach the cottage and the long, rural views beyond. Through that timbered porch, a sprightly, brave and unpretentious lady will lead you into her big, wood-floored and ceilinged country dining room - warmed in winter by the old granite fireplace, it is uncluttered and soberly French. Bedrooms are simple and unfussy too, with sloping ceilings and soft rugs, roof windows or dormers; her garden is tended with love and pride and produces vegetables for dinner, when you can enjoy intelligent and wide-ranging conversation (in French) with an interesting companion.

Rooms: 1 triple with shower & wc; 1 double, 1 single sharing continental bath & separate wc.

Price: €41 for two; €53 for three.

Meals: Dinner €14.

Closed: Never.

From Rennes N137 S exit Poligné D47 4km; left to L'Aubrais; right into and across farmyard, down lane 20m, cottage on right.

Yvette Guillopé
Épineu
35890 Bourg des Comptes
Ille-et-Vilaine
Tel: (0)2 99 52 16 84

Entry No: 264   Map: **2**

Sheer delight for lovers of the utterly personal, even eccentric. In this miniature museum of a house where the stunningly-draped orange dining room leads to an elegant yellow *salon*, the infectiously vibrant Rhona will introduce you to her wiggly Chinese sofa, her husband's regimental drum, an 18th-century looking-glass (one of a remarkable collection) and other cherished household gods. A home like no other, unsurpassed hospitality, a remarkable garden (climb up to the second terrace with a book), a comfortable bed (one has a glass door onto its fine bathroom), a generous and elegant breakfast. Unforgettable.

Rooms: 2 doubles, both with bath, shower & wc.

Price: €53 for two.

Meals: Wide choice of restaurants close by.

Closed: 1 November-28 February.
From Dinan central square, take Rue de Lehon, through Porte St Louis, follow road down, bear left below ramparts, straight across into Rue de Coëtquen.

Rhona Lockwood
53/55 rue de Coëtquen
22100 Dinan
Côtes-d'Armor
Tel: (0)2 96 85 23 49
Fax: (0)2 96 87 51 44

Entry No: 265   Map: **2**

There's no other like it: an extraordinary, rather crumbly old château (the Viscount's ancestor built it in 1373), the sea at the bottom of the drive, vast and wonderful guest rooms, a lively, lovable couple of aristocratic hosts, bent on riding, hunting and entertaining you. You breakfast in the upstairs *salon*, or downstairs, through the low stone arch, in the room with the boar's head and other bits of personality - such fun. Madame is applying energy and good taste to renovating some of the 30 rooms. One suite is pink, another blue and yellow. Beds are canopied, windows high, portraits ancestral, rugs cotton - atmosphere unreal yet utterly alive. *Gîte space for 4 people.*

Rooms: 2 suites, 1 double, all with bath or shower & wc.

Price: €68.50-€114.50 for two; €24.50 per extra person

Meals: Good choice of restaurants 5km.

Closed: October-April.

From St Brieuc N12 for Lamballe, exit Yffigniac-Hillion; left D80 to Hillion; D34 for Morieux for about 200m to roadside cross on left by château gates.

Vicomtesse Louis du Fou de Kerdaniel
Château de Bonabry
22120 Hillion
Côtes-d'Armor
Tel: (0)2 96 32 21 06
Fax: (0)2 96 32 21 06

Entry No: 266   Map: **1**

Brittany

So very aristocratic; a 15th-century manor of such character and history: tower, turrets, monumental fireplaces, worn spiral staircase, ancestral portraits, fine furniture. The bedrooms have space, taste, arched doors, good bathrooms and the great Breton breakfast can be brought to your room if you wish. Madame planted the lovely garden some 40 years ago and still tends it; Monsieur is gracious and well-travelled. Their welcome is elegant, their conversation intelligent, their house a delight and their son breeds racehorses on the other half of the estate. *Minimum stay two nights.*

Rooms: 2 twins, both with bath & wc.

Price: €76 for two.

Meals: Choice of restaurants 7-10 km.

Closed: November-Easter

Here is a long, low Breton house built on hard Breton granite, guarded by a soft Breton Spaniel and kept by a relaxed and friendly Breton woman whose family has owned it for generations and who lives in the little house. Old wood is everywhere - ceilings, wardrobes, beams, beds; there are fabrics and fancies: gingham cloths, floral curtains, lace cushions. Breakfasts and evening meals (which must be booked ahead) are cooked on a wood-fired range and served on attractive rough pottery at separate tables in the guests' dining room.

Rooms: 3 doubles, 1 twin, 1 triple, 1 double & bunks, all with bath or shower & wc.

Price: €39-€41 for two.

Meals: Dinner €15, including wine & coffee.

Closed: Never.

From N12 exit Bégard/ Plouaret (between Guingamp & Morlaix) to Plouaret; D11 for Lannion to Kerauzern; D30 left towards St Michel en Grève/Ploumilliau, cross railway & cont. 3km; left at sign 100m, left again to end.

From Dinard, D168 to Ploubalay & D768 to Plancoët; D19 to St Lormel; left opposite school at far end of village; follow signs for 1.5km.

M & Mme Gérard de Bellefon
Manoir de Kerguéréon
Ploubezre
22300 Lannion
Côtes-d'Armor
Tel: (0)2 96 38 91 46

Évelyne Ledé
La Pastourelle
Saint Lormel
22130 Plancoët
Côtes-d'Armor
Tel: (0)2 96 84 03 77
Fax: (0)2 96 84 03 77

Entry No: 267   Map: 1

Entry No: 268   Map: 2

Inside the enclosed courtyard you discover the charms of this 17th-century grey stone presbytery. Walled gardens and an orchard for picnics complete the peaceful, private mood. The interestingly-furnished rooms have lots of personal touches, particularly the biggest which is high and stylish and has an amazing, 50's deco, bathroom. The cosy, cottagey, low-beamed attic rooms have small shower rooms (not for taller types). A comfy lived-in feel pervades this house. Madame knows the area "like her pocket" and has itineraries for your deeper discovery of secret delights (two or three days?). Good food but make sure your dinner booking is firm. *Gîte space for 6 people.*

Rooms: 1 double, 2 twins, all with bath or shower & wc.

Price: €50 for two.

Meals: Dinner €20, including wine & coffee.

Closed: Never.

A genuine Breton château with a larger-than-life Countess, Kermezan has been in the family for 600 years. Its 17th-19th-century version is a masterpiece of understated elegance: high ceilings, generous windows, a granite-hearthed, tapestry-walled guest sitting room where old books and family portraits remind you this is "just an ordinary family house". Madame, dynamic and adorable, loves her visitors. All the rooms, varying in size and character, are fascinating, though we preferred *La Jaune* for its panelling and lovely view. Worth every penny. *Gîte space for 10.*

Rooms: 3 doubles, 2 twins, all with bath, shower & wc.

Price: €76.50–€100 for two.

Meals: Crêperie in village; excellent restaurant nearby.

Closed: Never.

From Guingamp N12 towards Morlaix, exit Louargat. From Louargat church, D33 to Tregrom (7km). House in village centre opp. church (blue door in wall).

From St Brieuc N12 to Guingamp; D8 towards Tréguier. At Pommerit Jaudy left at lights; signposted.

Nicole de Morchoven
L'Ancien Presbytère
22420 Plouaret
Côtes-d'Armor
Tel: (0)2 96 47 94 15
Fax: (0)2 96 47 94 15

Comte & Comtesse de Kermel
Château de Kermezen
22450 Pommerit Jaudy
Côtes-d'Armor
Tel: (0)2 96 91 35 75
Fax: (0)2 96 91 35 75
E-mail: micheldekermel@kermezen.com

Entry No: 269   Map: **1**

Entry No: 270   Map: **1**

The grand 15th-century Breton *longère*, that has been in the Beaupère family for four generations, is now a perfect place for golfers with a nine-hole golf course plus all the trappings (clubhouse, lessons, socialising) - and the added charm of a farm atmosphere, a cosy house and carp ponds for those with rods. Madame, who paints, has a flair for decorating with velvet and florals, plants, paintings, sculptures and photographs - her rooms are very comfortable and she is charming. The old Breton bread oven is working again for the baking of bread or even, occasionally, the roasting of sucking pig.

Rooms: 2 twins, 2 doubles, all with bath or shower & wc.

Price: €48 for two.

Meals: Restaurants nearby.

Closed: Never.

Breakfast in the big traditional dining room includes gentle piped music and Breton pancakes. As well as tending her immaculate garden, Madame collects dolls and other bits of folklore that peek out from nooks and corners. Great carved mirror-fronted wardrobes are standard, beds are firm and comfortable, floors are polished wood, bathrooms are modern and the dominant colour is blue (even the radiators). There is a kitchen annexe for self-catering, climbing frames for children in the front field and bikes are available. You will feel well looked after in this quiet country place with direct, genuine farming folk. *Gîte space for 25 people.*

Rooms: 2 doubles, 1 triple, all with bath or shower & wc.

Price: €37 for two.

Meals: Choice of restaurants in Yffiniac 4km; self-catering possible.

Closed: Never.

From N12 exit Yffiniac (NOT Yffiniac Gare) into village. Go 1km then left towards Plédran, through La Croix Orin; Le Grenier is down hill on left, 3.5km from Yffiniac centre.

From Dinan N176 for St Brieuc. At Plélan le Petit D19 right to St Michel de Plélan. House sign left 1km after village.

Odile & Henri Beaupère
La Corbinais
22980 Saint Michel de Plélan
Côtes-d'Armor
Tel: (0)2 96 27 64 81
Fax: (0)2 96 27 68 45
E-mail: corbinais@corbinais.com
Web: www.corbinais.com

Marie-Reine & Fernand Loquin
Le Grenier
22120 Yffiniac
Côtes-d'Armor
Tel: (0)2 96 72 64 55
Fax: (0)2 96 72 68 74
E-mail: le.grenier@wanadoo.fr
Web: www.le.grenier.com

Entry No: 271   Map: **2**

Entry No: 272   Map: **1**

The everyday becomes remarkable in these people's hands: modern houses have a hard time getting into this book but Malik sailed in. Clad in red cedar, open-plan to provide space for six children, its wood, metal and glass are in perfect harmony; only the best materials are used and every tiny detail has been taken care of: plain white covers on beds, Eastern-style cushions and wall hangings on plain walls, superb beds and towels, shower pressure just right. Breakfast, beautiful and *un peu brunch*, is as carefully thought out as the house. Lovely people and an exquisite, serene house that seems to hug its garden to its heart.

Rooms: 1 suite for 2 with *salon*, 1 suite for 4 (2 bedrooms), both with shower & wc.

Price: €52 for two.

Meals: Restaurants within walking distance.

Closed: December-March.

From Dinan N176 W for St Brieuc for about 12km. Exit right to Plélan le Petit. Follow signs to Centre/Mairie; at Mairie right for St Maudez, then 2nd right.

Martine & Hubert Viannay
Malik
Chemin de l'Étoupe
22980 Plélan le Petit, Côtes-d'Armor
Tel: (0)2 96 27 62 71/
(0)6 09 92 35 21
E-mail: martineviannay@nomade.fr
Web: perso.infonie.fr/malikhotes

Entry No: 273   Map: 2

Enter and you will understand why we chose this modernised house: the ever-changing light of the great bay shimmers in through vast swathes of glass. In guest rooms too you can sit in your armchair and gaze as boats go by. Or take 10 minutes and walk to the beach. Guy chose the house so he could see his small ship at anchor out there (lucky guests may be taken for a sail) and Marie-Clo has enlivened the interior with her talented patchwork and embroidery. It is calm, light, bright; they are attentive and generous and breakfast is seriously good. *Gîte space for 4 people.*

Rooms: 2 doubles, both with sitting area, sea view, shower & wc.

Price: €50 for two.

Meals: Lots of restaurants in Perros Guirec.

Closed: Never.

From Lannion D788 N to Perros Guirec; follow signs to Port; coastal road round bay for approx. 1km; left at sign. (Will fax map or collect you from railway station.)

Marie-Clo & Guy Biarnès
41 rue de la Petite Corniche
BP 24
22700 Perros Guirec, Côtes-d'Armor
Tel: (0)2 96 23 28 08
Fax: (0)2 96 23 28 23
E-mail: guy.biarnes@wanadoo.fr
Web: perso.wanadoo.fr/corniche/

Entry No: 274   Map: 1

The sheltered, flowered courtyard fills the windows of the guest rooms in the converted stables behind the main farmhouse. They are spotless and stylish in that slightly stark classic French way, softened by books, plants and personal touches, antiques and the odd deco piece. Great bathrooms and a small guest sitting room, too. Breakfast - home-made croissants and jams - is served at individual tables in the owner's chandeliered living room. Both Édith and Jean-Claude were born in Paris but have Breton roots. Édith runs the house and is friendly, chatty and elegant. Quiet countryside 4km from the sea.

Rooms: 2 doubles, 1 twin, 1 apartment for 4/5.

Price: €53 for two.

Meals: Good restaurants 4km.

Closed: 16 November-Easter.

Squarely planted in its Breton soil, this is totally a family house open to guests, not a purpose-converted affair. The children run the farm and the Gralls, genuine Breton-speaking Bretons, have time for visitors. After a blissful night - rooms have warm traditional décor, excellent mattresses, neat modern bathrooms - and a bucolic awakening to birdsong in the fields, come down to Madame's home-made crêpes or *far breton* at their square Breton table beside the deeply-carved sideboard. She's an expansive soul, gentle and chatty. Family antiques, family warmth, peace and unity that reassure and relax.

Rooms: 2 doubles, 1 twin, all with shower & wc.

Price: €40 for two.

Meals: Restaurant 2.5km.

Closed: Never.

From St Malo D168 towards St Brieuc. At first roundabout after Ploubalay D26 towards Plessix Balisson for 4km to hamlet - house on right, signposted.

From St Pol de Léon D10 W to Cléder. Arriving in Cléder, take road to sea for 2km; left following signs to Ferme de Kernévez.

Édith & Jean-Claude Rey du Boissieu
Le Clos Saint Cadreuc
22650 Ploubalay
Côtes-d'Armor
Tel: (0)2 96 27 32 43
Fax: (0)2 96 27 32 43
E-mail: jc.reyduboissieu@mail.dotcom.fr

François & Marceline Grall
Kernévez
29233 Cléder
Finistère
Tel: (0)2 98 69 41 14
Web: www.ifrance.com/kernevez

Crow's Rock Manor has always had these big, airy, wood-floored, lofty-ceilinged, chandeliered rooms with their superb views of the generous grounds. Built in the 1840s by well-travelled writer/merchant Corbière (his better-known poet son Tristan was a protégé of Verlaine's), it has been admirably restored by your young and sociable hosts and is definitely a special place with its air of old-style, refined but not overstated luxury. For a modern touch, step up to your marble bath to gaze out to hills and woods on two sides. Breakfast may include *far breton* and crêpes, strawberries and home-made jam.

Rooms: 3 twins, all with bath & wc.

Price: €67 for two.

Meals: Restaurants nearby.

Closed: Never.

Above ancient Breton rocks, sea and pine trees, this modern house hides fine old pieces, ancestral portraits, family trees. Your hosts, a great mix of French aristocracy and American academe, are cultured, polyglot, eager to share their love of Brittany. Bedrooms, cosily clothed in velvet and patchwork, decorated with unusual pictures (worth asking about) and good furniture, have a colourful bathroom each, one on a different floor, one containing two bunk beds! (An independent wc and basin allow parents to ablute while offspring sleep.) The big, light, blue and yellow kitchen is a warm place for meals; garden and sea beckon on the doorstep.

Rooms: 1 suite, 1 double, 1 twin, all with bath & wc.

Price: €65 for two.

Meals: Dinner €15-€23, including wine & coffee.

Closed: November-Easter.

From Morlaix follow right bank of river N, take SECOND right signed Ploujean (hairpin bend) for 500m. Right towards Ploujean; house 3rd on right.

From Morlaix D64 for 'Lannion par la Côte'; Locquirec is 21km from Morlaix, 22km from Lannion. In village, towards 'Sables Blancs'. House on this road.

Étienne & Armelle Delaisi
Manoir de Roch ar Brini
29600 Morlaix Ploujean
Finistère
Tel: (0)2 98 72 01 44
Fax: (0)2 98 88 04 49
E-mail: rochbrini@aol.com
Web: www.brittanyguesthouse.com

Comte & Comtesse Hubert de Germiny
Villa Germiny
11 rue de Keraël
29241 Locquirec, Finistère
Tel: (0)2 98 67 47 11
Fax: (0)2 98 67 47 11
E-mail: lorraine-de-germiny@wanadoo.fr

Entry No: 277   Map: **1**

Entry No: 278   Map: **1**

Yolande is a smiling, helpful mother of five, Charlick the most sociable workaholic you could find. Having beautifully renovated their old Breton weavers' house, they are converting other ruins as well as running the small *auberge* that serves traditional dishes and meats grilled on the open fire. They are active, artistic (he has momentarily set his darkly expressive painting aside) and fun. The rooms have clever layouts, colour schemes and fabrics and brilliant use of wood, all informed by an artist's creative imagination - superb in their rustic elegance. All is gentle and soft and there are animals and swings for children's delight. *Minimum stay 2 nights in summer.*

Rooms: 3 quadruple, 2 double, all with bath or shower & wc.

Price: €42-€60 for two.

Meals: Dinner €17; wine €9-14.

Closed: Christmas-New Year.

On the fascinating, desolate heath of the Monts d'Arée, in the *Arée* National Park, Kreisker stands in a tiny, quiet hamlet - a sensitive, utterly Breton conversion, all local stone, slate roofs and giant slabs of schist from the old floors. Inside it's scrubbed wood, more stone, ethnic rugs, fresh cotton and pretty china. The independent guest room has a lovely blue/grey-clothed brass bed and a fine bathroom. After the feast that is breakfast, your ears ringing with Madame's knowledgeable talk of Breton culture, go and explore this ancient land. *Children welcome if you bring a child's bed. Gîte space for 8 people.*

Rooms: 1 double with bathroom.

Price: €39 for two.

Meals: Crêperies & restaurants 2.5-7km; book ahead.

Closed: Never.

From St Brieuc N12 for Morlaix, exit 'Plouigneau' to Plougonven; cont. for Plourin lès Morlaix 5km. House on right, sign.

Charlick & Yolande de Ternay
La Grange de Coatélan
29640 Plougonven
Finistère
Tel: (0)2 98 72 60 16

From Morlaix, D785 for Quimper. At La Croix Cassée, D42 to Botmeur. 200m after town hall head for Feuillée; 1st right.

Marie-Thérèse & Jean-Bernard Solliec
Kreisker
29690 Botmeur
Finistère
Tel: (0)2 98 99 63 02
Fax: (0)2 98 99 63 02
E-mail: msol@club-internet.fr

The two most memorable things here are Marie-Christine's smile as she talks about her native Brittany and the sympathetic use of wood on floor, ceilings and walls. Guest rooms are in the old cider-press - pretty and fresh with skylight windows and handsome antiques. Breakfast, perhaps with Breton music in the background (to make the Breton dresses dance?), is prepared in the guest dayroom and eaten at the long refectory table there, with views of the garden and books all around. It is quiet and comfortable and you can be quite independent. Dinner with Madame's daughter can be arranged.

Rooms: 1 double, 1 triple, both with shower & wc.

Price: €41 for two.

Meals: Dinner €14, including wine & coffee; restaurants nearby.

Closed: Never.

From Morlaix D785 towards Quimper for about 35km. 800m before Brasparts, turn right (on bend) & follow signs.

Marie-Christine Chaussy
Domaine de Rugornou Uras
Garz ar Bik
29190 Brasparts
Finistère
Tel: (0)2 98 81 47 14/
     (0)2 98 81 46 27
Fax: (0)2 98 81 47 99

Entry No: 281   Map: 1

The bewitching name (of the warring knight who became first baron in 1010), the splendidness of the place, its vast, opulent rooms and magnificent grounds, seduced us utterly: a powerful experience, grand rather than intimate, but unforgettable. Built with stones from the 11th-century fortress, it is a jewel of 18th-century aristocratic architecture, inside and out. M Davy, the latest descendant, is passionate about buildings, his ancient family seat in particular, and gives all his energy and intelligence to restoring château and park, planting thousands of bulbs and bushes and getting visitors to share his passion. Deeply interesting and unusual. *Gîte space for 5 people.*

Rooms: 4 doubles, 2 suites, all with bath or shower & wc.

Price: €115-€140 for two; suite €170-€200.

Meals: Choice of restaurants nearby.

Closed: Never; book ahead in winter.

From Quimper D765 W for 5km; left D784 for Landudec 13km; left & follow signs.

Philippe Davy
Domaine du Guilguiffin
29710 Landudec
Finistère
Tel: (0)2 98 91 52 11
Fax: (0)2 98 91 52 52
E-mail: chateau@guilguiffin.com
Web: www.guilguiffin.com

Entry No: 282   Map: 1

Brittany

From the terrace in front of your quarters, the view across fields and wooded hills is perfectly wonderful. In a converted outbuilding, separate from the owners' house, each smallish room has a double-glazed door-window onto that long terrace where chairs await. The modern-furnished rooms and bathrooms are identically impeccable. Breakfast, with crêpes or croissants, is in a big modern veranda room where a richly-carved Breton wardrobe takes pride of place. Madame is efficient, full of information about Breton culture, and very purposeful. *Only suitable for older children who can sleep alone.*

Rooms: 4 doubles, 2 twins, all with shower & wc.

Price: €40 for two.

Meals: Dinner €14, including wine & coffee.

Closed: Never.

Madame is a darling: quiet, serene and immensely kind, she really treats her guests as friends. The long, low, granite house has been in the family for all of its 300 years, enjoying the peace of this wind-blown, bird-sung spot just five minutes from the sea and that gorgeous coastal path. And standing stones in the garden! Most of the building is gîtes; the *chambres d'hôtes* are tucked into the far end - small, impeccably simple, like the dining room, with some handsome Breton furniture. With charming Port Manech and good beaches nearby, it is a wonderful holiday spot. *Gîte space for 14.*

Rooms: 2 doubles, 2 twins, all with shower & wc.

Price: €40 for two.

Meals: In village, within walking distance.

Closed: Never.

From Quimper D765 towards Rosporden. At St Yvi left to Kervren; at very end of lane (2.5km).

From Pont Aven, D77 for Port Manech; right just before sign Port Manech; 1st left. Signed Chambres d'Hôtes.

Odile Le Gall
Kervren
29140 Saint Yvi
Finistère
Tel: (0)2 98 94 70 34
Fax: (0)2 98 94 81 19

Yveline Gourlaouen
Kerambris
Port Manech
29920 Nevez
Finistère
Tel: (0)2 98 06 83 82
Fax: (0)2 98 06 83 82

Entry No: 283   Map: 1

Entry No: 284   Map: 1

Here is a Breton house with naturally hospitable Breton owners, Breton furniture and a huge Breton brass pot once used for mixing crêpes. Madame is welcoming and chatty (in French), Monsieur has a reassuring earthy calmness; they love having children to stay. The large, light, country-style rooms are all merrily painted in sunny yellow, fresh green, orange or pink. Copious breakfasts include those crêpes (though not mixed in the brass pot) and home-grown kiwi fruit in season. An authentic rural haven between *Armor*, the land by the sea and *Argoat*, the land of the woods. *Gîte space for 8.*

Rooms: 3 doubles, 1 twin, all with shower & wc.

Price: €40 for two.

Meals: Restaurant 4km.

Closed: Never.

From Scaër, D50 for Coray Briec; after 3km, left at 'Ty Ru' and follow signs for Kerloaï.

Louis & Thérèse Penn
Kerloaï
29390 Scaër
Finistère
Tel: (0)2 98 59 42 60
Fax: (0)2 98 59 05 67

Entry No: 285   Map: **1**

A stupendously atmospheric place: the embracing enclosure, the ruin, the arched door through to the hugely-paved hall. And inside, more ancient stones and timbers, a generous 16th-century staircase, large and exquisitely-renovated rooms with just enough period furniture, soft, rich textures, modern beds and excellent bathrooms. Peter and Clarissa have breathed new life into their Breton home. Relaxed and knowledgeable hosts, they organise seasonal fungus hunts and love communicating their feel for 'real' Brittany. Walk the canal path, visit the beautiful hinterland and return, perhaps, to a refined dinner made with home-grown organic vegetables.

Rooms: 2 doubles, 2 twins, 1 family for 4, all with bath or shower & wc.

Price: €42-€53 for two.

Meals: Dinner €21, including wine & coffee; restaurants nearby.

Closed: October-Easter.

From Carhaix Plouguer, take N164 southern bypass; turn off at traffic lights by "Cycles le Cam". Follow signs to Prévasy.

Peter & Clarissa Novak
Manoir de Prévasy
29270 Carhaix
Finistère
Tel: (0)2 98 93 24 36
Fax: (0)2 98 93 24 36

Entry No: 286   Map: **1**

Brittany

The setting is out of this world, the welcome just right and the youth of the house is immaterial. You can boat on the lake with the wild duck, walk by the babbling stream through woods and wild rhododendron, sit on the bank under the palm tree and gaze cross the valley to the distant hills. And you can barbecue in the orchard. Hospitality comes naturally to this serene retired couple who are happy to share their truly privileged environment in a quiet hamlet. The rooms are perfectly adequate in their ubiquitous pink and blue, the atmosphere incomparable.

Rooms: 1 triple, 1 double, both with shower & wc.

Price: € 37 for two.

Meals: Good choice of restaurants 1.5km.

Closed: Never.

A heavenly place, cradled in a quiet hamlet 200 yards from the river in a very lovely corner of Brittany. Delightful people: Martine looks after old folk and young Melissa, Philippe pots and teaches aikido; both have lots of time for guests. In an outbuilding, you have your own sitting/breakfast room and kitchen and two big, superbly-converted, uncluttered attic rooms, decorated with flair in subtle pastels and fitted with good shower rooms. Birds sing. The cat is one of the best ever. The dog will love you. A genuine welcome and possibly a different kind of cake for breakfast every day. Readers' letters are full of praise.

Rooms: 2 twins, both with shower & wc.

Price: € 36 for two.

Meals: Wide choice of restaurants in St Nicolas 3km; self-catering.

Closed: November-Easter, except by arrangement.

From Quimperlé D790 towards Le Faouët 9km; left to Querrien; continue towards Mellac. 1km after village, 1st left to Kerfaro; left after stone house; last house in lane.

From Pontivy D768 S for 12km; exit to St Nicolas des Eaux; right imm'ly after bridge; follow signs Chambres d'Hôtes & Poterie for 3km.

Renée & Yves Le Gallic
Kerfaro
29310 Querrien
Finistère
Tel: (0)2 98 71 30 02 /
(0)6 85 17 96 43
Fax: (0)2 98 71 30 02

Martine Maignan & Philippe Boivin
Lezerhy
56310 Bieuzy les Eaux
Morbihan
Tel: (0)2 97 27 74 59
Fax: (0)2 97 27 74 59
E-mail: boivinp@wanadoo.fr
Web: perso.wanadoo.fr/poterie-de-lezerhy/

Meadows of wild flowers and woods surround the enchanting old farmhouse - it feels miles from anywhere. Bare stonework rubs shoulders with whitewashed walls, potted plants and dried flowers throng. The open-plan living room, warmly beamed and berugged, has comfy sofas round an open fire, all shared with your attentive hosts who love dining here with guests. Steep stairs - go carefully - lead to simply-decorated rooms where bright fabrics set off stone walls under sloping rafters. If not relaxing in the garden or strolling the fields, you can play ping-pong, badminton or croquet, go fishing or paddle a canoe. *Gîte space for 5 people.*

Rooms: 2 doubles, 1 twin, all with shower & wc.

Price: €38 for two.

Meals: Dinner €14, including wine & coffee.

Closed: Never.

The stones of this fine manor farm sing with 500 years of deepest Breton history. The pigeon-wall displays the lord's wealth, the vastly-fireplaced *salon*, where he sat in justice, declares his status. Tower and Master bedrooms are well named: oak floors, high beamed ceilings, stone fireplaces, big windows, pretty ground-floor bathrooms. The darker ground-floor room has a small shower room. All are big with oodles of character. Yann has expertly restored, replumbed, rewired this beautiful place, Michèle has lovingly decorated and furnished it. They are intelligent, humorous and full of enthusiasm for guests, house and garden with its discreet and heated pool.

Rooms: 1 double, 1 triple, 1 quadruple, all with shower or bath & wc.

Price: €58-€69 for two.

Meals: Choice of restaurants in Josselin, 3km.

Closed: Never.

From Pontivy D768 S for 12km; exit for St Nicolas des Eaux then Talvern Nenez; follow for Golf de Rimaison; right opp. golf course for 1km; left and follow signs.

From Josselin D126 towards Guégon. Take 4th right AFTER Guégon turning. House 150m up, on left.

Marie-Thérèse Vannier
La Baratte
Lelfaux
56310 Bieuzy les Eaux
Morbihan
Tel: (0)2 97 27 74 11

Yann Bourdin & Michèle Robic
Manoir du Val aux Houx
56120 Guégon
Morbihan
Tel: (0)2 97 22 24 32
Fax: (0)2 97 75 42 65
E-mail: yann.bourdin@wanadoo.fr

Before converting Kerreo for the privileged few, including you, Gérard used his skills as a chef for the wealthy of this world (châteaux-hotels) and the deprived (catering schools for troubled youths). The B&B is all his: Nelly works in town. He has revived the old bread oven in the lush little garden, renovated and decorated the 'cottage' with great flair and faithfulness - the rooms, named after Breton fairies, are enchanting. He is quietly welcoming and the whole family is deeply Breton, doing *Fest-Noz* with costumes, dances, bagpipes and songs, with a dash of foreign in the odd moonlight game of *boules* or darts.

Rooms: 4 doubles, 1 twin, all with bath or shower & wc.

Price: €46-€50 for two.

Meals: Dinner €17, including wine/cider & coffee.

Closed: Never.

From Lorient N165 E for 39km; exit D24 N for about 8km; left at sign to Chaumière de Kerreo: thatched house with fuschia paintwork at hamlet crossroads.

Gérard Grevès & Nelly Le Glehuir
Chaumière de Kerreo
56330 Pluvigner
Morbihan
Tel: (0)2 97 50 90 48
Fax: (0)2 97 50 90 69

Entry No: 291   Map: 1

Dreams drift over Keraubert where the pond mirrors the dragonflies' precious dance and one of those semi-tropical Breton gardens luxuriates. Your hosts have created a welcoming, comfy atmosphere, Bernard's paintings grace many walls and he and Jacqueline quickly convey their refreshing optimism and warm delight in the place. Each pretty but untwee guest room has a garden door with iron table and chairs for two. The deeply pink room is small and cosy with garden views; the thoroughly blue room is bigger, in revived 1930s style, with less view. It is unashamedly romantic with an authentic homey feel and the owners are a lovely couple.

Rooms: 2 doubles, both with shower & wc.

Price: €43 for two.

Meals: Restaurants within walking distance.

Closed: Never.

From Rennes N24 for Lorient, exit Baud/Auray on D768 for Vannes 4km; D24 right for Landevant 10km; entrance on left before Malachappe.

Bernard & Jacqueline Belin
Keraubert
56330 Pluvigner
Morbihan
Tel: (0)2 97 24 93 10
Fax: (0)2 97 24 93 10

Entry No: 292   Map: 1

The standing stones of Carnac are minutes away, beaches and coastal pathways close by. Kerimel is a handsome group of granite farm buildings in a perfect setting among the fields. The bedrooms are beauties: plain walls, some panelling, patchwork bedcovers and pale blue curtains, old stones and beams, sparkling shower rooms and fluffy towels. The dining room is cottage perfection: dried flowers hanging from beams over wooden table, tiled floor, vast blackened chimney, stone walls. Gentle, generous, elegant people... "We talked of flowers", wrote one guest.

Rooms: 5 doubles/twins, all with shower & wc.

Price: €60-€68 for two.

Meals: Good restaurants 3km.

Closed: Never.

Yes, it's an oyster farm, bang there on the quayside! All bedrooms have the view so close that you might want to stay here alone with paint and brushes to soak up and capture that lovely, limpid atmosphere - almost Cornish? - while drinking coffee on the balcony, smelling the sea and listening with utter contentment to the chugging of fishing boats. Madame, from northern France, was a legal advisor to businesses in England, Germany and USA - alert, efficient and chatty, she came to Brittany to help François farm oysters, and never looked back. He'll take you out there too, if you ask. Unusual and very welcoming. *Gîte space for 10 people.*

Rooms: 1 twin, 1 triple, 1 apartment for 3, all with shower & wc.

Price: €46-€61 for two.

Meals: Restaurant 500m.

Closed: Never.

From N165 exit for Quiberon/Carnac on D768, 4km; right to Ploemel; D105 W for Erdeven; house signed on right, 1.5km.

From Auray D28/D781 to Crach & La Trinité sur Mer; right at lights before bridge across to La Trinité; house 400m along on left, signed 'François Gouzer'.

Babeth & Pierre Malherbe
Kerimel
56400 Ploemel (Carnac)
Morbihan
Tel: (0)2 97 56 84 72
Fax: (0)2 97 56 84 72
E-mail: elisabeth.malherbe@wanadoo.fr
Web: kerimel.free.fr

Christine & François Gouzer
Kernivilit
Saint Philibert
56470 La Trinité sur Mer
Morbihan
Tel: (0)2 97 55 17 78
Fax: (0)2 97 30 04 11
E-mail: fgouzer@club-internet.fr

Entry No: 293   Map: **1**

Entry No: 294   Map: **1**

Beyond garden and terrace, gaze at the ever-changing blue-green sea from the three attractive simply-furnished ground-floor bedrooms of this well-designed modern house. A vast carved four-poster reigns imposingly in the first-floor bedroom that leads to an even more startling dayroom with billiard table, books all round, an oak altar, a 1950's juke box, a telescope, a child-size Louis XV armchair - all neatly arranged as if in a stately home. Madame, brisk and practical, has a style that features marked contrasts - you will warm to her. There are oyster beds nearby and a little beach at the end of the garden for shallow high-tide bathing.

Rooms: 1 double with bath; 3 doubles with basin & bidet sharing 2 showers; all sharing 6 wcs.

Price: €47-€56 for two.

Meals: Restaurants in Larmor Baden, 1.5km.

Closed: Mid-July & August.

From Auray D101 S to Baden; D316 S to Larmor Baden; through village N/NE to Locqueltas: small white sign on right - house 10m along on right.

Mme MC Hecker
Locqueltas
56870 Larmor Baden
Morbihan
Tel: (0)2 97 57 05 85
Fax: (0)2 97 57 25 02

Entry No: 295   Map: 1

BOOKING

Rooms
We have witnessed unhappy travellers arriving out of the blue at *chambres d'hôtes* at 7pm or later and being dismayed to be told there was no room for them. In your own interest as well as that of your hosts, do take the precaution of 'phoning beforehand. If a house is already full, the owners can usually suggest other places nearby but turning up without warning at the end of the day is asking for disappointment.

Dinner
Please remember that *chambres d'hôtes* are not hotels and *table d'hôtes* is never automatic - it absolutely has to be arranged ahead. Very few owners offer dinner every day so do organise it in good time. Secondly, once you have arranged with your hosts to dine in, it is a question of common courtesy to turn up and partake of the meal prepared for you. These occasions can be wonderful experiences of both food and company in an utterly authentic French family atmosphere. Others are more formal and some hostesses have given up eating with their guests for reasons of health and silhouette...

Backed against the fortifications of beautiful, medieval Guérande, this Breton house with original mosaic and parquet floors, huge granite fireplace and wide wooden staircase feels older than its 140 years. Valérie's superb sense of colour, choice of fabrics and fine attention to detail blend its traditional solidity with contemporary lightness - her bedrooms are breathtaking (she herself lives mostly in another house). In the green and tranquil garden, you can breakfast in the company of 100-year-old trees and entertaining modern sculpture. Smiling and friendly, Valérie sells local produce and crafts from a shop on the ground floor.

Rooms: 4 doubles, 1 triple, 1 suite for 4, all with bath or shower & wc.

Price: €54-€77 for two.

Meals: Good restaurants within walking distance.

Closed: Never.

From Nantes/Vannes follow signs to Guérande; enter through La Porte Vannetaise (north town gate), first house on right.

Valérie Lauvray
La Guérandière
5 porte Vannetaise
44350 Guérande, Loire-Atlantique
Tel: (0)2 40 62 17 15
Fax: (0)2 51 73 04 17
E-mail: la.guerandiere@wanadoo.fr
Web: www.hotelsudbretagne.com/laguerandiere.htm

Western Loire

The great waterway moves slowly seawards through lands where Catholic Royalists battled bitter against Revolution while the precious, hand-gathered salt travelled upstream in flat, flop-sailed *gabares*.

You can expect an authentic taste of life with the French country aristocracy here. Your graceful, cultured hosts always dine with you: dress for it, and enjoy a game of billiards afterwards. It may seem rather endearingly formal, with breakfast at 9am sharp and a touch of old-fashioned primness about table manners but they are good company and enjoy introducing guests to each other. Inevitably, the bedrooms are magnificent. The château has its own lake and 100 hectares of superb parkland... all within the Brière Regional Park where water and land are inextricably mingled and wildlife abounds. *Gîte space for 10 people.*

Rooms: 2 doubles, 1 twin, all with bath or shower & wc.

Price: €85-€95 for two.

Meals: Dinner €40, including wine & coffee; auberges nearby.

Closed: Never.

These are the sweetest people, even if their somewhat kitschy taste is not everyone's cup of tea! They really do "treat their guests as friends". Madame, bright and sparkling with a smiling open face, is proud to show you her decorated books, musical scores and hats with the dried flower and gold spray touch; Monsieur is a retired farmer, less chatty but equally friendly. The house is warm (log fire in winter), cosily country-furnished, the smallish rooms are soft and welcoming (mind your head on the way up) with much attention to detail and there's a summer kitchen. Breakfast is served in pretty little baskets at the long table. *Gîte space for 3 people.*

Rooms: 2 triples, each with shower & wc; 1 triple (double + single) sharing bath & separate wc.

Price: €43 for two.

Meals: Good restaurant 3km; self-catering in summer.

Closed: Never.

From N165, exit 15 towards La Baule to Herbignac (10km); fork left D47 towards St Lyphard for 4km; house on right.

From Rennes N137 for Nantes 63km. Exit at Nozay N171 for Blain for 8km. At bottom of hill, left at roadside cross; signposted.

François & Cécile de la Monneraye
Château de Coët Caret
44410 Herbignac
Loire-Atlantique
Tel: (0)2 40 91 41 20
Fax: (0)2 40 91 37 46
E-mail: coetcaret@multimania.com
Web: welcome.to/coetcaret.com

Yvonne & Marcel Pineau
La Mercerais
44130 Blain
Loire-Atlantique
Tel: (0)2 40 79 04 30

Entry No: 297   Map: **2**

Entry No: 298   Map: **2**

Le Plessis is deeply connected: it once belonged to the Roche family who crossed with William in 1066, settled in Fermoy, Ireland, then returned to France. Now very Breton, it has velvet curtains and high-backed chairs in the *salon*; silver coffee pots and freshly-squeezed orange juice at breakfast; 3,000 rosebushes in the garden and bedrooms of huge character. The Belordes bought back the family seat after decades of "alien owners". Her father was in London with de Gaulle; she loves the English, enjoys cosmopolitan conversation (lots) and offers candlelit champagne dinners. Expensive but special. *Gîte space for 4*.

Rooms: 1 suite for 5, 1 double, 1 twin/quadruple, all with bath & wc.

Price: €95-€140 for two; reduction for 2 nights or more.

Meals: Dinner €45-€60, including wine & coffee, €70 with champagne.

Closed: Never.

This pretty old coaching inn with its big, sheltered courtyard for turning the carriages was actually built just before the motor came in and the horse went out, here in the middle of the flat Muscadet country. Your ever-charming hosts have brought their fine carved armoires from their old B&B in Normandy to add some character to the rather heavily renovated interior. Madame's dynamism and sense of fun are, of course, intact. The guest rooms, two in an annexe with kitchenette and a steep, uneven staircase, have parquet floors and good new bathrooms; fresh flowers and peace are the keynotes. *Gîte space for 6 people.*

Rooms: 4 doubles, 1 twin, all with shower & wc.

Price: €40 for two.

Meals: Choice of restaurants 6km; self-catering in annexe.

Closed: Never.

From Nantes leave A83 ringroad on D85 past airport. At T-junction at Champ de Foire left through Pont St Martin & follow signs to Le Plessis.

From Nantes N249 for Poitiers, exit Vallet for Loroux Bottereau/ Le Landreau for 5km; 600m before Le Landreau right; signs to La Rinière (3km).

M & Mme Belorde
Château du Plessis-Atlantique
44860 Pont Saint Martin
Loire-Atlantique
Tel: (0)2 40 26 81 72
Fax: (0)2 40 32 76 67
E-mail: josiane.belorde@wanadoo.fr

Françoise & Louis Lebarillier
Le Relais de La Rinière
44430 Le Landreau
Loire-Atlantique
Tel: (0)2 40 06 41 44
Fax: (0)2 51 13 10 52
E-mail: riniere@netcourrier.com
Web: www.riniere.com

Entry No: 299 Map: 2

Entry No: 300 Map: 2

A feeling of Renaissance nobility extends everywhere except to the bathrooms - they are reassuringly modern. The lofty dining room has massive beams, a massive table, massive old flags; the panelling took 500 hours to restore, fine period furniture gleams - Monsieur is passionate about buildings and an avid auction-goer. Madame seems charmingly eccentric and, under daughter Gaëlle's management, the estate produces a Muscadet from the surrounding vineyards that is served as an aperitif at about seven, before you sally forth for dinner. *Gîte space for 10.*

Rooms: 5 doubles, all with bath or shower & wc.

Price: €74-€104 for two.

Meals: Wide choice of restaurants within 5 minutes.

Closed: November-March, except by arrangement.

The friendly, unobtrusive Desbrosses particularly enjoy the company of foreign vistitors to their typical long low 18th-century house - it's a perfect setting for a quiet escape. In the guest wing, you may choose one of their many books and withdraw to a deep leather chair by the monumental drawing-room fireplace. Guest rooms and bathrooms are frilly and old-fashioned - so are some of the beds. The excellent breakfast and occasional dinner are served on matching blue and yellow plates in the blue and yellow dining room - Madame is a delightful potter and the strong colours are her own, successful choice.

Rooms: 1 suite, 1 double, both with bath & wc.

Price: €49 for two.

Meals: Dinner €22, including wine.

Closed: Never.

From Nantes N249 for Poitiers; right N149 for Le Pallet; 1km before Le Pallet D7 right to Monnières; left for Gorges; château 1km on left.

Annick & Didier Calonne
Château Plessis-Brezot
44690 Monnières
Loire-Atlantique
Tel: (0)2 40 54 63 24
Fax: (0)2 40 54 66 07
E-mail: a.calonne@online.fr
Web: www.chateauplessisbrezot.com

From Nantes D937 for La Roche sur Yon. At Rocheservière D753 to Legé centre; towards Touvois. Left after Le Paradis restaurant. Signed Richebonne.

Christine & Gérard Desbrosses
La Mozardière
Richebonne
44650 Legé, Loire-Atlantique
Tel: (0)2 40 04 98 51
Fax: (0)2 40 26 31 61
E-mail: christine@lamozardiere.com
Web: www.lamozardiere.com

Entry No: 301   Map: 2

Entry No: 302   Map: 11

Hurry! Here is a lovely, quiet family with cows that they know by name and a love of the land that is becoming rare. Michelle does the B&B, Gérard and their son run the farm. The hub is the huge living room where you all relax after a gorgeous dinner of regional dishes made with their own produce (guest sitting room upstairs too). Bedrooms are not large but comfortable in French country style, the two in the separate old sheepfold ideal for a family; the big garden has games for children and an immaculate *potager*. Come for these wonderful, kind hosts and her superb cooking rather than the rooms.

Rooms: 2 doubles, 2 triples, all with shower & wc; 1 family with bath & wc.

Price: €42 for two.

Meals: Dinner €14, including wine & coffee.

Closed: November-April.

The Pikes' simple, old-fashioned, easily-renovated 1900s farmhouse has a big garden where children play and adults barbecue; then climb the outside stairs to the two quiet, comfortable rooms for restful seclusion after a day at the seaside. Your lively, welcoming hosts and their two sets of identical twin teenage sons (*la fraternité*) came from farming in England and are thoroughly integrated here. Ian manages the farm, Janty helps with lambing and eggs (pheasant), they all enjoy having guests, will point you towards the hidden treasures of the area they have come to love - and take you to see the sheep if you're interested. *Gîte space for 6 people.*

Rooms: 1 double with bath, shower & wc; 1 twin with shower & wc.

Price: €38 for two.

Meals: Good restaurant 3km.

Closed: Mid-September-mid-June.

From Challans D948 to St Christophe du Ligneron; opposite baker's right D2 for Palluau for 4km; left at sign for house.

From La Roche sur Yon D948 25km through Aizenay; at Bel Air hamlet D94 left for Commequiers 1km (signs to La Fraternité); left for Maché, house imm'ly on right.

Michelle & Gérard Loizeau
L'Hubertière
85670 St Christophe du Ligneron
Vendée
Tel: 02 51 35 06 41
Fax: 02 51 49 87 43
E-mail: michelle.loizeau@terre-net.fr

Janty & Ian Pike
La Fraternité
Maché
85190 Aizenay, Vendée
Tel: (0)2 51 55 42 58
Fax: (0)2 51 60 16 01
E-mail: ian.pike@libertysurf.fr
Web: www.chez.com/lafraternite/

Entry No: 303   **Map:** 11

Entry No: 304   **Map:** 11

An unusual study in *chiaro e oscuro*: light outside and dark inside. The vertical reach of the planking takes the eye up beyond the everyday to a place where realism and practicality are, thank Heavens, not needed. Yet the interplay of new and old wood, light and dark again, is exciting in an age of the bland exteriors of warehouse and supermarket architecture. The owners have a casual approach to hospitality, it must be admitted, leaving you the raw materials to construct your own bed and furniture. But you may come and go and indulge in whatever whimsical behaviour you wish - nobody will object.

Rooms: Well, 'room' really. An ensuite, open-plan, unobstructed multi-purpose 'space' (or lack thereof).

Price: Unaffordable, but well worth it.

Meals: Meals 'de trolley' do the occasional roll-by.

Closed: Owners just can't keep people away.

The delightful Bertins, former bistro-owners, are wild about their lovely house beside the River Vendée - a glorious setting, with all the flavour of this watery area where the sea once lapped, and a fisherman's paradise. Thierry knows the historical depths and will illustrate his fascinating talk with appropriate videos. There are two boats for exploring the river, a terrace for dry observation, a walled garden for seclusion, superb rooms for guests: exquisite rugs on polished floors, antique washstands and armoires, brand new bedding, excellent bathrooms. And moreover, Martine cooks divinely with all organic produce. *Gîte space for 4* .

Rooms: 3 triples, 2 family, all with bath or shower & wc.

Price: €51 for two.

Meals: Dinner €19, including wine & coffee; ferme auberge 6km.

Closed: 30 November-31 January.

Past Poitiers, then left after road on right. Once in the complex, this unit is fifteenth on Avenue de la Différence.

From Fontenay le Comte D938ter for 13km; right D25. Le Gué de Velluire is 4.5km on; left at end of village; beside river.

M & Mme Hutte
Sans Abri
Allée Chaque
85555 Place Carré
Tel: Ext. 87.
Fax: In main office.
E-mail: always@loggerheads.fr
Web: www.à-chaque-son-shack.fr

Martine & Thierry Bertin
Le Logis d'Elpénor
5 rue de la Rivière
85770 Le Gué de Velluire
Vendée
Tel: (0)2 51 52 59 10
Fax: (0)2 51 52 57 21

Entry No: 305   Map: 11

Entry No: 306   Map: 11

At the bottom of the lane by the lazy, winding river, Massigny is a secret corner of marshy Vendée. The rooms are as handsome as you'll find: Jean-Claude teaches cabinet-making and his delight in wood is evident. Add beds made for deep sleep, unfussy fabrics, papers and painted beams for aesthetic satisfaction, a guest sitting room with two carved armoires and a lovely copper tub for plants, a sensitively-landscaped secret hillside garden where hoopoes nest, and all you need is to sit with these caring, open people and share their wide-ranging conversation. Remarkable value in a memorable and unsung spot.

Rooms: 1 double, 1 family room, both with shower & wc.

Price: €43 for two.

Meals: Choice of restaurants 3-10km.

Closed: November-March.

Serendipity - a fine French house, inside and out, a glorious garden, seeded by Rabelais five centuries ago with lettuce and raspberry, 70 varieties of iris, a lawn to the stream, a punt to drift you deep into the *Marais* (known as *Venise Verte* here), its own fishing spot. Liliane, a vivacious and enthusiastic local guide, and her doctor husband are great hosts. Bedrooms: parquet floors, photos of the *Marais*, an old four-poster with views of the water, a beam-thronged bathroom. Downstairs: books, chess, a splendid stone-walled conservatory. All rather poetic and very special.

Rooms: 3 doubles, 1 triple, 1 twin, all with bath or shower & wc.

Price: €59.50 for two.

Meals: Restaurants in village.

Closed: Never.

From A83 exit Fontenay le Comte D938ter for La Rochelle 6km; right at small sign to Massigny; 1st house on left entering hamlet.

From Fontenay le Comte N148 for Niort 9km; right D15 to Maillezais; follow signs for Abbaye; house on left, signposted.

Marie-Françoise & Jean-Claude Neau
Massigny
85770 Velluire
Vendée
Tel: (0)2 51 52 30 32
Fax: (0)2 51 52 30 32

Mme Liliane Bonnet
69 rue de l'Abbaye
85420 Maillezais, Vendée
Tel: (0)2 51 87 23 00
Fax: (0)2 51 00 72 44
E-mail: liliane.bonnet@wanadoo.fr
Web: www.marais-poitevin.com/heberg-ch/bonnet/bonnet.html

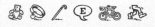

A rare survivor of Cholet's imperial past (they manufactured handkerchiefs then), this elegant town house was the orangery of a long-gone château. Nothing imperial about Édith though, who loves to make guests feel at home. The bedrooms are light and beautiful with fine period furniture and gleaming modern bathrooms. Two give onto the quiet street, the suite looks over the rose-filled, tree-shaded garden. There are two pretty *salons* and a glass-roofed dining room in the sunken courtyard - excellent dinners here. French style and hospitality at its best.

Rooms: 2 doubles, 1 suite, all with shower or bath & wc.

Price: €61 for two; suite €107 for four.

Meals: Dinner €23, including wine & coffee; restaurants 50m.

Closed: Never.

Rue nationale is a one-way street through Cholet centre. No 28 200m down on right.

Édith & Jean-René Duchesne
Demeure l'Impériale
28 rue Nationale
49300 Cholet, Maine-et-Loire
Tel: (0)2 41 58 84 84
Fax: (0)2 41 63 17 03
E-mail: demeure.imperiale@wanadoo.fr
Web: demeure-imperiale.com

Entry No: 309   Map: 11

This 15th-century semi-moated *gentilhommière* has been in the same family for generations. With its mellow terracotta tiles, oak beams, rough-cast ochre walls, old family furniture, log fires and Madame's easy-going, cheerful vivacity, the house glows with warmth and humour. In the large sitting room, a friendly circle of assorted upholstered chairs (Madame also teaches upholstery) and the cheerful clutter of family memorabilia speak of happy gatherings. The bedrooms are two charming adjoining rooms behind a massive old oak door, the smaller one with a canopied bed and dreamy views over moat and woodland. An enchanting place and a wonderful hostess. *Gîte space for 6-8 people.*

Rooms: 1 suite for 4 with bath & wc.

Price: €61 for two; suite €107 for four.

Meals: Restaurants nearby.

Closed: Never.

From Angers D748 to Brissac, Martigné-Briand & Vihiers. Stay on D748 towards Bressuire. Approx 5km after Vihiers right D167. Through St Paul & right for Coron. House 2km along this road.

Béatrice de Seguins-Ricour
La Gaubertière
49310 Saint Paul du Bois
Maine-et-Loire
Tel: (0)2 41 75 81 87
E-mail: charles.ricour@infonie.fr

Entry No: 310   Map: 11

The Migons, who couldn't be nicer, have expertly renovated their long-faced, 8-metre-thick house with its barn-enclosed courtyard, two towers and covered terrace. Big, north-facing bedrooms are pretty, elegant and comfortable behind their shutters. There's a good mix in the reception rooms: contemporary leather sofas and a suit of armour; antique dining-room furniture beneath blue and green painted beams; two billiard tables, a piano, a set of drums in the games room. Monsieur has a collection of veteran cars and plays bass guitar - promises of entertaining evenings. Superb grounds with a fishing pond and an 'aperitif gazebo'.

Rooms: 1 twin, 3 doubles, 2 doubles/twins all with bath or shower & wc.

Price: €70–€100 for two.

Meals: Dinner €25, including wine & coffee.

Closed: Never.

From A11 exit 20 on D923. Cross Loire to Liré on D763; right D751 to Drain; left D154 for St Laurent des Autels. In Drain, house 3.5 km after church on left.

Brigitte & Gérard Migon
Le Mésangeau
49530 Drain
Maine-et-Loire
Tel: (0)2 40 98 21 57
Fax: (0)2 40 98 28 62
E-mail: le.mesangeau@wanadoo.fr
Web: www.anjou-et-loire.com/mesangeau

Entry No: 311   Map: 2

The great playwright Racine was made Prior here by an uncle but was removed by a Bishop: this inspired *Les Plaideurs*. Your hosts are lovely people, interesting, amusing and educated. Bernard likes to cook dinner for guests occasionally with the emphasis on simple recipes using the best local ingredients. The main house has a friendly family kitchen and a dining room with stacks of books and a pianola in the fireplace. The duplex guest rooms in a converted outbuilding are well but simply furnished and the old chapel is now a garden room for breakfast. There's a big garden with a swimming pool, too.

Rooms: 2 suites for 4, both with bath & 2 wcs; 1 twin with bath & wc.

Price: €65 for two.

Meals: Dinner €25, including wine & coffee.

Closed: 15 September-1 May.

From Angers N23 for Nantes for 13km; through St Georges; cont. about 1.5km; left after garage. Pass château: house on left. Park outside, walk through gate.

Bernard & Geneviève Gaultier
Prieuré de l'Épinay
49170 Saint Georges sur Loire
Maine-et-Loire
Tel: (0)2 41 39 14 44
Fax: (0)2 41 39 14 44
E-mail: bgaultier@compuserve.com

Entry No: 312   Map: 2

This is a charming, friendly 200-year-old farmhouse run by an extremely welcoming young couple who have twin sons and guest-loving dogs. The cheerful, cosy sitting room with its open fire immediately sets the tone. Many readers have praised the hospitality shown to both young and old and the excellent traditional food - served in the lovely light, tiled dining room. Bedrooms, up steep stairs, are delightfully plain and simple with pale floral curtains and bedcovers and showers behind curtains, and French (small!) towels. *Please arrive after 4pm if possible - still in time for a swim.*

Rooms: 2 doubles, 2 twins, all with shower, sharing 2 separate wcs.

Price: € 38.50 for two.

Meals: Dinner € 19, including wine & coffee.

Closed: November-mid-April.

This couple have lovingly preserved their typical old Segré farmhouse with its long deep roof and curious *outeau* openings (some might have put in modern dormers). You cannot fail to warm to Madame's easy vivacity and infectious laugh. She virtually lives in her kitchen (in the house just opposite), making jams, pastries and bread in the old bread oven. The living room has great beams, a big brick fireplace, exposed stone walls and new country furniture. Rooms are deliciously rustic: crochet, terracotta, pine, sloping ceilings. The woods are full of birdlife and the cows graze peacefully under the children's window.

Rooms: 2 quadruples, 1 double, all with bath or shower & wc.

Price: € 34-€ 36 for two.

Meals: Choice of restaurants 2-5 km; picnic in garden possible.

Closed: Never.

From Angers N162 towards Laval. At Lion d'Angers, D770 W towards Candé; pass garden centre; after 1.5km left at big wooden cross; signposted.

From Angers N162 to Lion d'Angers; cont. towards Rennes/Segré on D863 for 3km. Left at Chambres d'Hôtes sign; house 1km along on left.

M & Mme Patrick Carcaillet
Le Petit Carqueron
49220 Le Lion d'Angers
Maine-et-Loire
Tel: (0)2 41 95 62 65

Jocelyne & François Vivier
Les Travaillères
49220 Le Lion d'Angers
Maine-et-Loire
Tel: (0)2 41 61 33 56/
(0)6 77 86 24 33

Entry No: 313 Map: 2

Entry No: 314 Map: 2

The whole family is delightful and Madame, an elegant former teacher, is a great source of local knowledge (old slate mines, model villages, river trips...). Their converted farm building, in the grounds of the Château du Teilleul, has a big, convivial, cedar-panelled sitting room. The guest room, charmingly decorated and beamed with a sloping roof, has a clever arrangement with the bath behind a bookcase/bar and its own loo in the corridor. This is a splendid home, full of heirlooms - you feel embraced by the place the moment you walk in and the setting is totally calm (the garden has a 'real' English lawn, cut to a carpet!).

Rooms: 1 twin with bath & basin, wc down corridor.

Price: €46 for two.

Meals: Dinner €19, including wine & coffee.

Closed: Never.

The original 18th-century town house was "cloned" by a 19th-century owner for his daughter! The austere topiaried spinning-tops flanking the drive belie the warm, quietly elegant, sunny rooms inside. Richard has a book shop in Angers, Florence paints and runs art courses at home, and the house breathes books, art and music. Built on the ramparts of the old fortified village, there are wonderful views over open countryside from the pretty 'hanging' garden and two of the delightfully decorated bedrooms, while sunny yellow and lime-green fabrics and hand-painted butterflies brighten up the north-facing room. A very special place.

Rooms: 2 twins, 1 double, 1 suite for 4, both with bath & wc.

Price: €46 for two; suite €69 for four.

Meals: Dinner €17, including wine & coffee.

Closed: Never.

From St. Sauveur D923 direction Segré. Driveway on right, 200m after village.

From Angers N162 to Le Lion d'Angers; D863 to Segré; D923; left D863 to l'Hôtellerie de Flée; D180 to Châtelais. 1st left on entering village.

Marie-Alice & Michel de Vitton
Le Domaine du Teilleul
49500 Saint Sauveur de Flée
Maine-et-Loire
Tel: (0)2 41 61 38 84
Fax: (0)2 41 61 38 84
E-mail: domainevitton@wanadoo.fr

Richard & Florence Sence
Le Frêne
22 rue Saint Sauveur
49520 Châtelais
Maine-et-Loire
Tel: (0)2 41 61 16 45
Fax: (0)2 41 61 16 45

Entry No: 315   Map: 2

Entry No: 316   Map: 2

The wide river flows past the large, lush riverside garden, cheeky red squirrels run along the stone balustrade: it feels like deep country but this handsome manor has urban elegance in its very stones. Panels, cornices, mouldings, subtly-muted floor tiles bring grace while traditional French furnishings add softness. In these formal surroundings Madame, energetic, relaxed and communicative, adores having guests and pampering them with luxury. Monsieur is jovial and loves fishing! Fine, plush bedrooms, three with river views, all with superb bathrooms. Walking and cycling paths are marked.

Rooms: 2 doubles, 2 twins, all with bath/shower & wc.

Price: €58-€73 for two.

Meals: Dinner €26, including wine & coffee; restaurants 4-15km.

Closed: Never.

A neo-Gothic surprise with a bucolic stork-nested, deer-roamed park that runs down to the river and an interior worthy of Hollywood: the sitting room is wildly mock-medieval, the panelled drawing room was taken whole from an 18th-century château. This was once a fully self-sufficient country estate and there are the remains of a chapel, dovecote and mill (swimming and rowing in the river). Any proper château has a Bishop's Room, of course: you can sleep in this one; the corner room has a splendid four-poster. An elegantly warm welcome from people who fill the house with friends and family and might even play bridge with you.

Rooms: 1 triple, 3 doubles, all with bath or shower & wc.

Price: €61-€65 for two.

Meals: Dinner €23, including wine & coffee.

Closed: November-Easter.

From Angers, N162 for Lion d'Angers. At Grieul (20km) right D291 to Grez Neuville. At church (1.5km), Rue de l'Écluse towards river on left.

From Angers, N23 north. At Seiches sur Loir, D74 towards Châteauneuf sur Sarthe for 5.5km. Château on right as you leave Montreuil village.

Jacqueline & Auguste Bahuaud
La Croix d'Étain
2 rue de l'Écluse
49220 Grez Neuville, Maine-et-Loire
Tel: (0)2 41 95 68 49
Fax: (0)2 41 18 02 72
E-mail: croix.etain@anjou-et-loire.com
Web: www.anjou-et-loire.com/croix

Jacques & Marie Bailliou
Château de Montreuil
49140 Montreuil sur Loir
Maine-et-Loire
Tel: (0)2 41 76 21 03
E-mail: chateau.montreuil@anjou-et-loire.com
Web: www.anjou-et-loire.com/chateau

Entry No: 317   Map: 2

Entry No: 318   Map: 2

Age-old peace and youthful freshness breathe from the old farmhouse, transformed from tumbledown dereliction to rural idyll for this cultured, artistic, unpretentious couple and their four children. Rooms are decorated with flair and simplicity - using some strong, warm colours, sea-grass flooring and good fabrics. Wonderful meals - Regina's regional recipes are very sought after. A perfect retreat too for music, art and nature lovers. This is the family estate: join the Tuesday choir practice at the château, take singing lessons with a sister. And fish, boat or walk in the unspoilt countryside. A very special place.

Rooms: 1 twin, 1 double, 1 triple, all with bath or shower & wc.

Price: €58 for two.

Meals: Dinner €23, including wine & coffee.

Closed: Never.

What a splendid woman she is! Down to earth, fun-loving and decent, offering authentic farmhouse hospitality. They are both delighted to show you their exclusively grass-fed brown oxen, even sell you beef direct. You breakfast in the simple dining room which is alive with the desire to please. The attic has been converted into three good, honest rooms and a children's room. Great old roof timbers share the space with new rustic-style beds and old armoires. It is simple and clean-cut with discreet plastic flooring, pastel walls, sparkling new shower rooms. They have two lively kids, there are toys and games and swings for yours.

Rooms: 2 triples, 1 twin, all with shower & wc.

Price: €34 for two.

Meals: Choice of restaurants 5km.

Closed: Never.

From Angers towards Lion d'Angers. At Montreuil Juigné right on D768 towards Champigné. 500m after x-roads at La Croix de Beauvais right up drive to La Roche & Malvoisine.

From Angers N23 to Seiches sur le Loir; right on D766 towards Tours for 9km; right into Jarzé on D59 towards Beaufort en Vallé. House on left 700m after Jarzé.

Patrice & Regina de La Bastille
Malvoisine
49460 Écuillé, Maine-et-Loire
Tel: (0)2 41 93 34 44 /
    (0)6 88 90 15 76
Fax: (0)2 41 93 34 44
E-mail: bastille-pr@wanadoo.fr
Web: www.malvoisine-bastille.com

Véronique & Vincent Papiau
Le Point du Jour
49140 Jarzé
Maine-et-Loire
Tel: (0)2 41 95 46 04
Fax: (0)2 41 95 46 04

This is a fine house and a gateway to a variety of cultural influences. Set proudly on the Loire embankment, the house has an unbeatable view of the mighty river but the road is busy (little traffic at night). Guests have a cobblestoned kitchen/diner whence the original slate stairs lead up to the house and four well-furnished double-glazed rooms (two with Loire views). Other, pretty rooms are in the old stables, alongside the architecturally-correct dog kennel. Young and lively, Claudine offers a monthly cultural event: take one of her mystery tours, join a traditional Songs-of-the-Loire dinner or a story-telling cocktail party.

Rooms: 1 suite for 4, 2 triples, 2 doubles, 1 twin, all with shower & wc; 2 have kitchenettes.

Price: €51-€59 for two.

Meals: Dinner €22, including wine & coffee.

Closed: Never.

A nose for fine wine brought Françoise and Paul-Hervé from the world of the Paris media to this organic wine-growing estate. A whiff of Cabernet accompanies you from the open kitchen-cum-sitting area up to your bedrooms in the loft over the old wine-press. They blend frill-free contemporary design with traditional natural materials. The yellow room is large and luminous, the green room has its own outside stone stairs. Paul-Hervé loves to explain the mysteries of fine-wine-making, and you can borrow bicycles to explore the local vineyards, or relax with a book in the big shady garden.

Rooms: 1 double & 2 twins, all with bath or shower & wc.

Price: €55-€65 for two.

Meals: Good restaurant in Thouarcé, 10km.

Closed: November-April.

From Angers, D952 for Saumur. House is on left-hand side of road (signposted) as you enter St Mathurin.

From Angers N260 towards Niort-Poitiers; exit towards Brissac D748 for 5km; right towards Homois for 150m; right towards Clabeau; cont. downhill 2km; left after bridge.

Mme Claudine Pinier
La Bouquetterie, 118 rue du Roi René
49250 St Mathurin sur Loire
Maine-et-Loire
Tel: (0)2 41 57 02 00
Fax: (0)2 41 57 31 90
E-mail: cpinier@aol.com
Web: www.anjou-et-loire.com/bouquetterie

Entry No: 321   Map: **2**

Françoise & Paul-Hervé Vintrou
Domaine des Charbotières
Clabeau
49320 Brissac Quincé, Maine-et-Loire
Tel: (0)2 41 91 22 87
Fax: (0)2 41 66 23 09
E-mail: contact@domainedescharbotieres.com
Web: www.charbotieres.com

Entry No: 322   Map: **2**

The keynotes here are serenity, harmony, peace. Not the most spectacular countryside, perhaps, but the house is utterly tranquil in its little hamlet and for excitement Monsieur will guide beginners in the art of billiards if they wish. Madame is shy but kind, spontaneously welcoming and properly proud of her pretty, unfussy rooms where pastel colours, tiled floors and oriental rugs sit well under old rafters and stones and all is perfectly kept. Breakfast, with home-made jams, can be in the garden on fine mornings and you can picnic there too or bicycle down to the banks of the Loire.

Rooms: 2 doubles, 1 triple, all with shower & wc.

Price: €41 for two.

Meals: Dinner €17.50, including wine & coffee.

Closed: Never.

The air carries a heady scent and the design of this farm is most pleasing: the gentle green paintwork and the stone arches soften the square symmetry of the courtyard, which has virtually no farm mess to spoil it. Yet these intelligent farmers work hard, growing fields of lupins, hollyhocks and thyme for seed. Your hosts' wing (and yours while you stay - other family members live in other wings) has been done with simple good taste; each room has a personal touch; there are landing chairs for guests to watch farmyard life go by. Martine, young, dynamic and thoroughly likeable, is conscious of what B&B enthusiasts really want. *Gîte space for 18.*

Rooms: 1 double with shower & wc; 1 double, 1 twin, both with shower, sharing 2 wcs (showers behind curtains). One large room on ground floor also.

Price: €38.50-€46 for two.

Meals: Good restaurants 3-7km.

Closed: Never.

From Angers N761 towards Brissac & Doué. At Les Alleuds left on D90 towards Chemellier. Hamlet 3km on left.

From Angers, N260 for Cholet; D748 for Poitiers. After Brissac, D761 for Poitiers. House signposted on left after 2km, at end of avenue of chestnut trees.

Éliette Edon
Chambres d'Hôtes
49320 Maunit Chemellier
Maine-et-Loire
Tel: (0)2 41 45 59 50
Fax: (0)2 41 45 01 44

Jean-Claude & Martine Colibet
La Pichonnière
Charcé Saint Ellier
49320 Brissac Quincé, Maine-et-Loire
Tel: (0)2 41 91 29 37 (mealtimes)
Fax: (0)2 41 91 96 85
E-mail: gite-brissac@wanadoo.fr
Web: www.gite-brissac.com

Entry No: 323   Map: **2**

Entry No: 324   Map: **2**

Alternative could be the word: it is unusual, and great for the informal. Joyce, a relaxed, welcoming aromatherapist, has an organic kitchen garden, cooks good veggie food, receives art, yoga and meditation workshops (lovely meditation room) and may invite you to "come and join in". In its soft, leafy stand of poplars, the 300-year-old farm has beams everywhere - take care going to bed. One room has steps down to the courtyard, the other looks over the pond, both have warm-hued furnishings in harmony with the old wood and stone. Old rural it feels, mature alternative it sings. Small camping site, lots of animals. *Gîte space for 6 people.*

Rooms: 1 triple, 1 double, sharing bath & wc.

Price: €46 for two.

Meals: Vegetarian dinner €13, including wine & coffee.

Closed: Never.

The atmosphere here is artistic, relaxed, convivial. Madame loves decorating her wonderful house, making sure you love it too. Monsieur is an artist: his hand is visible everywhere. In a quiet wooded spot, the house is a Victorian extravaganza; the little tower, once dovecote and chapel, is older. Inside, it's a study in disorganised elegance, masses of antiques, *brocante* and modernities - sophisticated and fun. There are relaxation sessions, billiards, piano, and coffee-roasting on the spot; a sense of magic in the park, the odd statue peering from the vegetation, a pond fed by a reputedly miraculous spring. Good food, too.

Rooms: 1 suite for 5, 4 doubles, all with bath & wc.

Price: €68.50 for two.

Meals: Dinner €23, including wine & coffee.

Closed: January-February.

From Le Mans N23 to La Flèche. There D37 to Fougeré; N217 for Baugé, 1.5km. Behind poplars on left.

From A11 left on A85 towards Tours. Exit at Longué on D938 towards Baugé for 5km. Right on D62 towards Mouliherne. House 5km along on right.

Joyce Rimell
La Besnardière
Route de Baugé
49150 Fougeré
Maine-et-Loire
Tel: (0)2 41 90 15 20
Fax: (0)2 41 90 15 20

Françoise & Michel Toutain
Le Prieuré de Vendanger
49150 Le Guédeniau
Maine-et-Loire
Tel: (0)2 41 67 82 37
Fax: (0)2 41 67 82 43
E-mail: info@vendanger.fr
Web: www.vendanger.fr

Impeccable - this conversion of farm and outbuildings is superbly done and Mireille's sense of style and attention to detail are everywhere: perfectly co-ordinated colour schemes with her own stencilling, new beds, good linen, nice big towels and a living area with refrigerator and microwave for guests - meals are served here or outside. The Métiviers want you to be comfortable and relaxed; they love to chat and are fascinating about local history and the environment; but they'll fully understand if you prefer to eat alone. A lovely garden too - all utterly restful. *Children under two free.*

Rooms: 2 doubles with extra single bed, both with shower & wc, 1 wc separate.

Price: €47.50 for two.

Meals: Dinner €14, including wine & coffee.

Closed: 2 weeks in summer.

They are a refreshingly young, enthusiastic, welcoming family and their 18th-century barn has modern eyes in the back of its head - huge windows onto the garden - and is full of light. Lovingly-restored original beams, tiles and stones (Monsieur restores houses - very well) are the perfect backdrop for simple old armoires and bedheads. Each room has its own entrance, the suites have steep stairs up to the children's rooms, everything is in unpretentious good taste and the old *pressoir* (wine press) is now the ping-pong and pool house. You all eat together at the long table - Madame is sociable, easy-going, and a good cook!

Rooms: 1 double, 1 twin, 1 triple, 2 suites, all with bath or shower & wc.

Price: €46-€54 for two.

Meals: Dinner €19, including wine & coffee.

Closed: Never.

From Angers N147 towards Saumur; 3km after Corné D61 left towards Baugé for 2km past dairy & agricultural co-op; 2nd left at sign. House 1st on right.

From Saumur N147 N/NW 15km past Longué; D938 right towards Baugé for 2.5km; left to Brion. House signposted in village opposite church.

Mireille & Michel Métivier
Le Haut Pouillé
La Buissonnière
49630 Mazé, Maine-et-Loire
Tel: (0)2 41 45 13 72
Fax: (0)2 41 45 19 02
E-mail: labuissonniere@mageos.com
Web: www.labuissonniere.fr.st

Anne & Jean-Marc Le Foulgocq
Le Logis du Pressoir
Villeneuve
49250 Brion, Maine-et-Loire
Tel: (0)2 41 57 27 33
Fax: (0)2 41 57 27 33
E-mail: lepressoir@wanadoo.fr
Web: www.lepressoir.fr.st

Entry No: 327   Map: 7

Entry No: 328   Map: 7

Michael and Jill are fun, good talkers and good listeners; with their two lively children, their guinea pigs, cats, chickens and ponies, the whole place has a friendly family atmosphere that brings new cheer to the old French house. Bedrooms are big, bright and comfortable: the double, up characterfully creaky stairs, has a green 'marbled' fireplace, garden views and two deep armchairs from which to survey the scene; the quadruple, under the beamed roof and with rugs on parquet floors, has those same views through low windows, a large sofa and a small shower room. Everything is clean and tidy without being oppressively so. *Gîte space for 4 people.*

Rooms: 1 double with private bath & wc, 1 family with shower & wc.

Price: €50 for two.

Meals: Dinner €20, including wine & coffee.

Closed: Never.

This Neo-Gothic folly is inhabited by a couple of charming, un-selfconscious aristocrats and lots of cheerfully active children. There's a properly dark and spooky baronial hall, light, elegant reception rooms with ancestors on the walls, lots of plush and gilt. If you splurge on the 'suite' (in fact, one vast room), you will have a sitting area and a library corner in an alcove. The smaller double has its shower up in a turret, its loo in another along the corridor. Both are elegantly, unfussily decorated with period French pieces and some modern fabrics. The park is huge, wild boar roam, boarlets scamper in spring. An amazing experience.

Rooms: 1 double with shower & private wc (only July-August); 1 suite with bath & wc.

Price: €75-€200 for two.

Meals: Dinner €46; wine €17-€26.

Closed: Never.

From La Flèche D308/D938 to Baugé; follow signs for Tours & Saumur; right at traffic lights on D61 to Le Vieil Baugé. Signposted after 2km.

From A85 exit 'Saumur' on D767 for Le Lude. After 1km, left on D129 to Neuillé. Signposted.

Michael & Jill Coyle
La Chalopinière
49150 Le Vieil Baugé
Maine-et-Loire
Tel: (0)2 41 89 04 38
Fax: (0)2 41 89 04 38
E-mail: rigbycoyle@aol.com

Monica Le Pelletier de Glatigny
Château de Salvert
Salvert
49680 Neuillé, Maine-et-Loire
Tel: (0)2 41 52 55 89
Fax: (0)2 41 52 56 14
E-mail: info@salvert.com
Web: www.salvert.com

Nothing pretentious about this quiet village house but a genuine warm welcome from your nature-loving hosts - Carmen, a sprightly retired English teacher, and ex-chef Hervé who cooks excellent traditional French dinners. The bedrooms are in the old farmhouse in the shady courtyard – two, with their own entrances, are simply but pleasantly decorated - one has a magnificent stone fireplace and an old school desk with small shower rooms. The third, up outside stairs, has old beams, stone walls and pretty yellow and white fabrics. Trees almost engulf the house, and the sunny conservatory dining room looks over a bosky garden. *Gîte space for 4.*

Rooms: 2 doubles, 1 triple, all with private shower or bath & wc.

Price: €38-€43 for two.

Meals: Dinner €18, including wine.

Closed: Never.

A wonderful woman greets you, a gentle artist and nature-lover with a sure and personal approach to interiors, both house and human. The suite is superb in dramatic red, white and blue (yes, it works!), the children's room deeply child-friendly. Woodwork has been stripped back, walls are richly clothed (all Madame's work), the furniture is old but not wealthy, the light pours in and you bask in the harmony of warm, authentic, timeless comfort. The magical lush green haven surrounding the rambling 19th-century château is a 10-acre oasis of semi-wild vegetation where endangered flora and fauna take refuge. Out of this world.

Rooms: 1 double, 1 triple, 1 suite for 5, all with bath or shower & wc.

Price: €53-€76 for two; suite €122 for five.

Meals: Good restaurants in Saumur, 9km.

Closed: Never, open by arrangement in winter.

Leave A85 at exit 2 (Longué); N147 for Saumur; at Super U r'bout D53 to St Philbert. House on right on entering village.

From Saumur N147 for Longué. At La Ronde D767 for Vernantes; left D129 for Neuillé. 1km before Neuillé follow Fontaine Suzon; signposted.

Carmen & Hervé Taté
La Closerie
Le Bourg
49160 Saint Philbert du Peuple
Maine-et-Loire
Tel: (0)2 41 52 62 69

Mme Monique Calot
Château du Goupillon
49680 Neuillé
Maine-et-Loire
Tel: (0)2 41 52 51 89
Fax: (0)2 41 52 51 89

Here, between town and country, is a thoroughly French family house. As well as this solid old manor, the energetic Bastids have a health-food shop, four lovely children and an open, welcoming attitude. Their generous reception rooms, furnished with antiques and heirlooms, are elegant but not imposing. The pleasant guest rooms are altogether simpler (two shower rooms are just curtained off) with quaint touches, such as an old stone sink and a wallpapered safe as bedside tables, while the big bosky garden is a good barrier against the road. On request, all diets can be catered for at breakfast. *Gîte space for 2-5 people.*

Rooms: 1 suite, 1 triple, 1 double, all with bath or shower & wc.

Price: €38–€56 for two.

Meals: Wide choice of restaurants in Saumur.

Closed: Occasionally.

From Saumur Tourist Office N147 for Angers. Cross Loire (2 bridges) & railway; straight on 500m; left Ave des Maraîchers; 400m, right Rue Grange Couronne; house 1st on right.

Catherine & Emmanuel Bastid
La Bouère Salée, Rue Grange Couronne
49400 St Lambert des Levées, Saumur
Maine-et-Loire
Tel: (0)2 41 67 38 85/(0)2 41 51 12 52
Fax: (0)2 41 51 12 52
E-mail: manubastid@aol.com
Web: www.ifrance.com/labouere/

Entry No: 333   Map: 7

The flattish countryside round the traditional farmhouse gives little inkling that under your feet are deep quarries and underground caves, transformed by Carole and Michel into a maze of terraced gardens and courtyards. One cave is now a kitchen for guests and another a gallery for Carole's stained-glass works. Three bedrooms open onto the sunny, Mediterranean-style courtyard, the others look down onto a sunken garden. All are simply but most attractively decorated, while mouth-wateringly vibrant colours give an exotic feel to the dining room. Your young artist hosts are delightful and attentive. Fascinating and unusual. We loved it. *Children over seven welcome.*

Rooms: 3 doubles, 1 suite, all with shower & wc.

Price: €44–€58 for two.

Meals: Dinner €20, including wine & coffee; use of kitchen extra; restaurants 3-13 km.

Closed: Never.

From Saumur, D960 to Doué-la-Fontaine. There 1st right on D214, to Forges. Through the village; fork left at crucifix. House signposted on left.

Carole Berréhar & Michel Tribondeau
L'Estaminet de la Fosse, La Fosse
49700 Forges-Meigné sous Doué
Maine-et-Loire
Tel: (0)2 41 50 90 09
E-mail: info@chambrehote.com
Web: www.chambrehote.com

Entry No: 334   Map: 7

House and hostess are refined but relaxedly welcoming - a perfect balance. Once the servants' quarters of the château (they housed their servants grandly...), it is in a deep and secluded valley, right on the GR3 long-distance path and the Loire Valley walk. The bedrooms are under the high exposed roof beams, elegantly and discreetly done and with good antiques, matching wallpaper and flowery English-style fabrics, impeccable bathrooms and loos. Breakfast is beautifully served, with linen table napkins and silver teapot; and you can picnic in the garden later if you wish. *Gîte space for 4 people.*

Rooms: 1 twin/triple, 1 suite for 4, both with shower & wc.

Price: €61 for two.

Meals: Wide choice of restaurants in the area.

Closed: Never.

From Saumur D751 W for 15km. In Gennes D69 towards Doué la Fontaine, up hill, past church & police station. At r'bout take road past Super U; drive to house is 500m along on left.

Annick & Jean-Baptiste Boisset
Le Haut Joreau
49350 Gennes
Maine-et-Loire
Tel: (0)2 41 38 02 58
Fax: (0)2 41 38 15 02
E-mail: joreau@fr.st
Web: joreau.fr.st

Entry No: 335   Map: 7

Sketches of Maria Callas greet you in the conservatory-like hall of this elegant unstuffy mansion and Rossini may accompany candlelit dinner in the big-windowed dining room. Everywhere there are books, unusual objects and pictures collected by Jean-Jacques, who is your lively, entertaining host in Didier's weekday absence. In the quiet, comfortable bedrooms, stylish contemporary fabrics contrast with large 70's bathrooms. The Loire flows tantalisingly nearby, hidden by jungly woodland that threatens to engulf the tended garden, while a theatrical curtain of trailing ivy conceals massive *caves* and their memories of past winemaking days.

Rooms: 2 doubles, both with bath & wc; 1 suite with bath & separate wc.

Price: €69 for two; €114 for four.

Meals: Dinner €30, including wine & coffee.

Closed: Never.

From Saumur D947 towards Chinon. Entrance on right 2km after Gratien & Mayer cellars.

Didier Jehanno
La Cour Pavée
374 route de Montsoreau
49400 Dampierre sur Loire
Maine-et-Loire
Tel: (0)2 41 67 65 88
Fax: (0)2 41 51 11 61
Web: www.cour-pavee.com

Entry No: 336   Map: 7

What a full life! A convent in the 1500s, a courtier's residence in the 1600s, a police station in the 1900s, it is now a B&B, still with its superb stone staircases. The *Suite Blanche* (an orange room leads to the white room) has beams, tiles, mirrors, fireplaces, carved armoires. Other rooms are big too, a little less stunning, and maintenance may be needed. But the glorious living room with its mystifying high-level door, high beamed ceiling and old built-in cupboards is worth the visit by itself. Monsieur restored antiques - his house speaks well of his former trade; Madame is pleasant and efficient; restoration continues.

Rooms: 2 suites, 1 triple (with kitchenette), all with bath or shower & wc (very occasionally sharing).

Price: €55 for two.

Meals: Choice of restaurants in town or self-catering.

Closed: November-February.

The owners are Franco-British, the breakfast sometimes 'Scandinavian', the house indisputably French and the squirrels on the green sward red. In this haven of quiet, Denis will fill you with tales of their days as foreign correspondents. Patricia has plenty of stories too and is a passionate gardener - it shows, out there. For you, there are good beds in country décor, a cosy sitting room with the old bread oven, a complete kitchen and a lovely path down to the stream. After visiting villages, walking the trails, dreaming in the rolling country, return to good conversation and real hospitality.

Rooms: 2 doubles/twins, both with bath & wc.

Price: €52 for two.

Meals: Auberge in village; good restaurants nearby; guest kitchen available.

Closed: 1 November-Easter.

From Saumur, D147 for Poitiers. In Montreuil Bellay, follow signs to Les Petits Augustins la Joie Vivante; entrance to house near chapel.

From Mayenne N12 for Alençon for 5km; left D34 for Lassay. In Montreuil Poulay, left D160; house 700m along.

Monique & Jacques Guézénec
Demeure des Petits Augustins
Place des Augustins
49260 Montreuil Bellay
Maine-et-Loire
Tel: (0)2 41 52 33 88
Fax: (0)2 41 52 33 88
E-mail: moniqueguezenecbb@minitel.net

Denis & Patricia Legras-Wood
Le Vieux Presbytère
53640 Montreuil Poulay
Mayenne
Tel: (0)2 43 00 86 32
Fax: (0)2 43 00 81 42
E-mail: 101512.245@compuserve.com

Entry No: 337   Map: 7

Entry No: 338   Map: 2

Prize-winning cows in the fields, prize-winning owners in the house. They are an exceptionally engaging, relaxed couple and their conversation is the heart and soul of this marvellous place. At dinner, everything from pâté to *potage* to *patisserie* is home-made *Normand* and attractively presented. Breakfast is a feast at which you help yourself to eggs, cheese and buckets of coffee. The refurbished, Japanese grass-papered bedrooms have a few antiquey bits and bobs and pretty window boxes. Good rooms, creative cooking, excellent people.

Rooms: 1 triple, 1 double, 1 twin, all with shower or bath & wc.

Price: €43 for two.

Meals: Good choice of restaurants nearby.

Closed: December-March.

This unusual and proudly-restored 15th-century manor has a staircase tower to the upstairs bedroom to lend an air of mystery, a bread oven and a fine dining room where breakfast is served to the chiming of the church clock. The Nays' old family home, it is well lived in and they love sharing it with guests. Rooms are elegant with antiques and decent bathrooms. They can teach you French, weave baskets, make music and radiate enthusiasm. A wonderful atmosphere in delectable countryside. Readers have loved the "real character of the place".

Rooms: 1 double, 1 triple, both with bath or shower & wc.

Price: €38 for two.

Meals: Restaurants in village or 3km.

Closed: Never.

From Fougères N12 east for Laval 15km; farm signposted on right.

From Laval N157 for Le Mans; at Soulgé sur Ouette D20 left to Evron; D7 for Mayenne. Signs in Mézangers.

Maurice & Thérèse Trihan
La Rouaudière
Mégaudais
53500 Ernée
Mayenne
Tel: (0)2 43 05 13 57
Fax: (0)2 43 05 71 15

Léopold & Marie-Thérèse Nay
Le Cruchet
53600 Mézangers
Mayenne
Tel: (0)2 43 90 65 55
E-mail: bandb.lecruchet@wanadoo.fr

Entry No: 339   Map: 2

Entry No: 340   Map: 2

In the heart of the town, here are *chambres d'hôtes* on the grandest of scales in a splendid mansion, a fine park with formal French box garden and romantic 'English' landscaped section – and exquisitely courteous hosts (Monsieur speaks perfect English). The magnificently châteauesque rooms are large and light, each in individual, inimitably French, style. There's an easy mix of luxury and comfort in the cavernous bathrooms, marble fireplaces and beautiful panelling, some of it delicate blue against striking yellow curtains and bedcovers. Exceptional position, style and attention to detail.

Rooms: 3 doubles, 1 suite, all with bath & shower & wc.

Price: €90–€100 for two.

Meals: Good choice of restaurants in Laval.

Closed: December & January.

Monsieur le Comte is the sprightly patriarch of this very close family which will extend to include you: Loïk and Hélène, the younger generation, give a wonderfully relaxed welcome to their guests. This exceptional place has innumerable expressions of history, taste and personality: oval windows, canopied beds, sunken marble bath, children's room, lift to bathroom, ancient oaks, bread oven, ice house, endless reception rooms, magnificent stone staircase, pool like a 'mini-Versailles'. Teresa Berganza stayed and practised at the grand piano - she too enjoyed that gracious and natural sense of hospitality.

Rooms: 2 doubles, 1 twin, 3 singles, all with bath or shower & wc. Extra space for children.

Price: €140 for two.

Meals: Restaurants in village.

Closed: Mid-December-mid-January.

In Laval follow signs to Mairie then brown signs to Le Bas du Gast - opp. 'Salle Polyvalente' and 'Bibliothèque' (about 1km from Mairie).

From Château Gontier, N171 to Craon. Château clearly signposted as you enter town. 30km south of Laval.

M & Mme François Williot
Le Bas du Gast
6 rue de la Halle aux Toiles
53000 Laval
Mayenne
Tel: (0)2 43 49 22 79
Fax: (0)2 43 56 44 71
E-mail: chateaubasdugast@wanadoo.fr

Comte Louis de Guébriant, Loïk & Hélène de Guébriant
Château de Craon
53400 Craon, Mayenne
Tel: (0)2 43 06 11 02
Fax: (0)2 43 06 05 18
E-mail: guebrian@club-internet.fr
Web: www.chateaudecraon.com

Entry No: 341   Map: **2**

Entry No: 342   Map: **2**

Here beside the luminous fast-flowing river reigns the easy atmosphere of genuine class - you are welcomed by Madame's gentle intelligence and Monsieur's boundless energy. The house has been much added to since the family arrived 400 years ago but each of the objects, antiques and pictures tells a story. The 1st-floor double and big light bathroom are full of interest and comfort; the 2nd-floor suite is ideal for families with its four-poster double and choice of other rooms. The large, formal sitting room is pure 'château' while across the hall/piano room there's an elegant dining room with separate tables for breakfast.

Rooms: 1 double, 1 twin, 1 suite, all with bath & wc.

Price: €76 for two.

Meals: Restaurants nearby.

Closed: Never.

This vastly old, characterful farmhouse with its amazing oak staircase is now home to the delightful young fifth generation who juggle cattle, children and guests with skill and a light, humorous touch: the iron man in the *salon*, the secret *grog flambé* recipe are reminders of ancestral traditions. In the big, soft rooms, every bed is canopied, except the single box-bed which is carved and curtained to a tee. There are nooks, crannies, crooked lines and angles; terracotta floors, half-timbered walls, antiques - and pretty shower rooms. Ducks paddle in the enchanting pond, cows graze in the fields, apples become cider - bucolic peace. *Gîte space for 6 people.*

Rooms: 2 doubles, 1 triple, 1 family, all with shower/small bath & wc.

Price: €38.50-€43 for two.

Meals: Dinner €12.50, including aperitif & coffee, €7 for wine.

Closed: Never.

In Château Gontier N162 N for Laval. Entrance on left 50m after last r'bout as you leave town.

From Laval N162 towards Château Gontier for 14km; left through Villiers Charlemagne to Ruille Froid Fonds; left C4 towards Bignon for 1km. Signposted.

Brigitte & François d'Ambrières
Château de Mirvault-Azé
53200 Château Gontier
Mayenne
Tel: (0)2 43 07 10 82
Fax: (0)2 43 07 10 82
E-mail: bfljc@hotmail.com

Christophe & Christine Davenel
Villeprouvé
53170 Ruille Froid Fonds
Mayenne
Tel: (0)2 43 07 71 62
Fax: (0)2 43 07 71 62
christ.davenel wanadoo.f

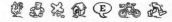

Entry No: 343   Map: 2

Entry No: 344   Map: 2

The old stairs wind up through the subtly-lit interior to fairly sophisticated rooms with lovely furniture, beams and low doorways, plenty of sitting areas, rooms off for your children or butler - your Franco-Irish hosts' beautiful restoration of this ancient priory, mostly 14th and 15th century, is a marvel (famous people get married in the chapel). They are a friendly, humorous couple of horse and hunting enthusiasts who enjoy their new B&B activity. The huge grounds lead to open country unspoilt by 20th-century wonders, that big pond is full of carp for keen fishers and there's a tennis court.

Rooms: 1 double, 1 family, 1 suite for 5, all with bath & wc; 1 double with shower & wc.

Price: €53.50-€91.50 for two.

Meals: Dinner €23, including wine & coffee.

Closed: 1 May-15 September.

From Chateau Gontier D28 for Grez en Bouère; at Gennes right D15 for Bierné; in St Aignan right before church; house 3km on left.

Ghislain & Françoise Drion
La Gilardière
53200 Gennes sur Glaize
Mayenne
Tel: (0)2 43 70 93 03
Fax: (0)2 43 70 93 03
E-mail: lagilar@hotmail.com

Entry No: 345   Map: 2

All who stay at the Logis du Ray are sure to be beautifully looked after – the dozen or so fine draught horses by Jacques, B&B guests by Martine. From their previous life in Paris as antique dealers comes a love of beautiful things to add to their natural hospitality, but if you can tear yourself away from the beautiful bedrooms, the homely sitting room or the delightful cottage garden, there are riverside walks and unspoilt countryside to explore on foot or by pony and trap (your hosts run a carriage-driving school). Our readers love it.

Rooms: 1 double, 2 triples, all with shower & wc.

Price: €58-€65 for two; €90 for three.

Meals: Good restaurants in village.

Closed: Never.

From Sablé sur Sarthe D309/D27 for Angers; entering St Denis, 1st left at 'Renov' Cuir' sign. House 100m along; signposted.

Martine & Jacques Lefebvre
Le Logis du Ray
53290 Saint Denis d'Anjou
Mayenne
Tel: (0)2 43 70 64 10
Fax: (0)2 43 70 65 53

Entry No: 346   Map: 2

The door stands open to welcome all comers or for waving excitedly to the little steam train - this happy, active couple run three teenagers and a farm and keep a truly hospitable house, he the handyman, she the decorator and mosaic-layer (superb pool in converted barn). Dinner is a lengthy, gregarious, joyful affair - wonderful for lovers of French family cooking. The guest quarters in the outbuildings, endearingly French, may show signs of the passing of time... and the family cats, but you will like the Langlais a lot. And her 150 eggcups. *Well-behaved pets with watchful owners only. Gîte space for 6 people.*

Rooms: 2 doubles, 1 twin, 1 triple, plus 1 suite in 'La Petite Maison', all with shower & wc.

Price: €42 for two.

Meals: Dinner €18, including wine or cider & coffee.

Closed: One week at Christmas.

A house of huge character and charm, it has exciting memories of the 100 Years War and a turret turned into a four-bed children's delight - a round stone nest with a magical little doorway, narrow windows and a fireplace. Other rooms have period country furniture, endless views across the beautiful Sarthe countryside, space and parquet floors. Madame is an utterly delightful hostess and an excellent cook of regional specialities; Monsieur is quietly, humorously supportive; the atmosphere of the house is one of simple, unaffected hospitality.

Rooms: 1 quadruple with bath & wc; 1 triple, 1 double with shower, sharing wc.

Price: €42-€46 for two.

Meals: Dinner €16, including wine & coffee.

Closed: Never.

From Alençon N138 S for 4km; left D55 through Champfleur for Bourg le Roi; farm sign 1km after Champfleur.

Denis & Christine Langlais
Garencière
72610 Champfleur
Sarthe
Tel: (0)2 33 31 75 84
Fax: (0)2 33 27 42 09
E-mail: denislanglais@wanadoo.fr

From Mamers D3 for Le Mêle for 6km - do not go into Aillières; farm on left.

Marie-Rose & Moïse Lorieux
La Locherie
Aillières
72600 Mamers
Sarthe
Tel: (0)2 43 97 76 03

Entry No: 347   Map: **3**

Entry No: 348   Map: **3**

Parts of this old French farmhouse can be traced back to the 11th century but until recently Claude and Ginette spent 20 years rearing 20th-century chickens for the local market. They now cook delicious meals for their guests, *poulet à l'estragon* being one of Claude's specialities. The bedrooms, which have sloping ceilings and exposed beams, are comfortable, attractively decorated and furnished. One has a fine white iron bedstead, another a tiny window at floor level. But what beats everything is the view from the dining room - the surrounding countryside is luscious. *Gîte space for 4 people.*

Rooms: 3 doubles, all with shower & separate wc.

Price: €43 for two.

Meals: Dinner €19.50, including wine & coffee.

Closed: Never.

Your hosts are the nicest, easiest of aristocrats, determined to keep the ancestral home alive in a dignified manner - 19 generations on. A jewel set in rolling parkland, sheep grazing under mature trees, horses in the paddock, swans on a bit of the moat, peacock, deer, boar... it has antiques on parquet floors and modern beds; bathrooms and loos in turrets, cupboards, alcoves; an elegant dining room with family silver, a sitting room with log fire, family portraits, a small book-lined library - and do ask to see the chapel upstairs. Hunting trophies, timeless tranquillity, lovely people.

Rooms: 1 suite for 3, 4 doubles, 1 twin, all with bath or shower & wc.

Price: €82-€107 for two.

Meals: Dinner €37, including wine & coffee.

Closed: Never.

From Mamers D311 towards Alençon for 7km; right D116 towards Villaines la Carelle; enter village towards St Longis. Gîtes de France sign on left.

From Alençon N138 S for Le Mans about 14km; at La Hutte left D310 for 10km; right D19 through Courgains; left D132 to Monhoudou; signs.

Claude & Ginette Pelletier
Le Fay
72600 Villaines la Carelle
Sarthe
Tel: (0)2 43 97 73 40
Web: assoc.wanadoo.fr/bunia/lefay/

Michel & Marie-Christine de Monhoudou
Château de Monhoudou
72260 Monhoudou, Sarthe
Tel: (0)2 43 97 40 05
Fax: (0)2 43 33 11 58
E-mail: monhoudou@aol.com
Web: www.monhoudou.com

In the family tradition, Marie is a good, helpful hostess. Laurent is in motor racing and buffs flock for Le Mans. Theirs is so French a château, not overwhelming, just peaceful loveliness with farmland and woods beyond. Some rooms look onto an amazing 400-year-old cedar, others have wonderful garden views, all have interesting furniture and are being redone (50 windows to replace!). The long panelled sitting room feels like the inside of an old ship and it is all unpretentious with some gratifyingly untidy corners, small, pretty shower rooms and much unselfconscious good taste. *Gîte space for 6.*

Rooms: 2 doubles/triples, 3 suites for 4/5, all with bath or shower & wc; 2 separate wcs.

Price: €49-€58 for two.

Meals: Dinner €19 with wine & coffee.

Closed: Never, please book ahead.

From Le Mans N23 for La Flèche to Cérans Foulletourte; D31 to Oizé; left on D32; signposted on right.

Madame, determined, energetic and most hospitable, is a perfectionist. Her creeper-clothed house is extremely and prettily flowery. Her rooms have flower names that inspire the décor of floral patterns, cushions, bedcovers, friezes; all sorts of chairs and side tables found in *brocante* shops then lovingly restored and painted with... flowers. Her garden blooms as wonderfully as her house, the rich and copious breakfast is served in the old-tiled, wood-fired extension and she runs the whole show with the help of her friendly, well-behaved Alsatian.

Rooms: 1 suite (triple & single), 1 double, 1 twin, 1 quadruple, all with bath or shower & wc.

Price: €43-€58 for two.

Meals: Choice of restaurants 3-7 km.

Closed: 1 October-1 April, except by arrangement.

From Le Mans D147 S to Arnage (8km); left fork D307 for 15km; right D77 for Mansigné for 5km; Route de Tulièvre is tiny road on left, 3km after Requeil.

Laurent Sénéchal & Marie David
Château de Montaupin
72330 Oizé
Sarthe
Tel: (0)2 43 87 81 70
Fax: (0)2 43 87 26 25
E-mail: chateaudemontaupin@oreka.com

Marie-Dominique Blanchard
La Maridaumière
Route de Tulièvre
72510 Mansigné
Sarthe
Tel: (0)2 43 46 58 52
Fax: (0)2 43 46 58 52

The plain face on the street hides another world behind: a beautifully-decorated 17th-century house, guest rooms with masses of personality in a 14th-century outbuilding round a lily-pond courtyard, a lovely garden with 300 trees and a properly-concealed pool, all stretching back from the street. Once in the garden, you'll scarcely know you're in town. The rooms are nicely independent - the suite, in a building of its own, even has kitchenette and washing machine - while convivial meals are shared in the dining room. Monsieur prides himself on his choice of Loire wines from small, unpublicised wine-growers. Charming house, host and region. *Gîte space for 4 people.*

Rooms: 1 double, 1 triple, 1 suite for 4/5 with small kitchen, all with shower & wc.

Price: €46-€56 for two.

Meals: Dinner €14, including table wine (Loire wines €8).

Closed: Never.

From Le Mans D147 to Arnage; D307 to Pontvallain; house in town centre; signposted.

Guy Vieillet
Place Jean Graffin
72510 Pontvallain
Sarthe
Tel: (0)2 43 46 36 70
Fax: (0)2 43 46 36 70

A picture of a place: a three-acre, tree-reflecting pond full of fish, frogs and ducks, a group of low buildings, views to a hilltop village - peace and space for all. There are games (croquet, table tennis, *pétanque*), a boat, even a sauna. Smallish, well-fitted rooms have mixed modern and old furnishings and separate entrances: you have a degree of independence, somewhat at the price of homeliness perhaps. Madame loves feeding guests and chatting. Monsieur twinkles and gets on with the garden. They are a charming, caring couple. Breakfast includes cheese and cold meats. Dinner is an important event, so indulge! "The kids were in seventh heaven."

Rooms: 2 triples, 2 doubles, 1 twin, all with shower & wc.

Price: €43 for two.

Meals: Dinner €14, including wine & coffee.

Closed: 15 November-1 March.

From Le Mans D304 to Grand Lucé and La Chartre. Left on D305 through Pont de Braye. Left on D303 to Lavenay & follow signs (2km).

Monique & Jacques Déage
Le Patis du Vergas
72310 Lavenay
Sarthe
Tel: (0)2 43 35 38 18
Fax: (0)2 43 35 38 18

Marie-Claire and Martin, an ardent Anglophile, have converted this 18th-century watermill brilliantly - a labour of love, down to the cogwheels that turn in the great kitchen where breakfast is served at the huge oak table. She is so relaxed, such good adult company, so unflappably efficient that it's hard to believe she has four children under 10 - other kids love it here. The double-height sitting room is full of books and videos for all; simple, attractive rooms have good beds, old tiled floors, bare stone walls. The atmosphere embraces you, the country sounds of stream, cockerel and Angelus prayer bells soothe, the unsung area brims with interest.

Rooms: 2 doubles, 1 family, all with bath or shower & wc.

Price: €43 for two.

Meals: Restaurant opposite.

Closed: Never.

Bushels of history pour from the beams and vaulted ceilings of the moated priory, snug beneath its old church: built in the 12th, extended in the 16th, it had monks into the 20th century. Christophe loves telling the history, Marie-France does the decorating, brilliantly in keeping with the elegant old house: oriental rugs on old tiled floors, pale-painted beams over stone fireplaces, fine old paintings on plain walls and good modern beds under soft-coloured covers. They are attentive, intelligent hosts, only too happy to share their vaulted dining room, antique furniture and peaceful garden, and the road is not an inconvenience.

Rooms: 1 twin, 2 doubles, 1 suite, all with bath, shower & wc.

Price: €84-€99 for two; suite €114 for three.

Meals: Auberge opposite & restaurants nearby.

Closed: 1 November-31 January, unless booked in advance.

From Tours N138 towards Le Mans to Dissay sous Courcillon (35km). In village, left at lights; mill is just past church.

From Tours or Le Mans N158 to Dissay sous Courcillon - Le Prieuré signposted in village.

Marie-Claire Bretonneau
Le Moulin du Prieuré
3 rue de la Gare
72500 Dissay sous Courcillon
Sarthe
Tel: (0)2 43 44 59 79

Christophe & Marie-France Calla
Le Prieuré
1 rue de la Gare
72500 Dissay sous Courcillon
Sarthe
Tel: (0)2 43 44 09 09
Fax: (0)2 43 44 09 09
E-mail: ccalla@club-internet.fr

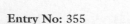

Inside this good old house, oak panelling is set off by touches of aquamarine: a tablecloth in the breakfast room, a wall behind the ornate carved staircase. Bedrooms are large, elegant and truly French, two with antique sleigh beds. We really loved the children's room: no cartoon characters, just pale striped walls, white furniture and a starched cotton bedspread. Anne left banking in Paris to move here with Jean-Pierre when their son, now 19, was born, found peace at last, and started bed and breakfast seven years ago. The grounds are large and peaceful, too, with a couple of holes of golf.

Rooms: 1 double, 1 suite for up to 4, both with bathroom & wc.

Price: €85–€95 for two.

Meals: Choice of restaurants locally.

Closed: Never.

From Verneuil sur Avre D941 towards La Ferté Vidame. Just before La Ferté, take tree-lined drive on left.

Jean-Pierre & Anne Jallot
Manoir de la Motte
28340 La Ferté Vidame
Eure-et-Loir
Tel: (0)2 37 37 51 69
Fax: (0)2 37 37 51 56
E-mail: manoir.de.la.motte.lfv@wanadoo.fr

Loire Valley

Oh gentle living that was here – and deep, dark intrigue – when the Renaissance blossomed by the banks of France's mightiest river and kings and courtiers rode out to hunt the noble stag.

Entry No: 357   Map: **3**

This was Roger and Dagmar's country cottage until they left Paris eight years ago to live here. He's a retired chef, she left her native Germany and adopted France many moons ago. They are friendly and hospitable and will probably join you for breakfast where there will be hot croissants - or you could make it a huge meal, with ham, smoked salmon and cheese. If you time it right, the walls are covered with roses: it looks a cosy place to stay, even from outside. One bedroom is wood-panelled, the other more typical with sloping rafters; fabrics are flowered and the varnished wooden floors are symmetrically rugged.

Rooms: 1 double, 1 suite for 3, both with bath & wc.

Price: €39-€51 for two.

Meals: Dinner €19, including wine & coffee.

Closed: January-February.

Jean-Marc is golf mad, Catherine is horse crazy: her mare is as understanding as a dog (together they'll take you walking or cycling) and she runs a horse-blanket laundry service; he does golf training for all ages, all levels; their enthusiasm is infectious. In a quiet little village, behind high gates, they, their son, Labrador and Great Dane receive you with alacrity in the big beamed kitchen and send you up the steep barn stairs to sleep in simple white-walled, Italian-tiled rooms where patches of bright colour - cushions, lampshades, towels, toothmugs - punctuate the space most effectively.

Rooms: 1 double, 2 twin, 2 family, all with bath & wc.

Price: €58-€76 for two; €108 family room for four.

Meals: Restaurants in Nogent le Roi & Maintenon.

Closed: Never.

From Chartres D939 NW towards Verneuil sur Avre; through Châteauneuf en Thymerais; right D133 towards Blévy; follow signs to Chambres d'Hôtes.

From Paris A13, A12, N12, exit Gambais for Nogent le Roi. Entering Coulombs, left at lights for Chandelles; left at crossroads 1.5km; house on right.

Roger Parmentier
2 route des Champarts
28170 Blévy
Eure-et-Loir
Tel: (0)2 37 48 01 21
Fax: (0)2 37 48 01 21
E-mail: parti@club-internet.fr

Catherine & Jean-Marc Simon
Les Chandelles
19 rue des Sablons, Chandelles
28130 Villiers le Morhier, Eure-et-Loir
Tel: (0)2 37 82 71 59
Fax: (0)2 37 82 71 59
E-mail: info@chandelles-golf.com
Web: www.chandelles-golf.com

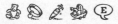

Loire Valley

Only 15 minutes from the soaring glory of Chartres, the house is wrapped about by fields worked single-handedly by Bruno. No typical farmer, he went to the Lycée Français in London, so conversation can be in either language. Rooms here are blissfully quiet and deeply comfortable - good linen and a satisfying mix of old-fashioned and modern. Dinner is generally good - try Nathalie's goat cheese as a starter perhaps followed by *porc avec pruneaux* - and the family eat with you, except during harvest time. Simple sitting/dining room, easy access to the garden, nice children, relaxed, refined people.

Rooms: 2 doubles, 1 twin, all with bath or shower & wc.

Price: €45-€53 for two.

Meals: Dinner €15, including wine & coffee.

Closed: Never.

Up two steep spirals to the attic (fear not, Monsieur will carry your bags), across the family's little prayer room, which is your sitting room, and the mood is set: the bedroom feels rather like a church with unexpectedly comfortable beds, lots of books, and a good shower on the floor below. There are reminders of pilgrimage and religion everywhere - all very appropriate so close to the great Cathedral. Madame is gently friendly, Monsieur is a charmer and enjoys a chuckle. A slightly eccentric and welcoming place in a timeless spot.

Rooms: 1 twin with shower & wc.

Price: €43 for two.

Meals: Choice of restaurants at your doorstep.

Closed: Never.

In Chartres N154 N for Dreux; after Chartres right D133 for Fresnay; signs for Chambres d'Hôtes to Levéville.

Arriving in Chartres, follow signs for IBIS Centre; park by Hotel IBIS (Place Drouaise); walk 20m along Rue de la Porte Drouaise to Rue Muret (approx. 100m car to house).

Nathalie & Bruno Vasseur
Ferme du Château
Levéville
28300 Bailleau l'Évêque
Eure-et-Loir
Tel: (0)2 37 22 97 02
Fax: (0)2 37 22 97 02

Jean-Loup & Nathalie Cuisiniez
Maison JLN
80 rue Muret
28000 Chartres
Eure-et-Loir
Tel: (0)2 37 21 98 36
Fax: (0)2 37 21 98 36
E-mail: jln.cuisiniez@wanadoo.fr

A beautiful painted sign points to the well-restored yet somewhat quaint old house. Madame is matronly and trusting and the house has a warm, family, lived-in air, with old pieces of furniture and pets ensconced on sofas. The three cosy, white guest rooms and one very large ground-floor room have excellent bedding. Birdsong soothes your ear - your hosts know all about the various bird species - and wheat fields sway before your eye as you rest in the pretty garden. In summer there is a children's pool. Eulogies for these people have reached us. *Bookings not confirmed by 5pm on day of arrival may be re-allocated.*

Rooms: 1 double, 1 triple, 2 quadruples, all with shower & wc (some on landing).

Price: €41.50 for two.

Meals: Choice of restaurants 7km.

Closed: Never.

Michel is a farmer with a difference, he has a rare expertise of which he is very proud: he grows poppies for use in pharmaceuticals. Géraldine's lively manner and easy welcome into her delightful family relieve the dreariness of the ever-flat Beauce. The farm is set round a quiet, tidy courtyard where rabbits and hens lead their short lives, the good guest rooms are light and pleasantly if simply furnished, the bathrooms pristine. "Remarkable value. Real people. They've got it just right," said one reader, but don't expect designer décor or gourmet food at these amazing prices - it's just gentle and genuine. *Gîte space for 5 people.*

Rooms: 1 triple, 2 doubles, 1 twin, all with shower & wc.

Price: €33 for two.

Meals: Dinner €11, including wine, by arrangement only.

Closed: Never.

From A11 exit Thivars; N10 towards Châteaudun for 15km; left to Moriers; D153 to Pré St Martin; signposted.

Bernadette & Jean-Baptiste Violette
Le Carcotage Beauceron
8 rue Saint Martin
28800 Pré St Martin, Eure-et-Loir
Tel: (0)2 37 47 27 21
Fax: (0)2 37 47 38 09
E-mail: carcotage.beauceron@wanadoo.fr
Web: www.carcotage.com

From A10 Allaines exit on D927 towards Châteaudun to La Maladrerie; D39 to Loigny. Signposted opp. church.

Géraldine & Michel Nivet
8 rue Chanzy
28140 Loigny la Bataille
Eure-et-Loir
Tel: (0)2 37 99 70 71
Fax: (0)2 37 99 70 71

Loire Valley

Here is a taste of real French provincial aristocratic style, with much horsiness: the suite is over the stables, other rooms are full of equine reminders, including Toulouse-Lautrec lithographs. You sleep in great comfort under period rafters, dine *en famille* by candlelight (outside in summer), and breakfast whenever you like - "people are on holiday", says Madame generously. Both your hosts were members of the French National Carriage-Driving team and offer rides in their prize-winning equipage. Lots of other outdoor activities are to be found in the huge forest which surrounds the quietly elegant building.

Rooms: 3 doubles, 1 suite, all with bath & wc.

Price: € 115 for two.

Meals: Dinner € 35, including wine & coffee.

Closed: Never.

This elegant 18th-century canalside townhouse has inherited an expansive atmosphere from its wine merchant builders. They were loading their wine onto barges on the canal which flows under the windows until the 1930s. So much for the past. For the present: you will dine with your refined hosts in the antique-furnished, chandeliered dining room, sleep in good, very individual rooms, breakfast off ravishing Gien china with fruit from the garden, meet Lucia the black Labrador who helps her owner welcome guests over a glass of local white wine. Madame is happy to arrange visits to wine growers.

Rooms: 1 apartment for 4, 1 triple, both with bath & wc; 1 apartment for 5 with bath & wc downstairs.

Price: € 50 for two.

Meals: Dinner € 25, including wine & coffee.

Closed: Never.

From Montargis N7 for Paris 6km; right through forest to Paucourt; entering village 1st right Route Grotte aux Loups for 200m; house on left, ivy on wall.

From Orléans N60 E towards Montargis/Nevers, exit to Fay aux Loges; through Fay, cross canal, left D709; house 1st on left arriving in Donnery.

Émmanuelle & Antoine de Jessé Charleval
Domaine de Bel Ébat
45200 Paucourt, Loiret
Tel: (0)2 38 98 38 47/
    (0)6 81 34 68 99
Fax: (0)2 38 85 66 43
E-mail: belebat@wanadoo.fr

Nicole & Jacques Sicot
Les Charmettes
45450 Donnery
Loiret
Tel: (0)2 38 59 22 50
Fax: (0)2 38 59 26 96
E-mail: nsicot@mail.club-internet.fr

Entry No: 364   Map: **8**

Entry No: 365   Map: **8**

Sologne used to be the hunting ground of kings. Your bubbling, smiling hostess is keen on hunting and horses: hence horses and dogs outside, horns and antlers in. Hers is a typical brick and stone Solognote house with great beams and lovely flagstones, the talking telly in contemporary contrast. The double room is brilliantly done, small but cosy, with steeply sloping ceilings - no good for the over-stretched; the suites are larger (one is 60m²); all are differently furnished - this is very much a family house. Madame, genuinely eager to please, cooks only occasionally but will happily drive you to and from the restaurant.

Rooms: 1 double, 1 suite for 4, both with bath or shower & wc.

Price: €54-€77 for two.

Meals: 2 restaurants 1km; self-catering possible.

Closed: Never.

A vast estate by the Loire, a house for guests, another for family, exotic pheasants and peacocks swanning around the splendid garden, even a private hunting reserve (long-stay guests may visit it). Your welcoming young hosts - he is a vet, she looks after the house, their small children and you - make it feel friendly despite the grand appearance. The rooms are carefully decorated and have lovely old furnishings. Breakfast is in the *salon* (games and hi-fi) or on the flowered terrace. *Gîte space for 3 people.*

Rooms: 2 doubles, all with shower or bath & wc; 1 suite for 3 with bathroom & kitchen.

Price: €44-€52 for two.

Meals: Good restaurants in Briare or Gien 4km; self-catering in suite.

Closed: Never.

From Orléans N60 E to Châteauneuf sur Loire. Through town centre, over bridge to Tigy; D83 through Vannes; house about 1km on right.

Agnès Celerier
Domaine de Sainte-Hélène
Route d'Isdes
45510 Vannes sur Cosson
Loiret
Tel: (0)2 38 58 04 55
Fax: (0)2 38 58 28 38
E-mail: celerierloiret@hotmail.com

From A6 onto A77 towards Nevers, exit Briare; D952 towards Gien. Between Briare and Gien: signposted by nurseries.

Mme Bénédicte François
Domaine de la Thiau
45250 Briare
Loiret
Tel: (0)2 38 38 20 92
Fax: (0)2 38 67 40 50
E-mail: lathiau@club-internet.fr
Web: perso.club-internet.fr/lathiau

There's a barge restaurant in summer just a stroll from the house and you must see the great 19th-century canal bridge over the Loire at Briare - a stupendous alliance of engineering and nature. The canal flows gently past this handsome old village house but you may hear the less gentle road in the morning. Guest rooms are rustic-furnished and very good-looking - the suite in the loft in the main house with its exposed beams is particularly handsome - and there are two cosy self-contained cottages with kitchens. Nicole and her husband are kind, well-educated and welcoming: their breakfast room is decorated with lots of pretty, personal knick-knacks. *Gîte space for 4 people.*

Rooms: 1 double, 1 suite for 3, both with shower & wc.

Price: €41 for two.

Meals: Restaurants nearby.

Closed: Never.

The whole house is full of worldwide travel memories and there's a romantic and shady walled garden where you can breakfast in traditional French fashion on brioches, croissants and garden fruits in season. The guest rooms are furnished with elegance, taste and those touches of luxury which make you feel pampered. You may be greeted with a glass of Sancerre in the wonderful *salon*, whose old tiles continue into the bedrooms of this 15th-century *logis*. And fluent English, too: Madame is married to an Englishman and her artistic daughter, who clearly inherited her talent from her mother, studied in Manchester. *Gîte space for 4 people.*

Rooms: 1 double, 1 twin, sharing shower & wc; 1 double with bath, shower & wc.

Price: €53.50 for two.

Meals: Choice of restaurants 10km.

Closed: 15 September-15 April.

From Gien (D952) cross Loire for Poilly lez Gien; left D951 to Châtillon sur Loire; signs.

Nicole Lefranc
La Giloutière
13 rue du Port
45360 Châtillon sur Loire
Loiret
Tel: (0)2 38 31 10 61

From Cosne sur Loire D55 W to Ste Gemme & on to Subligny (13km). House just beneath church in walled garden.

Agnès Singer
La Chenevière
18260 Subligny
Cher
Tel: (0)2 48 73 89 93
Fax: (0)2 48 73 89 93
E-mail: agnes.singer@universal.fr

Fantastic bedrooms! In a pretty outbuilding, the double, with a green iron bed, old tiled floor and bold bedspread, is on the ground floor looking onto the garden; the twin has the same tiles underfoot, beams overhead and high wooden beds with an inviting mix of white covers and red quilts. The Count and Countess, who manage forests, farm and hunt but are relatively new to B&B, are charming and thoroughly hospitable. If you would like to eat in, you will join them for dinner in the main house. Members of the family run a vineyard in Provence, so try their wine. *Children under five free. Gîte space for 6 people.*

Rooms: 1 suite for 2-4, with bath, shower & 2 wc.

Price: €99 for two; €145 for four; reduction for 3 nights or more.

Meals: Dinner €15-€22, including wine & coffee; self-catering possible.

Closed: Never.

18th-century stones and 20th-century design have married to turn the old stables into brilliant guest quarters. Pale timber clothes the space with architectural features such as a double-height staircase, 14-foot wooden columns and sliding shutters. The breakfast room is a union of new wood and antique treasures; in the bedrooms, contemporary fabrics couple perfectly with lacy linen and crocheted covers. The house is full of light, the garden, where guests have a terrace, has an abundance of green and flowery things. Meals are delicious, we are told, and Madame quietly and graciously looks after you.

Rooms: 3 doubles, 2 twins, all with bath or shower & wc (2 on ground floor).

Price: €50 for two.

Meals: Dinner €18.50, including wine & coffee.

Closed: 15 November-1 March.

From Bourges D940 to Chapelle d'Angillon; D12 to Ivoy le Pré. At church left D39 for Blancafort, Oizon, Château de la Verrerie for 2.5km; gate on right.

From Sancerre D955 towards Bourges for 16km; D44 left to Montigny and 5km beyond; signposted.

Étienne & Marie de Saporta
La Verrerie
18380 Ivoy le Pré
Cher
Tel: (0)2 48 58 90 86
Fax: (0)2 48 58 92 79
E-mail: desaporta@dactyl-buro.fr

Élisabeth Gressin
La Reculée
18250 Montigny
Cher
Tel: (0)2 48 69 59 18
Fax: (0)2 48 69 52 51
E-mail: e.gressin@terre-net.fr

Sober and solid, this was the village notary's house; the present owner's tastes show in her room names: *Monet, Picasso, Van Gogh*, each decorated to suit. Marie-Christine is into painting and decorating too: the panelling of the dining hall is punctuated by stencilled columns with flowerpots atop - the whole room is a *tour de* painting *force*. Her warm welcome and her colour schemes are worthy of the hospitable Monet: you can breakfast in the garden on fine days and she will even babysit - an extra that Monet probably wouldn't have offered: Picasso possibly? The less agile should ask for *Monet* which has no mezzanine.

Rooms: 1 double, 2 quadruples, all with shower & wc.

Price: €43-€46 for two.

Meals: Good family restaurant 200m.

Closed: Never.

Your hosts came to this rustic haven, where the natural garden flows into woods and fields, deer roam and birdlife astounds, to bring up their new family. Jean is a kindly young grandfather, Chantal teaches infants and the house reflects their travels to distant places: Indian rugs and Moroccan brasses in the pleasant ground-floor guest rooms; a collection of fossils in a vast glass cabinet in the duplex; African memorabilia and lots of old farmhouse stuff everywhere, nothing too sophisticated. Jean will give you a light history lesson if you like. Return after contemplating Bourges to meditate in this corner of God's harmonious garden.

Rooms: 2 triples, 1 quadruple, all with shower & wc; 1 duplex for 4/5 with bath & wc.

Price: €40 for two.

Meals: Dinner €13, including wine & coffee.

Closed: Never.

From N7 exit towards Sancerre. Cross river, turn left & follow canal S to Herry. House signposted on village green.

From Bourges D944 towards Orléans. In Bourgneuf left at little roundabout; immed. right and follow signs 1.5km.

Marie-Christine Genoud
10 place du Champ de Foire
18140 Herry
Cher
Tel: (0)2 48 79 59 02
Fax: (0)2 48 79 59 02
E-mail: imaghine@wanadoo.fr

Jean Malot & Chantal Charlon
La Grande Mouline
Bourgneuf
18110 Saint Eloy de Gy
Cher
Tel: (0)2 48 25 40 44
Fax: (0)2 48 25 40 44

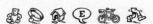

Entry No: 372   Map: 8

Entry No: 373   Map: 8

In deepest Berry, the heartland of rural France, this articulate husband-and-wife team run their beef and cereals farm, taxi their children to school and dancing classes, make their own jam and still have time for their guests. Laurence is vivacious and casually elegant and runs an intelligent, welcoming house. The big, simple yet stylishly attractive bedrooms of her superior 18th-century farmhouse are of pleasing proportions - one of them in an unusual round brick-and-timber tower. Guests may use the swimming pool, set discreetly out of sight, at agreed times. *Gîte space for 9.*

Rooms: 2 doubles, 1 twin, 1 triple, 1 quadruple, all with bath or shower & wc.

Price: €46-€49 for two.

Meals: Restaurants in village or choice 6km.

Closed: Never.

A venerable 15th-century guesthouse round a leafy, secret, garden courtyard, a dining room where ancient timbers, niches, cupboards have been exposed in all their mixed-up glory, unspoilt, old-style bedrooms with antique furniture and new mattresses, and eager new owners who have renewed all the bathrooms and will be gradually redecorating. The family live just across the courtyard with their two small daughters. Add the privilege of sleeping beneath that unsurpassed Cathedral and it feels like a gift from the angels.

Rooms: 2 suites for 3/4, both with bath & wc; 2 doubles, both with bath or shower & wc.

Price: €57-€65 for two.

Meals: Full choice of restaurants within walking distance.

Closed: Never.

From Vierzon N76 towards Bourges through Mehun sur Yèvre; D60 right to Berry Bouy and beyond for about 3km; farm on right.

In the centre of Bourges, at foot of Cathedral. Park in yard if space permits.

Laurence & Géraud de la Farge
Domaine de l'Ermitage
18500 Berry Bouy
Cher
Tel: (0)2 48 26 87 46
Fax: (0)2 48 26 03 28

Nathalie Llopis
Les Bonnets Rouges
3 rue de la Thaumassière
18000 Bourges
Cher
Tel: (0)2 48 65 79 92
Fax: (0)2 48 69 82 05
Web: bonnets-rouges.bourges.net

Entry No: 374   **Map:** 8

Entry No: 375   **Map:** 8

Quiet country folk with tanned faces, clear eyes and much gentle reality, the Chambrins are the most honest, no-fuss, genuinely hospitable couple you could hope for. Special touches, such as great swathes of creeper outside and dried flowers and an old iron cot inside, give character to this simple old farmhouse set among the sunflower fields. The kitchen-cum-breakfast room, with its carved dresser, is small and intimate. Rooms are comfortable, though not huge, and there is a nice guests' sitting area on the landing with well-worn, quilt-thrown sofas, books and games. *Gîte space for 5 people.*

Rooms: 1 double, 1 twin, 1 triple, all with shower & wc.

Price: €31 for two.

Meals: Good choice of restaurants 1-6km.

Closed: Never.

The Claudes inspire remarks like: "I learned heaps about Art Deco and gardening", "a wonderful lanky couple full of life, laughter and intelligence", "lovely, artistic and wacky". Conversation flows effortlessly over glass and ashtray. Their 1940s manor is entirely Art Deco and has an eclectic collection of modern art. You find original art and good beds in the rooms, can learn how to make a properly formal French garden and breakfast whenever you want. Dine - until the small hours - beneath the huge collage in the congenial, bohemian, fun-loving atmosphere created by your down-to-earth hosts (both called Claude). Out of the ordinary - we love it.

Rooms: 2 doubles, 1 twin, all with bath, shower, wc.

Price: €61-€76 for two.

Meals: Dinner €23-€30, including wine & coffee.

Closed: Never.

From Bourges, N144 to Levet; then D28 towards Dun sur Auron. After 2km turn right. House 300m from junction.

From St Amand Montrond, D951 towards Sancoin & Nevers. At Charenton Laugère, D953 towards Dun sur Auron; house is 300m on left.

Marie-Jo & Jean Chambrin
Bannay
18340 Saint Germain des Bois
Cher
Tel: (0)2 48 25 31 03
Fax: (0)2 48 25 31 03

M & Mme Claude Moreau
La Serre
18210 Charenton Laugère
Cher
Tel: (0)2 48 60 75 82
Fax: (0)2 48 60 75 82

Entry No: 376   Map: **8**

Entry No: 377   Map: **8**

In the family for over 200 years, this is a beautifully proportioned house, standing in its large, shady garden. The sitting room is a cool blue/grey symphony, the dining room smart yellow/grey with a most unusual maroon and grey marble table - breakfast is in here while dinner *en famille* is in the big beamed kitchen. Each room has individual character, both elegant and comfortable, and Madame has a fine eye for detail. She is charming, dynamic, casually elegant and genuinely welcoming. Visitors have heaped praise: "Quite the most beautiful house we've ever stayed in", "a unique experience of French hospitality and taste". *Gîte space for 6 people.*

Rooms: 1 double, 2 twins, all with bath or shower & wc.

Price: €42-€49 for two.

Meals: Dinner €18, including wine & coffee.

Closed: Never.

As is the way with watermills, this place is pure delight to look at and the ground-floor double has its own door to the stream-side terrace - the soothing sound of water should drown out any overhead floorboard creaks or noise from lorries on the road at the bottom (ask for a room at the back). Pretty rooms all, with antiques and lace, a good sitting room with the wonderful beam structure of the former milling area (look out for old graffiti on the stone walls) and breakfast feasts. The owners have done a sensitive restoration, are genuinely interested and caring and have a flexible approach to your needs.

Rooms: 1 double, 1 triple, 1 suite for 4, all with shower & wc.

Price: €40 for two.

Meals: Dinner €19, including wine & coffee.

Closed: Mid-October-May.

From A71 exit 8; at roundabout D925 W towards Lignières & Châteauroux. House signposted 500m on right.

From Loches N143 S towards Châteauroux for 16km. On entering Fléré, village square is on right; Moulin clearly signed at bottom of square.

Marie-Claude Dussert
Domaine de la Trolière
18200 Orval
Cher
Tel: (0)2 48 96 47 45
Fax: (0)2 48 96 07 71

Danielle Aumercier
Le Moulin
36700 Fléré la Rivière
Indre
Tel: (0)2 54 39 34 41
Fax: (0)2 54 39 34 93
E-mail: lemoulindeflere@wanadoo.fr

Entry No: 378   Map: **8**

Entry No: 379   Map: **7**

A stylish home of simple sophistication and a relaxed atmosphere has been created here by your charming, talented, partly-Parisian hosts - one a window-dresser, the other a theatre hair-and-make-up artist. The elegant, well-proportioned rooms have canopied beds, subtle/intense colour schemes (*Les Mûriers* just avoids being blackberry-lurid), good bathrooms. The white-walled sitting room is furnished with good country antiques, encompassing sofas, fascinating *objets* and paintings. Enjoy the lime-tree-shaded garden, its roses, lavender and wisteria and your hosts' genuine hospitality. Interesting terms for long stays.

Rooms: 1 double, 1 twin, both with shower & wc; 1 suite for 4 with bath & wc.

Price: €55-€56.50 for two; suite €84 for four.

Meals: Restaurant in village.

Closed: Mid-Sept-mid-June; open winter weekends by arrangement.

From Loches N143 S towards Châteauroux for 16km, through Fléré; 1km beyond, right D13a for Cléré du Bois; signposted.

Claude Renoult
Le Clos Vincents
36700 Fléré la Rivière
Indre
Tel: (0)2 54 39 30 98
Fax: (0)2 54 39 30 98

Entry No: 380   Map: 7

One guest comes every year for the dragonflies to this most striking house in its large park where protected species thrive. Your hostess fell in love with it too and renounced her beloved Paris, but she needs lots of people to make it hum. Relaxed and sociable, she prefers doing to tidying, collects egg cups, will treat you as family and may take you to look for deer. The generous rooms have beams and good old French furniture, the ochre-walled hall is a homely clutter of riding gear, the dining room feels definitely lived in and the open view across parkland to the woods beyond is supremely tranquil. *Gîte space for 4*.

Rooms: 1 double, 1 double/twin, 1 suite for 4, all with bath or shower & wc.

Price: €49 for two.

Meals: Dinner €18, including wine.

Closed: November-March.

From Poitiers N151 60km to Le Blanc; right before river D10 to Bélâbre; left D927 towards St Gaultier for 5km; house on right.

Aude de la Jonquière-Aymé
Le Grand Ajoux
36370 Chalais
Indre
Tel: (0)2 54 37 72 92
Fax: (0)2 54 37 56 60
E-mail: grandajoux@aol.com
Web: members.aol.com/grandajoux

Entry No: 381   Map: 7

This brave and endearing young English couple came to farm in France, with their rabbit-eared sheep (they have two children, and cattle, too) and now invite you to drive 2km through the woods for a taste of rural French tranquillity with an English flavour. Their house still has some old beams and a stone fireplace. Rooms are big, pale-floored, simply-furnished, supremely peaceful: pilgrims to Compostela often stay here. Alison will take good care of you and Robin may tell you tales of shearing French sheep and settling into this other land. He can also show you where to gaze on rare orchids. Argenton, 'Venice of the Indre', is a must.

Rooms: 1 double with bath & wc; 2 doubles, 1 family, sharing bathroom & separate wc.

Price: €46 for two.

Meals: Dinner €15, including wine & coffee.

Closed: January-March.

A retired teacher and enthusiastic hurdy-gurdy player deeply involved in local folk music, Solange Frenkel has converted her 18th-century *grange* (barn) into one of the friendliest *chambre d'hôtes* we know. In the remote rural area where George Sand held her salons and consorted with Chopin, it has high ceilings, huge beams, a vast fireplace in the sunken cosy living room 'pit' and pretty bedrooms with garden entrances. You can have unlimited breakfast while Lasco the Labrador waits patiently to take you walking. One reader simply wrote, "The best". Another: "A lovely person".

Rooms: 1 double, 1 twin, both with bath or shower & wc.

Price: €44 for two.

Meals: Dinner €15, including wine; good restaurant 4km.

Closed: Never.

From Châteauroux A20 exit 16 to Tendu; 1st left into village. Pass Mairie, fork left at church towards Chavin & Pommiers. House 2km up track.

From Bourges N144 for Montluçon to Levet; D940 for La Châtre to Thevet St Julien; D69 for St Chartier for 2km; left for 1km; left again. Signs.

Robin & Alison Mitchell
La Chasse
36200 Tendu
Indre
Tel: (0)2 54 24 07 76

Solange Frenkel
La Garenne
36400 Thevet Saint Julien
Indre
Tel: (0)2 54 30 04 51
Fax: (0)2 54 30 04 51

Entry No: 382   Map: 7

Entry No: 383   Map: 8

A gem - grand hunting lodge rather than château, it stands in acres of parkland before a vast private lake (boating and safe swimming). Karin has lived here for decades and lovingly tends every inch of it, including the vast picture window that seems to bring the lake into the sitting room. The hall carries a surprising display of religious statuary and a great staircase up to the 'Austrian baroque' room with its sloping ceilings, gorgeous rugs and super-luxy bathroom. The pretty 'modern' room on the ground floor has yellow walls and masses of cupboards. Karin is delicious, nothing is too much for her and the area is full of interest. *German, Spanish and Dutch also spoken. Gîte space for 2 people.*

Rooms: 2 doubles, with shower or bath & wc.

Price: €54 for two.

Meals: Dinner €19, including wine.

Closed: Never.

From Châteauroux D943 to Ardentes; left on D14 for St Août 8km; left at château sign 400m; entrance on right.

Karin Verburgh
Château de la Villette
Saint Août
36120 Ardentes
Indre
Tel: (0)2 54 36 28 46

In this house of tradition and great originality, you are instantly one of the family, which is Hector the gentle giant hound, Persian Puss, two fine horses, a bright and friendly little girl, her congenial artist father and her relaxed linguist mother. Rooms - two in the main house, two in the garden house, where you can also study painting or French - are subtly colourful with good family furniture, vibrant bathrooms and... Jean-Lou's works on the walls. Some Aubusson tapestry cartoons too, and understated elegance in the sitting and dining rooms. A joy of a garden, interesting, fun-loving hosts and a big welcoming table in the evening.

Rooms: 4 doubles, all with bath & wc.

Price: €53.50 for two.

Meals: Dinner €23, including wine & coffee.

Closed: Never.

From Blois D956 to Contres; D675 to St Aignan; over bridge; D17 right to Mareuil sur Cher. House on left in hamlet La Maison des Marchands (just before cat breeder sign) before main village.

Martine & Jean-Lou Coursaget
Le Moutier
13 rue de la République
41110 Mareuil sur Cher, Loir-et-Cher
Tel: (0)2 54 75 20 48
Fax: (0)2 54 75 20 48
E-mail: lemoutier.coursaget@wanadoo.fr
Web: perso.club-internet.fr/vilain/lemoutier

Loire Valley

It's a delight for the eyes: stunning ancient buildings outside, Madame's decorating flair inside. The 13th-century chapel, still used on the village feast day, and the newer manor house (1500s…), drip with history, 16th-century antiques, tapestries and loveliness - huge sitting and dining rooms, smallish cosy bedrooms. One has a large stone fireplace, painted beams and very successful Laura Ashley fabrics. The setting is superb, fine mature trees shade the secluded garden and you can put your horse in the paddock. And you'll like your hosts and their estate wine. They can arrange wine tastings too.

Rooms: 1 suite with bath, shower & wc; 2 doubles, all with shower & wc.

Price: €61 for two; suite for four €137; suite for five €150.

Meals: Wide range of restaurants locally.

Closed: Never.

Sophie, who speaks fluent English, left glamorous theatre management in Paris to devote her energy to her new B&B project where the emphasis is on simple living and organic food (*cuisine bio*). Breakfast bread, from the organic bakery, is made with milk and *fromage blanc* and her imaginative dinner menus, 95% organic too, use home-grown ingredients or stuff from the local organic co-operative. Rooms are attractive and functional with bright bedspreads, original sketches and paintings. She's passionate about British history and particularly loves talking to British guests. *She also speaks some Spanish and German.*

Rooms: 3 doubles, 1 twin, all with shower & separate wc; 1 twin with shower & wc.

Price: €41-€45 for two.

Meals: Dinner €16, including wine & coffee.

Closed: November-January and occasionally.

St Georges is between Chenonceau & Montrichard on N76. In town centre, up hill to 'La Chaise' (signs); cont. up Rue du Prieuré. No 8 has heavy wooden gates.

From Blois D764 to Montrichard for 18km. In Sambin, house up lane between church and grocer's.

Danièle Duret-Therizols
Prieuré de la Chaise
8 rue du Prieuré
41400 St Georges sur Cher, Loir-et-Cher
Tel: (0)2 54 32 59 77
Fax: (0)2 54 32 69 49
E-mail: prieuredelachaise@yahoo.fr
Web: www.prieuredelachaise.com

Sophie Gélinier
Chambres d'Hôtes du Prieuré
23 rue de la Fontaine Saint Urbain
41120 Sambin
Loir-et-Cher
Tel: (0)2 54 20 24 95
Fax: (0)2 54 20 24 95
E-mail: sophie.gelinier@libertysurf.fr

Entry No: 386   Map: 7

Entry No: 387   Map: 7

Loire Valley

An amazingly quiet place, La Quantinière. The drive is a half-mile pine-lined tunnel; the garden disappears into fields which disappear into woods... yet there are wine cellars and châteaux galore to be visited just down the road (even the 'big house' next door has a moat). Your dynamic, youthfully-retired hosts are eager to make your stay just right in their converted 19th-century 'stables' (horses clearly lived like kings). The big living room with its fine fireplace is a splendid space, guest rooms are big, simple and attractively furnished and the welcome is warmly genuine.

Rooms: 2 doubles, 1 twin, 2 family rooms, all with bath or shower & wc.

Price: €50 for two.

Meals: Dinner €21, including wine & coffee.

Closed: January-March.

A treat of a place - a house of endless happy discoveries. Easy-going, chatty Marie-France has created an oasis of sophisticated rusticity and enjoys playing shepherdess – she has some sheep and hens and loves to take children on fresh egg hunts – and working in the garden in combat gear. The house itself – open, airy and connected to the bedrooms by a glass walkway, has a soft, attractive feel (despite the marble tiles!) and a gorgeous woodsy view of the valley. There is an astonishing cylindrical shower in the centre of one of the double bedrooms – and another room sports a billiard table.

Rooms: 2 doubles, 1 family suite, all with shower & wc.

Price: €64-€84 for two; suite €130 for five.

Meals: Restaurants 3-7km.

Closed: November-March.

From Amboise D23 for 3km to Souvigny; D30 to Vallières les Grandes; D27/D28 right towards Montrichard; lane 2nd left after water tower; house just after manor house.

From Blois D751 13km to Candé, left after bridge towards Valaire. Pass War Memorial & grain silo. Keep right at next fork; left at sign Le Chêne Vert; house on left after small bridge.

Annie & Daniel Doyer
Ferme de la Quantinière
41400 Vallières les Grandes
Loir-et-Cher
Tel: (0)2 54 20 99 53
Fax: (0)2 54 20 99 53
E-mail: fermequantiniere@minitel.net
Web: www.france-bonjour.com/la-quantiniere/

Marie-France Tohier
Le Chêne Vert
41120 Monthou sur Bièvre
Loir-et-Cher
Tel: (0)2 54 44 07 28
Fax: (0)2 54 44 17 94

Entry No: 388   Map: 7

Entry No: 389   Map: 7

Didier, a French chef with cross-Channel experiences, speaks lovely English with accents as needed (Scots, London...) to colour his humour. He will take you mushrooming, as well as cooking dinners with things like rabbit stew with... wild mushrooms, home-smoked salmon, chocolate mousse. Anita is charmingly Dutch and takes good care of her guests. The three impeccably clean, attractively-furnished bedrooms have high dormer windows overlooking fields towards the forest and firm comfortable beds. Add a shallow swimming pool well away from the house and, if you like, cookery lessons.

Rooms: 2 suites, 2 doubles, 1 twin, all with bath or shower & wc.

Price: €56-€75 for two.

Meals: Dinner €22, including wine; choice of restaurants 2-6km.

Closed: January.

Mary, brimming with energy and optimism, teaches English to French businessmen. Patrick, soft-spoken with a lovely sense of humour, has renovated the house and now finds much enjoyment in running the B&B. They are Irish, delighted to be very much part of their French village and will look after you very well. Rooms, up narrow stairs under the old rafters, with lots of floral patterns and pictures, are a good size, with rather small bathrooms. The garden apartment is nicely independent. You all breakfast together in the warm-hearted Crehans' cheerful dining room. Super spot for walking and bird-watching.

Rooms: 2 doubles, 1 apartment for 4/5, all with bath or shower & wc.

Price: €43-€53 for two.

Meals: Choice of restaurants in village.

Closed: Never.

From A10 exit Blois for Vierzon; join D765 to Cheverny then D102 for Contres; lane to farm on right about 1.5km after Cheverny château; signs.

From A71 exit 3 onto D923 through La Ferté Beauharnais to Neung sur Beuvron; through village; house on right just after turning to La Marolle.

M & Mme Merlin
Ferme des Saules
41700 Cheverny
Loir-et-Cher
Tel: (0)2 54 79 26 95
Fax: (0)2 54 79 97 54
E-mail: merlin.cheverny@infonie.fr
Web: www.chez.com/fermedessaules

Mary Ellen & Patrick Crehan
Breffni Cottage
16 rue du 11 novembre
41210 Neung sur Beuvron
Loir-et-Cher
Tel: (0)2 54 83 66 56
Fax: (0)2 54 83 66 56
E-mail: breffni65@hotmail.com

In the 17th century, Queen Marie de Médicis used to take the waters here, hence the miniature Italianate villa; the fine garden still has a hot spring and the River Loire flows regally past behind the trees. Muriel, a flower-loving perfectionist of immaculate taste, has let loose her considerable decorative flair on the interior. It is unmistakably French in its careful colours, lush fabrics and fine details - fresh flowers too. Carved wardrobes and brass beds grace some rooms. The suite is a wonderful 1930s surprise and has a super-smart bathroom. You will be thoroughly coddled in this very elegant and stylish house.

Rooms: 1 suite, 1 quadruple, 2 doubles, 2 twins, all with bath or shower & wc.

Price: €66 for two.

Meals: Dinner €30, including wine & coffee.

Closed: Never; open by arrangement in winter.

Macé is 3km north of Blois along N152 towards Orléans. Enter village & follow signs; house 500m on right before church.

Muriel Cabin-Saint-Marcel
La Villa Médicis
Macé
41000 Saint Denis sur Loire
Loir-et-Cher
Tel: (0)2 54 74 46 38
Fax: (0)2 54 78 20 27

Entry No: 392 Map: 7

A house of style, originality and lovely surprises; fascinating and delightful people. Madame, an art historian, talks exuberantly about everything and creates beauty with her hands, including shimmering patchwork quilts. Monsieur has a great sense of fun too, yet their house hums with serenity. Rooms are period-themed with family pieces: the *1930s* has an old typewriter, a valve radio and an authentic, garish green bathroom; the *1900s* has a splendid carved bed. The romantic garden is a mixture of French geometric and English informal; the house is set back enough for the road not to be a problem and the Loire is a short step from the garden gate.

Rooms: 1 double, 1 twin, 1 triple, 1 single, all with bath or shower & wc.

Price: €55-€60 for two.

Meals: 2 restaurants in village.

Closed: November-March, except by arrangement.

From A10 exit 16 & follow signs to Chambord, crossing Loire river at Mer. After bridge right on D951; house on right at end of village.

Francis & Béatrice Bonnefoy
L'Échappée Belle
120 rue Nationale
41500 Saint Dyé sur Loire
Loir-et-Cher
Tel: (0)2 54 81 60 01
E-mail: fbonnefoy@libertysurf.fr
Web: perso.libertysurf.fr/fbonnefoy

Entry No: 393 Map: 7

With luck you'll be greeted by the house mascot - a fine white duck, symbol of friendship. Inside, a warmly sensitive atmosphere radiates from the beautiful old floor tiles, fabulous timbered ceilings, lovely family furniture. Madame uses her innate feeling for history to advise on places to see and both your hosts are quietly, gently caring about their guests' well-being. Bedrooms, each in a different style, are big, harmonious in fabric and colour, and look over the rambling, peaceful garden; the ground-floor bathroom looks straight onto the mill wheel, restored by Monsieur. Huge selection of teas for breakfast.

Rooms: 2 doubles, 2 triples, 1 suite, all with bath or shower & wc.

Price: €54-€76 for two.

Meals: Excellent choice of restaurants within 7km.

Closed: Never.

From A10 exit 16 on N152 towards Blois. 3.5km after Mer, right towards Diziers - follow Chambres d'Hôtes signs.

Marie-Françoise & André Seguin
Le Moulin de Choiseaux
8 rue des Choiseaux
41500 Suèvres, Loir-et-Cher
Tel: (0)2 54 87 85 01
Fax: (0)2 54 87 86 44
E-mail: choiseaux@wanadoo.fr
Web: www.choiseaux.com

Entry No: 394   Map: 7

The 18th-century house stands in seven acres of woodland that cut out all sight of the nuclear power station. Ideal for Chambord and the Sologne area, it's a quiet, leafy place to rest after your sightseeing exertions: one owner went through Revolution, Restoration, Napoleon, three prisons, three death sentences... and died here in his bed. Traditionally-furnished bedrooms are light, sunny, attractive: there are fine old things everywhere, including grandfather's paintings. Madame, who speaks little English, shares her time between guests and her family, who breakfast separately - her welcome is appropriately formal.

Rooms: 2 doubles, 1 triple, all with shower & wc.

Price: €50 for two.

Meals: Restaurant in village; choice 8km.

Closed: Never.

From Orléans, D951 for Blois. On entering St Laurent, follow signs to Chambres d'Hôtes.

Catherine & Maurice Libeaut
L'Ormoie
26 rue de l'Ormoie
St Laurent des Eaux
41220 St Laurent Nouan, Loir-et-Cher
Tel: (0)2 54 87 24 72
Fax: (0)2 54 87 24 93
E-mail: maurice.catherine.libeaut@wanadoo.fr

Entry No: 395   Map: 7

An old townhouse with a country feel, a pretty garden, a majestic towering chestnut and miniature trees at the bottom to screen the outbuildings. Madame will be found in the picture-framing workshop; her jovial husband farms and will serve your breakfast in the dining room among an array of pictures, samplers and *objets*. Up the characterful sloping-treaded stairs, the light, simple rooms are decorated in understated good taste and pale colours. There are beams, polished parquet or tiled floors, billiards in the sitting room and a kitchenette for guests. A lovely place to stay. *Gîte space for 6 people.*

Rooms: 1 double/twin, 3 triples, 1 suite, all with bath or shower & wc.

Price: €45-€61 for two.

Meals: Choice of restaurants in Mer.

Closed: January.

"A little gem of a B&B", as one reader said, with its sweeping farmyard, its pond and such a welcome. You can see for miles across fields filled with lark song and cereals. The owners are a smiling couple who give you their time without invading your space but are delighted to show you their immaculate farm, orchard and vegetable garden if you're interested. Their rooms have gentle colours, soft materials and firm mattresses. The furniture is simple and rustic, the bedrooms and bathrooms are deeply raftered, the old farmhouse breathes through its timbers. It is peaceful, pretty and a place for picnics.

Rooms: 1 double with shower & wc; 2 doubles sharing bath & wc.

Price: €35-€41 for two.

Meals: Dinner €13, including wine & coffee; restaurant 6km.

Closed: Never.

From N152 enter Mer and park by church. House is short walk up main street; entrance in picture-framing shop on left. (Car access details on arrival.)

From Vendôme D957 for Blois 6km. Right at sign to Crucheray & Chambres d'Hôtes. House 4km from turning; signposted.

Joëlle & Claude Mormiche
9 rue Dutems
41500 Mer
Loir-et-Cher
Tel: (0)2 54 81 17 36
Fax: (0)2 54 81 70 19
E-mail: mormiche@wanadoo.fr
Web: www.france-bonjour.com/mormiche/

Élisabeth & Guy Tondereau
Les Bordes
41100 Crucheray
Loir-et-Cher
Tel: (0)2 54 77 05 43
Fax: (0)2 54 77 05 43

The history lesson on the old school room ceiling covers the Creation, Noah's Ark, the Kama Sutra. Artists, writers, musicians love this place. Your hosts, both wordsmiths, are articulate and delightfully relaxed: children come and go to his parents' house via a ladder over the wall; conversations turn on ancestral recipes and climate change. The unspoilt schoolhouse has white rooms and bright paintwork, original paintings and myriad *objets*. Woods and fields lie beyond the semi-wild garden where you can sit in a live willow *gloriette*. Home production is king here: hams, sheepskins, dandelion jelly... *Small dogs welcome.*

Rooms: 1 double, 1 twin, 1 triple, all with bath or shower, sharing wc.

Price: € 33 for two.

Meals: Dinner € 13.50, including wine & coffee.

Closed: Occasionally.

From Vendôme N10 for Tours 19km; right D71 to Villechauve; in village, house on right just after church.

Claude & Ariane Laballe
La Lune et les Feux
Le Bourg
41310 Villechauve
Loir-et-Cher
Tel: (0)2 54 80 37 80

Entry No: 398   Map: 7

A very friendly, open couple, new to B&B and loving it. Grégoire has restored this fairy-tale manor house, complete with Renaissance façade, with help from Véronique when she wasn't working in Paris (she can fill you in on the political scene). The guest rooms are reached via the wonderful turret, draped with Indian fabrics. 4-metre high ceilings, two four-poster beds, antique furniture and interesting *objets*. Guests also have a truly majestic sitting room. An amazing place to stay in the most beautiful, peaceful surroundings: you can breakfast, laze, sketch the Barbary ducks or fish in the grounds - rods are provided.

Rooms: 1 triple, 1 suite for 6, both with bath & wc.

Price: € 45-€ 48 for two.

Meals: Wide choice of restaurants 5km.

Closed: 30 October-1 April.

From Vendôme D917 to Montoire; cross Loir; D10 for Couture sur Loir 1.5km; right at signpost for 2.5km; house 4th on left (with tower).

Grégoire Lucien-Brun & Véronique Debeaumont
Manoir de la Chevalinière
41800 Saint Martin des Bois
Loir-et-Cher
Tel: (0)2 54 72 53 94
Fax: (0)2 54 72 53 94
E-mail: gregoirelucienbrun@hotmail.com

Entry No: 399   Map: 7

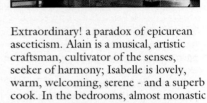

Fabienne is a charming, sociable hostess who genuinely wants you to get the most out of your stay. A lot of the decorative detail is hers and the pretty rooms are named after the flowers she loves and tends in her garden. Light floods in through the big windows of the dining room and there's always home-made jam and cake for breakfast. Fabienne may go with you on local walks or bike rides to make sure you don't miss anything. The troglodyte village of Trôo is just 4km away and it's 6km to the craft centre of Poncé where you can watch potters and glass-blowers at work. *Gîte space for 6 people.*

Rooms: 1 family suite (2 separate doubles) sharing bath & separate wc; 1 double with shower & wc.

Price: €35-€38 for two.

Meals: Good restaurant in Pont de Braye, 2km.

Closed: November-Easter.

From Vendôme D917 for Montoire & Trôo. Sougé is 4 km after Trôo. House on left at entrance of village.

Fabienne & Alain Partenay
La Mulotière
10 rue du Bourg Neuf
41800 Sougé sur Braye
Loir-et-Cher
Tel: (0)6 80 33 72 55
Fax: (0)2 54 72 46 97

Entry No: 400 Map: 7

Extraordinary! a paradox of epicurean asceticism. Alain is a musical, artistic craftsman, cultivator of the senses, seeker of harmony; Isabelle is lovely, warm, welcoming, serene - and a superb cook. In the bedrooms, almost monastic in their simplicity, nothing distracts from the natural warmth of old tiles and Alain's beautiful furniture: all is light, space, harmony. The magnificent room under the rafters is used for recitals and furniture display. Isabelle's vegetable garden centres on a lily pond and there's a little path through the 'wild' wood beyond: this house is a meeting of market place and wilderness - humans grow here.

Rooms: 1 double, 2 triples, 1 suite for 6/7, all with bath or shower & wc.

Price: €40-€45 for two.

Meals: Dinner €19, including wine & coffee.

Closed: November-Easter.

From Le Mans N157 for Orléans 52km; left D921 to Mondoubleau; Carrefour de l'Ormeau is central village junction; house on corner opp. Ford garage.

Alain Gaubert & Isabelle Peyron
Carrefour de l'Ormeau
41170 Mondoubleau
Loir-et-Cher
Tel: (0)2 54 80 93 76
Fax: (0)2 54 80 88 85

Entry No: 401 Map: 7

This simple characterful old farmhouse has its touches of fun: a couple of parrots perch in the children's room, for example. Madame is charming, clearly delighting in her role as hostess; Monsieur quietly gets on with his gardening. Now retired, they are both active in their community, a caring and unpretentious couple. Traditionally furnished, the rooms have subtle, well-chosen colour schemes, the bathroom is new and clean. Breakfast is served in the dining room with home-made jams and crusty bread. Surrounded by chestnut trees, the house backs onto the gardens of the château and is wonderfully quiet.

Rooms: 1 triple, 1 twin, 1 suite for 5, all with bath or shower & wc.

Price: €40 for two.

Meals: Auberge 300m.

Closed: Never.

From Tours D29 to Beaumont la Ronce. House signposted in village.

Michel & Andrée Campion
La Louisière
37360 Beaumont la Ronce
Indre-et-Loire
Tel: (0)2 47 24 42 24
Fax: (0)2 47 24 42 24

Entry No: 402 Map: 7

Intimate and romantic: in the lovely, unsung Loir valley you have the little old house in the garden to yourselves. All recently renovated, it has a kitchen and a bathroom downstairs, two little bedrooms up a steep staircase and its own piece of flower-filled garden for private breakfasts. Or you can join Madame at the long check-clothed table in her light and cheerful kitchen where baskets hang from the beams. She is friendly, cultivated and dynamic, very involved in the local music festival and tourist activities so an excellent adviser for guests, and also a great maker of jams. It's not luxurious, but elegantly homely, quiet and welcoming.

Rooms: 2 doubles in cottage, sharing bathroom.

Price: €46 for two.

Meals: Dinner €18, including wine & coffee.

Closed: 1 November-31 March.
From Tours/La Membrolle N138 towards Le Mans. At Neuillé Pont Pierre D68 to Neuvy le Roi. House on road; blue front door, opposite turning to Louestault.

Ghislaine & Gérard de Couesnongle
20 rue Pilate
37370 Neuvy le Roi
Indre-et-Loire
Tel: (0)2 47 24 41 48
E-mail: de-couesnongle-neuvy@caramail.com

Entry No: 403 Map: 7

High on a cliff above the Loire, it looks over the village, across the vines and the valley to a château. It may be 'modern imitating old' but we chose it for Madame's superb, generous, 5-star hospitality. The house is immaculate and meticulously kept - one room is in repro Louis XIV, plus orangey carpet and flowery paper. There is a big dining/sitting area with tiled floor and rugs, an insert fireplace and views over the large sloping garden - the oldest bit, a troglodyte dwelling, is beneath the lawn! Mountain bikes to borrow, giant breakfasts, wonderful welcome - great value for the Loire.

Rooms: 1 suite, 3 doubles, all with bath & wc.

Price: €43-€49 for two; suite €78 for four.

Meals: Several restaurants in village.

Closed: Never.

A smart, almost lavish château with its listed garden (stupendous trees) and an attentive new owner who serves a magnificent breakfast buffet in the new wrought-iron conservatory overlooking the garden. Three rooms are in the château (lots of stairs to the top room but what a view), three in the *Closerie*, one with a dramatic oval window onto the setting sun. Superb décor with lovely materials, subtle colours, fine furniture, attention to origins. One 'monastic' room (plain walls, exposed brick and timber) contrasts pleasingly with the classy plushness. And a heated outdoor swimming pool! A treat worth paying for.

Rooms: 1 suites for 4, 2 doubles, 2 triples, 1 twin, all with bath, shower & wc.

Price: €95-€170 for two.

Meals: Dinner €40, including apéritif & coffee.

Closed: Never.

From Tours A10 for Paris; cross Loire; exit 20 to Rochecorbon. In village left at lights and right up steep narrow lane; signposted.

From Tours N152 for Blois 4km. Left at St Georges; follow signs 1km to château.

Mme Jacqueline Gay
7 chemin de Bois Soleil
37210 Rochecorbon
Indre-et-Loire
Tel: (0)2 47 52 88 08
Fax: (0)2 47 52 85 90
E-mail: jacqueline.gay2@wanadoo.fr

Laurent Gross
Château de Montgouverne
37210 Rochecorbon
Indre-et-Loire
Tel: (0)2 47 52 84 59
Fax: (0)2 47 52 84 61
E-mail: info@montgouverne.com
Web: www.montgouverne.com

Loire Valley

Swim in the beautiful pool then carouse over dinner in the lovely old room with its beams and large open fireplace; the meal, very much *en famille*, starts after the evening's milking - this is a working goat farm producing its own delicious cheese. The atmosphere around the table, the unusual and lovely setting and the interesting conversation of your easy, good-natured hosts make the fairly basic rooms, out in the converted pighouse, utterly acceptable. Bits of the house are 13th century: it was built by a glass-maker, a very superior trade in those days, and overlooks the extraordinary ruins of a large castle.

Rooms: 2 doubles, 1 twin, 1 family, all with shower & wc.

Price: €39 for two.

Meals: Dinner €13, including wine & coffee. Good value restaurants 400m.

Closed: 16 October-31 March.

Surrounded by forest, standing in a big 'English' garden (Madame is passionate about her flowers, both inside and out), this imposing lodge has a harmonious, mellow feeling despite being built so recently - but in 17th-century Angevin style with old materials from the château next door. An unusual and refreshingly natural place, it reflects the family's plan to return to country simplicity. They are gentle, caring, cultivated and creative, as proved by the delightful, carefully-designed and decorated bedrooms. There's a lovely new 'pigeon loft' room with half-timbered walls and a round window - very enticing. *Children over 10 welcome.*

Rooms: 1 double, 2 twins, all with shower (1 behind curtain) & wc.

Price: €53.50 for two.

Meals: Restaurant in village.

Closed: 20 December-5 January.

From Château la Vallière D34 towards Langeais - first right, right again, past ruined castle: house at top of track.

Gérard & Martine Ribert
Vaujours
37330 Château la Vallière
Indre-et-Loire
Tel: (0)2 47 24 08 55
Fax: (0)2 47 24 19 20
E-mail: rib007@aol.com

Entry No: 406   Map: 7

From Tours N152 towards Saumur to St Patrice; D35 to Bourgueil; D749 to Gizeux; D15 to Continvoir. In village, left on D64; signposted.

Michel & Claudette Bodet
La Butte de l'Épine
37340 Continvoir
Indre-et-Loire
Tel: (0)2 47 96 62 25
Fax: (0)2 47 96 07 36

Entry No: 407   Map: 7

A genuine French family house: *Oncle Vincent*'s room has two big single beds, one made for Vincent with matching wardrobe and chest of drawers, the other, brass-knobbed and not matching the cane chair... *Tante Angèle* did the samplers in HER room, and Madame is properly proud of her fine linen. The cottage snuggles demurely in its *Jardin Secret*, rose scent wafts, Monsieur takes you to his favourite wine growers and craftsmen. They love having guests and opening doors onto unknown Loire treasures.

Rooms: 1 double with bath, 1 twin with shower, sharing wc. Cottage for 3.

Price: € 37-€ 48 for two.

Meals: Auberge 50m, choice 7km.

Closed: Christmas Day.

From Chinon, D16 to Huismes. Under arch between church and large house, 1st left: house 2nd on right.

Anne & Jean-Marc Bureau
Le Clos de l'Ormeau
37420 Huismes
Indre-et-Loire
Tel: (0)2 47 95 41 54
Fax: (0)2 47 95 41 54

Entry No: 408 Map: 7

Traditional materials - soft Touraine stone, lime render, wood - and old furniture, biscuit and oatmeal colours and lots of light make the old slate-topped house a welcoming haven by the Cher where the birdsong drowns out the trains. Here live Anne, Éric, their four children, various horses, cats, doves and ducks. They are charming, love meeting people, have lots of local lore for you and concoct wonders with things from their miniature 'Villandry' flower and vegetable garden. Anne loves looking for new recipes, new bits of antiquery (your bedhead in the lovely guest room is an adapted Breton *lit clos*) and attends lovingly to every detail. *Spanish spoken.*

Rooms: 1 double with shower & wc.

Price: € 49 for two; reduction 3 nights or more.

Meals: Dinner € 15, including wine & coffee.

Closed: Never.

From Tours D7 to Savonnières (9km); right across bridge; left for 3.5km; house on left.

Anne & Éric Gaudouin
Le Chat Courant
37510 Villandry
Indre-et-Loire
Tel: (0)2 47 50 06 94
E-mail: lechatcourant@netcourrier.com
Web: www.le-chat-courant.com

Entry No: 409 Map: 7

Éric, an energetic, artistic Anglophile with a sense of fun and a real interest in people, delights in his superb garden and the beautifully-finished details of his house: just the person to consult on buying antiques. Four bedrooms have stone beams, fireplaces and their own terraces; upstairs, the gentle grey and white room has a big balcony, the other is full of powerful florals; all have classy bathrooms and a stylish use of colour. Hall and dining room are splendiferous in their 18th-century elegance - crystal chandeliers, gilt-framed mirrors, statues - and there's a cosy sitting room. The whole place is a haven of history, culture, peace - magical.

Rooms: 2 triples, 1 twin, 2 doubles, 1 suite (1 double & 1 twin), all with bath or shower & wc.

Price: €92 for two.

Meals: Dinner €20, including wine & coffee.

Closed: February-March.

From Tours D7 to Savonnières; left at Hôtel Faisan D7 for Ballan Miré; up hill about 1km. House on left; signs.

Éric & Christine Salmon
Prieuré des Granges
15 rue des Fontaines
37510 Savonnières, Indre-et-Loire
Tel: (0)2 47 50 09 67
Fax: (0)2 47 50 06 43
E-mail: salmon.eric@wanadoo.fr
Web: prieuredesgranges.com

Entry No: 410   Map: 7

All this in one place? Heron and duck, wild boar and deer - and three tame mallards; plus a 9-hole golf course; plus a grass tennis court, a rarity in France, plus 14 hectares of grounds. And moreover, Mark, a Gallicised Englishman, and Katia, an Anglicised Frenchwoman, great travellers come to rest, are so enthusiastic about their new life here. The old farmhouse is done, naturally, with a mix of English and French: pleasing antiques, crisp bright bedrooms beneath their typical old beams, dinners of fresh seasonal things such as gentle local asparagus. And the splendours of the Loire just down the road. *Golf, 9 holes. Tennis in summer.*

Rooms: 3 doubles, all with shower & wc (one with bath also).

Price: €55-€70 for two.

Meals: Dinner €22, including wine & coffee.

Closed: December-January.

From A10 exit 18 on D31 for Amboise to Autrèche; left D55 to Dame Marie les Bois; right D74; 1st house on left after woods.

Mark & Katia Foster
Le Clos du Golf
Fleuray
37530 Cangey, Amboise
Indre-et-Loire
Tel: (0)2 47 56 07 07
Fax: (0)2 47 56 82 12
E-mail: closdugolf@wanadoo.fr

Entry No: 411   Map: 7

Even the pool is special: a 'Roman' bath hewn out of the hillside with a fountain and two columns, it lies on one of several garden levels, the crowning glory being the vines where chemical-free grapes are grown by natural methods. The new young owners, recently back from Italy with their small children, brim with enthusiasm for their elegant, history-laden château, built in 1518 to gaze across the Loire at Amboise. Every detail has been treated with taste and discretion. Rooms, two in the main house, one smaller in an outbuilding, are light and fresh in their delightful pale colours. Fine dinners with a hint of Italian finish the picture.

Rooms: 2 doubles with bath & wc; 1 double with shower & wc.

Price: €85-€90 for two.

Meals: Dinner €23, including wine & coffee.

Closed: Christmas Day & New Year's day.

From A10 exit 18 for Amboise 12km; right D1 to Pocé/Cisse & Nazelles Négron; in village centre, take narrow Rue Tue la Soif between Mairie & La Poste.

Véronique & Olivier Fructus
Chateau de Nazelles
16 rue Tue la Soif
37530 Nazelles, Indre-et-Loire
Tel: (0)2 47 30 53 79
Fax: (0)2 47 30 53 79
E-mail: info@chateau-nazelles.com
Web: www.chateau-nazelles.com

Entry No: 412   Map: 26

From common street to stately courtyard magnolias to circular marble domed staircase and you have a *Monument Historique*, a miniature Bagatelle Palace, a bachelor's folly with a circular *salon*. The light, airy, elegant rooms, small and perfectly proportioned, are softly pink-and-grey; lean out and pick a grape from the vine-clad pergola. Monsieur was a pilot and still flys vintage aircraft. Madame was an air hostess and English teacher and is casually sophisticated and articulate about her love of fine things, places and buildings. Wonderful, and a stone's throw from Chenonceaux.

Rooms: 1 double, 1 suite for 4, both with shower & wc.

Price: €53.50-€61 for two; extra bed €15.50.

Meals: Good choice of restaurants within walking distance.

Closed: December-March, except by arrangement.

From Amboise D31 to Bléré through Croix en Touraine; over bridge (Rue des Déportés opp. is one-way): left, imm'ly right, 1st right, right again. OR collection from private airport 5km.

Dominique Guillemot
Le Belvédère
24 rue des Déportés
37150 Bléré, Indre-et-Loire
Tel: (0)2 47 30 30 25
Fax: (0)2 47 30 30 25
E-mail: jr.guillemot@wanadoo.fr
Web: www.multimania.com/lebelvedere

Entry No: 413   Map: 7

Loire Valley

A narrow meandering track leads you through a gorgeous 'lost valley' to this light and airy house where the lawns run down to the banks of the Cher with not a neighbour in sight. The whole place is being beautifully restored by the present owners, refugees from the Parisian bustle. Using traditional *Tuffeau* stone, typical of the region, they have created a magnificent dining room. The garden-level bedroom has an African theme with terracotta tiling; another, at the top of the house, has an enormous full tester bed, which looks big enough to sleep four.

Rooms: 1 double, 2 triples, all with bath & wc.

Price: €46-€62 for two.

Meals: Dinner €22, including wine & coffee.

Closed: Never.

This is an especially tranquil place - it feels as old as the hills (actually the Middle Ages), with the fortified farm in the background that was used as a hunting lodge by Lafayette. There are ornamental geese and ducks on the lake and places to sit, read or paint in the neatly-tended garden. Brightly-decorated bedrooms blend well with antique furniture and lake views. The old milling machinery in the breakfast area still works - ask and Monsieur will turn it on for you - and there are relics from the days when this was a working mill, including original flour sacks from Azay. Amazing. *Gîte space for 6 people.*

Rooms: 2 doubles, 2 suites, all with bath & wc.

Price: €57 for two.

Meals: Good auberge in village, 500m.

Closed: Never.

From Tours N76 towards Bléré; pass sign for Athée sur Cher, continue to Granlay; immed. left to Vallet.

From Tours N143 for Loches; left D58 to Reignac; D17 to Azay sur Indre; left opp. restaurant; at fork, left (over two bridges); mill below fortified farm on right.

Denise & Augustin Chaudière
Le Pavillon de Vallet
4 rue de l'Acqueduc
37270 Athée sur Cher
Indre-et-Loire
Tel: (0)2 47 50 67 83
Fax: (0) 2 47 50 68 31
E-mail: pavillon.vallet@wanadoo.fr

Mme Danie Lignelet
Moulin de la Follaine
37310 Azay sur Indre
Indre-et-Loire
Tel: (0)2 47 92 57 91
E-mail: moulindelafollaine@wanadoo.fr
Web: www.multimania.com/moulindefollaine

Entry No: 414   Map: 7

Entry No: 415   Map: 7

Pure magic for all *Wind in the Willows* and other watermill fans. Three old mills side by side on a great sweep of the Indre, a boat for just messing about in, wooden bridges to cross from one secluded bank to another, a ship-stern view of the river from the terrace as you share a civilised dinner with your amusing, well-travelled hosts. The airy, elegant, uncluttered rooms have stunning river views (fear not - the sound of rushing water is limited to a gentle murmur at night), in styles to suit a Lieutenant, a Colonel and a Prior (in ascending order!).

Rooms: 2 doubles, all with shower & separate wc; 1 twin with bath & wc.

Price: €76-€90 for two.

Meals: Dinner €22, including wine & coffee.

Closed: Occasionally.

Once home to the *Boher*, who trained knights for medieval jousting tournaments, it is now a peaceful, flowery place - Madame really loves flowers and her summer garden is glorious. She is relaxed and keen to make you feel at home in her pretty farmhouse among the sunflower fields. Rooms, predictably flower-themed and fresh-flower decorated, are smallish but bright and cheerful, the guests' dayroom opens onto the terrace and the family dining room is most welcoming. And how about enjoying a spot of billiards practice before dinner?

Rooms: 1 double, 1 twin, 2 triples, all with bath or shower & wc.

Price: €40-€43 for two.

Meals: Dinner €14, including wine & coffee (available Mon-Fri only).

Closed: Never.

From Tours N143 towards Loches for 12km; 500m after Esso garage, right D17 for 1.3km; left to Vontes; left to Bas-Vontes. House at end of road.

From Tours N143 towards Loches; 10km after Cormery, left at Massy-Ferguson garage for Azay sur Indre/Chambres d'Hôtes; house 700m along, signposted.

Odile & Jean-Jacques Degail
Les Moulins de Vontes
37320 Esvres sur Indre
Indre-et-Loire
Tel: (0)2 47 26 45 72
Fax: (0)2 47 26 45 35
E-mail: info@moulinsdevontes.com
Web: www.moulinsdevontes.com

Marie-Agnès Bouin
La Bihourderie
37310 Azay sur Indre
Indre-et-Loire
Tel: (0)2 47 92 58 58
Fax: (0)2 47 92 22 19
E-mail: mignes.bouin@freesbee.fr

Entry No: 416   Map: 7

Entry No: 417   Map: 7

Philosopher Bruno and Titian-haired Nancy, an engaging couple with four young children, have turned his family château into a delightful refuge for the world-weary traveller. The demands of children to be taken to dancing lessons and guests needing intellectual and physical sustenance are met with quiet composure and good humour. Generations of sliding children have polished the banisters on the stairs leading to the large, light bedrooms, freshly decorated round splendid brass bedsteads and family memorabilia. On fine summer evenings, you can take a supper tray to picnic *à la* Glyndebourne in a favourite corner of the vast grounds.

Rooms: 2 doubles, 1 twin, all with bath/shower & wc.

Price: €84-€92 for two.

Meals: Dinner €29, including wine & coffee.

Closed: Occasionally.

A well-converted stable block of an elegant stone house bathing in the inimitable limpid light of the Loire Valley on the edge of a quiet little village - you are welcome in this protected wetland area between the Loire and Vienne rivers. The guest quarters have ancient beams, stone walls and new floors, space to sit or cook, even a little terrace. The uncluttered, sizeable rooms have the same happy mix of old and new with some fine pieces of furniture. The hospitable, gentle owners are proud of their house and area and will direct you to less obvious places of interest. "Very clean, very friendly, very good food", say readers' letters.

Rooms: 2 triples, both with bath & wc; 1 double with shower & wc.

Price: €36-€43 for two.

Meals: Dinner €15.50, inc. wine & coffee. Self-catering possible.

Closed: 15 December-15 January.

From Tours D751 for Chinon 5km. In Ballan Miré, right at lights before level crossing. Sign; entrance opp. golf course.

From Chinon D749 for Bourgueil for 6km. Left for Savigny en Véron; follow signs to 'Camping'. House 1km after campsite on right.

Monsieur Bruno Clément
Château du Vau
37510 Ballan Miré
Indre-et-Loire
Tel: (0)2 47 67 84 04
Fax: (0)2 47 67 55 77
E-mail: chateauduvau@chez.com
Web: www.chez.com/chateauduvau

Marie-Françoise & Michel Chauvelin
Cheviré
11 rue Basse
37420 Savigny en Véron
Indre-et-Loire
Tel: (0)2 47 58 42 49
Fax: (0)2 47 58 42 49

Entry No: 418   Map: 7

Entry No: 419   Map: 7

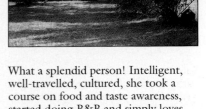

Monsieur, a man of many talents - wine grower, antique dealer, genial host - and Madame, delightfully down-to-earth and genuine, speak excellent English and organise memorable wine-tasting gourmet evenings involving a ritual aperitif and game of *boules* before a 5-course dinner round a jolly family table in their typical country kitchen (booking essential). Simple bedrooms, some larger than others, are light and cheerful with old features such as marble fireplaces, old floor tiles, the odd antique; the guest sitting room is endearingly lived-in with comfortable sofas and books; the whole feel is utterly welcoming.

Rooms: 2 doubles, 3 triples, 1 family, all with bath, shower & wc.

Price: €45-€52 for two.

Meals: Dinner €20, wine €7.

Closed: November-March.

From Langeais N152 for Saumur 7km; right D35 for Bourgeuil 5km; in Ingrandes right D71 Rue de l'Ouche; 2nd right Rue St André.

Michèle & Michel Pinçon
Le Clos Saint André
37140 Ingrandes de Touraine
Indre-et-Loire
Tel: (0)2 47 96 90 81
Fax: (0)2 47 96 90 81
E-mail: mmpincon@club-internet.fr

Entry No: 420 Map: 7

What a splendid person! Intelligent, well-travelled, cultured, she took a course on food and taste awareness, started doing B&B and simply loves bringing people together over an excellent meal where all her interests are nourished. And what a sensitive restoration of her old farmhouse (some of it 15th-century). A big fire crackles in the sitting room, the old tiles and timbers glow rich and mellow, summer dinners are in the little walled courtyard, the shady garden has private corners, rooms play variations on the theme of good fabrics and furniture (the small, lower-priced room is real value). Swathes of conviviality and light envelop the place. *Gîte Panda.*

Rooms: 4 doubles, all with bath or shower & wc.

Price: €38-€50 for two.

Meals: Good restaurants nearby.

Closed: January

From Chinon D749 for Bourgueil; Beaumont roundabout 3rd exit for La Roche Honneur; left at sign to Grézille.

Antoinette Degrémont
La Balastière, Hameau de Grézille
37420 Beaumont en Veron
Indre-et-Loire
Tel: (0)2 47 58 87 93
Fax: (0)2 47 58 82 41
E-mail: balastiere@infonie.fr
Web: perso.infonie.fr/balastiere/

Entry No: 421 Map: 7

Back in Chinon after many years in Paris, Jany and Jean create a thoroughly civilised atmosphere where guests bask in refined but unpretentious comfort. Their well-renovated 19th-century townhouse stands on the bank of the stately River Vienne with the little streets of medieval Chinon mounting up behind it to the old castle. Both bedrooms (*Iris* and *Loriette*) overlook the water and have Jany's unmistakable personal touch. Jean sings in the local choir and his amazing CD and record collection covers two walls of his study. They are an articulate, music- and art-loving couple, and excellent hosts.

Rooms: 2 doubles, both with shower or bath & wc.

Price: €52-€57 for two.

Meals: Good choice of restaurant within walking distance.

Closed: October-March.

This solid wine-grower's house sings in a subtle harmony of traditional charm and contemporary chic under thoroughly modern Martine's touch. Terracotta sponged walls, creamy beams and colourful modern fabrics breathe new life into rooms with old tiled floors and stone fireplaces. Windows are flung open to let in the light and the stresses of city living are forgotten in cheerful, easy conversations with your hostess. There is a baby grand piano in the elegant sitting room for the musical, a pool for the energetic, and wine-tastings at the vineyard next door. A great place.

Rooms: 2 doubles, 1 suite, all with bath & wc.

Price: €76 for two.

Meals: Dinner €25, including wine & coffee.

Closed: Never.

Entering Chinon on D751 from Tours, along river past bridge and Rabelais statue. House just after Post Office.

Jany & Jean Grosset
84 quai Jeanne d'Arc
37500 Chinon
Indre-et-Loire
Tel: (0)2 47 98 42 78

From Chinon D749 for Richelieu; 1km after r'about D115 right for 'Ligré par le vignoble' 5km; left to Le Rouilly; left at Dozon warehouse; house 800m on left.

Martine Descamps
Le Clos de Ligré
Le Rouilly
37500 Ligré
Indre-et-Loire
Tel: (0)2 47 93 95 59
Fax: (0)2 47 93 06 31
E-mail: martinedescamps@hotmail.com

Entry No: 422   Map: 7

Entry No: 423   Map: 7

In a magical garden on a steep secluded slope where troglodytes once lived (the cave with its original fireplace now contains pans and preserves), the pretty little creeper-covered old house and its renovated outbuilding housing two excellent guest rooms make a gentle retreat from the crowds visiting the châteaux. One room has a superbly carved Norman bridal bed (doves and sheaves for peace and prosperity), the other has a fine family armoire, both are softly furnished and have good bathrooms. Madame, relaxed, cultivated and welcoming, is most knowledgeable about her beloved Loire Valley.

Rooms: 2 doubles, both with shower & wc.

Price: €44 for two.

Meals: Wide choice of restaurants within 5km.

Closed: November-February.

A tree-shaded garden shields this old walnut farm-turned antique dealer's. Inside, a cornucopia of exotica mingles well with traditional antique furniture in splendid oak-beamed, book and stone-clad rooms. The stylishly-decorated bedrooms are a good size, one bathroom is big enough to dance in, the suite has its own large sitting room downstairs with a huge open fireplace. And if you find your antique carved bedhead irresistible, you may be able to buy it! Barbara, articulate and efficient, believes in mollycoddling her guests – there are hand-embroidered linen sheets on the beds and sumptuous breakfasts served on the best china.

Rooms: 2 doubles, 1 suite for 2/4, all with bath & wc.

Price: €80-€90 for two.

Meals: Auberge in village; good choice in Chinon, 12km.

Closed: Never.

From Saumur D947 for Chinon to Montsoreau; D751 through Candes & St Germain sur Vienne. 500m after church, at Goujon Frétillant restaurant, right; follow signs for 1.5km.

From Tours D751 to Chinon; D21 to Cravant les Côteaux. Pallus is approx. 1.5km after village on right, at sign 'Bernard Chauveau – Antiquaire'.

Anne Dubarry
7 La Vallée des Grottes
37500 Saint Germain sur Vienne
Indre-et-Loire
Tel: (0)2 47 95 96 45

Barbara Chauveau
Domaine de Pallus
37500 Cravant les Côteaux
Indre-et-Loire
Tel: (0)2 47 93 08 94
Fax: (0)2 47 98 43 00
E-mail: bcpallus@clubinternet.fr

Entry No: 424 Map: 7

Entry No: 425 Map: 7

Dug into the hillside with the engulfing forest behind and a wide-angle view of vines, fields and sky in front, this 'traditional' wine-grower's manor successfully pretends it was built in the 1800s rather than the 1980s, with its venerable oak beams gnawed by generations of woodworm and stone cut by troglodyte stonemasons. The furniture in the bedrooms is antique too – a superb carved wooden bedhead, a big puffy eiderdown, old prints. Only the pool, elegant bathrooms and guests' functional sitting and utility rooms show the owners' thoroughly contemporary concern for luxury and comfort. And there is wine to taste and buy. *Gîte space for 4 people.*

Rooms: 1 suite for 3/4 in main house, 2 doubles in pool-side cabin, all with bath or shower & wc.

Price: €61-€76 for two.

Meals: Choice of restaurants 5km.

Closed: Never.

Éliane is a most welcoming, enthusiastic hostess who loves talking to people about their interests and her own. New to B&B, she is constantly looking for ideas to improve her rooms, the pink, mezzanined quadruple in her pretty old farmhouse and the other larger triple in a converted outbuilding. Parts of the house are 17th century with massive beams, good mixes of new and old furniture, wild and dried flowers, colours and fabrics. A goose wanders about the little garden and it is all deliciously cosy.

Rooms: 1 quadruple, 1 triple, both with shower & wc.

Price: €36-€40 for two.

Meals: Auberge nearby.

Closed: Never.

From Chinon, D21 to Cravant les Côteaux. Continue towards Panzoult; house on left after 2km.

Exit Ste Maure de Touraine from A10; N40 for Tours. After 6km right to St Catherine de Fierbois. In village D1 for Bossé 3km. House 3km further.

Marie-Claude Chauveau
Domaine de Beauséjour
37220 Panzoult
Indre-et-Loire
Tel: (0)2 47 58 64 64
Fax: (0)2 47 95 27 13
E-mail: domainedebeausejour@wanadoo.fr
Web: www.domainedebeausejour.com

Mme Éliane Pelluard
La Tinellière
37800 Sainte Catherine de Fierbois
Indre-et-Loire
Tel: (0)2 47 65 61 80

The Miévilles (he English, she French) came to the Loire Valley from Paris in search of a better quality of life. They once lived in Spain too, and are interested in the cultural differences between countries. They have turned this lovely 15th-century watermill into a colourful and cosy home full of flowers and scatter cushions, and have kept much of the original machinery in the mill room, where you have breakfast. The garden around the millpond with its own little island is gorgeous, with plenty of shade for those hot summer days and public footpaths close by. *Spanish spoken.*

Rooms: 2 doubles, 2 triples, all with bath & wc.

Price: €55-€58 for two.

Meals: Good restaurants locally.

Closed: November-March.

Do you dream of living in a watermill? Your charming young hosts have converted theirs, near the magnificent château of Montrésor, in stylish and simple good taste as befits the old building: a wooden staircase leading to the coconut-matted landing, super colours (green/gold, blue/white, yellow/cream), good linen. The atmosphere is welcoming, very warm, with lots of original features... and quiet flows the water over the wheel beneath the glass panel in the dining room - wonderful! Madame is as educated as she is travelled and her family has been in the château for 200 years - no-one stands on ceremony and there is a sense of timeless peace here, off the beaten track.

Rooms: 1 double, 1 twin, 2 triples, all with bath or shower & wc.

Price: €50-€55 for two; under 4s free. Reduction for 4 nights or more.

Meals: Choice of restaurants within 5km.

Closed: Never.

From Blois D764 through Montrichard towards Genillé-Loches. Just before Genillé, D10 right towards St Quentin sur Indrois. Mill on left.

From Loches D760 to Montrésor; left towards Chemillé; mill on left; signposted.

Josette & Clive Mieville
Le Moulin de la Roche
37460 Genillé
Indre-et-Loire
Tel: (0)2 47 59 56 58
Fax: (0)2 47 59 59 62
E-mail: clive.mieville@wanadoo.fr
Web: www.moulin-de-la-roche.com

Sophie & Alain Willems de Ladersous
Le Moulin de Montrésor
37460 Montrésor
Indre-et-Loire
Tel: (0)2 47 92 68 20
Fax: (0)2 47 92 74 65
E-mail: alain.willems@wanadoo.fr

Entry No: 428   Map: 7

Entry No: 429   Map: 7

Sue's welcome has been vastly praised. So have Andrew's cooking (he's a friendly host too), the setting, the décor, the fun. Their deliciously watery home, a carefully restored mill on an island, is all ups and downs, nooks and crannies, big rooms and small, character and variety with skilful use of Sue's stencils and sponging. Plus a restful shady garden, private waterside spot, the added temptation of about 1,000 paperbacks - and a brilliant blue and yellow macaw! And now a heated swimming pool. *Not really suitable for young children.*

Rooms: 3 doubles, 1 triple, 1 twin, all with bath or shower & wc.

Price: €60-€70 for two.

Meals: Dinner €25, including wine & coffee.

Closed: December-February.

From Loches N143 for Châteauroux; pass Perusson; left at sign to St Jean St Germain; house is last over bridge on left.

Andrew Page & Sue Hutton
Le Moulin
Saint Jean Saint Germain
37600 Loches
Indre-et-Loire
Tel: (0)2 47 94 70 12
Fax: (0)2 47 94 77 98
E-mail: millstjean@aol.com

Entry No: 430   Map: 7

Gourmets: the Dallais Restaurant opposite has a Michelin star! People come to the tiny village and stay in this unassuming B&B just for that special dinner (the village has a more modest eating house too). But there's more: Natacha, a busy, bubbly, intelligent young mother, is sweetly attentive; her quiet, affable husband is grounded here in his family goat-cheese business (almost 200 goats 3km away - guests can visit); Le Grand Pressigny, 10km away, has a superb museum of prehistory. The fairly basic bedrooms (French cheap 'n' cheerful) are in a separate wing with a good dayroom and real disabled facilities in one room.

Rooms: 4 doubles, all with shower & wc.

Price: €35 for two.

Meals: In village, 1 restaurant Michelin starred, 1 simple 'family'.

Closed: Never.

From Châtellerault D725 through La Roche Posay & Preuilly sur Claise. 1km after Preuilly left on D50/D41 to Le Petit Pressigny. House in centre opp. Restaurant Dallais.

Bernard & Natacha Limouzin
La Pressignoise
37350 Le Petit Pressigny
Indre-et-Loire
Tel: (0)2 47 91 06 06
E-mail: natacha.limouzin@wanadoo.fr

Entry No: 431   Map: 7

In a quiet street in this historic, grid-based town designed by Cardinal Richelieu, the street door opens into a charming courtyard with an unusual nut bladder tree, banana plants and a pocket-handkerchief of lawn. Tim teaches the piano and English and is endlessly helpful. Marion is the creative force behind the beautifully-decorated rooms. The two in the main house are charming – a large cool blue double, a prettily pink single with sloping ceiling and low window looking onto the courtyard. The twin and family rooms opposite have their own mini-kitchens. Bountiful breakfasts are served in the elegant but homely dining/sitting room.

Rooms: 1 single, 1 double, 1 twin, 1 family, all with bath or shower & wc.

Price: € 57 for two.

Meals: Self-catering possible; wide choice of restaurants within 200m; picnic & barbecue possible.

Closed: Never.

From A10, Richelieu exit. After entering Richelieu, 2nd left. House 300m down on right.

Marion & Tim Lawrence
L'Escale
30 rue de la Galère
37120 Richelieu
Indre-et-Loire
Tel: (0)2 47 58 25 55
Fax: (0)2 47 58 25 55

Entry No: 432   Map: 7

CANCELLING

Please always telephone to cancel as soon as you realise you are not going to take up your booking, even if it is late in the day. The owners may still be able to let the room for that night and will at least not stay up until the small hours wondering whether you have had an accident and when they should give up and go to bed.

By the same token, if you discover that you are going to arrive later than planned, do let your hosts know in time to prevent them from worrying or, worse, from deciding you're not coming at all and giving your room to someone else.

These essential politenesses, as among friends, keep the machine oiled and running smoothly.

Poitou-Charentes

The old family seat, a picture-book chateau in a large park, has period pieces galore, family portraits and trees - your hosts having added twigs to those trees in the form of 11 grandchildren. Monsieur is a genial, English-speaking field sportsman; Madame has a sprightly elegance and will greet you like a long-lost friend in intelligent if slightly impeded French. Rooms and washing arrangements are also rather eccentric but have a timeless charm - showers in cupboards, a sometimes quirky use of antiques. Your hosts will gladly discuss visits to Loire châteaux, Futuroscope and other fascinations.

Rooms: 1 triple, 1 double, both with shower; 1 single with basin; 2 wcs for all (1 on another floor).

Price: €36.50-€46 for two.

Meals: Dinner €15, including wine & coffee.

Closed: Never.

That heady golden liquid is distilled near ancient wetlands where for centuries fugitives have hidden from tyranny, flat-bottoms have carried hunters and waterfowl have risen wild.

From Loudun, D759 for Thouars 7km; left D19 to Arçay 1km; château on right behind big gates as you enter village (no signs).

Hilaire & Sabine Leroux de Lens
Château du Puy d'Arçay
86200 Arçay
Vienne
Tel: (0)5 49 98 29 11

Poitou-Charentes

After 20-odd years of B&B, your hosts still enjoy their guests enormously so come and experience daily life in a small hilltop village with a fine 12th-century church. He, a jovial retired farmer (their son now runs the farm), knows his local lore; she smiles quietly and gets on with her cooking in the big homely kitchen - they are the salt of the earth. Up the superb, old, solid oak staircase, bedrooms are clean and bright with good beds, curtained-off showers and separate loos. A warm and generous welcome is guaranteed plus masses of things to do and see.

Rooms: 3 doubles, 1 with extra bed for child, all with shower & wc.

Price: €35 for two.

Meals: Dinner €12, including wine & coffee.

Closed: Never.

Such a lovely old farmhouse, built in the late 15th century, proudly set at the end of its drive. Five generations of Picards have lived here, serenely. They are quiet, welcoming, if busy, cereal farmers who will treat you as part of the family. Overlooking the chestnut-treed garden are the generous bedrooms where good furnishings include handsome wardrobes and firm new mattresses. Sunlight streams into the huge sitting room with its well-matched beams, white walls and terracotta floor. Breakfast is in the yellow dining room or on the leafy terrace and there are now simple cooking facilities for guests.

Rooms: 2 doubles, 1 twin, all with shower & wc.

Price: €43 for two.

Meals: Dinner 600m, self-catering possible.

Closed: Never.

From Loudon towards Thouars; D60 for Moncontour. From Mouterre Silly church, house 50m for Silly, signposted 'Chambres d'Hôtes'.

From Richelieu D7 towards Loudun for 4km; right into drive lined with lime trees.

Agnès & Henri Brémaud
Le Bourg
86200 Mouterre Silly
Vienne
Tel: (0)5 49 98 09 72
Fax: (0)5 49 98 09 72

Jean & Marie-Christine Picard
Le Bois Goulu
86200 Pouant
Vienne
Tel: (0)5 49 22 52 05
Fax: (0)5 49 22 52 05

Entry No: 434   Map: 7

Entry No: 435   Map: 7

Nothing austere or forbidding about this imposing, lovingly-restored, 15th-century fortified castle. A wide spiral stone staircase leads to the beautifully-decorated, comfortable rooms where old family furniture, vast stone fireplaces and beds with richly-textured canopies, finely stitched by your talented hostess, preserve the medieval flavour, while bathrooms are state-of-the-art. From the stone window seats where ladies of yore tatted and gossiped you can admire the view over the surrounding countryside. There is an elegant dining room for breakfast and dinner and a huge, high-ceilinged, light-filled sitting room for enlightened conversation with your cultured and charming hosts. And much more.

Rooms: 1 twin, 1 triple, 2 suites, all with bath & wc.

Price: €53-€99 for two.

Meals: Dinner €23, including wine & coffee.

Closed: November-Easter.

From Paris A10 exit Chatellerault Nord; at r'bout after toll for Usseau 5km; D749 for Richelieu; D75 to Usseau.

Jean-Marie & Marie-Andrée Bardin
Château de la Motte
86230 Usseau
Vienne
Tel: (0)5 49 85 88 25
Fax: (0)5 49 85 89 85
E-mail: j-marie.bardin@wanadoo.fr

Entry No: 436 Map: 7

You will be mollycoddled by these delightful, good-humoured people with their remarkable attention to detail. One room in a converted woodshed has beams, pretty curtains, blue and yellow tiled floor and view over the large, rambling garden with its meandering frog pond (hence *Grenouillère*). Two rooms are upstairs in a house across the courtyard where Madame's mother, a charming lady, lives and makes a phenomenal collection of jams. Pleasant, comfortable rooms, a most attractive group of buildings, meals on the shaded terrace in summer and messing about in the small rowing boat.

Rooms: 2 triples, 3 doubles, all with bath or shower & wc.

Price: €42-€45 for two.

Meals: Dinner €18, including aperitif & wine.

Closed: Never.

From Tours N10 S for Châtellerault 55km. In Dangé St Romain, right at 3rd traffic lights, cross river, keep left on little square. House 200m along on left; signs.

Annie & Noël Braguier
La Grenouillère
17 rue de la Grenouillère
86220 Dangé Saint Romain
Vienne
Tel: (0)5 49 86 48 68
Fax: (0)5 49 86 46 56

Entry No: 437 Map: 7

Poitou-Charentes

They are a charming young couple, have young children, are frank, sociable and very good company, spending time with guests after dinner when family demands allow. They have converted a fine big barn into guest quarters - older than the main house, it has been very well done, muted colour schemes in the largish rooms harmonising with ethnic rugs. The superb cobbled terrace that runs the full length of the building invites you to sit on balmy evenings gazing across the wide landscape, listening to the music of the wind in the poplars. With a nature reserve on the doorstep, this is a little-known corner waiting to be discovered.

Rooms: 1 triple, 2 doubles, all with bath & wc.

Price: €46 for two.

Meals: Dinner €14, including wine.

Closed: Never.

So close to the lovely, lively old city of Poitiers and even closer to the high-tech Futuroscope, yet only the ping-pong of the little white ball or the splish-splash of swimmers disturbs the hush of the tiny village. Madame, vivacious and dynamic, is delighted to welcome you to sleep in her simple, pretty rooms in the converted outbuilding and to breakfast so copiously in courtyard or dining room that children are given doggy bags. The two rooms sharing cooking facilities have good, traditional French furnishings. The duplex, with its two smallish rooms, is more 'rustic' with an intriguing window layout. All are excellent value.

Rooms: 1 double, 1 triple, 1 duplex for 4/5, all with bath or shower & wc.

Price: €42-€45 for two.

Meals: Choice of restaurants 3km; self-catering, excluding duplex.

Closed: Never.

From Châtellerault D749 to Vouneuil sur Vienne; left in church square & follow Chambres d'Hôtes signs. Last house on right in hamlet of Chabonne.

From A10 exit 28 onto D18 W for Avanton for about 2km. Signposted in hamlet of Martigny.

Florence & Antoine Penot
Chabonne
86210 Vouneuil sur Vienne
Vienne
Tel: (0)5 49 85 28 25
Fax: (0)5 49 85 22 75

Annie & Didier Arrondeau
La Ferme du Château de Martigny
86170 Avanton
Vienne
Tel: (0)5 49 51 04 57
Fax: (0)5 49 51 04 57
E-mail: annie.arrondeau@libertysurf.fr
Web: www.lafermeduchateau.fr

Entry No: 438   Map: 7

Entry No: 439   Map: 7

Begun in the 1400s, 'finished' in the 1700s, the château has a properly aged face. From the dramatic dark-panelled, orange-walled hall up the superbly bannistered staircase, through a great carved screen, you reach the *salon* gallery that runs majestically the length of the house. Here you may sit, read, write, dream of benevolent ghosts. Off the gallery, the bedrooms are loaded with personality. Madame's hand-painted tiles adorn a shower, her laughter accompanies your breakfast. Monsieur tends his trees and knows all there is to do in the area. A great couple in a genuine family château. *Gîte space for 4 people.*

Rooms: 1 suite, 2 twins, all with bath or shower & wc. Extra children's room.

Price: €61-€69 for two.

Meals: Auberge nearby; good choice 10km.

Closed: Never.

From A10 Futuroscope exit D62 to Quatre Vents r'bout; D757 to Vendeuvre; left D15 through Chéneché. Labarom 800m on right after leaving Chéneché.

Eric & Henriette Le Gallais
Château de Labarom
86380 Chéneché
Vienne
Tel: (0)5 49 51 24 22/
(0)6 83 57 68 14
Fax: (0)5 49 51 47 38
E-mail: chateau.de.labarom@wanadoo.fr

Monsieur once resuscitated cars for a living - he now takes far more pleasure in reviving tired travellers; Madame cares for every detail. Their house is on the old ramparts and the pretty garden looks directly over the boulevard below where you would expect a moat (quiet enough at night). The two rooms are neat, with good beds and old armoires. One has surprising big-flower wallpaper, the smaller is plain blue; both have space and the shower room has been prettily retiled. Breakfast is in high-backed chairs at the long table in the converted stables beneath the old hay rack. An utterly delightful couple who cannot do enough for you.

Rooms: 2 twins, both with shower or bath & wc.

Price: €37 for two.

Meals: Restaurants in village.

Closed: Never.

From Châtellerault D725 towards Parthenay for 30km. In Mirebeau, left immed. after Gendarmerie traffic lights; No 19 about 50m on right.

Jacques & Annette Jeannin
19 rue Jacquard
86110 Mirebeau
Vienne
Tel: (0)5 49 50 54 06
Fax: (0)5 49 50 54 06

A quiet village, a fine 18th-century coaching inn, a charming courtyard, large garden and mature trees: it is an oasis of green peace - Vivaldi would have loved it. Attractively restored by Monsieur Flambeau and his vivaciously welcoming English/French wife, the immaculate rooms: *Spring* - very French with its old cherrywood bed, *Summer* - brass four-poster, *Winter* - snow-white canopied bed, *Four Seasons* - almost English with old-style pine furniture, pretty children's room and peach-pink double, have beautifully-tiled bathrooms to match and guests have a sitting room in the old stables. *Baby-sitting available.*

Rooms: 1 suite for 4, 3 triples, 1 double, all with bath or shower & wc.

Price: €40-€50 for two.

Meals: Dinner €20.50, including wine & coffee.

Closed: Mid-November-February.

In the big flagstoned kitchen of the crag-perched château, friends and family chat over the jam-making. Hunting trophies and family portraits, including a mob-capped great-grandmother, in the sunny breakfast room; comfortable, freshly-decorated bedrooms with old family furniture - every object tells a tale; charming un-snobbishly aristocratic hosts, hugely knowledgeable about local Romanesque art, tell stories of monks and brigands. 15th-century castles didn't have en suite loos: there are chamber pots in case you can't face the stairs! *Gîte space for 4 people.*

Rooms: 1 double/twin, 1 double, 1 suite, all with shower or bath & wc.

Price: €56 for two.

Meals: Restaurants 3km.

Closed: Never.

From Poitiers N149 W towards Nantes for 14km; at Vouillé left D62 to Latillé. House is largest in main village square. (24km total.)

From A10 exit Poitiers Nord N149 for Nantes 12km; at bottom of hill left for Masseuil.

Yvonne Flambeau
La Demeure de Latillé
1 place Robert Gerbier
86190 Latillé, Vienne
Tel: (0)5 49 51 54 74
Fax: (0)5 49 51 56 32
E-mail: latille@chez.com
Web: www.chez.com/latille

Alain & Claude Gail
Château de Masseuil
86190 Quinçay
Vienne
Tel: (0)5 49 60 42 15
Fax: (0)5 49 60 70 15

Who says you can't have a honeymoon every year? This is the perfect spot for all honeymoons. It's a ravishing 17th-century château where sophisticated, simple luxury is the keynote and each bedroom is named after the marble used in its bathroom. Michel, a retired lawyer, has not lost his professional gift of the gab and Monique is an inspired interior designer. You may eat locally-grown and often home-reared food (including *foie gras*) by candlelight, sleep in a four-poster under a magnificent beamed ceiling and breakfast hugely the next morning in the garden.

Rooms: 2 doubles, 1 twin, all with bath & wc.

Price: €90–€120 for two.

Meals: Dinner €30, including wine & coffee.

Closed: Never.

In a clearing in the woods this long stone house stands in quiet seclusion: you know at once that you will be welcomed like family by utterly liveable, likeable people. She is delightful and caring with a lovely smile, he is quieter and friendly, their house is deliciously, sunnily, genuinely French. The old tiles shine with wax, armchairs are pink plush, low ceilings are beamed and wallpapers floral. The sitting part of the suite is a cosy den with beautiful fitted cupboards and board games, bedrooms are calmly pretty. It is safe, soft and comfortable and all guests, including families, will feel at ease.

Rooms: 1 double, 1 suite for 3, both with shower & wc.

Price: €40–€46 for two; suite €55 for three.

Meals: Restaurant 5-15km; picnic possible.

Closed: Never.

From Poitiers N147 for Limoges; first left for Savigny l'Évescault; first right D89 for 5km. First right on entering village.

From Poitiers N147 for Limoges for 12km; right for Nieul; house on right before village.

Monique & Michel Tabau
Château de la Touche
86800 Savigny l'Évescault
Vienne
Tel: (0)5 49 01 10 38
Fax: (0)5 49 56 47 82
E-mail: infos@chateaudelatouche.com
Web: www.chateaudelatouche.com

Jacques & Marie-Thérèse Lacroix
La Petite Thimotte
86340 Nieul L'Espoir
Vienne
Tel: (0)5 49 42 06 00
Fax: (0)5 49 42 54 66

Poitou-Charentes

In the generous château outbuildings, the guest quarters are decorated with a wonderful flair for fabrics and colours - mats and tablecloth match crockery, bathrooms match bedrooms. It's smart yet utterly welcoming, as befits a converted château bakery. The largest room, finely renovated with exposed beams, stones and thick white curtains, holds the old bread oven. Your hosts are well-travelled, sociable people who will happily chat (Monsieur in perfect English) in the pleasant sitting area about all the things in the cultural treasure-chest that is the Poitou.

Rooms: 2 rooms for 3/4, 2 doubles, 2 twins, all with bath, shower & wc.

Price: €54-€68 for two.

Meals: Restaurants 2-8km; self-catering possible.

Closed: Never.

It is naturally, unstiltedly, aristocratically French, this former orangery in the fine château park - so are its owners. The stone-flagged *salon* has a fine jumble of ten French chairs, bits of ancient furniture, pictures, ornaments, lamps. The dining room has traditional elegance. Everywhere, objects shout out their stories, there are statues indoors and out; bedrooms are large, bursting with character; bathrooms too. The family is lively and fun with many interests: Monsieur's are history and his family, Madame's are art and life - they combine unselfconscious class with flashes of southern non-conformism. And this is a dog-friendly house.

Rooms: 2 doubles, 1 twin, 1 suite, all with bathrooms (1 on separate floor).

Price: €61 for two.

Meals: Dinner €11, including wine & coffee.

Closed: Never.

From A10 exit 29 Rocade Est (ring road). Limoges & Châteauroux 5km; exit left D3 dir. Montamisé 3km; right D18 for 2.5km. Château on right.

From A10, Poitiers Nord exit, N10 direction Limoges. After 7km, left to Bignoux; follow signs to Bois Dousset.

Daniel & Agnès Vaucamp
Château de Vaumoret
Rue du Breuil Mingot
86000 Poitiers
Vienne
Tel: (0)5 49 61 32 11
Fax: (0)5 49 01 04 54

Vicomte & Vicomtesse Hilaire de Villoutreys de Brignac
Logis du Château du Bois Dousset
86800 Lavoux
Vienne
Tel: (0)5 49 44 20 26
Fax: (0)5 49 44 20 26

Entry No: 446   Map: 7

Entry No: 447   Map: 7

A bee farm! The humble bee reigns royal here where honeys and other bee products are made - the small shop is a hive of activity. Jacky does the bee-tending while vivacious Charline welcomes you with a genuine smile. She is excellent at explaining (in French) the ancient complicity between man and insect over breakfast in the separate guest building. Two bedrooms are in the converted pigsty; downstairs has ivy-framed windows, upstairs has big skylights, colourful décor and plenty of space. The third room is behind the main house - smallish and cosy with its own tiny garden. Great for children too.

Rooms: 2 doubles, 1 twin, all with bath or shower & wc.

Price: € 39.50 for two.

Meals: Restaurant in St Savin. Barbecue available.

Closed: November-February.

After a splendid tree-lined drive, the lovely entrance hall is very striking in black and white tiles, black and white prints; elsewhere, original paintings and antiques add intensity to this clever marriage of French style and English comfort. Delight in the elegantly green French dining room, wallow in the clubby leather and English chintz of the sitting rooms, enjoy a good bathroom and sleep deeply beneath your classy half tester. Deby is a charming hostess, Richard revels in his pretty, natural garden, their children welcome others and the GR48 footpath goes past the house. What more could nature-lovers ask? *Gîte space for 8 people.*

Rooms: 2 doubles, 2 twins, all with bath or shower & wc.

Price: €64 for two.

Meals: Dinner €14, including wine & coffee.

Closed: Never.

From Chauvigny, N151 for St Savin. 2km before St Savin, left to Siouvre; signs.

From Chauvigny D54 to Montmorillon; D727 for La Trimouille 10km; house on right.

Charline & Jacky Barbarin
Siouvre
86310 Saint Savin
Vienne
Tel: (0)5 49 48 10 19
Fax: (0)5 49 48 46 89
E-mail: charline.barbarin@wanadoo.fr
Web: perso.wanadoo.fr/hebergementmiel/

Richard & Deby Earls
La Boulinière
Journet
86290 La Trimouille, Vienne
Tel: (0)5 49 91 55 88
Fax: (0)5 49 91 72 82
E-mail: jr-earls@interpc.fr
Web: www.interpc.fr/jr-earls/bbweb.htm

Entry No: 448   Map: 7

Entry No: 449   Map: 7

True farming folk (their son now 'does' the goats) with deep roots in village life, they sing in the choir, act with the drama group, Madame shows her embroidery, Monsieur has been elected Mayor. And they love sharing their simple, stylish house with intelligent, cultured, like-minded guests. The suite is in the converted coach house, its kitchen in the old bread oven. All rooms, with their good fabrics and Madame's exquisite samplers, blend harmoniously with the garden and woodlands (golden orioles, hoopoes, wild orchids...). You may visit the goats, watch cheese being made, fish in their big lake.

Rooms: 2 doubles, 1 suite for 4/5 with kitchen/diner, all with bath or shower & wc. Extra room for children.

Price: €44 for two.

Meals: Dinner €16, including wine & coffee.

Closed: Never.

From Poitiers N147 SE to Lussac les Châteaux; D727 E for 21km; left D121 to Journet. In village, N towards Haims; house 1km on left.

Jacques & Chantal Cochin
Le Haut Peu
86290 Journet
Vienne
Tel: (0)5 49 91 62 02
Fax: (0)5 49 91 59 71

Entry No: 450   Map: 7

Jean-Louis, a genial twinkly man, used to farm but now sticks to vegetables, chickens and a role in numerous local events. Geneviève is a keen artist. Their home is a traditional Poitevin farmhouse, rendered a sunny shade of orange, with a corridor running the width of the house and rooms opening off either side. You come to it from the back, up a long tree-lined drive, so will be surprised to find it is in fact in the middle of the village. Rooms are freshly decorated, furniture is suitably old: the canopy over one bed was made for Madame's great-grandmother's wedding. Real and comforting.

Rooms: 1 twin with shower & separate wc; 1 quadruple with shower & wc.

Price: €38-€40 for two.

Meals: Dinner €10-13, including wine & coffee.

Closed: Never.

Exit A10 Poitiers Sud N10 towards Angoulême to Vivonne; 2nd exit Champagne St Hilaire/Sommières du Clain; right towards Civray: Champniers 8km on left - Chambre d'hôtes signs.

Geneviève & Jean-Louis Fazilleau
Le Bourg
86400 Champniers
Vienne
Tel: (0)5 49 87 19 04
Fax: (0)5 49 87 96 94
E-mail: jeanlouis.fazilleau@free.fr

Entry No: 451   Map: 7

The Salvaudons are educated, intelligent farmers - he energetic and down-to-earth, she gentle and smiling - committed to the natural way ("there's more here than the Futuroscope"), who like swapping travellers' tales and sharing simple, lasting values. Their house is relaxed and genuine too, with decent guest rooms. All the farm produce is organic: don't miss the chance to try Madame's Limousin specialities - lamb, chicken cooked in honey, vegetable pies - round the family table. The sheep farm lies in rolling, stream-run country beloved of fisherfolk and Monsieur will take children to meet the sheep. *Gîte space for 6 people.*

Rooms: 2 doubles, both with shower & basin, sharing wc.

Price: € 31 for two.

Meals: Dinner € 13, including wine & coffee.

Closed: Never.

The picture tells it all - moat, keep, drawbridge, dreams. Up two spiral stone flights is "the biggest bedroom in France" - solid granite windowsills, a giant fireplace, a canopied bed and the shower snug in the former *garde-robe* (water closet). Breakfast under the five-metre guardroom vault, your feet on the original 14th-century flagstones. The old stones are exposed, the furniture sober and the fires always laid, just like olden times. Indeed, the whole place is brilliantly authentic, the magnificent gardens glow from loving care and Pippa is eager and attentive - flowers, bubbly, fishing in the moat - all on the house! *Gîte space for 5 people.*

Rooms: 1 double, 1 suite for 4, both with shower & wc.

Price: € 110-€ 130 for two.

Meals: Restaurant 4km; choice 9km.

Closed: Christmas-March.

From Poitiers D741 to Civray; D148 east and D34 to Availles; D100 towards Mauprévoir for 3km; signposted.

From A10 exit 29 on N147; N149 W to Parthenay; round Parthenay northbound; cont. N149 for Bressuire; 7km north of Parthenay right at sign for château.

Pierre & Line Salvaudon
Les Écots
86460 Availles Limousine
Vienne
Tel: (0)5 49 48 59 17
Fax: (0)5 49 48 59 17

Nicholas & Philippa Freeland
Château de Tennessus
79350 Amailloux
Deux Sèvres
Tel: (0)5 49 95 50 60
Fax: (0)5 49 95 50 62
E-mail: tennessus@csi.com
Web: www.tennessus.com

Entry No: 452   Map: 7

Entry No: 453   Map: 7

Your hosts are a splendid team and excellent company - she teaches, he cooks, lots of home-produced things, popping in and out of the kitchen in his apron to chat - the atmosphere is very easy. Up the fine staircase, the suite is big and attractive; in an attached building, the apartments, simply but nicely furnished, have their own corner kitchens. In this old Protestant area, the nearby *Marais Poitevin*, a common hiding place for both sides during religious strife, is worth a visit. Excellent value in a pretty, welcoming house in wooded grounds on the edge of the village.

Rooms: 2 suites for 4, 1 triple, all with shower & wc.

Price: € 38 for two.

Meals: Dinner € 14 , including wine & coffee.

Closed: Never.

From A10 exit Niort Centre or A83 Niort Est; D7 for Mougon 1km; left D5 for La Mothe St Héray 7km; right for Prailles. Sign on left entering village; cont. & right to house.

Michel & Marie-Claude Duvallon
Le Colombier des Rivières
79370 Prailles
Deux Sèvres
Tel: (0)5 49 32 84 43

It is delightfully, aristocratically eccentric, the river glimmers in the garden, a beautiful Japanese maple looks into the big bedroom and the slightly shambolic state of the rooms quite won us over. Madame is husky-voiced from smoking *Gauloises*. Her family snapped the house up after the Revolution and women loom large among the portraits in the big, cluttered sitting room. Monsieur uses a limpidly charming French. A most likeable pair who serve splendid dinners, enjoy good conversation and may suggest a game of bridge. Children love the enormous park and the boat.

Rooms: 1 triple with bath, shower & wc; 1 triple sharing shower & wc; 1 double with shower, sharing wc; 2 children's rooms.

Price: € 38-€ 61 for two.

Meals: Dinner € 19, including wine & coffee.

Closed: Never.

From Poitiers N10 for Angoulême 3km; N11 for Niort; at Lusignan D950 3km; after Melle right D301; through St Romans; house in valley just before church.

M & Mme Rabany
Le Logis
79500 Saint Romans lès Melle
Deux Sèvres
Tel: (0)5 49 27 04 15
Fax: (0)5 49 29 18 37

The idyllic riverside setting has views out to the River Sèvre Niortaise and evening peace once the trippers have gone. Monsieur, who is most knowledgeable about the utterly fascinating *Marais* area, will escort guests on trips in his boat (at reasonable rates). Madame is justifiably proud of this pretty single-storey house where she was born and which has a charming old-world atmosphere, rooms crammed with a lifetime's collection of objects, solid repro furniture and is good value in a touristy area. Families welcome, preferably without toddlers (unfenced water).

Rooms: 1 double, 1 triple, both with shower & wc.

Price: €40 for two.

Meals: Restaurants within walking distance.

Closed: Never.

From Coulon centre, D23 towards Irleau. At end of village, immed. left along bank of River Sèvre which is Rue Élise Lucas.

Ginette & Michel Chollet
68 rue Élise Lucas
79510 Coulon
Deux Sèvres
Tel: (0)5 49 35 91 55/42 59

Entry No: 456   Map: **11**

The old farmhouse, lovingly restored and decorated, is simple, pristine, with biggish, comfortable rooms overlooking a pretty garden where you may picnic (there's a useful guest kitchen too). They are an interesting young couple of Anglophiles. Madame knows about nutrition and serves generous breakfasts with home-made jam, cheese, yogurt and cereals, all on local pottery. Monsieur teaches engineering in beautiful historic La Rochelle: follow his hints and discover the lesser-known treasures there. They love children of any age - there's some baby kit, table tennis and country peace. Good value. *No pets in rooms.*

Rooms: 1 suite for 4 with bath, shower, wc & possible extra room for 2; 1 triple with shower & wc.

Price: €45-€50.50 for two.

Meals: Dinner occasionally available €18.50, including wine & coffee; restaurants within 5 minutes drive.

Closed: Never, but must book ahead.

From La Rochelle N11 E for 11km; north on D112 to Longèves; in village, right at 'Alimentation', first left, past Mairie; house 700m on left.

Marie-Christine Prou
43 rue du Marais
17230 Longèves
Charente-Maritime
Tel: (0)5 46 37 11 15
Fax: (0)5 46 37 11 15
E-mail: mcprou@wanadoo.fr
Web: perso.wanadoo.fr/17longeves

Entry No: 457   Map: **11**

A lively young family who enjoy having guests: the parents cook together (lots of organic ingredients) while the three children entertain young visitors - an excellent team. In their lovingly-restored old house, old and modern each have their place. Antique armoires and big new beds, a collection of old scales and full disabled facilities (in the more modern-décor cottage), lots of treasures and a tennis court. The air is full of warm smiles, harmony breathes from the old walls and woodwork. They have thought of everything to make you comfortable and families are positively welcome.

Rooms: 1 triple, 1 suite for 6, 1 cottage for 5, all with bath or shower & wc.

Price: €60 for two.

Meals: Dinner €23, including wine & coffee.

Closed: Never.

A wonderful old house and sure-footed hosts who grow endives - what more could one ask? Built in 1600, renovated in 1720, the house stands in a garden of mature trees reaching to the River Boutonne: walk in peace, swim in clean shallow water, or play in the huge guest sitting room among antiques, armchairs and a French billiard table. In clean, fresh bedrooms are good beds and big armoires. Indeed, the whole place has a totally French country feel to it: you might be staying with your favourite granny, though Monsieur has a wicked sense of humour. There are good bike trails to spin off on and fabulous Romanesque churches to visit in the area.

Rooms: 1 double/twin with shower & wc; 1 suite for 4 with bath & wc.

Price: €43 for two.

Meals: Dinner €15, including wine & coffee.

Closed: Never.

From Surgères Gendarmerie & fire station, D115 NW towards Marans & Puyravault following signs for 5km.

From the Gendarmerie in St Jean d'Angély, D127 NE towards Dampierre for 8km. In Antezant, first right.

Brigitte & Patrick François
Le Clos de la Garenne
9 rue de la Garenne
17700 Puyravault, Charente-Maritime
Tel: (0)5 46 35 47 71
Fax: (0)5 46 35 47 91
E-mail: info@closdelagarenne.com
Web: www.closdelagarenne.com

Pierre & Marie-Claude Fallelour
Les Moulins
17400 Antezant
Charente-Maritime
Tel: (0)5 46 59 94 52
Fax: (0)5 46 59 94 52

Entry No: 458   Map: 11

Entry No: 459   Map: 11

The Deschamps just love doing B&B and it shows. Madame delights in cooking delicious meals for her guests and Monsieur enjoys talking to them. In the dining room, dotted with family treasures, the atmosphere round the big table is legendary and their generosity has been sung by many a returning guest (they once delayed going to a friend's party to dine with late-arriving guests), so what matter a slightly unkempt façade? Huge wardrobes dominate the bright-papered bedrooms, beds and bedding are traditional French and the recently re-decorated double has three lovely windows. A very special place.

Rooms: 1 double, 2 suites, all with bath or shower & wc.

Price: €42 for two.

Meals: Dinner €15, including wine & coffee.

Closed: November-15 April.

Here is a professional couple who left Paris for the country – and what country it is. With Romanesque wonders galore, Cognac nearby, the beaches of Ré and Oléron islands not too far, and even the well-known 'free-range' zoo of La Palmyre, you find culture and beauty as well as a warm, relaxing place to stay. The creamy local stone of the old farmhouse - part 17th, part 19th-century - is a perfect foil for flowers and Madame, an enthusiastic gardener, grows organic veg too. There are hand-painted touches plus a kitchen designed so she can cook and entertain guests at the same time. Welcome! *Gîte space for 4.*

Rooms: 2 doubles, both with bath or shower & wc, 1 twin to make family 'suite' with double.

Price: €46 for two.

Meals: Dinner €17, including wine & coffee.

Closed: Never.

From St Jean d'Angély D939 towards Matha. About 3km after crossroads to Varaize, D229 towards Aumagne. House 0.8km on left.

From A10 exit 34 for St Jean d'Angély. E on D939 to Matha (20km). In Matha, right for Thors. Before entering Thors, turn left; Le Goulet on right.

Éliane & Maurice Deschamps
La Clé des Champs
17770 Aumagne
Charente-Maritime
Tel: (0)5 46 58 23 80
Fax: (0)5 46 58 23 91

Frédérique Thill-Toussaint
Le Clos du Plantis
1 rue du Pont
Le Goulet, 17160 Sonnac
Charente-Maritime
Tel: (0)5 46 25 07 91
Fax: (0)5 46 25 07 91
E-mail: auplantis@wanadoo.fr

Entry No: 460   Map: 11

Entry No: 461   Map: 11

A totally French house, a thoroughly English couple. Jenny gardens and writes, with pleasure; John builds his boat for crossing the Atlantic, with dedication; together they have caringly restored their *Charentais* farmhouse and delight in creating a sociable atmosphere and welcoming their guests to dine *en famille*. Or feel free to go your own way (separate guest entrance). The beautifully-landscaped garden with its pretty windmill (let separately) has an English feel - and a croquet lawn - but the 'sense of place' remains unmistakably French. And St Savinien is a painters' delight - this really is a lovely part of the country. *Gîte space for 2.*

Rooms: 1 room for 2-4 with bath & wc.

Price: €40-€46 for two.

Meals: Dinner €15, including wine & coffee.

Closed: Christmas.

From St Savinien bridge D114 along river, under railway, left D124 towards Bords for 2km; 2nd left after Le Pontreau sign; house 200m on right.

John & Jenny Elmes
Le Moulin de la Quine
17350 Saint Savinien
Charente-Maritime
Tel: (0)5 46 90 19 31
Fax: (0)5 46 90 19 31
E-mail: elmes@club-internet.fr

Entry No: 462   Map: 11

Behind its modest, wisteria-covered mask, this 17th-century former wine-grower's house hides such a pretty face and a magnificent garden that flows through orchard and *potager* (freshest fruit and veg for your 5-course dinner) into the countryside. Outstanding bedrooms too: light, airy and immaculate, every detail just so, they are beautifully done with luxurious bathrooms. The room for disabled guests is the best we have ever seen. Your hosts, recently retired from jobs in agricultural safety and country tourism, have given their all to make house and garden as near perfect as possible and you will find them wonderfully attentive.

Rooms: 2 doubles, 1 suite for 4, all with bath, shower & wc.

Price: €44-€49 for two.

Meals: Dinner €14, including wine & coffee.

Closed: Never.

From A10 exit 34 on D739 to Tonnay Boutonne; left D114 to Archingeay; left for Les Nouillers - house just after turning.

Marie Therese & Jean-Pierre Jacques
Chambres d'Hôtes
17380 Archingeay
Charente-Maritime
Tel: (0)5 46 97 85 70
Fax: (0)5 46 97 61 89
E-mail: jpmt.jacques@wanadoo.fr

Entry No: 463   Map: 11

Your hosts have lavished care, money and time on their superb farmhouse since settling here after years in Morocco - you can tell they love it. A delightful couple: Anne-Marie is a talented artist whose stylish painted furniture, patchwork, painstakingly-constructed rag rugs and co-ordinated colour schemes adorn the house; her husband is the mayor; they share good breakfasts and dinners with their guests in the dining room or by the swimming pool. Their gardens are landscaped, terrace paved, flowers blooming and bedrooms big. *Quiet children over six welcome.*

Rooms: 4 doubles, all with bath & wc.

Price: €60 for two; extra bed €15.

Meals: Dinner €23, including wine & coffee.

Closed: Never.

Arrive at La Jaquetterie and step back in time: the old virtues of having time for people and living at a gentler pace are here in this well-furnished, old-fashioned house, and it is so comfortable. These kindly farmers are really worth getting to know: Madame keeps a good home-produced table; Monsieur organises outings to distilleries and quarries; both enjoy their guests, especially those who help catch escaping rabbits. Great old armoires loom in the bedrooms, lace covers lovely antique sleigh beds, and one of the bathrooms is highly modern-smart. An authentic country experience with genuinely good people.

Rooms: 1 triple on ground floor, 1 suite for 2-4, both with shower & wc.

Price: €46 for two.

Meals: Dinner €15, including wine & coffee.

Closed: Never.

From Saintes N150 W for 5km; fork right N728 for 29km; right D118 to St Sornin. In centre, Rue du Petit Moulin opposite church door.

From A10 exit Saintes N137 towards Rochefort/La Rochelle for about 11km; D119 to Plassay. House on left on entering village.

Anne-Marie Pinel-Peschardière
La Caussolière
10 rue du Petit Moulin
17600 St Sornin, Charente-Maritime
Tel: (0)5 46 85 44 62
Fax: (0)5 46 85 44 62
E-mail: caussoliere@wanadoo.fr
Web: www.caussoliere.com

Michelle & Jacques Louradour
La Jaquetterie
17250 Plassay
Charente-Maritime
Tel: (0)5 46 93 91 88

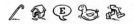

Entry No: 464   Map: **11**

Entry No: 465   Map: **11**

It's an enormous, intriguing old château with dark walls, weapons on the walls, fabulous antiques - and lots of light: it's just one room thick. Your hostess, a beautiful, laughing extrovert, has lived here for decades, knows the history deeply and is addicted to receiving guests. Appropriately old-fashioned bedrooms are furnished with taste and flair (plumbing a bit old-fashioned too) and the open-fired original kitchen, where you step over and under priceless objects, is a gem, ideal for cold-weather breakfast. Artists and musicians love the long thin house and its fine gardens but Madame is unforgettable.

Rooms: 1 double, 1 triple, both with shower & wc; 2 twins, sharing shower & wc.

Price: €46-€53 for two.

Meals: Dinner at neighbouring farm; restaurants 5-12km; picnic possible.

Closed: November-March.

Your quarters are a huge, many-beamed barn: there's sitting space with a big log fire, billiards and rocking chairs downstairs, gallery access to bedrooms above. These, called *Agatha Christie*, *Picardie*..., have books, lace bedcovers and garden views. Madame, a likeable, lively person, interested in people (that includes you), and Monsieur, a wizard on local tourist info, really care for your comfort. They love to chat with guests about the best places to explore in this beautiful area. We have heard of "breakfasts on the sunlit terrace with home-made jams" - and you may use Madame's kitchen (leave it tidy!).

Rooms: 3 doubles, 1 twin, all with shower & wc.

Price: €43.50 for two.

Meals: Restaurants 1.5-7km.

Closed: Mid-November-April.

From Saintes N137 for La Rochelle 10km; D119 to Plassay; house on right as enter village, signposted.

From Saintes N137 towards Rochefort for 6km; left D127 to St Georges. Rue de l'Église in village centre - house on left.

Alix Charrier
Le Logis de l'Épine
17250 Plassay
Charente-Maritime
Tel: (0)5 46 93 91 66

Anne & Dominique Trouvé
5 rue de l'Église
17810 Saint Georges des Coteaux
Charente-Maritime
Tel: (0)5 46 92 96 66
Fax: (0)5 46 92 96 66

Entry No: 466   Map: **12**

Entry No: 467   Map: **11**

Sue's talent for watercolours springs from the same sense of style and colour she has brought to revitalising this handsome farmhouse - prettily-decorated bedrooms, bright and fresh and furnished with French antique-style pieces; new shower rooms with sensibly big towels. There's plenty of choice at breakfast and if you've arranged dinner there will be home-grown vegetables, or there's a barbecue for you to do your own. Beyond the large garden are vineyards and, in summer, fields of sunflowers. This is good walking and cycling country and it's a 20-minute drive to the beach and to Cognac.

Rooms: 1 twin, 2 doubles, all with bathroom & wc.

Price: €55 for two.

Meals: Dinner €20, including wine & coffee.

Closed: Occasionally.

This grand house lords it over a tiny hamlet surrounded by superb walking country and tantalising views. Claude's ravishing collection of ornaments and antique furniture is on display in every room: the big bedrooms, one of which has a particularly beautiful ormolu wardrobe, are magnificently decorated and scattered with oriental rugs. The huge hall and staircase give a great feeling of space. Look at the floor tiles in the *salon*: they were left to dry outside in the woods where they collected imprints of the feet of foxes, badgers and birds, before being laid in a church. Wonderful stuff.

Rooms: 2 doubles, 1 twin, all with bath, shower & wc.

Price: €58-€66 for two.

Meals: Dinner €21, including coffee & wine.

Closed: Occasionally.

From A10 exit 36 for Pons; after toll bear right; right for Gémozac 1.5km; left for Tanzac & Givrezac; centre of Givrezac left at garage; house last on left.

From A10 exit 37 towards Mirambeau. At r'bout pass 'Marché U'; D254 1st right to St Georges des Agoûts; right at church D146; first junction left & follow Chambres d'Hôtes signs.

Sue & Phillip Capstick
La Belle Maison
Route de Belluire
17260 Givrezac
Charente-Maritime
Tel: (0)5 46 49 06 66
Fax: (0)5 46 49 06 66

Dinah & Claude Teulet
Les Hauts de Font Moure
17150 Saint Georges des Agoûts
Charente-Maritime
Tel: (0)5 46 86 04 41
Fax: (0)5 46 49 67 18
E-mail: cteulet@aol.com
Web: www.fontmoure.com

Poitou-Charentes

The genuine château works: gilt, marble, mouldings and period furniture to match the 1850s building. Both house and garden are being brilliantly restored. Monsieur, who was a designer and teaches history of art, has a natural feel for colour and fabric; he loves arches too, and has put one over each bath; rooms, large and finely-proportioned, overlook the park where guests can picnic and admire the botanical wonders - it is all superb, as are his fascinating talk about bringing his château back to life, his piano-playing and his candlelit dinners of traditional regional dishes in a most congenial atmosphere.

Rooms: 3 doubles, all with bath, shower & wc.

Price: €75-€85 for two.

Meals: Dinner €35, including wine & coffee.

Closed: Occasionally.

Gordon is from London, Laure from Paris, both are ex-market researchers and they thoroughly enjoy people. Laure cooks (rather well) because she loves it. The two big guest rooms in the annexe are pretty and welcoming, with plenty of stone and wood - all kept spotlessly clean. Everyone can use the hosts' sitting room with its fireplace, or the chairs by the pool, and the kitchen door is always open. Once a modest inn for train travellers, the house still overlooks the old station, now an attractive place to live. Their brochure says: 'La Font Bétou is one of those very rare places in the world that does not pretend but just is.' It is.

Rooms: 1 split-level double, 1 twin, both with shower & wc + sitting space downstairs.

Price: €50-€55 for two.

Meals: Dinner €23, including wine & coffee.

Closed: January.

From A10 exit 37 to Mirambeau Centre. Ave de la République is after & opposite Tourist Office & swimming pool, behind trees on your right.

From Angoulême N10 S for 45km; left D730 towards Montguyon. 1km after Orignolles, right to house, signposted.

René Ventola
Le Parc Casamène
95 avenue de la République
17150 Mirambeau
Charente-Maritime
Tel: (0)5 46 49 74 38
Fax: (0)5 46 49 74 38
Web: www.homestead.com/mirambeau/

Laure Tarrou & Gordon Flude
La Font Bétou
17210 Orignolles
Charente-Maritime
Tel: (0)5 46 04 02 52
Fax: (0)5 46 04 02 52
E-mail: tarrou@la-font-betou.com
Web: www.la-font-betou.com

Entry No: 470   Map: **11**

Entry No: 471   Map: **11**

A real family affair: when Christine is dealing with her young daughters, her parents welcome guests to their 18th-century village house, just yards from the beautiful cloisters of the Royal Abbey where Eleanor of Aquitaine was born and her mother buried - you can see the church from the lovely walled garden. The rooms, in subdued, slightly impersonal rustic taste, are simple and serene (the loft is the most appealing) and look over the garden. You breakfast in the old stable block and sit comfortably in the former wash-house where Christine will make up a fire if it's cold.

Rooms: 2 triples, 1 double, 1 twin, all with shower & wc.

Price: €41-€44 for two.

Meals: Restaurant & crêperie 100m.

Closed: October-April.

What an interesting, unexpected place - a paradise for children. Pretty, fresh guest rooms, one large, one smaller, are in a converted outbuilding - from the front window you see deer by the lake, from the back door, llamas and wallabies. And there are ostriches: if you want to try some, ask for dinner; sitting on the ostrich-skin sofa, you will be offered a glass of local *Pineau des Charentes*. Alex left hectic London for French farming with a difference and is thoroughly enjoying his new life. Hélène loves pergolas so there are plenty of spots to sit and enjoy the fascinating surroundings. Fun and hugely welcoming. *Gîte space for 4.*

Rooms: 1 quadruple, 1 triple, both with bath or shower & wc.

Price: €40 for two.

Meals: Dinner €16, including coffee (wine €8).

Closed: Never.

From Niort N148 for Fontenay le Comte 20km; after Oulmes right to Nieul sur l'Autise; head for Abbey: house just beyond on left.

From Poitiers D741 S towards Confolens for 50km. 10km after Pressac, left on D168 for St Germain de Confolens; signed after 2km.

Christine Chastain-Poupin
Le Rosier Sauvage
1 rue de l'Abbaye
16310 Nieul sur l'Autise
Charente
Tel: (0)2 51 52 49 39
Fax: (0)2 51 52 49 46

Alex & Hélène Everitt
Le Pit
Lessac
16500 Confolens
Charente
Tel: (0)5 45 84 27 65
Fax: (0)5 45 85 41 34
E-mail: everitt16@aol.com

Entry No: 472   Map: 11

Entry No: 473   Map: 7

This prosperous-looking country house is home to young English farmers, their family antiques and their bilingual children (excellent company for small visitors, who are positively welcomed). They grow corn, sunflowers, ostrich and turkey: they are busy but happy to sit and talk round the big table at informal, family-style meals. From the panelled dining hall with its polished wood, soft colours and floor-to-ceiling doors, a splendid staircase leads up to the simple rooms. The big one has a romantic air and a claw-footed bath; others are smaller but all have good lighting and towels and are excellent value.

Rooms: 2 doubles, both with bath & wc; 1 double with shower & sharing wc; 1 twin with shower & wc.

Price: €40 for two.

Meals: Dinner €14, including wine & coffee; choice of restaurants Confolens.

Closed: Never.

From Confolens D948 for Limoges for 4km; signposted on road.

Stephen & Polly Hoare
Lesterie
Saint Maurice des Lions
16500 Confolens
Charente
Tel: (0)5 45 84 18 33
Fax: (0)5 45 84 01 45
E-mail: polly.hoare@libertysurf.fr

Entry No: 474   Map: 7

Do look up as you enter the guest house in the old stables: the hall ceiling is marvellous. Breakfast is served here if it isn't fine enough to sit outside. Rooms are good too: white paint and exposed stone make a stunning setting for fine antiques and old beds fitted with new mattresses. Madame, busy breeding horses (gorgeous foals in summer), is full of smiles and always has time to help you plan your day, arrange cognac-distillery visits or invite you to relax in a hammock after a bit of badminton. Monsieur is most sociable and offers a local aperitif to guests of an evening in this peaceful wooded spot where the local red stone walls glow. *Gîte space for 8 people.*

Rooms: 1 double, 1 twin, both with shower & wc.

Price: €46 for two.

Meals: Good restaurant at St. Adjutory.

Closed: Never.

From Angoulême, N141 to La Rochefoucauld; right at 3rd traffic light on D162 to St Adjutory; in village 2nd right & follow signs.

Sylviane & Vincent Casper
La Grenouille
16310 Saint Adjutory
Charente
Tel: (0)5 45 62 00 34
Fax: (0)5 45 63 06 41

Entry No: 475   Map: 7

There's an old-fashioned, well-lived-in, much-loved air to this interesting house. The bedrooms have parquet floors, old-style wallpapers, pretty old beds with new mattresses; bathrooms have been modernised. Madame's regional cooking is highly appreciated and dinner is worth coming back for. A conservatory has been built to seat more people round a bigger table where your hosts stay and chat if not too busy serving you. They'll also show you the fascinating old cognac still and on winter weekends you may be able to help with the distilling process. *Camping possible too.*

Rooms: 2 triples, 2 doubles, 1 twin, all with shower & wc.

Price: € 37 for two.

Meals: Dinner € 13, including wine & coffee.

Closed: Never.

This is a gem, perfect for those who definitely do not want a hotel. Béatrice inherited the exquisitely French neo-Gothic château and she lovingly protects it from the worst of modernisation (though the hurricane took its toll in the garden and trees have had to be replanted). Sleep between old linen sheets, sit in handsome old chairs and wallow in a superb bathroom. The sitting room has that unusual quirk, a window over the fireplace, the dining room a panelled ceiling studded with plates. Béatrice, a teacher, and Christopher, a lecturer in philosophy, like eating with their guests.

Rooms: 1 family suite, 2 doubles, 1 twin, all with bath or shower, sharing 2 wcs on guest room floor & 1 downstairs.

Price: € 46 for two.

Meals: Dinner € 12, including wine & coffee.

Closed: Never.

From A10 Pons exit D700 for Barbezieux Archiac. After Echebrune D148 (1st left) for Lonzac-Celles; right D151 & follow signs.

From A10 exit 36 to Pons, Archiac & Barbezieux (D732/D700/D731); D731 towards Chalais for 12km. After Passirac, 1st right at roadside cross; up leafy drive.

Micheline & Jacky Chainier
Le Chiron
16130 Salles d'Angles
Charente
Tel: (0)5 45 83 72 79
Fax: (0)5 45 83 64 80

Mme Béatrice de Castelbajac
Le Chatelard
Passirac
16480 Brossac
Charente
Tel: (0)5 45 98 71 03
Fax: (0)5 45 98 71 03
E-mail: c.macann@wanadoo.fr

Entry No: 476   Map: **11**

Entry No: 477   Map: **12**

Aquitaine

The first artists painted their powerful magic underground; then stilted shepherds led their flocks through the swamps; then pine forests drained the land; so stilts now dance for consumers at high-class wine fairs.

Such a special place. Antoine, a cookery teacher, loves to whip up feasts in his sensational kitchen and offer good wines from his 'trade contacts'. Dinner is at a giant round table, made from an outsize wine barrel, in a 19th-century barn with a cantilevered gallery and a superb two-storey fireplace; good-quality rooms are interestingly different; children are spoilt: sandpit, climbing frame, huge shallow-ended pool, horses to feed, three Laborde children to play with. Canoeing, trips on the lovely Canal du Midi, fishing, riding, cycling are all possible. Readers write reams of praise.

Rooms: 3 doubles, 1 triple, 1 twin, all with bath and/or shower & wc.

Price: € 52 for two.

Meals: Dinner € 20, including wine & coffee.

Closed: Occasionally.

From A62 exit 4 onto D9; left towards Bazas-Grignols; over motorway bridge; 1st left, 250m after bridge; follow signs Chambres d'Hôtes 3km.

Claire & Antoine Laborde
La Tuilerie
33190 Noaillac
Gironde
Tel: (0)5 56 71 05 51
Fax: (0)5 56 71 05 51
E-mail: claire.laborde@libertysurf.fr

Entry No: 478   Map: **12**

A modest exterior? Don't be fooled - you go through the main buildings and splendour strikes! Discover delightful gardens and a great pool enclosed by charming guest quarters: your dynamic hosts have done a brilliant conversion of the old stables. They have kept much of the original wood and added elegant antique furniture to each of the large, individually-decorated bedrooms. Attention to detail includes armoires lined with sophisticated fabrics that match curtains and wallpaper, good bathrooms, superb breakfasts. Overall, excellent value. *Gîte space for 6 people.*

Rooms: 2 doubles, 1 twin, all with bath or shower & wc.

Price: €69 for two.

Meals: Restaurant 300m.

Closed: Never.

Food and wine buffs love it here with these kind, courteous people: Madame is an excellent cook who can cater for special diets (with advance warning) and Monsieur is a wine expert - enjoy it all in the Art Déco dining room with its modern pictures and *two* fireplaces. Set among fields and vineyards, their farmhouse is attractively furnished and the beamed, wallpapered guestrooms are big and comfortable. The family room is particularly lovely: it has a more contemporary feel with its mezzanine and sitting area overlooking the garden. Kind, courteous people, they offer wine courses and vineyard trails all over the Bordelais, and you can buy their preserves.

Rooms: 1 double, 1 triple, 1 family; all with bath, shower & wc.

Price: €53 for two.

Meals: Dinner €8-€30.

Closed: 16 October-31 December.

From Libourne D670 S 45km to La Réole; left N113 for Agen; house on left on edge of town opp. Automobile Museum.

From Libourne D670 S for 31km; left D230 to Rimons; at sawmill on right, first left - signposted.

Christian & Danielle Henry
Les Charmettes
Henry's Lodge
33190 La Réole
Gironde
Tel: (0)5 56 71 09 23
Fax: (0)5 56 71 25 13

Dominique & Patrick Lévy
Le Grand Boucaud
Rimons
33580 Monségur, Gironde
Tel: (0)5 56 71 88 57
Fax: (0)5 56 61 43 77
E-mail: grandboucaud@free.fr
Web: grandboucaud.free.fr

Born in Senegal, Monsieur has been in Madagascar, Tahiti and many other places: quantities of fascinating souvenirs tell the tale. But this immaculate and comfortable 1750s farmhouse was his family holiday home for years. Madame, pleasant and attractive, was a nursery school teacher and is eager to please her guests: we were naturally offered coffee and cakes on the terrace. Beautiful bedrooms, simple yet not stark, have white or clean stone walls, built-in cupboards often with genuine wall-to-wall doors. Excellent for fishing, canoeing or riverside walking (50m to the River Dordogne) and St Emilion just 7km away. *Gîte space for 2-4 people.*

Rooms: 1 double/twin, 1 suite for 2/4, both with bathroom.

Price: €44-€51 for two.

Meals: Restaurants nearby.

Closed: Never.

From Bordeaux D936 E for 36km. 4km after Branne right on D670 towards Agen. At Lavagnac (1km) left after Boucherie/Charcuterie; house on left.

France Prat
Le Refuge du Peintre
3 chemin de Courbestey
Lavagnac
33350 Sainte Terre, Gironde
Tel: (0)5 57 47 13 74
E-mail: france.prat@wanadoo.fr
Web: perso.wanadoo.fr/france.prat

Entry No: 481   Map: **12**

Tradition has deep, proud roots here; you sense it in the ancient walls and Monsieur's wine knowledge is vast. He is a kind, gentle man, his big farmhouse has stood for three centuries, his vines, now tended by the next generation, are mature, his wine superb; the lovely linen, patchwork and lace are family heirlooms and the family has a strong, lively presence. The country-style, stone-walled, old-furnished bedrooms and their small bathrooms are immaculate, though great beams and attic ceilings may reduce your space. You have your own living room and kitchen (ideal if you're daunted by local restaurant prices) but the beautiful breakfast table is in the cosy family dining room.

Rooms: 2 doubles, 2 twins, 1 triple, all with bath or shower & wc.

Price: €46-€49 for two.

Meals: Choice of restaurants locally; self-catering possible.

Closed: 15 January-15 February.

From Libourne D243 towards St Émilion; pass Château Girard Bassail on right; 3km before St Émilion left D245 towards Pomerol; house 300m on right.

Claude Brieux
Château Millaud-Montlabert
33330 Saint Émilion
Gironde
Tel: (0)5 57 24 71 85
Fax: (0)5 57 24 62 78

Entry No: 482   Map: **11**

You appreciate good wine? Believe you can absorb the knowledge by osmosis? Then you will enjoy this coolly restrained, very beautiful manor among the vines. It has been in the family for nine generations though the owners live in another Grand Cru château, leaving nephew and pleasantly relaxed manager to run this one. They come every day and will invite you to taste the goods in the cellars - an easy if busy couple. Rooms, with plain sandstone or painted walls and simple antiques, offer sober quiet and the shrubby garden has an arch of trees that gives dappled shade as you walk towards the distant statue.

Rooms: 5 doubles, 1 twin, all with shower & wc.

Price: €55-€84 for two.

Meals: Restaurants nearby.

Closed: Never.

In an amazing, historic town yet utterly quiet in its large walled garden where the shutters match the oleander flowers, the elegant townhouse has properly classy furnishings - superb antiques set off by unfussy fabric and grasspaper walls, beautiful rugs on polished floors, lustrous chests, paintings and prints of real quality and an astounding quantity of tapestry work done by Monsieur himself. The smallest (cheapest) room is fine enough, the others are sheer luxury. Your hosts, smart and highly hospitable retired professionals, know the local winegrowers and can guide you round. A high-class house, in the town yet not of it.

Rooms: 1 suite, 1 twin, both with shower & wc; 1 double with separate, private bathroom.

Price: €60-€90 for two.

Meals: Dinner €30, including wine.

Closed: Christmas & New Year.

From A10 exit St André de Cubzac through Libourne for Bergerac; 3km after Bigaroux left D234E for St Laurent; right before railway for St Hippolyte; house on left.

From Libourne D243 to St Émilion; roundabout right to Hôtel de Ville. Park in square: Rue Abbé Bergey leads off this.

Bernard & Béatrice Rivals
Château Monlot Capet
Saint Hippolyte
33330 Saint Émilion, Gironde
Tel: (0)5 57 74 49 47
Fax: (0)5 57 24 62 33
E-mail: mussetrivals@belair-monlot.com
Web: www.belair-monlot.com

François & Élisabeth Musset
3 rue Abbé Bergey
33330 Saint Émilion
Gironde
Tel: (0)5 57 24 70 12
Fax: (0)5 57 24 70 12

In the 12th century, pilgrims rested gratefully at this welcoming priory. Susie's warm personality (she does personal development workshops) and the serenity of the setting now make it a refreshing haven for 20th-century guests. Lie in a hammock under the walnut tree, let the fantail pigeons coo you into a blissful siesta and the nightingales serenade your dawn. The house is decorated with a sophisticated combination of good antiques and modern pieces, opulent curtains and cheerful bedcovers. No routine - breakfast served whenever it suits, candlelit dinners on request. *Gîte space for 6 people. Minimum stay 2 nights July-August in apartment.*

Rooms: 2 doubles with shower, bath & wc, 1 apartment with 2 doubles.

Price: €91 for two; apartment €129 for two-four.

Meals: Ask if chef is around; restaurant 3km.

Closed: Never.

Here you will find three good and very big bedrooms, a stone entrance hall, a wrought-iron balcony terrace for a glass of their own dry white Semillon wine, and decorative bantams all over the garden. They are a hard-working young couple in an 18th-century château without quite enough money to make it over-stylish, thank heavens. It is relaxed and easy - even busy - with three young children, and deer in the woods. Breakfast is on the terrace, wine-tasting in the magnificent *salle de dégustation*. The small pool is for evening dippers rather than sun-worshippers.

Rooms: 2 triples, both with shower & wc; 1 family with bath, shower & wc.

Price: €53 for two; €91.50 for four.

Meals: Choice of restaurants in Bourg.

Closed: February & 1 week in August.

From Bordeaux D936 for Bergerac; exactly 1km after St Quentin de Baron, house sign on right.

From A10 exit 40a or 40b through St André de Cubzac; D669 through Bourg for Blaye; quickly right D251 for Berson for 1km; sign on right up lane.

Susie de Castilho
Le Prieuré
33750 Saint Quentin de Baron
Gironde
Tel: (0)5 57 24 16 75
E-mail: stay@stayfrance.net
Web: www.stayfrance.net

M & Mme Bassereau
Château de la Grave
33710 Bourg sur Gironde
Gironde
Tel: (0)5 57 68 41 49
Fax: (0)5 57 68 49 26
E-mail: chateau.de.la.grave@wanadoo.fr
Web: www.chateaudelagrave.com

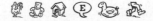

Entry No: 485   Map: 11

Entry No: 486   Map: 11

From Brazil, New Zealand, the New Hebrides, the Sahara, Michèle came home to the hacienda-style house built when her family's old winegrowing farm crumbled away. The imitation zebra and tiger skins in the living room fit strangely well with all the memorabilia and African sculptures; bedrooms are good traditional, with fine views across oceans of vines. It is relaxed and exotic and Michèle, lively and intelligent, knows all there is to know about this area - ask her about the roses planted at the ends of the vines - and its great wines. Their own wine comes with dinner and the nearby ferry comes from Blaye and Royan.

Rooms: 1 double with bath & wc; 1 twin with shower & wc.

Price: €46-€49 for two.

Meals: Dinner €23, including wine & coffee.

Closed: Never.

Old meets new here in a successful mixture of both. Rooms have modern fabrics alongside fine old pieces of furniture, Philippe is Cellar Master for a *Grand Cru Classé* steeped in tradition, and an Internet convert; Monika, who is German and nursed in Vietnam for a while, may give you home-baked bread and muesli for breakfast. They are urbane, helpful, well-travelled polyglots and can obtain entry to most big wine châteaux for their guests: ideal for wine lovers. The large fish-and-lily pond adds a note of serenity. You may breakfast on the terrace and the beach is just 20 minutes away. *Gîte space for 4 people.*

Rooms: 1 double/twin, 1 double, 1 suite, all with bath or shower & wc.

Price: €40-€58 for two.

Meals: Restaurant 7km.

Closed: Never.

From Bordeaux bypass exit 7 on D1 to Castelnau; N215 through St Laurent; 4km, D104 to Vertheuil; abbey on right, over level crossing, house 1km on left.

From Bordeaux ring road exit 7 N215/D1 41km; right D104 to Cissac; right at War Memorial Rue du Luc; house 1km on left, after water tower.

Michèle Tardat
Cantemerle
9 rue des Châtaigniers
33180 Vertheuil Médoc
Gironde
Tel: (0)5 56 41 96 24
Fax: (0)5 56 41 96 24

Philippe & Monika Achener
Le Luc
6 route de Larrivaux
33250 Cissac Médoc, Gironde
Tel: (0)5 56 59 52 90
Fax: (0)5 56 59 51 84
E-mail: ph.achener@gmx.net
Web: www.travel.to/medoc

In its secluded setting, their miniature château rejoices in a fine chestnut staircase with iron banister, a veranda paved with rare Bidache stone, high ceilings, old prints, a glimpse of the Pyrenees and the call of a peacock. Madame is a gem, gracious and charming - she teaches yoga, paints, is a long-distance walker and a committed vegetarian; her husband is gently reserved; Braco the dog loves company. Children can roam the 20 hectares of parkland freely - they love it. The rooms, large and properly decorated, have gorgeous parquet floors and relatively little 'château' furniture. We think the smaller ones give better value.

Rooms: 3 doubles, 1 twin, all with shower or bath & wc.

Price: €46-€77 for two.

Meals: Good restaurant in village.

Closed: November-March, except by arrangement.

"The whole place is stunning, inside and out! Astounding furniture, captivating house, brilliant décor." Our inspector was obviously moved by this house with prodigious original panelling (1610), whose contents have been accumulated by Colette's family for 14 generations: portraits from the 12th century onwards; spectacular bedrooms with canopied antique beds, strong colours, wonderful furniture; three with open fireplaces. Dining room and *salon* are handsome, too: more antiques, terracotta tiles and a huge stone fireplace. Colette is elegant, attentive, helpful and hugely resourceful. An exceptional place.

Rooms: 4 doubles, all with bath or shower & wc.

Price: €43-€56.50 for two.

Meals: Dinner €17, including wine & coffee.

Closed: Never.

From A10 or A63 exit St Geours de Maremne to Orist. Or, from A64 exit Peyrehorade to Dax. In both cases, 10km to Monbet.

From Dax D947 for Pau/Orthez 10km; on D947 ignore sign for Mimbaste; take NEXT right D16; follow discreet yellow signs to house.

M & Mme Hubert de Lataillade
Château du Monbet
40300 Saint Lon les Mines
Landes
Tel: (0)5 58 57 80 68
Fax: (0)5 58 57 89 29

Colette Dufourcet-Alberca
Maison Capcazal de Pachioü
40350 Mimbaste
Landes
Tel: (0)5 58 55 30 54
Fax: (0)5 58 55 30 54

Entry No: 489   Map: 16

Entry No: 490   Map: 16

An atmosphere of dream-like tranquillity wafts over this grand and appealing old French country house and its original oak floors. Just outside the park gates is the beautiful River Adour, rich in bird and wildlife - every 10 years or so it comes up and kisses the terrace steps. The two south-facing bedrooms overlook the river and a great spread of communal meadows where animals graze freely. There is a vast choice for 'flexitime' breakfast on the terrace or in the dining room. Madame, an attractively energetic and interesting hostess, was a publisher in Paris for many years. *Spanish spoken.*

Rooms: 3 doubles, 1 triple, all with bath or shower & wc.

Price: €60 for two.

Meals: Wide choice of restaurants 2-5km.

Closed: Never.

From A63 exit 8 to St Geours de Maremne; D17 S for 5km to Saubusse; right just before bridge; château 800m on right.

Claude Dourlet
Château de Bezincam
Route de l'Adour
Saubusse les Bains
40180 Dax
Landes
Tel: (0)5 58 57 70 27
Fax: (0)5 58 57 70 27

Entry No: 491   Map: **16**

It is a cliché, but - hey, they built houses to last in those days. Were a bright young modern architect to come up with the idea of one central supporting structure, and make it work, the media would drivel. This structure has stood every test that Nature and Man have conspired to throw at it. Not a penny has ever been spent on maintenance. The roof is as sound now as it was long before Asterix tugged the Roman beard. The decision to do without windows was far-sighted - again, no maintenance. It may be uncomfortable and of little use to man or beast, but it satisfies our key criteria: it is unusual, interesting, attractive and - it has soul.

Rooms: More like nooks, crannies and crevices really, stony yet snug and without excessive softness or pattern.

Price: Only flint-based currencies & barter accepted.

Meals: Back to trapping - all part of the experience.

Closed: Never, but occasionally jealously guarded.

From Landes, turn left and make way up nearest hillock. At top, realise it's the wrong hillock, but you'll be able to see the one you should be on.

M & Mme U'Shroom
Dun Dolmen
Petit Marché
44444 Ville en Pierre en Haut, Landes
Tel: Cup and string.
Fax: Stone tablet, chalk.
E-mail: throw@carrier_pigeon.fr
Web: www.libertyturf.fr

Entry No: 492   Map: **16**

A house to satisfy your soul: lost in a forest, its windows onto endless young oaks and pines with duck pond and river beyond. Madame, a lovable person, teaches yoga (for guests too); her artist son's hand-painted decoration (marbling, stencilling, trompe l'œil) brings originality without offence to old stone and brickwork (he also teaches); grandchildren live next door, all in harmony with nature, and summer walks yield wildflower treasures. The simple rooms are not large but there is real family space at the piano or around the huge kitchen fireplace during delicious dinners.

Rooms: 1 double, 1 twin, 1 triple, all with shower & wc (& 2 small family rooms).

Price: €33.50-€38 for two.

Meals: Dinner €12.50, including wine & coffee.

Closed: Never.

Heather, warmly communicative, Desmond, a retired architect with a great sense of fun: an exceptional couple who have brilliantly restored Agnos and do all the cooking. Bedrooms come in various sizes, the most impressive being Henri IV (antique gilt beds) and François I (black and white bathroom & antique cast iron bath). Admire the high ceilings framing remarkable mirrors, paintings set into panelling, fine period furniture, the black marble dining room fountain... François I is said to have escaped by a secret tunnel (can you find it?), there's a medieval kitchen and an old prison. It's huge and you will feel completely at home. *Children over 12 welcome. Gîte space for 14 people.*

Rooms: 3 suites, 1 double, 1 twin, all with bath and/or shower & wc.

Price: €60-€110 for two.

Meals: Dinner €18.50, wine €10.

Closed: 2 weeks in February & November.

From Mont de Marsan N134 NW to Garein; left D57 for Ygos & Tartas; follow signs: 1km of lane to house.

From Pau N134 for 35km to Oloron Ste Marie; through town; N134 for Zaragoza 1km. In Bidos, right for Agnos.

Mme Liliane Jehl
Moulin Vieux
40420 Garein
Landes
Tel: (0)5 58 51 61 43
Fax: (0)5 58 51 61 43

Heather & Desmond Nears-Crouch
Château d'Agnos
64400 Agnos
Pyrénées-Atlantiques
Tel: (0)5 59 36 12 52
Fax: (0)5 59 36 13 69
E-mail: chateaudagnos@wanadoo.fr

Landscape painters love it. From the terrace you can see for ever into the great Pyrenees - sunlit snowy in winter, awesomely coloured in summer: the Brownes own the land around so no danger of encroaching uglies. They have converted the old gîte for three delightful cosy bedrooms - exposed stonework, beams and a living room - with a fourth in the main house, built in 1727, all with good bathrooms. Your hosts are multinational (Polish, French, South African), they and their children are a happy, relaxed and thoroughly integrated family. It is informal, easily friendly - and the food is delicious.

Rooms: 3 doubles (2 can be triple), 1 twin, 1 family; all with bath or shower & wc.

Price: €47 for two.

Meals: Dinner €23, including wine & coffee.

Closed: Never.

The owners and their grand 18th-century village house are quiet, elegant, sophisticated. Dinner is a chance to pick their well-stocked brains about the region and you can delve into their extensive library (she binds books). They have completely renovated the house since finding it and this sleepy village in the Pyrenean foothills. The bedrooms are light and airy with interesting old furniture and lovely wooden floors. *La Rose* is very chic and *La Verte* is a dream - enormous, beautifully furnished, with views of the mountains and a 'waltz-in' bathroom. Readers are ecstatic.

Rooms: 2 doubles, both with shower or bath & wc.

Price: €46 for two.

Meals: Dinner €16, including wine & coffee.

Closed: Never.

From Pau N134 S for Saragosse to Gan; right D24 for Lasseube 9km; left D324. Follow Chambres d'Hôtes signs; cross 2 small bridges; house on left up hill.

From Navarrenx D2 for Monein to Jasses; right D27 for Oloron Ste Marie; in Lay Lamidou, left, first right, 2nd house on right.

Simon & Isabelle Browne
Maison Rancesamy
Quartier Rey
64290 Lasseube
Pyrénées-Atlantiques
Tel: (0)5 59 04 26 37
Fax: (0)5 59 04 26 37
E-mail: missbrowne@wanadoo.fr

Marie-France Desbonnet
Chambres d'Hôtes
64190 Lay Lamidou
Pyrénées-Atlantiques
Tel: (0)5 59 66 00 44/(0)6 86 22 02 76
Fax: (0)5 59 66 00 44
E-mail: desbonnet.bmf@infonie.fr
Web: www.ifrance.com/chambrehote/

One of those sturdy Béarn houses with solid old furniture and traditional decoration where Marie-Christine has added her own good furniture and decorative touches over the years: colourful wallpapers in the bedrooms, small, modern bathrooms, and everything is immaculate. She is elegant and energetic, doing nearly all the work here herself and longing to show you her remarkable garden. It has huge old trees, magnolia, azalea, rhododendron, with benches discreetly placed for quiet reading... and the Pyrenees as a backdrop. There's a table tennis table and the new spa centre in Salies is good for swimming all year. *Gîte space for 10.*

Rooms: 2 twins, 1 double, 1 suite, all with bath or shower & wc.

Price: €46–€52 for two.

Meals: Dinner €15, including wine & coffee.

Closed: Never.

Sylvianne lives on a hill in a typical old Basque farmhouse full of timbers, pictures, carved country furniture and her own skillfully-orchestrated patches of colour - she loves colour! Up the twisty old staircase, each super room has its strong chromatic vibration: Pamplona rippling blue and yellow with an open timber frame in the middle; Seville vigorously orange and green; Cordoue fresh blue and acid green; bits and bobs, bouquets and bows finish the effects and bathrooms are good. Downstairs, you will be generously received by your smilingly bright young hostess who knows the area and cooks very well.

Rooms: 1 quadruple, 3 triples, both with shower & wc

Price: €50 for two.

Meals: Dinner €20, including wine & coffee.

Closed: Never.

From A64 exit 7; right for Salies '<5 tonnes'; next right to Le Guilhat for 1.8km; house on left beside nurseries at junction with Chemin des Bois.

From A64 exit 4 towards Urt; right D123; through Labastide Clairence towards St Palais for 3km. House on left on top of hill - signposted.

Marie-Christine Potiron
La Closerie du Guilhat
64270 Salies de Béarn
Pyrénées-Atlantiques
Tel: (0)5 59 38 08 80
Fax: (0)5 59 38 08 80
E-mail: guilhat@club-internet.fr

Sylvianne Darritchon
Lacroisade
64240 La Bastide Clairence
Pyrénées-Atlantiques
Tel: (0)5 59 29 68 22
Fax: (0)5 54 29 62 99
E-mail: sylvianned@aol.com

Entry No: 497 Map: 16

Entry No: 498 Map: 16

You are up above the village in a 14th-century Basque farmhouse: the vast lintel stones, the original heart-of-oak staircase, the split levels, nooks and crannies speak of great age, the distant hills echo the message. A huge hall leads to the *salon*; leather chairs wait round the open fireplace. The former attic, restored with imagination and colour by Isabelle, successfully combines old and contemporary. Indulge in daughter Charlotte's delicious desserts, hear tales of yore from Isabelle, who has adopted her new land by training as a native storyteller, and visit the prehistoric caves of Isturitz for a taste of things more ancient still.

Rooms: 2 doubles, 3 triples, all with shower & wc.

Price: €43-€49 for two.

Meals: Dinner €17, including wine & coffee.

Closed: 1-15 February.

A lovely face among all the lovely faces of this superb listed village, the 16th-century Basque farmhouse, resuscitated by its French/Irish owners, is run with well-organised informality. Dinners, of excellent local dishes, around the great oak table are lively. Rooms are big, light, well decorated with hand-stencilling and pretty fabrics, beams and exposed wafer bricks, country antiques and thoughtful 'extras' like good books and bottled water. Breakfast is on the terrace in warm weather. And Gilbert will laugh and teach you *pelote basque*.

Rooms: 1 triple, 4 doubles, all with bath or shower & wc.

Price: €46-€56 for two.

Meals: Dinner €20, including wine & coffee.

Closed: Occasionally.

From A64 Briscous exit D21 to Hasparren; left D10 for Labastide Clairence for 3km; right D251 through Ayherre to Isturitz. Signposted.

From A64 junc. 4 for Urt/Bidache; right on D123 to La Bastide Clairence. House on main street, opp. bakery.

Isabelle & Charlotte Airoldi
Urruti Zaharria
64240 Isturitz
Pyrénées-Atlantiques
Tel: (0)5 59 29 45 98
Fax: (0)5 59 29 14 53
E-mail: urruti.zaharria@wanadoo.fr
Web: www.urruti-zaharria.fr

Valerie & Gilbert Foix
Maison Marchand, Rue Notre Dame
64240 La Bastide Clairence
Pyrénées-Atlantiques
Tel: (0)5 59 29 18 27
Fax: (0)5 59 29 14 97
E-mail: valerie.et.gilbert.foix@wanadoo.fr
Web: perso.wanadoo.fr/maison.marchand

Entry No: 499   Map: **16**

Entry No: 500   Map: **16**

The house cornerstone, the magnificent magnolia, the towering pines were all planted on one day in 1881. The Mallor family's welcome is as generous as they: an enchanting couple with teenage children who have lived and fished in southern seas. Their deeply sensitive restoration includes a Blue Marlin room, canopied pine beds, modern fittings and respect for the original chestnut panelling. They know about good food and wine too: Krystel ran a restaurant, Philippe's cellar is brilliant - do dine with them. There's a trompe-l'œil in the kitchen, Espelette for stocking up on spice, great walking, a sauna for afterwards, donkeys, children, church bells and lots more. *Spanish spoken.*

Rooms: 3 doubles, 2 triples, all with shower & wc.

Price: €60 for two.

Meals: Dinner €20, including wine & coffee; restaurants 700m.

Closed: Never.

From A63 exit on D932, continue through Ustaritz/Cambo les Bains; left into Louhossoa; straight over crossroads. House 500m on right.

Krystel & Philippe Mallor
Domaine de Silencenia
64250 Louhossoa
Pyrénées-Atlantiques
Tel: (0)5 59 93 35 60
Fax: (0)5 59 93 35 60
E-mail: domaine.de.silencenia@wanadoo.fr
Web: perso.wanadoo.fr/silencenia

Entry No: 501   Map: 16

Hear the electronic gate click behind you and 29 hectares of forested peace and quiet are yours with their fabulous wildlife. Draw your beautiful curtains next morning and you may see deer feeding; lift your eyes and feast on long, long vistas to the Pyrenean foothills; come down to the earthly feast that is Basque breakfast. Shyly attentive, Isabelle manages all this impeccably and keeps a refined house where everything is polished and gleaming, floors are chestnut, bathrooms marble, family antiques of high quality. A beautifully manicured haven - worth staying several days for serious cossetting.

Rooms: 1 twin, 2 doubles, all with bath & wc.

Price: €92-€107 for two; reduction 2 nights or more.

Meals: Restaurant 7km.

Closed: Never.

From Biarritz railway station to Bassussary & Arcangues; D3 for St Pée; 8km after Arcangues house on left; signs.

Isabelle Ormazabal
Bidachuna
Route Oihan Bidea D3
64310 Saint Pée sur Nivelle
Pyrénées-Atlantiques
Tel: (0)5 59 54 56 22
Fax: (0)5 59 47 31 00

Entry No: 502   Map: 16

Walk through the entrance hall into the handsome country kitchen and thence onto the lawns that roll towards those views. Or stay there and dine: it has a big fireplace, pottery pieces, sculpture, and a lot of flowers. In the sitting room, terracotta tiles and kilim rugs, a fireplace and grand piano give a comfortably smart air. Adriana is Swiss, Jocelyn South African, and they tend to do things well. Relatively new to B&B, they are hugely committed, creating lush bedrooms with a touch of luxury in the bathrooms. The abiding memory will be of terracotta tiles, attention to detail and great food. *Gîte space for 8.*

Rooms: 2 suites, both with bathroom & wc.

Price: €67-€82 for two.

Meals: Dinner €15, including wine & coffee.

Closed: Never.

18th-century elegance in an unspoilt village, it overlooks the old market place, has a walled garden, and a terrace with breathtaking country views at the back. Fiona is Scottish, Leif is Danish, with a cosmopolitan background in film and interior design - Leif a wonderful raconteur, Fiona an inspired cook and their house is stuffed full of paintings, antiques, props from film and theatre productions. The beige and white luxury extends to the bedrooms - white-painted floors, sumptuous raw Irish linen fabrics, fine furniture. *Gîte space for 2 people.*

Rooms: 1 double, 2 twins, all with bath or shower & wc.

Price: €53-€58 for two.

Meals: Dinner €20, including wine; picnic basket possible.

Closed: Never.

From A10 exit St André de Cubzac to Ste Foy La Grande; D708 to Duras; 4km after Duras left C1 to St Pierre sur D.

From Marmande D708 for Duras 17km to Levignac; bear left; head for Centre Ville; house on left behind market hall: two bay trees & white front door.

Jocelyn & Adriana Cloete
Manoir de Levignac
Saint Pierre sur Dropt
47120 Duras
Lot-et-Garonne
Tel: (0)5 53 83 68 11
Fax: (0)5 53 93 98 63
E-mail: cloete@lokace-online.com

Leif & Fiona Pedersen
La Maison de la Halle
47120 Lévignac de Guyenne
Lot-et-Garonne
Tel: (0)5 53 94 37 61
Fax: (0)5 53 94 37 66
E-mail: maison.de.la.halle@wanadoo.fr
Web: www.lamaisondelahalle.com

Tired of working too hard in Monte Carlo and New York, the Peyres moved here for a quieter life, then thought of B&B as a way of sharing their love of the place. The double rooms are not large but have French windows to their own terrace and splendid valley views to a small lake. The huge twin room has rugs on the original wood floor and sleigh beds in proper French country house style. Then there are the glorious main rooms and the vast yellow-tiled kitchen. Stunning furniture, a remarkable solid brass candelabra, a piano, a billiard room, handmade carpets... the list goes on. Most civilised in its casualness. *Gîte space for 4 people.*

Rooms: 2 doubles, 1 twin, all with shower & wc.

Price: €65-€85 for two.

Meals: Dinner €19, including wine & coffee.

Closed: 15 December-March.

From Bergerac D933 S towards Marmande. Approx. 1.5km after Eymet left on C1 towards Agnac-Mairie; château 500m on left.

Françoise & Henri Peyre
Château de Péchalbet
47800 Agnac
Lot-et-Garonne
Tel: (0)5 53 83 04 70
Fax: (0)5 53 83 04 70
E-mail: pechalbet@caramail.com

Entry No: 505   Map: **12**

This many-gloried place, a 17th-century family château, has 15 fabulous hectares of garden and woodland where red squirrels and deer cavort, wild orchids glow and the Babers nurture 400 new trees. Their furniture from Scotland sits graciously in these French rooms, white carpeting spreads deep luxury in the lovely suite, family antiques grace the guest sitting room and they invite you to share their welcoming manor. Breakfast generously in the huge kitchen or on the terrace then roam, relax or play: there's a carp lake for fishing, a tennis court, a 16m child-friendly pool. Great hosts, rooms, local markets, restaurants and wines. *Gîte space for 8.*

Rooms: 2 doubles, 1 family suite, all with bath & wc.

Price: €52.50-€73.50 for two.

Meals: Several good restaurants in Castillonnès (5 mins).

Closed: Christmas & New Year.

From Bergerac N21 for Villeneuve. 1.5km after Castillonnès, pass 'Terres du Sud' on left. After 50m, drive signposted on right before crest of hill.

James Petley, Patricia & David Baber
Domaine des Rigals
47330 Castillonnès
Lot-et-Garonne
Tel: (0)5 53 41 24 21
Fax: (0)5 53 41 24 79
E-mail: babersrig@aol.com
Web: www.ccu.co.uk/rigals

Entry No: 506   Map: **12**

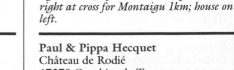

Within striking distance of three famous *bastides*, this old farm grows tobacco, maize and sunflowers and there's a château thrown in for the view. The house is a converted pigeon tower (hawks and owls nest in the holes outside); there are good bedrooms, a log-fired, country-style sitting room, high chair, bottle-warmer and games for children, a fine swimming pool for all. Horses are a passion with this family and you will often find them out riding. Madame has an infectious energy and speaks fluent English; her affable husband is quieter. Readers are enthusiastic. *Gîte space for 8 people.*

Rooms: 2 doubles, both with shower & wc, 1 with mini-kitchen.

Price: €51 for two.

Meals: Dinner €18, including wine & coffee; self-catering €9 per day.

Closed: Never.

From Villeneuve sur Lot, D676 to Monflanquin and D272 for Monpazier. 1.5km after crossroads to Dévillac, left before bridge; house is 3rd on right.

Michel & Maryse Pannetier
Colombié
47210 Dévillac
Lot-et-Garonne
Tel: (0)5 53 36 62 34
Fax: (0)5 53 36 04 79
E-mail: colombie@wanadoo.fr

Brash modernities are hidden (the telephone lurks behind a model ship). Paul and Pippa did most of the triumphant restoration themselves, with two small children and a passionate commitment to the integrity of the 13th/16th-century building. It is breathtaking: an elaborate *pisé* floor set in cabalistic patterns and lit only with candles, two stone staircases, patches of fresco, a vast hall with monumental fireplace and giant table - the welcome is to scale. The tower room is unforgettable, as is the pool. This family is veggie-friendly and pro-organic; dinner may feature home-reared lamb and often lasts hours; people simply love it. *Gîte space for 9 people.*

Rooms: 3 doubles, 2 suites, all with bath, shower & wc.

Price: €69-€99 for two.

Meals: Dinner €18, including wine & coffee.

Closed: Never.

From Fumel D102 to Tournon; D656 for Agen 300m; left to Courbiac, past church, right at cross for Montaigu 1km; house on left.

Paul & Pippa Hecquet
Château de Rodié
47370 Courbiac de Tournon
Lot-et-Garonne
Tel: (0)5 53 40 89 24
Fax: (0)5 53 40 89 25
E-mail: Chateau.Rodie@wanadoo.fr

Aquitaine

The impressive 3-acre garden of this surprising salmon-shuttered château has some foreign trees - olive and palm - and some ancient natives, as well as a rose bower and a fish pond. Ann, who is often working in the States, knows her design and uses unusual paint techniques for her colourful walls. You'll find open fires, high windows, polished wooden floors, some Empire furniture - and a fitness room; superb bedrooms that are large, light, individual, well-mattressed - and a Rice Bed from Ann's native South Carolina. Dinner is delicious, with a relaxed yet efficient host. *Security provided by electronically operated park gates.*

Rooms: 1 duplex for 5 with shower room & bathroom; 4 doubles, all with bath or shower & wc.

Price: € 105 for two; reduction 2 nights or more.

Meals: Dinner € 23, including wine & coffee.

Closed: Never, please book ahead.

From A62 exit 6 towards Aiguillon; 2nd right D642 towards Buzet; château on right, signposted just before Buzet.

Ann & Alain Doherty Gelix
Château de Coustet
47160 Buzet sur Baïse
Lot-et-Garonne
Tel: (0)5 53 79 26 60
Fax: (0)5 53 79 14 16
E-mail: reservations@coustet.com
Web: www.coustet.com

Entry No: 509   Map: **12**

French B&B *par excellence.* A wonderfully welcoming hostess (Monsieur runs the farm), brilliant big unflouncy bedrooms in best French provincial style looking across the garden to meadows and woods, opulent but unostentatious white bathrooms, acres of parkland for walks from the door, space for 8,000 free-range chickens and myriad other animals: sheep, horses, ducks, dogs (and no cats). Despite its size, the 17th-century château is a comfortable, informal home, ideal for children. You can play billiards, table tennis, croquet, *boules.* Breakfast - with eggs of course - and dinner are very much *en famille.*

Rooms: 1 double, 1 twin, 1 suite, all with bath or shower & wc.

Price: € 52-€ 60 for two; suite € 90 for four.

Meals: Dinner € 20, including wine & coffee; € 10 for children.

Closed: Never.

From Marmande D933 S towards Casteljaloux for 10km. Château signposted on right opposite D289.

M & Mme de La Raitrie
Château de Cantet
Samazan
47250 Bouglon
Lot-et-Garonne
Tel: (0)5 53 20 60 60
Fax: (0)5 53 89 63 53
E-mail: jb.delaraitrie@wanadoo.fr

Entry No: 510   Map: **12**

A deliciously rustic hamlet where you will experience true French *paysan* hospitality in the Durieux' converted barn. Furniture is properly dark, bathrooms authentically simple, Madame's regional cuisine (you can watch her cook) a daily marvel. She uses fine ingredients, many home-produced: vegetables, nuts, honey, fruit and free-range chickens. The history-charged area has ancient caves and stately châteaux; add spice to sightseeing with a sprinkling of local folklore, available courtesy of Monsieur who acts, if requested, as a knowledgeable guide and plies guests with his own fruit liqueurs when they return.

Rooms: 2 triples, both with shower & basin behind screens, sharing wc.

Price: € 37.50 for two.

Meals: Dinner € 11.50, including wine & coffee.

Closed: Never.

From Angoulême, D939 south. After Dignac D23 to Villebois Lavalette, D17 to Gurat; D102 for Vendoire 2km; left for Le Bouchaud.

André & Pierrette Durieux
Le Bouchaud
24320 Vendoire
Dordogne
Tel: (0)5 53 91 00 82
Fax: (0)5 53 91 00 82

Entry No: 511   Map: **12**

The peaceful, long-viewed stone cottage standing in two acres of woods and fields was once a lovers' retreat. Your hostess paints, plays the flute, teaches French, shares her library and also, drawing on a long and interesting life, her talent for good conversation. Her house, filled with Belgian antiques and exceptional paintings, has a split-level sitting room opening onto a sun terrace, modest but adequate bedrooms, big open fires and a large heated pool. Madame welcomes single visitors for week-long rest cures, French language immersion and excellent guided tours of the area - enquire about full-board terms. *Gîte space for 4 people.*

Rooms: 1 double, 1 twin, sharing bath, shower & wc (2nd wc on ground floor).

Price: € 46 for two.

Meals: Dinner € 15, including wine & coffee.

Closed: Never.

From Angoulême D939 S 29km; right D12/D708 22km to Bertric Burée. D106 for Allemans 3km; right for Chez Marty 1km, left at junction; house at end of lane on left.

Anne Hart
La Fournière
Chez Marty
24320 Bertric Burée
Dordogne
Tel: (0)5 53 91 93 58
Fax: (0)5 53 91 93 58

Entry No: 512   Map: **12**

The bright, rustic dining room with its limed walls, white tablecloths and ticking chair covers, the level changes upstairs, the bedrooms with their berugged wooden floors and simple furnishings (good taste and African throws), the inviting bathrooms - we love this place. The cool, overflowing stone plunge pool in the green and pleasant garden is unforgettable (there's a shallow one for children). Delightful, energetic Jane creates a relaxed atmosphere, offers superb and imaginative food and early supper for children in this lovely tranquil spot. And John "is a joy to be with". *Gîte space for 4 people.*

Rooms: 2 doubles, 1 twin, all with shower & wc; 1 double, 1 twin sharing bath & wc.

Price: €46-€53 for two.

Meals: Dinner €17, including coffee. Wine €8.

Closed: Never.

David and Alison have created such a pretty garden - you eat, separately from your hosts, under a wooden pergola covered in roses, honeysuckle and vines and the pool looks out over heavenly countryside. Convinced vegetarians, they also produce their own vegetables, eggs, honey and jam for their excellent meat-free dinners. The two large uncluttered bedrooms, with sloping ceilings and massive beams, are in a converted barn where they share a dayroom furnished with pieces made by David, a first-rate carpenter. And it's a great place for children who adore the donkeys, goats, chickens and cats. *German spoken. Gîte space for 8 people.*

Rooms: 1 double, 1 twin, both with shower & wc.

Price: €46 for two.

Meals: Dinner (vegetarian or vegan) €15, including wine & coffee.

Closed: Christmas Day.

From Angoulême D939 for Périgueux 29km; right D12 for Ribérac to Verteillac; left D1 for Lisle 5 km; right D99 for Celles for 400m; sign to left.

From D675 (Nontron to Brantôme), take D98 east. La Roche on right about 3km from D675.

Jane & John Edwards
Pauliac
Celles
24600 Ribérac, Dordogne
Tel: (0)5 53 91 97 45
Fax: (0)5 53 90 43 46
E-mail: pauliac@infonie.fr
Web: www.pauliac.fr

David Allison & Alison Coutanche
La Roche
24530 Champagnac de Belair
Dordogne
Tel: (0)5 53 54 22 91
Fax:
E-mail: allisons@club-internet.fr
Web: perso.club-internet.fr/allisons/

Entry No: 513   Map: **12**

Entry No: 514   Map: **12**

Fascinating people, they are committed to the rural heritage movement. Their sensitive restoration of this lovely, listed group of ancient buildings, with a shingle-roofed bread oven, illustrates that commitment. Bedrooms, at opposite ends of the long building, have odd layouts: one has the shower in a (big) cupboard next to the fireplace, an antique washbasin that tips straight into the drain (genuine period feature) and a 120cm brass bed. They founded the local music and dance festival, are very involved in the cultural life of the community and go to Glyndebourne whenever they can.

Rooms: 1 suite for 4 with bath & wc; 1 double with shower & wc.

Price: €50-€55 for two.

Meals: Restaurant 1.5km; picnic possible.

Closed: Mid-October-early-November; January.

A touch of Alsace in the Dordogne? This *moulin* in a valley is like a Swiss mountain inn. Levels change, steep original stairs rise, brilliantly-chosen colours give huge character, Alsace rugs and antiques warm the atmosphere - as does the sitting room fireplace - and if bedrooms are on the small side the welcome from your easy-going hostess is huge. The whole effect is rich and brave. Add fully organic home-grown ingredients for delicious dinners and you have excellent value.

Rooms: 1 twin (& child's room), 1 double, all with shower & wc.

Price: €39 for two.

Meals: Dinner €16, including coffee.

Closed: November-February.

From Périgueux N21 N to Sarliac sur l'Isle; D705 to Coulaures; right D73 to Tourtoirac. Right after bridge, left D67 towards St Orse; house 1km on left.

In Mussidan, at church, towards Villamblard 4km; follow blue signs left for St Séverin 2km, blue sign on right.

Danièle & Jean-Pierre Mougin
Bas Portail
Tourtoirac
24390 Hautefort
Dordogne
Tel: (0)5 53 51 14 35
E-mail: bestofperigord@perigord.com
Web: www.best-of-perigord.tm.fr

Jacques & Ginette Kieffer
Le Moulin de Leymonie du Maupas
24400 Issac
Dordogne
Tel: (0)5 53 81 24 02

Entry No: 515   Map: 12

Entry No: 516   Map: 12

The whole family are involved: Madame has handed the daily management of auberge and B&B to her two daughters, Monsieur runs the mixed farm producing fruit, vegetables, poultry and wine, and they all thrive. The two bedrooms, in Grandmother's old house over the road from the auberge, are simple and good, perfect for two couples travelling together who could have the whole house. People come quite a way to eat here, the food is so good (open every day for lunch - leave time for a siesta afterwards - and dinner). With a brand new pool in the kempt little garden, it's a real bargain.

Rooms: 2 doubles, both with own shower & wc.

Price: €38 for two.

Meals: Dinner €14-€24, including wine & coffee.

Closed: October-April.

Carine, half-Greek, easy-going and helpful, makes you feel very welcome in the sunny kitchen of her restored farmhouse. She enjoys cooking French and international dishes, with local ingredients where possible, and sometimes organises barbecues round the swimming pool. Each new-bedded, newly-decorated, modern-bathroomed bedroom in the converted barn has its own terrace onto the shady garden (the pool is far enough away not to disturb your siesta), the unfussy style relies on exposed stonework and beams, fresh paintwork and local country furniture. Spend two or three nights and get to know the area.

Rooms: 2 doubles, both with shower & wc; 2 twins, both with bath & wc.

Price: €44.50-€47.50 for two.

Meals: Dinner €14, including wine & coffee.

Closed: January.

From Périgueux N21 for Bergerac. 4km after Bordas left to St Maime; continue for Vergt and immediately left for Castagnol. Follow Auberge signs.

From Le Bugue go to Ste Alvère; at main crossroads there, D30 towards Trémolat. House 2nd right, 500m after sign Le Maine at top of hill.

Laurence & Ghislaine Gay
La Petite Auberge
Castagnol
24380 Saint Maime de Péreyrol
Dordogne
Tel: (0)5 53 04 00 54
Fax: (0)5 53 04 00 54

Carine Someritis
Les Hirondelles
Le Maine
24510 Sainte Alvère
Dordogne
Tel: (0)5 53 22 75 40
Fax: (0)5 53 22 75 40

Entry No: 517　　　Map: **12**

Entry No: 518　　　Map: **12**

Being Robert and Stuart's guests in their charming watermill, where they serve their own spring water, is a delight. Views over a perfect landscape of willow-dotted meadow, green lawns, stream coursing under house and reedy lake can be drunk from the ever-immaculate, smallish rooms in the separate guest house and the good dayroom has a white piano. Breakfast tables are set out here or on the idyllic, vine-shaded little terrace beside the old bread oven. It is all lovingly tended, nearby is unspoilt Paunat with its huge church and here is peace, perfect peace. *Small pets by arrangement; children must be carefully supervised - unfenced water.*

Rooms: 3 doubles, 2 twins, 1 triple, all with bath or shower & wc.

Price: €74 for two.

Meals: Good choice of restaurants nearby.

Closed: Never.

In a tiny, peaceful hamlet in a particularly lovely area, La Licorne is three old buildings with a stream bounding the pretty courtyard. Claire and Marc are from the Alps - she teaches skiing, he works in tourism and is an experienced cook - and are keen to make their new home a relaxing, easy place to be. Clutter-free rooms, one in the 13th-century barn overlooking the nut trees and garden, are small, white, with modern furniture and the occasional old carved cupboard door. The dining room is superb with its big fireplace and gallery at each end; food is light and vegetable-orientated. *Please arrive after 5pm.*

Rooms: 2 doubles, 1 suite for 4, all with bath or shower & wc.

Price: €53.50-€56.50 for two.

Meals: Dinner €18, including wine & coffee; restaurants 500m-6km.

Closed: Mid-November-March.

From Le Bugue D703/D31 through Limeuil. At x-roads D2 for Ste Alvère 100m; fork left; house on left 2km along; drive leads down from small x-roads.

From Montignac D65 south for 6km; left on minor road to Valojoulx. House in centre of hamlet, left of Mairie.

Robert Chappell & Stuart Shippey
Le Moulin Neuf
Paunat
24510 Sainte Alvère
Dordogne
Tel: (0)5 53 63 30 18
Fax: (0)5 53 63 30 55
E-mail: moulin-neuf@usa.net

Claire & Marc Bosse
La Licorne
Valojoulx
24290 Montignac Lascaux
Dordogne
Tel: (0)5 53 50 77 77
Fax: (0)5 53 50 77 77

Entry No: 519   Map: **12**

Entry No: 520   Map: **12**

The perfect site, with lovely wide rural views, was carefully chosen to transplant this lovely old barn - once the garden has matured, you'll think it's been here for centuries. Marie-Ange and Philippe's country furniture looks just right on the old floor tiles beneath the old oak beams - all is bright and uncluttered, ancient and modern mix and match, the fresh young bedrooms have views, stylish fabrics and superior mattresses. Sit on the rose-covered terrace and contemplate a spot of fishing - they have their own lake - horse riding or touring; another member of the family runs stables nearby. *Gîte space for 12 people.*

Rooms: 2 doubles, 1 twin, all with shower & wc.

Price: €42 for two.

Meals: Good choice of restaurants 3km.

Closed: Never.

All power to this deeply united family and their desire to keep local tradition alive while breeding poultry and hand-crafting pâtés and *foie gras*. Marie-Jeanne and her son and daughter-in-law (a brilliant cook and teacher, though not for vegetarians) share the B&B tasks. Marie-Jeanne will welcome you with her natural good humour, settle you into your pure French Rustic room, give you time to admire the view then drive you the 7km across the Dordogne River to her son's lovely old house for a memorable dinner. One of France's most exquisite areas and an exceptional experience of genuine French country warmth. *Gîte space for 5 people.*

Rooms: 1 double, 1 triple, 1 quadruple, all with shower & wc (1 curtained).

Price: €44 for two.

Meals: Dinner €18, including wine & coffee.

Closed: December-February.

From Libourne N89 to Monpon Ménestérol; right D708 for Ste Foy la Grande 8km. Right in St Rémy, opp. Chez Sam, D33 for St Martin/ Villefranche; follow signs.

From Bergerac D32 towards Ste Alvère; after 10km look for signpost 'Périgord - Bienvenue à la Ferme'.

Marie-Ange Caignard
Domaine de la Mouthe
24700 Saint Rémy sur Lidoire
Dordogne
Tel: (0)5 53 82 15 40
Fax: (0)5 53 82 15 40
E-mail: hebergement@pays-de-bergerac.com

Marie-Jeanne & Marie-Thérèse Archer
La Barabie
Lamonzie Montastruc
24520 Mouleydier
Dordogne
Tel: (0)5 53 23 22 47
Fax: (0)5 53 22 81 20

Aquitaine

Your Belgian hosts know their adopted region "like their pocket" and are keen that you discover hidden treasures not just oversubscribed star sights. Their fine set of Périgord buildings sits high on a wooded, hawk-hunted hill and the big, solar-heated pool is a decent distance from the beautifully-restored house - the garden is taking shape too. In the biggest room, you sleep under a soaring timber canopy - a hymn to the carpenter's art - supporting a crystal chandelier. Easy décor, good furniture, a friendly welcome and the run of the kitchen. You may even be able to paint your own souvenir tile. *Gîte space for 6.*

Rooms: 1 double, 1 triple, 1 quadruple, all with bath & wc.

Price: €40-€50 for two.

Meals: Auberge 4km; choice of restaurants in Bergerac, 9km; use of kitchen possible.

Closed: 30 October-14 March.

If the curvy roof, the entrance arch, the rough old beams and the wafer bricks round the fireplaces are well-preserved old friends that we are always happy to see again, the first-floor alcove enclosing the original long-drop privy is infinitely rarer. Splendid main rooms combine simplicity and taste, antique and modern furniture; smaller, tempting bedrooms have hand-stencilled doors. Your hosts, two easy, articulate former *Parisiennes,* may offer you their irresistible chocolate courgette cake, a browse in their library and a chance to share their genuine pleasure in people. *Gîte space for 6.*

Rooms: 3 doubles, 1 twin & 1 family suite, all with bath or shower & wc.

Price: €53.50 for two.

Meals: Dinner €19, including wine & coffee.

Closed: Never.

From Bergerac N21 towards Périgueux. 4km after Lembras, Les Rocailles sign on right.

From Bergerac D660 for Lalinde & Sarlat; right over R. Dordogne at Pont de Couze (still D660); at Bayac right D27 for Issigeac 2 km; at top of hill house on left.

Marcel Vanhemelryck & Nicole Denys
Les Rocailles de la Fourtaunie
24520 Lamonzie Montastruc
Dordogne
Tel: (0)5 53 58 20 16
Fax: (0)5 53 58 20 16
E-mail: lesrocailles@wanadoo.fr

Francine Pillebout & Odile Calmettes
Le Relais de Lavergne
Lavergne
24150 Bayac
Dordogne
Tel: (0)5 53 57 83 16
Fax: (0)5 53 57 83 16
E-mail: relaisdelavergne@wanadoo.fr

Entry No: 523   Map: **12**

Entry No: 524   Map: **12**

These proud, unspoilt farmers with their old sense of values and priorities make no concessions to modernity. It's all waxed floorboards and antimacassars, dark country antiques and browny orange wallpapers: pure, simple tradition (with proper bathrooms). There are walnuts galore, dairy cows, a kitchen garden and you can visit the prune ovens. Indeed, food looms large and the pivot of the house is the big family kitchen where succulent regional dishes are shared. Altogether an excellent and welcoming place to learn about real French farming life. "Huge fun but don't talk while the weather report is on," said one reader. *Gîte space for 5.*

Rooms: 2 doubles, 1 triple, all with bath or shower & wc.

Price: € 35 for two; half-board € 63 for two.

Meals: Dinner € 14, including wine & coffee.

Closed: Never.

From Beaumont du Périgord, D660 5km for Montpazier; 2nd farm on right after sign for Petit Brassac.

Gilbert & Reine Marescassier
Petit Brassac
Labouquerie
24440 Beaumont du Périgord
Dordogne
Tel: (0)5 53 22 32 51
Fax: (0)5 53 22 32 51

Entry No: 525   Map: **12**

A dream château hard by medieval Sarlat, it is much visited (free tour for B&B guests). Painted beams draw the eye, the carved stone staircase and the ancient floors call hand and foot, history oozes from every corner (there may be a ghost). All furniture is authentic 17th-century Perigordian - no concessions to 20th-century chic. The twin? two four-posters; the suite? one perfect Louis XVI room with claw-footed bath behind curtains and loo in an archer's turret, the other room clothed in classic red Jouy fabric, slightly showing its age. Madame is elegant, friendly, very French; her son, who helps in the château, speaks good English; both are delightful. *Gîte space for 10 people.*

Rooms: 1 twin (& single), 1 suite, both with bath, shower & wc.

Price: € 115 for two.

Meals: Good restaurant 5km; choice in Sarlat.

Closed: November-March.

From Sarlat D47 towards Les Eyzies for 8km. Château signposted regularly.

Comte & Comtesse de Montbron
Château de Puymartin
24200 Sarlat la Canéda
Dordogne
Tel: (0)5 53 59 29 97
Fax: (0)5 53 29 87 52
E-mail: xdemontbron@wanadoo.fr

Entry No: 526   Map: **12**

Mombette, built in the 1600-1700s by the same family, has the simple, harmonious elegance that natural style brings to an organically-grown family house. From its hilltop it looks across to the splendid medieval fortifications of Domme. Madame is fittingly welcoming and easy, has travelled a lot, especially to North Africa, and may even enjoy a game of bridge with you. The character of her house is made of fine, generous spaces and good regional antiques, an attractive library and very lovely gardens. Rooms are comfortable, light and airy and you are within reach of all the delights of the Dordogne. Most relaxing.

Rooms: 1 twin, 1 triple, 1 double, all with bath, shower & wc.

Price: €83 for two.

Meals: Restaurants nearby.

Closed: 15 November-1 April.

Come for the opulent 'marbled halls' of the main rooms, for the poolside set-up, for Richard, half-Spanish, half-Bordelais, who encourages deer and donkeys, has hens and ponies running loose, grows fruits and nuts to bursting point, makes his own oil. He's a young, enthusiastic, ex-hotelier; he paints too. Isabelle is a part-time air-hostess and they will share their imaginatively-cooked dinner with you if you are a small group. Simple bedrooms with plain beds and white walls are in calming contrast to the spectacular style below. Breakfast consists of fresh eggs and anything you want. Definitely special. *Gîte space for 5.*

Rooms: 3 doubles, 2 twins, all with shower or bath & wc (2 connect for family use).

Price: €53-€69 for two.

Meals: Dinner €16-€23, wine €9-€19.

Closed: Never.

From Sarlat D46 to Cénac et St Julien; D50 right for St Cybranet for 300m; left and follow signs.

Mme Michèle Jahan
Château de Mombette
24250 Cénac et Saint Julien
Dordogne
Tel: (0)5 53 28 30 14
Fax: (0)5 53 28 30 14
E-mail: michele.jahan@wanadoo.fr

From Périgueux D710 S for Belvès. At roundabout do NOT take right fork to Belvès, stay on D710 500m then turn left - signs. House 600m on left.

Richard & Isabelle Ginioux
Le Branchat
24170 Belvès
Dordogne
Tel: (0)5 53 28 98 80
Fax: (0)5 53 28 90 82
E-mail: le.branchat@wanadoo.fr
Web: www.perigord.com/belves/lebranchat

Entry No: 527   Map: **12**

Entry No: 528   Map: **12**

Once a charterhouse, this good-looking Périgord house sits squarely in 10 hectares of parkland and peace, a tribute to the rich, sober taste of the area. Inside reflects outside: the same dark timbers against pale stone and the new owners have redecorated the bedrooms most charmingly. They are gradually replacing the modern furniture with country antiques and the feel is warmly authentic. And moreover, they used to run a restaurant - it's well worth dining here. Sitting at the big table for house guests, you may find other gourmets in the beamed dining room: a few outsiders are occasionally allowed! *Gîte space for 6 people.*

Rooms: 2 quadruples, 1 triple, 1 twin, 1 double, all with bath or shower & wc.

Price: €59-€92 for two.

Meals: Dinner €21.

Closed: 2 November-1 April.

From Sarlat take D46 to Cénac St Julien. At end of village continue for Fumel. House 3rd turning on right.

Brigitte & Christophe Demassougne
La Guérinière
Baccas
24002 Cénac et St Julien, Dordogne
Tel: (0)5 53 29 91 97
Fax: (0)5 53 30 23 89
E-mail: contact@la-gueriniere-dordogne.com
Web: www.la-gueriniere-dordogne.com

Entry No: 529   **Map: 12**

Once a wreck, now a village manor again thanks to your hosts' hard labour and touch of easy elegance. In the living room overlooking the sweeping lawn, warm bright colours reflect Madame's sunny, Latin personality and you're welcome to play the piano and read the books. The tower suite and small double have a modern feel, the three other rooms are more traditional, huge and high-ceilinged; all have very good modern comforts. There are children's games, a free beach nearby on the Dordogne, good food (neighbours' produce) if you dine in, plenty of choice out and riding stables next door that make it really special.

Rooms: 3 doubles, 1 double/twin, 1 suite, all with bath or shower & wc.

Price: €69-€86 for two.

Meals: Dinner €18.50, including wine & coffee; good restaurants nearby.

Closed: Never.

From Sarlat D57 to Beynac; D703 to St Cyprien; 7km beyond, right to Coux et Bigaroque; through village, left after Mairie; house on right after about 1km, just past wayside cross.

Ghislaine & Marc Oréfice
Manoir de la Brunie, La Brunie
24220 Le Coux et Bigaroque
Dordogne
Tel: (0)5 53 29 61 42
Fax: (0)5 53 28 62 35
E-mail: marc.orefice@wanadoo.fr
Web: www.abscisse.com

Entry No: 530   **Map: 12**

Aquitaine

Graham, who's English, and Anne, who's American, share a deep love of the French way of life. They are charmingly outgoing and caring people, always concerned for guests' welfare. They have virtually gutted this elegantly arch-windowed, mid-19th-century manor house, saving every original feature possible - panelling, old oak doors, a variation on the theme of the baronial double entrance - and creating four excellent bedrooms as well as the library and sitting room they share with guests. It is all furnished with good taste and fine antiques.

Rooms: 1 double, 1 twin, each with bath & wc; 2 twins, each with shower & wc.

Price: €69 for two.

Meals: Dinner €17, including wine & coffee.

Closed: December-mid-January.

On a quiet road with its land stretching behind it, the château is mostly 14th and 17th centuries with a superb 12th-century tower. In the four very fine château bedrooms antiques and old paintings mix perfectly with more contemporary pieces. Shower rooms are less grand but perfectly adequate. There's a baronial-style dining room - Monsieur prepares dinner for four or more guests - and a dignified *salon* with red brocade chairs and memories of Imperial China. The gardens below the swimming pool are charming, you can bicycle or walk through the woods and there's so much to visit close by. *Gîte space for 18 people.*

Rooms: 4 doubles, all with shower & wc.

Price: €84 for two.

Meals: Dinner €23; restaurants 400m.

Closed: December-January.

From Sarlat D703 for Bergerac; exit for Siorac at r'bout; right over Dordogne; 1st right D703. House 1st on right.

From Sarlat D704 Gourdon for 3.5km; left D704a towards Souillac to Cazoulès; opp. bakery, left beside restaurant; château up hill on left.

Graham & Anne Templeton
Le Hêtre Rouge
24220 Coux et Bigaroque
Dordogne
Tel: (0)5 53 31 14 29
Fax: (0)5 53 31 27 31
E-mail: anne@perigord.com

Michèle & William Vidal d'Hondt
Château du Pas du Raysse
24370 Cazoulès
Dordogne
Tel: (0)5 53 29 84 41
Fax: (0)5 53 59 62 16
Web: www.chateauduraysse.com

Wonderful French value, really interesting hosts - French country cooking enthusiasts, including vegetarians, sing the praises of Mother's meals made with home-grown vegetables, lamb, duck, pigeon and rabbit (delicious pâtés): she just loves to cook (try her tomato jam too). Myriam has lots of time for guests while Pierre looks after the 20 sheep and works hard on house improvement. The 18th-century farmhouse, with its magnificent wooden staircase, original beams and timber framing, has country antiques, functioning fireplaces, peacefully simple bedrooms, a garden full of toys, and... excitement on a microlight.

Rooms: 1 double, 1 triple, 2 family, all with shower & basin, 1 wc in corridor; 1 triple with shower & wc.

Price: € 31 for two.

Meals: Dinner € 13, including wine & coffee.

Closed: November-January.

In Bellac follow signs to Limoges; just before leaving Bellac D3 right towards Blond. 4km to Thoveyrat. House signposted on left.

Pierre & Myriam Morice
Thoveyrat
87300 Blond
Haute-Vienne
Tel: (0)5 55 68 86 86
Fax: (0)5 55 68 86 86
E-mail: chambrehote@freesurf.fr

Limousin

In a leaf-green paradise, ancestral tribes buried their dead beneath great smooth stones, early saints sowed the seeds of Romanesque arches and strong castles gentle troubadours.

Entry No: 533   Map: 7

Limousin

The serene 18th-century château stands proud for all to see on the site of an ancient fortification, and the sun sets over the lake. Bedrooms are mostly vast, traditionally furnished and regally wallpapered. Bathrooms have all mod cons. Madame, full of energy, charm and enthusiasm, is re-establishing the formal gardens and also organises cookery courses. The atmosphere in the spectacular west-facing dining room, with pale blue and yellow panelling, high-backed tapestried chairs and a fine dining table may be informal but the surroundings do impose civilised dressing for dinner.

Rooms: 3 doubles, 1 twin, all with bath & wc.

Price: €100 for two.

Meals: Dinner €25, including wine & coffee.

Closed: November-June.

Eight centuries ago Knights Templar farmed here; four centuries ago dashing King Henri IV hunted wolves here; the same family has always owned these 750 acres and pilgrims have always passed through on the way to Compostela - such is the tapestry of history that your intelligent, sociable host weaves for you beneath the Aubusson or across the grand dinner table. He is absolutely the right mix of friendly and formal. All rooms are properly period-furnished, but pay the extra for the superb suite and enjoy its mighty bathroom (shower rooms are smaller).

Rooms: 1 suite for 4, 1 double, 2 twin, all with bath or shower & wc.

Price: €62-€77 for two; suite €100 for four.

Meals: Dinner €20, including aperitif; wine €4-€20.

Closed: December-February.

From Poitiers N147 towards Limoges, through Bellac; left D96 towards St Junien les Combes. First left in village towards Rancon for about 1km.

From A20 exit 24 on D27 to Bersac & on for Laurière; left after railway bridge; follow signs to château 3km.

Comte & Comtesse Aucaigne de Sainte Croix
Château de Sannat
Saint Junien les Combes
87300 Bellac, Haute-Vienne
Tel: (0)5 55 68 13 52
Fax: (0)5 55 68 13 52
E-mail: labeljack@aol.com

Éric Perrin des Marais
Le Château du Chambon
Le Chambon
87370 Bersac sur Rivalier
Haute-Vienne
Tel: (0)5 55 71 47 04
Fax: (0)5 55 71 47 04
E-mail: desmarais@infonie.fr

Here is a really super, nature-loving, chemical-free house where natural materials come into their own: wood everywhere including under the tiles, cork insulation, organic food that includes meat and home-made bread, and they've been doing it for 30 years! The central heating is carried by steam ducts leading from the cooking-pot over the open fire. He is a painter, of Italian extraction; she made all the upholstery, bedheads and patchworks; rooms have soothing, simple, successful colour schemes and lots of wood. And there are more fabulous colours, and walks, to be found outside.

Rooms: 2 doubles, 1 triple, all with shower & wc.

Price: €42-€46 for two; reduction 2 nights or more.

Meals: Dinner €16, including wine & coffee.

Closed: Never.

Your own wisteria and rose-clad entrance leads to a kitchen area with stairs up to the appealing bedroom: white walls, off-white carpet, sea-grass wallpaper and wide view. The other is a useful overflow bedroom. You have your own rather fine living room too, with an open fire. (It can all be let as a gîte.) The house is lovely, splashed with colour and imaginative gestures, and the big garden makes further demands upon a willing but busy pair of owners. Néline, a gently direct and energetic hostess, will bring your breakfast in a basket if you prefer your own company. *Dutch & German spoken.*

Rooms: 1 double/twin, 1 twin, sharing shower, wc & small kitchen with dishwasher & washing machine (same group only).

Price: €45 for two; reduction for 2 nights or more.

Meals: Self-catering.

Closed: Never.

From A20 exit 25 D44 for St Sylvestre; left D78 for Grandmont & St Léger la Montagne; through Grandmont; right for Les Sauvages after 200m.

From Limoges N141 to St Léonard; D39 for St Priest 5km; right for Lajoumard; first left and follow signs.

Lorenzo & Edith Rappelli
Les Chênes
Les Sauvages
87240 Saint Sylvestre, Haute-Vienne
Tel: (0)5 55 71 33 12
Fax: (0)5 55 71 33 12
E-mail: les.chenes@wanadoo.fr
Web: www.haute-vienne.com/chenes.htm

Mme Néline Jansen de Vomécourt
La Réserve
Bassoleil
87400 Saint Léonard de Noblat
Haute-Vienne
Tel: (0)5 55 56 18 39
E-mail: vomecourt.jansen1@libertysurf.fr

Entry No: 536   Map: 7

Entry No: 537   Map: 7

Definitely different, with a glorious touch of eccentricity. The 400-year-old multi-part house has been in the family for generations and, true to type, your host doggedly nurtures his passions and projects - jazz piano, model railway, restoration. You may share a bath or creep down a floor for the loo, but one room is authentic Charles X and all are deeply evocative. The main house has a spectacular stone staircase with Egyptian vases pillaged from a Pharaoh's tomb, huge bedrooms and modern bathrooms. The great dining hall has wood panelling but breakfast is in a small guest *salon* or in the cottage kitchen. Most unusual. *Gîte space for 6 people.*

Rooms: In gatehouse: 1 double with shower, 2 doubles sharing bathroom, all 3 sharing wc; in main house: 1 triple, 1 suite, both with bath & wc.

Price: €46-€69 for two.

Meals: Dinner €15, including wine & coffee.

Closed: Never.

From Limoges D979 for Eymoutiers; Fougeolles on left just before entering Eymoutiers, Chambres d'Hôtes signs.

Jacques du Montant
Fougeolles
87120 Eymoutiers
Haute-Vienne
Tel: (0)5 55 69 11 44

A cannon-ball forge once stood here, then a mill; now they make pâtés and *confits* by the great mill pond, keep animals (Lusitanian horses are a hobby) and two children, all very much part of farm life and the atmosphere is easy and *familiale*. Nothing fancy about the bedrooms - they are just cosy and comfortable. A huge sitting room with enormous hearth, stone walls, tatty sofa, and the nicest possible people. Stay for dinner: most ingredients are home-grown (super *potager*) or home-raised. Boating on the lake. Guests love it all. *Ask about pets when booking.*

Rooms: 3 doubles, all with shower & wc.

Price: €39 for two.

Meals: Dinner €17, including wine & coffee.

Closed: 15 November-15 March.

From A20 exit 39 to Pierre Buffière; cross river D15/D19 for St Yrieix for 15km. At Croix d'Hervy left D57 for Coussac Bonneval; mill on left after lake (7km).

Valérie & Renaud Gizardin
Moulin de Marsaguet
87500 Coussac Bonneval
Haute-Vienne
Tel: (0)5 55 75 28 29
Fax: (0)5 55 75 28 29

Entry No: 538   Map: 7

Entry No: 539   Map: **12**

These utterly real farmers aim to be as bio-dynamic (respectful of natural life systems) and self-sufficient as possible, so meals are home-grown and nourishing. The four rooms share a living room with kitchen, but dine with your hosts if you can: they are completely unpretentious, very good company and know their region intimately. Two rooms are on the ground floor, two in the roof, with pine-clad sloping ceilings, white walls and roof windows. The farm is surrounded by woods (superb walking), and children love helping to milk the goats and collect the eggs. So do some adults.

Rooms: 3 doubles, 1 triple, all with shower & wc.

Price: €38 for two.

Meals: Dinner €14, including wine & coffee, 1 July-15 August only; self-catering possible.

Closed: Never.

In a lively yet relaxed atmosphere, things here are more traditional than the photo suggests. Michel's modern sculptures add magic to the garden and his work is everywhere: handmade door handles, towel rails, shelf supports... mainly in brass and steel. Bedrooms and bathrooms are biggish and the house glories in an extravagant use of materials: opulent floor-length curtains, off-white material instead of wallpaper and a tented ceiling of it in the dayroom (all Madame's work). The living and dining rooms have a studio feel with 'works in progress'. He loves showing his forge and studio, she loves making cakes - a very likeable couple.

Rooms: 2 doubles, both with shower & wc.

Price: €47 for two.

Meals: Dinner €15, including wine & coffee.

Closed: January-March.

From A20 exit 41 to Magnac Bourg; D215 (between Total service station & Brasserie des Sports) SW & follow signs 4km to La Chapelle.

From Eymoutiers D30 for Chamberet. House in village of La Roche, 7km beyond Eymoutiers.

Patrick & Mayder Lespagnol
La Chapelle
87380 Château Chervix
Haute-Vienne
Tel: (0)5 55 00 86 67
Fax: (0)5 55 00 70 78
E-mail: lespagno@club-internet.fr

Michel & Josette Jaubert
La Roche
87120 Eymoutiers
Haute-Vienne
Tel: (0)5 55 69 61 88
Web: clos.arts.free.fr

Entry No: 540   Map: **12**

Entry No: 541   Map: **12**

This infectiously enthusiastic American couple decided to give up globe-trotting at last and get to work, a lot of work, on a château hung on the cliffside of the Dordogne. Using their hands and all their new-world energy, they have done a fabulous job. Each bedroom faces the sensational view, each is differently, richly decorated, every detail perfect - one has deep red walls and a hand-carved reproduction of Empress Josephine's bed. Dane and Terry want you to love it as much as they do, encourage you to add your comment or drawing to the cellar mural, offer champagne to celebrate the day. And water from their own spring.

Rooms: 4 doubles, 1 triple, all with bath, shower & wc.

Price: €115-€133 for two.

Meals: Dinner €55, including wine & coffee.

Closed: Never.

It's all very cosmopolitan here, where Jacquie, half-French, and Ian, half-Hungarian, are fervent Francophiles. Their renovation of this old village house is an achievement to be proud of, with remarkable bathrooms and Laura Ashley-style décor. They are very organised and will tell you everything about the locality and its people, history, flora and building regs. A professional chef, Ian produces superb food which he serves with a flourish and wines from his own cellar. Aperitifs and dinner *en famille* are occasions for stimulating conversation - not a time for shrinking violets.

Rooms: 2 doubles/twins, 1 twin, all with bath or shower & wc.

Price: €28-€31 for two.

Meals: Dinner €13, including wine & coffee.

Closed: Never.

From Beaulieu sur Dordogne cross bridge, 1st left D41 for Aurillac; pass Château du Doux; drive is 200m further on left, château 1km up drive.

From Tulle N120 to Forgès. Left into Place de la Mairie, park in church square behind.

Dane & Terry Earnheart
Château de Chauvac
Beaulieu sur Dordogne
19430 Bassignac le Bas, Corrèze
Tel: (0)5 55 91 50 58
Fax: (0)5 55 91 50 58
E-mail: info@chateauchauvac.com
Web: www.chateauchauvac.com

Ian & Jacquie Hoare
La Souvigne
1 impasse La Fontaine
19380 Forgès, Corrèze
Tel: (0)5 55 28 63 99
Fax: (0)5 55 28 65 62
E-mail: souvigne@wanadoo.fr
Web: perso.wanadoo.fr/souvigne

Entry No: 542   Map: **12**

Entry No: 543   Map: **12**

Come stay a while, live the life of the farm and understand why Madame, born in the area, has no desire ever to move away. In what is now a conservation area, with its expanse of grass within eyesight, canoes for hire and fishing down on the River Dordogne (ask about their own piece of river bank) and a proper kitchen for guests, Saulières is ideal for families and has a superbly 'family, friends and farming' atmosphere. They are a highly likeable couple - he raises beef cattle and grows walnuts while she makes pretty curtains, soft bedcovers and paints pictures for the guest rooms, which are in the modern extension. *Gîte space for 8.*

Rooms: 1 quadruple, 1 triple, 1 double, 1 twin, all with shower & wc.

Price: €40 for two.

Meals: Self-catering possible; good choice of restaurants, 2km.

Closed: Never.

From Tulle N120 to Argentat; D12 along River Dordogne towards Beaulieu, past Monceaux to Saulières (6km from Argentat).

Marie-Jo & Jean-Marie Lafond
Saulières
Monceaux sur Dordogne
19400 Argentat
Corrèze
Tel: (0)5 55 28 09 22
Fax: (0)5 55 28 09 22

Entry No: 544   **Map: 13**

The Lardners were born to do B&B: interested in others, they genuinely love having visitors, their enthusiasm for their adopted area is infectious, Anne's cooking is superb - good wine too. The kitchen is a wonderful place, full of farm things and Anne's sunny presence - she delights in texture, smell and colour, her cooking reflects her pleasure and you catch the vibes easily. Their house restoration, done under Jim's caring guidance, is a form of perfection. Many local farmers are friends and visits can be arranged, proof of thorough integration among the rolling hills of rural France. Deep peace and really excellent value. *Gîte space for 2 people.*

Rooms: 2 twins with bath or shower & wc. Extra room for children.

Price: €32 for two.

Meals: Dinner €15, including wine & coffee.

Closed: Never.

From Argentat N120 for Tulle; left D921 for Brive. Pass sign to Albussac; 300m on; left to Le Prézat; through hamlet; house on right with lawn.

Anne & Jim Lardner
Le Prézat
19380 Albussac
Corrèze
Tel: (0)5 55 28 62 36
Fax: (0)5 55 28 62 36
E-mail: jlardner@libertysurf.fr

Entry No: 545   **Map: 12**

This pretty converted school has three fresh and simply-decorated bedrooms downstairs (one with a mezzanine), sharing a living room and kitchenette. The upstairs suite, more traditional, also has its own living room - the headmistress's study perhaps? A flower-covered loggia leads to the dayroom: it is entirely glazed on one side to let in the beautiful garden, which also produces vegetables for excellent dinners. Béatrice and Henry are delightful, happy to talk in French or English and keen to help you discover their fascinating area. Guided flora and fauna tours and boats for hire too.

Rooms: 1 double, 1 twin, 1 quadruple, 1 suite, all with shower or bath & wc.

Price: €42 for two.

Meals: Dinner €14, including wine & coffee.

Closed: 15 December-2 January.

From A20 exit 22 to La Souterraine; D951 through Dun le Palestel; right D15 to La Celle Dunoise; left after tennis courts for Anzême about 4km; sign.

Beatrice & Henry Nguyen
L'École Buissonnière
23800 La Celle Dunoise
Creuse
Tel: (0)5 55 89 23 49
Fax: (0)5 55 89 27 62
E-mail: ecolebuissonniere@wanadoo.fr
Web: www.ecole-b.com

Surprisingly, your jolly, genuine hostess and her delightful husband, who live in amiable confusion, both used to be in *haute couture.* If the quaint, quirky and creative appeal to you, come to this 18th-century house on the edge of town. The bouncy dog, the exquisite handmade patchwork quilts contrast with fading wallpaper; the cluttered terrace has stunning views of medieval Boussac castle. Good clean rooms (ask for one with a view) and a new triple with a kitchenette. It's all a totally French experience and ideal for exploring town and country. *Gîte space for 4 people.*

Rooms: 2 doubles, 1 triple, 1 suite, all with bath or shower & wc.

Price: €46 for two.

Meals: Dinner €14, including wine & coffee.

Closed: October.

From A71 exit 10 on D94 W for 15km; right D916 to Boussac; in main square, take road to left of Mairie; left again at butcher's; house on right.

Françoise Gros & Daniel Colsenet
La Courtepointe
3 rue des Loges
23600 Boussac, Creuse
Tel: (0)5 55 65 80 09
Fax: (0)5 55 65 80 09
E-mail: courtepointe@wanadoo.fr
Web: perso.wanadoo.fr/courtepointe

Brigitte's house is a breath of fresh air, a place of organised chaos where paintings by friends old and new, carvings from Borneo, antiques from her native Belgium and Bauhaus steel-and-leather armchairs sing together in artistic harmony: objects of interest are everywhere. Bedrooms are vast, inviting and full of yet more original works - the two scenes of life in Zimbabwe are wonderful. Even the bathrooms are full of stylish character. Brigitte, a fabric designer, travelled a lot with her husband and is happy to be receiving appreciative guests in this old 1800s wine merchant's house, the first in a land of cider.

Rooms: 2 doubles with bath or shower & wc.

Price: €40-€46 for two.

Meals: Dinner € 15, including wine & coffee.

Closed: Never.

From A20 exit 23 to Guéret; N145 to Gouzon; D997 to Boussac; D71 for Clugnat 4km; D13 for Domeyrot; 1.4km left D77. At 'Les Montceaux' on hill, right before chestnut tree. First house on right.

Brigitte-Marie Van de Wege
Les Montceaux
23600 Toulx Sainte Croix
Creuse
Tel: (0)5 55 65 09 55
Fax: (0)5 55 65 09 55
E-mail: brigitte.van-de-wege@wanadoo.fr
Web: perso.wanadoo.fr/chez.brigitte

Entry No: 548   Map: **8**

REGIONAL FOOD STYLES

*À la manière de…/*In the manner of…
À l'Alsacienne - With sauercraut and sausage.
À l'Américaine - A corruption of *À l'Àrmoricaine, Armor* being the Celtic name for Brittany; with tomato sauce and shallots.
À l'Anglaise - Plain boiled.
À l'Ardennaise - With juniper berries.
À l'Auvergnate - With cabbage and bits of bacon.
À la Basquaise - With onions, sweet peppers, rice and possibly Bayonne cured ham.
À la Bordelaise - Bordeaux style, with red wine, onions, mushrooms and bacon.
À la Bretonne - With leeks, celery and beans (cf. Américaine above for another *Bretonne*).
À la Dauphinoise - With cream, garlic and sometimes cheese.
À la Dijonnaise - With mustard sauce.
À la Flamande - Flemish style: cooked in beer or vinegar.
À la Lyonnaise - With onions, wine, vinegar, and often sausage.
À la Niçoise - With anchovies and olives.
À la Normande - With cream.
À la Périgourdine - With goose liver and truffles.
À la Provençale - With tomatoes, garlic, olive oil.
À la Savoyarde - With cream and cheese.

And four supra-regional manners:-

À la Bonne Femme - Good Woman style, with white wine, shallots and mushrooms.
À la Bourgeoise - Townswoman style, with a sauce of carrots, onions and bacon.
À la Ménagère - Housewife style, with onions, potatoes, carrots, turnips, peas.
À la Paysanne - Peasant Woman-Country Woman style, with vegetables!

The Montaignacs are elegant, immaculate and gracious and, like their dining room with its panelling, breakfast silver and great looming ancestor, are the epitome of Old France. Choose the ground-floor, original-parqueted, fireplaced suite or glide up the fine stone staircase past more ancestors to the twin room. Both welcome you with antiques, old engravings, personality. Monsieur knows books-worth of fascinating history; Madame is quietly attentive. Peaceful at the end of its long drive, this is a wonderful place, albeit more formal than some.

Rooms: 1 suite for 2-4 people, 1 twin, both with bath or shower & wc.

Price: €93 for two.

Meals: Good choice of restaurants within 9km.

Closed: Never, but advance bookings only.

From Montluçon, N371 for Chamblet; signposted on the right.

Yves & Jacqueline de Montaignac de Chauvance
Château du Plaix
03170 Chamblet
Allier
Tel: (0)4 70 07 80 56

Auvergne

On the wild plateau, protected by a multitude of medieval castles, the ancient hardwoods share the land with mild cows, hardy sheep and a few farmers – their ancestors ate those chestnuts, their pigs those acorns.

Entry No: 549   Map: **8**

The 14th-century origins of this gloriously isolated house, once a fortified manor, are still evident but it is a far cry from the ruin your hosts bought some 30 years ago. They have restored it beautifully, making big, cosy, subtly-lit rooms that are lovingly decorated with family antiques and memorabilia and reached by a wonderful spiral staircase - a treat. Their sheep graze safely in the the fields which surround the house - here, you can walk, fish and hunt mushrooms in season. The easy, good-natured Raucaz open their hearts and dining table to all; this is really somewhere you can feel at home and relax.

Rooms: 1 double, 1 twin, 2 triples, all with bath or shower & wc.

Price: €40 for two.

Meals: Dinner €16, including wine & coffee.

Closed: Never.

Opulent are those gilded curlicues, marble fireplaces and ornate mirrors; light pours in through the tall *salon* windows, bouncing off the glowing floor; even the games room is panelled. A fine mansion, built by a devout family whose bricks were refused for a church, it is now owned by a descendent of Corot and there's good art in every room as well as a small gallery. Lovely knowledgeable hosts who also have an excellent eye for colour. Their rooms are good enough for the glossies yet it remains an unpretentiously welcoming family house.

Rooms: 2 doubles, 1 triple, all with shower & wc; 1 triple with bath & wc; 1 suite for 4 with shower & wc.

Price: €67-€73 for two.

Meals: Dinner €17-€23, including wine & coffee.

Closed: Never.

From Nevers N7 S 22km; right on D978a to Le Veudre; there D13 then D234 to Pouzy Mésangy. Signposted.

From Moulins N9 S 20km; in Châtel de Neuvre left to La Ferté Hauterive; house on right.

Claire Raucaz
Manoir Le Plaix
Pouzy Mésangy
03320 Lurcy Levis
Allier
Tel: (0)4 70 66 24 06
Fax: (0)4 70 66 25 82

Jérôme & Annick Lefebvre
Demeure d'Hauterive
03340 La Ferté Hauterive
Allier
Tel: (0)4 70 43 04 85
Fax: (0)4 70 43 00 62
E-mail: auhauterive@val-de-sioule.com
Web: www.demeure-hauterive.com

Entry No: 550   Map: **8**

Entry No: 551   Map: **8**

A generous and handsome family house: the volcanoes gave their lava for dining room and staircase floor slabs; ancestors gave their names for bedrooms where their faded photographs and intricate samplers hang on the walls; others left some fine old *objets* and pieces of furniture and built the stupendous brick barns that shelter the garden; Élisabeth applied all her flair to the décor, marrying vital colour harmonies and soft fabrics. She is dynamic, intelligent and full of wry humour, once a trace of shyness has worn off, and serves her deliciously wholesome breakfast in the flower-decked garden in summer.

Rooms: 3 doubles, all with shower & wc.

Price: €51-€58 for two.

Meals: Good restaurants 9km.

Closed: Never; open by arrangement Nov-March.

From A71, Riom exit, N144 for Combronde/Montluçon. 2.5km after Davayat, right onto D122 to Chaptes.

Mme Élisabeth Beaujeard
8 route de la Limagne
Chaptes
63460 Beauregard Vendon
Puy-de-Dôme
Tel: (0)4 73 63 35 62

Entry No: 552　　　　**Map: 8**

A fairy-tale castle that was English during the Hundred Years' War, Vaulx has been in the family for 800 years. Creak along the parquet, pray in the chapel, swan around the *salon*, sleep in one tower, bath in another. Room names are as evocative as furnishings are romantic - worthy of Sleeping Beauty, who would surely have woken up for breakfast of home-hive honey, brioche, yogurt, eggs, cheese. Get to know your delightfully entertaining hosts, visit the donkey or, if you're feeling homesick, have a drink in Guy's *petit pub* with its impressive collection of beer mats. A dream of a place! *Gîte space for 5.*

Rooms: 2 triples, 1 double, all with bath or shower & wc.

Price: €46-€61 for two.

Meals: Dinner €16, including wine & coffee; auberge 3km.

Closed: Never.

From A72 exit 3 on D7 through Celles sur Durolle to Col du Frissonnet. Château is the first right after the Col.

Guy & Régine Dumas de Vaulx
Château de Vaulx
63120 Sainte Agathe
Puy-de-Dôme
Tel: (0)4 73 51 50 55
Fax: (0)4 73 51 50 55

Entry No: 553　　　　**Map: 8**

La Closerie, a modernised typical old stone-walled, stone-shingled house sits among the ancient volcanoes of Auvergne where great rivers rise. Françoise, known as Manou, is a delight, as generous with her time as with her breakfasts, served in the impressive dining room or the garden: ham, cheese, three kinds of bread, brioches, home-made jam - embroidered napkins give an idea of her attention to detail. Bedrooms are hung with silk, writing tables await your deathless prose, hairdryers hide in bathrooms; in short, every modern comfort against a timeless backdrop of drama and character. *Book ahead. Gîte space for 4/8 people.*

Rooms: 2 doubles, 1 twin, 2 triples, all with shower & wc.

Price: €53.50 for two.

Meals: Several good restaurants in village.

Closed: November-December; January-February.

From A71/75 exit 6 on D978/D996 W to Le Mont Dore (53km). Continue D996 W past Mairie then 5km to Le Genestoux. House signposted in village.

Françoise-Marie Larcher
La Closerie de Manou
Le Genestoux
63240 Le Mont Dore
Puy-de-Dôme
Tel: (0)4 73 65 26 81
Fax: (0)4 73 65 58 34

The solid reality of this magical tower is deeply moving. Michel's renovation skill (well, reconstruction from near-ruin), Anita's decorating talent, their passionate dedication, have summoned a rich and sober mood that makes the 15th-century *chastel* throb with authenticity: only 'medieval' materials (stone, brick, timber, cast iron, lime wash); magnificent deep-tinted fabrics, many designed by Anita; antique tapestries, panelling and furniture - nothing flashy, all simply true to the density of the place. Spectacular bedrooms, amazing bathrooms of antique-faced modern perfection and a generous breakfast - this is a must. *Minimum stay 2 nights July-August.*

Rooms: 3 doubles, all with bath/shower & wc.

Price: €84-€122 for two.

Meals: Auberge & traditional restaurants 1-4km.

Closed: January-February.

From A75 exit 6 for St Nectaire; through Champeix to Montaigut le Blanc; follow signs up to château.

Anita & Michel Sauvadet
Le Chastel Montaigu
63320 Montaigut le Blanc
Puy-de-Dôme
Tel: (0)4 73 96 28 49
Fax: (0)4 73 96 21 60

Whichever of the splendid rooms is yours, you will feel grand: here a canopied bed, there an exquisite little dressing room, or Louis Philippe in yellow, everywhere shimmering mirrors, fabulous views of acres of parkland, ancient trees, the Puy-de-Dôme. The vast, panelled, period-furnished drawing and dining rooms are quite dramatic. A perfect hostess, Madame makes you feel immediately at ease and helps you plan your day over a delicious breakfast. She will show you the 14th-century vaulted chapel, the walled garden and how to make lace (*dentelle du Puy*). Really very special.

Rooms: 3 doubles, 1 twin, 1 suite, all with bath and/or shower & wc.

Price: €61-€87 for two.

Meals: Excellent restaurants 2km.

Closed: November-March.

From Clermont Ferrand A75 exit 13 to Parentignat; D999 towards St Germain l'Hermite for 6km; signposted on right. (8km from A75 exit.)

Henriette Marchand
Château de Pasredon
63500 Saint Rémy de Chargnat
Puy-de-Dôme
Tel: (0)4 73 71 00 67
Fax: (0)4 73 71 08 72

Entry No: 556   **Map: 13**

Built on the ramparts of the ancient town, just below the medieval Abbey whose August music festival draws thousands, the old house has been lovingly filled with flowers, in every fashion and form - carpets, curtains, quilts - reflected in wooden floors, country antiques and some lovely old looking-glasses. It is a soft French boudoir where mother and daughter welcome their guests to sleep in cosy bedrooms with firm-mattressed divan beds and good little bathrooms - some even have wonderful views out to the hills - and enjoy true Gallic cuisine enhanced by bone china and Bohemian crystal before the huge stone fireplace.

Rooms: 2 triples, 1 double, 1 twin, all with bath or shower & wc.

Price: €49 for two.

Meals: Dinner €19, including wine & coffee.

Closed: Never.

From Brioude D19 to La Chaise Dieu. Head for Centre Ville; facing Abbey, right to Place du Monument. Park here; house is off the square: bottom right-hand corner then down on left.

Jacqueline & Carole Chailly
La Jacquerolle
Rue Marchédial
43160 La Chaise Dieu
Haute-Loire
Tel: (0)4 71 00 07 52

Entry No: 557   **Map: 13**

Here where the forest laps up to the edge of the hilltop village, *Valentin* lives on: Bill and Catherine left the bright lights of show biz to save the old inn from ruin and make it theirs while sensitively preserving its identity. As well as the original façade, Bill has painted murals and cupboards for the four seasons rooms - appropriately - in the converted barn overlooking the little wooded valley. They are big, light, fresh-coloured and furnished with warmly pale English country pieces. Beneath the main living room, the old forge has become a superbly original dark green and dusky pink suite.

Rooms: 1 suite for 4, 3 doubles, 1 twin, all with bath or shower & wc.

Price: €48-€53 for two.

Meals: Dinner €19, including wine & coffee; super restaurant next door.

Closed: Never.

From Clermont Ferrand, A75 to Issoire exit 13 on D999 to La Chaise Dieu; S on D906 for Le Puy; after 100m left D20; signs for 6km.

Bill & Catherine Hays
Chambres d'Hôtes 'Valentin'
Le Bourg
43160 Bonneval
Haute-Loire
Tel: (0)4 71 00 07 47

Entry No: 558   Map: **13**

Lively, intelligent Béatrice took over this gorgeous old farmhouse and moved from Lyon a year ago; she's German, speaks excellent English and French, adores cooking and plans international menus (dance and language courses are in the pipeline too). The country elegant atmosphere of the panelled *salon* still greets you; the character and individuality of the bedrooms are unchanging; the décor simply freshened. Bathrooms are excellent. Walk out and explore those remote, green-wooded hills and secret streams; maybe you'll return to a blazing log fire in the great stone fireplace and dinner in the former stables where a magnificent 15m tree carries the ceiling.

Rooms: 3 doubles, 2 twins, all with shower & wc (2 adjoining, 3 separate).

Price: €48 for two.

Meals: Dinner €19, including wine & coffee.

Closed: Never.

From Le Puy en Velay N102 for Brioude, D906 for La Chaise Dieu; D1 through Craponne D498 for Pontempeyrat, 3km; follow signs, left up hill, house 1st on left.

Béatrice Knop
Paulagnac
43500 Craponne sur Arzon
Haute-Loire
Tel: (0)4 71 03 26 37
Fax: (0)4 71 03 26 37
E-mail: celivier@infonie.fr

Entry No: 559   Map: **13**

Simple, unaffected people and keen walkers love Rosa, her somewhat dated décor and her fabulous home-grown, home-made food which oozes genuine natural goodness. A real old soldier, she manages the flock of milk-producing sheep, is surrounded by grandchildren and welcomes all-comers with a 'cup of friendship' before her great granite hearth. The house is warm, the rooms basic but perfectly adequate, the hostess unforgettable. And walkers can join a circuit here and walk from B&B to B&B in this superbly unspoilt area; or cross-country ski it in winter.

Rooms: 1 double, 1 twin, 1 triple, all with shower & wc.

Price: € 30.5-€ 34 for two; reduction for children.

Meals: Dinner € 10, including wine & coffee.

Closed: November-February.

On the southern slope of Europe's largest extinct volcano, where nine valleys radiate starlike for fabulous walking, stands a rustic 18th-century château guarded by an 11th-century tower. Here are two gasp-worthy vaulted bedrooms, one with four-poster, for feudal dreamers and lovers of 'memory stones'. The very elegant twin has the right furbelows and drapery and in the glorious kitchen - vast inglenook, beams supporting gigantic blocks of lava - Sophie serves home-smoked ham and veg from her organic garden. She and Michel are fascinating, cultured, bilingual hosts. You play an instrument? bring it with you. Bridge? bring your tricks. And dream on. *Gîte space for 7.*

Rooms: 2 doubles, 1 twin, all with bath or shower & wc.

Price: €47-€61 for two.

Meals: Dinner € 23, including wine & coffee; super restaurant in Laguiole.

Closed: Never.

From Le Puy en Velay, D589 to Saugues then D585 for Langeac, turning left onto D32 to Venteuges.

From Clermont Ferrand A75 to St Flour; right D921 for 10km; right D990 through Pierrefort to St Martin. Right for Brezons; château 3km on right.

Rosa Dumas
Le Bourg
43170 Venteuges
Haute-Loire
Tel: (0)4 71 77 80 66

Michel Couillaud & Sophie Verhulst
Château de Lescure
15230 Pierrefort
Cantal
Tel: (0)4 71 73 40 91
Fax: (0)4 71 73 40 91
E-mail: michel.couillaud@wanadoo.fr
Web: www.multimania.com/psvlescure

Entry No: 560   Map: **13**

Entry No: 561   Map: **13**

Your young hosts escaped from heaving, stressful Paris to this rural paradise where their brilliant conversion of an old Cantal farmhouse has preserved the original scullery ledge and sink, made of vast slabs of stone, the beams, the inglenook fireplace. They now aim to convert their neighbours to better environmental (get the scrap metal off the hillside) and social (more respect for your woman?) attitudes. The rooms are well and simply done with good colours and fabrics and no unnecessary frippery, the meals are feasts, the Balleux a most interesting and happy couple.

Rooms: 1 double, 1 suite for 2 in main house; 2 suites & 1 double in cottage; all with bath or shower & wc.

Price: €38-€49 for two; half-board €30-€38.50.

Meals: Dinner €12, including wine & coffee.

Closed: Never.

From Aurillac D920 to Arpajon; left on D990 for 10km (don't go to St Etienne de Carlat) left for Caizac; signs.

Francine & Jacky Balleux
Lou Ferradou
Caizac
15130 St Etienne de Carlat
Cantal
Tel: (0)4 71 62 42 37
Fax: (0)4 71 62 42 37
E-mail: fballeux@m6net.fr

Entry No: 562   Map: **13**

A treat, an experience from another age. The deliciously organic old château in pure Cantal style surveying the panorama has been in the family for ever and is utterly lavish. The courtroom (the lord of the manor was chief justice) panelled and dazzlingly painted; the fine and formal dining room (do dress for dinner); the Aubusson-hung, chandeliered *salon*; the Louis XV guest room with its lovely carved fireplace, the extraordinary four-postered Troubadour room and another painted ceiling, a remarkable Dinky Toy collection, and more. Come and enjoy the company of gentle, caring hosts. *Gîte space for 2.*

Rooms: 2 doubles, 1 twin, 1 triple, all with bath & wc.

Price: €112 for two.

Meals: Dinner €34, including wine & coffee.

Closed: November-Easter.

From Clermond-Ferrand N89 to Tulle; left N120 to Argentat; left D980 then D880 through Pleaux to Ally. Signs.

Bruno & Anne du Fayet de la Tour
Château de la Vigne
15700 Ally
Cantal
Tel: (0)4 71 69 00 20
Fax: (0)4 71 69 00 20
E-mail: la.vigne@wanadoo.fr
Web: perso.wanadoo.fr/chateau.de.la.vigne

Entry No: 563   Map: **13**

Midi-Pyrénées

Passionate eager hosts, a refined old manor in an idyllic setting, magnificent rooms, meals cooked by a master (in winter they run an Alpine restaurant). Abel and Anna's restoration is caring and sophisticated, rooms and bathrooms are statements of simple luxury, the great kitchen, where cookery demonstrations and meals happen, is a dream, its cooker a wonder to behold, fireplace massive, ceiling vaulted. There is space for togetherness and privacy, your hosts are unintrusively present and Anna can offer a professional massage after Abel's demanding wine-tastings. You get more than you pay for - enjoy it to the hilt.

Rooms: 4 doubles, all with bath & wc.

Price: €92 for two.

Meals: Dinner €31, including wine & coffee.

Closed: Mid-October-May.

A20 exit 53 for Cressensac; left 1st dual carriageway; left immed. for Cuzance & Église de Rignac; right at cemetery & stone cross; house 800m on right.

Anna & Abel Congratel
Manoir de Malagorse
46600 Cuzance
Lot
Tel: (0)5 65 27 15 61
Fax: (0)5 65 27 14 78
E-mail: acongratel@manoir-de-malagorse.fr
Web: www.manoir-de-malagorse.fr

Wielding the shepherd's favourite Laguiole blade over a shaggy flock, the guardian goose will in turn have to give his fatted liver to the knife and gourmet gullets beneath the ruins of heaven-seeking Cathar castles.

Entry No: 564   Map: **12**

Now that the Bells have accomplished that labour of love called restoration, the old farmhouse is quaint and inviting with its steep roofs and light-coloured stone. The original character of beams, old floors and twisty corners has been preserved, furnishing is simple with cast-iron beds, original paintings and, in the huge living-kitchen, an open hearth and a closed stove. It's not smart, just family-comfortable and relaxed. Gavin, an artist and potter, and Lillian, a happy (and excellent) cook, left South Africa to live with their young son in this quiet setting where they'll give you a great welcome. *Gîte space for 10 people.*

You instantly feel at home in Madame's converted 18th-century barn with its great Lot views. She spent many years in America and returned an avid patchworker: her creative touch is everywhere, including the garden and terrace, full of shrubs and ferns and secluded spots. The open-plan living room, where old skylights deliver splashes of sky, is full of artistic character with oak floors, old stove and pretty antiques beneath paintings of all periods. The airy ground-floor guest room has its own antique writing table, watercolours and a glazed stable door onto the garden.

Rooms: 1 triple, 1 double & bunks, 1 suite for 3, all with bath or shower & wc.

Price: €39 for two.

Meals: Dinner €15.50, including wine & coffee.

Closed: Never.

Rooms: 2 twins sharing bath & wc.

Price: €43 for two.

Meals: Dinner €16, including wine & coffee.

Closed: Never.

From Brive N20 S for 10 km; N140 for Rocamadour; D36 left to Rignac; at church, left then right; D36 for Lavergne 50m; left for Pouch 2km; first house, blue shutters.

From Figeac N140 24km towards Gramat; before Thémines exit, right for Le Bout du Lieu; house 200m on left with large wooden gates & blue sign.

Gavin & Lillian Bell
Pouch
46500 Rignac
Lot
Tel: (0)5 65 33 66 84
Fax: (0)5 65 33 71 31
E-mail: lilianbel@aol.com

Élisabeth de Lapérouse-Coleman
La Buissonnière
Le Bout du Lieu
46120 Thémines
Lot
Tel: (0)5 65 40 88 58
Fax: (0)5 65 40 88 58

Entry No: 565   Map: **12**

Entry No: 566   Map: **12**

The lovely ancient mill which your hosts have restored to make space for you and space for them, stands in colourful gardens with the stream running round it. Nearly all the guestrooms, with their sand/lime-rendered or old stone walls and fine wall hangings, lead off a ground-floor corridor and have French windows onto the garden. A new barn conversion includes kitchen, TV room, *salon* and dining conservatory for guests. Here, you will eat Madame's fine food and view Monsieur's paintings of typical local houses. Their near-professional welcome is superb, the area full of fascinating treasures such as Rocamadour and the Gouffre du Padirac.

Rooms: 4 doubles, 1 family, all with shower & wc.

Price: €50.50-€67 for two.

Meals: Dinner €18.50, including wine.

Closed: November-March.

From Gramat N140 for Figeac; after 500m, left small road leading to mill.

Gérard & Claude Ramelot
Moulin de Fresquet
46500 Gramat
Lot
Tel: (0)5 65 38 70 60
Fax: (0)5 65 33 60 13
E-mail: moulindefresquet@ifrance.com
Web: www.moulindefresquet.com

Entry No: 567   Map: **12**

A multi-talented, cosmopolitan couple keep house here in the summer and live in Japan in the winter. Charles cooks - the huge kitchen/entrance hall is his domain - and meals, French or Franco-Japanese, are memorable. Kako paints - even the wooden coat hangers bear her flowers. The house is French and spotless. All bedrooms, in the older, lower part of the house, have an exceptionally tranquil rolling view, superb mattresses and lush bathrooms; the oldest has an ancient stone fireplace and the original stone sink. They are delightful people and Figeac is said to be "one of the best-renovated towns in Europe".

Rooms: 2 twins, 1 suite for 3, all with bath or shower & wc.

Price: €44 for two.

Meals: Dinner €17, including wine & coffee.

Closed: November-May.

From Gramat N140 towards Figeac 17km; through Le Bourg, sharp left imm'ly after small bridge on edge of village. House signed on left, 1km.

Kako & Charles Larroque
Mas de la Feuille
46120 Le Bourg
Lot
Tel: (0)5 65 11 00 17
Fax: (0)5 65 11 00 17
E-mail: larroquecharles@club-internet.fr

Entry No: 568   Map: **13**

In the hills between Figeac and Rocamadour, Isabelle and her son live in a beautiful barn with one of those plunging rooflines. The superb conversion, with very green bathrooms, centres on a wonderful beamed living/eating area which opens out through big barn doors onto a pretty garden. Isabelle is an open-hearted person with great energy and enthusiasm. Meals at the big convivial table are good Périgord style and she grows her own vegetables. A relaxed atmosphere, intelligent conversation and guidance on things to see in the Lot.

Rooms: 1 double, 3 triples, all with shower & wc.

Price: €38.50 for two.

Meals: Dinner €14, including wine & coffee.

Closed: Never.

From Figeac N140 towards Gramat for 21.5km, left D38 to Théminettes; signposted, 1st left 400m after N140.

Isabelle N'guyen
La Gaoulière
Friaulens Haut
46120 Théminettes
Lot
Tel: (0)5 65 40 97 52
Fax: (0)5 65 40 97 52

You will be made hugely welcome at Montsalvy. There are five hectares of garden, a vast swimming pool with a 'summer kitchen' where you can make yourself lunch, a tennis court and swings for children. Guy and Gilou will even play a game of tennis with you if you wish. The beautiful terrace has wonderful views, perfect for warm summer dinners. Everything has been newly done for B&B so the mattresses are good, the comfort is perfect and there's a children's bedroom with two beds and a platform in the *pigeonnier*. *Gîte space for 4 people.*

Rooms: 2 doubles, both with shower & wc; extra room for children available.

Price: €46 for two.

Meals: Dinner €16, including wine & coffee.

Closed: Never.

From Gourdon D673 towards Fumel; left D6 to Dégagnac; follow SNCF station signs; after football ground, 2nd right; at top of hill right to Domaine de Montsalvy.

Guy & Gilou Nodon
Domaine de Montsalvy
Montsalvy
46340 Dégagnac, Lot
Tel: (0)5 65 41 51 57
Fax: (0)5 65 41 51 57
E-mail: gnodon@aol.com
Web: domaine-de-montsalvy.com

Once the laundry house of the 16th-century château that rises above it in this perfect medieval village, it is old, tiny, three-levelled, and full of small surprises. The bedroom under the eaves is richly decorated with a mix of French antiques and treasures from faraway places (Egypt, China...). You can fish in the river at the bottom of the garden, which has a beach, or chat to delightful Françoise. Breakfast when you like on fresh bread and croissants from the local bakery. Very special. *Gîte space for 4.*

Rooms: Cottage for 6: 2 doubles & 2 twins, shower & wc, kitchen.

Price: €46 for two.

Meals: Dinner €12, including wine & coffee; self-catering €8; restaurants in village.

Closed: Never.

Dr Rouma, a distinguished local figure and Consul General, built the house in the 1850s. It was almost a ruin before the Arnetts found it on their return from Japan and restored it, keeping as much of the original as possible, including the wallpaper in the hall, where the winding staircase is such a delight. The décor has an oriental tendency, particularly in the enormous dining room. The setting just couldn't be better; there are stunning views over the river and the pretty old town - famous for its medieval music festival which climaxes, by the way, with the "largest firework display in France".

Rooms: 2 doubles, 1 twin, all with bath, shower & wc.

Price: €45.50 for two.

Meals: Choice of restaurants nearby.

Closed: Never.

From Cahors D911 30km to Puy l'Évêque; at r'bout go towards bridge; before bridge, right Rue des Teinturiers. Park by river between plane trees & take steps up to house.

From Cahors D911 towards Fumel & Villeneuve sur Lot. At Puy l'Évêque take Rue du Dr Rouma to bridge: house last on right before bridge.

Mme Françoise Pillon
4 rue des Mariniers
46700 Puy l'Évêque
Lot
Tel: (0)5 65 36 56 03
Fax: (0)5 65 36 56 47
E-mail: fanfan2.@wanadoo.fr

Bill & Ann Arnett
Maison Rouma
2 rue du Docteur Rouma
46700 Puy l'Evêque, Lot
Tel: (0)5 65 36 59 39
Fax: (0)5 65 36 59 39
E-mail: williamarnett@hotmail.com
Web: www.puyleveque.com

Entry No: 571   **Map:** 12

Entry No: 572   **Map:** 12

A heart-warming and very French experience, staying with this lovely cheerful couple who are always ready for a drink and a chat (in French) - their wonderful love of life is infectious. Use the peaceful terrace where your hosts are happy for you to sit all day over your breakfast, revelling in the setting, the vast views and the flowering garden. Inside, the décor is in keeping with the old farmhouse: floral papers and family furniture. No dinner but lots of home-grown wine and aperitif, fruit from their trees and *gâteau de noix* (walnut cake) with their own honey - flowing as if you were in paradise. *Gîte space for 6 people.*

Rooms: 1 double with curtained-off shower & wc.

Price: € 38 for two.

Meals: Good restaurant 2km.

Closed: Never.

The Italian ambassador, homesick for Florence, built this house and its balustraded terrace overlooking the river in 1805. It has a beautiful garden and a swimming pool in a flowery corner of the lawn (for guests in the mornings) but inside, the first word that comes to mind is 'dramatic'. The library is raspberry with a zebra throw over the black leather sofa while the big, white beamed dining room – once the kitchen perhaps? – is dominated by a vast fireplace, bold still lifes and red and white checks. A teacher, who loves to talk to people, Claude is due to retire soon and thought B&B the perfect solution.

Rooms: 3 doubles, all with shower & wc.

Price: € 46 for two.

Meals: Choice of restaurants nearby.

Closed: Never.

From Cahors D8 for Pradines 8km; at sign for Flaynac, follow Chambres d'Hôtes sign on right, then right and right again.

From Cahors D8 to Pradines; right at roundabout; house 100m down on right through big gates.

M & Mme Jean Faydi
Flaynac
46090 Pradines
Lot
Tel: (0)5 65 35 33 36

Claude Faille
Valrose - Le Poujal
46090 Pradines
Lot
Tel: (0)5 65 22 18 52
E-mail: claude.faille@libertysurf.fr
Web: perso.libertysurf.fr/valrosc

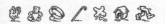

Entry No: 573   Map: **12**

Entry No: 574   Map: **12**

The golden Lot stone glows, there are stunning views over two valleys, the pool is solar-heated and salt-purified, so what matter if rooms are smallish with limited storage and the atmosphere sometimes a little chaotic? The Scotts labour ever on at their little empire, restoring the 17th-century farmhouse and outbuildings to their original character and adding modern comforts for gîtes and B&B. Zoé will charm you, see you have a good time, serve breakfast at any time. Dinner, sometimes a poolside barbecue, is fun, relaxed and informal and Peter plays the guitar. Pool-house kitchen and fridge for picnic lunches. *Gîte space for 22.*

Rooms: 1 double with bathroom; 1 suite for 2 with bathroom & wc.

Price: €40–€55 for two.

Meals: Dinner €15, including wine & coffee.

Closed: Never, please book ahead.

Quiet Gilbert will take you egg-hunting or goose-feeding of a morning. Soft, smiling and big-hearted, Michèle loves doing B&B, has won prizes for her recipes, invents sauces and makes her own aperitif. The quaintly old-fashioned rooms are comfortable (beware waist-low beams) but food is definitely the priority here. Fishing rods on loan for use in the pond; footpaths out from the gate; proper hiking trails a bit further away; the treasures of Moissac, lovely villages, caves, all within easy reach. This is exceptional farm B&B. *Small pets welcome. Gîte space for 4 people.*

Rooms: 2 doubles, 2 twins, all with bath, shower & wc.

Price: €38 for two.

Meals: Dinner €14, including wine & coffee; restaurant 5km.

Closed: Never.

From Cahors for Toulouse; at r'about D653 for Agen 16km; at junction right D656; through Villeseque, Sauzet, Bovila; on for St Matré 2km; sign on left.

From Moissac D7 for Bourg de Visa about 14km; before Brassac, just before a bridge, right for Fauroux; farm 2km; signposted.

Peter & Zoé Scott
Mondounet
46800 Fargues
Lot
Tel: (0)5 65 36 96 32
Fax: (0)5 65 31 84 89
E-mail: scotsprops@aol.com

Gilbert & Michèle Dio
La Marquise
Brassac
82190 Bourg de Visa
Tarn-et-Garonne
Tel: (0)5 63 94 25 16
Fax: (0)5 63 94 25 16

Entry No: 575   Map: **12**

Entry No: 576   Map: **12**

They have a flock of 120 milking sheep! The Sellars are warm country people who left big-scale farming in Sussex for a smallholding in deepest France where they breed sheep, goats, poultry and rabbits using natural, traditional methods (no pesticides, no heavy machines). Their enthusiasm and guts - it's hard hard work - have earned them the respect of the local community and their recipe for a simple, rewarding way of life includes receiving guests under the beams and by the open hearth. Julie will welcome you to her kitchen, too, where she creates feasts fit for farmers (organic veg and home-made goodies of course).

Rooms: 1 family for 3-4, 1 double, both with shower & wc.

Price: €36 for two.

Meals: Dinner €15, including wine & coffee.

Closed: Never.

As lovingly restored as the dreamy hamlet with its wonderful church, this 19th-century stone farmhouse is owned by a Franco-Dutch couple who enjoy sharing their summers here with guests. Madame teaches Spanish, is extrovert and energetic, Monsieur is calm, diplomatic and in business and they offer delicious dinners at their long, convivial table - regional and exotic dishes and an excellent cheeseboard. The honeysuckled courtyard and tall-treed garden are lovely, the rooms are fresh and light with good prints, local art, old wardrobes, terracotta tiles - a happy marriage of old and new.

Rooms: 1 suite for 2-4, 1 double, both with bath & wc.

Price: €43 for two.

Meals: Dinner €14, including wine & coffee.

Closed: September-June.

From A62 exit 8 on D953 for Cahors (round Valence d'Agen) 21km; at Lamothe left: Chambres d'Hôtes signs for 2km.

From A62 exit 8 for Gramont; follow signs to Lachapelle; entering village house on right.

Julie & Mark Sellars
Tondes
82400 Castelsagrat
Tarn-et-Garonne
Tel: (0)5 63 94 52 13

M & Mme Van den Brink
Au Village
82120 Lachapelle
Tarn-et-Garonne
Tel: (0)5 63 94 14 10 or
(0)1 39 49 07 37
E-mail: lachapelle_vdb@hotmail.com

Entry No: 577   Map: **12**

Entry No: 578   Map: **12**

The Gorges de l'Aveyron here are worth a big detour - a paradise of clear water, cliffs, wildlife, canoeing and rugged scenery. Johnny and Véronique, suitably, are sports teachers - all tan and dynamism, they encourage the active-holiday idea with great enthusiasm. They have renovated their house beyond the constraints of its origins - its rooms are simple, modern and functional, with little that is memorable or quintessentially French. But the food is good and generous and so are your friendly hosts. Very busy in summer so don't expect family intimacy then.

Rooms: 2 doubles, 2 twins, 1 family, all with bath or shower & wc.

Price: €49-€53 for two; €41.50 for two, out of season.

Meals: Dinner €15, including wine & coffee; restaurant 2km.

Closed: Never.

These two have buckets of enthusiasm for their new project. Having catered in many places but never in France, though Françoise is half French, they are loving it all: the elegant simplicity of this renovated 13th-15th-century townhouse with its sense of light and space in the airy hall and great spiral staircase; its views through to the garden courtyard; its original tiles and stone walls; its big, beautifully-decorated rooms, one with its own terrace; "the delightful guests who have already been to share it all with us," - and baby Travis. Seriously into food, they do an excellent *table d'hôtes* with everything home-made. A lovely young couple.

Rooms: 4 doubles, 2 twins, all with bath & wc.

Price: €61-€69 for two.

Meals: Dinner €18, including wine & coffee.

Closed: Never.

From Cahors, N20 to Caussade; D964 for Gaillac. At Montricoux, D115 for Nègrepelisse; after 500m, signposted.

From Montauban N20 22km to Caussade; right D926 for 7km; right D5 to Saint Antonin Noble Val (12km); follow signs.

Johnny & Véronique Antony
Les Brunis
82800 Nègrepelisse
Tarn-et-Garonne
Tel: (0)5 63 67 24 08
Fax: (0)5 63 67 24 08

Françoise & Richard Green
La Résidence, 37 rue Droite
82140 Saint Antonin Noble Val
Tarn-et-Garonne
Tel: (0)5 63 68 21 60
Fax: (0)5 63 68 21 60
E-mail: laresidence@compuserve.com
Web: www.laresidence-france.com

Here is complete rural Frenchness. Your hosts, lively and empathetic, share their home easily, without fuss; the rustic, cluttered dayroom has a warm open fire; bedrooms are simply furnished, pleasing and spotless, breakfast coffee is in a bowl and, with the loveliest smile, Madame takes you in as family; her dogs and cats are as friendly as she is and she greeted us from the milking shed, her hands dripping with the evidence: Le Gendre is a working farm with roaming chickens, ducks and pigs. Go lightly on lunch: dinner is uncompromisingly, deliciously 'farmhouse' with portions suitable for a hard-working farmer.

Rooms: 1 double, 1 suite for 4, both with shower & wc.

Price: € 35 for two.

Meals: Dinner € 13, including wine & coffee.

Closed: Never.

No splashing, no screaming - no pool! Peace reigns in the big garden; the gently rolling, wooded and brooked countryside beckons; wild orchids and woodpecker thrive in the clean air. Once a professional cook, Rosie still loves cooking, knows about vegetarian as well as local cuisine and uses virtually organic veg and eggs from Sam's fine *potager*. The late 19th-century house has wood-burning stoves and comfortable, relaxing furniture; bedrooms have polished wooden floors, big windows and impeccable bathrooms. And the area bursts with temptation for the gourmet and the *sportif*.

Rooms: 1 triple, 1 double, 1 twin, all with shower & wc.

Price: € 50.50 for two; special terms for long stays.

Meals: Dinner € 15.50, including wine & coffee.

Closed: Never.

N20 south from Cahors to Caussade. Left D926 through Septfonds. 3km beyond, left for Gaussou. Farm 1km on; sign.

From Agen D931 to Condom; D15 to Castelnau; right for 'Centre Ville'; right at Post Office D43 for St Pé & Sos about 5km; house first on left past landslip.

Françoise & Jean-Louis Zamboni
Ferme du Gendre
82240 Lavaurette
Tarn-et-Garonne
Tel: (0)5 63 31 97 72

Rosie & Sam Bennett
Les Colombiers
Bournic
32440 Castelnau d'Auzan
Gers
Tel: (0)5 62 29 24 05
Fax: (0)5 62 29 24 05
E-mail: rabennett@talk21.com

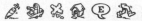

Built snug against the 13th-century hilltop village fortifications, the 18th-century house has a lovely terraced garden shaded by masses of scented old-fashioned climbing roses and perfect for breakfast - Madame loves gardening and it shows. She has also successfully preserved original features such as floorboards, fireplaces and door fittings. Colour schemes are mostly pale, with plenty of blue and grey making for elegant yet unpretentious rooms. There's a kitchenette for longer-stay guests: it's really worth settling in to explore this historic, little-visited area. Good footpaths close by.

Rooms: 1 double, 1 twin, 1 triple, all with shower & wc. 1 twin with bath & wc.

Price: €43-€54 for two.

Meals: Several good restaurants, 4km.

Closed: 4 January-4 February.

From Auch N21 for Tarbes. At le Trouette D2 to l'Isle de Noé; D943 to Montesquiou. Through village past church on left; house on right.

Mme Kovacs
Maison de la Porte Fortifieé
32320 Montesquiou
Gers
Tel: (0)5 62 70 97 59
Fax: (0)5 62 70 97 59
Web: www.france-bonjour.com/gascogne/

Noailles rejoices in a very French and delightfully secluded setting of gentle hills, crops and pastures. Madame has lived here all her life and her son now runs the busy farm. The house, full of French *paysan* warmth, is as genuine as your kindly hostess. Breakfast is outside or at a long table by a huge open hearth and there's a useful guests' kitchen area too. The bedrooms open onto the balcony overlooking the courtyard, have super old rickety wooden floors and some endearing features like Granny's wedding furniture (beds are old as well but have first-class mattresses). It is all down-to-earth and clean with proper country charm.

Rooms: 1 double, 1 triple, 1 suite ideal for families, all with bathrooms.

Price: €35 for two.

Meals: Self-catering possible.

Closed: Never.

From Auch, N21 towards Tarbes. 6km after Mirande, house signposted on left.

Marthe Sabathier
Noailles
32300 Saint Maur
Gers
Tel: (0)5 62 67 57 98

On a clear day you can see the Pyrenees... and every day the rolling fields beyond the wooden terrace outside your window. Youthful and natural, Mireille is an inspired cook and a delight to be with; Olivier, though somewhat disenchanted with farming in the modern age, still enjoys his smallholding. They grow Christmas trees and cereals, fill their cosy house with antique plates, prints, pictures and furniture and create a relaxed and happy family home with the essential dogs and cats and a swimming pool. Perfect for children. *Gîte space for 10 people.*

Rooms: 1 double (+ 1 small double for 2 children) with bathroom.

Price: €44 for two.

Meals: Dinner €14, including wine & coffee.

Closed: Never.

The sober, secret-looking buildings round the rose garden give no inkling of the explosion inside. 80 years ago, an Italian painter spread his heart and love of colour on ceilings and doors. 'His' suite has vast space, fine antiques, a dream of a bathroom and paintings to dazzle you for days. Theresa and Ian fell for the romantically wild house and park and left high-pressure London jobs to save them from dereliction. Their enthusiasm and sensitive intelligence show in every room. And the waterfall, the island, the Italian garden, the wild bit - there's no other place like it; and that's before you've stepped inside, or tasted Theresa's cooking. *Gîte space for 21 people with separate pool.*

Rooms: 2 suites, both with bath & wc.

Price: €65-€100 for two.

Meals: Dinner €23, including wine & coffee.

Closed: Never.

From Auch N21 for Tarbes 2km; left D929 for Lannemezan; in Masseube, left for Simorre 4km; left for Bellegarde; 1st left, before church and castle.

Mireille & Olivier Courouble
La Garenne
Bellegarde
32140 Masseube
Gers
Tel: (0)5 62 66 03 61
Fax: (0)5 62 66 03 61

From Auch, south on N21 for 3km; left D929 towards Lannemezan; in Pavie, left after Mairie, cross old bridge, bear right at fork; house 1km on left.

Theresa & Ian Martin
Domaine de Peyloubère
Le Gers, Pavie
32550 Pavie, Gers
Tel: (0)5 62 05 74 97
Fax: (0)5 62 05 75 39
E-mail: martin@peyloubere.com
Web: www.peyloubere.com

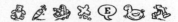

Entry No: 585   Map: **12**

Entry No: 586   Map: **12**

Having worked in exotic places, Maria, an Italian architect, and Andrew, an English hotelier (luxury safari camps included), a most interesting couple, are now serenely happy at Tail with their children. They have created two drawing rooms and put antiques everywhere; there are three four-posters draped in acres of flowers, a well-stocked library, the beautiful Bread Basket of France to explore (this is more Gers than Pyrénées), delicious international cuisine to share at dinner. Definitely affordable luxury, and child-friendly.

Rooms: 1 suite, 1 triple, 1 twin, 1 double, all with bath, shower & wc.

Price: €58-€85 for two.

Meals: Dinner €20, including wine & coffee; restaurant 5km.

Closed: Never, but booking essential in winter.

The main bedrooms have ornate wooden furniture, striped wallpaper, old linen and embroidered pillow cases - echoes of the 'Victorianisation' of a 17th-century house, they're fun and spotless; bathrooms are no-nonsense modern. The smaller double is on the mezzanine above the tiled and beamed living room where Luc and Marie-Françoise love sitting and chatting with guests. There's a good deal of cosy knick-knackery: dried flowers, gingham and floral fabrics, brasses and ornaments - it's all rather comforting and your hosts so warm and friendly. Son Pascal is a guide - mountaineering, caving and canoeing.

Rooms: 1 double, 3 triples, all with bath & wc.

Price: €46 for two.

Meals: Good restaurants 150m-3km.

Closed: Never.

From Tarbes D935 N for 40km. In Castelnau, château 500m from centre; well signposted.

Andrew & Maria Hedley
Château du Tail
65700 Castelnau Rivière Basse
Hautes-Pyrénées
Tel: (0)5 62 31 93 75
Fax: (0)5 62 31 93 72
Web: sudfr.com/chateaudutail

Entry No: 587   Map: **12**

From Lourdes D937 for Pau 8km to St Pé de Bigorre; facing Mairie take road on right. La Calèche 100m on right.

Luc & Marie-Françoise L'Haridon
La Calèche
65270 Saint Pé de Bigorre
Hautes-Pyrénées
Tel: (0)5 62 41 86 71
Fax: (0)5 62 94 60 50
E-mail: turon.immobilier@wanadoo.fr

Entry No: 588   Map: **12**

You could weep, this valley is so beautiful. And so are the house, its story, garden, owners. A doctor built it (see the cadduceus on the great newel post), then fostered one Bishop Laurence, who 'proved' Bernardette's miracles and set Lourdes up for glory. Arlette, a miracle of industry and human warmth, sews, decorates, cooks brilliantly (you'll never want to eat out) and still finds plenty of time for guests; quiet, attentive Robert will take you hiking and fishing in that gorgeous valley (Pyrenean high-mountain trout are the best, naturally). A very special place.

Rooms: 3 doubles, 1 triple, with bath or shower & wc.

Price: € 38 for two.

Meals: Dinner € 15, including wine & coffee; restaurants in Lourdes.

Closed: Never.

Madame prepares dinners and cooks the local speciality *gâteau à la broche* (cake on a spit), in the big open fireplace. Monsieur cheerfully does breakfast. She was a costume designer for the Paris Opera House and her needlework makes the cosy, perfectly decorated bedrooms, complete with electric blankets, exceptional; brilliant bathrooms too. He is both ski instructor and mountain guide so there's good advice on hand. They both like dining with their guests. All this in a traditional Pyrenean building in the oldest part of the village. Perfect in summer or winter.

Rooms: 3 doubles, all with bath & wc.

Price: € 54 for two.

Meals: Dinner € 16, including wine & coffee.

Closed: November-15 January.

From Lourdes N21 S for 2km; left at bridge; immediately left again D26 to Juncalas; house in village centre on right.

From Lourdes N21 towards Argelès-Gazost for; 3km right D13 towards Ossen & Omex. House signposted.

Arlette & Robert Assouère
Maison de L'Évêque
Impasse Monseigneur Laurence
65100 Juncalas
Hautes-Pyrénées
Tel: (0)5 62 42 02 04
Fax: (0)5 62 94 13 91

Mme Murielle Fanlou
Les Rocailles
65100 Omex-Lourdes
Hautes-Pyrénées
Tel: (0)5 62 94 46 19
Fax: (0)5 62 94 33 35
E-mail: muriellefanlou@aol.com

Entry No: 589   Map: **12**

Entry No: 590   Map: **12**

In rolling farmland on the Gers border - a wildlife haven an hour from the mountains - this is the most relaxed house you could wish for: 18th-century bones, 20th-century flesh. Dominique's decorative talent runs to cleverly-used bright colours, her own fantasy patchwork and great flair at auction sales. Nick cooks with French, Thai, Latin American flourishes and is a great entertainer. They have three teenage children, are a well-travelled, thoughtful couple, involved in the local music festival, concerned with the countryside - evenings on the terrace can be stimulating. Great walks, super food, easy living.

Rooms: 2 doubles, 1 triple, all with shower & wc.

Price: €50 for two.

Meals: Dinner €20, including wine & coffee.

Closed: Never.

The Hindu greeting *namaste* is the name, slightly exotic is the feel of this comfortable 18th-century farmhouse. The Fontaines restored it, polished the floors and created a lasting air of harmony. One of the two ground-floor guest rooms has doors onto a semi-secluded corner of the garden and a fine big shower room. The two new rooms upstairs will be ideal for people doing yoga, dance or art workshops here. In cold weather, enjoy the huge open fire in the comfortable *salon* and always enjoy Jean's dinners at the long communal table: he likes doing veggie food and using organic ingredients.

Rooms: 1 quadruple with bath & wc; 1 triple with shower & wc.

Price: €43 for two.

Meals: Dinner €15.50, including wine & coffee.

Closed: Never.

From Tarbes D632 to Trie sur Baïse; through village onto D939 for Mirande 1km; house up little road signed on left.

From A64 exit 16 on D939 through Lannemezan to Galan; from village square/church, Rue de la Baïse towards Recurt; house 500m on left.

Nick & Dominique Collinson
Jouandassou
65220 Fontrailles
Hautes-Pyrénées
Tel: (0)5 62 35 64 43
Fax: (0)5 62 35 66 13
E-mail: nick@collinson.fr
Web: www.collinson.fr

Jean & Danielle Fontaine
Namaste
13 rue de la Baïse
65330 Galan, Hautes-Pyrénées
Tel: (0)5 62 99 77 81
Fax: (0)5 62 99 77 81
E-mail: namaste_65@libertysurf.fr
Web: www.namaste-pyrenees.com

Madame is so gracefully down to earth, her *domaine* an oasis of calm and plain class where you may share her delight in playing the piano or golf (3km) and possibly make a lifelong friend. Built in Napoleon's time, her house has an elegant hall, big, airy bedrooms and great bathrooms, while fine furniture and linen sheets reflect her pride in her ancestral home - a combination of uncluttered space and character. The huge quadruple has space to waltz in and the smallest bathroom; a beautifully-presented breakfast comes with civilised conversation. Come to unwind - you may never want to leave for this is a remarkable place.

Rooms: 1 double, 1 triple, 1 quadruple, all with bath & wc.

Price: €45 for two.

Meals: Good restaurants 5-7 km.

Closed: Never.

Set among 300-year-old cedars, it has majestic gardens, a pond-blessed orchard attracting woodpeckers, owls, hoopoes and deer, a heated swimming pool and big breakfasts till noon. The higher things in life are lavishly worshipped: there's a baby grand, an elegant library and a fabulous antique clock collection. Arnold is English and was 'in clocks', Denise is Swiss, both have adopted France with alacrity. They are good company, their rooms are big and comfortable and they love having guests. So close to skiing, golfing, fishing and Toulouse's new opera house - but why go anywhere when Soulès (meaning 'sun') is here? *Gîte space for 8.*

Rooms: 3 triples, 1 double, all with bath or shower & wc; some connecting.

Price: €60 for two.

Meals: Restaurants nearby.

Closed: New Year.

From A64 exit 16 to Lannemezan; there, N117 for Toulouse 5km; at Pinas church D158 for Villeneuve. House on right 1km.

From Toulouse N20 S to Pins Justaret (10km); fork right on D4 for 26km to Lézat sur Lèze. Continue 3km after Lézat; château entrance on right.

Mme Marie-Sabine Colombier
Domaine de Jean-Pierre
20 route de Villeneuve
65300 Pinas
Hautes-Pyrénées
Tel: (0)5 62 98 15 08
Fax: (0)5 62 98 15 08
E-mail: marie.colombier@wanadoo.fr

Denise & Arnold Brun
Château de Soulès
09210 Saint Ybars
Ariège
Tel: (0)5 61 69 20 12
Fax: (0)5 61 69 21 68
E-mail: arnold.brun@wanadoo.fr

Entry No: 593   Map: **12**

Entry No: 594   Map: **12**

More than a farmhouse, a whole renovated hamlet facing the Pyrenees. You could plan your stay during one of Dutch Jeanne's weekend art courses - she's a wonderful sculptor - and stop a while: forget the maps and itinerary and enter a world of ceramics, watercolours, weaving, sculpture... and wide-open spaces. The rooms feel right, light, not over-decorated and are adorned with Jeanne's handiwork. Guests have their own living room and fridge but dinner - cooked rather well by Guy - is *en famille* in a relaxed and friendly atmosphere. *Ask about summer art courses. Gîte space for 7 people.*

Rooms: 1 double, 2 triples, all with bath or shower & wc.

Price: € 38 for two.

Meals: Dinner € 14, including wine & coffee.

Closed: Never.

Nick, a fauna and flora guide who really knows his stuff, lists about 200 different birds and over 50 orchids, though people do come to look for just one type. He and Julie, who's a midwife, are a thoroughly likeable pair. Their tiny hamlet has breathtaking views up to the mountains and across miles of fields, farms and forests - it is ineffably lovely. The simple and pretty renovated house has smallish rooms and a cosy family living room. They'll collect you from the airport as part of a week's package. Great value.

Rooms: 2 doubles, 1 twin, all with shower & wc.

Price: € 37 for two.

Meals: Dinner € 13, including wine & coffee.

Closed: November-April

From Toulouse A66/N20 S exit Belpech. D11 for 8km, right for La Bastide de Lordat, through village for Gaudies. Before Gaudies bear right, cross river. Certes farm near top on left.

From St Girons D117 E for 7km; just before fork for Mas d'Azil left at Chambres d'Hôtes sign; follow signs up tiny, metalled track for 2km.

Jeanne & Guy Gosselin
Certes
09700 Gaudies
Ariège
Tel: (0)5 61 67 01 56
Fax: (0)5 61 67 42 30

Nick & Julie Goldsworthy
La Baquette
Lescure
09420 Rimont, Ariège
Tel: (0)5 61 96 37 67
Fax: (0)5 61 96 37 67
E-mail: goldsnj@aol.com
Web: www.ariege.com/lodging/goldsworthy.html

Entry No: 595   Map: **12**

Entry No: 596   Map: **12**

A wonderful working farm: they raise sheep, pigeons, ducks, turkeys, chickens, pigs and geese (for *foie gras*). Plus donkeys and a great cage of parrots - heaven for children, as is the fenced rose-scented garden with its soft, roll-worthy lawn. François, a tall distinguished farmer, and Danielle, his helpful smiling wife, are generous, trusting country people who love their foreign guests. The big, freshly-decorated bedrooms in the converted barn have lovely armoires, fresh flowers and extraordinary long views over forested hills to the distant Pyrenees. *Martin Guerre* was filmed in this beautiful valley.

Rooms: 1 twin, 2 doubles, eall with shower & wc; 1 family suite with shower & 2 wcs.

Price: €41.50 for two.

Meals: Dinner €14.50, including wine and coffee.

Closed: 15 November-15 March.

From Toulouse south on E80; N20 towards Foix for 3.5km; right onto D4; D919 to Artigat; 2km further; right signed 'Chambres d'Hôtes le Touron'.

Danielle & François Denry
Ferme du Touron
09130 Lanoux
Ariège
Tel: (0)5 61 67 15 73
Fax: (0)5 61 67 55 41

Great for the artistic: soul-stretching landscapes away to the Pyrenees, a well-travelled, talented Belgian artist who plans to hold workshops here and fills her converted farmhouse with books and paintings. There are echoes of eastern culture everywhere, a meditation and yoga room, a big, tranquil, uncluttered living room, cool in summer, log-fired in winter, and a many-beamed dining room. The unpretentious, wood-ceilinged bedrooms vary in size: the tiny single is adorable with its day bed and huge corner bath; all have rich Indian bedcovers and compact shower rooms. And a hiking path on the doorstep. *German spoken.*

Rooms: 1 double, 1 twin, both with shower, sharing wc; 1 double with shower & wc; 1 single with bath, shower & wc.

Price: €50 for two.

Meals: Dinner €22, including wine & coffee; BBQ possible.

Closed: Never.

From Toulouse N20 exit Varilhès to Verniolle; left to Bénagues; up hill; right at top; past water tower; narrow left fork, 1km. House on left.

Christine van Roggen
Moulet
Saint Bauzeil
09100 Pamiers
Ariège
Tel: (0)5 61 60 40 05
Fax: (0)5 61 60 40 05
E-mail: moulet@rubiscem.net

Down on the Cathar Trail, how about breakfast in a Protestant Temple? Well, remains of, turned into a pretty patio by twinkling, down-to-earth John and lively, sociable Lee-anne - Australians restoring this elegant mansion and loving it. Graciously high ceilings, a sweeping spiral staircase, lovely great windows: a fine and formal house in an oasis of ancient, stream-kissed oaks made relaxed and welcoming by your hard-working, fun-loving hosts. Guest rooms are generous too, in pastels and just enough antiques; one even has the vast original claw-footed bath.

Rooms: 1 triple with bath, shower & wc; 3 doubles, 1 suite for 4, all with bath or shower & wc.

Price: €53.50-€58 for two; suite €107 for four.

Meals: Dinner €18, including aperitif; wine €6-€10; restaurant 200m.

Closed: Never.

From Toulouse N20 for Foix; exit D119T to Mirepoix; D625 for Lavelanet for 11km; at Aigues-Vives left for Léran D28.

John & Lee-anne Furness
L'Impasse du Temple
09600 Léran
Ariège
Tel: (0)5 61 01 50 02
Fax: (0)5 61 01 50 02
E-mail: john.furness@wanadoo.fr
Web: www.chezroo.com

Entry No: 599   Map: **18**

Bring your hiking boots to this magical valley where nails were once made. Beds are softer but don't expect silver or lace: it is simple and honest, the room is white and pine with a little sitting corner, the shower small. There's a lovely terrace, two adorable furry-eared donkeys to delight young and old, the rushing water for trout (in season) and to lull you to sleep after that great walk. Your hospitable hosts, who love to chat but don't flutter, will gladly harness a horse for a day in the foothills with a picnic lunch. And you have a private kitchen. *Gîte space for 4 people.*

Rooms: 1 twin with shower & wc. Kitchenette available.

Price: €32 for two.

Meals: Good restaurant in St Pierre de Rivière 2km.

Closed: January.

From Foix D21 to Ganac. After 5km take route to Micou 'Les Carcis'; right just after small bridge.

Sylviane Piednoël & Guy Drouet
Les Carcis
09000 Ganac
Ariège
Tel: (0)5 61 02 96 54
Fax: (0)5 61 65 52 28

Entry No: 600   Map: **17**

"Enchanting!" The setting is spectacular, the reception rooms generously fireplaced, the antique chests, tables and desks genuine and in superb condition, the bedrooms big, airy and elegant and the bathrooms excellent. Michel, a restaurateur for 30 years, is still the finest chef within 100km and loves cooking for half a dozen. He takes his daily inspiration from the market, has twinkling eyes, says he is temperamental but may let you into his sanctum. What a welcome! And moreover, Unac Church, just next door, is an early Romanesque jewel. *Well-behaved children over 5 welcome.*

Rooms: 1 double, 1 triple, both with bath & wc.

Price: €64 for two.

Meals: Dinner €28, including wine & coffee.

Closed: Never.

Come walking. Once you've reached the house, you'll never need to get into your car again: 80km of hiking trails, from easy to tough, lead straight from the door into a paradise for botanists, bird-watchers and tree insect fanatics, and your kindly hosts know those paths intimately. Layrole's most memorable features are the greenery, the riot of flowers all round the south-facing terrace and the sound of water in the background. The guest room has an immaculate new bed, a mass of books and central heating while the Orient Express loo will appeal to train buffs. A very pretty village and good homely dinners.

Rooms: 1 double with shower & wc.

Price: €34 for two.

Meals: Dinner €14, including wine & coffee.

Closed: Mid-October-mid-April.

From Foix N20 S 33km through Tarascon to Luzenac; left D2; follow signs to Unac; 2nd entrance to Unac; house just down from church, 100m on right.

From Foix N20 S to Tarascon; D618 for St Girons; 2.5km after the café/bar at Saurat, right up steep road for Cabus; house 700m on right.

Michel & Simone Descat
L'Oustal
09250 Unac
Ariège
Tel: (0)5 61 64 48 44

Roger & Monique Robert
Layrole
09400 Saurat
Ariège
Tel: (0)5 61 05 73 24

High up on a remote edge of the world, surrounded by 70 hectares of breathtaking forested Pyrenean foothills, the setting is out of this world, the house has tons of character - local stone, beams, low windows, uneven ceilings, all excellently renovated - and your hosts know what real *chambres d'hôtes* means. They raise horses and Newfoundlands, will let you join their picnics, ride their horses (if you are an experienced rider), live in their space for a while and hear their stories, in several languages, of sailing the Atlantic or the Caribbean: don't miss dining with them. Good rooms and excellent value. *Gîte space for 6 people.*

Rooms: 2 doubles, 1 twin, 1 triple, 1 quadruple (summer only), all with shower & wc.

Price: €37-€40 for two. Book early.

Meals: Dinner €12, including wine & coffee.

Closed: 1 October-Easter.

From Foix D17 for Col de Marrous 9km; in La Mouline left at Chambres d'Hôtes sign for 1.5km, right C6, tiny but easy track, to house.

Bob & Jenny Brogneaux
Le Poulsieu
Serres sur Arget
09000 Foix
Ariège
Tel: (0)5 61 02 77 72
Fax: (0)5 61 02 77 72
Web: www.france-bonjour.com/le-poulsieu/

Entry No: 603   **Map:** 17

They are a delightful family and their home has real heart. After years of renovation your weaver hosts have made this rural idyll what it is today. Samples of their work, using only natural dyes from local plants, are everywhere and fit well with the exposed stone and woodwork of the old house. Bedrooms are rustic-warm with good views. Dine *en famille* in a huge living/dining room (village dances were held here!) and share the Loizances' local knowledge. Perfect for summer walking and winter cross-country skiing - the tiny hamlet is perched 900m up on the side of a National Park valley and the valley above is virtually unpopulated.

Rooms: 3 doubles, 1 triple, all with shower & wc.

Price: €40 for two.

Meals: Dinner €14, including wine & coffee.

Closed: Never.

From Foix D17 for Col des Marrous 15km; do not follow for Le Bosc on left: 'Hameau de Madranque' sign on right.

Birgit & Jean-Claude Loizance
Madranque
09000 Le Bosc
Ariège
Tel: (0)5 61 02 71 29
Fax: (0)5 61 02 71 29

Entry No: 604   **Map:** 17

From the lovely dining room you see straight across to a great snowy peak, a spectacular view for breakfast. Impressionist Henri Duran hid here during the war, understandably. Inside are pretty fabrics and your hosts' own works (from July to September they stage a special exhibition). Goan Teresa was educated in England and paints; Alpine-born, Paris-educated Bernard is an expert on water mammals, sculpts and draws. A very special couple. And this tiny village (pop. 60) feels almost Alpine. *Children over five or babies only (ladder to mezzanine). Gîte space for 4.*

Rooms: 1 double, 1 single, with bath & wc.

Price: €39 for two.

Meals: Choice of restaurants 1.5km.

Closed: Never.

From A64 exit 20 to St Girons; right D618 for Castillon 12km; tiny D404 on left to Cescau. Park below church on left.

Teresa & Bernard Richard
Chambres d'Hôtes
09800 Cescau
Ariège
Tel: (0)5 61 96 74 24
E-mail: tizirichard@caramail.com

Entry No: 605   Map: **17**

The happy family who live down this quiet lane have decorated their 18th-century manor in peaceful good taste with antiques (every piece chosen because it is the right one), lovely bed linen, pretty bath tiles and their blue-and-white valentine theme - not sky or baby or royal but Brigitte's favourite French (Williamsburg to Americans) blue. It is soft, mellow, uncluttered; she is smiling, enthusiastic, young; the daughters are adorable and helpful. A dreamy, comfortable, happy house, where you appreciate the skill of the hard-working kitchen gardener when you sit down to dinner.

Rooms: 1 double, 1 twin sharing shower & wc. 1 double with shower & wc.

Price: €40 for two.

Meals: Dinner €14, including wine & coffee.

Closed: Last week in August.

From Toulouse N117 SW for about 50km; exit S D6 to Cazères; over River Garonne, right D62, follow for Camping Planturel; house 2nd left after Camping.

Brigitte & Bruno Lebris
Les Pesques
31220 Palaminy
Haute-Garonne
Tel: (0)5 61 97 59 28
Fax: (0)5 61 98 12 97

Entry No: 606   Map: **12**

Midi-Pyrénées

Fire roars and stream flows, bedding and bathrooms excel, French country furniture glows, rugs are oriental and colours simple. Steve is a wonderful cook, Kris a man of the theatre, together they have achieved this splendid restoration of their remote old mill. They are deeply involved in the local environment, preserving trees, encouraging wildlife, helping farmers and still dreaming of a turbine to make heat from the river (so rooms may be a little chilly in winter). A very special spot, great value... and so near the Pyrenees.

Rooms: 2 triples, both with bath/shower & wc; 1 double & 1 triple sharing shower & wc.

Price: €42 for two.

Meals: Dinner €14, including wine & coffee.

Closed: Never.

From Toulouse A64 to Boussens (exit 21); D635 to edge of Aurignac; right D8 for Alan 3km; left to Samouillan (7km); D96; signposted.

Stephen Callen & Kris Misselbrook
Le Moulin
Samouillan
31420 Aurignac, Haute-Garonne
Tel: (0)5 61 98 86 92
Fax: (0)5 61 98 60 77
E-mail: kris.steve@free.fr
Web: www.moulin-vert.net

Entry No: 607   Map: **12**

Madame Fieux's visitors are immersed in the French way of life, sleep in fine rooms with views across the green oaks, enjoy her warm and genuine interest in people, manifested with "a mix of the formidable and the lovable, the dignified and the mischievous" and she gets full marks for the beauty of her reception rooms: they are big, warm and dignified in the elegant patina of age. Her house is full of old pictures, books, comfortable chairs and antiques. Step out on a summer's morning for breakfast - often with home-made cakes - in the large, lush garden. When the temperature soars head for those oaks. Lake and tennis court next door.

Rooms: 3 doubles, 1 family, all with bath or shower & wc.

Price: €76 for two.

Meals: Restaurant 4km.

Closed: Never.

From Toulouse A68 for Albi; exit 3 Montastruc 1km; right D30 for Lavaur 4.5km; right D30E for Verfeuil & follow for Stoupignan; 1km on left.

Claudette Fieux
Stoupignan
31380 Montpitol
Haute-Garonne
Tel: (0)5 61 84 22 02
Fax: (0)5 61 84 22 02

Entry No: 608   Map: **12**

Gérard taught philosophy, Chantal taught English and theirs is a well-stocked library. They love music, too. Formerly a working farm, the house still has its hay loft, well and bread oven and you will gape, astounded, at the scale of the inglenook fireplace with all its attendant oak beams plus a nail where *Grand'mère* used to hang her money among the washing. A large terrace overlooks the hills (kites available), a vine-covered pergola gives shade, a grassy courtyard has a barbecue, table tennis and home-made exercise machines. No antiques, but we loved it for its unpretentious simplicity and the intelligent company.

Rooms: 3 triples, 1 double & bunk, all with bath or shower & wc.

Price: €37-€41 for two; €49-€53 for three.

Meals: Dinner available locally.

Closed: Never.

Birds, bees and sheep will serenade you in this lovely and largely undiscovered part of France, so close to Albi and its fascinating red-brick Cathedral. Your Anglo-French hosts are welcoming and helpful - the bright, unfussy rooms may be small but the hospitality is great and their deeply converted 200-year-old farmhouse is a deliciously secluded place to stay and walk or bike out into the country. Local sheep farmers (who supply Roquefort with milk) will show you their milking sheds if asked. The Wises grow their own vegetables and summer dinners are on the terrace overlooking the lovely Tarn valley.

Rooms: 1 twin, 1 triple, all with shower & wc; 1 twin sharing bathroom.

Price: €35 for two.

Meals: Dinner €14.50, including wine & coffee.

Closed: Never.

From A68 exit 3 to Montastruc; D30 for Lavaur for 5km; left D30c to Azas; cont. 2km; sign for Garrigue (D22g).

From Albi D999 for Millau 25km; at La Croix Blanche left to Cambon du T., up to La Barthe on D163; right; house on left.

Chantal & Gérard Zabé
En Tristan
31380 Azas
Haute-Garonne
Tel: (0)5 61 84 94 88
Fax: (0)5 61 84 94 88
E-mail: gerard.zabe@free.fr
Web: en.tristan.free.fr

Michèle & Michael Wise
La Barthe
81430 Villefranche d'Albigeois
Tarn
Tel: (0)5 63 55 96 21
Fax: (0)5 63 55 96 21
E-mail: mx2wise@aol.com
Web: www.angelfire.com/la/wise

Entry No: 609   Map: **12**

Entry No: 610   Map: **13**

Ian & Penelope's good furniture, books and paintings are thoroughly at home now in this seriously old, history-laden house (the watchtower is 13th-century) and all is serene and inviting. Each freshly-decorated room has its own private entrance, balcony or terrace and stupendous views. The house is on the southern slope of the hilltop village of Cordes (only five minutes from both the top and the bottom), the swimming pool is big enough for real exercise and there's a poolside barbecue, kitchen and dining area. Cosy in winter too. Enough to entice you to stay a while and try the special three-day deal?

Rooms: 1 suite for 4, 1 double, 2 twin, all with bath or shower & wc.

Price: €50-€64 for two.

Meals: Wide choice of restaurant in Cordes, within easy walking distance. Barbecue & summer kitchen available.

Closed: January-February.

From Albi D600 to Cordes; up 'Cité' road on right of 'Maison de la Presse' for 500m; fork left for Le Bouysset; left at hairpin bend marked Rte de St Jean; Aurifat 200m on right.

Ian & Penelope Wanklyn
Aurifat
81170 Cordes sur Ciel
Tarn
Tel: (0)5 63 56 07 03
Fax: (0)5 63 56 07 03
E-mail: aurifat@wanadoo.fr
Web: www.jcjdatacomm.co.uk/france

Entry No: 611   **Map: 13**

The old house glows with the sensitive, loving care it has received. A magnificent hallway and sweeping staircase bring you to fine, airy rooms that have original fireplaces, beams, interesting pictures, views of Cordes and are beautifully furnished (matt satin is very fitting). Your hosts are a gentle couple, maybe a little reserved at first but their dry humour warms up over dinner - most of which they'll proudly tell you they produced themselves. Children are welcome; there are games, a small park where you can picnic if you wish, and Leonard the friendly donkey. A small corner of delight on the edge of Cordes.

Rooms: 1 twin, 2 doubles, 1 triple, 1 quadruple, all with shower & wc.

Price: €48-€55 for two.

Meals: Dinner €17, including wine & coffee.

Closed: Never.

From Albi D600 to Cordes; there follow signs 'Parking 1 & 2'; signposted.

Annie & Christian Rondel
Les Tuileries
81170 Cordes sur Ciel
Tarn
Tel: (0)5 63 56 05 93
Fax: (0)5 63 56 05 93
E-mail: christian.rondel@wanadoo.fr

Entry No: 612   **Map: 13**

Like its owners, Mas de Sudre is a warm friendly house. George and Pippa are ideal B&B folk - relaxed, good-natured, at ease with people, adding lots of little extras to make you comfortable and enthusiastic about their corner of France. *Dégustations* (wine-tastings) can be arranged and there's a large shady garden set in rolling vineyards and farmland where you can sleep off any excesses. For the more energetic there are bikes, a pool, a tennis court, badminton and table tennis. Guests are encouraged to treat the house as their own. *Gîte space for 10 people.*

Rooms: 2 doubles, 2 twins, all with shower & wc.

Price: €55 for two.

Meals: Good choice of restaurants locally.

Closed: Never.

From Gaillac for Cordes; over railway; fork imm'ly left D964 for Castelnau de Montmiral 1km; left D18 for Montauban 400m; right D4 1.5km; 1st left, 1st house on right.

Pippa & George Richmond-Brown
Mas de Sudre
81600 Gaillac
Tarn
Tel: (0)5 63 41 01 32
Fax: (0)5 63 41 01 32
E-mail: georgerbrown@free.fr

Entry No: 613   Map: **13**

Come for an absolutely fabulous French bourgeois experience: huge cool entrance hall, massive stone staircase, trompe-l'œil marble alcoves, high ceilings and southern colours - deep blue shutters, white walls. It is almost colonially grand. Add the owners' passion for Napoleon III furniture, oil paintings and ornate mirrors and the mood, more formal than family, is unmistakably French. Bedrooms, some with cathedral, some with rooftop views, are antique-furnished and very comfortable, breakfast is on the terrace overlooking the cathedral square. It's good to be in a town with utterly French people. And Madame has a keen sense of humour.

Rooms: 1 suite, 4 doubles, 1 twin, all with bath or shower & wc.

Price: €43 for two.

Meals: Plenty of choice in town.

Closed: Never.

In centre of Gaillac, directly opposite St Michel abbey church as you come in across bridge from A68 Toulouse-Albi road.

Lucile Pinon
8 place Saint Michel
81600 Gaillac
Tarn
Tel: (0)5 63 57 61 48
Fax: (0)5 63 41 06 56

Entry No: 614   Map: **13**

Madame, who runs her family château with boundless energy and infectious *joie de vivre*, serves breakfast in her big kitchen in order to chat more easily to you while preparing dinner - she's a delight. The good, lived-in bedrooms still have their original 19th-century charm, including a rare 1850s wallpaper - and turning walk-in cupboards into showers or loos was a stroke of brilliance. The antique-filled sitting rooms are totally French and the little reading room holds hundreds of books. A country house in the style of days gone by, now comfortably worn around the edges and with a tennis court you're welcome to use.

Rooms: 1 suite, with shower & wc; 1 double with shower, sharing wc.

Price: €60-€75 for two.

Meals: Dinner €21, including wine & coffee.

Closed: Never.

A child's dream become an adult's paradise of history, culture and peace: inside those forbidding walls you climb old stone stairs to the open sentry's gallery, enter your chamber and gasp at the loveliness of the room and the depth of the view. Beyond the fine old timbers and stonework, glowing floor, furniture and fabrics, your eyes flow out over luscious gardens and woods. Alan is a softly-spoken Scot, Laurence a charming Parisienne, both are passionate about their prize-winning restoration - original materials, expert craftsmen - and other delights: they have musical evenings and produce excellent wine. A remarkable place. *Gîte space for 3 people.*

Rooms: 1 twin, 1 double, both with bath, shower & wc.

Price: €69 for two.

Meals: Restaurants within 5km.

Closed: 20 December-28 February.

From Revel D622 for Castres for 9km; left D12 to Lempaut; right D46 for Lescout - La Bousquétarié on left.

Monique & Charles Sallier
La Bousquétarié
81700 Lempaut
Tarn
Tel: (0)5 63 75 51 09
Fax: (0)5 63 75 51 09

Entry No: 615   Map: **13**

From Gaillac D964 for Castelnau de Montmiral; at junction D15 to Château de Mayragues, signposted.

Laurence & Alan Geddes
Château de Mayragues
81140 Castelnau de Montmiral
Tarn
Tel: (0)5 63 33 94 08
Fax: (0)5 63 33 98 10
E-mail: geddes@chateau-de-mayragues.com
Web: www.chateau-de-mayragues.com

Entry No: 616   Map: **12**

Nothing is too much trouble, even picnics can be arranged - Catherine runs her 19th-century manor farmhouse with charm and efficiency. There's table tennis, *pétanque*, a swimming pool and a big, peaceful garden to roam or relax in. Bedrooms are immaculate with prettily co-ordinated colour schemes, good linen and mattresses and meals are served either in the bright, pleasant dining room or on the terrace. Perfectly placed for the extraordinary Cathedral at Albi, walking, cycling and riding in the Grésigne forest or outings to the nearby lake complex with all its sporting possibilities.

Rooms: 1 double, 2 triples, all with bath or shower & wc.

Price: €48 for two.

Meals: Dinner €17, including wine & coffee.

Closed: Never.

Drive through the imposing gates and up the gravel drive - you know this is special. This magnificent house is shamelessly luxurious - wonderful stained glass windows in the dining room, interesting paintings, pottery and exotic rugs everywhere, each bedroom and bathroom stylishly decorated with unusual attention to detail in superb furnishings and linens, embroidered towels and bathrobes. The sprawling gardens are filled with birdsong, the large swimming pool is discreetly distant, your cosmopolitan hosts generate a lively, relaxed atmosphere.

Rooms: 2 doubles, 2 twin, 1 suite, all with bath or shower & wc.

Price: €57.50-€75 for two.

Meals: Dinner €28, including wine & coffee.

Closed: Never.

From Gaillac D964 N to Castelnau de Montmiral, right at bottom of village for 100m; right at sign Croix du Sud; fork left for Mazars; house on left.

From A68 Toulouse-Albi exit 6. At Saint Sulpice D13 towards Coufouleux for about 3km. House on left, clearly signed.

Catherine Sordoillet
La Croix du Sud
Mazars
81140 Castelnau de Montmiral, Tarn
Tel: (0)5 63 33 18 46
Fax: (0)5 63 33 18 46
E-mail: guillaume.sordoillet@libertysurf.fr
Web: www.la-croix-du-sud.com

Tony & Marianne Silver
Le Manoir de la Maysou
81800 Coufouleux
Tarn
Tel: (05) 63 33 85 92
Fax: (05) 63 40 64 24
E-mail: tonysilver@compuserve.com
Web: www.manoir-maysou.8m.com

Genuine human warmth and refined luxury are the keynotes of this beautifully-restored house and its superb gardens. 43 big ebony beams (brought from Madagascar in the family's repatriation luggage...) went into the renovation. The atmosphere is happily, humorously family with many traces of those years on exotic shores, in the cooking as well as the bathrooms. The large, pretty bedrooms are immaculate, the cultured, people-loving owners are most unusual, both refined and down-to-earth, country-comfortable and artistic. *If they haven't heard from you by 8pm they may re-let the room.*

Rooms: 1 double, 1 twin, both with bath or shower & wc.

Price: €50 for two.

Meals: Dinner €15, including wine & coffee. Plenty of restaurants in the area.

Closed: Mid-December-mid-January.

A gem, both house and garden, in the post-industrial waste of this old mining area. You are received by a lively hostess who, deeply interested in art and furniture, loves decorating her beamy old house with style and poise that reflect her personality, tending her garden of plenty - three secret sitting corners - and gathering the fruit that hangs richly around - yes, you may. A stream runs at the bottom, forests march along the edge, you are æons away from the ugliness down the road. Bedrooms, bearing bookish names, are painted white with colour trimmings and lots of wood (beams, floors, antiques) - delightful.

Rooms: 1 twin, 2 doubles, all with shower & wc.

Price: €43 for two.

Meals: Light supper €9, wine €1.50; restaurant 1km.

Closed: Never.

From Rabastens D12 for Coufouleux; cross River Tarn; left at lights D13 for Loupiac. Just before village right by cemetery; skirt cemetery, fork right, follow signs for La Bonde 1km.

From A20 or N20, N140 for Figeac/ Decazeville; just before Decazeville right to Viviez; over railway; sign.

Maurice & Bernadette Crété
La Bonde-Loupiac
81800 Rabastens
Tarn
Tel: (0)5 63 33 82 83
Fax: (0)5 63 33 82 83
Web: www.labonde81.com

Mireille Bernard
Joany
12110 Viviez
Aveyron
Tel: (0)5 65 43 42 90
Web: www.joany.org

Midi-Pyrénées

A mini-hamlet in the calm green Aveyron where there is so much space. Two rooms, in the main house, each with a little terrace, look out over a typical medieval château; the third, in an outbuilding, has a mezzanine; all are welcoming, two have cooking facilities. The garden is full of flowers, the view stupendous, your hosts solicitous and keen to help, providing for all your needs. The food is "outstanding and imaginative" - Pierre and Monique used to run a restaurant. *Well-behaved children and pets welcome. Gîte space for 8 people.*

Rooms: 2 doubles, both with bath or shower & wc. In separate house: 2 doubles, bath & wc.

Price: €38-€46 for two.

Meals: Dinner €16, including wine & coffee; restaurant 1km.

Closed: 2 weeks in September.

From Villefranche D922 towards Albi; at entrance to Sanvensa, follow signs on right to Monteillet Chambres d'Hôtes.

Monique & Pierre Bateson
Monteillet-Sanvensa
12200 Villefranche de Rouergue
Aveyron
Tel: (0)5 65 29 81 01
Fax: (0)5 65 65 89 52
E-mail: pbc.@wanadoo.fr

Entry No: 621   Map: 13

The ever-welcoming Riebens have exchanged a cosy northern village with paddocks by the garden for a swathe of southern Auvergne - farmhouse, fields, woods, a lake and... paddocks for Jacques' beloved horses. Views from the terrace merit several hours of gazing; or get out there and discover the walks and the wildlife. House and furniture are properly old-fashioned and quaint (bathrooms are recent) and the décor respects them utterly: stripped wooden floors, original beams, good old beds, soft colours and plenty of little pieces to give it the personal touch. Your hosts love their new home - so will you. *Gîte space for 10 people.*

Rooms: 1 double, 2 family, all with bath & wc.

Price: €43 for two; €69 for four.

Meals: Dinner €15, including wine & coffee; restaurant 5km.

Closed: Never.

From Villefranche de Rouergue for Rodez D911; exit Rieupeyroux for Rodez 2km; right D85 to Tayrac. At La Rode right for La Salvetat Peynalés; towards Montarsès; sign.

Jo & Jacques Rieben
Montarsès de Tayrac
12440 La Salvetat Peyralés
Aveyron
Tel: (0)5 65 81 46 10
Fax: (0)5 65 81 46 10

Entry No: 622   Map: 13

An energetic, lovable couple run relaxation courses in this astonishing old place, built on a hillside before a heart-stopping view. Inside, you go from level to delightful level: the ancient frame holds brilliantly-restored rooms done in a simple, contemporary style that makes the old stones and timbers glow with pride. The emphasis is on communal living, of course - superb dining and sitting rooms with original paving, huge organic *potager*, great atmosphere - but there are little terraces and a library for quiet times. Lovely guest rooms are big (except the singles), pale or bright. An exceptional place on all accounts.
Children over 4 welcome. Gîte space for 6.

Rooms: 5 twins with shower & wc, 2 singles with shower & separate wc.

Price: € 55 for two.

Meals: Dinner € 15, including wine & coffee.

Closed: Never.

A simple unpretentious home with a real family feel. The house is modern, the rolling Languedoc hills are wild and very ancient. You can put on your wings and join the paragliders and hang-gliders who launch themselves off a nearby cliff, or you can watch them from the safety of your breakfast table in the garden. It matters little that Henriette speaks no English: she is kind and welcoming and you can get a long way with smiles and sign language. The immaculate, simply and attractively furnished bedrooms include a suite which is perfect for a family.

Rooms: 1 double, 1 suite for 4, both with shower & wc.

Price: € 37-€ 40 for two.

Meals: Choice of restaurants Millau, 3km.

Closed: Never.

From Millau D992/D999 for Albi; at St Pierre D902 right for Réquistay; 3km after Faveyrolles left through Salelles; La Grande Combe signposted.

From Millau D911 towards Cahors. Just after leaving city limits right at 'Chenil' and 'Auberge' crossroads. Signposted. Follow small road for about 2km.

Hans & Nelleke Versteegen
La Grande Combe
12480 Saint Izaire
Aveyron
Tel: (0)5 65 99 45 01
Fax: (0)5 65 99 48 41
E-mail: grande.combe@wanadoo.fr
Web: www.la-grande-combe.nl

Mme Henriette Cassan
Montels
12100 Millau
Aveyron
Tel: (0)5 65 60 51 70

Vast pastures slope away, a castle towers on a rock: it's ideal for outdoors lovers - orchids to hunt, canoeing, climbing, hang-gliding to practise - though with less of a family feel than some. The 16th-century guest *bergerie* has shiny terracotta floors, old beams and white walls; Jean, your friendly farmer host, made a lot of the pine furniture. There are tapestries and antiques smelling of years of polish in the dining room where Véronique's excellent meals of home-grown organic meat and veg are served. Worth staying some time.

Rooms: 2 twins, 2 doubles, 1 triple, 1 room for 4/5, all with bath or shower & wc.

Price: €43 for two; reductions for longer stays.

Meals: Dinner €14.50-€17; good choice of restaurants in Millau.

Closed: Mid-November-March.

From Millau N9 to Aguessac; on way out, D547 right to Compeyre, left in village, follow signs for 2km.

Jean & Véronique Lombard-Pratmarty
Quiers
12520 Compeyre, Aveyron
Tel: (0)5 65 59 85 10
Fax: (0)5 65 59 80 99
E-mail: quiers@wanadoo.fr
Web: www.ifrance.com/quiers

GETTING TO KNOW YOU

Owners and guests both find huge satisfaction in longer stays. You have the time to make real contact with them, their family and their way of life; they have the time to let you into the secrets of their area and point you to the hidden treasures that don't appear in guide books or tourist office literature.

Entry No: 625   Map: **13**

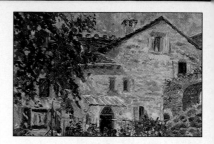

Languedoc-Roussillon

Rugby rouses great passions here, as do corridas and high dramas enacted beneath the Roman arches; down on the coast, traditional water-jousters get less emotional but much wetter.

In an unsung, beautiful part of France, cross the lovely old bridge over the Tarn into Quézac. You'd never guess Marius was a new house, it fits in so perfectly with its old stones, beams and doors and its warm, lived-in feel. Dany and Pierre clearly adore embellishing their home - delightful country-print fabrics for chairs and curtains, a mural of birds flying up the stairs - and spoiling their guests with an amazing array of delicacies, from home-made brioche to home-grown organic veg to their speciality: *gâteau de noix* made with their own walnuts. *Gîte space for 12 people.*

Rooms: 3 doubles, all with shower & wc; 1 twin with bath, shower & wc.

Price: €43-€61 for two.

Meals: Dinner €20, including wine & coffee.

Closed: Never.

From A75 exit 39 on N88 E for 25km; right N106 for Alès 25km; at Ispagnac right to Quézac; signs in village.

Danièle Méjean & Pierre Parentini
La Maison de Marius
8 rue du Pontet
48320 Quézac
Lozère
Tel: (0)4 66 44 25 05
Fax: (0)4 66 44 25 05

Entry No: 626   Map: **13**

Languedoc-Roussillon

Built 200 year ago by Madame's great-grandfather, the fine old *bastide* (fortified farmhouse) stands proudly on the Ardèche River by its own beach. Rooms, some reached by the superb stone staircase, look over the romantic and much-painted ruined bridge or the squirrelly, tall-treed park where shade invites summer lingerers. Madame paints furniture, most prettily, and one room has hand-painted frieze and ceiling; Monsieur can accompany you on canoe trips (you may spot an otter) - an attractive, sociable couple who enjoy their guests. *Gîte space for 8.*

Rooms: 1 quadruple, 1 triple, 2 doubles, 1 twin, all with shower & wc.

Price: €55 for two.

Meals: Good restaurants in village.

Closed: Never.

Your hosts have created a home for themselves and their three children in this fine rambling house. Built in the 18th century as a silkworm farm, it has old stones, arched terraces, a lovely courtyard and is done in their own friendly, informal image: delightful Isabelle is an artist, her touch evident in the imaginative treatment of indoor and outdoor spaces. Breakfast is home-made jams and delicious breads on the shady terrace in summer. You dine here too. Isabelle is interested in cookery from all round the Mediterranean and includes North African and Greek dishes in her repertoire - all very exciting (and the road shouldn't impinge).

Rooms: 2 twins, 1 triple, 1 quadruple, all with shower & wc.

Price: €51 for two.

Meals: Dinner €18, including wine & coffee.

Closed: Never.

From A7 Bollène exit D994 to Pont St Esprit; N86 for Bourg St Andéol; sign before bridge across river.

From Alès D16/D579 NE through Barjac for Vallon Pont d'Arc; 300m after Gendarmerie house on right, arched doorway.

Mme de Verduzan
Pont d'Ardèche
30130 Pont Saint Esprit
Gard
Tel: (0)4 66 39 29 80
Fax: (0)4 66 39 51 80

Antoine & Isabelle Agapitos
Le Mas Escombelle
La Villette
30430 Barjac, Gard
Tel: (0)4 66 24 54 77
Fax: (0)4 66 24 54 77
E-mail: mas-escombel@wanadoo.fr
Web: perso.wanadoo.fr/mas-escombel/

Out among the almond trees of the scented *garrigue*, delicate, energetic Sylvie has restored the old sheep and silk farm with flair and sensitivity. The house is full of secret corners - and hearts (*cœurs*), collected over 20 years and discreetly integrated here; there are garden spaces for all where a fountain fiddles; her marriage of old stones and colour, beams and wall hangings, simple southern furniture and gentle lighting is one of love and good taste - and then she serves tempting Mediterranean meals on the leafy terrace. She adores people, and also knows where to get superior lavender essence.

Rooms: 1 suite for 4 with shower & wc; 1 apartment for 3 with mini-kitchen, shower & wc.

Price: €76 for two.

Meals: Dinner €23, including wine & coffee; restaurants 5-10km.

Closed: Never.

Cassandra's house is in the heart of a delectable 17th-century village. Here she took refuge from Switzerland a while ago - and stayed, delighting in the old stones of her sheltered courtyard, the pergola on the sunny terrace where gentle (canine) Pastis may join you for a glass, the cool vaulted dining room, the pure white walls, superb beds and simple, good furniture of the bedrooms - Swiss design sense and French atmosphere in perfect balance. Good shower rooms too. You will enjoy her direct vivacity and her ability to respect your privacy.

Rooms: 3 doubles, all with shower & wc.

Price: €54 for two.

Meals: Restaurants within walking distance.

Closed: November-March.

From A9 exit Nîmes Ouest N106 to Alès; right D6 for Bagnols/Cèze 19km; D356 left 2km; left to Saussines; house 1st on right.

From A7 exit Bollène for Pt St Esprit & Bagnols/Cèze 19km; left D980 for Barjac 16km; right to St André de R.; park Place de la Mairie: house 20m away.

Sylvie Sommer
Maison Cœurs
Saussines
30580 Bouquet
Gard
Tel: (0)4 66 72 97 53
Fax: (0)4 66 72 81 86
E-mail: shappy@wanadoo.fr

Cassandra Branger
Chez Cassandra
Rue du Four Banal
30630 St André de Roquepertuis
Gard
Tel: (0)4 66 82 19 21
E-mail: chez.cassandra@wanadoo.fr
Web: www.avignon-et-provence.com/bb/cassandra

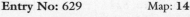

Languedoc-Roussillon

Climb the steps straight into the huge old kitchen to find a long wooden table on an uneven stone floor, an old sideboard along one whitewashed wall, the old stone sink along another. Touches of bright blue and splashes from pretty ochre-yellow plates punctuate the picture. This happy, intelligent couple chat easily, are warm, informal and welcoming. Bedrooms are big and uncluttered; the house is family-relaxed; dinner is good value and a chance to talk about lots of things including local culture and... wine!

Rooms: 2 doubles, 1 suite, all with shower & wc.

Price: €50-€55 for two.

Meals: Dinner €15, including wine & coffee.

Closed: Never.

From Alès D6 E 27km; left D979 beyond Lussan for Barjac 1km; left D187 to Fons sur Lussan; entering village right at fountain; house up on left opp. church.

Michèle Dassonneville
La Magnanerie
30580 Fons sur Lussan
Gard
Tel: (0)4 66 72 81 72
E-mail: la-magnanerie@wanadoo.fr

Entry No: 631   Map: **14**

Ideal for hikers, culture lovers and potters. Madame is delightful and an excellent cook. Monsieur is a very competent *potier* - lovely pottery around the house and a little gallery to buy from. They run a pottery workshop as well as their *chambres d'hôtes* so the atmosphere is busy and creative with lots of interesting people about. The guest rooms, separate from the main house, are simply furnished and guests have a sitting room with a fireplace. Breakfast and dinner (on request) are served on the terrace or in the dining room. Lovely landscape of rolling hills and woods, music festivals and theatrical happenings locally. *Gîte space for 16.*

Rooms: 1 double with shower & wc.

Price: €44 for two.

Meals: Dinner €14, including wine & coffee.

Closed: Never.

From Alès, D16 through Le Saut du Loup. 7 km after Le Saut left D241 for St Julien de Cassagnas; signs.

Michel & Françoise Simonot
Mas Cassac
30500 Allègre
Gard
Tel: (0)4 66 24 85 65
Fax: (0)4 66 24 80 55
E-mail: mas.cassac@online.fr
Web: www.ceramique.com/Mas-Cassac

Entry No: 632   Map: **14**

Languedoc-Roussillon

A sense of distant Britain inhabits the old *mas* upon its Cévennes hillside - books, pictures, trinkets, a certain kind of comfort - but the colours and spaces are so carefully thought out, the dining room so pleasant with its Turkey rugs, that we think you'll like it too. Breakfast is worth being on time for, as generous as the rooms are comfortable; and children are as welcome as you are: Edna is a big-hearted grandmother. The viewful pool and the bountifully-flowered garden are reason enough to stay here, so is the shady pergola for reading beneath... miles from any hassle.

Rooms: 2 doubles, both with bath, shower & wc; 1 double, 1 twin, both with shower & basin, sharing wc.

Price: €60-€75 for two.

Meals: Wide choice within 10km.

Closed: Never.

Sit in the château's large drawing room where a dozen French chairs open their arms. Or wander onto the balcony with panoramic view across river, dramatic viaduct and red-roofed village to the terraced hills beyond. The big beautiful bedrooms have a perfect château feel with their strong-coloured walls setting off the family furniture. Madame, one of an old French silk family who have lived here for several generations, is as elegant and charming as her house - a good cook, too. She will show you where to find really good walks, exciting canoeing, tennis, riding, interesting wildlife spots and ancient buildings to visit nearby.

Rooms: 1 twin, 2 doubles, all with bath or shower & wc.

Price: €58-€74 for two.

Meals: Dinner €22, including wine & coffee.

Closed: Never.

From Alès N110 S; right D910 for Anduze 500m; left D24 to Canaules via Lézan; right D149 to St Nazaire des G., right at railway bridge to Mairie; left; house at bottom on left.

From Millau S on N9 for 19km to La Cavalerie; left D7 for Le Vigan about 50km to Bez; before bridge, sign on left.

Edna & Ted Price
Mas de la Fauguière
30610 Saint Nazaire des Gardies
Gard
Tel: (0)4 66 77 38 67
Fax: (0)4 66 77 11 64

Françoise du Luc
Château Massal
Bez et Esparon
30120 Le Vigan
Gard
Tel: (0)4 67 81 07 60
Fax: (0)4 67 81 07 60

Entry No: 633   Map: **14**

Entry No: 634   Map: **13**

John is a charmer: open-minded, fun and generous, he runs a deliciously relaxed house where either B&B guests share the quiet with him or groups meet for yoga and music workshops. It's a beautiful set of buildings that he is still restoring, as well as working on a film, cooking meals for long, talk-filled, wine-flowed evenings and soaking up the songs of birds, bees and wind in the trees. Rooms are simple and perfect in their white walls, Indian cotton bedcovers for a splash of colour and a mix of French farm antiques and English stripped pine and there's space for all on the various levels of garden that disappear out into the countryside. *Studio with piano available. Gîte space for 8 people.*

Rooms: 1 double, 1 twin sharing shower & wc; 1 triple, 1 family both with shower & wc.

Price: €46-€61 for two.

Meals: Dinner €14, including wine & coffee; restaurants 10km.

Closed: Never.

From Nîmes D999 to St Hippolyte du Fort; D39 towards La Salle for about 10km; house signposted on left.

John Macdonald
Domaine de Bagard
30460 Lasalle
Gard
Tel: (0)4 66 85 25 51
Fax: (0)4 66 85 25 51
E-mail: johnmacdonald@minitel.net

Entry No: 635　　Map: **13**

Philippe 'receives' at his *hôtel particulier*, his private mansion, with warm refinement. His rooms, all very separate and private, each named after a different local luminary (including our own Lawrence Durrell) are in traditional Provençal style: highly-polished floors, white bedcovers, a different and beautiful wall-hanging over each bed; super big bathrooms too. The magic secluded terrace garden with views over the roofs of the old town is where you have breakfast, which to Philippe is a very important moment of the day. Guests have filled the visitors' book with ecstatic comments; yours to come?

Rooms: 4 doubles, 1 twin, 1 triple, all with bath or shower & wc.

Price: €58-€76 for two. Special winter prices.

Meals: Dinner €21.50 including wine & coffee.

Closed: Never.

From Nîmes D40 W 28km to Sommières. Château clearly signed from town centre; park in front.

Philippe de Frémont
Hôtel de l'Orange
Chemin du Château Fort
30250 Sommières, Gard
Tel: (0)4 66 77 79 94
Fax: (0)4 66 80 44 87
E-mail: hotel.dorange@free.fr
Web: hotel.delorange.free.fr

Entry No: 636　　Map: **14**

There is a slightly Moorish feel to the rooms that Marion has so lovingly put together in her 17th-century house. With a natural sense of style, she has placed beautiful pieces of furniture and paintings just where they enhance the rooms' generous proportions. Her cooking also has a North African influence as well as the Provençal specialities one would expect. Candlelit dinner under the pergola in a lovely walled garden, huge breakfast the next morning including cold meats, cheese and local *fougasse* (a soft delicate bread), and the usual French delicacies - bliss! A truly special place.

Rooms: 2 double, each with shower & wc; 1 suite with bath & wc.

Price: €65-€95 for two.

Meals: Dinner €25, including wine & coffee.

Closed: Never.

From A9 exit 26 S to Aimargues Centre. Cross roundabout with fountain down lane of plane trees for 300m. Entrance Rue de la Violette (3 cypresses behind garden wall).

Marion Escarfail
26 boulevard Saint Louis
30470 Aimargues
Gard
Tel: (0)4 66 88 52 99
Fax: (0)4 66 88 52 99
E-mail: marionmais@aol.com
Web: members.aol.com/marionmais

A path through the woods leads from the house to the river by the Pont du Gard, a World Heritage site - the setting is truly wonderful. Indoors, the décor is fulsome, definitely idiosyncratic - a net canopy over one of the beds, hanging hats, splayed fans, silk flowers, etc. The rooms are themed. *La Provençale* has a small connecting room with bunk beds and soft toys for the younger guest. Monsieur works in Nîmes but gives all his remaining time to welcoming and caring for his guests. The swimming pool is an added enticement and bedrooms have air-conditioning. *Gîte space for 11 people.*

Rooms: 1 suite, 2 doubles, 2 twin with bath or shower & wc.

Price: €80 for two.

Meals: Dinner €24-€32, including wine & coffee.

Closed: October-March.

From Remoulins follow signs for Pont du Gard 'Rive Droite'. Signposted on right.

Gérard Cristini
La Terre des Lauriers
Rive Droite - Pont du Gard
30210 Remoulins, Gard
Tel: (0)4 66 37 19 45
Fax: (0)4 66 37 19 45
E-mail: gerard.cristini@laterredeslauriers.com
Web: www.laterredeslauriers.com

John, who will welcome you with exuberance to the 19th-century *maison de maître* he has restored with Michel, is a joiner who also has an excellent eye for interior design and decoration while Michel does the cooking and the garden. They are a delightful couple. From the classic black and white tiles of the entrance hall to the carefully-planned lighting in the bedrooms, every detail has been attended to. A very generous breakfast is served under the chestnut trees or by the pool; afterwards you can wander off to join in lazy Provençal village life, visit Avignon, Uzès or nearby Lussan, the fortified Cévenol village.

Rooms: 2 doubles, 1 twin, all with bath or shower & wc; 1 large twin with bath, shower & wc.

Price: €85-€95 for two.

Meals: Dinner €30, including wine & coffee.

Closed: Never.

Lovely, long stone buildings enfold the two-tier courtyard, great trees give generous shade, the Cévennes hillsides march away behind. It is enchanting. Your young and welcoming Dutch hosts are still renovating but the garden and lawn around the pool, the glowing old furniture are already a triumph. Bedrooms are simple: light and white, very separate from each other round the courtyard. Esther really loves cooking - good regional dishes, outside or in their beautiful dining room. *Her sister has another B&B nearby. Minimum 2 nights stay in winter. Gîte space for 6.*

Rooms: 3 doubles, all with shower & wc.

Price: €52-€65 for two.

Meals: Dinner €21.

Closed: Never.

From A9 exit 23 W to Uzès 19km. D979 N 7.5km; right D238 to La Bruguière. House on big square next to Mairie (vast Micocourier tree in front).

From Uzès D981 to Montaren for 6km; right D337 to St Médiers; in village cont. up & around to right. House on left.

John Karavias & Michel Comas
Les Marronniers
30580 La Bruguière
Gard
Tel: (0)4 66 72 84 77
Fax: (0)4 66 72 85 78
E-mail: les.marronniers@12stay.co.uk
Web: www.les.marronniers.12stay.co.uk

Léonard Robberts & Esther Küchler
Mas d'Oléandre
Hameau St Médiers
30700 Montaren et St Médiers, Gard
Tel: (0)4 66 22 63 43
Fax: (0)4 66 03 14 06
E-mail: oleandre@provence-sud.com
Web: www.provence-sud.com/oleandre

A magical, mostly 17th-century moated château (parts are 12th-century) with its very own ghost, *la Dame à la Rose*. Towers overlook the monumental courtyard where Mary Stuart (later Queen of Scots) once walked. Madame runs a cultural centre and stages a summer music festival; this is a château that works. Breakfast is in the courtyard or in the dining room. The vast bedrooms, some with round tower bathrooms, have been renovated with colourful details such as bright new satin canopies. Thoughtfulness like 'no lawn-mowing during siesta-time' is typical of the attitude here.

Rooms: 3 doubles, 2 quadruples, 1 twin, all with bath & wc.

Price: €84 for two.

Meals: Plenty of restaurants nearby.

Closed: Never.

Helen and Jacques met while working in Africa, where she was a nurse and Jacques an agriculturist - they are an interesting and concerned couple (10% of their B&B income goes to development projects) and the house has many African mementoes and lots of pine. Theirs is a simple village home where guests have space in their vaulted ground-floor suite and, although it's right on the street, there's very little traffic in enchanting Pujaut. The pretty, peaceful, terraced garden now has a summer kitchen for guests but is not really suitable for adventurous toddlers. Super folk with whom to share good conversation over delicious suppers.

Rooms: 1 suite for 4 with shower & wc.

Price: €40 for two.

Meals: Dinner €12.50, including wine & coffee.

Closed: Never.

From Avignon, N580 for Bagnols/Cèze. At junction in L'Ardoise, left D9 for Laudun; signs.

From Avignon N580 for Bagnols/Cèze; right D377 & D177 to Pujaut. In village head for Mairie; Saba'ad 300m into old village from Mairie & church.

Gisèle & Jean-Louis Bastouil
Château de Lascours
30290 Laudun
Gard
Tel: (0)4 66 50 39 61
Fax: (0)4 66 50 30 08
E-mail: chateau.de.lascours@wanadoo.fr

Helen Thompson & Jacques Sergent
Saba'ad
Place des Consuls
30131 Pujaut
Gard
Tel: (0)4 90 26 31 68
Fax: (0)4 90 26 31 68

Go through high double doors in a peaceful Provençal village to find this lovely converted barn and small house. The Rousseaus are warm, friendly people and really enjoy having guests to stay. Joël paints watercolours and Michèle is a keen and good cook. Meal times are flexible, the atmosphere relaxed and the sheltered courtyard or cosy dining room very conducive to lingering chat. The cottagey, beamed bedrooms have good solid furniture, wooden floors, plants, patchwork counterpanes and sensible bathrooms. An easy place to be, 10 minutes from Avignon, 20 minutes from Nîmes and in excellent rosé wine, olive and fruit country.

Rooms: 1 double with bath & wc.

Price: €43 for two.

Meals: Dinner €12, including wine & coffee.

Closed: Never.

A village or not a village? It feels like one and is a perfect place to stay when Avignon itself is heaving with people. A former stable block, the house is next door to *La Chartreuse de Villeneuve*, a beautiful 13th-century monastery, now a European Centre for Literature and Theatre. Pascale runs the Écuries as a B&B but you really have a fully equipped studio, so can opt to be independent. But don't think she doesn't want you! She is on hand with breakfast, information and magazines you can borrow, and an aperitif before you head out for the evening.

Rooms: 2 doubles, 1 suite, all with bath, shower & wc.

Price: €60-€84 for two.

Meals: Good choice of restaurants nearby.

Closed: Never.

From Avignon & Villeneuve N580 for Bagnols/Cèze; right on D377 & D177 to Pujaut. House opp. town hall; large wooden door.

From Avignon cross the Rhône for Nîmes/ Villeneuve lès A. Just after bridge right for Villeneuve centre, Rue de la République. House next to La Chartreuse.

Joël & Michèle Rousseau
Les Bambous
Rue de la Mairie
30131 Pujaut
Gard
Tel: (0)4 90 26 46 47
Fax: (0)4 90 26 46 47
E-mail: rousseau.michele@wanadoo.fr

Pascale Letellier
Les Écuries des Chartreux
66 rue de la République
30400 Villeneuve lès Avignon, Gard
Tel: (0)4 90 25 79 93
Fax: (0)4 90 25 79 93
E-mail: ecuries-chartreux@avignon-et-provence.com
Web: www.avignon-et-provence.com/ecuries-chartreux

Entry No: 643   Map: **14**

Entry No: 644   Map: **14**

In these superbly wild, pastoral surroundings with great walking and climbing trails, you bathe in simplicity, stream-babble and light. Your hosts, hard-working walnut and chestnut growers, have carefully transformed their barn for guests: country antiques, old cotton lace curtains, new bedding and soft blue tones relax the eye; there's a fireplace and a full kitchen too. Monsieur has a real, friendly handshake, Madame is gentle and welcoming - they are lovely people running a genuine B&B despite the separate quarters. Breakfast on the shady terrace includes cheese or walnuts or honey.

Rooms: 2 doubles, 1 single, all with bath & wc.

Price: €43 for two.

Meals: Self-catering; restaurants nearby.

Closed: December-March except by arrangement.

The shyly friendly Dutch owners of the elegant Cerisaie came to visit, fell in love with it and bought it, lock, stock and furniture. Honorah serves a fabulous lunch buffet from 12 till 5pm: catch it early before or late after a long wild walk. She has also hung lots of her attractive paintings, a personal touch these classically-proportioned rooms really respond to. Breakfast is in the soft yellow-painted, green-panelled dining room. A proud old staircase mounts to the bedrooms which are just right - light, roomy, marble-fireplaced, old-furnished, double-glazed against the road, with super views of hills and the truly lovely garden. *Gîte space for 4.*

Rooms: 3 doubles, 2 twins, 1 suite for 2 with kitchenette, all with bath or shower & wc.

Price: €59.50-€74.50 for two.

Meals: Lunch à la carte; Dinner €19.50 Wednesdays. Good restaurant nearby.

Closed: 1 November-Easter.

From Mazamet N112 towards St Pons de Thomières. At Courniou, left to Prouilhe; farm on left.

From A9 exit Béziers Ouest; D64 then N112 for Castres/Mazamet/St Pons; 1km before St Pons right D908 to Riols; house on left leaving Riols.

Éliane & Jean-Louis Lunes
La Métairie Basse
Hameau de Prouilhe
34220 Courniou
Hérault
Tel: (0)4 67 97 21 59
Fax: (0)4 67 97 21 59

Honorah & Albert Jan Karsten
La Cerisaie
1 avenue de Bédarieux
34220 Riols
Hérault
Tel: (0)4 67 97 03 87
Fax: (0)4 67 97 03 88
E-mail: cerisaie@wanadoo.fr

In an enchanting village, this fine house has been revivified by a New Zealander who runs cookery courses and an English photographer. The red door opens onto a high cool hall, old stone stairs lead past a trompe-l'œil scene to delicately decorated bedrooms in mainly modern style with good new shower rooms and some super views to the hillside. One room glories in an incongruous baronial fireplace; one is on the ground floor. You can walk, ride, climb rocks; swim, canoe in the river; follow Denis's wine trail; visit the unusual succulent garden - and return drunk with exertion and beauty for a superb, civilised meal on the terrace with your delightful hosts. *Gîte space for 4.*

Rooms: 2 doubles, 2 twins, 1 suite, all with shower & wc.

Price: €65-€72.50 for two.

Meals: Dinner €27, including wine & coffee.

Closed: November.

From Béziers N112 W for St Pons for 1-2km; right D14 through Maraussan, Cazouls lès Béziers, Cessenon to Roquebrun; signs in village.

Denis & Sarah La Touche
Les Mimosas
Avenue des Orangers
34460 Roquebrun, Hérault
Tel: (0)4 67 89 61 36
Fax: (0)4 67 89 61 36
E-mail: la-touche.les-mimosas@wanadoo.fr
Web: perso.wanadoo.fr/les-mimosas/

Entry No: 647   Map: 13

"The exotic appearance of the vegetation matches the anachronism of the architecture adding to the impression of a theatrical décor". How's that for a start? "Vast, amazing" - the brochure lies not. Towers, turrets, troubadour style – yet a very simple welcome from Marie-France and her children; she is a remarkable and courageous woman. Crystal chandeliers, grand piano, original wallpapers, cavernous rooms with great beamed ceilings, lovely inner courtyard, delightful gardens, defensive walls – it is all 19th century, has adopted the comforts of this century and retained the traditions of hospitality of another. Worth every penny. *Gîte space for 7.*

Rooms: 2 doubles, 1 twin, all with bath & wc.

Price: €94.50-€102.50 for two; suite €149.50 for four.

Meals: Dinner €15.50, including wine & coffee.

Closed: Never.

From A75 exit 35 Béziers; Château on D909, 20km south of Bédarieux.

Mme Marie-France Lanson
Château de Grézan
34480 Laurens
Hérault
Tel: (0)4 67 90 28 03
Fax: (0)4 67 90 05 03
E-mail: chateau-grezan.lanson@wanadoo.fr

Entry No: 648   Map: 13

Dominating the little town spread in rings below it, the splendid 15th-century château has vastly thick walls and ungrand châteauesque bedrooms, much favoured for wedding nights. They are decorated in loving and careful detail by Marie-Laure with rich, soft-coloured fabrics and just enough good furniture. She washes and irons the antique hand-embroidered bed linen herself and has found some lovely china for her special breakfasts in the highly-furnished dining room or the pretty courtyard, planted by its delightful, devoted new owners. Lots to do here: canoeing, wine-tasting, super medieval fête in July.

Rooms: 1 double, 2 triples, 1 suite for 3, all with shower & wc.

Price: €70 for two.

Meals: Restaurants nearby; self-catering possible.

Closed: Never.

From A9 exit 35 for Centre Ville; at 1st & 2nd r'abouts: head for Bédarieux; 3rd r'about: for Corneilhan/Murviel; château in Murviel centre.

Augustin Rousselet & Marie-Laure Bernard
Château de Murviel
1 place Georges Clémenceau
34490 Murviel lès Béziers, Hérault
Tel: (0)4 67 32 35 45
Fax: (0)4 67 32 35 25
E-mail: chateau-de-murviel@wanadoo.fr
Web: www.murviel.com

The famous, tree-lined, much-cycled Canal du Midi runs through this lovely medieval village and the old townhouse looks pretty grand. Yet nothing prepares you for its château-like interior: ceilings magnificent in their 18th and 19th-century paintings, walls frescoed with Languedoc scenes, a superb marble staircase spiralling up a medieval tower - all reminders of four centuries of grandeur. Big, comfortable rooms have two-metre beds, power showers and much attention to authentic detail; your friendly Australian hostess is genuinely welcoming; and you are only 5 km from the sea. *Gîte space for 2 people.*

Rooms: 2 doubles, 2 twins, all with bath or shower & wc.

Price: €50 for two.

Meals: Dinner €18, including wine & coffee.

Closed: Never.

From A9 exit Béziers Est to Villeneuve; N112 then D37 to town centre; house opp. Hôtel de Ville.

Jennifer-Jane Viner
7 rue de la Fontaine
34420 Villeneuve lès Béziers
Hérault
Tel: (0)4 67 39 87 15
Fax: (0)4 67 32 00 95
E-mail: anges-gardiens@wanadoo.fr

Languedoc-Roussillon

Madame, an artist and sculptor, is an open, fun person who loves getting to know her guests, showing them her work, even teaching them to sculpt (do enquire). Her modern house has lots of artistic atmosphere and big, simply-furnished rooms, each with a few lovely things, good fabrics and a private outside space onto the green garden. The surroundings are worth the trip too: you are up on the hillside, protected by umbrella pines, above the magnificent Salagou lake - perfect sailing and swimming on those long, hot summer's days, wonderful biking, walking and riding in winter. Definitely worth staying two nights or more.

Rooms: 2 doubles, both with bath or shower & wc.

Price: €43-€50 for two.

Meals: 2 restaurants 3.5km.

Closed: Never.

A9 exit 34 on D13 N 10km; N9 to Clermont l'Hérault; D156 left for Lac du Salagou 3km; left to Liausson; 700m along last house on right before woods.

M & Mme Neveu
La Genestière
Route de Liausson
34800 Clermont l'Hérault, Hérault
Tel: (0)4 67 96 30 97/(0)4 67 96 18 46
Fax: (0)4 67 96 32 56
Web: www.mediatisse.com/Lac-du-Salagou/genestie/genestie.htm

Entry No: 651　　　　Map: **13**

A vast and lovely stone winery is the guest wing on this old family property. Your host's sensitive conversion uses old tiles, doors and beams; high bedrooms are designed for comfort and privacy, each with an excellent shower room, superb bedding and French windows onto the well-caressed garden courtyard. Jean-François and his mother happily share their living space: go through the big hall, hung with some fine prints, to breakfast in the pleasing living room where a cabinet of treasures will intrigue. Outside, a discreet pool glimmers under a vast umbrella pine.

Rooms: 4 doubles, all with shower & wc.

Price: €66 for two.

Meals: Restaurants 3-12km.

Closed: Never.

From Clermont L'Hérault N9 r'about D4 for Brignac 3.5km; house on right entering village.

Jean-François Martin
La Missare
9 route de Clermont
34800 Brignac
Hérault
Tel: (0)4 67 96 07 67
Fax: (0)4 67 50 14 11
E-mail: la.missare@free.fr

Entry No: 652　　　　Map: **13**

Languedoc-Roussillon

A perfect B&B on a superb estate with mulberry-lined drive, hills, vineyards and a real family atmosphere: simplicity, space, peace, fine big rooms and a genuine welcome. The delightful, hard-working owners have four children of their own and run an inn in their beautifully-restored old family house. In a separate building, guest rooms have soft-coloured walls, generous mezzanines, pretty shower rooms. The big dining room has old honey-coloured beams - a dream - and gives onto the terrace and rows of vines beyond: just the place to try a glass of estate wine followed by an authentic auberge dinner.

Rooms: 4 double/quadruples, all with shower & wc.

Price: €54 for two.

Meals: Dinner €19, including wine & coffee; pizzeria & brasserie 3-5km.

Closed: Last week in October.

On the edge of a wild, unspoilt forest, in a green oasis flooded with mimosa, hibiscus and iris where 36 tortoises roam freely, it's hard to believe you're just 3km from lively Montpellier. The house is recent, built with old materials, its young vegetation already thick and rich, the swimming pool set among atmospheric stone 'ruins'. You sleep in rooms full of family furniture and colourful fabrics which share a very good bathroom. Your hostess, once a city girl in public relations, loves this place and her tortoises passionately (she knows each one by name), talks easily and is excellent company. *Gîte space for 2.*

Rooms: 2 doubles, sharing shower & separate wc.

Price: €58-€88.50 for two.

Meals: Montpellier 3km.

Closed: Never.

From Gignac east towards Montpellier; at the edge of town 'Hérault Cuisines' on right; turn right and follow signs for 3km.

Isabelle & Baudouin Thillaye de Boullay
Domaine du Pélican
34150 Gignac
Hérault
Tel: (0)4 67 57 68 92
Fax: (0)4 67 57 68 92

From Mairie in Castelnau le Lez take Rue Jules Ferry; 5th left Chemin de la Rocheuse; last house on left.

Dominique Carabin-Cailleau
289 chemin de la Rocheuse
34170 Castelnau le Lez
Hérault
Tel: (0)4 67 72 63 08
Fax: (0)4 67 72 63 08
E-mail: dpcc@libertysurf.fr
Web: www.multimania.com/castlecottage

Entry No: 653   Map: **13**

Entry No: 654   Map: **13**

Off the typical sun-drenched sleepy village street with its arched doorways and shuttered windows, the big gates open onto a fine old village house. At the back, your eye leaps straight out to the parallel vines and uneven hills - a festival of flaming colour in autumn. Monsieur is English; Madame is French and an artist. She is good company and has done up her house with great sympathy for its original spaces and stone floors. Her works are a bonus on the walls. It is a privilege to be her only guests, enjoy the big ground-floor bedroom that gives onto the garden and step out into the morning light for home-made fig jam.

Rooms: 1 double with bathroom & wc.

Price: €54 for two.

Meals: Choice of restaurants 5km.

Closed: Never.

In an exquisitely peaceful, leafy garden, here is a dream house, beautifully restored, with elegant old features including a mosaic tiled hallway, fine wooden chevron floors, old radiators and wood-panelled ceilings. Enormous, immaculate bedrooms have been renovated and decorated in individual styles with tremendous attention to detail and the finer creature comforts, such as candles in the bathrooms. The multi-lingual owners, originally from Belgium, adore meeting people, making them feel at home and chatting around a welcome drink. No wonder people keep coming back for more.

Rooms: 4 doubles, 1 suite, both with shower and/or bath & wc.

Price: €60-€70 for two.

Meals: Restaurants in village.

Closed: November-March.

From A9 exit 27 on D34 Sommières; left to St Christol; main road right of post office for Cave Coopérative; left at r'bout before small bridge, right for 800m, left Av. des Bruyères then Rue de l'Église.

From A61 exit Lezignan-Corbieres for Fabrezan 6km; yellow signs to Chambres d'Hôtes.

Monique Sykes-Maillon
La Ciboulette
221 rue de l'Église
34400 Saint Christol, Hérault
Tel: (0)4 67 86 81 00
Fax: (0)4 67 86 81 00
E-mail: happy@stchristol.com
Web: www.stchristol.com

Mieke Machiels & Jan Wouters
Lou Castelet
Place de la République
11200 Fabrezan, Aude
Tel: (0)4 68 43 56 98
Fax: (0)4 68 43 56 98
E-mail: lou.castelet@bigfoot.com
Web: lou.castelet.free.fr

The big inviting bedrooms, called *Syrah, Chardonnay...* to reflect Jacques' passion for his wild and wonderful Cathar country and its wines - have a superb feeling of space and light. Divine smells rise from the kitchen where Françoise is baking cakes for tomorrow's breakfast to be served on the stone terrace that leads to the garden. She so clearly loves having guests to cook for and chat to. Wide stone stairs, old pieces of furniture and soothing colours, all well thought out, plus the owners' big smiles make this house most comfortable and welcoming. "A little corner of Paradise", reported one guest - and excellent value. *Gîte space for 6 people.*

Rooms: 4 doubles, 1 twin, with bath or shower & wc.

Price: €61-€65 for two.

Meals: Dinner €23, including wine & coffee.

Closed: Never.

From A61 exit 25 for Lezignan; D212 for Fabrezan (back over A61); D106 to Ferrals les Corbières; D161 to Boutenac; signposted in village.

Françoise & Jacques Camel
La Bastide des Corbières
17 rue de la Révolution
11200 Boutenac, Aude
Tel: (0)4 68 27 20 61
Fax: (0)4 68 27 62 71
E-mail: bastide.corbieres@wanadoo.fr
Web: perso.wanadoo.fr/bastide.corbieres

Entry No: 657   **Map: 13**

Art-lovers are happy here for bubbly energetic Martine and her husband are passionate about art and the house is full of his paintings and sculptures. Tea-lovers too, for she has more than 40 types on offer. It's a comfortable place, endearingly faded around some edges, with strong colours and dark furniture in the bedrooms. Meals are on the terrace or in the kitchen by the massive marble-topped open fireplace. There's tennis in the village and the Canal du Midi 200m away. *Gîte space for 4 people.*

Rooms: 2 doubles, both with shower & wc.

Price: €46 for two.

Meals: Dinner €17, including wine & coffee (not July or August).

Closed: November-mid-March.

From Narbonne N113 to Capendu; left at 1st traffic light to Marseillette; right after bridge over the Aude; house 100m on right.

Martine de Roulhac
Demeure La Fargue
16 avenue de la Belle Aude
11800 Marseillette
Aude
Tel: (0)4 68 79 13 88
Fax: (0)4 68 79 13 88

Entry No: 658   **Map: 13**

Languedoc-Roussillon

Sally has thrown her energies into turning her 17th-century coaching inn into a well-balanced marriage of solid old French base and modern inspiration. Having lived in England and America, where she was an interior designer, she has completely adopted France and her sense of style permeates the old house in a comfortable mix of antique and contemporary pieces. She is also a superb cook, making delicious Mediterranean-inspired dishes with the best local produce, provides all possible goodies in her big, well-furnished bedrooms and loves to share her passion for, and books on, history and travel. *Children over 12 welcome. 2 nights minimum June-September.*

Rooms: 2 doubles, 1 suite for 4, all with bath & wc.

Price: €61 for two.

Meals: Dinner €30, including wine & coffee.

Closed: Never.

From Carcassonne N113 to Trèbes; left D610 to Homps; left D910 to Olonzac; follow signs to Pépieux - blue shuttered house next to church.

Sally Worthington
Le Vieux Relais
1 rue de l'Étang
11700 Pépieux, Aude
Tel: (0)4 68 91 69 29
Fax: (0)4 68 91 65 49
E-mail: sally.worthington@wanadoo.fr
Web: perso.wanadoo.fr/carrefourbedbreakfast/

Entry No: 659   **Map: 13**

Coming in from the magnificent gardens, you catch a wonderful smell of herbs as you walk through the house. The happy new owners, educated, well-travelled and charming, moved here from east France for a more relaxing way of life and climate. Using exquisite taste, they have combined original 18th-century elegances with new necessities in big bedrooms and bathrooms of pure luxury, each with its own lovely colour scheme. Outside, there are shaded spots for all, a superb 150-year-old cedar, olive trees and a salt-water swimming-pool surrounded by roses with covered terrace for relaxing. A place of great beauty.

Rooms: 1 twin, 3 doubles, 1 suite for 4, all with bath, shower & wc.

Price: €77-€130 for two.

Meals: Dinner €23, including wine & coffee; restaurants in Carcassonne.

Closed: January-February.

From A61 exit 23 for Mazamet; at r'about D620 for Villalier; after 1.5km, towards Villedubert; house on right, through wrought iron gates.

Christophe & Catherine Pariset
Domaine Saint Pierre de Trapel
11620 Villemoustaussou
Aude
Tel: (0)4 68 77 00 68
Fax: (0)4 68 77 01 68
E-mail: cpariset@trapel.com
Web: www.trapel.com

Entry No: 660   **Map: 14**

The House is on a Hill overlooking medieval Carcassonne, just a short kilometre through the vines. A quiet and sumptuous haven from bustling postcard sellers, it is ablaze with colour inside and out, full of pictures, lovely old furniture and treasures (hats, handmade pots, straw sandals). The wonderfully festooned bedrooms have bathrooms to match - one with a two-body shower. Madame is open and generous, serves a fantastic array of home-made jams at breakfast on the terrace and is helped by her daughter who also made the striking coffee table of polished cement and iron. *Gîte space for 4 people.*

Rooms: 4 doubles, 1 apartment for 4, all with shower or bath & wc.

Price: €54-€92 for two.

Meals: Dinner €23, including wine & coffee.

Closed: January-February.

Go to Carcassonne Cité main gate, pass cemetery on right; follow Chambres d'Hôtes signs for 1km along narrow lane through vineyards. Well signposted.

Mme Nicole Galinier
La Maison sur la Colline
Sainte Croix
11000 Carcassonne
Aude
Tel: (0)4 68 47 57 94
Fax: (0)4 68 47 57 94
E-mail: nicole.galinier@wanadoo.fr

Entry No: 661   Map: **13**

Rigby has lovingly renovated the old pharmacy, preserving the elegant oak staircase where old theatre posters clothe the red walls, the sitting-room marble fireplace (music scores on these walls), the beautiful wooden fireplace in the warm green dining room. Masses of antiques and works of art, but the house feels very lived in. French windows lead to the oh-so-peaceful garden, a two-part paradise: swimming pool on one side and formal box hedging on the other with deep borders, shingle paths, shady trees and the relaxing sound of running water. Rigby is intelligent, amusing and incredibly artistic - you will enjoy being here.

Rooms: 1 twin, 3 doubles, all with bath or shower & wc.

Price: €45-€55 for two.

Meals: Dinner €28, including wine & coffee; restaurant 1km.

Closed: Never.

From A61 exit 22 to Bram. At r'about follow signs for Centre Ville; right at traffic lights; house 200m on right.

Rigby Holmes Field
Le Lierre
2 avenue Ernest Léotard
11150 Bram, Aude
Tel: (0)4 68 76 52 01
Fax: (0)4 68 76 60 30
E-mail: lelierrebram@aol.com
Web: www.lelierre.com

Entry No: 662   Map: **13**

There are space and air galore in this 19th-century gentleman-farmer's house - the freshly-decorated bedrooms are vast, comfortably furnished (plus good mattresses) and impeccably clean and the restful gardens cover one whole hectare. A generous breakfast is served on the terrace in fine weather. Madame, open and welcoming, willingly chats to guests in her big warm kitchen and enjoys their travellers' tales. You are in the country yet so near the buzz of Carcassonne while the dreamy Canal du Midi and the vineyards offer their seductively parallel alternatives. *Gîte space for 5 people.*

Rooms: 1 double, 1 triple, 1 suite for 4/5, all with shower & wc.

Price: €50-€58 for two.

Meals: Choice of restaurants nearby.

Closed: Never.

Resplendent in huge beams, an open fireplace and impeccable taste throughout, the beautifully-converted farmhouse has five pretty rooms (one for disabled), utter quiet to relax into and wonderful walks around. Diana is lively, attentive and a superb cook, though meals, served in the enormous dining room or outside, have been known to run late. She and Chris revel in the area, its birdlife, wild flowers, history and wine. They have lovely children (and well-behaved large dogs) and give language courses in winter. And all this just 5km from Carcassonne, 10km from an 18-hole golf course. *Minimum stay 2 nights May-September.*

Rooms: 3 doubles, 1 twin, 1 triple, all with bath or shower & wc.

Price: €55.50-€64 for two.

Meals: Dinner €25, including wine & coffee.

Closed: January & November.

On A61 exit Carcassonne-West to Salvaza airport; stay on D119 for approx. 4km more. House signposted on left.

From Carcassonne D142 to Cazilhac. Left opp. Mairie D56 for Villefloure (bear left at cemetery); right fork at wine bottle for 2km; left at Sauzette sign.

Isabelle Clayette
Domaine des Castelles
11170 Caux et Sauzens
Aude
Tel: (0)4 68 72 03 60
Fax: (0)4 68 72 03 60

Chris Gibson & Diana Warren
Ferme de la Sauzette
Route de Villefloure, Cazilhac
11570 Palaja, Aude
Tel: (0)4 68 79 81 32
Fax: (0)4 68 79 65 99
E-mail: info@lasauzette.com
Web: www.lasauzette.com

Entry No: 663   Map: **13**

Entry No: 664   Map: **13**

Languedoc-Roussillon

There are donkeys and goats roaming around and as this is definitely Cathar country, the rooms are named after Cathar castles. They are ordered rather than cosy but the cool impression of alarm clocks and televisions is dispelled by the Ropers' warm personal attention and the library of 1,000 books, many on the Cathars, many on cookery. Breakfast is hearty with several types of bread, honey, cheese, home-made cakes and jams. Supper could be grilled salmon with lemon sauce and Madame's crème caramel. Nearby are fortified Carcassonne, medieval Foix and Mirepoix. Wonderful setting.

Rooms: 2 doubles, 1 twin, all with shower & wc (& children's room).

Price: €53-€56 for two. Discount on stays of more than 3 days.

Meals: Dinner €20, including wine & coffee.

Closed: Never.

This well-travelled, cosmopolitan Scottish family have turned their house into a perfect Pyrenean haven among some of Europe's wildest, remotest landscapes. It has a magical garden full of lush vegetation and intimate sitting areas among the trees, dazzling views past snow-capped mountains down to the sea, romantic and comfortable rooms decorated with original works of art and bright scatter cushions. Two rooms offer the private bliss of walking from bed to terrace for breakfast, delivered by Kim - she is an exceptionally warm and lovely person. *Children welcome with parental supervision (pool).*

Rooms: 3 doubles, 1 twin, 1 suite all with shower & wc.

Price: €84-€130 for two.

Meals: Excellent restaurant 400m or choice in village; barbecue available.

Closed: December-January.

From Limoux D620 for Chalabre 7km; fork right D626 for Mirepoix to Peyrefitte. Signposted from village.

A9 to Spain, last exit before border; into Céret for Centre Ville then for Hôtel La Terrasse au Soleil. House 300m after hotel, on left.

Jean-Pierre & Marie-Claire Ropers
Domaine de Couchet
11230 Peyrefitte du Razès
Aude
Tel: (0)4 68 69 55 06
Fax: (0)4 68 69 55 06
E-mail: jean.pierre.ropers@fnac.net

Kim & Gill Bethell
La Châtaigneraie
Route de Fontfrède
66400 Céret, Pyrénées-Orientales
Tel: (0)4 68 87 21 58
Fax: (0)4 68 87 68 16
E-mail: kimmie@club-internet.fr
Web: www.ceret.net

Entry No: 665   **Map: 13**

Entry No: 666   **Map: 18**

This typical Catalonian farmhouse has stood dramatically on its hillside of Mediterranean *maquis* and vineyards for 200 years. Your hosts have built an extension and made it a perfect place for all lovers of nature, walking and good food. Lucie is a passionate cook with a repertoire, using lots of organics, that reflects her cosmopolitan, polyglot background. Breakfast is remarkable, too. She and Jacques radiate warm, intelligent hospitality and the common rooms in the old house are the expressions of their personalities. The superbly-equipped bedrooms in the modern block are less romantic but utterly comfortable.

Rooms: 1 double, 1 twin, 2 triples, 1 family, all with shower & wc.

Price: €53 for two.

Meals: Dinner €21, including wine & coffee.

Closed: October-March.

From A9 exit 42 on D612 to Thuir; D615 W for 5km; left just before D58 for 1.5km; drive on right (1km, steep, winding, paved).

Lucie & Jacques Boulitrop
Le Mas Félix
66300 Camelas
Pyrénées-Orientales
Tel: (0)4 68 53 46 71
Fax: (0)4 68 53 40 54
E-mail: lucie.boulitrop@wanadoo.fr

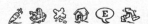

Entry No: 667   Map: **18**

It feels almost Moroccan, this old Catalan house, as it unfolds onto its exposed stone and beams, pine floors and terracotta tiles. The walled pool is perfect; the surrounding wild hills are the garden. Big, airy, well-equipped bedrooms and the upstairs *salon* (music and books) look out to those great hills, to the sea, or to the vineyards. Your host, an ex-professional trumpet player, really knows his regional wines, which are served with dinner (he's an excellent cook). It's perfect after the delights of Collioure, cloisters and Cathar castles (Spain, sea and mountains are all 40 minutes away). *Main house occasionally available to rent. Gîte space for 2-12.*

Rooms: 1 double, 1 triple, 1 suite for 4, all with shower or bath & wc.

Price: €50 for two.

Meals: Dinner €20, including wine & coffee.

Closed: Never.

From A9 exit 42 on D612 west for Thuir. Just before Thuir D615 south to Fourques; D2 west 11km to Caixas (on right). First house on left.

Ian Mayes
Mas Saint Jacques
66300 Caixas
Pyrénées-Orientales
Tel: (0)4 68 38 87 83
Fax: (0)4 68 38 87 83
E-mail: masstjacq@aol.com

Entry No: 668   Map: **18**

The drive up is spectacular so do take your time. Arrive for a drink on the terrace, a gasp at the view across the valley and time to stay and unwind. Judas trees enchant, bright flowers tumble over terraces, the 400-year-old house has nooks and crannies around a small courtyard, cosy bedrooms, a magnificent vaulted sitting room, plus heated pool, sauna, telescope, music system, stupendous walking... Henri is smiling and positive, Jacote quieter and twinkly; they are good, interesting hosts and provide excellent food (home-made sorbets are a real treat) with locally-made ingredients (also for sale).

Rooms: 3 doubles, 1 twin, 2 family rooms, all with shower & wc.

Price: €59.50-€72 for two.

Meals: Dinner €20, including wine & coffee.

Closed: December-April, except by arrangement.

Rhône Valley-Alps

In the valley where once horn-helmetted Gauls harassed Roman legions, the country's greatest chefs now reign and among the chilly peaks the marmot warms his furry cockles with Savoy's richly gooey *fondue*.

From Joyeuse D203 towards Valgorge. At Pont du Gua cross bridge and take narrow paved road up hillside to La Roche (10 hairpins in 3km!).

Henri & Jacote Rouvière
La Petite Cour Verte
07110 La Roche Beaumont
Ardèche
Tel: (0)4 75 39 58 88
Fax: (0)4 75 39 43 00
E-mail: henri.rouviere@wanadoo.fr
Web: www.lapetitecourverte.com

Entry No: 669   **Map: 14**

How to describe paradise in one short paragraph? The setting: high, rural, hidden, silent. The views: long, of mountain peaks, inspiring. The house: lovingly restored, of stone, and wood from the surrounding chestnut forests, light, open, lovely. Bedrooms: just right. Food: organic, home-grown, imaginative... and there's lots of honey. Your hosts are warm and trusting, quickly your friends. Gil is a carpenter in winter and a beekeeper in summer. Come up the long narrow road to walk, talk, and believe us.

Rooms: 1 suite for 5, 1 triple, 1 double, all with shower & wc.

Price: €45 for two.

Meals: Dinner €17, including wine & coffee.

Closed: Christmas.

This is such a glorious setting, let the wild Ardèche landscape be your playground or the backdrop for total relaxation. Take walking boots, jodhpurs, bike, canoe, hang-glider, or just yourselves, and you'll be warmly welcomed. Surrounded by almond trees, fields of lavender and mountains, this peaceful farmhouse is truly lost in the countryside. Monsieur has elevated 'home brew' onto a new plane, making aperitifs and *digestifs* to go with Madame's local dishes, eaten *en famille*. Simply-furnished rooms, each with its own entrance, vary in size and style and there's a charming stone-vaulted dayroom.

Rooms: 1 family room, 3 doubles, all with shower & wc.

Price: €43 for two.

Meals: Dinner €14, including wine & coffee.

Closed: Never.

From Aubenas N102 W for Le Puy for 8.5km. At Lalevade left to Jaujac. By Café des Loisirs, cross river & follow signs 4km along narrow mountain road.

From Bourg St Andéol D4 to St Remèze then D362 for Gras. Signposted on right.

Marie & Gil Florence
Les Roudils
07380 Jaujac
Ardèche
Tel: (0)4 75 93 21 11
Fax: (0)4 75 93 21 11

Sylvette & Gérard Mialon
La Martinade
07700 Saint Remèze
Ardèche
Tel: (0)4 75 98 89 42
Fax: (0)4 75 04 36 30
E-mail: sylvetlm@aol.com
Web: www.angelfire.com/la/lamartinade/

The high-walled garden is a dream where hibiscus, oleander, mallows and vines rampage, nothing is too kempt and statues can take you by surprise. It has secret corners and a perfect breakfast terrace with splendid pots against the pale stone wall. Indoors, Madame plays soothing classical music so the antics of Ivan the dachshund don't impinge. A gently friendly hostess, she brought her children up here and creates a family atmosphere. The guest room's fireplace can be lit in winter to make it cosy over the fine red and blue-tiled floor, its antique bookshelves are stuffed with books, the touch of damp due for repair. A good hideaway.

Rooms: 1 double with shower & wc.

Price: €46 for two.

Meals: Regional restaurant 150m, 3 in village.

Closed: Never.

Ten minutes and a world away from the motorway, this pretty and impressive old building on the main village square, originally a hotel, is now a real family house where guests can share one of Madame's much-praised dinners with their hosts under the lime tree as the evening fades. Bedrooms are big, warm, lightly floral with very French beds, be they brass or sleigh, fine armoires and good bathrooms. Windows look over the walled garden behind or to the square in front; there's space and a sense of old-time comfort. And your friendly hosts have collected quantities of coffee grinders and *carafes* - mind-boggling.

Rooms: 1 twin, 2 doubles, with bath or shower & wc; 1 triple with bath, shower & separate wc.

Price: €40-€46 for two.

Meals: Dinner €15, including wine; restaurants in town.

Closed: October-June.

From A7 exit Bollène to Pt St Esprit; N86 for Bourg St Andéol; in St Just, Rue de Versailles opp. church; house (big gates) 100m on right.

From A72 exit 4 (Noirétable-Les Salles) for Noirétable for 500m; left D73 through St Julien la Vêtre to St Didier - house on main square.

Jacqueline Crozier
Quartier Versailles
07700 Saint Just d'Ardèche
Ardèche
Tel: (0)4 75 04 60 52

Dany & Michelle Trapeau
La Closerie
Le Bourg
42111 Saint Didier sur Rochefort
Loire
Tel: (0)4 77 97 91 26
Fax: (0)4 77 97 91 26

Entry No: 672   Map: **14**

Entry No: 673   Map: **8**

Once upon a time, kindly Anne-Marie lived in a big town. One day she found her dream house in the Auvergne near deep mysterious woods and babbling brooks so she left the city, lovingly restored her house, installed her old family furniture and opened the door so that visitors could share her dream. So, after a delicious supper, before the roaring fire, Anne-Marie may treat you to a fairy tale of her own making. (She also offers breathing and relaxation courses.) Thus you will all live happily ever after and never forget this exceptional woman.

Rooms: 2 triples, 2 twins, 1 double, all with shower & wc.

Price: €42-€57 for two.

Meals: Dinner €16, including wine & coffee.

Closed: Never.

Do stay a few days in this charmingly typical Napoleon III manor house, square and confident in its five acres of parkland (with tennis court) and the famous Troisgros restaurant just 8km away. There are fine walks (all levels of difficulty) to help work up an appetite for the local gastronomy. You are guests in a family home, your antique-furnished bedroom has its own character, the bath is a claw-footed marvel (plenty of towels and bathrobes to go with it) and Madame a gentle friendly widow. She loves sharing a welcome cup of something with new people and guiding them to the hidden delights of this lovely area. *Ask about pets. Gîte space for 2-3 people.*

Rooms: 1 double with shower & wc; 1 suite for 3/4 with bath & wc.

Price: €63 for two; suite €98.

Meals: Choice of restaurants within 3km, or in Roanne, 8km.

Closed: 15 November-15 March.

From A72 exit 4 D53 E to Champoly. D24 E to St Marcel d'Urfé; D20 S for St Martin la Sauveté and follow signs.

From Roanne D53 for 8km. Right into village & follow signs.

Anne-Marie Hauck
Il fut un temps
Les Gouttes
42430 Saint Marcel d'Urfé, Loire
Tel: (0)4 77 62 52 19
Fax: (0)4 77 62 52 19
E-mail: anne-marie.hauck@wanadoo.fr
Web: www.eazyweb.co.uk/ilfut

Mme Gaume
Domaine de Champfleury
42155 Lentigny
Loire
Tel: (0)4 77 63 31 43
Fax: (0)4 77 63 31 43

Entry No: 674   Map: **8**

Entry No: 675   Map: **8**

Come and join this family's charming, authentically aristocratic life: no prissiness (two screened-off bathrooms) in their big townhouse, just unselfconscious style. The richly-decorated golden *salon* has a piano, books and open fireplace. The richly-stocked garden has a pool, a summerhouse, a large terrace, 150 species of trees, an organic vegetable garden and a statue of Grandpère. Madame is too busy cooking to eat with guests but welcomes company as she's preparing dinner. Children love it - there are toys and the hosts' own children to play with.

Rooms: 2 doubles, 2 twins, all with bath or shower & wc.

Price: €65 for two.

Meals: Dinner €20, including coffee; wine €12.

Closed: Never.

An Egypto-Roman obelisk amid the topiary in the garden, wine from the vines which surround the château and beautiful 17th-century beams to sleep under. What more could you want? Your hosts, much-travelled, polyglot and sophisticated, are genuinely keen to share their enthusiasm for the area and its wines (and will organise wine-tastings). The vast rooms, some with fine carved door frames, are eclectically and elegantly furnished (Olivier's brother is an antique dealer) and breakfast, with home-made jams, can be followed by a visit to the winery. If you want to sample *le grand style*, this is for you.

Rooms: 3 doubles, 2 suites, all with bath & wc.

Price: €96 for two.

Meals: Dinner €32, including wine & coffee.

Closed: Never.

From A6 exit Macon Sud or Belleville; N6 to Romanèche and Lancié. In village head for Fleurie into Square Les Pasquiers.

From A6 exit 'Belleville'; N6 for Lyon 10km; right D43 to Arnas. Go through village; château on right after 1.5km.

Jacques & Laurence Gandilhon
Les Pasquiers
69220 Lancié
Rhône
Tel: (0)4 74 69 86 33
Fax: (0)4 74 69 86 57
E-mail: ganpasq@aol.com

Alexandra & Olivier du Mesnil
Les Jardins de Longsard
Château de Longsard
69400 Arnas
Rhône
Tel: (0)4 74 65 55 12
Fax: (0)4 74 65 03 17
E-mail: longsard@wanadoo.fr

Entry No: 676   Map: **9**

Entry No: 677   Map: **9**

Inimitably fine... An amazing avenue of lime trees conducts you to this wholly exceptional house and hostess. Madame is a live wire, laughing, enthusing, giving - unforgettable. The house is as elegant as she is. Climb the old wooden stairs to your splendidly decorated and furnished room, revel in Persian carpets, trompe-l'œil, antiques, fresh flowers. Beside the complete works of Shakespeare, Madame pours tea from silver into porcelain and artfully moves the breakfast butter as the sun rises; at night she'll light your bedside lamp, leaving a book open at a carefully chosen page for you to read after a game of (French) Scrabble.

Rooms: 1 double with bathroom & wc; 1 double, 1 twin, sharing shower & wc.

Price: €79 for two.

Meals: Good restaurant 3km.

Closed: Never.

A revelation to those who expect farms to be a bit scruffy, the light, harmonious air in this old Savoyard farmhouse is created by stone and wood, white paint, dried flowers and country antiques - and it matches Madame's delightful, energetic presence. Now virtually retired from farming, Monsieur happily shares his great knowledge of the area, wines and mushrooming; they will do anything for you. Your sitting room has a half-moon window at floor level (the top of the old barn door), your big light bedroom has antique, new-mattressed, lace-covered beds and spotless glass-doored shower. A super place.

Rooms: 1 double, 2 twins, all with shower & wc (1 behind curtain).

Price: €55 for two; reduction for longer stays.

Meals: Dinner available occasionally; BBQ possible; Savoyard restaurant 3-4km.

Closed: Never.

From Bourg en Bresse, N83 for Lyon. At Servas right on D64 for Condeissiat 5km; left at sign Le Marmont into plane-tree avenue. Don't go as far as St André.

From Annecy N201 for Geneva. 1km after Cruseilles, left D27 through Copponex; left at cemetery; signs to Chambres d'Hôtes Châtillon. House on left.

Geneviève & Henri Guido-Alheritiére
Manoir de Marmont
01960 Saint André sur Vieux Jonc
Ain
Tel: (0)4 74 52 79 74

Suzanne & André Gal
La Bécassière
Châtillon
74350 Copponex
Haute-Savoie
Tel: (0)4 50 44 08 94
Fax: (0)4 50 44 08 94

A no-frills place, simple and clean, with relaxed, friendly hosts - locals who know their area well, the possibility of baby-sitting and a kind micro-climate: the nearby mountains apparently attract the clouds, leaving the sun to beat a clear path to your door. Breakfast only is provided but the Martins recommend restaurants and provide a kitchen for the two rooms in the guest chalet. The rooms are fairly small and furnishings are plain and simple but the garden is a pleasant surprise with swings and ropes for youngsters and there are fabulous walks to be taken. Only 10km from Annecy. *Gîte space for 6 people.*

Rooms: 2 doubles (& sofa bed) in cottage, both with shower & wc.

Price: €45 for two.

Meals: Self-catering possible.

Closed: Never.

"Luxury without ostentation" is the aim here and this house flourishes with the loving care its owners lavish upon it. They are passionate about interior decorating, gourmet cuisine and entertaining so you're definitely in for a treat. A vast brunch for all and four or five-course dinners on request: French-Canadian Denyse is a food journalist. The rooms are all different: the blue *Albanaise*, the raspberry *Aixoise*, the oak-beamed, four-postered *Écossaise*. You choose. Bathrooms are superb too. Beautiful Annecy with its gleaming lake, Chamonix-Mont Blanc, the towering Alps, swinging Geneva, are all nearby. *Gîte space for 3 people.*

Rooms: 2 doubles, 1 twin, all with bath or shower & wc.

Price: €115 for two.

Meals: Dinner €40, including wine & coffee.

Closed: Never.

From A41 exit Annecy Sud for Chambéry; at junction D16 right for Rumilly for 10km; enter Marcellaz Albanais, imm'ly left D38 towards Chapeiry for 1km; right for Chaunu; house 200m on right.

From A41 exit Alby/Rumilly, N201 for Chambéry. In St Félix, at church take D53; 300m past cemetery; left (sign for Mercy) to statue, right and immed. left, past farm & through gate.

Claudie & Jean-Louis Martin
Chemin de Chaunu
74150 Marcellaz Albanais
Haute-Savoie
Tel: (0)4 50 69 73 04

Denyse & Bernard Betts
Les Bruyères
Mercy
74540 St Félix
Haute-Savoie
Tel: (0)4 50 60 96 53
Fax: (0)4 50 60 94 65

Jenny came to France from South Africa 40 years ago, fell in love with the place and stayed ever after; a warm, friendly person, she is deliriously happy in her small chalet among the high Alpine meadows where waterfalls abound. There's walking for all levels in spectacular scenery, white water rafting on the river running through the village, or sleepy people-watching with the locals. The bedsitter is in fact the wood-lined lower floor of the chalet with just enough room for a kitchenette, shower, loo and sofa bed - all perfectly finished and charmingly warm with a little terrace outside its private entrance. *Skiing available.*

Rooms: 1 double (sofabed) with shower, wc & kitchenette.

Price: €49 for two.

Meals: Savoyard restaurants within walking distance.

Closed: Never.

From Samoëns D907 to Sixt Fer à Cheval; over 2nd bridge D29 opp. war memorial; after Les Vagruys chairlift, 2nd right at sign 'Maison Neuve' to end; No. 14 last on right.

Jenny Vanderplank
Chalets de Sixt 14
Maison Neuve
74740 Sixt Fer à Cheval, Haute-Savoie
Tel: (0)4 50 34 10 55
Fax: (0)4 50 34 10 55
E-mail: jennyvplank@wanadoo.fr
Web: www.pour-les-vacances.com/shanti

The Brownes have built a hymn to wood, outside and in, plus lovely fabrics and furniture to make this brand new traditional chalet warm and reassuring. It has panoramic views south across the valley to rising green Alpine pastures and great rocky mountains. Guests have a floor to themselves, a room with doors to the garden and that fabulous view. Your hosts, retired contented travellers, are great fun, energetic and enthusiastic about their house, the 135km of marked mountain trails, and their lovely Labradors who enjoy the walking too. Delightful Annecy is just two dozen kilometres and a few bends away; Geneva is one hour. And the skiing's great.

Rooms: 1 twin with shower & wc.

Price: €50 for two.

Meals: Dinner €17, including wine & coffee.

Closed: Never.

From Annecy D909 to Thones; D12 for Serraval & Manigod; very shortly after, D16 to Manigod; through village, 1st left to Les Murailles; house 4th on right.

Colin & Alyson Browne
Les Murailles
74230 Manigod
Haute-Savoie
Tel: (0)4 50 44 95 87
Fax: (0)4 50 44 95 87
E-mail: colin.browne@worldonline.fr

Madame has boundless energy, is a great walker, adores her mountain retreat in this lovely valley and cooks very well indeed. Her chalet rooms, all wood-clad of course, are bright and welcoming in blue, white and orange; they have unusually high ceilings, good storage and plenty of space. The open-plan living area looks out of big windows to the small garden and the mixture of old and modern furniture plus bits and pieces of all sorts gives the whole place a comfortable, family feel. With Annecy so close and Geneva just an hour away, it's ideal for a mountain holiday.

Rooms: 1 double with shower & separate wc; 2 doubles share bathroom & separate wc.

Price: €40 for two.

Meals: Dinner €13, including wine & coffee; restaurant 800m.

Closed: Never.

From Annecy D909 to Thones; D12 for Serraval & Manigod; 200m after 'Welcome to Manigod' sign, left at cross; chalet on left.

Josette Barbaud
Proveyroz
74230 Manigod
Haute-Savoie
Tel: (0)4 50 44 95 25
Fax: (0)4 50 44 95 25

Entry No: 684   Map: **10**

Anne-Marie, outgoing and a delight to talk to, makes this place - come if you want to bathe in genuine French mountain hospitality, don't come if you need spotless mod cons and new bedding. She speaks English, keeps horses, organises treks to the Alpine pastures. Exceptional walking: you may see chamois and marmots if you go far enough. The chalet has a 'museum' of olden-day Alpine farm life. Dinner (served late to allow you time to settle) is eaten at the long wooden table, with grand-mama's recipes cooked on a wood-fired stove: "simple ingredients well prepared; delicious cheeses" - and the half-board formula includes absolutely everything.

Rooms: 1 triple with shower & wc; 4 doubles sharing 2 showers & 2 wcs.

Price: Half-board only €33.50 per person.

Meals: Breakfast, dinner with aperitif, wine & coffee included in price.

Closed: Never.

From Thonon les Bains, D26 for Bellevaux. House 2km before Bellevaux on left; sign.

Anne-Marie Félisaz-Denis
Le Châlet
La Cressonnière
74470 Bellevaux
Haute-Savoie
Tel: (0)4 50 73 70 13
Fax: (0)4 50 73 70 13

Entry No: 685   Map: **10**

Overlooking the valley, vineyards and distant peaks, the 18th-century house, once the château's cottages and stables, has been a country cottage for years. Simone and Henry did some sensitive renovation, using old materials and recreating an authentic atmosphere, then they started doing B&B. They are still feeling their way, learning how much contact or privacy their guests expect, hunting for little tables and pieces of character to add to their very well-finished, mezzanined guest rooms - each has a small sitting area. Breakfast is in the pretty courtyard garden in summer. Excellent hosts and good value. *Gîte space for 4 people.*

Rooms: 1 twin, 1 double, both with bath & wc.

Price: €60 for two.

Meals: Good choice of restaurants 2-10 km.

Closed: 31 October-Easter.

A41 exit Aix les Bains D991 to Viuz; D56 right for Ruffieux; at r'about head for Chessine & Chambres d'Hôtes.

Simone & Henry Collé
Chessine
73310 Ruffieux
Savoie
Tel: (0)4 79 54 52 35
Fax: (0)4 79 54 52 35
E-mail: chessine@noealexinfo.com
Web: www.chessine.fr.st

Entry No: 686   Map: **9**

Château life is yours, once you have greeted the gentle giant Danes and taken in the scale of La Terrosière. In the luxuriously-converted stable block there are vast antique-furnished bedrooms (you may need a mounting block for the four-poster), brilliant bathrooms, a softly embracing living room with open fire, staff to wait on you and a *châtelaine* of charm and wit to make fine food, bring superb wines from her cellar and keep you company at table. Horses exercise in the school; a tennis court, fishing lake and heated spring-water pool beckon on the 100-acre estate. You won't regret a cent. Oh, and it's brunch, not breakfast.

Rooms: 2 suites, 1 twin, all with bath and shower & wc.

Price: €122-€137 for two.

Meals: Dinner €53, including wine & coffee.

Closed: August & Christmas, except by arrangement.

From Chambéry N504 N via Le Bourget du Lac through small tunnel to Chevelu; left D921 to St Paul. After r'bout, 1st left. House on right about 1km along (large iron gates).

Mme Jeannine Conti
La Terrosière
73170 Saint Paul sur Yenne
Savoie
Tel: (0)4 79 36 81 02
Fax: (0)4 79 36 81 02

Entry No: 687   Map: **9**

Cows graze in the foreground, mountains march into Italy beyond. Myriam, bubbly and easy, adores having guests and everyone joining in the lively, lighthearted family atmosphere at La Touvière. In their typical old unsmart farmhouse, the cosy family room is the hub of life. Marcel is part-time home improver, part-time farmer (he just has a few cows now). One guest room has a properly Alpine view across the valley, the other overlooks the owners' second chalet, let as a gîte; both are small but not cramped, simple but not basic. This is a perfect place whence to set out into the walkers' paradise that surrounds it. And it's remarkable value. *Gîte space for 8 people.*

Rooms: 2 doubles, both with shower & wc.

Price: € 34 for two.

Meals: Dinner € 14, including wine & coffee.

Closed: Never.

A year-round Alpine dream... In summer it's all flowers, birds and rushing streams. In winter you can ski cross-country, snow-walk or take the ski lift, just 500m away, to the vast ski field of Les Arcs. La Plagne and Val d'Isère are quite close too. Cooking takes place in the outside wood oven and the cuisine is as good and honest as your dynamic and friendly young hosts. Children are catered for with early suppers, son Boris and daughter Clémence are playmates for them and Claude will baby-sit in the evening. Guests have their own comfortable dayroom with a refrigerator. *Discount on ski hire and passes.*

Rooms: 1 suite for 4/5, 1 double for 2/3, both with shower & wc.

Price: € 40 for two.

Meals: Dinner € 14, including wine & coffee.

Closed: Never.

From Albertville N212 for Megève 21km; after Flumet, left at Panoramic Hotel & follow signs to La Touvière.

From Albertville N90 to Moutiers; cont. for Bourg St Maurice. Right D87E to Peisey Nancroix; left to Peisey Centre ; follow green arrows. 9km from main road to house.

Marcel & Myriam Marin-Cudraz
La Touvière
73590 Flumet
Savoie
Tel: (0)4 79 31 70 11

Claude Coutin & Franck Chenal
Maison Coutin
T12 Peisey
73210 Peisey Nancroix, Savoie
Tel: (0)4 79 07 93 05/(0)6 14 11 54 65
Fax: (0)4 79 04 29 23
E-mail: maisoncoutin@aol.com
Web: www.maison-coutin.fr.st

Perched on the edge of a mountain, you have a superb view of peaks above and villages below, be you in your room, in the jacuzzi, or rolling in the snow after your sauna. Blazing fires, natural wood - all pure *Savoyard*. Plus big rooms and luxury bathrooms - such a treat. The televisions and the cardphone in the hall give a slight 'hotelly' feel, but what matter? After a hearty breakfast your Franco-American hostess will gladly help you map out your itinerary - mountain-lake fishing in summer, skiing in winter, superb walking all year. *Gîte space for 9.*

Rooms: 3 suites for 4, 3 doubles (queen or king-size beds), all with bath or shower & wc.

Price: €100-€150 for two.

Meals: Dinner €30, including wine & coffee.

Closed: October-November; May-June.

The ground floor of the tower is the original 17th-century kitchen complete with wood-fired range, stone sink and cobbled floor. Hélène makes her own bread, honey and jams and prepares meals using vegetables from her garden; she even makes her own aperitifs (the *vin d'orange* is superb). You will also be offered wine from the Rossis' own vineyard near Montpellier. The house has loads of character with enormous rooms, high heavy-beamed ceilings and large windows overlooking the valley, and the bedrooms are reached up an ancient stone spiral staircase which sets the imagination reeling.

Rooms: 2 doubles, 2 twins, 1 family, all with bath or shower & wc.

Price: €52 for two.

Meals: Dinner €17, including wine & coffee. Self-catering possible.

Closed: Never

From Bourg St Maurice D902 for Val d'Isère through Ste Foy Tarentaise. After La Thuile left for Ste Foy Station and follow wooden signs.

From Grenoble A51 or N75 for Sisteron 25km to roundabout; follow signs to St Martin de la Cluze. Château signs in village.

Nancy Tabardel
Yellow Stone Chalet
Bonconseil Station
73640 Sainte Foy Tarentaise, Savoie
Tel: (0)4 79 06 96 06
Fax: (0)4 79 06 96 05
E-mail: yellowstone@wanadoo.fr
Web: limelab.com/yellowstone

Jacques & Hélène Rossi
Château de Paquier
38650 Saint Martin de la Cluze
Isère
Tel: (0)4 76 72 77 33
Fax: (0)4 76 72 77 33
E-mail: hrossi@club-internet.fr
Web: chateau.de.paquier.free.fr

Such care, attention and unbridled luxury, including space, superb beds and great bathrooms, may not make for a 'homely' atmosphere but this is a superbly-kept French house, a place for a real treat without the children. A brilliant mix of satin cushions, swags, curly legs and oriental pictures adorns the living room: your perfectionist but fun-loving hosts brought their standards from the Riviera and you will want for nothing. Breakfast is a banquet of home-made jams, brioche, cake, and more. The half-acre garden provides rest or badminton and... flowers for indoors.

Rooms: 3 doubles, 1 twin, 2 suites, all with bath & wc.

Price: €68.50-€84 for two.

Meals: 2 restaurants 5 minutes' walk.

Closed: Never.

Although this is not a working farm, it might as well be. The Garniers adore animals. They have seven Camargue horses (for stroking, not riding), ducks, chickens, turkeys, guinea fowl, a pig, two dogs and a cat! Albert is French, Jean-Margaret is English, she loves cooking and grows all her own vegetables. She also has a large collection of dolls from around the world. The classic Dauphinoise house is a thoroughly welcoming family home decorated in French country style with some modern pieces and a pretty garden; all this near a ramblingly attractive old village in rolling wooded countryside.

Rooms: 1 triple, 1 twin, both with shower & wc.

Price: €41.50-€44 for two.

Meals: Dinner €14, including wine & coffee.

Closed: Never.

From Lyon, A43 Chimilin/Les Abrets exit towards Les Abrets & follow signs.

From A43 exit La Tour du Pin to N6; right at r'bout for Aix les Bains; left at lights St Clair de la T. 3km for Dolomieu; Chambres d'Hôtes signs.

Christian & Claude Chavalle Revenu
La Bruyère
38490 Les Abrets
Isère
Tel: (0)4 76 32 01 66
Fax: (0)4 76 32 06 66
E-mail: carbone38@aol.com
Web: members.aol.com/carbone38/

Jean-Margaret & Albert Garnier
Le Traversoud
38110 Faverges de la Tour
Isère
Tel: (0)4 74 83 90 40
Fax: (0)4 74 83 90 40

The Barrs are Scottish and Irish but have lived in France for more than 25 years so are pretty well French too. Mary, an easy, relaxed person, loves flowers and helps Greig with his wooden-toy business in winter. They have renovated their old farmhouse to give it an English feel yet preserve its utterly French character: the atmosphere is light, airy and warm as well as solid and reassuring. In the big guest rooms, the beds have excellent mattresses, the views are rural, the super bathroom (across the landing but private) is blue and white with lots of pretty china bits. A very civilised place to stay.

Rooms: 2 twins/doubles with bath & wc.

Price: €46 for two.

Meals: Dinner €23, including wine & coffee.

Closed: September-December.

These are the most caring and endearing of B&B owners: he, warmly humorous and humble about his excellent cooking abilities; she, generous and outgoing with lots of interesting talk. Built in 1646 as a fort, high on a hill, beside a spring that still runs through the shrubby garden, their superb old house is wrapped round a big green-clad courtyard. Inside, levels change, staircases abound, vast timbers span the dining room, guest rooms have separate entrances and floral papers, plush chairs and country antiques, impeccable bathrooms - and a bedhead from Hollywood in the best room. A deep country refuge just 15 minutes from Lyon.

Rooms: 3 doubles, 1 duplex, all with bath & wc.

Price: €85-€115 for two.

Meals: Dinner €31, including wine & coffee.

Closed: Never.

From A43 exit 8 on N85 to Nivolas; left D520 for Succieu. After 2km left 56D for Succieu. Through Succieu for St Victor 3km; last house at top of steep hill; sign.

From A7, A46 or A47 exit Chasse-Rhône; through large Centre Commercial; under railway; left for Trembas. (Will fax map or guide you to house.)

Mary & Greig Barr
Longeville
38300 Succieu
Isère
Tel: (0)4 74 27 94 07
Fax: (0)4 74 92 09 21
E-mail: mary.barr@free.fr

M & Mme Fleitou
Domaine de Gorneton
712 chemin de Violans
38670 Chasse sur Rhône, Isère
Tel: (0)4 72 24 19 15
Fax: (0)4 72 24 19 15
E-mail: gorneton@wanadoo.fr
Web: www.gorneton.com

Madame alone is worth the detour: her kindliness infuses her home - one that, at first glance, is coy about its age or charms; her eventful life has nourished a wicked sense of humour but no bitterness and she is a natural storyteller (she'll show you the photographs too). The slightly fading carpets and small shower rooms become incidental after a short while. Enjoy, instead, the pretty bedrooms, the peace of the lush leafy garden which shelters the house from the road and relish breakfast - organic honeys, home-made jams and cake, cheese - where the table is a picture in itself.

Rooms: 2 twins, 1 single/twin, all with shower & wc.

Price: €39-€45 for two.

Meals: Restaurants 2-7km.

Closed: Never.

From A7 Valence Sud exit A49 for Grenoble. Exit 33 right on D538a for Beaumont 2.6km; right at sign Chambres d'Hôtes/Chambedeau; house 600m on right, tarmac drive.

Mme Lina de Chivré-Dumond
Chambedeau
26760 Beaumont lès Valence
Drôme
Tel: (0)4 75 59 71 70
Fax: (0)4 75 59 75 24
E-mail: linadechivredumond@minitel.net

Entry No: 696   Map: 14

There's a time-warp feel to this 1970s villa high above the valley outside Valence: dark floral wallpaper covers hall, stairs and bedrooms, animal skins cover floors and modern sofas, interesting modern sculptures call from *salon* and stairs. Your hostess is interesting, enthusiastic and hugely welcoming, a gift inherited from Armenian parents. Enjoy breakfast of hot croissants and home-made organic jam on the terrace and admire the magnificent chalk escarpments of the Vercors range (beyond less attractive Saint Marcel). Little traffic noise can be heard. *Careful: this is the B&B on the left-hand side of the road.*

Rooms: 1 twin with shower & wc; 1 double with bath & wc.

Price: €45-€51 for two.

Meals: Vast choice of restaurants in Valence, 5km.

Closed: Never.

From A7 exit Valence Nord; through Bourg lès Valence; left on N532 for Grenoble; exit to St Marcel. At 'Place de la Mairie' left to Stop, straight across, under bridge, straight on up hill (total 400m) - house on LEFT round hairpin.

Marie-Jeanne Katchikian
La Pineraie
383 chemin Bel Air
26320 Saint Marcel lès Valence
Drôme
Tel: (0)4 75 58 72 25
E-mail: marie.katchikian@minitel.net

Entry No: 697   Map: 14

Opt for the simple country life at this friendly farm which has been in the family for more than a century and has returned to *biologique* (organic) methods which Madame calls "acupuncture for the land" - she's also interested in feng shui. Meals of regional recipes are served family-style and include home-produced vegetables, fruit and eggs. Monsieur has a collection of old farming artefacts and Madame, although always busy, makes time to chat with guests. The bedrooms are in a separate wing with modern interiors, interesting antique beds, floral, lace and candlewick fabrics. The setting, at the foot of the Vercors range, is very peaceful.

Rooms: 1 twin, 1 double, 1 triple, all with shower or bath & wc.

Price: € 40 for two.

Meals: Dinner € 13, including wine & coffee; restaurants 3km.

Closed: Never.

Madame is the grandmother we all dream of, a delightful woman who cossets her guests, putting flowers, sweets and fruit in the bedrooms. This old stone farmhouse facing the Vercors mountains is definitely a family home and meals of regional dishes with local wine, prepared by daughter Élisabeth, can be very jolly with family, friends and guests all sharing the long wooden table in the kitchen. The roomy, old-fashioned, much-loved bedrooms have handsome walnut armoires and a comfortable, informal feel. The whole place has a timeless appeal.

Rooms: 3 triples, both with bath or shower & wc.

Price: € 36 for two.

Meals: Dinner € 14, including wine & coffee.

Closed: Never.

From Romans D538 towards Chabeuil. Leaving Alixan left by Boulangerie on D119; left again, Chambres d'Hôtes St Didier signs for 3km; farm on left.

From A6 exit Valence Sud on D68 to Chabeuil. There, cross river; left on D154 for Combovin 5km; signs.

Christiane & Jean-Pierre Imbert
Le Marais
26300 St Didier de Charpey
Drôme
Tel: (0)4 75 47 03 50
E-mail: imbert.jean-pierre@wanadoo.fr

Mme Madeleine Cabanes
Les Péris
D154 - route de Combovin
26120 Châteaudouble
Drôme
Tel: (0)4 75 59 80 51
Fax: (0)4 75 59 48 78

This artistic, caring couple are deeply concerned with social and ecological issues. They have renovated their farmhouse with sensitivity and an eye for detail, using nothing but authentic materials. Art lovers will enjoy Madame's beautifully-made china dolls, and the summer exhibitions and courses (it's a great place for seminars for up to 15 who can self-cater or be catered for). Guest quarters, in a separate building, have good rooms and handsome carpentry by Mado's son. Organic meals with home-grown vegetables and fruit in season are served in the vaulted guest dining room or on the terrace. A special house with a very special atmosphere. *Minimum stay 2 nights. Gîte space for 15.*

Rooms: 3 doubles, 1 suite for 4, all with bath or shower & wc.

Price: €42-€60 for two.

Meals: Dinner €15, including wine & coffee.

Closed: Never.

Blacons is different: shining views of the Vercors, an enchanting park designed by Le Nôtre, a stream, exotic fowl and an exhibition of contemporary art. Evelyne, herself an artist, loves creative people and opens her lively château (on an occasionally busy road) to groups doing meditation, music and massage. The big uncluttered bedrooms, château or arty style, have some good antiques and simple bathrooms, the food is naturally delicious and vegetarian dishes are no problem. House and outbuildings can sleep large groups during courses - B&B guests are informed ahead. Do stay long enough to explore this ravishing area. *Minimum stay 3 nights.*

Rooms: 1 double, 2 twins, all with shower & wc.

Price: €52 for two.

Meals: Dinner €14, including wine & coffee.

Closed: Never; please book ahead.

From Chabeuil, D538 for Crest 5km (ignore signs for Montvendre). Left at sign Les Dourcines; house 700m on right next to Auberge-Restaurant sign.

From Crest D93 to Mirabel et Blacons; château on left on leaving village: sign Galerie Arbre de Vie on wall.

Mado Goldstein & Bernard Dupont
Les Dourcines
26120 Montvendre
Drôme
Tel: (0)4 75 59 24 27
Fax: (0)4 75 59 24 27

Evelyne Latune
Château de Blacons
Mirabel et Blacons
26400 Crest
Drôme
Tel: (0)4 75 40 01 00
Fax: (0)4 75 40 04 97
E-mail: chateaudeblacons@caramail.com

Entry No: 700   Map: **14**

Entry No: 701   Map: **14**

The stone cross-vaulting in the dining room is wonderful and Francis has renovated the rest of the house with huge care, giving new life to old beams and tiles. He was once an engineer and knows about structures. Jackie is immediately likeable, an artist who really goes out of her way to make people feel at home. There is an organic vegetable garden, producing the basics, plus fruit and eggs, for some superb meals. The rooms are perfectly simple, with tiled floors and Provençal print fabrics, and have their own entrance. Lively and charming people living in lovely countryside.

Rooms: 2 triples, 1 double, 1 twin, all with bath or shower & wc.

Price: €52-€60 for two.

Meals: Dinner €19, including wine & coffee.

Closed: Rarely.

The ever-delightful Prothons have done a fine renovation job on their 17th-century coaching inn. The impressive, high hay barn has been put to superb use: each guest room has a mezzanine and views through one normal and one roof window to the magnificent countryside, though stairs are VERY steep. Lots of friendly old furniture, and one room has one of the antique loos from the old house. Meals, in the family dining room or outside, are made with products from the younger Prothons' farm; there are truffle weekends in winter and a welcoming fireplace. A hard-working and wonderfully friendly place. *Gîte space for 5 people.*

Rooms: 3 family rooms, all with shower & wc.

Price: €49 for two.

Meals: Dinner €18.50, including wine & coffee.

Closed: 15 December-15 January.

From Montélimar D540 E to La Batie Rolland (10km). In village left onto D134 for 2km towards St Gervais; signposted on right.

From A7 exit 18, N7 S for Avignon 2km, left on D133 for Grignan 5km. Just before Valaurie, right for Clansayes (D133) 2km; house on right 200m from road.

Francis & Jackie Monel
La Joie
26160 La Batie Rolland
Drôme
Tel: (0)4 75 53 81 51
Fax: (0)4 75 53 81 51
E-mail: f.monel@infonie.fr

Marie-Claire (Mick) & François Prothon
Val Léron
26230 Valaurie
Drôme
Tel: (0)4 75 98 52 52
Fax: (0)4 75 98 52 52
E-mail: ls.vacher@free.fr

Entry No: 702   Map: **14**

Entry No: 703   Map: **14**

If you enjoy people who love country life and are without pretension, then go and stay with this well-educated, relaxed couple in their creeper-clad, wisteria-hung farmhouse in this forgotten corner of the Drôme. Breakfast and dinner include home-made jams, eggs, vegetables from their superb kitchen garden and, in season, truffles hunted in their own secret ways. The Pagis are generous and off-beat, their guest rooms in the next-door barn are simple, the bathroom and kitchen really basic - but it's not the 'facilities' that make this place special, it's the people. And Jean-Jacques plays trumpet in the local salsa band.

Rooms: 1 double, 1 quadruple, sharing kitchen, bath & wc.

Price: € 34 for two.

Meals: Dinner € 12, including wine & coffee; self-catering possible.

Closed: December-February.

From Vaison la Romaine, D938 for Malaucène 4km. Left on D13 8km. Right on D40 to Montbrun les Bains, right for Sault. House 1km on left.

Jean-Jacques & Agnès Pagis
Le Chavoul
Reilhanette
26570 Montbrun les Bains
Drôme
Tel: (0)4 75 28 80 80
E-mail: antoine3@wanadoo.fr

FRENCH PASTRIES & BREAKFAST TREATS
Delights to be found in pastry shops (*pâtisseries*) at teatime; some also appear regularly or exceptionally - on high days and holy days - at breakfast.

Viennoiseries - Flaky and puffy pastries.
Croissant - Flaky crescent. Usually, the curved ones are made with margarine, the straighter ones with butter.
Pain au chocolat - Flaky pastry wallet enfolding a soft chocolate bar.
Chausson aux pommes - 'Apple slipper': a semi-circle of flaky pastry folded over stewed apples to keep them warm.
Choux - 'Cabbages': little light puffy balls filled with cream or chocolate; as a wedding cake: piled into a pyramid and dribbled with caramel *croquembouche*.
Religieuse - 'Nun': two large *choux* originally crowning the wedding pyramid, a ruff of cream at her neck, a robe of choux to her feet.
Éclair - An elongated cream or chocolate-iced *chou* to be eaten in an instant, like lightning (*éclair*).
Paris-Brest - Created for the first Paris-Brest bicycle race in 1891: a wheel of éclair spokes filled with cream and almond flakes.
Mille-feuilles - 'One thousand leaves' of flaky pastry spread with fine sweet custard and powdered with icing sugar.

Cakes and specialities
Quatre-quarts - Four equal parts of eggs, sugar, butter, flour make this classic sponge.
Madeleine - Little soft rounded oval cake with a light orange or lemon flavour, made famous by Marcel Proust for whom it triggered volumes of memories.
Diplomate - Like its namesake, a cake of many talents: shortbread then stewed fruit, a light custard then a glacé cherry.
Financier - Created by a Paris Stock Exchange pastrycook in the shape and colour of a gold ingot, it hides a soft sweet centre.
Saint-Honoré - Dedicated to the patron saint of baker-pastrycooks: shortbread holding a puff-pastry ring filled with whipped cream.

Provence –
Alps – Riviera

The best *bouillabaisse* ingredients swim among the white Mediterranean horses; on shore, the native white ponies carry their dashing *gardians* over the Camargue, herding the great black bulls.

Jean-Marc and Jacqueline are keen walkers, quite able to plan a whole walking holiday for you. You can walk or ski straight out onto the mountains from this dramatically-set house with its wonderful views over to Italy. Jean-Marc designed and built the house (he's a retired architect) with the bedrooms snugly under the eaves. There is a self-contained apartment with its own garden; the third person does have to sleep in the kitchen/living room, but has sole use of the microwave and the magnificent view. *Advance booking essential.*

Rooms: 2 doubles, sharing shower & wc; 1 twin with shower & wc; 1 apartment with bath & wc.

Price: €51-€64 for two.

Meals: Choice of restaurants in Briançon, 4km.

Closed: 1 April-24 May; 9 September-20 December; 5 January-2 February.

From Gap N94 to Briançon. Entering town, left at first traffic light for Puy St André. In village, house 3rd on left.

Jacqueline & Jean-Marc Laborie
Le Village
Puy Saint André
05100 Briançon, Hautes-Alpes
Tel: (0)4 92 21 30 22
Fax: (0)4 92 21 30 22
E-mail: jlabalastair@club-internet.fr

Entry No: 705   Map: **15**

Come to ski across country or down hills, rent your snow shoes on the spot, do some exceptional summer walks, hang-glide or just bathe in splendour. Michel, who took a half-ruined farmhouse and turned it into this atmospheric, country-warm house of welcome with small, no-frills rooms that have all you could want, is a burly, good-natured host who loves the convivial evenings around the communal table. Claude's artistry is seen in the décor, her kindness is in the air. Your first taste of the magnificent scenery here is the drive up - you should not be disappointed.

Rooms: 1 double, 2 quadruples, 2 twins, 1 suite, all with shower & wc.

Price: €40-€46 for two.

Meals: Dinner €16, including wine & coffee.

Closed: Never, but telephone to check.

From Gap N94 for Briançon; right just before Embrun D40 10km. Follow 'Station des Orres' down hill; house in hamlet, on left just before bridge.

Michel & Claude Hurault
La Jarbelle
Les Ribes
05200 Les Orres
Hautes-Alpes
Tel: (0)4 92 44 11 33
Fax: (0)4 92 44 11 23
E-mail: lajarbelle@wanadoo.fr

Entry No: 706   Map: **15**

History and mystery ooze from the ancient bits of this village château. Plays based on high spots of 'French history at Montmaur' are enacted on summer Fridays, the exhibition room has a five-metre-high fireplace, the breakfast room - family silver on a magnificent Provençal cloth - has superb old beams and your energetic hostess is kindness itself; she will also give you a guided tour. Guest rooms, not in the château proper, are somewhat dim and cramped with unremarkable furnishings. But romantics at heart come for the ghostly splendour of it all.

Rooms: 3 triples, all with shower & wc.

Price: €76 for two. 10% reduction for 2 nights.

Meals: Choice of restaurants, 4-10km.

Closed: October-April.

From Gap, D994 for Veynes. 4km before Veynes, take D320 for Superdévoluy; Montmaur 2km on, visible from road. Drive along château wall then towards church.

Élise Laurens
Château de Montmaur
05400 Veynes
Hautes-Alpes
Tel: (0)4 92 58 11 42
Fax: (0)4 92 58 11 42
E-mail: chateau.de.montmaur@wanadoo.fr

Entry No: 707   Map: **14**

Esparron has been in the same family since the 1400s. Vast bedrooms, reached by a superb stone staircase, are lovingly decorated: plain walls and fresh flowers, tiles and fine designer fabrics, good antiques and lots of lamps. The garden is small - for a château - but prettily planted. Slender, apple-blossom Charlotte-Anne and her two beautiful children come straight from a Gainsborough portrait (she IS English). She is attentive to everyone: husband, children, staff and guests. Bernard, with suntan, impeccable clothes and manners and pipe, adds a touch of 1930s glamour. Wonderful family, splendiferous house, vast breakfast...

Rooms: 3 doubles, 1 twin, 1 suite, all with bath & wc.

Price: €107-€198 for two.

Meals: Restaurant 5 minutes' walk.

Closed: November-March.

From Aix en Provence A51 exit 18 onto D907; D82 to Gréoux les Bains; follow signs on D952 & D315 to Esparron. Stop and ring at château gates (once past, it's impossible to turn).

Bernard & Charlotte-Anne de Castellane
Château d'Esparron
04800 Esparron de Verdon
Alpes-de-Haute-Provence
Tel: (0)4 92 77 12 05
Fax: (0)4 92 77 13 10
E-mail: bernard.de.castellane@wanadoo.fr
Web: www.provenceweb.fr/04/ukEsparron.htm

Entry No: 708   Map: **14**

Every day, Josiane puts a fresh yellow rose in the yellow rooms, a pink one in the pink room. Everything in this remarkably converted 14th-century barn - once the abbey farm - is as stylish and caring as that. Scented air, arched oak doors, lovely floors, simple iron furniture, a fine use of colour (desert red and white bathrooms), an inner terrace where lemons grow - it has a sense of peace and space (shame about nocturnal barking). Josiane, kind and intelligent, lives with her husband in the château next door where the magical pool hides in a walled garden. *The whole house can be rented on a weekly basis.*

Rooms: 2 doubles, 1 twin, all with shower & wc.

Price: €54 for two; reduction for longer stays.

Meals: Restaurants within walking distance.

Closed: Never, but book ahead in winter.
From Apt D22/D51 for Banon 24km; left into Simiane; house on right just before village nameplate.

Josiane Tamburini
Les Granges de Saint Pierre
04150 Simiane la Rotonde
Alpes-de-Haute-Provence
Tel: (0)4 92 75 93 81
Fax: (0)4 92 75 93 81
Web: www.luberon-news.com/granges-st-pierre.html

Entry No: 709   Map: **14**

Venerable stones in the remote thyme-wafted air of a hillside village: an apparently modest old house unfolds into a place of grandeur with a vast flourish of a dining hall, a tower for the fairytale touch, a pigeon loft for... pigeons, and well-travelled, fascinating hosts with a fine mix of shyness, extroversion and humour for company. The courtyard is wisteria-clad, the garden sheltered, the food superb. Two rooms on the 17th-century lower level charm with their simple ancientness, the canopy bed lies in splendour below serried beams; they overflow with character if not with hanging space. And there are two lovely terraces. A divine place. *Gîte space for 5-6 people.*

Rooms: 1 double with shower, bath & wc; 2 doubles with shower & wc.

Price: € 68.50 for two.

Meals: Dinner € 28-€ 30, including wine & coffee.

Closed: Never.

Madame and her house both smile gently. It's a simple, authentic Provençal farmhouse that has escaped the vigorous renovator, its courtyard shaded by a lovely lime tree. Madame, who grows chemical-free vegetables and fruit, considers dinners with her guests, in dining room or courtyard, as the best part of B&B - her meals are showcases for local specialities. The interior is a bright version of traditional French country style with old family furniture and tiled floors. Set among vineyards below the Montmirail hills, it has soul-pleasing views across the surrounding country and unspoilt villages.

Rooms: 1 family, 1 double, 3 twins, all with shower & wc.

Price: € 39 for two.

Meals: Dinner € 13, including wine & coffee.

Closed: November-March.

From Forcalquier N100 towards Apt; at 1st r'about D950 right to Banon; D51 to Montsalier; house at entrance of village behind Mairie.

From Carpentras D7 N through Aubignan & Vacqueyras; fork right (still D7) for Sablet; right 500m after 'Cave Vignerons Gigondas'; signposted.

Mme Karolyn Kauntze
Montsalier
04150 Banon
Alpes-de-Haute-Provence
Tel: 04 92 73 23 61
Fax: 04 92 73 23 61
E-mail: montsalier@infonie.fr

Sylvette Gras
La Ravigote
84190 Gigondas
Vaucluse
Tel: (0)4 90 65 87 55
Fax: (0)4 90 65 87 55

A great spot for exploring Provence. The big old house, surrounded by its vineyards, and within harmless earshot of a road, is very handsome and Madame brings it to life with her special sparkle and enthusiasm for what she has created here. The decoration is all hers - more 'evolved French farmhouse-comfortable' than 'designer-luxurious'. She loves cooking, herbs and flowers; you may be offered her elderflower aperitif and have home-made cakes at breakfast. Nothing is too much trouble - walkers' luggage can be transferred, picnics can be laid on, or wine, or honey tastings...

Rooms: 2 doubles, 1 triple, 1 suite (4), 1 suite (6), all with bath or shower & wc.

Price: €72 for two.

Meals: Dinner €20, including wine & coffee.

Closed: Never.

A stone jewel set in southern lushness and miles of green vines and purple hills. Country furniture (a seductive choice of Provençal chairs) is polished with wax and time; big, luminous bedrooms are prettily uncluttered: moss-coloured *Birds* sings to the tune of the aviary outside, *Elephant* has Indian fabric and... elephants, *Camargue*, in the mezzanined old barn, has a balcony and a *gardian's* hat. John rightly calls himself a Provençal Englishman, Monique is warmly welcoming too - theirs is a happy house. *German spoken.*

Rooms: 1 double with bath & wc; 1 double, 1 family with shower & wc.

Price: €45-€50 for two.

Meals: Restaurant in village. Self-catering possible.

Closed: Mid-November-Easter.

A9 exit Bollène for Carpentras 18km; leaving Cairanne, head for Carpentras 1.5km; house right-hand turn.

From A7 exit Bollène for Nyons D94; D20 right for Vaison & Buisson; cross River Aygues then left for Villedleu/Cave la Vigneronne D51 and D75 for 2.2km.

Élisabeth & Jerry Para
Domaine du Bois de la Cour
Route de Carpentras
84290 Cairanne, Vaucluse
Tel: (0)4 90 30 84 68
Fax: (0)4 90 30 84 68
E-mail: infos@boisdelacour.com
Web: www.boisdelacour.com

Monique Alex & John Parsons
L'École Buissonnière, D75
84110 Buisson, Vaucluse
Tel: (0)4 90 28 95 19
Fax: (0)4 90 28 95 19
E-mail: ecole.buissonniere@wanadoo.fr
Web: www.guideweb.com/provence/bb/ecole-buissonniere

Entry No: 712   Map: 14

Entry No: 713   Map: 14

Narrow, cobbled streets lead to this fascinating, impeccably-furnished house that was once part of the 17th-century Bishop's Palace. The Verdiers are charming, cultivated people - he an architect/builder, she a teacher - with a keen interest in antiques and modern art. There's an impressive poster collection in the cosy guest sitting room and bedrooms have an appealing Provençal feel. Well-presented breakfasts on the terrace come complete with French and English newspapers and, best of all, the magnificent view over to the Roman bridge.

Rooms: 1 double, 2 twins, 1 suite for 3, all with bath or shower & wc.

Price: €66-€73 for two; suite €98 for three.

Meals: Good choice of restaurants in Vaison.

Closed: 2 weeks in November.

Michael still has many plans for this handsome, rambling old house and garden in prime walking and cycling country. The mood inside is relaxed and comfortable: plenty of fresh, bright colours, stripped and be-rugged wooden floors, interesting *brocante* pieces, original fireplaces and the odd period bath and basin. Breakfast at nine, often outside under mature trees with vineyards and distant mountain views, on local bread and home-made jam. Dinner should be good too; Michael is English and an imaginative chef. *Gîte space for 2/3 people.*

Rooms: 1 suite for 4, 3 doubles, all with bath or shower & wc.

Price: €65 for two.

Meals: Dinner €27.50, including wine & coffee.

Closed: November-March.

From Orange, D975 to Vaison. In town, follow 'Ville Médiévale' signs.

From Vaison la Romaine D938 N for Nyons, 5km; right on D46 for Buis les Baronnies, 4km. On entering Faucon, house on right at crossroads with D205 (blue gate).

Aude & Jean-Loup Verdier
L'Évêché
Rue de l'Évêché
84110 Vaison la Romaine, Vaucluse
Tel: (0)4 90 36 13 46
Fax: (0)4 90 36 32 43
E-mail: eveche@aol.com
Web: eveche.free.fr

Michael Berry
Les Airs du Temps
84110 Faucon
Vaucluse
Tel: (0)4 90 46 44 57
Fax: (0)4 90 46 44 57
E-mail: michaelaberry@hotmail.com

Entry No: 714   Map: **14**

Entry No: 715   Map: **14**

Built on the foundations of a 12th-century watermill, this solid old aristocratic *bastide* (manor farmhouse) has thick stone walls which keep rooms cool in the fiercest heat. There is also a big pool, with fountains, in the landscaped, tree-filled garden surrounding it. The house is full of interesting mementoes of the owners' time in various North African countries; bedrooms are traditionally furnished with good mattresses and bathrooms. Breakfast includes home-made jam out on the terrace or in the dining room and dinners feature Madame's Provençal specialities. She and her family create a very relaxed, easy atmosphere here.

Rooms: 2 doubles, 2 family suites, all with bath or shower & wc.

Price: €56 for two.

Meals: Dinner €21, including wine & coffee.

Closed: Never.

From Carpentras, D974 for Bédoin/Mont Ventoux; stay on this road, do NOT enter Crillon village. Mill is on left below signpost.

Bernard & Marie-Luce Ricquart
Moulin d'Antelon
Route de Bédoin
84410 Crillon le Brave, Vaucluse
Tel: (0)4 90 62 44 89
Fax: (0)4 90 62 44 90
E-mail: moulin-dantelon@wanadoo.fr
Web: www.art-vin-table.com

Entry No: 716   Map: **14**

Sincere, charming, animated hosts: Monsieur is a keen cook and prepares Provençal dishes using local produce and herbs while Madame makes the desserts and also gives Feldenkrais (conscious movement) sessions. Their 19th-century farmhouse, built around a courtyard shaded by a spreading lime tree, is in great walking country among spectacular fields of lavender with vast views. The family living/dining room is homely and warm with a large table and a fireplace for cooler weather. The comfortable, light-filled rooms are carefully decorated in an unpretentious mix of new and old. Stay long enough to taste ALL these pleasures.

Rooms: 1 suite for 4, 1 suite for 3, 3 triples, all with bath or shower & wc.

Price: €65-€85 for two.

Meals: Dinner €22, excluding wine.

Closed: January & February.

From Carpentras, D941/D1 to Sault (41km); D942 for Aurel. Just before Aurel, left at sign.

Christian & Visnja Michelle
Richarnau
84390 Aurel
Vaucluse
Tel: (0)4 90 64 03 62
Fax: (0)4 90 64 03 62
E-mail: c.richarnau@accesinter.com
Web: richarnau.free.fr

Entry No: 717   Map: **14**

The Lawrences couldn't be nicer and thoroughly enjoy their role as hosts - they offer an open-hearted welcome and a real guest room in a real home. The room has its own dressing room, an extra mezzanine single and a newly-tiled shower; guests have use of a fridge and are welcome to picnic. Theirs is a modern house built of old stone in traditional local style and is surrounded by hills, woods and vineyards with lovely views across the valley towards Goult and the Lubéron. The Lawrences worked overseas for 40 years and the house is full of attractive *objets* from their travels. *Gîte space for 16 people.*

Rooms: 1 triple with shower & wc.

Price: €46 for two.

Meals: Good choice of restaurants 5km.

Closed: Never.

A totally revamped 18th-century silkworm farm, it's a handsome building with a clever mix of old and new: big, country-elegant bedrooms, gnarled beams, old stonework and armoires, then modern touches such as glass-topped tables, good bedding, linen and bathrooms. In the stylish guest sitting room you can enjoy an open fire, comfy sofa, books, games and bits of Provençalia - bunches of dried lavender, candles... Add feast-like breakfasts and dinners, great views from the pool, a boules court and a terraced garden with a backdrop of cherry trees. Very appealing. *Minimum stay 2 nights.*

Rooms: 2 double, 1 twin, 2 triple, all with bath, shower & wc.

Price: €70-€80 for two.

Meals: Dinner €26, including wine & coffee.

Closed: 12 November-February.

From Avignon N100 for Apt. At Coustellet, D2 for Gordes. After Les Imberts right D207/D148 to St Pantaléon; pass church; D104 for 50m; left small hill; 3rd drive on right.

A7 exit Cavaillon for Apt through Robion; D3 right for Ménerbes; at foot of village head for Bonnieux for 3km; house 200m, sign.

Pierrette & Charles Lawrence
Villa La Lèbre
Saint Pantaléon
84220 Gordes
Vaucluse
Tel: (0)4 90 72 20 74
Fax: (0)4 90 72 20 74

Natalie & Vincent Rohart
La Magnanerie
Le Roucas
84560 Ménerbes, Vaucluse
Tel: (0)4 90 72 42 88
Fax: (0)4 90 72 39 42
E-mail: magnanerie@aol.com
Web: www.magnanerie.com

Entry No: 718   Map: **14**

Entry No: 719   Map: **14**

Summer evenings are spent beneath the ancient spreading plane tree as the setting sun burnishes the vines beyond the slender cypresses and the old stones of this 17th-century *mas* breathe gold. With the eager help of six-year-old Marie for any children you may bring, your hosts, simple, smiling and unpretentious, will welcome you happily into their traditional interior: lots of wood, almond-green paintwork, a lavishly yellow and orange dining room, warmly plain farm furniture. Bedrooms are in quietly gentle pastels with pretty bedcovers. And good Provençal cooking at the big, convivial table.

Rooms: 4 doubles, 1 family, all with bath or shower & wc.

Price: €73-€84 for two.

Meals: Dinner €24, wine €5; restaurants nearby.

Closed: Never.

From Carpentras D4/39 to St Didier; D28 right for Pernes; house sign on left before Pernes.

Jean-Pierre & Françoise Faure-Brac
Mas Pichony
Chambres d'Hôtes
1454 Route de St Didier D28
84210 Pernes les Fontaines, Vaucluse
Tel: (0)4 90 61 56 11
Fax: (0)4 90 61 56 33
E-mail: mas-pichony@wanadoo.fr
Web: www.eurobandb.com/gites/pichony_f.htm

Entry No: 720   Map: **14**

Young hosts - with a passion for wine and a great collection of carpets - who've escaped here from their city pasts. Their guest bedrooms in this converted farmhouse are all very different: one white and cream with a blue and white bathroom, a twin with Senegalese bedspreads and a Paris Metro-tiled bathroom; a family room with a big brass double bed and, on a separate floor, three singles. The land here is flat with a high water table so the garden, sheltered by trees and the surrounding tall maize in summer, is always fresh and green - a perfect retreat after a hard day's sight-seeing. *Gîte space for 5 people.*

Rooms: 1 double, 1 twin, 1 family for 5, all with bath, shower & wc.

Price: €61-€70 for two.

Meals: Choice of restaurants 6km.

Closed: November-March, by arrangement.

From A7 exit 23; after toll right at r'bout for Carpentras/Entraigues; 1st exit to Vedène D6 to St Saturnin lès Avignon; left to Le Thor D28 for 2 km; right Chemin du Trentin.

Frédéric & Emmanuelle Westercamp
Le Mas de Miejour
117 chemin du Trentin
84250 Le Thor
Vaucluse
Tel: (0)4 90 02 13 79
Fax: (0)4 90 02 13 03
E-mail: mas.miejour@free.fr
Web: mas.miejour.free.fr

Entry No: 721   Map: **14**

We need pages to do justice to this gem. The Gouins, a real Provençal family, grow grapes and cherries and Madame is a renowned cook. For breakfast she may serve her special *galette de pommes* and her evening meals are outstanding. The beauty of the interior - sunshine yellows, fresh flowers, natural stone, charming furniture - is partnered by the stunning exterior, a well-planted, shade-dotted garden, a field of sunflowers (in July) and views of the Lubéron. The apartment is ideal for families, with three rooms and a jacuzzi! (It also brings numbers up quite a lot.) Simply arrive, absorb and wonder what on earth you did to deserve it. *Children over 12 welcome.*

Rooms: 1 suite, 2 quadruples, 2 doubles, 1 apartment for 6 (2 nights minimum), all with shower & wc.

Price: €92-€122 for two; apartment €182.

Meals: Dinner €25, including wine & coffee.

Closed: November & February.

From Avignon, N7; D22 Apt (approx. 29km total). After Le Petit Palais, sign on right.

Isabelle & Rolland Gouin
La Ferme des 3 Figuiers
Le Petit Jonquier
84800 Lagnes
Vaucluse
Tel: (0)4 90 20 23 54
Fax: (0)4 90 20 25 47

According to one of our readers, "Madame is a star with a lovely sense of humour"; fortunately she is up and shining during the daytime as well. She and her family - a gently shy husband and two teenage children - create a genuine Provençal atmosphere round the table. The fare is traditional, with home-grown vegetables. The dining room, with its tile floors and old beams, used to be the carthorse stable and country simplicity is the theme throughout this recently-restored farmhouse. Its clean and basic rooms include good beds with Provençal covers and views over the fields.

Rooms: 5 doubles, all with bath or shower & wc.

Price: €45 for two.

Meals: Dinner €14, including wine & coffee.

Closed: 1 January-9 February.

From Apt, N100 for Avignon. At Lumières, D106 for Lacoste; right D218 for Ménerbes; 2nd farm on left.

Maryline & Claude Chabaud
Mas Marican
84220 Goult
Vaucluse
Tel: (0)4 90 72 28 09

Genuine country class is here. Michel, who lives nearby, is part of a true Provençal community: his family has lived here for generations, his father runs the farm; vineyards and cherry trees march past, honey is combed for breakfast (and what breakfasts...), a friend deals with the wine and Sophie looks after guests, superbly. The irrigation pond has rippled with southern light for 250 years, the old house has been carefully restored with properly colour-washed walls, old doors and floor tiles and is pleasantly uncluttered. But modernity takes a bow with superb bathrooms and a streamlined pool.

Rooms: 2 doubles, 2 twins, 1 triple, all with bath & wc.

Price: €61-€76 for two.

Meals: Restaurants within 2km.

Closed: 16 November-end March.

From Cavaillon D973 E for 30km. Left then right, through Lauris on D27 and on towards Puyvert/Lourmarin; signposted after 1km.

Michel Cuxac
La Carraire
84360 Lauris
Vaucluse
Tel: (0)4 90 08 36 89
Fax: (0)4 90 08 40 83
E-mail: infos@lacarraire.com
Web: www.lacarraire.com

Entry No: 724   Map: **14**

Just what a house in Provence should be: wonderful furniture, fabrics, tiles and beams, it is all exquisite refinement. It is a former 17th-century staging post, yet its garden is an oasis of coolness, right in the centre of pretty Lourmarin. Madame, a cultivated and interesting person and a keen cyclist, is ready to advise on routes and leads such an active life that she may just not be there to greet you or dust your room! She is now running the Villa with her daughter - and her young granddaughter, who speaks perfect English. There are bikes for guests' use and for the less athletic - or the saddle-sore - there's that shady garden.

Rooms: 2 doubles, 3 twins, all with bath or shower & wc.

Price: €55-€70 for two.

Meals: Restaurants nearby.

Closed: Never.

From Aix en Provence, N96 & D556 to Pertuis. There, D973 to Cadenet; D943 for Bonnieux to Lourmarin.

Mme & Mlle Lassallette
Villa Saint Louis
35 rue Henri de Savornin
84160 Lourmarin
Vaucluse
Tel: (0)4 90 68 39 18
Fax: (0)4 90 68 10 07
E-mail: villasaintlouis@wanadoo.fr

Entry No: 725   Map: **14**

On an old cobbled street right in the heart of old Tarascon, this *maison de maître* has ancient origins. It has been beautifully, artistically renovated without losing any of the lovely patina of stone walls and old tiles. Built round a typical ochre-hued courtyard where breakfast is served, and candles lit in the evening, it exudes Mediterranean age and history. The impeccable, stylish rooms have fine old furniture and beams, excellent bathrooms and linen. While both you and they can be totally independent, your charming hosts receive guests in the most relaxed, friendly way and thoroughly enjoy the contact. A really lovely, atmospheric place. *Minimum stay 2 nights July-August.*

Rooms: 4 doubles, 1 twin, all with bath or shower & wc.

Price: €64-€76 for two.

Meals: Choice of restaurants in town.

Closed: November-20 December, except by arrangement.

In Tarascon centre take Rue du Château opposite the château (well signposted). No. 24 is along on right.

Yann & Martine Laraison
24 rue du Château
13150 Tarascon
Bouches-du-Rhône
Tel: (0)4 90 91 09 99
Fax: (0)4 90 91 10 33
E-mail: ylaraison@wanadoo.fr
Web: www.chambres-hotes.com

Entry No: 726   Map: **14**

The calm of the elegant manor is enhanced by Marie-Pierre's refined, pastel, almost baroque décor. She is passionate about art and books, Christian loves music and making furniture. Both journalists travelled the world before settling here; they organise concerts in the barn, and painting classes.. The stylish, well-furnished bedrooms, one in the tower wing, one with a carved mezzanine, all with great personality, have stone walls and beams, fine old armoires and polished floors, excellent bathrooms and wonderful views of the Provençal hills beyond. Interesting hosts, a flower-bordered pool, much peace. *Gîte space for 4.*

Rooms: 2 doubles, 1 triple, 1 suite, all with shower or bath & wc.

Price: €85-€100 for two.

Meals: Dinner €29, including wine & coffee.

Closed: Never.

From Avignon D570 to Tarascon; leave road to Arles to left; now on D970: under bridge; 2km beyond, left on bridge through white gate.

Marie-Pierre Carretier & Christian Billmann
Le Mas d'Arvieux, Route d'Avignon
13150 Tarascon, Bouches-du-Rhône
Tel: (0)4 90 90 78 77
Fax: (0)4 90 90 78 68
E-mail: mas@arvieux-provence.com
Web: www.arvieux-provence.com

Entry No: 727   Map: **14**

Sophisticated simplicity is here: white walls and fine pale fabrics, old beds and cupboard doors that glow venerably in the sunlight filtering through the greenery outside - Bassette is an ethereal picture of pure Provence. Your hosts are as quiet and charming, gentle and generous as their 15th-century *mas* and its magical great garden where the swimming pool hides among big potted plants and wooden furniture. Big bedrooms are perfect: one picture and one framed text chosen by Marie for each, old terracotta tiles and wicker chairs, thick towels and soap in a basket. Superb value, utter peace.

Rooms: 2 doubles, both with bath, shower & wc.

Price: €70-€90 for two.

Meals: Good retaurants 5-20km.

Closed: Never.

Madame, who owns an antique shop, has used her knowledge and imagination to furnish this smart townhouse on one of Fontvieille's busy main streets with every attention to detail. Everything here is refined and in impeccable order. Both bedrooms have beautiful antiques as well as thick woollen carpets, fine linens and large bathrooms; both overlook the small garden. There is a large, very handsome guest *salon* and breakfast is served on old silver, a typically elegant touch. Your enthusiastic hosts enjoy sharing their love of music and Provence.

Rooms: 1 double, 1 triple, both with bath, shower & wc.

Price: €100 for two.

Meals: Restaurants in village.

Closed: Never; please book ahead.

From Tarascon D35 to Barbentane; head for 'Abbaye du Frigoulet'; at big car park on right, left into Chemin des Moulins; first right when see mill; left at crucifix.

From Arles, D17 to Fontvieille; head for 'Regalido' Hotel; after 50m right onto Route du Nord which becomes Av. F Mistral. House on right. On-street parking.

Marie & François Veilleux
Mas de Bassette
13750 Barbentane
Bouches-du-Rhône
Tel: (0)4 90 95 63 85
Fax: (0)4 90 95 63 85
E-mail: bassette@club-internet.fr

Jean-Marie & Édith-Claire Ricard Damidot
Le Mas Ricard
107 avenue Frédéric Mistral
13990 Fontvieille
Bouches-du-Rhône
Tel: (0)4 90 54 72 67
Fax: (0)4 90 54 64 43

Entry No: 728   Map: **14**

Entry No: 729   Map: **14**

A manicured farmhouse whose interior is as southern cool as the welcome from its owners is sincerely Franco-Irish - John is big and relaxed, Christiane is trim and efficient. Natural stone, oak beams, terracotta floors and cool colours give a wonderfully light and airy feel to the house while bedrooms are carefully elegant with small, functional shower rooms. Outside, a delectable garden, centuries-old plane trees, a vine tunnel, three hectares of cypresses and horses (why not head for the Alpilles mountains?) add to the magic. An oft-tinkled piano is there for you to play. *Minimum stay 6 nights July & August.*

Rooms: 3 doubles, 2 twins, all with shower & wc.

Price: €85-€95 for two.

Meals: Choice of restaurants in St Rémy.

Closed: November-Easter.

If you want to share a *grillade* in the garden with this charming, vivid and genuine couple or listen for hours to Monsieur's humorous talk of arcane Provençal traditions and tales, start practising your French now - *Risoulet,* the previous owner's name, means *smiling man* in patois and is utterly appropriate. Their rooms are as colourful as they are in their flowery, joyous decoration - the sky blue, the almond green, the yellow with its special sunflower-shaped brass beds and little sitting area under the roof. Such authenticity is rare in the area and the traffic does die down at night.

Rooms: 1 twin, 2 doubles, all with shower & wc.

Price: €46-€53 for two.

Meals: Good restaurants in Eyragues & Châteaurenard.

Closed: Never.

From St Rémy D571 for Avignon; over 2 r'bouts, left before 2nd bus stop (Lagoy), opp. 2nd yellow Portes Anciennes sign, Ch. de Velleron & P.; house 6th on right.

From A7 exit Avignon south for Tarascon 8km; left D34 for La Crau, Eyragues, St Rémy 2km; at La Crau sign on right.

Christiane & John Walsh
Mas Shamrock
Chemin de Velleron & du Prud'homme
13210 Saint Rémy de Provence
Bouches-du-Rhône
Tel: (0)4 90 92 55 79
Fax: (0)4 90 92 55 80

Charly & Colette Bertrand
Le Mas le Risoulet
4122 D34
13160 Châteaurenard
Bouches-du-Rhône
Tel: (0)4 90 94 71 38
Fax: (0)4 90 90 02 92

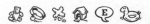

Entry No: 730   Map: **14**

Entry No: 731   Map: **14**

Provence – Alps – Riviera

Float in the pool and watch the sun set over the Alpilles before strolling to the large, picture-hung kitchen where Madame's mother may be imparting her knowledge of Provençal food and gardening - there are always home-made cakes. Built by great-grandfather in 1897, up a quiet lane, surrounded by fields and fruit trees, this *mas* blends modern with rustic Provence. Quarry-tiled rooms with colourful local fabrics open onto terrace and garden. Madame, a former teacher, will help you choose the ideal walk or restaurant or you can use the guest kitchen/dining/reading room or the pretty veranda.

Rooms: 1 double, 1 suite for 4, both with shower & bath.

Price: €58-€61 for two; suite €92-€100 for four.

Meals: Good restaurants nearby; self-catering available.

Closed: Never.

Receiving strangers comes naturally to Michael: he began with refugees and finds endless time for his guests, offering home-made croissants, cookery classes with olive oil straight from his trees, jogging companionship, airport pick-up. His fine pink villa is filled with Provençal antiques, Berber carpets, works by local sculptors and piles of books - a discovery at every turn. Plus tennis and croquet on the spot, sailing, swimming, trekking, bicycling a step away. Superior prices for superior attention: "What you seek is here", he proclaims in Latin over the door. Come and try his charmingly generous and individual house.

Rooms: 2 triples, both with bath & wc.

Price: €115 for two.

Meals: Dinner €30, including wine & coffee.

Closed: Never.

From Avignon, N7 for Aix-Marseille, exit for Plan d'Orgon - Cavaillon. House shortly before church on left (arrow signposts).

Magali Rodet
Mas de la Miougrano
447 route des Écoles
13750 Plan D'Orgon, Bouches-du-Rhône
Tel: (0)4 90 73 20 01
Fax: (0)4 90 73 20 01
E-mail: lamiougrano@net-up.com
Web: perso.net-up.com/lamiougrano

From A54 exit 13 on D19 for Miramas; in Grans D16 right to St Chamas; just before r'way bridge, left for Cornillon, up hill 2km; house on right before tennis court. Map faxed on request.

Michael Frost
Mas de la Rabassière
Route de Cornillon
13250 St Chamas, Bouches-du-Rhône
Tel: (0)4 90 50 70 40
Fax: (0)4 90 50 70 40
E-mail: michaelfrost@rabassiere.com
Web: www.rabassiere.com

Entry No: 732   Map: **14**

Entry No: 733   Map: **14**

An enormous 1850s *bastide aixoise*, decorated in local period style - the ceiling in the huge dining room, painted by Coulange-Lautrec (distant relative of Toulouse?), is remarkable. Monique is quite an expert on Provençal culture, custom and dress. Her special talent is making Nativity cribs and there is a wonderful *crèche* in the sitting room which she redecorates every Christmas. Bedrooms are comfortable, peaceful and simply furnished. Everywhere there are hints of the house's aristocratic past: family portraits, antiques, vases of dried and silk flowers. Fascinating.

Rooms: 2 doubles, both with shower & wc; 1 suite for 4 with bath, shower & wc.

Price: €61 for two; suite €100 for four.

Meals: Dinner €20, including wine & coffee.

Closed: November-March.

The Babeys are relaxed and easy, their modern, Provençal-style house sits above the surrounding vineyards and orchards as if in a Cézanne: the view of the Montagne Sainte Victoire is loaded with breathtaking references. Their cosy, rustically-furnished guest cottage or *cabanon* (illustrated), just below, has one large bedroom with mezzanine and a separate kitchen/sitting room with south-facing terrace. There's a fine pool, table tennis, boules, the sea 45 minutes away and lovely old Aix within easy reach. *Check pool availability.*

Rooms: Cottage for 4: 1 double/twin on ground floor, 1 double on mezzanine, bathroom & kitchenette.

Price: €61 for two.

Meals: Self-catering; restaurants in village, 2km.

Closed: Never.

From Aix N8 for Marseille through Luynes; at large r'bout right for Gardanne 600m; D59B right for Bouc Bel Air. House on left about 1200m after x-roads, 300m back from road.

From Aix, N7 Nice for approx. 15km; left just after Château Bégude for Puyloubier; Ch. des Prés 20m on right. House at end.

Monique & Henri Morand
La Lustière
442 Petit Chemin d'Aix
13320 Bouc Bel Air
Bouches-du-Rhône
Tel: (0)4 42 22 10 07
Fax: (0)4 42 94 13 42
E-mail: morand.monique@wanadoo.fr

Jean-Pierre & Sophie Babey
Les Bréguières
Chemin des Prés
13790 Rousset
Bouches-du-Rhône
Tel: (0)4 42 29 01 16
Fax: (0)4 42 29 01 16

Entry No: 734   Map: **14**

Entry No: 735   Map: **14**

The 18th-century manor farmhouse dominates its little hilltop on the edge of pretty Peynier. Pull the old cowbell, pass the big wooden doors and its solid red-shuttered mass surges up from a rose-filled garden. Beautifully restored *à la Provençale*, it once belonged to painter Vincent Roux and memories of his friend Cézanne live on. 'Roux' room (the best) has a delicious garden view, beams, terracotta tiles, a fantastic ochre/green bathroom down the corridor. The others are good too, though more functional, but the *salon* is a lovely spot. The atmosphere created by your gracious hostess is much praised. *Older children welcome.*

Rooms: 3 doubles, all with bath or shower & wc.

Price: €60 for two.

Meals: Restaurants in village; summer kitchen available for lunches.

Closed: First 3 weeks in August.

From Aix on D6, 4km before Trets, right D57 to Peynier. There, up hill to Trets/ Aubagne road; left D908; right between Poste & Pharmacie. House 50m.

Mme Jacqueline Lambert
Mas Sainte Anne
3 rue Auriol
13790 Peynier
Bouches-du-Rhône
Tel: (0)4 42 53 05 32
Fax: (0)4 42 53 04 28

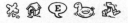

Entry No: 736   Map: **14**

These are happy, civilised people who enjoy having guests in their beautiful rambling stone property, leaving them in peace and cooking them delicious dinners. You sleep in rooms of timeless simplicity in the ancient tower (once a dovecote): exposed stones and old tiles breathe in the coolness, smart bedcovers glow, each room has its own entrance - it's almost monastic. Meals, with home-grown fruit and vegetables, are in the family dining room (separate tables) or on the terrace. There is a majestic peacock, a friendly dog, lots of pure-bred Arab ponies and... a child. Botanic walks, riding and visits to local wine cellars can be arranged.

Rooms: 3 suites for 3, 1 triple, 1 twin, all with bath or shower & wc.

Price: €50 for two.

Meals: Dinner €18, including wine & coffee.

Closed: December-March.

From Ginasservis D23 for Rians, 1.5km; left D22 for Esparron, 1km. Sign on left.

Fatia & Michel Lazès
Aubanel
83560 Ginasservis
Var
Tel: (0)4 94 80 11 07
Fax: (0)4 94 80 11 04
E-mail: aubanel-lazes@wanadoo.fr

Entry No: 737   Map: **14**

Jean-Yves and Alain have tackled their new careers here with panache, bringing their own inimitable sense of style, their noble black Labrador and some lovely new paintings, furniture and *objets* to an already fine house, a bust of Marie-Antoinette to the dining room and a touch of freshness to the uncluttered, stylish bedrooms - five of which have private terraces. The gardener cares for the lavender, herbs and organic vegetables in front of the house. Breakfast can be brought to your room between 8am and midday; dinners are imaginative and delicious. Not to be missed.

Rooms: 4 triples, 2 doubles, all with shower & wc.

Price: €70 for two.

Meals: Dinner €23, including wine & coffee.

Closed: November.

The Mediterranean garden here is spectacularly beautiful with its tall trees, flowering shrubs and manicured lawn. Indeed, the whole place is thoroughly manicured. Monsieur, an architect, designed the large, luxurious family villa, thoughtfully integrated into its surroundings - the pool is well concealed. Rooms are decorated in Provençal style with lovely Salernes bathroom tiles and are extremely comfortable; one has its own garden with table and chairs. Monsieur is shyly welcoming, Madame smilingly efficient and the nearby medieval village of Castellet is definitely worth a visit. *Gîte space for 4 people.*

Rooms: 2 doubles, 1 twin, 1 suite for 4, all with bath or shower & wc.

Price: €69 for two.

Meals: Restaurant in village.

Closed: Never.

In St Maximin D28 for Bras/le Val 3km to sign on right. From here follow narrow road for further 3km.

From Toulon N8 for Aubagne; in Le Beausset cross 2 r'bouts; right opp. Casino supermarket; imm'ly into Chemin de la Fontaine; house on left 1.5km, signed.

Alain Van't Hoff & Jean-Yves Savina
Domaine de Garrade
Route de Bras
83470 St Maximin la Ste Baume, Var
Tel: (0)4 94 59 84 32
Fax: (0)4 94 59 83 47
E-mail: garrade@aol.com
Web: www.provenceweb.fr/83/garrade

Charlotte & Marceau Zerbib
Les Cancades
1195 Chemin de la Fontaine
83330 Le Beausset
Var
Tel: (0)4 94 98 76 93
Fax: (0)4 94 90 24 63
E-mail: charlotte.zerbib@wanadoo.fr

Entry No: 738   Map: **14**

Entry No: 739   Map: **14**

Simply welcoming, your hosts were born in this unspoilt part of the Var where beautiful, distant views of the Pre-Alps - and genuine human warmth - await you at their modernised farmhouse (19th-century foundations). The smallish bedrooms feature typical Provençal fabrics and antiques, and other personal touches like dried-flower arrangements; the bathrooms are kept spotless. Over breakfast, brought to you on the private terrace or in the dining room - with wholemeal bread, local honey and apple juice - Madame will happily help you plan your day. She couldn't be kinder and thoroughly enjoys chatting with her guests. *Gîte space for 4 people.*

Rooms: 1 triple, 1 double, 1 twin, all with shower & wc.

Price: €48-€79 for two.

Meals: Restaurants 1-3 km. Barbecue available.

Closed: Never.

Readers write: "Armelle is wonderful". Breakfast is the highlight of her hospitality, when she dispenses intelligent conversation and ideas for excursions and Monsieur, an historian, happily shares his vast knowledge of the area. Theirs is a warm, lively family: a delightful, cultivated couple, four lovely children; their working vineyard has a timeless feel to it. The first-class, authentically Provençal bedrooms and the breakfast room (with mini-kitchen) are in a separate wing but, weather permitting, breakfast is on the terrace. Peace and privacy in a beautiful old house, superb walking country, seriously good value. *Gîte space for 4 people.*

Rooms: 2 twin/doubles & 1 suite for 4, all with bath or shower & wc.

Price: €49-€58 for two.

Meals: Self-catering; good restaurant nearby.

Closed: November-March.

From Aups, D9 and D30 to Montmeyan; D13 for Quinson. House is on left of road, 1km along; signposted.

From A8 exit St Maximin/Ste Baume D560 to Barjols; cont. D560 2km for Draguignan; entrance opp. D60 turning for Pontevès.

Dany & Vincent Gonfond
Mas Saint Maurinet
Route de Quinson
83670 Montmeyan
Var
Tel: (0)4 94 80 78 03
Fax: (0)4 94 80 78 03

Guillaume & Armelle de Jerphanion
Domaine de Saint Ferréol
83670 Pontevès
Var
Tel: (0)4 94 77 10 42
Fax: (0)4 94 77 19 04
E-mail: saint-ferreol@wanadoo.fr

Entry No: 740   Map: **15**

Entry No: 741   Map: **15**

The land is ancient Provence, the olive grove is young, the two houses are new, and it works. The Artauds left their village bistro to do B&B on this herby hillside and are entertaining, warm-hearted hosts. In the guest house, three rooms have single-bed mezzanines, the fourth has a vast window behind the bed – its fun. They are done in simple contemporary taste - plain calico curtains, seriously comfortable beds, spanking showers - with the odd bistro table or bit of *brocante* and works by artist friends. You eat on the terrace above the olive grove - Maryse makes delicious Provençal dishes. Supremely peaceful spot though rooms may lack sound-proofing.

Rooms: 3 triples, 1 double, all with own shower & wc.

Price: €61 for two.

Meals: Dinner €23, including wine & coffee.

Closed: 2-3 weeks in January.

Half of this gorgeous, well-restored 18th-century *bastide* (manor farmhouse) is yours: yours the light, airy, vineyard-view bedrooms, simply Provençal-furnished with a happy mix of antique and modern, yours the big bourgeois sitting room (little used because it's usually too lovely outside), yours the kitchen for picnic-making and laundry, yours a share in the great spring-watered tank for delicious natural swims. Gently confident, Jean-François runs the vineyard and the tastings. Enthusiastic and efficient, Nathalie cares for three children - and you - with sweet-natured ease. Very close to perfection, we thought.

Rooms: 3 doubles, 1 twin, all with bath or shower & wc.

Price: €54-€60 for two.

Meals: Dinner €18, including wine & coffee.

Closed: November-February.

From Cotignac D50 for Entrecasteaux 1km - entrance to house signposted on left.

Maryse & Richard Artaud
La Radassière
Route d'Entrecasteaux
83570 Cotignac, Var
Tel: (0)4 94 04 63 33
Fax: (0)4 94 04 66 99
E-mail: radasse@club-internet.fr
Web: www.sejour-en-provence.com/radas01.htm

From A8 Brignoles exit north D554 through Le Val; D22 through Montfort sur Argens for Cotignac. 5km along left; sign.

Nathalie & Jean-François Roubaud
Domaine de Nestuby
83570 Cotignac
Var
Tel: (0)4 94 04 60 02
Fax: (0)4 94 04 79 22
E-mail: nestuby@wanadoo.fr

The Counts of Provence lived here in the 1100s: they had style; so does Michel Dyens, a civilised, sociable gentleman. Panache too. In the quiet heart of the old town, the châteauesque side over the little street, the other over the walled garden, trees and fountain; the house feels almost colonial. Enter on original honeycomb tiles and under a grand, arched, embossed ceiling. The elegant comforts of your big, beautifully-furnished bedroom include headed paper with the house's 17th-century front door logo. In winter you can nestle by a log fire and read in peace.

Rooms: 3 large doubles, 1 twin, 1 triple, all with bath/shower & sep. wc.

Price: €62–€91.50 for two.

Meals: Dinner €23, including wine & coffee; restaurants in Brignoles.

Closed: November-March.

From A8 exit Brignoles; over river for Centre Ville, imm'ly right for Hôtel de Claviers; round Pl. Palais de Justice; right Av. F. Mistral; Rue des Cordeliers on left.

Michel Dyens
La Cordeline
14 rue des Cordeliers
83170 Brignoles, Var
Tel: (0)4 94 59 18 66
Fax: (0)4 94 59 00 29
E-mail: lacordeline@ifrance.com
Web: ifrance.com/lacordeline

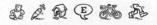

Entry No: 744   Map: **15**

The warm-hearted, tireless Didiers seem to have been born to run a happy and hospitable B&B and they do so, enthusiastically, in their quiet 1960s villa with its backdrop of vineyards and hills. Two spotlessly clean bedrooms with real attention to comfort - good cupboards and bedside lights, for example - share the modern shower room and are hung with Amélie's fine paintings. The guest dining room leads to a private outside terrace and thence to the peaceful, beautiful garden; ideal for relaxing after the day's visit, maybe by boat to one of the Iles d'Hyères.

Rooms: 1 suite (1 double, 1 twin), sharing bath, shower & wc.

Price: €60 for two; €100 for four.

Meals: Simple restaurants nearby; choice in Le Lavandou.

Closed: Never.

From Le Lavandou D559 E to La Fossette. Arriving in village, left Ave Capitaine Thorel, left again Chemin des Marguerites. If lost, telephone for help!

Robert & Amélie Didier
21 chemin des Marguerites
La Fossette
83980 Le Lavandou
Var
Tel: (0)4 94 71 07 82
Fax: (0)4 94 71 07 82

Entry No: 745   Map: **15**

A reassuringly unusual place built with ancient stones just 60-odd years ago as the second home of a wealthy Marseille family. Morning views as the mist rises over the parasol pines and the Massif des Maures beyond are stunning. Edwardian-style bedrooms have antique and retro furniture, or Provençal, or Modern with original paintings (many Madame's own). Breakfast simply, and preferably not too early, alone or at a big communal table, in the lovely garden, or in the glorious 100m² *salon* if it's cold. Madame also organises walking, biking and golfing parties. *Children over five welcome.*

Rooms: 2 doubles, 2 triples, all with bath & wc.

Price: €61 for two.

Meals: Good auberge 800m.

Closed: January.

Built in 1760 as a silkworm farm, this delicious old manor house still has mulberry trees shading the wonderful terrace that gives onto a mature walled garden. Plus a meadow area with children's games, a summer pool and a stupendous view to the distant hills. Inside it is just as authentic: old tiles with good rugs, beams, white walls and simple, comfortable antique furniture. Unlike our other owners, organised, warm-hearted Nicola is here four months of the year only; her vivacious, multi-lingual Norwegian friend, Randi, receives you, in perfect English, at other times.

Rooms: 1 double, 1 twin, both with shower & wc; 1 double, 1 twin, sharing shower/bath & wc.

Price: €85-€95 for two.

Meals: Wide choice within walking distance.

Closed: Never.

From A8 exit 'Le Luc' D558 for La Garde Freinet & St Tropez; house signposted on right after 4km.

From A8 exit 13 on N7 E to Vidauban; left D48 to Lorgues. In main street, post office on right: right, right again; at T-junction left Pl. Arariso. Leave square on left into Rue de la Canal; house on left.

Mme Monique Fauvet
La Gîthomière
Route de Saint Tropez
83340 Le Cannet des Maures
Var
Tel: (0)4 94 60 81 50
Fax: (0)4 94 60 81 50

Nicola d'Annunzio
La Canal
177 rue de La Canal
Quartier le Grand Jardin
83510 Lorgues, Var
Tel: (0)4 94 67 68 32
Fax: (0)4 94 67 68 69
E-mail: lacanallorgues@aol.com

Entry No: 746   Map: **15**

Entry No: 747   Map: **15**

Georges is retired and runs the B&B with enthusiasm and warmth, keeping the house, with its surprising touches of colour and imagination, immaculately. The bedrooms are indisputably pretty; one, the much larger of the two, has floral curtains on a brass rod, peach-coloured 'dragged' walls and a painted bed. Hard to imagine anyone not liking it, especially the doors onto the private terrace. Half a mile up a rough stony track, it is all immensely peaceful, there's a splendid pool, views across the tree-laden countryside and generous windows to let the Provençal light stream in. We wanted to stay for a week! *Gîte space for 5 people.*

Rooms: 2 doubles, both with shower or bath & wc.

Price: €70 for two.

Meals: Good restaurants nearby.

Closed: Never.

What a view! Sit here each morning, gazing past palms and pool to the plunging sea and enjoying Yvette's speciality of the day (tart, crumble...). She is a wonderful woman, sprightly and endlessly caring; Guy, a gentle and invaluable member of the team, collects the fresh bread and helps you plan your stay; they have travelled lots and simply love people. All three pretty, pastel guest rooms lead off a delightful bright, Moroccan-touched landing - brass lamps, hand-painted mirror - and have lovely Moroccan rugs on honeycomb-tile floors. The biggest room is definitely the best. And a sandy beach is just ten minutes down the cliff.

Rooms: 1 twin, 1 double, both with shower & wc; 1 double with bath & wc.

Price: €75-€105 for two.

Meals: Restaurants in Les Issambres.

Closed: October-May.

From A8 exit Le Muy for Ste Maxime & St Tropez. About 5km before Sainte Maxime right D74 to Plan de la Tour; entering village left D44 for Grimaud.

From Ste Maxime N98 E through San Piere; after Casino supermarket, 4th left Av Belvédère; right Av Coteaux; left Corniche Ligure; house on junction.

M & Mme G. Ponselet
Le Petit Magnan
Quartier Saint Sébastien
83120 Plan de la Tour
Var
Tel: (0)4 94 43 72 00
Fax: (0)4 94 43 72 00
E-mail: lepetitmagnan@worldonline.fr

Yvette & Guy Pons
Les Trois Cyprès
947 boulevard des Nymphes
83380 Les Issambres, Var
Tel: (0)4 98 11 80 31
Fax: (0)4 98 11 80 32
E-mail: gyjpons@mac.com
Web: homepage.mac.com/gyjpons/

Entry No: 748   Map: **15**

Entry No: 749   Map: **15**

Looking out over ancient hillsides studded with gnarled olive trees, this modern house is a place to rest between sophisticated Monte Carlo and the wild Verdon gorges. Your kindly, hospitable hosts are doing B&B for the sheer pleasure of it - feel the difference. Monsieur will tell you all about everything (in French), and may then take you walking in the 'red' hills of Esterel. Madame is quieter with the sweetest smile. The double room is excellent, simply but thoughtfully furnished, has good storage space and lighting and shares the large shower room with the much smaller twin room. Very good value.

Rooms: 1 twin, 1 double, sharing bathroom & wc.

Price: €40-€46 for two.

Meals: Choice of restaurants in Montauroux, 4km.

Closed: Never.

Breakfast in Paradise on Michèle's finely-laid spread before a vast and magic sea view, birdsong thrilling from the lush subtropical vegetation and Beethoven from the house. The terraced garden drops down to the sheltered pool, the house is done with antiques and taste. Your hosts, a devoted couple who adore children, make all who come near them feel happier: he, a partially blind former soldier, makes olive-wood carvings and fascinating conversation; Madame, a management consultant of charm and intelligence, is now Cultural Attachée to the Mairie. Wonderful hosts, super dog Oomba.

Rooms: 1 double with bath, shower & wc; 1 family suite with bath & wc.

Price: €70-€110 for two; under 10s free.

Meals: Dinner €15, including wine & coffee; restaurants in village.

Closed: Occasionally in winter.

From A8 exit 39 on D37 N for 8.5km; cross D562; continue 200m; Chemin Fontaine d'Aragon on right; signs.

From A8 exit St Laurent du Var; over r'bout for Zone Ind.; over 2nd r'bout; left at 3rd r'bout D118 to St Jeannet; through village to top, Rue St Claude. (Owners will send map.)

Pierre & Monique Robardet
Chemin de la Fontaine d'Aragon
Quartier Narbonne
83440 Montauroux
Var
Tel: (0)4 94 47 71 39
Fax: (0)4 94 47 71 39
E-mail: p.robardet@wanadoo.fr

Guy & Michelle Benoît Sère
L'Olivier Peintre
136 rue Saint Claude
06640 Saint Jeannet
Alpes-Maritimes
Tel: (0)4 93 24 78 91
Fax: (0)4 93 24 78 77

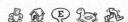

Blushes of pelargonium and cascades of bougainvillea, beloved by colour-loving Riviera gardeners, tumble over this 1930s villa and grapes dangle into your hand at breakfast. From the pretty garden, you enter your delightful little sitting room with its country antiques, then through a basic shower room to a rather cramped and minimalist bedroom. But your hosts as so genuinely, generously welcoming - fresh flowers in the rooms, delicious breakfast - and take such great care of you that this is a minor thorn among the roses. It is remarkably quiet and, although this is a dull piece of suburbia, sweet old seaside Antibes is only a 20-minute walk away. *Minimum stay 2 nights.*

Rooms: 1 double with small sitting room, shower & wc.

Price: €68 for two.

Meals: Wide choice of restaurants in Antibes.

Closed: Never.

In Antibes centre from Pl. de Gaulle take Rue Aristide Briand; left at r'bout, follow railway 600m; right impasse with barrier marked 'Privé'; house at end on right.

Martine & Pierre Martin
Villa Maghoss
8 impasse Lorini
06600 Antibes
Alpes-Maritimes
Tel: (0)4 93 67 02 97
Fax: (0)4 93 67 02 97

Entry No: 752   **Map: 15**

Panko is a riot of colour: the sheltered (no-smoking) garden has clumps of orange, mauve and scarlet flowers; real and fake flowers invade every bit of the living room and fight with the cheerful pictures that cover the variegated walls; upstairs are rainbow sheets, patchwork bedcovers, painted furniture and *objets* galore, fine big towels and myriad toiletries; big outdoor breakfasts on colourful china. Madame's energy drives it all - she'll organise your stay to a tee, galleries and museums a speciality. It is quiet, exclusive, six minutes from several small beaches - superb! *Book early. Minimum stay 5 nights April-October.*

Rooms: 2 double/twin, both with bath & wc; 2 extra beds.

Price: €100-€115 for two.

Meals: Good choice of restaurants 10 minutes' walk.

Closed: Christmas, New Year, 2 weeks August.

From Antibes for Cap d'Antibes; palm-tree r'bout for Cap d'Ant. Direct; next junction for Cap d'Ant.; 1st right Chemin du Crouton; 1st left into cul-de-sac. At end, left on drive. At no. 17, 2nd house on right.

Clarisse & Bernard Bourgade
Villa Panko
17 chemin du Parc Saramartel
06160 Cap d'Antibes
Alpes-Maritimes
Tel: (0)4 93 67 92 49
Fax: (0)4 93 61 29 32

Entry No: 753   **Map: 15**

Provence – Alps – Riviera

The paradise of a garden, blending into the pine-clothed hillside, is a lesson in Mediterranean flora, æons away from the potteries and madding fleshpots of nearby Vallauris, and Madame makes marmalade with the oranges. The Roncés restored this old building on a terraced vineyard after leaving hectic Paris: they understand the value of peace. Pamper yourself by the pool, relax to the sound of chirruping cicadas. The bedrooms - one large, one smaller, one with a view, one with less - have in common their comfort and clever use of cheerful colours and good fabrics. Your hosts may seem rather distant - is it shyness or a desire not to intrude?

Rooms: 1 double with bath & wc; 1 twin with shower & wc.

Price: €67-€76 for two.

Meals: Good bistro walking distance; choice in town.

Closed: Never.

From A8 Antibes exit to Vallauris; D135 Rte de Grasse; over 2 r'bouts, slow after hairpin bend; left down track signed Mas du Mûrier. Ring if lost.

M & Mme G. Roncé
Mas du Mûrier
1407 route de Grasse
06220 Vallauris
Alpes-Maritimes
Tel: (0)4 93 64 52 32
Fax: (0)4 93 64 23 77

Entry No: 754   **Map: 15**

Ève, a fascinating Medieval History specialist, has decorated her large and spotlessly clean, cool villa in her own personal 'retro' style. She and Henri, a doctor, provide a generous breakfast that is usually served in the lovely garden under the spreading palm tree (self-service before 8am); one of the ground-floor rooms actually opens onto the garden and the top bedrooms have a big private balcony. The house is only 15 minutes' walk from old Cannes and its famous star-crossed Croisette (they close during The Festival to avoid the curling faxes strewn on the floor at 4am) and your hosts are really worth getting to know.

Rooms: 1 double, 2 twins, 1 triple, all with bath & wc.

Price: €73-€95 for two.

Meals: Restaurants 5 minutes' walk.

Closed: Never.

From A8 exit 'Cannes Centre' Bd Carnot. At 69 Bd Carnot (Le Kid café) right Rue René Vigieno; up hill 150m; house on right on small r'bout; entrance at back.

Ève & Henri Daran
L'Églantier
14 rue Campestra
06400 Cannes
Alpes-Maritimes
Tel: (0)4 93 68 22 43
Fax: (0)4 93 38 28 53
Web: www.bnbnet.com/bfr/fr00042.html

Entry No: 755   **Map: 15**

This very appealing Provençal-type villa is a happy marriage of modern technique and traditional design; the setting is entrancing, with umbrella pines, palms, the southern skies and Mediterranean heat. In the cool interior all is well-ordered and smart. Your charming, efficient and enthusiastic hosts have created old out of new, paved their generous terrace with lovely old squares, and furnished the rooms with an appropriate mix of the antique and the contemporary. There is an excellent dayroom/kitchen for guests and a beautifully-tended green garden (and 10 golf courses within a 5km radius.)

Rooms: 2 doubles/twins, 1 double, all with bath & wc.

Price: €54-€70 for two.

Meals: 2 excellent restaurants 300m.

Closed: Never; please book ahead.

Annick, a well-travelled, kind and restful person, is a former riding instructress, now better at helping people into hammocks than onto horses. Her peaceful garden, with its awesomely ancient olive trees, like old men with a few wisps of hair dotted about the terraces and among the lush grass, is ideal for a siesta. Over this looks the garden suite, a treat for those who want to self-cater: its delightful kitchen is light-filled and quarry-tiled. The smaller blue room is charming with its own entrance, a vast antique wardrobe and an old wooden bed. If it's too hot for the terrace, breakfast is in the lovely saffron-yellow living room.

Rooms: 1 double with shower & wc; 1 double with bath, wc & kitchenette.

Price: €55-€70 for two.

Meals: Restaurants in village; self-catering available.

Closed: November-mid-December.

From A8 exit for Antibes D103; over Bouillides r'bout for Valbonne village 3km; 100m after Bois Doré rest't, before Petite Ferme bus stop, ring at iron gate No. 205; up lane, house on left at top.

From Grasse D2085 to Le Rouret; through village, left D7 for Cagnes; on leaving village, hard right down steep track; house on right.

Alain & Christine Ringenbach
Le Cheneau
205 route d'Antibes
06560 Valbonne
Alpes-Maritimes
Tel: (0)4 93 12 13 94
Fax: (0)4 93 12 91 85
E-mail: ringbach@club-internet.fr

Annick Le Guay
Les Coquelicots
30 route de Roquefort
06650 Le Rouret
Alpes-Maritimes
Tel: (0)4 93 77 40 04
Fax: (0)4 93 77 40 04

Entry No: 756   Map: **15**

Entry No: 757   Map: **15**

Utterly welcoming, bubbling with joy, radiating serenity, Marianne told her dogs and cat to "say *bonjour* to the lady" and all four smiled in greeting. About twenty years ago there was a little stone sheepshed on 5,000m² of land. Then an open-plan villa took one stone wall as its attractive fireplace and the rest became a semi-independent cottage, now beautifully equipped for guests, its small scale in total contrast to the vast living and terrace areas of the villa. Marianne's breakfasts are a feast; Éric will initiate longer stayers into scuba diving; tennis and golf are nearby. Wonderful people; lovely house. *Sensible dogs welcome.*

Rooms: Duplex with sitting room, double bedroom, shower & wc.

Price: €61-€69 for two.

Meals: Choice of restaurants within easy drive.

Closed: 1 November-31 March.

From A8 exit 47 D2085 for Grasse 17km. About 1km after Le Rouret, hard left before Mercedes garage, imm'ly right Ch. Reinards 800m, right Ch. Clamarquier, right to No. 34 in cul-de-sac.

Marianne & Éric Prince
34 chemin de Clamarquier
06650 Le Rouret
Alpes-Maritimes
Tel: (0)4 93 77 42 97
Fax: (0)4 93 77 42 97

Entry No: 758   Map: **15**

Both Alain and Michelle, a delightfully happy and enthusiastic couple, are fiercely and rightly proud of this very pretty old house which they saved up for while working for *France Télécom*. In an ideal setting on the upper fringe of a very pretty village, the house and garden have been lovingly renovated to create a really super place to stay. The bedrooms, each with its own terrace onto the garden, are separate from yet cleverly integrated with the rest of the house. Dinners are amazing and they claim they charge "the lowest prices on the Côte d'Azur". Ask Alain about his vintage wines.

Rooms: 1 double, 1 suite for 4, both with shower, bath & wc.

Price: €46-€52 for two.

Meals: Dinner €16, including wine & coffee.

Closed: 15 December-30 January.

From Cagnes sur Mer centre D18 to La Gaude; left 600m after La Gaude sign & cupola. Park Pl. des Marroniers; walk up behind grocer's, Rue des Marroniers to house. (Alain will fetch luggage.)

Alain & Michelle Martin
13 Montée de la Citadelle
06610 La Gaude
Alpes-Maritimes
Tel: (0)4 93 24 71 01
Fax: (0)4 93 24 71 01

Entry No: 759   Map: **15**

You can see the sea from this huge, Italianate villa smothered in bougainvillea and set in a big, peaceful garden way up above Nice, beyond the lowly quarters. The drive up is part of the adventure and your reward is a warm welcome; if necessary, Monsieur will park your car for you in the tiny space. Madame, new to B&B, is enthusiastic and attentive. Served on the sunny terrace, her breakfast of cheese and *charcuterie*, cereals and fruit, a variety of breads and jams, is not for picking at. Rooms are big, each one individually decorated with comfort unmatched by any hotel we know and the sparkling bathrooms sport myriad toiletries.

Rooms: 2 doubles, 1 suite for 4, all with bath, shower & wc.

Price: € 100 for two.

Meals: Vast choice in town, 2km (walk down, taxi back?).

Closed: Never.

Such warm and engaging hosts - a game of *pétanque*, a chat about horticulture, help with planning your trip - nothing is too much trouble. And what a classic Côte d'Azur setting... gaze out from your elegantly-furnished bedroom (the suite has its own terrace) over immaculate lawns and palms imported from Egypt. Heaps of Provençal style, though the atmosphere is not the least intimidating, with family antiques, Persian carpets on marble floors and pristine modern bathrooms (even a double bath). Breakfast can be either full English or Continental. "Super inside, super outside and super people". *Open by request during carnival. Minimum 2 nights stay all year round.*

Rooms: 2 doubles, 1 suite, all with bath & wc.

Price: € 100 for two; suite € 167 for four.

Meals: Restaurants in Nice.

Closed: 30 October-15 March.

Near Nice station. From Pl. St Philippe, under expressway, left Av. Estienne d'O. 600m, over level crossing, after sharp right-hand bend, hard back left private track climbing to house.

From Nice Route Grenoble for airport; continue past Leroy Merlin shopping centre; right at Agencement Cuisine sign.

Martine Ferrary
Le Castel Enchanté
61 route de Saint Pierre de Féric
06000 Nice
Alpes-Maritimes
Tel: (0)4 93 97 02 08
Fax: (0)4 93 97 13 70
E-mail: castel.enchante@wanadoo.fr

Jean-Claude & Brigitte Janer
La Tour Manda
682 route de Grenoble
06200 Nice
Alpes-Maritimes
Tel: (0)4 93 29 81 32
Fax: (0)4 93 29 81 32
E-mail: latourmanda@wanadoo.fr

Entry No: 760   Map: **15**

Entry No: 761   Map: **15**

Madame, an elegant, much-dreamt traveller and a lively, talented painter, loves her house to bits and enjoys sharing it. It is like a dolls' house; indeed, the small single room is full of antique dolls. The main bedroom, also quite small, looks onto the rambling, lushly Mediterranean, statue-decorated, terraced garden with many reading corners whence you can see the sea. It has delightful French antiques, a good kitchenette and a small modern shower room. Amazing quiet so near Nice, with good walking and cycling paths nearby. *Minimum stay 2 nights.*

Rooms: 1 suite (double & single) with shower & wc.

Price: €64 for two.

Meals: Restaurants 3-7km.

Closed: Never.

Paul, who is French, and his English wife Dorothy have been here since the '60s and have made the most of every square inch of the steep site. He is very proud of his handiwork: his latest creation is a Japanese-style bridge over the water garden. The views - of wooded valley leading to distant sea - are stupendous and make it entirely worth braving the narrow approach roads through the outskirts of Old Menton. Bedrooms all open off a south-facing terrace, have satin bedspreads, simple furniture and functional bathrooms. Breakfast may be on that pretty shaded terrace and it's deliciously breezy by the pool in summer. *Gîte space for 13 people.*

Rooms: 4 doubles, all with bath & wc.

Price: €54 for two.

Meals: Wide choice of restaurants in Menton.

Closed: December & January, except by arrangement.

From A8 exit 54 Nice Nord D14 for Gairaut and Aspremont for 4km; left at T-junction for Aspremont; Ave Panéra 500m on left; house 50m on right.

Mme Pia Malet-Kanitz
Villa Pan'É Râ
8 avenue Panéra - Gairaut Supérieur
06100 Nice
Alpes-Maritimes
Tel: (0)4 92 09 93 20
Fax: (0)4 92 09 93 20

From Menton D24 for Castellar (not Ciappes de Castellar). Follow numbers (odds on left) and park above house.

M & Mme Paul Gazzano
151 route de Castellar
06500 Menton
Alpes-Maritimes
Tel: (0)4 93 57 39 73
E-mail: natie06@yahoo.fr

Entry No: 762   Map: **15**

Entry No: 763   Map: **15**

Looking east over the yacht-studded bay, south over the onion domes of a *fin de siècle* Persian palace, here is a warmly human refuge from the fascinating excesses that are Monaco. Michelle's sober, white-painted flat is decorated with wood, marble and lots of contemporary art, her own and friends'. Living room: arched doors, little fireplace, little breakfast table, wide balcony; guest room: white candlewick bedcover, big gilt-framed mirror, sea view; bathroom: gloriously old-fashioned beige. Space everywhere, and Michelle is as good a hostess as she is an artist.

Rooms: 1 double/twin with bath & wc.

Price: €80 for two. Children under 2 free.

Meals: Wide choice of restaurants in Monaco.

Closed: August.

From A8 exit 56 Monaco for centre (tunnel); past Jardin Exotique; on rt. hand bend (pharmacie on corner) turn left; left at end Malbousquet; park opp. No. 26 to unload.

Michelle Rousseau
Villa Nyanga, 26 rue Malbousquet
98000 Principauté de Monaco
Tel: (00) 377 93 50 32 81
Fax: (00) 377 93 50 32 81 Please note this includes code for Monaco.
E-mail: michelle.rousseau@mageos.com
Web: www.bbfrance.com/rousseau.html

Entry No: 764   Map: **15**

The Little Earth Book
A fascinating read. The earth is now desperately vulnerable; so are we. Original, stimulating mini-essays about what is going wrong with our planet, and about the greatest challenge of our century: how to save the Earth for us all. It is pithy, yet intellectually credible, well-referenced, wry yet deadly serious.

Alastair Sawday is also an environmentalist. For over 25 years he has campaigned, not only against the worst excesses of modern tourism and its hotels, but against environmental 'looniness' of other kinds. He has fought for systems and policies that might enable our beautiful planet - simply - to survive. He founded and ran Avon Friends of the Earth, has run for Parliament, and has led numerous local campaigns. He is now a trustee of the Soil Association, experience upon which he draws in this remarkable book.

The Little Earth Book is a clarion call to action, a mind-boggling collection of mini-essays on today's most important environmental concerns, from global warming and poisoned food to economic growth, Third World debt, genes and 'superbugs'. Undogmatic but sure-footed, the style is light, explaining complex issues with easy language, illustrations and cartoons. Ideas are developed chapter by chapter, yet each one stands alone. It is an easy browse.

The Little Earth Book is as important as it is original. Learn about the issues and join the most important debate of this century.

Alastair Sawday Publishing

Price £5.99

French words and expressions

French words and expressions used in this book
Types of houses:

Chambre d'hôtes - B&B

Table d'hôtes - dinner with the owners of the house

Gîte Panda: may be either a *chambre d'hôtes* or a self-catering house in a national or regional park; owners provide information about flora and fauna, walking itineraries, sometimes guided walks and will lend you binoculars, even rucksacks

Château - a mansion or stately home built for aristocrats between the 16th and 19th centuries

Bastide has several meanings : it can be a stronghold, a small fortified village or, in Provence, it can simply be another word for *mas*

Longère - a long, low farmhouse made of Breton granite

Maison bourgeoise and *maison de maître* are both big, comfortable houses standing in quite large grounds and built for well-to-do members of the liberal professions, captains of industry, trade, etc

Mas - a Provençal country house, usually long and low and beautifully typical in its old stone walls, pan-tiled roof and painted shutters

Other words and expressions:
Bergerie - sheep fold, sheep shed

Brocante - secondhand furniture, objects, fabric, hats, knick-knacks

Le confit - parts of goose or duck, preserved in their own fat, then fried

Châtelain/e - Lord/lady of the manor

Clafoutis - fruit flan

Garrigue - typical scrubby vegetation on Mediterranean hillsides

Jouer aux boules, pétanque - bowling game played with metal balls on a dirt surface

Lavoir - public washing place

Mairie and *Hôtel de Ville* mean town and city hall respectively

Marais - marsh or marshland

Maquis - wild shrubland

Moulin - a mill - water or wind

Notaire - Notary

Objets/objets trouvés - objects/finds (lost property)

Paysan - not peasant in the English sense, but smallholder, modest farmer

Pelote - Basque ball game, with similarities to squash

Porte-monnaie - purse

Potage/potager - vegetable soup/vegetable garden

Pressoir - Press for olives/grapes/apples

Salle de chasse - gun room

Viennoiserie - literally 'things from Vienna' - covers all those relatively plain flaky-pastry concoctions served for breakfast or tea: *croissants, pains au chocolat,* etc.

Tips for travellers in France

- If you are not wedded to a mobile phone buy a phonecard (*télécarte*) on arrival; they are on sale at post offices and tobacconists' (*tabac*).

- Be aware of public holidays; many national museums and galleries close on Tuesdays, others close on Mondays (e.g. Monet's garden in Giverny) as do many country restaurants, and opening times may be different on the following days:

New Year's Day (1 January)   **May Day** (1 May)
Liberation 1945 (8 May)   **Bastille Day** (14 July)
Assumption (15 August)   **All Saints** (1 November)

2002 dates:

Easter Sunday	31 March
Ascension Thursday	24 May
Whit Sunday & Monday (Pentecost)	19 & 20 May

- Beware also of the mass exodus over public holiday weekends, both the first day - outward journey - and the last - return journey.

Medical and Emergency procedures

- If you are an EC citizen, have an E111 form with you for filling in after any medical treatment. You will subsequently receive a refund for only part of your payment, so it is advisable to take out private insurance.

- French emergency services are: the public service called SAMU or the Casualty Department - Services des Urgences - of a hospital; the private service is called SOS MÉDECINS.

Roads and driving

- Current speed limits are: motorways 130 kph (80 mph), RN national trunk roads 110 kph (68 mph), other open roads 90 kph (56 mph), in towns 50 kph (30 mph). The road police are very active and can demand on-the-spot payment of fines.

- One soon gets used to driving on the right but complacency leads to trouble; take special care coming out of car parks, private drives, narrow one-lane roads and coming onto roundabouts.

Directions in towns

The French drive towards a destination and use road numbers far less than we do. Thus, to find your way *à la française*, know the general direction you want to go, i.e. the towns your route goes through, and when you see *Autres Directions* or *Toutes Directions* in a town, forget road numbers, just follow towards the place name you're heading for or through.

Avoiding cultural confusion

En suite

'En suite' is not used in France to describe bathrooms off the bedroom and to do so can lead to confusion. To be clear, simply ask for a room *'avec salle de bains et wc'*.

Greetings and forms of address

We drop far more easily into first-name terms than the French. This reluctance on their part is not a sign of coldness, it's simply an Old National Habit, to be respected, we feel, like any other tribal ritual. So it's advisable to wait for the signal from them as to when you have achieved more intimate status.

The French do not say *"Bonjour Monsieur Dupont"* or *"Bonjour Madame Jones"* - this is considered rather familiar. They just say *"Bonjour Monsieur"* or *"Bonjour Madame"* - which makes it easy to be lazy about remembering people's names.

À table

Breakfast

There may be only a bowl/large cup and a teaspoon per person on the table. If so, you are expected to butter your bread on your hand or on the tablecloth (often the kitchen oilcloth) using the knife in the butter dish, then spread the jam with the jam spoon.

A well-bred English lady would never dream of 'dunking' her croissant, toast or teacake in her cup - it is perfectly acceptable behaviour in French society.

Lunch/dinner

Cutlery is laid concave face upwards in 'Anglo-Saxon' countries; in France it is proper to lay forks and spoons convex face upwards (crests are engraved accordingly). Do try and hold back your instinctive need to turn them over!

To the right of your plate, at the tip of the knife, you may find a knife-rest. This serves two purposes: to lay your knife on when you are not using it, rather than leaving it in your plate; to lay your knife *and* fork on (points downwards) if you are asked to *'garder vos couverts'* (keep your knife and fork) while the plates are changed - e.g. between starter and main dish.

Cheese comes *before* pudding in France - that's the way they do it! Cut a round cheese as you would cut a round cake - in triangular segments. When a ready-cut segment such as a piece of Brie is presented, the rule is to 'preserve the point', i.e. do not cut it straight across but take an angle which removes the existing point but makes another one.

Quick reference indices

WHEELCHAIR FRIENDLY

These owners have told us that they have facilities for people in wheelchairs.

Alsace
87

Burgundy
125 • 128

Normandy
171 • 185

Brittany
255

Western Loire
301

Loire Valley
431

Poitou - Charentes
437 • 458 • 463

Aquitaine
478 • 524 • 532

Languedoc - Roussillon
664

Rhône Valley - Alps
676 • 702

Provence - Alps - Riviera
742

LIMITED MOBILITY

These houses have bedrooms and bathrooms that are accessible for people of limited mobility. Please check details.

The North
10 • 12 • 13 • 14 • 20 • 26 • 38

Picardy
43 • 44 • 47 • 49 • 51 • 52 • 53 • 59 • 65

Champagne-Ardenne
67 • 72 • 75

Lorraine
83 • 84

Franche Comté
94 • 95

Burgundy
105 • 106 • 118

Paris - Ile-de-France
135 • 137 • 151

Normandy
161 • 165 • 172 • 183 • 192 • 194 • 201 • 204 • 205 • 207 • 208 • 225 • 227 • 231 • 237 • 240 • 246 • 249

Brittany
254 • 283 • 290

Western Loire
298 • 302 • 303 • 305 • 308 • 311 • 312 • 314 • 319 • 321 • 323 • 324 • 327 • 328 • 331 • 334 • 337 • 340 • 342 • 347 • 353 • 354 • 355

Loire Valley
366 • 367 • 371 • 374 • 375 • 383 • 385 • 387 • 388 • 389 • 390 • 394 • 398 • 401 • 406 • 410 • 411 • 412 • 413 • 414 • 415 • 417 • 420 • 421 • 424 • 426 • 427 • 432

Poitou - Charentes
434 • 438 • 439 • 442 • 445 • 446 • 447 • 448 • 461 • 462 • 464 • 473

Aquitaine
493 • 503 • 504 • 505 • 507 • 510 • 511 • 518 • 525 • 526 • 527

Limousin
533 • 537 • 543 • 547

Auvergne
549 • 551 • 553 • 559 • 560

Quick reference indices

ORGANIC
Owners use organic produce.

NO CAR?
These owners have told us that their B&B can be reached by public transport and/or that they are happy to collect you from the nearest bus or train station - please check when booking. (Other owners not on this list may be just as helpful, so do ask.)

Quick reference indices

Quick reference indices

What is Alastair Sawday Publishing?

A dozen or more of us work in two converted barns on a farm near Bristol, close enough to the city for a bicycle ride and far enough for a silence broken only by horses and the occasional passage of a tractor. Some editors work in the countries they write about, e.g. France and Spain, others work from the UK but are based outside the office. We enjoy each other's company, celebrate every event possible, and work in an easy-going but committed environment.

These books owe their style and mood to Alastair's miscellaneous career and his interest in the community and the environment. He has taught overseas, worked with refugees, run development projects abroad, founded a travel company and several environmental organisations - many of which have flourished. There has been a slightly mad streak evident throughout, not least in his driving of a waste-paper-collection lorry for a year, the manning of stalls at impoverished jumble sales and the pursuit of causes long before they were considered sane.

Back to the travel company: trying to take his clients to eat and sleep in places that were not owned by corporations and assorted bandits he found dozens of very special places in France - farms, châteaux etc - a list that grew into the first book, *French Bed and Breakfast*. It was a celebration of 'real' places to stay and the remarkable people who run them.

The publishing company is based on the unexpected success of that first and rather whimsical French book. It started as a mild crusade, and there it stays - full of 'attitude', and the more appealing for it. For we still celebrate the unusual, the beautiful, the individual. We are passionate about rejecting the banal, the ugly, the pompous and the indifferent and we are passionate too about promoting the use of 'real' food. Alastair is a trustee of the Soil Association and keen to promote organic growing and consuming by owners and visitors.

It is a source of deep pleasure to us to have learned that there are many thousands of people who share our views. We are by no means alone in trumpeting the virtues of standing up to the destructive uniformity of so much of our culture.

We are building a company in which people and values matter. We love to hear of new friendships between those in the book and those using it, and to know that there are many people - among them farmers - who have been enabled to pursue their lives thanks to the extra income the book brings them.

Alastair Sawday's
Special Places to Stay series

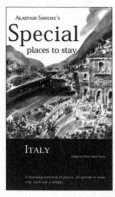

ALASTAIR SAWDAY'S

Special
places to stay

ITALY

A stunning selection of places, all special in some way, each one a delight.

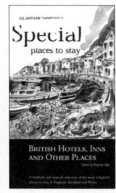

ALASTAIR SAWDAY'S

Special
places to stay

BRITISH HOTELS, INNS
AND OTHER PLACES

A brilliant and unusual selection of the most delightful places to stay in England, Scotland and Wales

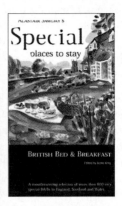

ALASTAIR SAWDAY'S

Special
places to stay

BRITISH BED & BREAKFAST

A mouthwatering selection of more than 600 very special B&Bs in England, Scotland and Wales

ALASTAIR SAWDAY'S

Special
places to stay

FRENCH HOTELS, INNS &
OTHER PLACES

Over 200 furnishingly lovely, hugely appealing places to stay throughout France - each one special in some way

ALASTAIR SAWDAY'S

Special
places to stay

PARIS HOTELS

A really select place to be, gracious to be spent in this setting hotel

ALASTAIR SAWDAY'S

Special
places to stay

IRELAND

From the sublime to the eccentric, the sophisticated to the simple? Here is the best of Ireland's best.

ALASTAIR SAWDAY'S

Special
places to stay

SPAIN

A host of over 400 wonderful places all over mainland Spain and its Islands.

ALASTAIR SAWDAY'S

Special
places to stay

PORTUGAL

From the sublime to the eccentric, the sophisticated to the simple? Here is the best of Ireland's best.

ALASTAIR SAWDAY'S

Special
places to stay

GARDEN BED & BREAKFAST

Gardens with buds? Well - scan of. Ninety-nine very special houses with gardens to match. Sleep and smell as poem.

www.specialplacestostay.com

Order Form UK

All these books are available in major bookshops or you may order them direct. Post and packaging are FREE.

	Price	No. copies
***Special Places to Stay:* Portugal**		
Edition 1	£8.95	
***Special Places to Stay:* Spain**		
Edition 4	£11.95	
***Special Places to Stay:* Ireland**		
Edition 3	£10.95	
***Special Places to Stay:* Paris Hotels**		
Edition 3	£8.95	
***Special Places to Stay:* Garden Bed & Breakfast**		
Edition 1	£10.95	
***Special Places to Stay:* French Bed & Breakfast**		
Edition 7	£14.99	
***Special Places to Stay:* British Hotels, Inns** and other places		
Edition 3	£11.99	
***Special Places to Stay:* British Bed & Breakfast**		
Edition 6	£13.95	
***Special Places to Stay:* French Hotels, Inns** and other places		
Edition 2	£11.99	
***Special Places to Stay:* Italy**		
Edition 2	£11.95	
***Special Places to Stay:* French Holiday Homes**		
Edition 1 (available January 2002)	£11.99	
The Little Earth Book	£5.99	

Please make cheques payable to: **Alastair Sawday Publishing**   Total [   ]

Please send cheques to: Alastair Sawday Publishing, The Home Farm Stables, Barrow Gurney, Bristol BS48 3RW. **For credit card orders call 01275 464891 or order directly from our website www.specialplacestostay.com**

Name:

Address:

Postcode:

Tel: Fax: FBB7

If you do not wish to receive mail from other companies, please tick the box ❑

Order Form USA

All these books are available at your local bookstore, or you may order
direct. Allow two to three weeks for delivery.

	Price	No. copies
Special Places to Stay: **Portugal**		
Edition 1	$14.95	
Special Places to Stay: **Ireland**		
Edition 3	$17.95	
Special Places to Stay: **Spain**		
Edition 4	$19.95	
Special Places to Stay: **Paris Hotels**		
Edition 3	$14.95	
Special Places to Stay: **French Hotels, Inns** and other places		
Edition 2	$19.95	
Special Places to Stay: **British Bed & Breakfast**		
Edition 6	$19.95	
Special Places to Stay: **Garden Bed & Breakfast**		
Edition 1	$17.95	
Special Places to Stay: **Italy**		
Edition 2	$17.95	
Special Places to Stay: **British Hotels, Inns and other places**		
Edition 3	$17.95	

Shipping in the continental USA: $3.95 for one book,
$4.95 for two books, $5.95 for three or more books.
Outside continental USA, call (800) 243-0495 for prices.
For delivery to AK, CA, CO, CT, FL, GA, IL, IN, KS, MI, MN, MO, NE,
NM, NC, OK, SC, TN, TX, VA, and WA, please add appropriate sales tax.

Please make checks payable to: The Globe Pequot Press   **Total**

To order by phone with MasterCard or Visa: (800) 243-0495. 9am to 5pm
EST; by fax: (800) 820-2329, 24 hours; through our web site:
www.globe-pequot.com; or by mail: The Globe Pequot Press, P.O. Box 480,
Guilford, CT 06437.

Name: Date:

Address:

Town:

State: Zip code:

Tel: Fax:

FBB7

Report Form

Comments on existing entries and new discoveries

If you have any comments on entries in this guide, please let us have them.
If you have a favourite house, hotel, inn or other new discovery, not just in
Britain, please let us know about it.

Book title: _____ Entry no: _____ Edition: _____

New recommendation ☐ Country: _____

Name of property: _____

Address: _____

_____

Postcode: _____

Tel: _____

Date of stay: _____

Comments: _____

_____

_____

_____

_____

_____

From: _____

Address: _____

_____

Postcode: _____

Tel: _____

Please send the completed form to: **Alastair Sawday Publishing,
The Home Farm Stables, Barrow Gurney, Bristol BS48 3RW** or go to
www.specialplacestostay.com and click on contact.

Thank you.

Reservation form

À l'attention de:
To:

Date:

Madame, Monsieur

Veuillez faire la réservation suivante au nom de:
Please make the following booking for (name):

Pour	*nuit(s)*	*Arrivant le jour:*	*mois*	*année*
For	night(s)	Arriving:day	month	year
		Départ le jour:	*mois*	*année*
		Leaving: day	month	year

Si possible, nous aimerions		*chambres, disposées comme suit:*
We would like		rooms, arranged as follows:

À grand lit	*À lits jumeaux*	
Double bed	Twin beds	
Pour trois	*À un lit simple*	
Triple	Single	
Suite	*Appartement*	*ou autre*
Suite	Apartment	or other

Nous sommes accompagnés de enfant(s) *âgé(s) de* ans.
Avez-vous un/des lit(s) supplémentaire(s), un lit bébé; si oui, à quel prix?
Our child is/children are years old. Please let us know if you
have an extra bed/extra beds/a cot and if so, at what price.

Notre chien/chat sera-t-il le bienvenu dans votre maison? Si oui, y a-t-il un
supplément à payer?
We are travelling with our dog/cat. Will it be welcome in your house?
If so, is there a supplement to pay?

Nous aimerions également réserver le dîner pour personnes.
We would also like to book dinner for people.

Veuillez nous envoyer la confirmation à l'adresse ci-dessous:
Please send confirmation to the following address:

Nom: Name:

Adresse: Address:

Tel No: E-mail:

Fax No:

www.specialplacestostay.com

Adrift on the unfathomable and often unnavigable sea of accommodation pages on the Internet, those who have discovered www.specialplacestostay.com have found it to be an island of reliability. Not only will you find a database full of honest, trustworthy, up-to-date information about over a thousand *Special Places to Stay* across Europe, but also:

- Direct links to the web sites of hundreds of places from the series.
- Colourful, clickable, interactive maps.
- The facility to make most bookings by email - even if you don't have email yourself.
- Online purchasing of our books, securely and cheaply.
- Regular, exclusive special offers on books from the whole series.
- The latest news about future editions, new titles and new places.
- The chance to participate in the evolution of both the guides and the site.

The site is constantly evolving and is frequently updated. By the time you read this we will have introduced an online notice board for owners to use, where they can display special offers or forthcoming local events that might tempt you. We're expanding our European maps, adding more useful and interesting links, providing news, updates and special features that won't appear anywhere else but in our window on the world wide web.

Just as with our printed guides, your feedback counts, so when you've surfed all this and you still want more, let us know - this site has been planted with room to grow!

Russell Wilkinson, Web Editor
editor@specialplacestostay.com

Index by surname

Index by surname

Index by surname

Index by surname

Index by surname

Index by surname

Index by surname

Index by place name

Index by place name

Index by place name

Index by place name

Index by place name

Index by place name

Exchange rate table

Euro	Franc	US $	£ Sterling
5	33	4.60	3.16
10	66	9.19	6.31
20	131	18.38	12.62
30	197	27.57	18.93
40	262	36.76	25.34
50	328	45.97	31.56
60	394	55.17	37.87
70	459	64.38	44.18
80	525	73.58	50.49
90	590	82.77	56.80
100	656	92.02	63.07
150	984	138.08	94.67

Rates correct at time of going to press September 2001

COMPETITION

All our books have the odd spoof hidden away within their pages. Sunken boats, telephone boxes and ruined castles have all featured. Some of you have written in with your own ideas. So, we have decided to hold a competition for spoof writing every year.

The rules are simple: send us your own spoofs, include the photos, and let us know for which book it is intended. We will publish the winning entries in the following edition of each book. We will also send a complete set of our guides to each winner.

Please send your entries to:

**Alastair Sawday Publishing, Spoofs Competition,
The Home Farm Stables, Barrow Gurney,
Bristol BS48 3RW.**

Explanation of symbols

Treat each one as a guide rather than a statement of fact and check important points when booking:

 Working farm.

 Children are positively welcomed, with no age restrictions, but cots, high chairs etc are not necessarily available.

 Pets are welcome but may have to sleep in an outbuilding or your car. Check when booking.

 Vegetarians catered for with advance warning. All hosts can cater for vegetarians at breakfast.

 Most, but not necessarily all, ingredients are organic, organically grown, home-grown or locally grown.

 Full and approved wheelchair facilities for at least one bedroom and bathroom and access to all ground-floor common areas.

 Basic ground-floor access for people of limited mobility and at least one bedroom and bathroom accessible without steps, but not full facilities for wheelchair-users.

 No smoking anywhere in the house.

 This house has pets of its own that live in the house: dog, cat, duck, parrot...

 Credit cards accepted; most commonly Visa and MasterCard.

 Swimming pool on the premises.

 Smoking restrictions exist usually, but not always, in the dining room and some bedrooms. For full restrictions, check when booking.

 You can either borrow or hire bikes here.

 Your hosts speak English, whether perfect or not.

 Good hiking from house or village.